The Conservative Government
and the End of Empire
1951–1957

The British Documents on
the End of Empire Project
gratefully acknowledges
the generous assistance of
the Leverhulme Trust.

BRITISH DOCUMENTS ON THE END OF EMPIRE

General Editor S R Ashton
Project Chairman D A Low

Series A Volume 3

The Conservative Government and the End of Empire 1951–1957

Editor
DAVID GOLDSWORTHY

Part I
INTERNATIONAL RELATIONS

Published for the Institute of Commonwealth Studies
in the University of London

LONDON : HMSO

© *Crown copyright 1994*
Introduction copyright David Goldsworthy 1994
Applications for reproduction should be made to HMSO
First published 1994

ISBN 0 11 290535 8 ✓

British Library Cataloguing in Publication Data

A CIP catalogue record for this book
is available from the British Library

Write to PC11C, Standing Order Service, HMSO Books, PO Box 276,
LONDON SW8 5DT quoting classification reference 040 30 017 to
order future volumes from the British Documents on the End of
Empire project.

HMSO publications are available from:

HMSO Publications Centre
(Mail, fax and telephone orders only)
PO Box 276, London, SW8 5DT
Telephone orders 071-873 9090
General enquiries 071-873 0011
(queuing system in operation for both numbers)
Fax orders 071-873 8200

HMSO Bookshops
49 High Holborn, London, WC1V 6HB
(counter service only)
071-873 0011   Fax 071-873 8200
258 Broad Street, Birmingham, B1 2HE
021-643 3740   Fax 021-643 6510
33 Wine Street, Bristol, BS1 2BQ
0272 264306   Fax 0272 294515
9–21 Princess Street, Manchester, M60 8AS
061-834 7201   Fax 061-833 0634
16 Arthur Street, Belfast, BT1 4GD
0232 238451   Fax 0232 235401
71 Lothian Road, Edinburgh, EH3 9AZ
031-228 4181   Fax 031-229 2734

HMSO's Accredited Agents
(see Yellow Pages)

and through good booksellers

Printed in the United Kingdom by HMSO
Dd294237   C7   4/94

Contents

Foreword

The main purpose of the British Documents on the End of Empire Project (BDEEP) is to publish documents from British official archives on the ending of colonial and associated rule and on the context in which this took place. In 1945, aside from the countries of present-day India, Pakistan, Bangladesh and Burma, Britain had over fifty formal dependencies; by the end of 1965 the total had been almost halved and by 1985 only a handful remained. The ending of Britain's position in these formal dependencies was paralleled by changes in relations with states in an informal empire. The end of empire in the period at least since 1945 involved a change also in the empire as something that was more than the sum of its parts and as such formed an integral part of Britain's domestic affairs and international relations. In publishing official British documents on the end of empire this project is, to a degree, the successor to the two earlier series of published documents concerning the end of British rule in India and Burma which were edited by Professors Mansergh and Tinker respectively.[1] The successful completion of *The transfer of power* and *The struggle for independence*, both of which were based on British records, emphasised the need for similar published collections of documents important to the history of the final stages of Britain's association with other dependencies in Africa, the Middle East, the Caribbean, South-East Asia and the Pacific. In their absence, scholars both from sovereign independent states which emerged from colonial rule, as well as from Britain itself, lack an important tool for understanding and teaching their respective histories. But BDEEP is also set in the much wider context of the efforts made by successive British governments to locate Britain's position in an international order. Here the empire, both in its formal and informal senses, is viewed as an instrument of the domestic, foreign and defence policies of successive British governments. The project is therefore concerned with the ending of colonial rule in individual territories as seen from the British side at one level, and the broader political, economic and strategic considerations involved in that at another.

BDEEP is a sequel, not only to the India and Burma series but also to the still earlier series of published Foreign Office documents which continues as Documents on British Policy Overseas (DBPO). The contemporary volumes in DBPO appear in two parallel series covering the years 1945 to 1955. In certain respects the documents published in the BDEEP volumes will complement those published in DBPO. On issues where there is, or is likely to be, direct overlap, BDEEP will not provide detailed coverage. The most notable examples concern the post-Second World War international settlements in the Far East and the Pacific, and the immediate events of the Suez crisis of 1956.

---

[1] Nicholas Mansergh et al, eds, *Constitutional relations between Britain and India: the transfer of power 1942–47*, 12 vols, (London, 1970–1983); Hugh Tinker, ed, *Constitutional relations between Britain and Burma: the struggle for independence 1944–1948*, 2 vols, (London, 1983–1984).

Despite the similarities, however, BDEEP differs in significant ways from its predecessors in terms both of presentation and content. The project is of greater magnitude than that undertaken by·Professor Mansergh for India. Four major differences can be identified. First, the ending of colonial rule within a dependent empire took place over a much longer period of time, extending into the final years of the twentieth century, while having its roots in the Second World War and before. Secondly, the empire consisted of a large number of territories, varying in area, population, wealth and in many other ways, each with its own individual problems, but often with their futures linked to those of neighbouring territories and the growing complexity surrounding the colonial empire. Thirdly, while for India the documentary record for certain matters of high policy could be encapsulated within a relatively straightforward 'country' study, in the case of the colonial empire the documentary record is more diffuse because of the plethora of territories and their scattered location. Finally, the documents relating to the ending of colonial rule are not conveniently located within one leading department of state but rather are to be found in several of them. As the purpose of the project is to publish documents relating to the end of empire from the extensive range and quantity of official British records, private collections and other categories of non-official material are not regarded as principal documentary sources. In BDEEP, selections from non-official material will be used only in exceptional cases to fill gaps where they exist in the available official record.

In recognition of these differences, and also of the fact that the end of empire involves consideration of a range of issues which operated at a much wider level than that normally associated with the ending of colonial rule in a single country, BDEEP is structured in two main series along with a third support series. Series A represents the general volumes in which, for successive British governments, documents relating to the empire as a whole will be published. Series B represents the country or territory volumes and provides territorial studies of how, from a British government perspective, former colonies and dependencies achieved their independence, and countries which were part of an informal empire regained their autonomy. In addition to the two main documentary series, a third series – series C – will be published in the form of handbooks to the records of the former colonial empire which are deposited at the Public Record Office (PRO). The handbooks will be published in two volumes as an integral part of BDEEP and also as PRO guides to the records. They will enable scholars and others wishing to follow the record of the ending of colonial rule and empire to pursue their inquiries beyond the published record provided by the general studies in series A and the country studies in series B. Volume One of the handbooks, a revised and updated version of *The records of the Colonial and Dominions Offices* (by R B Pugh) which was first published in 1964, is entitled *Records of the Colonial Office, Dominions Office, Commonwealth Relations Office and Commonwealth Office*. It covers over two hundred years of activity down to 1968 when the Commonwealth Office merged with the Foreign Office to form the Foreign and Commonwealth Office. Volume Two, entitled *Cabinet, Foreign Office, Treasury and other records*, focuses more specifically on twentieth-century departmental records and also includes references to the records of inter-departmental committees, commissions of inquiry and international organisations. These two volumes have been prepared under the direction and supervision of Dr Anne Thurston, honorary research fellow at the Institute of Commonwealth Studies in the

University of London.

The criteria which have been used in selecting documents for inclusion in individual volumes will be explained in the introductions written by the specialist editors. These introductions are more substantial and contextual than those in previous series. Each volume will also list the PRO sources which have been searched. However, it may be helpful to outline the more general guiding principles which have been employed. BDEEP editors pursue several lines of inquiry. There is first the end of empire in a broad high policy sense, in which the empire is viewed in terms of Britain's position as a world power, and of the inter-relationship between what derives from this position and developments within the colonial dependencies. Here Britain's relations with the dependencies of the empire are set in the wider context of Britain's relations with the United States, with Europe, and with the Commonwealth and United Nations. The central themes are the political constraints, both domestic and international, to which British governments were subject, the economic requirements of the sterling area, the geopolitical and strategic questions associated with priorities in foreign policy and in defence planning, and the interaction between these various constraints and concerns and the imperatives imposed by developments in colonial territories. Secondly, there is investigation into colonial policy in its strict sense. Here the emphasis is on those areas which were specifically – but not exclusively – the concern of the leading department. In the period before the administrative amalgamations of the 1960s,[2] the leading department of the British government for most of the dependencies was the Colonial Office; for a minority it was either the Dominions Office and its successor, the Commonwealth Relations Office, or the Foreign Office. Colonial policy included questions of economic and social development, questions of governmental institutions and constitutional structures, and administrative questions concerning the future of the civil and public services and of the defence forces in a period of transition from European to indigenous control. Finally there is inquiry into the development of political and social forces within colonies, the response to these and the transfer of governmental authority and of legal sovereignty from Britain to its colonial dependencies as these processes were understood and interpreted by the British government. Here it should be emphasised that the purpose of BDEEP is not to document the history of colony politics or nationalist movements in any particular territory. Given the purpose of the project and the nature of much of the source material, the place of colony politics in BDEEP is conditioned by the extent to which an awareness of local political situations played an overt part in influencing major policy decisions made in Britain.

Although in varying degrees and from different perspectives, elements of these various lines of inquiry appear in both the general and the country series. The aim in both is to concentrate on the British record by selecting documents which illustrate those policy issues which were deemed important by ministers and officials at the time. General volumes do not normally treat in any detail of matters which will be fully documented in the country volumes, but some especially significant documents do appear in both series. The process of selection involves an inevitable degree of

---

[2] The Colonial Office merged with the Commonwealth Relations Office in 1966 to form the Commonwealth Office. The Commonwealth Office merged with the Foreign Office in 1968 to form the Foreign and Commonwealth Office.

sifting and subtraction. Issues which in retrospect appear to be of lesser significance or to be ephemeral have been omitted. The main example concerns the extensive quantity of material devoted to appointments and terms of service – salaries, gradings, allowances, pension rights and compensation – within the colonial and related services. It is equally important to stress certain negative aspects of the official documentary record. Officials in London were sometimes not in a position to address potentially significant issues because the information was not available. Much in this respect depended on the extent of the documentation sent to London by the different colonial administrations. Once the stage of internal self-government had been reached, or where there was a dyarchy, the flow of detailed local information to London began to diminish.

Selection policy has been influenced by one further factor, namely access to the records at the PRO. Unlike the India and Burma series and DBPO, BDEEP is not an official project. In practice this means that while editors have privileged access (in the form of research facilities and requisitioning procedures) to the records at the PRO, they do not have unrestricted access. For files which at the time a volume is in preparation are either subject to extended closures beyond the statutory thirty years, or retained in the originating department under section 3(4) of the Public Records Act of 1958, editors are subject to the same restrictions as all other researchers. Where necessary, volume editors will provide details of potentially significant files or individual documents of which they are aware and which they have not been able to consult.

A thematic arrangement of the documents has been adopted for the general volumes in series A. The country volumes in series B follow a chronological arrangement; in this respect they adopt the same approach as was used in the India and Burma series. For each volume in both series A and B a summary list of the documents included is provided. The headings to BDEEP documents, which have been editorially standardised, present the essential information. Together with the sequence number, the file reference (in the form of the PRO call-up number and any internal pagination or numeration) and the date of the document appear on the first line.[3] The second and subsequent lines record the subject of the document, the type of document (letter, memorandum, telegram etc), the originator (person or persons, committee, department) and the recipient (if any). In headings, a subject entry in single quotation marks denotes the title of a document as it appears in the original. An entry in square brackets denotes a subject indicator devised by the editor. This latter device has been employed in cases where no title is given in the original or where the original title is too unwieldly to reproduce in its entirety. Security classifications and, in the case of telegrams, times of despatch and receipt, have generally been omitted as confusing and needlessly complicating, and are retained only where they are necessary to a full understanding. In the headings to documents and the summary lists, ministers are identified by the name of the office-holder, not the title of the office (ie, Mr Lyttelton, not secretary of state for the colonies).[4] In the same contexts, officials are identified by their initials and surname. Ambassadors,

---

[3] The PRO call-up number precedes the comma in the references cited. In the case of documents from FO 371, the major Foreign Office political class, the internal numeration refers to the jacket number of the file.

[4] This is an editorial convention, following DBPO practice. Very few memoranda issued in their name were actually written by ministers themselves, but normally drafted by officials.

governors, high commissioners and other embassy or high commission staff are given in the form 'Sir E Baring (Kenya)'. Footnotes to documents appearing below the rule are editorial; those above the rule, or where no rule is printed, are part of the original document. Each part of a volume provides a select list of which principal offices were held by whom, with a separate series of biographical notes (at the end) for major figures who appear in the documents. Minor figures are identified in editorial footnotes on the occasion of first appearance. Link-notes, written by the volume editor and indented in square brackets between the heading and the beginning of a document, are sometimes used to explain the context of a document. Technical detail or extraneous material has been extracted from a number of documents. In such cases omission dots have been inserted in the text and the document is identified in the heading as an extract. Occasional omission dots have also been used to excise purely mechanical chain-of-command executive instructions, and some redundant internal referencing has been removed, though much of it remains in place, for the benefit of researchers. No substantive material relating to policy-making has been excised from the documents. In general the aim has been to reproduce documents in their entirety. The footnote reference 'not printed' has been used only in cases where a specified enclosure or an annex to a document has not been included. Unless a specific cross-reference or note of explanation is provided, however, it can be assumed that other documents referred to in the text of the documents included have not been reproduced. Each part of a volume has a list of abbreviations occurring in it. A consolidated index for the whole volume appears at the end of each part.

One radical innovation, compared with previous Foreign Office or India and Burma series, is that BDEEP will reproduce many more minutes by ministers and officials.

All government documents are reproduced and quoted by permission of the Controller of HMSO. All references and dates are given in the form recommended in PRO guidelines.

*   *   *   *

BDEEP has received assistance and support from many quarters. The project was first discussed at a one-day workshop attended by over thirty interested scholars which, supported by a small grant from the Smuts Memorial Fund, was held at Churchill College, Cambridge, in May 1985. At that stage the obstacles looked daunting. It seemed unlikely that public money would be made available along the lines provided for the India and Burma projects. The complexities of the task looked substantial, partly because there was more financial and economic data with which to deal, still more because there were so many more territories to cover. It was not at all clear, moreover, who could take institutional responsibility for the project as the India Office Records had for the earlier ones; and in view of the escalating price of the successive India and Burma volumes, it seemed unlikely that publication in book form would be feasible; for some while a choice was being discussed between microfilm, microfiche and facsimile.

A small group nevertheless undertook to explore matters further, and in a quite remarkable way found itself able to make substantial progress. The British Academy adopted BDEEP as one of its major projects, and thus provided critical support. The Institute of Commonwealth Studies served as a crucial institutional anchor in taking responsibility for the project. The Institute also made office space available, and negotiated an administrative nexus within the University of London. Dr Anne Thurston put at the disposal of the project her unique knowledge of the relevant archival sources; while the keeper of the Public Records undertook to provide all the support that he could. It then proved possible to appoint Professor Michael Crowder as project director on a part-time basis, and he approached the Leverhulme Trust, who made a munificent grant which was to make the whole project viable. Almost all those approached to be volume editors accepted and, after consultation with a number of publishers, Her Majesty's Stationery Office undertook to publish the project in book form. There can be few projects that after so faltering a start found itself quite so blessed.

Formally launched in 1987, BDEEP has been based since its inception at the Institute of Commonwealth Studies. The work of the project is supervised by a Project Committee chaired by Professor Anthony Low, Smuts professor of the history of the British Commonwealth in the University of Cambridge. Professor Michael Crowder became general editor while holding a visiting professorship in the University of London and a part-time position at Amherst College, Massachusetts. Following his untimely death in 1988, Professor Crowder was replaced as general editor by Professor David Murray, pro vice-chancellor and professor of government at the Open University. Mrs Anita Burdett was appointed as project secretary and research assistant. She was succeeded in September 1989 by Dr Ashton who had previously worked with Professors Mansergh and Tinker during the final stages of the India and Burma series. Dr Ashton replaced Professor Murray as project director and general editor in 1993. When BDEEP was launched in 1987, eight volumes in series A and B were approved by the Project Committee and specialist scholars were commissioned to research and select documents for inclusion in each. Collectively, these eight volumes (three general and five country)[5] represent the first stage of the project which begins with an introductory general volume covering the years between 1925 and 1945 but which concentrates on the period from the Second World War to 1957 when Ghana and Malaya became independent.[6]

It is fitting that the present general editor should begin his acknowledgements with an appreciation of the contributions made by his predecessors. The late Professor Crowder supervised the launch of the project and planned the volumes included in stage one. The volumes already published bear lasting testimony to his resolve and dedication during the project's formative phase. Professor Murray played a no less crucial role in establishing a secure financial base for the project and in negotiating contracts with the volume editors and HMSO. His invaluable advice and expertise during the early stages of editing are acknowledged with particular gratitude.

---

[5] Series A general volumes: vol 1 *Colonial policy and practice 1924–1945*; vol 2 *The Labour government and the end of empire 1945–1951* (published 1992); vol 3 *The Conservative government and the end of empire 1951–1957* (published 1994).

   Series B country volumes: vol 1 *Ghana* (published 1992); vol 2 *Sri Lanka*; vol 3 *Malaya*; vol 4 *Egypt and the defence of the Middle East*; vol 5 *Sudan*.

[6] Plans are currently in preparation to commission new research for a second stage covering the period 1957–1964.

The project benefited from an initial pump-priming grant from the British Academy. Thanks are due to the secretary and Board of the Academy for this grant and for the decision of the British Academy to adopt BDEEP as one of its major projects. The principal funding for the project has been provided by the Leverhulme Trust and the volumes are a tribute to the support provided by the Trustees. A major debt of gratitude is owed to the Trustees. In addition to their generous grant to cover the costs of the first stage, the Trustees agreed to a subsequent request to extend the duration of the grant, and also provided a supplementary grant which enabled the project to secure Dr Ashton's appointment.

Members of the Project Committee, who meet annually at the Institute of Commonwealth Studies, have provided valuable advice and much needed encouragement. Professor Low, chairman of the Committee, has made a singular contribution, initiating the first exploratory meeting at Cambridge in 1985 and presiding over subsequent developments in his customary constructive but unobtrusive manner. In addition to the annual meeting of the Project Committee, the project holds an annual seminar to discuss issues arising from the research of the volume editors. Valuable comments have been received from academic colleagues attending the seminars by invitation. The director and staff of the Institute of Commonwealth Studies have provided administrative support and the congenial surroundings within which the general editor works. The editors of volumes in Stage One have profited considerably from the researches undertaken by Dr Anne Thurston and her assistants during the preparation of the records handbooks. Although BDEEP is not an official project, the general editor wishes to acknowledge the support and co-operation received from the Historical Section of the Cabinet Office and the Records Department of the Foreign and Commonwealth Office. He wishes also to record his appreciation of the spirit of friendly co-operation emanating from the editors of DBPO. Dr Ronald Hyam, editor of the volume in series A on *The Labour government and the end of empire 1945–1951*, played an important role in the compilation of the house-style adopted by BDEEP and his contribution is acknowledged with gratitude. Thanks also are due to HMSO for assuming publishing responsibility and for their expert advice on matters of design and production. Last, but by no means least, the contribution of the keeper of the records and the staff, both curatorial and administrative, at the PRO must be emphasised. Without the facilities and privileges afforded to BDEEP editors at Kew, the project would not be viable.

S R Ashton
Institute of Commonwealth Studies
October 1993

The Conservative Government and
the End of Empire 1951–1957

Schedule of contents: parts I–III

Abbreviations: part I

ADO	African Defence Organisation
AEF	Afrique Equatoriale française
ANZAM	Australia, New Zealand and Malaya
ANZUS	Australia, New Zealand, United States [Pact]
BBC	British Broadcasting Corporation
BDCC(ME)	British Defence Co-ordination Committee (Middle East)
BDEEP	British Documents on the End of Empire Project
BIS	British Information Service
CCTA	Commission for Technical Co-operation in Africa South of the Sahara
CDC	Colonial Development Corporation
CD(&)W	Colonial Development and Welfare (Act)
CDWF	Colonial Development and Welfare Fund
CIA	Central Intelligence Agency (US)
CIGS	chief of the imperial general staff
c-in-c	commander-in-chief
CINCAFMED	commander-in-chief, Africa and the Mediterranean
CINCPAC	commander-in-chief, Pacific (US)
CO	Colonial Office
COS	Chiefs of Staff
CRO	. Commonwealth Relations Office
CSIR	Council for Scientific and Industrial Research
cttee	committee
ECE	Economic Commission for Europe
ECOSOC	Economic and Social Committee (UN)
EDC	European Defence Community
EEC	European Economic Community
EFTA	European Free Trade Association

B

ENOSIS	Union of Cyprus with Greece
EOKA	National Organisation of Cypriot Fighters
EPU	European Payments Union
EURATOM	European Atomic Energy Commission
FO	Foreign Office
GATT	General Agreement on Tariffs and Trade
GPO	General Post Office
HBM	His/Her Britannic Majesty
HM	His/Her Majesty
HR	human rights
ICFTU	International Confederation of Free Trade Unions
ILI	International Labour Institute
ILO	International Labour Organisation
IMF	International Monetary Fund
IRD	International Relations Department (CO)
ISD	Intelligence and Security Department (CO)
IUS	International Union of Students
JIC	Joint Intelligence Committee
JPS	Joint Planning Staff (COS)
lt-gov	lieutenant-governor
maj	major
maj-gen	major-general
MEDO	Middle East Defence Organisation (also referred to as MEATO or METO, Middle East Treaty Organisation)
memo	memorandum
NATO	North Atlantic Treaty Organisation
NCO	non-commissioned officer
nsg's	non-self-governing territories
OAS	Organisation of American States
OEEC	Organisation for European Economic Co-operation
PRO	Public Record Office
PUSD	Permanent Under-Secretary's Department (FO)

RAF	Royal Air Force
SACEUR	Supreme Allied Commander, Europe
SEA	South-East Asia
SEACDT	South-East Asia Collective Defence Treaty
SEACOS	South-East Asia Chiefs of Staff
SEATO	South-East Asia Treaty Organisation
S of S	secretary of state
tel	telegram
UK	United Kingdom
UNESCO	United Nations Educational, Scientific and Cultural Organisation
UN(O)	United Nations (Organisation)
UNWRA	United Nations Works and Relief Agency
US(A)	United States (of America)
USSR	Union of Soviet Socialist Republics
WAITS	West Africa Inter-Terrritorial Secretariat
WEU	West European Union
WFDY	World Federation of Democratic Youth
WFTU	World Federation of Trade Unions

Principal holders of offices 1951–1957: parts I–III

1. *Ministers*

(a) *Cabinet ministers*

Prime minister	Mr W L S Churchill (KG 24 Apr 1953) (26 Oct 1951–5 Apr 1955) Sir Anthony Eden (6 Apr 1955–9 Jan 1957)
Lord president of the Council	Lord Woolton (28 Oct 1951) Marquess of Salisbury (24 Nov 1952–29 Mar 1957)
Chancellor of Exchequer	Mr R A Butler (28 Oct 1951) Mr M H Macmillan (20 Dec 1955–10 Jan 1957)
S of S foreign affairs	Mr R A Eden (KG 20 Oct 1954) (28 Oct 1951) Mr M H Macmillan (7 Apr 1955) Mr J Selwyn Lloyd (20 Dec 1955–27 July 1960)
S of S colonies	Mr O Lyttelton (28 Oct 1951) Mr A T Lennox-Boyd (28 July 1954–14 Oct 1959)
S of S Commonwealth relations	Lord Ismay (28 Oct 1951) Marquess of Salisbury (12 Mar 1952) Viscount Swinton (24 Nov 1952) Earl of Home (7 Apr 1955–27 July 1960)
Minister of defence	Mr W L S Churchill (28 Oct 1951) Earl Alexander (1 Mar 1952) Mr M H Macmillan (18 Oct 1954) Mr J Selwyn Lloyd (7 Apr 1955) Sir Walter Monckton (20 Dec 1955) Mr A H Head (18 Oct 1956–13 Jan 1957)

(b) *Cabinet Committees*

(i) *Committee on Commonwealth Membership*

The Committee was established by a Cabinet decision of 14 Apr 1953. It sat between May 1953 and Sept 1954.

S of S Commonwealth relations (chair), lord president, S of S colonies, minister of state, FO (Mr Selwyn Lloyd), minister of labour and national service (Sir Walter Monckton), parliamentary under-S of S Commonwealth relations (Mr J G Foster), secretary to Cabinet.

(ii) *Committee on Colonial Policy*

The Committee was established by the prime minister in Oct 1955. It continued into Macmillan's prime ministership.

Prime minister (chair), S of S foreign affairs, S of S Commonwealth relations, S of S colonies, minister of defence.

(c) *Junior ministers*

(i) *Colonial Office*

Minister of state	Mr A T Lennox-Boyd (2 Nov 1951)
	Mr H L D'A Hopkinson (7 May 1952)
	Mr J H Hare (20 Dec 1955)
	Mr J S Maclay (18 Oct 1956–16 Jan 1957)
Parliamentary under-secretary of state	Earl of Munster (5 Nov 1951)
	Lord Lloyd (18 Oct 1954–18 Jan 1957)

(ii) *Commonwealth Relations Office*

Parliamentary under-secretary of state	Mr J G Foster (3 Nov 1951)
	Mr A D Dodds-Parker (18 Oct 1954)
	Mr A H P Noble (20 Dec 1955)
	Lord J Hope (9 Nov 1956–18 Jan 1957)

(iii) *Foreign Office*

Minister of state	Mr J Selwyn Lloyd (30 Oct 1951–18 Oct 1954)
	Marquess of Reading (11 Nov 1953–17 Jan 1957)
	Mr H A Nutting (18 Oct 1954–3 Nov 1956)
	Mr A H P Noble (9 Nov 1956–9 Jan 1957)
Parliamentary under-secretary of state	Marquess of Reading (31 Oct 1951–11 Nov 1953)
	Mr H A Nutting (31 Oct 1951–18 Oct 1954)
	Mr A D Dodds-Parker (11 Nov 1953–18 Oct 1954; 20 Dec 1955–9 Jan 1957)
	Mr R H Turton (18 Oct 1954–20 Dec 1955)

2. *Civil servants*

(a) *Secretary to the Cabinet*	Sir Norman Brook (1947–1962)

(b) *Colonial Office*

(i) Permanent under-secretary of state	Sir Thomas Lloyd (1947–1956)
	Sir John Macpherson (1956–1959)

(ii) Deputy under-secretary of state

Sir Charles Jeffries (1947–1956)
Sir Hilton Poynton (1948–1959) } joint
Sir John Martin (1956–1965) } joint

(iii) Assistant under-secretary of state

J M Martin (KCMG 1952) (1945–1956)
A B Cohen (1947–1951)
C G Eastwood (1947–1952; 1954–1966)
W L Gorell Barnes (1948–1959)
J J Paskin (1948–1954)
J B Williams (1949–1953)
S E V Luke (1950–1953)
W B L Monson (1951–1964)
E Melville (1952–1961)
A R Thomas (1952–1964)
C Y Carstairs (1953–1962)
P Rogers (1953–1961)
H T Bourdillon (1954–1959)
A N Galsworthy (1956–1965)

(c) *Commonwealth Relations Office*

(i) Permanent under-secretary of state

Sir Percivale Liesching (1949–1955)
Sir Gilbert Laithwaite (1955–1959)

(ii) Deputy under-secretary of state

Sir Saville Garner (1952–1956)

(d) *Foreign Office*

(i) Permanent under-secretary of state

Sir William Strang (1949–1953)
Sir Ivone Kirkpatrick (1953–1957)

(e) *Treasury*

(i) Permanent secretary

Sir Edward Bridges (1945–1956)
Sir Norman Brook (1956–1963) } joint
Sir Roger Makins (1956–1960) } joint

(f) *Defence*

(i) Permanent secretary

Sir Harold Parker (1948–1956)
Sir Richard Powell (1956–1960)

3. *Chiefs of Staff*

First sea lord

Sir Rhoderick McGrigor (1951–1955)
Earl Mountbatten (1955–1959)

Chief of imperial general staff	Sir William Slim (1948–1952)
	Sir John Harding (1952–1955)
	Sir Gerald Templer (1955–1958)
Chief of air staff	Sir John Slessor (1950–1953)
	Sir William Dickson (1953–1956)
	Sir Dermot Boyle (1956–1960)

4. *Select list of ambassadors, high commissioners and governors*

Ambassador to the United States	Sir Oliver Franks (1948–1952)
	Sir Roger Makins (1952–1956)
	Sir Harold Caccia (1956–1961)
Ambassador to France	Sir Oliver Harvey (1948–1954)
	Sir Gladwyn Jebb (1954–1960)
Ambassador to the UN	Sir Gladwyn Jebb (1950–1954)
	Sir Pierson Dixon (1954–1960)
Ambassador to the North Atlantic Council	Sir Christopher Steel (1953–1957)
Commissioner-gen in South-East Asia	Mr M J MacDonald (1948–1955)
	Sir Robert Scott (1955–1959)
High commissioner in Malaya	Sir Gerald Templer (1952–1954)
	Sir Donald MacGillivray (1954–1958)
High commissioner in South Africa	Sir John le Rougetel (1951–1955)
	Sir Percivale Liesching (1955–1958)
Gov of Cyprus	Sir Andrew Wright (1949–1954)
	Sir Robert Armitage (1954–1955)
	Sir John Harding (1955–1957)
Gov of Gold Coast	Sir Charles Arden-Clarke (1949–1957)
Gov of Kenya	Sir Philip Mitchell (1944–1952)
	Sir Evelyn Baring (1952–1959)
Gov of Nigeria	Sir John Macpherson (1947–1954)
Gov-gen of Nigeria	Sir John Macpherson (1954–1955)
	Sir James Robertson (1955–1960)
Gov of Tanganyika	Sir Edward Twining (1949–1958)
Gov of Uganda	Sir Andrew Cohen (1952–1957)

Introduction

I. International relations

In the early 1950s Britain was still the world's third-ranking power. Its production was 50 per cent greater in value than West Germany's and 250 per cent greater than France's. Outside the superpowers it was the only country with nuclear capacity. The range of its overseas commitments and responsibilities greatly exceeded that of any other European power. The British world system of Commonwealth, colonial empire and informal empire still sprawled around the globe, its existence both signifying Britain's international influence and standing and helping to shape Britain's international roles.

This world system, however, was under challenge at many points, and not least in regions where Britain had interests it regarded as vital. Mossadeq of Iran had lately nationalised the Anglo-Iranian Oil Company. A communist guerrilla army was active in Malaya, the main source of the sterling area's dollar-earning primary exports. Meanwhile Britain's principal ally, the United States, did not seem altogether helpfully disposed. Harold Macmillan reflected: 'American aid is almost completely cut off, and they are doing all they can to force down the prices of rubber and tin. There is no hope of any short-term solution of the Persian question, and an immense loss to the balance of payments follows.'[1] It seemed indeed that a gamut of forces, from the superpowers to local nationalists (4, 6), was intent on sapping the British position. Another diarist, Mr Eden's private secretary C A E Shuckburgh, commented in January 1953:

> I ended today extremely gloomy about British prospects everywhere. In Kenya: the Mau Mau. In Egypt and Persia: the Americans refusing to support us. Even Iceland in process of destroying our deep-sea fishing industry. I see no reason why there should be any end to the surrenders demanded of us. International law and the temper of international opinion is all set against the things which made us a great nation, i.e. our activities outside our own territory.[2]

But no-one in the Churchill government had any intention of simply caving in to such pressures. Major power status was not negotiable. The real problem was how to maintain it at affordable cost. Over a lengthy period, and especially during the last decade, there had been a real and measurable diminution of the economic assets and economic performance which had long been integral to British power. Arriving in office in October 1951 during a balance of payments crisis, Conservative ministers had lost no time in appraising the realities. In the very first Cabinet memorandum to be placed before them, the chancellor, Mr Butler, pointed out that the external deficit was growing at a rate of £700 million a year. Coming even before the full financial impact of the rearmament programme ordered by the Labour government could be felt, this deterioration indicated both serious underlying weaknesses and a decline in foreign confidence in Britain's ability to deal with them. The essential problem was 'an overloaded economy' (358). In May 1952 Butler elaborated. 'With shrunken assets we have accepted commitments which are not only far greater than before the war, but many of which are non-productive'. Defence and social welfare were obvious cases in point. The fact was that the creditor nation of 1938 was now a major debtor, having been kept afloat in the late 1940s by an American loan. Despite much new investment, Britain in 1952 had still not recovered from wartime capital losses amounting to a quarter of the national wealth. Terms of trade were adverse; the pound was not strong. One of several essential tasks, in the face of all this, must be to review 'the whole field of our overseas commitments, covering both our present military layout and foreign policy and strategy on which it is based, and also our economic obligations both to Commonwealth and Colonies and to our foreign creditors'. All such commitments needed to be brought into line with Britain's real economic capacity to fulfil them (367; cf 368, 371).

The nature and extent of Britain's overseas commitments were spelt out a few weeks later by Mr Eden. There were three main kinds: those which arose from Britain's geography, such as the defence of Western Europe ('the first priority') and membership of NATO; those arising from the imperial heritage, which included the security of the Middle East, the security and development of colonial territories, and the maintenance of the global system of garrisons and bases; and those flowing from Britain's international position, including a share in resisting communist aggression in Korea and the obligations of membership in international organisations such as UNO and GATT. There were strong arguments against scaling down Britain's involvement in any of these areas. The risks of creating a vacuum which the Soviet Union might fill, or of undermining Britain's perceived value as an ally to America and Europe, were alike unacceptable. It was nevertheless clear, Eden agreed, that 'rigorous maintenance of the presently-accepted policies of Her Majesty's Government at home and abroad is placing a burden on the country's economy which it is beyond the resources of the country to meet'. The task must therefore be to determine how far external obligations could be reduced, shared or transferred 'without impairing too seriously the world position of the United Kingdom and sacrificing the vital advantages which flow from it'. Scrutiny of the options suggested only one, not very surprising, answer: Britain should seek to induce other countries, including Commonwealth allies but above all the United States, to assume a larger share of the common burden. This transfer should of course be effected 'gradually and inconspicuously' (3).

The Anglo-American alliance was the key to much of this. Britain had every interest in keeping the American forces in Europe and in trying to secure comparable military guarantees elsewhere, not least because such arrangements would help Britain to maintain its relatively independent role in the Middle East, the Mediterranean, Asia and Africa. Some ministers, such as the prime minister himself, envisaged a rather grander British role in the alliance. Churchill dreamed of summits where the Big Three would meet again. For him, the special relationship with the United States which had underpinned the wartime effort remained always special, the principal policy-making axis of the Free World—and all the more so after Eisenhower's accession to the presidency in January 1953 (13). Other policy makers had fewer illusions about British clout in Washington, and were sensitive to ways in which American attitudes were in practice distinctly unhelpful. For example, Washington evidently had no intention of offering any relief on interest payments on the

American loan, even though the sum that would be foregone meant *'nothing* in a material sense to the United States' (21; emphasis in original).

But it was plain enough that attempts to shift various burdens on to other shoulders would not get to the root of Britain's economic problems. The search for more thorough-going economic remedies became the dominant motif of Cabinet proceedings. A few ministers argued for expansionist approaches: Harold Macmillan, for example, who in 1952 put the case for an intensive fostering of sterling area trade as both feasible and preferable to restrictive measures (369). There was broad agreement that the main precondition for recovery was massively increased invest-ment in industrial production. But as the Treasury implacably argued, the surplus wealth was not there to be invested. Rather, wealth was being drained by excessive public expenditure at home and abroad. No minister, however, wished to sacrifice his own spending programmes. Macmillan, as minister for housing, was as adept as any at competing for budget share. Eden's specific proposals for economy in his 1952 paper were marginal at best. Indeed, Eden qualified his declared support for the chancellor's case by pointing out in the same paper that various overseas commit-ments, while expensive in themselves, helped generate economic returns in that they secured trade routes, protected investments, stimulated dollar earnings, and guaran-teed the supply of vital commodities such as oil (3). Thus the calculus was perhaps not so straightforward as Treasury accountancy might suggest. In like vein the colonial secretary, Mr Lyttelton, argued for expansion rather than contraction of expenditure in the colonial empire as being of long-term economic benefit to Britain (360). The Chiefs of Staff were similarly able to find grounds for arguing that defence expenditure had some positive economic consequences.[3]

It was defence spending that lay at the very centre of the debate. A huge rearmament programme was in train. There were defence establishments from Gibraltar to Singapore to be maintained. Virtually the entire army was meeting commitments abroad: in Germany, the Middle East, Malaya, Korea, Hong Kong. Successive chancellors argued the costs with successive defence ministers and service chiefs throughout the years of the Churchill and Eden governments. Their debate went to the heart of Britain's dilemma. 'We were all agreed when we took office', Butler declared in October 1952, 'that the defence programme which we inherited was beyond the nation's means. It was based on assumptions about American aid and the strength of our economy which have since been proved false' (9). In the foreseeable future the claims of defence, investment in industrial modernistion, and for that matter social expenditure, would necessarily be competi-tive. Butler prioritised export industry and pressed repeatedly for economies in defence (9, 11). So too, after 1955, did his successor Macmillan, himself a sometime defence minister (22, 23, 24). On their side, the defence ministers and the Chiefs of Staff posed stark alternatives: either the government must provide resources sufficient for supporting Britain's great power status or it must accept that trimming Britain's commitments would reduce that status. The latter alternative, the Chiefs of Staff argued on the basis of a region-by-region analysis, was no alternative at all since all major commitments were inescapable (10; cf 5, 8).

Year by year small defence economies were found, and towards the middle 1950s the end of the Korean war and an improving balance of payments helped ease the pressures somewhat. But there were always new defence contingencies requiring further hard decisions. Colonial crises were among them. By 1953 troops were required in Kenya and British Guiana as well as Malaya. Sir Harold Parker in Defence put it to his minister, Macmillan, that 'the Colonial Office gets into a mess and then asks the Army to help it out. Experience shows that this is a long and expensive business' (16). Macmillan himself believed that NATO's very success in countering the Soviet threat in Europe might lead to Soviet adventurism in the colonial world, and that 'If we are defeated here much of our effort in Western Europe will be wasted' (18). Cabinet agreed that the colonies' defences should be improved in order to reduce the demands on the British Army (15), and in 1955 agreed on a statement itemising 'the role of the colonies in war' (82); although ideas for using colonial troops in wider imperial defence were rejected as not just expensive but technically impracticable (1, 16).

Changes in military doctrine brought new issues into the debate. From 1954 Britain moved towards a defence policy based on the principle of nuclear deterrence, with concomitant reductions in the standing army; a policy which would receive its definitive public expression in the defence White Paper of 1957 (14, 17, 24). There were clear implications in this for the overseas bases and garrisons and hence for imperial responsibilities generally. Thus it was argued of the Suez base that such a 'conventional' military resource was not only destined for obsolescence; it not only tied down three divisions and prevented the buildup of the home reserve; by concentrating so much manpower and *matériel* in one place, it would be excessively vulnerable in the forthcoming nuclear age. Cyprus provided another key illustration of shifting attitudes. Up to 1954 no-one in government questioned the view that the Cyprus base was strategically vital to the defence of British and imperial interests (32, 43). By mid-1956 it was important rather than vital (49, 50). The governor, Sir John Harding, could suggest to the Chiefs of Staff that they might seek an opportunity to educate the Turkish General Staff 'on the effect of the development of weapons and aircraft on the future military value of Cyprus'.[4]

Yet the rethinking of defence policy for the new era did not fundamentally change the character of the economy-versus-strategy debate at Cabinet level. This emerged most clearly in June 1956 when Eden established a Policy Review Committee comprising himself, Macmillan, Selwyn Lloyd (foreign secretary), Sir Walter Monckton (minister of defence) and Lord Salisbury (lord president), to reconsider the whole range of Britain's commitments in the light of, first, the new strategic situation created by the advent of thermo-nuclear weaponry, and second, Britain's continuing economic travails. Placed before the committee was a major document, 'The future of the United Kingdom in world affairs', prepared by officials of the Treasury, the Foreign Office and the Ministry of Defence. Though it added little of substance to the arguments which Treasury ministers in particular had been putting to Cabinet for several years, this paper powerfully reinforced them with the cogency of its presentation and the bluntness of its message.

The paper stated flatly that Britain 'has ceased to be a first-class Power in material terms'. Materially it lagged far behind the United States and the Soviet Union, was in some respects now overtaken by Germany, and would in due course be materially outstripped even by such countries as Canada, China and India, which, unlike Britain, had vast untapped resources. Britain's international power and status had therefore to be based on something other than material strength. Essentially there were only two underpinnings: sterling, which was still the instrument of half the world's trade; and the British nuclear arsenal. But even these assets would not serve to maintain British power if present policies continued. The trouble was that ever since the war

> we have tried to do too much—with the result that we have only rarely been free from the danger of economic crisis. This provides no stable basis for policy in any field. . . . We must therefore concentrate on essentials and reduce other commitments.

Absolute priority had to be given to the maintenance of the international value of sterling. Success in this task would be 'the greatest single contribution we can make to the maintenance of our own position in world affairs and to the success of the policies which the free world is seeking to pursue'. Yet though this was 'a matter of life or death to us', Britain had for ten years run sterling on inadequate reserves 'and thus taken terrible risks'. It had therefore become essential to slash consumption and social investment at home, and to undertake yet another critical scrutiny of obligations abroad. Above all, given the new strategic situation created by thermo-nuclear deterrence, Britain might seek to substitute 'political, economic and information measures, which can be taken at comparatively low cost', for some at least of its foreign military involvements. Such a policy should be pursued in the Middle East and Asia and especially in Europe, where Britain's contribution of conventional forces to NATO constituted by far the most expensive component of its defence policy (21).

In a note of his own to the Policy Review Committee, Eden expressed the main theme a good deal more succinctly, if less apocalyptically: 'We must now cut our coat according to our cloth. There is not much cloth' (25).

Accepting the key assumption that 'the main threat to our position and influence in the world is now political and economic rather than military' (25), the committee focused from the beginning on the problem of reducing military expenditure. Officials were set to work to identify non-military methods of maintaining influence in the Middle East and Asia (27, 53, 66). Ministers concentrated chiefly on Europe, where the critical diplomatic task would be to persuade both Europeans and Americans that what Britain was proposing was actually redeployment in the collective interest, not unilaterial reductions in the British interest (21–24). It was essential to maintain Britain's reputation as a responsible ally, and to that end Monckton stressed the need for simultaneous cuts in social expenditure:

> Our Allies were inclined to believe that the United Kingdom could not at the same time discharge her obligations as a world power and maintain her high level of social security. It was important that we should not give the impression that, in order to preserve all our social expenditure, we were seeking to transfer our military burdens to our Allies (23).

Eden supported this argument. Yet whatever the 'impression' that Britain should or should not try to give, the reality was that a transfer of burdens was precisely what was being contemplated—and precisely what Eden himself had been advocating since his review paper of June 1952.

It is necessary now to look more closely at Britain's involvements—primarily, strategic involvements—in a number of important regions: Europe, the Middle East, Asia and Africa. All of these, in greater or lesser degree, were spheres of British influence. In all of them the relationship between 'influence' and 'commitment' was problematic. And in all of them the interplay of policy and events had implications for Britain's imperial role.

Europe

The defence of Europe, Eden said in 1952, was Britain's first priority. The British role in Europe was thus primarily a military one within the NATO framework. But Britain was also involved economically as a member of the Organisation for European Economic Co-operation, which had been set up as part of the Marshall Plan machinery, and as a member of the European Payments Union. Both these involvements, the military and the economic, would change considerably in later times. But up to the mid-1950s there seemed very little scope for modifying them: not that this prevented Cabinet from musing on the possibilities in the military sphere at least, as has just been noted.

From the very beginning of the government's term, however, Europe posed a wider political problem with large implications for British connections elsewhere. How should the government respond to the continent-based movement towards a 'united Europe'? In opposition some leading Conservative figures had made play with this notion, even as the Attlee government retreated from the prospect of British participation in the movement.[5] But once office was attained, Conservative enthusiasm became much qualified. Churchill argued that while Britain should be in favour of European federation, the European Defence Community and the Schuman Coal and Steel Plan, all of which would strengthen resistance to the Soviet Union while rendering another Franco-German war physically impossible, Britain's own role should be limited to encouraging the process; influence without entanglement. Churchill's sense of Britain's world role was clear: 'Our first object is the unity and the consolidation of the British Commonwealth and what is left of the former British Empire. Our second the "fraternal association" of the English-speaking world; and third, United Europe, to which we are a separate closely- and specially-related ally and friend' (2). To seek to enter Europe would be to compromise more important objectives, and to risk having the United States treat Britain as just another European state.

Yet there were always some ministers who felt that in the longer term the question of association with Europe might have to be reopened, though preferably in a way that permitted both a continuing imperial role and maximal British influence in European affairs. Macmillan in 1954 foreshadowed his own later approaches: ' "Federation" of Europe means "Germanisation" of Europe. "Confederation" (if we play our cards properly) should be British leadership of Europe'.[6] By 1956, with Churchill retired, changing circumstances were strengthening the hands of Macmillan and other conditional Europeanists such as Mr Thorneycroft (president of the Board of Trade) and Selwyn Lloyd. The growing dynamism of the continental economies was a major factor. In 1956 the Policy Review Committee was informed that Germany had re-established its economic position, currently had gold and dollar reserves fifty per cent greater than the central reserves of the whole sterling area, and was almost certainly a large net creditor on external account (21). Even in the early 1950s Britain had found itself losing overseas markets not only to America and Japan but also to continental exporters, Germany in particular. Britain's own industrial growth, into which so much investment had been directed since the late 1940s, depended in quite large measure upon meeting this formidable European competition—but also, perhaps, in gearing export industry much more than before towards the sophisticated markets of Europe itself, with their rapidly growing purchasing power.

The European economic challenge had taken on a new, institutionalised form in 1955 when the Six began their corporate economic life as the Messina Powers, looking ahead to the development of a customs union and other attributes of a common market. What should be the British response? Macmillan and Thorneycroft came up with Plan G, a proposal on suitably 'confederal' lines. There should be a European free trade area which would permit Britain to be associated with the continental European trading zone while not surrendering its preferential trade arrangements elsewhere, notably in the Commonwealth and colonies (387, 389–395). Commonwealth-minded ministers such as Lord Salisbury and Lord Home were uneasy; but Cabinet eventually accepted the case for making an overture to Europe in these terms, and in November 1956 Parliament provided broad bipartisan support.

In the interest of enhancing British influence the European connection was also being reconsidered in the politico-strategic sphere. This was in part a consequence of the post-1954 evolution of military doctrine. In January 1957 Selwyn Lloyd presented a Foreign Office plan for closer alliance with the Western European Union powers, entailing in particular the development of a joint nuclear weapons programme. Only by pooling technology and sharing costs in this way could Britain hope to remain 'a first-class Power with full thermo-nuclear capacity. . . . We should take our place where we now most belong, i.e. in Europe with our immediate neighbours'. This need not lead to any weakening of relationships with either the United States or the Commonwealth and empire; rather it would strengthen the overall Western alliance while also enhancing Europe's independent influence in regions such as Africa and the Middle East (28).

This intriguing vision met, however, a very much cooler reception in Cabinet than Plan G had done. In the last substantive policy debate of the Eden ministry (held in Eden's absence), ministers led by Lord Salisbury reasserted more Churchillian priorities: the preservation of the independent British nuclear deterrent; the maintenance—or rather the urgent repair, post-Suez—of the Anglo-American alliance; and the maintenance of Commonwealth ties (29). In strategic affairs rather more than economic, influence without entanglement seemed still to be the preferred doctrine on Europe.

The historic interest of these two Cabinet debates—the protracted economic one in 1956, the brisker strategic one in 1957—lies in the fact that they set a pattern for the ways in which Britain did, and did not, approach Europe in the years to come. The new Macmillan government made little effort to tighten the politico-strategic bonds, being manifestly more concerned to rebuild the American alliance; but it did pursue, with accelerating momentum, the goal of economic association. Both the 'confederal' EFTA proposal and the subsequent application for full-fledged EEC membership were, of course, rejected by President de Gaulle. But by the early 1970s British membership had been negotiated. Commonwealth and empire paid some of the price for this economic reorientation away from the agrarian South and towards the industrial North. By that time, however, Commonwealth and empire had long since been making alternative economic arrangements of their own.

The Middle East

Oil, the Suez Canal and Soviet proximity combined to make the Middle East a region of critical importance in which, in the early to middle 1950s, Britain was still the dominant foreign power (31, 45, 51, 52). The extent and penetration of British power in both the formal and informal empire were measured especially by Britain's military presence. There were the huge installations in the canal zone, with some 80,000 men occupying a base of some 200 square miles; the air bases maintained under treaty in Iraq; the naval facilities at Aden; and the British command over the Arab Legion in Jordan. There were long established rear bases in Cyprus and Malta. In Libya, following the ending of Britain's post-war administration, a treaty of 1953 established Britain's right to maintain military bases for twenty more years.[7] Further, there were British protectorates over the Persian Gulf sheikdoms.

Many of these positions, however, had lately come under threat of some kind. In May 1951 Mossadeq had nationalised the Anglo-Iranian Oil Company. In October of the same year Egypt had unilaterally abrogated the 1936 treaty (negotiated during Anthony Eden's first term as foreign secretary) under which the British were entitled to hold the Suez base until 1956; thereafter there was growing Egyptian harassment of base personnel and local labour became increasingly difficult to recruit and retain. Saudi Arabia was antagonistic towards the protectorates, and Yemen towards British control of Aden (41; cf 46, 48). The treaty with Iraq would shortly expire. Across the region Arab nationalism was a growing force, fuelled largely by hatred of Israel but directed also at Britain—both because of its obtrusive military-imperial presence and because it had played a part, of a kind, in Israel's creation.

It was not easy for policy makers in London to find appropriate responses. From a very early stage of the Churchill government some ministers argued that defence of the Middle East ought to become an American responsibility, in accordance with the Americans' own Truman doctrine (30). Churchill agreed on the importance of involving the Americans but seemed nevertheless unhappy at the thought of withdrawing from established positions, especially the Suez base: 'Surely we should now confront Neguib resolutely and insist on execution of the treaty till 1956. . . . Of course, what happens here will set the pace for us all over Africa and the Middle East' (35; cf 254). The Foreign Office view, however, in which Eden largely concurred, was that British interests would have to be protected increasingly by diplomatic agreements with the Arab states rather than by the imposition of armed force, and that sources of possible conflict must be minimised (38). The Suez base was at once the most expensive military commitment and the most likely source of local conflict. On the wider regional level, the FO hoped that an Egypt better disposed towards the United Kingdom by a Suez base deal might also take part in negotiations for some sort of Arab-Israeli accord. For these reasons Eden worked hard to reach agreement with Neguib and later Nasser on terms under which Britain could depart the base. His essential conditions were three: that Eygpt would agree to international control of the Suez Canal; that Egypt would join Britain in a multilateral treaty for defence of the Middle East against external (ie Soviet) threat; and that Eygpt would permit British reactivation of the base in an emergency (31, 33, 38, 39, 42). At the same time plans were drawn up for a Middle East Defence Organisation (MEDO) which, London hoped, the Americans would approve and take part in (42; cf 78, 81). And in December 1952 Cabinet decided to transfer Britain's regional military headquarters from Suez to Cyprus and to build up the defence facilities on the island even as Suez was scaled down (34; cf 43, 44, 49, 50).

The record of British achievement in all this was very mixed. Firstly, although the Americans did join Britain in bringing Iran back under Western influence, principally through a CIA-inspired coup against Mossadeq in 1953 and the subsequent installation of the Shah, the resulting commercial and political benefits flowed as much to the US as to Britain. Secondly, the Americans took the position that they would join in negotiations with Egypt only if invited by the Egyptians. No invitation transpired, but the US in any event seemed more interested in smoothing its own relations with the Arab world—by providing for example aid and weaponry to Egypt—than in supporting British objectives (36).[8] Thirdly, although the British did finalise a Suez evacuation agreement with Egypt in October 1954, it was without securing Egyptian accession to a MEDO.[9] Fourthly, when Britain finally managed to engineer the Baghdad Pact in 1955 it was a MEDO much reduced, with only Turkey and Iraq, and later Iran and Pakistan, acceding. The pact aroused the intense opposition of Nasser, who saw it as a British device to divide the Arab world and undermine Egyptian leadership of the region. At the same time it hardened him against participating in Arab-Israeli negotiations; thus one of Britain's regional policies undercut the other. Meanwhile the Americans remained aloof from the pact, greatly reducing its military credibility. Shuckburgh, by now the FO's under-secretary for the Middle East, noted their reasoning: 'First, they think the accession of Iran has made the Russians very sensitive to the Pact and very much afraid that Western air bases may be set up in this limitrophe country. Second, they set store on not driving Nasser more deeply into Soviet arms'.[10] This was two months after Nasser had arranged a weapons deal with Czechoslovakia.

In 1956, two Arab leaders in succession struck telling blows against the British position. On 1 March, under great pressure from Nasserite forces to distance himself from the British, the Hashemite King Hussein of Jordan dismissed General Glubb from his post as commander of the Arab Legion. Shuckburgh recorded Eden's reaction: 'A E took me aside and said I was seriously to consider reoccupation of Suez as a move to counteract the blow to our prestige which Glubb's dismissal means'. As Shuckburgh saw it, 'Everything in a mess, and the Arabs hating us more and more'.[11] In June, the Foreign Office was still advising the senior ministers on the Policy Review Committee that the preservation of British interests in the Middle East, and above all the security of oil supplies, 'depends more upon our being able to obtain the friendly co-operation of the producing and transit countries than upon the physical military strength we can deploy in the area. . . . It is increasingly a political rather than a military problem' (21). As noted above, this was a view Eden himself had frequently expressed, not least as a justification for closing the Suez base. But then on 26 July—only weeks after the last British troops had left Suez; only days after Britain and the United States had finally refused to fund construction of the Aswan high dam; and for that matter, only three days after the Policy Review Committee had received its report on 'non-military methods of promoting United Kingdom interests in the Middle East' (53)—Nasser nationalised the Suez Canal Company.

The policy review was shelved. For the better part of the next four months, the Suez issue absorbed virtually all of the time and energy of the most senior policy makers. Cabinet and its Egypt Committee appear to have adopted from the outset the view that this was a life or death issue for Britain as a great power, and to have accepted that military action might have to be taken—if necessary, by Britain going it alone (54). Eden's press adviser, William Clark, recorded him as saying in mid-August: 'people still talk about the danger of our alienating India, or worrying Africa, but the fact is that if we lose out in the Middle East we shall be immediately destroyed'.[12] Through August, September and October Britain, the United States and their major allies searched for diplomatic solutions. The Americans warned repeatedly against the use of force. But the Chiefs of Staff prepared contingency invasion plans, and reservists were mobilised. On 24 October the innermost group of British ministers reached covert agreement with the French and the Israelis on a French-devised plan for Israel to invade Egypt with Britain and France subsequently intervening to 'separate the combatants', occupy the Canal zone, and if possible overthrow Nasser. This plan went into effect with the Israeli attack of 29 October. During the following week Britain and France bombed Eygptian airfields, and in defiance of American, Soviet and United Nations calls for a ceasefire, went ahead with paratroop and seaborne troop landings. On 6 November the full weight of American disapproval made itself felt, in the form of a warning that unless there was a ceasefire by midnight the US would block an IMF loan which Britain needed in order to support the heavily threatened pound. Within hours, Britain and France had agreed to a ceasefire (56). Under continuing American pressure, Cabinet agreed on 30 November to an unconditional withdrawal. All British troops were evacuated by 22 December. Eden's premiership lasted another eighteen days.

Documentation of the aftermath of the Suez crisis lies beyond the scope of this volume.[13] But even before the end of the Eden premiership it was plain that Britain's international standing had been much damaged and that a major remedial effort would be required. At the United Nations there had been near-unanimous outrage and condemnation of the Anglo-French-Israeli action. International hostility was most vividly shown by the willingness of the United States to collaborate with the Soviet Union—this in the week of the Soviet invasion of Hungary—in an effort to curtail the operation. In the Middle East itself, Britain's position had obviously been weakened by the fact that Nasser had demonstrated, with such brutal clarity, what could be done. There was a significant difference here between Suez and earlier British reversals in the region. The abandonment of the Palestine mandate, the Iranian nationalisation, the dismissal of Glubb; in different ways all these events had exposed Britain as an emperor less than fully clad. What made Suez different was that this was the crisis in which the British, along with their collaborators, tried to re-establish a lost position by sheer force of arms. Failure at Suez was thus doubly humiliating.

And yet Britain's inability to crush its Egyptian tormentor did not signal to the policy makers of the day that Britain's *general* position in the Middle East had become untenable. Reviewing the strategic situation, the Chiefs of Staff concluded that although the value of the Cyrenaica facilities had been shown to be very limited, since Libya had not permitted their use in the crisis, the value of Cyprus and Malta (55) was if anything enhanced. EOKA notwithstanding, there seemed as yet no reason why the British position should not be maintained in these Mediterranean bases for as long as seemed necessary. In Jordan, Iraq, Aden and Kenya, bases, facilities and troop deployments remained in place (57). The Anglo-Jordan treaty continued. So did the Baghdad Pact. Influence in Kuwait and other Gulf sheikdoms seemed sufficient (47). Britain still had Middle Eastern policy cards it could play, for example the construction of a South Arabian federation (46). All these dispositions and plans were carried through into the post-Eden era.

Asia

Britain's strategic concerns in the Far East had to do primarily with countering the perceived threat of communism. Hong Kong, *entrepôt* and garrison city, was poised on China's flank—'the only British territory . . . contiguous with the Iron Curtain' (68)—and policy makers were deeply conscious of its vulnerability even as economic constraints and changing security doctrine led them secretly to plan reductions in the garrison (60, 68). But the main worries focused on South-East Asia. Singapore was of high strategic importance as a naval base and communications hub. Malaya, with its tin and natural rubber, had critical economic significance, enhanced by the Korean war which greatly increased international demand for these commodities. Malaya, however, was undergoing a war of its own, with the British army as yet unable to prevail over a guerrilla army of local Chinese communists. One of Mr Lyttelton's first actions as colonial secretary was to refashion Britain's approach to this war, notably through the appointment of General Templer as high commissioner and commander-in-chief with a brief to devise new counter-insurgency strategies (341, 342).

The government's policy for Malaya, Singapore and other colonial territories—Sarawak, Brunei, North Borneo—had also to take account of disturbing trends in the wider South-East Asian region. Burma, Thailand, French Indochina and Indonesia were all seen as unstable and under various degrees of threat from Chinese or local communism. 'The rice of Siam and Burma was of the greatest importance to our own territories, and for this and other reasons, Communist control . . . would make the situation in Malaya incomparably more difficult' (58; cf 405). By 1953 the military situation in Malaya was improving; but at the same time, that in Indochina was becoming critical. Ministers observed the deepening predicament of the French military with both concern and frustration. 'The root of the evil in Europe and Indo-China', Churchill felt, 'is the French refusal to adopt two years national service, and send conscripts abroad as we do. Their political infirmities have prevented them from doing this and they have so weak an army that they can neither defend their own country nor their Empire overseas' (59). A year later, with Dien Bien Phu on the brink, Lord Salisbury lamented the colonial powers' dilemma: by succumbing to pressures to grant self-government, they handed power to people who, however much they disliked communism, lacked the will to resist it (62). France was of course not only a fellow imperial power but Britain's most important ally in Europe. In 1953 Britain nevertheless refused to divert military manpower and resources from Malaya to assist the French, a decision deplored by the secretary of state for war but pragmatically endorsed by Churchill: 'we were quite right not to dissipate further our own limited and over-strained resources' (59).

Perforce, Britain's concerns over Indochina were expressed chiefly at the diplomatic level. By 1954 the future of Indochina was a major issue in Anglo-American relations and had become interlinked with plans for a collective defence treaty for the whole South-East Asian region. In contrast to the roles America and Britain would adopt in the Suez crisis two years later, America was by far the more hawkish of the two on Indochina, basically because of the intensity of the Americans' sinophobia. With the French army apparently beyond rescue, Mr Dulles could still propose a last-minute American military intervention and seek British collaboration in this adventure. British ministers would have none of it, looking rather to Geneva and a negotiated peace that would be underwritten by all five major powers including the Soviet Union and China (61). This was indeed Eden's agenda at the Geneva conference of April–July 1954, where he played a large part in securing an outcome which conceded the northern half of Vietnam to the Viet Minh as the price to be paid for peace in the country.

There could of course be no assurance that the peace would be a lasting one, or that the settlement in Vietnam might in some way contain the spread of communism in South-East Asia more generally. Hence the matter of constructing a multilateral regional defence pact was pursued with some urgency. Seeking to foster both its American and its Asian connections, Britain sought once again to play the role of moderating power. Certainly the British were convinced that a pact was necessary and that it should incorporate military planning machinery (64). They also thought it essential that Britain be fully involved in it, not least to compensate for their rather pointed exclusion from the ANZUS treaty of 1952.[14] Yet as the British commissioner-general in South-East Asia warned, the problem was not just to protect non-communist Asia from China and from local communist insurgents; it was also to check the growing 'misunderstanding and hostility' between Asia and the United States before their differences became 'irreconcilable' (63). Britain's role then was to support the creation of SEATO, which grouped America, Britain, France, Australia and New Zealand together with Pakistan, Thailand and the Philippines in a loose-knit defence treaty, while also seeking to conciliate the major neutralist countries of the 'Colombo powers' group, especially India. In this latter respect, however, British diplomacy was not altogether successful. The major Colombo countries were sharply critical of SEATO and went on to convene the Bandung conference of April 1955, which condemned imperialism and launched the non-aligned movement with India and Indonesia cast in leading roles (19).

But the South-East Asian epicentre, in the eyes of British strategists, was always Malaya. Securing Malaya was not only of the greatest importance in its own right. It also tied in with the global objective of demonstrating to the Americans Britain's determination to help itself, in which lay 'the greatest hope of securing United States co-operation in the long run' (64). At the same time, Malaya posed a classic late-colonial problem. As the Cabinet Defence Committee noted in December 1954, Britain had a 'declared policy of bringing about the independence of Malaya in due course'—but this could be seen as 'to some extent inconsistent with our strategic aim of building up the strength of Commonwealth forces in Malaya as a focal point for the defence of South-East Asia'.[15] Government acknowledged that doubts did exist, for example in Australia and New Zealand, about the long term strength of Britain's commitment to defence of the peninsula after decolonisation. But the commitment was real enough (347). The negotiation of Malaya's independence was linked with the negotiation of a defence agreement, independence being achieved in August 1957 and the agreement being concluded two months later.[16] Six years on British troops would find themselves once more on active service in Malaysia—not, in the event, against Chinese communism but against Indonesian *konfrontasi*.

'Burden sharing' remained an essential theme. Ensuring the security of Malaya meant, among other things, working towards involving the Australians, the New Zealanders and the Malayans themselves in Malaya's defence, and was seen in London as compatible with moves to reduce the size of Britain's own garrison (67). Eden's

1956 Policy Review Committee confirmed the objective of pruning military commitments in Eastern Asia as a whole. The corollary was to find ways in which interests might be preserved and influence exercised through other channels: representation, information services, training programmes, education programmes, and above all economic development schemes. An official committee pointed out to the Policy Review Committee that the Asian expenditures of CDC, CD(&)W and the Colombo Plan combined would amount to less than £5 million in 1956–57, compared with some £51 million of military expenditure (66). British governments of both parties had been enthusiastic about the Colombo Plan in its inaugural phase, seeing it as both a framework for development and a prophylactic against communism (397), but neither government had devoted substantial resources to it. According to the official committee, Britain had 'lost many opportunities' for involvement in Asian development: opportunities that the Soviet Union and China had been willing to exploit (66). Yet it would be far from easy to expand development spending, to judge by the attitude of the Treasury which under both Butler and Macmillan was forever trying to rein in expenditures under this head (423, 434). Whether or not the cuts in the defence budget which the new doctrine of deterrence would supposedly bring could help finance increases in the Commonwealth and colonial development budget was one of the many unresolved issues bequeathed by the Eden administration to its successor.

Africa
Africa south of the Sahara was clearly of lesser strategic importance than Europe, the Middle East or Asia. Nevertheless, in London's world view it was far from unimportant. Britain's formal imperial commitments were more diverse and territorially widespread in Africa than in any other continent, embracing, in the early 1950s, seventeen dependencies—a *mélange* of colonies, protectorates, trust territories, high commission territories and a condominium—whose joint populations comprised more than three-quarters of the population of the entire formal empire. In much of Africa Britain stood more or less alone as the major power, since of all Britain's traditional regions of interest this was the one in which the United States felt least need to play a part. And there were certainly strategic problems to worry about: the defence relationship with that difficult Commonwealth partner South Africa; the implications of Sudanese independence and the forthcoming Italian withdrawal from Somalia for local security; the possibility of Egyptian, and with it Soviet, influence spreading in Africa, especially as colonial territories acquired more responsibility for their own affairs. To a degree the general problems of African defence were linked, in British eyes, with the critical problem of Middle East defence, and this in itself enhanced their significance. These issues will now be briefly reviewed.

    South Africa had a powerful yet contradictory presence in London's thinking about Africa. On one hand, as a wartime ally, Commonwealth country, trading partner and the continent's strongest state economically and militarily, South Africa had always to be taken into account and sometimes into consultation. The close 'empire' bonding of the Smuts era was already some years in the past by the early 1950s; but responsible ministers in London, notably Lord Swinton, believed that the broad relationship with South Africa was still good (142, 143). On the other hand, British authorities had always feared that South African expansionism might erode their own power in the continent—whence a long-standing tradition of British policies intended to block the Union's regional ambitions (among other purposes). Conservative ministers such as Swinton, Lyttelton and Lord Ismay, no less than their Labour predecessors, were acting in this tradition when they endorsed the argument that Central African federation would help thwart Afrikaner imperialism (302); maintained the policy of keeping Seretse Khama in exile (303); and resisted South African pressures for the incorporation of the High Commission Territories (304).

The contradictory forces shaping the relationship could be seen most clearly in the matter of regional defence. Both sides wanted defence co-operation but each finally baulked at the other's key desideratum. On their side, the British sought above all a South African undertaking to provide troops for the defence of the Middle East if and when required. But this the South Africans were unwilling to give, being, as ministers saw it, 'obsessed with the dangers to internal security in the Union and neighbouring territories' and so preferring to keep their forces at home (80). Their counter-proposal was for an 'African defence organisation' in which South Africa and the colonial powers would jointly police the continent. Among senior British ministers only Swinton was attracted to this idea, thinking that it might 'get South Africa away from the Hertzog idea of neutrality' (72; cf 77). But the Foreign Office, the Ministry of Defence, the Colonial Office and their respective ministers combined in their distaste for a proposal which seemed likely to alienate Britain's European allies, upset Middle East policy, have unfortunate repercussions in colonial territories and be of scant military value anyway (73, 74, 76, 78, 81; cf 145, 148).

The issue which crystallised the argument was Simonstown. Both sides looked to an agreement which would transfer authority over the Simonstown naval base from Britain to South Africa, with Britain retaining a right to use the base. Churchill fretted at this weakening of a British position (one which he had himself settled by treaty with Smuts in 1921) 'at the same time as we are giving up the Suez Canal' (71), and it was true enough that the renegotiation of Simonstown was of a piece with the Suez withdrawal and other policies designed to transfer burdens and reduce costs. But the government's underlying objective was still to preserve Britain's status and protect its vital interests, and hence the British negotiators sought to exchange their concession of Simonstown for the desired South African commitment to Middle East defence. For their part, of course, the South Africans tried to link their own concession of residual British rights at Simonstown to their proposed African defence organisation. Stalemate was avoided because in 1955 both sides needed—as they had not in the 1951 negotiations[17]—to bring the Simonstown issue to a conclusion. And this they did. But in the end neither side proved able to budge the other on the broader issues; each had to settle for only a token version of what it wanted. Instead of a defence organisation, South Africa got the promise of a logistics and communications conference. No innovation this; there had been two such conferences already (69). But the British fared no better, securing merely a South African promise to set up a task force 'for use outside the Union' (80, 81).

For the British, the failure to achieve the larger goal was the more frustrating in that it compounded their other difficulties in sharing the burden of Middle East defence. Not only had the Americans stayed militarily aloof; by the mid-fifties even the closest Commonwealth allies, Australia and New Zealand, with all their economic and strategic interest in the canal, preferred, like the South Africans, to keep their forces in their own region.[18] And there was little compensatory comfort to be found in areas of Africa that lay closer to the Middle East. It was not practical logistics, or economics, to build up a substantial military force in Kenya (70, 75; cf 84). Britain did have a strategic interest in the Horn of Africa, specifically the Somaliland Protectorate which in May 1956 the Chiefs of Staff judged to be of increasing importance 'in view of recent developments in the Middle East' (90). But the British position in the Horn did not look especially secure. In 1954 the government had accepted Ethiopian claims to the Haud region and had withdrawn troops. This had created a minor power vacuum and opened up arguments over other disputed territories (97). The Italians were already committed to leaving Italian Somalia by 1960, thus significantly reducing the joint European presence (88, 89). Selwyn Lloyd explored, though with little hope of success, the idea of trying to persuade the Italians to stay on (94). For his part the colonial secretary, Mr Lennox-Boyd, revived Ernest Bevin's concept of a greater Somalia,[19] to be created by agreement between Britain, America, Italy, France and Ethiopia; yet another burden-sharing plan, in which the aim would be 'to maintain not *British* influence as such but *joint Western* influence' (97, emphases in original; cf 98). The Suez crisis diverted Cabinet's attention from this grand Colonial Office scheme. It was eventually considered in February 1957, but received short shrift from ministers who felt, much as Bevin's colleagues had done in 1946, that it would serve only to unite the Americans, French, Italians and Ethiopians in opposition to Britain's manoeuvres.[20]

The other main cause of anxiety among policy makers concerned with African security was the evidence of the Egyptians' efforts to spread their influence, and the possibility that this would open the way for Soviet penetration. The independence of the Sudan in January 1956, Lennox-Boyd felt, carried the risk that Egyptian influence might extend to the borders of British East Africa (83). The same fears applied in Islamic Somalia. In early to middle 1956 the African Department of the Foreign Office became convinced that the Soviets had a 'concerted plan', using Egypt as a bridge, to contact rebel movements and communist networks in French North Africa and penetrate 'southwards' (87; cf 85, 86, 91, 93). Over in West Africa there was already a Soviet presence in Liberia, and it had to be supposed that Moscow would seek diplomatic relations with independent Ghana (86). Britain had long since devised propaganda counter-measures against the Soviet propaganda offensive in African colonies (7, 12), but the new thrust appeared to indicate that the struggle might move onto the organisational plane with attempted Soviet infiltration of African parties, trade unions and other political institutions. This prospect sounded alarm bells in Washington and Paris as well as in London (86, 92, 99). Towards mid-year the State Department floated the idea of a committee of American, British, French and perhaps Belgian officials to consider how best to combat Soviet subversion in Africa. FO officials saw merit in this suggestion: 'It is to our advantage that the Americans should be encouraged to take an interest in the Colonial territories in Africa' (95). However the proposal foundered, interestingly enough, on resistance from the Colonial Office. 'We still have to educate the C.O. in the dangers of Communism!' observed one FO official.[21] But it seems distinctly unlikely that the CO's resistance to the American proposal reflected any complacency about Soviet activities, or about communism generally, in Africa. Indeed, reports in 1953 of growing communist influence in trade unions in the Gold Coast had been of major concern to CO officials. It was made plain to the governor, Sir Charles Aden-Clarke, that Lyttelton would not be able to recommend to Cabinet the adoption of the Gold

Coast White Paper on internal self-government until Nkrumah's government had dealt effectively with the alleged communist threat.[22] Much more likely is that the CO was acting upon its institutional interest in preserving exclusively British authority in British territories. It was partly, perhaps, in order to sort out such inter-departmental differences that an Official Committee on Counter-Subversion in Colonial Territories was established later in the year under the chairmanship of Sir Norman Brook, the Cabinet secretary.[23]

Thus stood security matters in Africa at the close of Eden's premiership. Even though Britain was perhaps more nearly in command of events in colonial Africa than in any other large region, new and potentially very serious security problems were emerging. Hence a firm policy was seen as essential. The official long term programme for colonies might be devolution of authority, but policy makers generally agreed that security and intelligence matters must be insulated from this process until the last possible minute—which might well be subsequent, rather than prior, to independence (82). Symptomatically, Lennox-Boyd was still refusing in mid-1955 to contemplate allowing Gold Coast ministers to take part in international discussions of African defence.[24]

Colonialism as a problem in international relationships

So far, this account of the international context of Britain's colonial policy has dealt mainly with high-policy strategic issues. But colonialism was itself an issue in Britain's international relationships. W G Wilson of the Colonial Office's International-al Relations Department argued in 1954 that the antipathy towards colonialism among many influential governments 'is such that it is a concrete and important factor affecting Her Majesty's Government's ability to maintain satisfactory foreign relations and to achieve the objectives of United Kingdom foreign policy'. Moreover, this antipathy had become so strong that colonial policy itself could not be pursued without taking it into account, especially because of its galvanising effects on indigenous nationalist politicians (136). For reasons that differed in different cases, colonialism was a complicating factor in relationships that mattered a great deal to Britain: with the major allies such as the United States and France, with Common-wealth partners such as India and South Africa, and with the United Nations.

The United States was historically anti-colonialist, as State Department officials regularly reminded Foreign Office and Colonial Office officials at the Anglo-American talks on colonial problems held in Washington each autumn. Certainly some senior Americans were receptive to British arguments, firstly that the empire was an important element in Britain's global power without which Britain would be a less effective ally, and secondly that premature decolonisation would create instabilities and opportunities for communist subversion in new nations. But as the Americans pointed out, their own revolutionary past disposed them sympathetically towards other peoples seeking self-determination. The United States could not openly support European colonialism if it was itself to win the confidence of new nations, or to play a brokerage role between colonial and anti-colonial powers (101, 102, 106, 108, 110). Dulles personally regarded European colonialism as an obstacle to the unity of the free world in the most important anti-colonial struggle of all, that against Soviet imperialism (107). Colonialism was in any event obsolescent. C H Phillips of the State Department explained to British officials in 1956 that in view of the force of nationalism and the weight of world opinion, the US had to work from the premise that colonialism 'could have only a limited duration. . . . Intelligent accommodation was the only answer'. It was preferable that Britain should act 'a little too early rather than a bit too late' (110).

Much of the discussion between officials of the two powers concerned policy towards the United Nations, where European colonialism was under persistent and bitter attack from the Arab-Asian and Soviet blocs. A Foreign Office official, C P Hope, noted in 1952 that whereas the Colonial Office's 'main anxiety' was 'to prevent the U.N. weakening our hold on our colonies', the Americans 'regard the United Nations as a major instrument of their foreign policy and they are anxious lest dissension on colonial questions will so divide the United Nations as to weaken it seriously' (100). The Americans thus played a double game. Under both Democrat and Republican administrations, they used the UN Trusteeship Council as an instrument for chiding the colonial powers and seeking friends among the Arab-Asian countries (109). But the diplomatic requirements of the Anglo-American alliance ensured that they generally refrained from attacking British colonialism in the most important public forums, the General Assembly and the Security Council.

They nevertheless argued that the European powers should be willing to defend their colonial policies in these major forums rather than hide behind their interpretation of Article 2(7), the 'domestic jurisdiction' clause. Thus in 1952 the Americans were prepared to concede the UN's competence to discuss French policy towards Tunisia (101), a decision which caused alarm in Whitehall and led to a Cabinet discussion.[25] And in spite of a personal plea from Churchill to Eisenhower (322), the Americans did not oppose the Greeks' inscription of the Cyprus issue on the General Assembly agenda in 1954 and later years.

It was not only in the UN, Hope observed, that 'the basic American dislike of colonialism . . . harms us'. Writing in 1952, he instanced the Persian oil dispute (100). In the immediately following years, the colonial problem on which American attitudes most worried British policy makers was Cyprus. The government's strategic plans for the Middle East and Mediterranean dictated an adamant refusal to contemplate self-determination for Cyprus (321).[26] It was hoped that Washington would broadly support the British position (106; cf 32). If only, Macmillan wrote, other nations would see that 'Cyprus is not and never has been a colonial problem' (327). But by the later part of 1954 it was plain enough that for reasons of both anti-colonial principle and State Department pragmatism (deriving for example from the need to maintain influence in Greece), the Americans were leaning towards the notion of ultimate self-determination for the island.[27] In a Cabinet memorandum written on his last day as foreign secretary, Eden was concerned that the US would 'find it increasingly difficult to support us as long as we refuse to pay homage to this principle [self-determination]', and raised the question of whether Britain should after all 'show that we do not exclude the prospect of self-determination for Cyprus'.[28] In subsequent discussions Cabinet began preparing the ground for this shift of policy, which was confirmed in the 1956 plans for a Cyprus settlement (328–333; cf 49–51). Though the primary reason for the shift probably lay in the government's own strategic rethinking, it is fair to suppose that sensitivity to American views also played some part.

The Americans did not wish to unsettle the broader alliance, and to some extent this consideration offset their irritation at the continuing imperial pretensions of the alliance's junior partner. But in the fraught circumstances of the Anglo-American rift of late 1956, American self-restraint was abandoned. Dulles attacked colonialism at length at a press conference on 1 October.[29] Eisenhower himself described Britain's Suez policy as 'extreme colonialism'. Some in the CO had earlier assessed the Republican administration as 'markedly more sympathetic' towards British colonial policy than the Democrats had been (105). The American anger over Suez could have left them with few such illusions.

With France, Britain's ally at Suez, colonialism created complications of very different kinds. France was of course the 'other' major colonial power; the question was how far co-operation, or at least consultation, on colonial problems should be attempted. Since an Anglo-French agreement of 1948, A B Cohen (head of the African Department) and other CO officials had held regular discussions with their French opposite numbers on matters of shared concern, especially in Africa where several British and French territories were contiguous (114). At France's request, these meetings were supplemented in 1952 by annual talks at ministerial level (113, 115, 116, 123). But the relationship was never very easy or productive. Practical Anglo-French collaboration in Africa seldom extended beyond fairly minor administrative, technical and economic matters, in spite of efforts, spearheaded on the British side by Cohen, to broaden the area of practical co-operation and to establish joint consultative machinery in the field (114, 118, 124). The main problem lay in the political gulf between the two powers' approaches to broad policy. The French took every opportunity to voice concern at the pace of political change in British West Africa and the Sudan, openly fearing repercussions in their own territories (113, 119). Whitehall recognised that Gold Coast policy in particular 'makes much more difficult the French policy of *l'union francaise*'.[30] But Whitehall itself was not altogether united. The FO, with an eye to the broader relationship, did not wish to antagonise the French unduly on colonial issues (117, 120–22, 129). The CO, however, was determined to resist French pressure for co-operation on larger colonial policy if that meant slowing the pace in West Africa; 'the whole idea of subordinating Colonial policy to foreign policy or of forming a defensive alliance with other Colonial powers is repugnant to us' (119).

Nor could Britain afford to let association with less liberal colonial powers—not just France but also Belgium, and even more, Portugal and Spain (126–128)—compromise its relationship with the United States. This was the reason why, in response to French and Belgian requests for multilateral talks with the Americans on colonial problems, CO and FO made common cause in insisting that bilateral talks were 'more effective'.[31] And yet the CO was quite prepared to exploit the illiberalism of other colonial powers when it suited it, especially in dealing with the UN. Unlike the British, the Belgians were always willing to mount intransigent defences of colonialism in the General Assembly; and as E G G Hanrott, a CO principal, noted, 'of course their intransigence suits us, since it adds an element of toughness to our common colonial position' (126).

Of all the powers with which Britain had close and important relationships, it was India which spoke out most vehemently against colonial 'toughness', and indeed against imperialism in any form. And no other critic had quite the same ability to get under Colonial Office skin. To Lyttelton, Nehru was a man 'in whom the term Colonial or Colonialism produces a pathological and not an intellectual reaction' (133). When in 1953 Nehru made an Amritsar day speech pledging India's moral support for the Mau Mau freedom fighters against their British oppressors, Sir

Thomas Lloyd, permanent under-secretary of state at the CO, expressed outrage: Nehru's 'calumny' was 'improper, provocative, and . . . intolerable'. Cabinet agreed that a strong official protest should be made (131, 132).

Yet Nehru had to be taken seriously. India was the influential leader of the non-aligned movement and, as Sir John Martin, assistant under-secretary of state at the CO, recognised, a formidable player of the UN game: 'the brains of the Arab/Asian bloc. . . . She has had so much intimate experience of our susceptibilities on Colonial issues that she is able to put a finger on our weak spots with unerring accuracy' (134). But more than that: London had to acknowledge that India's membership of the Commonwealth, together with the existence of Indian communities in East Africa, Central Africa, the West Indies and Fiji, gave New Delhi a legitimate interest in British colonial policy. In Whitehall the Commonwealth Relations Office in particular pointed this out (130, 139). Not unlike the FO in relation to France, the CRO believed that what was important was to avoid straining the overall relationship. Hence it sought to minimise confrontations with India over colonial issues (135). It thus played some part in moderating the CO's preference for a harder line. The CRO saw to it, for example, that the protest over Nehru's Amritsar speech was delivered privately, rather than publicly as the CO had wanted. It also toned down a Cabinet paper which the CO had initiated with the aim of providing an *exposé* of Indian anti-colonialism; after it had been through the CRO the paper dealt merely with Indian communities in the colonies and required no Cabinet decisions (136–138). The CRO was the relevant policy department for the Indian relationship, and there was little the CO could do to override it.

The other Commonwealth country which took an acute interest in colonial policy was South Africa. In general the South Africans perceived the Conservative government's colonial policy as much more acceptable than Labour's, or so British men on the spot reported (144). Nevertheless the South Africans could not be taken for granted. Trying to assess how they might react to the emergence of self-governing black states in Africa was a quite major preoccupation in the Whitehall of the 1950s. In 1951 Malan had signalled his perturbation at the speed of change in the Gold Coast.[32] During Churchill's government, successive Commonwealth relations secretaries invested diplomatic effort in explaining Britain's West African policy to Pretoria (142).[33] From 1952 it was thought also that the prospect of Sudanese self-government could become a sensitive issue for the South Africans, especially if the Sudan asked to join the Commonwealth: something to which South Africa, Swinton believed, 'would certainly not agree' (260). There were some characteristic differences in Whitehall over these matters. Some in the FO thought it important to avoid 'arousing the wrath' of South Africa over colonial policy.[34] In the CO, Cohen was 'horrified' by this attitude,[35] while deputy under-secretary of state Sir Charles Jeffries wrote, in a notably far-sighted minute, 'My own view is that the U.K. is already committed to the policy of a parti-coloured Commonwealth, and that if we have to choose between going back on that policy or losing South Africa from the Commonwealth we must face the latter' (259).

In the event it was not the Sudan that forced the issue, since the Sudan steered clear of the Commonwealth; it was the Gold Coast. From mid-1955 ministers and officials worked on the problem of how to propose the Gold Coast's admission to the Commonwealth while also ensuring that South Africa remained within the fold (146, 147). After a good deal of diplomatic sallying, enigmatic utterances by the South

African leaders and tactical moves at the Commonwealth prime ministers' conference in July 1956, this dual goal was achieved; though to Eden's considerable ire, Strijdom contrived to present his agreement to the Gold Coast's admission as acquiescence in a *fait accompli* rather than as freely given consent, thereby, no doubt, saving political face at home (149–154; see also 279).

The final matter to be considered in this section is Britain's general policy towards the United Nations, whose institutions, and indeed whose very existence, structured so much of the international debate on colonialism. Britain's essential aim was to prevent the establishment in UN doctrine of any principle of accountability of colonial powers to the UN. This had been the Labour government's policy and it was reaffirmed by the Conservative Cabinet in July 1952.[36] Conceding UN competence in colonial affairs would be to play into the hands of anti-colonial powers, encourage colonial agitators, and generally upset the delicate political process of devolution of power (157, 164). To forestall such threats, Britain and the other European colonial powers, with the not always welcome support of South Africa which had South-West Africa to consider (141, 166), took their stand on the principle that colonial policy was a matter of domestic jurisdiction. But, as H T Bourdillon, assistant under-secretary of state at the CO, told Portuguese officials, 'it was not certain that legal opinion would uphold this view and we were not anxious to have it tested in the International Court of Justice'. Britain had therefore found it 'tactically advantageous' to transmit technical information on non-self-governing territories and to work with the Trusteeship Council, the Committee on Information, and the Fourth Committee.[37] The government's working procedure, in short, was to accept the world's interest in colonial affairs as a fact of life and to co-operate with the UN, but only within limits strictly defined by the British.

Up to the mid-1950s, Britain's UN representatives were generally able to succeed in blocking any stratagems in the various UN bodies—on questions of self-determination or human rights, for example (155, 163)—whose outcome might have been to establish a principle of accountability, either *de jure* or *de facto*. Held in reserve was the weapon of 'walkout', to be used if the UN ever managed to outflank Britain's own manoeuvres and force a debate on an issue such as self-determination for Cyprus (159, 160, 168). But the governments of 1951–1957 had no occasion to use this weapon; somewhat to the relief of the Foreign Office, which considered it a device ill befitting a major power.

This is not to say that Britain's UN defences were impregnable. By the time of Eden's premiership there were ominous signs of change. The accession of seventeen new member states in 1955–1956 served mainly to strengthen the Arab-Asian group and the Soviet bloc. Britain countered by co-forming a 'European group' (167), but no longer found it easy to secure a blocking third in order to head off unwelcome discussions in the General Assembly. The FO, with its internationalist concerns, felt that Britain might have to learn 'to accept defeat gracefully' on colonial issues (170). This was not a view that the CO could welcome. But late in 1956 the CO finally succumbed to various pressures—especially from the Americans, but also from the British foreign secretary—to take the risk of mounting a defence of colonial policy in the Assembly, even though this might appear to be admitting accountability.

Then came the Suez invasion, and the exercise immediately became unthinkable again. As Bourdillon observed, 'any attempt to draw attention in the United Nations to our Colonial policy would merely result in a furious onslaught' (172; cf 169, 171).

Thereafter, Britain's position as a colonial power at the UN became increasingly embattled. One particular irony deserves mention. Ghana's forthcoming independence was to have been trumpeted in the General Assembly speech as proof of the virtues of British policy and as reason for other countries to moderate their criticism. In fact, Ghana's triumphal arrival on the international scene in March 1957 had a further galvanic effect on the anti-colonial lobby. And the irony compounded as time went on: the more that colonial policy was 'fulfilled' in the creation of new states, the more the attacks on that same policy gained international voice.

II. Politics and administration

Colonial policy and its context

At the time of the 1951 election the rationale of colonial policy was broadly settled and uncontroversial, having been outlined in a series of statements by both the wartime coalition government and the post-war Labour government. In essence the declared intention was to guide colonial territories towards responsible self-government within the Commonwealth while also ensuring that political advancement did not outpace economic and social progress. Within days of the Conservative election victory Cohen had advised Lyttelton to make a parliamentary statement pledging continuity along these lines, partly in order to allay fears in West Africa, and Lyttelton had agreed to do so (173, 174).

Policy was not just settled; it had an internal dynamic, premised on notions of what it was intrinsically about—good government, development, preparation. Virtually all of the CO's plans and decisions can be seen as resting on an adherence to such notions (see eg 199, 200, 201). But this is not to say that colonial policy was self-contained as a policy area or that its momentum was somehow self-sustaining. From Cabinet's point of view it was one rather minor element in the whole complex of policy-making, and the considerations which shaped it were, finally, considerations of national interest. Colonies were historically acquired appurtenances of Britain *qua* major power, and policy towards them was one aspect of Britain's continuing world role—interlinking with foreign and defence policies in ways which the first section of this essay has sought to illustrate, and with economic policy in ways which will be considered in the third section. This second section will focus more closely on colonial policy's 'internal dynamic', while still aiming to keep the broader policy framework in view.

The Conservative governments of 1951–1957 knew well enough that Britain's commitments had somehow to be tailored to match a contracting resource base. As Eden put it, 'there is not much cloth'. The problem was how to maintain major power status nevertheless. Within the colonial empire, British influence was unchallenged by other major powers. It was not, therefore, a sphere in which *Realpolitik* dictated any need to compromise British status. Several colonies played extremely important parts in Britain's global defence and communications systems, and for most of these self-government was simply not contemplated. Nor (occasional 'emergencies' aside) were colonies seen as an especially significant drain on resources—certainly not by comparison with the areas of truly massive spending, defence and social services. To the contrary: some colonies were seen as important net contributors to resources, through supplying the home market or by earning dollars for the sterling area. In general, then, colonial policy was not an area in which ministers went out of their way to find ways of diminishing Britain's role. The inevitability of political change in colonies was recognised but Cabinet thinking about it was rather negative, based largely on considerations of how to keep colonial political change 'under control' so that Britain's influence would not suffer damage.

It was a period in which not a single colonial territory actually arrived at independence. The only country to do so was the Sudan, a charge of the FO, and the timing of its independence (1 January 1956) reflected not the fulfilment of some process of tutelage but rather the exigencies of Middle East policy (254–261).[38] In this same period white settlerdom was given greater power over the Africans of Central Africa in a federation which, it was hoped, would evolve into a new 'British dominion' (302, 305–310). Policy makers in quest of more viable political and economic structures contemplated closer association of territories in several other regions even when local opinion seemed to be generally opposed to it: East Africa (281–283, 288–291), South-East Asia (345), the Caribbean (334, 335, 340), South Arabia (46), the Horn of Africa (97). Territories that gave trouble—Malaya (341, 342), Kenya (286, 287), Uganda (293, 294), British Guiana (336, 337), Cyprus (324, 326)—were dealt with by *force majeure*; the generally successful outcomes of the strong measures taken in these places seemed to confirm that British power still served as the final arbiter of events in the colonial empire.

It was in keeping with this general approach that when in October 1955 Eden decided to set up a standing Cabinet committee on colonial affairs, he defined the committee's task as 'to assist the Cabinet in controlling constitutional development in Colonial territories' (196). No less indicative was Cabinet's decision two months later that the word 'independence' should no longer be used in references to the constitutional development of colonies, since this term might encourage the idea that territories could in due course secede from the Commonwealth (197, 198). Lord Salisbury went on to argue, in a paper of May 1956, that governors must be given greater powers to control disorder so that change might be kept on the tightest possible rein (252, 253).

One factor underlying these attitudes was, no doubt, an adherence among some ministers to older imperialist values formed during Britain's heyday as a great power. Churchill himself had a strong sense of imperial nostalgia and was accordingly out of sympathy with the devolutionary aspects of post-war colonial policy. After his Cabinet made its first decision to transfer a small instalment of political authority (to the Gold Coast, in February 1952 (266)), Churchill proceeded to draft (though in the event he did not send) a telegram to the prime minister of South Africa: 'I hope you recognise that the decisions taken about the Gold Coast are the consequences of what was done before we became responsible'.[39] Towards the end of his premiership he still seemed to feel the same way, to judge by a brief which Brook wrote for him on the likely evolution of the Commonwealth: 'I recognise that this policy may be unpalatable to you. But . . . however much we may sigh for the past, we have to live in the present—and to plan for the future' (193). At the time, one of Churchill's own plans for the future was to extend Parliament Square in order to create 'a truly noble setting for the heart of the British Empire' (214).

Yet probably more important in determining attitudes across the government as a whole was a conviction that colonial stability was materially significant for both domestic economy and broad imperial strategy—a belief in which the Conservative Cabinet differed little from its Labour predecessor. Policy moves designed to accommodate nationalism, for example, had to be weighed against these broader considerations. It was from a Foreign Office perspective that Eden worried about the 'pretty dangerous political gallop' in West Africa (175). Eden endorsed in 1952 a Foreign Office paper written in the aftermath of the Iranian oil crisis and intended 'to suggest means by which we can safeguard our position as a world power, particularly in the economic and strategic fields, against the dangers inherent in the present upsurge of nationalism'—this force being seen as an 'attempted sapping at our position as a world power by less developed nations' (4). Though the CO believed that colonial nationalism, at least, needed to be sympathetically understood, and that it could be guided by British policy into broadly acceptable channels (6), Churchill's Cabinet would certainly have agreed with the FO's prescription that Britain must forestall 'nationalist demands which may threaten our vital interests' by whatever means seemed necessary.

There is another way in which the contextual constraints on colonial policy can be observed, and that is in the interaction of the CO with the rest of Whitehall. It was the given role of CO officials to argue for colonial innovation and the commitment of metropolitan resources to colonies. In these endeavours they frequently met bureaucratic resistance rooted in the different responsibilities of other departments. The CRO was concerned to look after the relationships with South Africa and the Central African Federation on one hand and India and Pakistan on the other, and was sometimes at loggerheads with the CO when these relationships impinged upon colonial policy. Likewise the FO in dealing, for example, with the United States, France, and the United Nations. Senior officials in Defence argued that far too much money was spent on 'social uplift' in colonies and far too little on security (16). The Home Office firmly resisted CO notions that it might take over responsibility for Malta on the Channel Islands model (317–319). Most significant of all was the Treasury, forever seeking to prune expenditure on colonial development and colonial services (384–386, 421–424, 433, 434, 449–451, 468–478). In general the Treasury did not believe that colonies, however distressed they might be financially, could have any privileged claim on the Exchequer, especially in a time of domestic stringency and dollar shortage. In the Treasury view it should in fact be a major aim of policy to wean colonies off metropolitan government funding altogether (194). Indeed, as will be discussed in section III, finance was in some ways the greatest of all the contextual constraints on policy.

To a degree, then, it might have seemed a wonder that colonial policy 'advanced', in accordance with its own devolutionary dynamic, at all. Yet the Conservative Cabinets of 1951–1957 did acquiesce, in their fashion, in the settled policy. From time to time it fell to the colonial secretary to argue in Cabinet that the moment had come for an instalment of devolution in, for example, the Gold Coast (265, 271, 275), Nigeria (271, 274), British Honduras (339), Malaya (348, 352), Singapore (355, 356), or Cyprus (330). With whatever reluctance in some quarters ('Alan shows signs of giving way all along the line', Lord Salisbury grumbled to Eden apropos Singapore in 1955 (351, note 1)), Cabinet accepted the colonial secretary's advocacy on each occasion that such matters came before it. Here, arguably, was colonial policy, as ideologically conceived, working itself out: these decisions were incremental steps towards a goal which no government would now repudiate.

Nevertheless, as was noted, Cabinets acquiesced 'in their fashion'. Generally, the government was much concerned to establish and demonstrate that devolution was not to be confused with abdication or with any loss of the will to rule. Devolutionary policy was much hedged about with qualifications. In a major Cabinet paper of 1954 it was argued that the only territories likely to be eligible for independence in the next ten to twenty years would be (in anticipated order of independence) the Gold Coast, Nigeria, the Central African Federation, a Malayan federation and a West Indian federation. At least twenty territories could never expect independence, so that devolution of power to them would never extend beyond some measure of internal self-government: the list included not only strategic outposts such as Malta, Cyprus and Aden, but also very poor countries such as Somaliland, and very small ones such as the Gambia and Fiji (192).

Qualifications and restrictions were evident also in the nature of the responsibilities actually transferred, at least up until about 1955. Here the case of the Gold Coast is instructive.[40] Though the Gold Coast was by no means the first British-ruled territory to gain independence in the post-war era (and not even the first in Africa), it was widely seen in the early 1950s as a pioneer, providing a kind of test case for CO methods of tutelage that had been formulated in some detail in the preceding few years. But the Cabinet in 1952 authorised the title of 'prime minister' for Nkrumah, and associated changes, on the understanding that this would amount to no more than 'an appearance' of greater authority for African politicians (265, 266). Lyttelton in 1953 conceived of the evolving Gold Coast constitution as a 'stucco facade' and the African leaders as 'nominal' ministers who should not necessarily have access to sensitive information such as intelligence reports (267). He believed that operational control of the police should remain in the governor's hands and was accordingly sceptical of CO proposals for graduated transfer of the police power, for example by way of a police commission on the British model. Certainly the CO shared ministerial worries about the future of the police, fearing that post-colonial governments might use the police politically—creating 'police states' rather than 'policed states' (244). Through the early 1950s Jeffries and other officials grappled with the problem of how to instil the British 'police idea', and hunted about, without much success, for administrative devices that would be acceptable both to the minister and to the incumbent British colonial police commissioners (244, 247–250).

The imperative of 'control' naturally carried greater weight in the areas of defence and internal security than anywhere else. The critical problem in any devolutionary policy—how and when to pass the point of no return on such important powers—was kept on the shelf during most of 1951–1957; which for the Gold Coast meant until the end of the dyarchy.

Qualifications and restrictions of a rather different kind were evident in policy for territories with minority British populations, in particular the 'settler' territories of East and Central Africa. In these places there could be no question of undiluted majority rule; rather, multi-racial power sharing must be the long term goal (296). Such a policy, Lennox-Boyd told Cabinet's Colonial Policy Committee, was necessary in order to save the European and Asian communities from being 'swamped' by Africans (led perhaps by demagogues), and 'offered the best hope in the end of maintaining European influence'. The committee granted Lennox-Boyd's request for authorisation to steer developments in East and Central Africa 'away from the early introduction of universal suffrage for Africans in the direction of systems of qualitative democracy', involving, for example, property franchises and communal rolls. This policy would undoubtedly come under attack from 'left-wing opinion' in

Britain and from countries such as India, but ministers were prepared to weather this.[41]

But the other face of the policy should also be noted. For multi-racialism to work properly, Europeans too would have to accept restrictions on their local political power. This quickly became a sensitive issue between the Conservative government and the European leaders of the Central African Federation which the government had established in 1953. Certainly Sir Godfrey Huggins, Sir Roy Welensky and their colleagues had many friends in the Conservative party and were regarded by Cabinet as rightfully in charge of the Federation's governance.[42] But Cabinet in 1956 accepted the advice of Home and Lennox-Boyd that European demands for early independence under virtually untrammelled white rule must be resisted. Instead Cabinet offered to 'enhance the status' of the Federation, but only in symbolic ways, and re-affirmed that the dispensation in Central Africa should remain in place at least until the federal review conference of 1960 (307–309). So palpably ambitious were the federal politicians, however, that in late 1956 some CO officials were already turning their minds to the question of how Britain should deal with a possible unilateral declaration of independence in Salisbury (312).

Thinking ahead

Policy makers in the early 1950s often remarked on the 'speed' of change in the Gold Coast (Eden's 'pretty dangerous political gallop'), and were sensitive to its possible impact on colonial politics elsewhere: in French Africa, as already noted, and more especially in British West Africa and East Africa (262, 264, 268–270). Sir John Macpherson, governor of Nigeria, had to be reassured that one reason why Britain did not simply apply 'sanctions' in the Gold Coast was that such measures 'would have even graver repercussions on our position in Nigeria than acquiescence (though it would not be tame acquiescence) in what we all of course recognise to be, theoretically, over-hasty political advance'.[43]

Yet the sense of speed was fairly localised. West Africa was *sui generis*. Across the broad range of the colonial empire there was no expectation that devolutionary policy was going to accelerate markedly. The time scale still seemed open ended.

Given this sense that there remained considerable time in hand, it is perhaps remarkable that policy makers engaged to the extent that they did in thinking about the major changes that must eventually come. For various reasons the early 1950s was a period of much official and ministerial rumination on such matters as the future of the Commonwealth, the future of the smaller territories, the future of the Colonial Service, and the future of the Colonial Office itself.

Of most concern at Cabinet level was the problem of Commonwealth evolution. The goal of colonial policy was not just self-government; it was self-government within the Commonwealth. Thus colonial and Commonwealth policies were always connected. The Commonwealth was regarded somewhat proprietorially as a major part of the British world system, and policy makers were quite frank in their view that the accession of ex-colonies to Commonwealth membership would enable a continuation of imperial-style power by other means. Indeed, to permit secession of new states from the Commonwealth on the Burma model 'would be tantamount to adopting a policy of deliberately weakening our own strength and authority in world councils by a series of self-inflicted wounds' (192).

Nevertheless some senior ministers, notably Churchill, Salisbury and Swinton,

D

were much concerned at the potential impact of new members on the *nature* of the Commonwealth. Its character had of course already been significantly altered by the accession of India, Pakistan and Ceylon, and by India's self-transformation into a non-aligned republic in 1950; Swinton lamented the retention of India in the fold 'on terms which not only exclude allegiance, but allow a critical neutrality. . . . I doubt if we shall ever escape the unhappy results of that fatal decision' (177).

Concern over these issues had been already ventilated during the Labour government.[44] In 1952–1953, however, some quite new factors brought the problem of Commonwealth evolution very much back on to the agenda. The realisation in 1952 that there might one day be a Sudanese application for membership concentrated minds wonderfully on the question of whether the Commonwealth might be altered beyond repair by an intake of African members (258–260). Cabinet was moved to set up a committee, with Swinton, Salisbury and Lyttelton as the major members, to consider the whole issue of criteria for Commonwealth membership.[45] Shortly afterwards, Malta abruptly demanded to be transferred from Colonial Office purview to the Commonwealth Relations Office. Lyttelton explained to Cabinet that the Maltese, 'as a European people boasting a civilisation older than our own, resent their "Colonial" status, more particularly their inclusion in the same constitutional category as the peoples of the African Colonies' (313). Malta was not perceived in London as a candidate for political independence, chiefly because of the great strategic significance of the Malta dockyards but also because of the island's tiny size. London was, however, well disposed to the idea of making some special arrangement for Malta, and the idea of integration into the United Kingdom, with administration perhaps handled by the Home Office, was seriously considered (314–320). But this issue served also to widen the concern about the Commonwealth's future, since it raised in acute form the question of what to do about the whole range of small, supposedly non-viable territories (202–207). Thus the possibility of developing some sort of multi-tiered Commonwealth structure to accommodate different 'classes' of member became a dominant item on the agenda of Swinton's committee and the supporting committee of officials under Brook (179, 180). The whole exercise provides another study in the government's felt need to maintain control and to prevent possible damage to British interests arising from the centrifugal forces that were beginning to emerge.

Swinton himself was much taken with the idea that the best way to preserve the essence of the old Commonwealth (and to keep South Africa in) was to create a lower form of membership for the lesser lights: 'a special class of Commonwealth country, which has complete control over all its internal affairs, but which leaves the United Kingdom Government responsible for its external affairs and its defence' (177). Lyttelton too favoured the idea of some sort of intermediate status, and told Swinton's committee that the colonies, or at least the political moderates therein, were unlikely to object strongly since they were 'principally interested in self-government. It was unlikely, for example, that the Gold Coast would wish to conduct its own foreign affairs' (179).

At the official level, the Colonial Office and Commonwealth Relations Office toyed with a variety of formulae that might meet these ministerial wishes and, it was hoped, satisfy the aspirations of the second-class members: they could be grouped under a special committee of the Privy Council, they could become 'States of the Commonwealth' or a 'Colonial Council' (203–206, 210, 211). Other departments were sounded out, and, over time, came up with predictable views on the criteria for first-class membership. For the Treasury, a country could be a full member only if it was not financially dependent on another member (194). For the Ministry of Defence, a full member should be willing and able to undertake some external defence commitment, such as the provision of a brigade 'for use in a major war'.[46]

This exercise was certainly revealing of contemporary attitudes. Even at the time, however, there were several who perceived it as quite unrealistic. Most of the senior officials were dubious of the two-tier idea from an early stage. Brook's official committee decided firmly against it in July 1953, chiefly on the ground (and with the Gold Coast much in mind) that 'to announce an inferior kind of membership would certainly cause resentment' and might well lead to countries preferring to take their independence outside the Commonwealth (186). Further, there would be many countries which did not clearly and obviously belong in one category rather than the other; distinctions in such cases would be even more invidious.

Officials then set out to persuade their ministers, on the basis of an interim report written by Brook. Lyttelton conceded the point fairly quickly. He had come to perceive that the West African politicians were after all 'showing an unwelcome interest' in defence and foreign affairs (183), and could see that it would be impossible to exclude them from these areas after independence. Swinton held out for several months longer. But his eventual acceptance of the officials' arguments left the way clear for Brook to write a lengthy final report that was essentially a recognition of the inevitable: Britain would simply have to live with a formally egalitarian Commonwealth having a majority of non-white members. But no doubt Britain would work more closely with partners of its own choosing in sundry respects, as was already the practice with regard, for example, to the sharing of military intelligence (187, 188, 192).[47]

In December 1954 Cabinet devoted an entire meeting to Brook's report. It is clear from the record of proceedings that there was deep disquiet: 'several Ministers said that they greatly regretted the course of Commonwealth development which was envisaged . . . It was unfortunate that the policy of assisting dependent peoples to attain self-government had been carried forward so fast and so far' (195). But in the end Cabinet accepted the report's recommendations, and it is fair to see this as a moment of some symbolic significance. Cabinet perceptions of 'the Commonwealth' would not be quite the same again (cf 26).

Related to this exercise was a continuing strain of official thinking on future administrative arrangements for handling Commonwealth and colonial affairs. An important stimulus was the prospect of a decline in career opportunities in the CO within the lifetime of officials currently employed. It was Jeffries who most clearly articulated the problem and was most fertile with ideas. One such idea was for a 'Commonwealth Services Office' which would effectively absorb CO personnel into the CRO bureaucracy. The CRO was not impressed (208, 209). Neither department much favoured the idea of a full amalgamation, although both sides increasingly recognised the administrative problems that were brewing (210, 211, 213, 215–218). In 1956 Brook reviewed the issue in a substantial report (215). But this nettle remained ungrasped at the end of Eden's premiership.

The question of the future of the Colonial Service came to seem more immediately urgent and more demanding of attention at top level. This was largely because of the manifest decline in Service morale and a wave of resignations in the pace-setter territories, the Gold Coast and Eastern Nigeria, where African ministers were increasingly exercising authority over British officials. The administratively distinct Sudan Political Service was similarly troubled. Jeffries again took the lead, with a plan for a 'British Overseas Service' which would make Colonial Service expertise available on contract to independent countries as well as colonial. Treasury resisted. A much watered-down version of the plan found administrative shape in Her Majesty's Overseas Civil Service, established in June 1954 (219–226). Colonial officials found little to reassure them in HMOCS, and in 1955 Jeffries returned to the charge. Under his new scheme redundant officials would be held on an unattached list at Treasury expense while alternative employment was sought. Jeffries was backed to the hilt by Lennox-Boyd who saw this as 'the most important issue of all' (240). An epic correspondence between Lennox-Boyd and successive chancellors resulted in another administrative compromise in mid 1956; again, it was not one which fully allayed the Service's fears (227–242).

The CO also tried to plan ahead on key administrative problems in the colonies such as indigenisation and the development of local government. This was not, however, a period which could compare with the late 1940s for sheer energy and creativity in officials' thinking about colonial administration.[48] By and large it was recognised that such matters were now moving beyond direct metropolitan purview. There was nevertheless a good deal of worrying among officials over the question of how far Britain should tolerate a decline in standards as these processes gained momentum (243, 245–246).

And this leads to a much larger question. Was that control over events which the Conservative Cabinet felt to be the *sine qua non* of colonial policy already something of an illusion? As devolution took its course, in however limited and qualified a fashion, how far could the policy makers remain confident that their plans for the colonial empire would remain on track; that theirs would be the decisions that counted?

Two answers are required here. The first is that up until the mid-1950s, Cabinet did appear generally to believe that it still held the whip hand on colonial policy. The multiple pressures generated by the domestic economy, international relationships and colonial nationalism were palpable enough. But they had not acquired the cumulative strength to force any basic policy reappraisal, or even a cost-benefit accounting of empire. It still appeared generally within Britain's power to contain the worst colonial crises militarily; as of 1955 this was the projection even for Cyprus (324, 326). In certain circumstances it was still possible for Cabinet to slow down the devolutionary process or even resume devolved powers if it saw fit, as was done in British Guiana in 1953 (336, 337) and in the new constitution offered to Cyprus in 1954 (321).

No basic reappraisal, then. But the second answer is that certain doubts were being voiced, probably more at official level than at ministerial, about Britain's capacity to prolong a 'firm' colonial policy indefinitely. Partly such doubts reflected the underlying problem of resources. As the wearisome haggling with the Treasury went on, some CO officials worried about the viability of what they saw as a chronically underfunded colonial policy (438). There was also a felt need to avert 'collisions' in colonies and an appreciation that 'sanctions' against restive national-ists were not always going to be a sufficient political device. Lloyd explained to Macpherson in 1953 that Nkrumah was being given more powers in order to 'avoid a head-on clash';[49] Macpherson was quite right to interpret this as a concession to nationalist pressure (269). Cohen in Uganda felt that 'the pace is determined far more by public pressure than by our own opinions of the stage when self-government should be granted' (295). Harding was convinced by 1956 that there was no prospect of securing the Cypriots' co-operation 'unless they had an assurance that the right of self-determination would at some future stage be conceded' (328). A governor's perception of need to come to terms with nationalists could suddenly arise in the most unexpected quarters, for example Tanganyika in late 1956 (298–301). The case for offering concessions rather than applying sanctions was usually clear enough. Sanctions were weapons of last resort and their use was, in effect, an admission of political failure. Moreover, resisting pressures for change could be counter-productive; more sapping of British authority than accommodation might be.

This is not to say that some sort of general argument about the pros and cons of 'resistance' and 'accommodation' was going on among the policy makers, let alone that they were dividing into camps over these problems. All would have agreed that the maintenance of British influence was a key objective. The question was more one of means to this end. Keeping the lid on, the approach for which Salisbury was the main Cabinet-level advocate (252, 253), was one possible means. But CO ministers, having the same objective in mind, were generally persuaded that a degree of flexibility would achieve better results. Thus Mr Hopkinson, writing on the Singapore constitutional crisis of 1955, saw the government's choice as lying between 'a refusal to make concessions with what the Colonial Secretary has described as "bloody and disastrous consequences" and meeting the demand for constitutional advances fast enough to keep the peace and retain a guiding influence over developments' (351, note).[50]

Not that Hopkinson's formulation really addressed the underlying issue of how far Britain remained 'actually' in charge of the agenda of colonial change. Cohen for one, to judge by his statement quoted above, believed that Britain could not have it both ways. Insistence on determining the agenda was becoming politically unrealistic. Further: as colonial politics took on a life of its own, so *a priori* British notions of stages of preparedness became rather marginal to the real issues being negotiated between governments and nationalists in the territories. An official much involved in Gold Coast policy, R J Vile, foresaw in 1954 that the decision on the timing of independence might have very little to do with the country's degree of preparedness; rather, 'the choice before us may well then be one of accepting independence at a certain date because its refusal would create worse conditions than its acceptance' (276). By the mid-1950s there seemed a growing sense in official circles that Britain, even while retaining the power of arbiter, was responding to colonial events at least as much as it was shaping them. Conservative ministers would not have taken much comfort in this; perhaps that is part of the reason why even those ministers who argued for accommodation still tended to use the *language* of control. But there was a major aspect of the problem that could not be ignored. If the precepts of 'preparation' and 'readiness' were not being altogether observed in the constitutional advance of pace-setter territories, did not devolutionary policy begin to look like an extremely risky leap into the dark?

In 1955 and 1956 the CRO's man in Accra, F E Cumming-Bruce, sent back some highly critical secret reports on the corruption, incipient authoritarianism and lack of ministerial calibre that he saw in Nkrumah's government: this after nearly a decade of 'preparation' (277). The Commonwealth relations secretary, Lord Home, was deeply worried by these and other reports and carried his worries right through to Ghana's independence, writing to John Hare in July 1956, 'I am frankly unhappy lest we should be taking too optimistic a view' (277, note), and to his new prime minister, Harold Macmillan, in January 1957, 'I am full of foreboding about the whole Gold Coast experiment'. Macmillan responded: 'I agree'.[51]

The whole idea of readiness was called into question by at least one senior policy maker, the philosophical Jeffries: 'I think there is too much tendency to consider whether these places [the smaller territories] are "ready". . . . Of course they are not, any more than the Gold Coast is "ready" for independence, or than one's teen-age daughter is "ready" for the proverbial latch-key'. Supporter though he was of the traditional policy of devolution by stages, Jeffries could see the force of the counter-argument that the policy could at best 'only maintain a state of uneasy equilibrium. Colonial politicians tend to concentrate attention on securing the next constitutional change instead of getting on with the job. Constitutions are in a state of continual flux and there is no stability' (204). In other words, the lack of readiness might be in part a function of the policy itself.

If so, government would have to base its decisions about transfer of power on criteria other than supposed readiness in the terms in which it had been traditionally understood: stability, maturity, viability. And some few years after Jeffries wrote, that would indeed be the manner in which the formal business of empire would be concluded.

III. Economic and social policies

Economic policies

The connections between Britain's economic problems and its overseas policy have already been noted at several points in this discussion. Butler's chancellorship began in a time of severe balance of payments difficulty and ended in another one. His early calls for retrenchment, and in particular for a review of 'the whole field of our overseas commitments' (367), were echoed in 1955 and Eden's Cabinet agreed to a major review of expenditure, both domestic and foreign, in search of economies.[52] The policy review set up in 1956 aimed to achieve similar goals. Sir Herbert Brittain, second secretary at the Treasury, informed the CO of the special need for restraining external expenditures that might run down the reserves or necessitate foreign borrowing, and stiffly rejected CO arguments that spending in colonies was a special case (384–386).

Besieged by slow growth, shortfalls of export revenue, debt and inflation, the Conservative government combined short-term austerity measures with efforts to stimulate production, especially through investment in the industrial sector. The governments of 1951–1957 were successful to the extent that no devaluation of sterling proved necessary; that in some years, notably 1954, exports did grow rapidly; and that there was a fair degree of domestic industrial reconstruction. Yet this did not mean that Britain's post-war decline *vis-à-vis* its competitors was being arrested. Other economies grew faster; British exports were being priced out of their traditional markets; balance of payments crises recurred. Stop–go tactics were forced upon Cabinet, preventing the implementation of a steady expansionist policy as advocated, for example, by Macmillan in the years before he became chancellor (369).

How, in this context, were the colonies seen? In the first place, they were seen as producers of commodities for the United Kingdom market. This was a role which had grown in importance in recent years, as signified by the post-war 'second colonial occupation' by agronomists, soil scientists, veterinarians and other technical experts whose mission was to boost colonial productivity. One of Lyttelton's earliest requests to his officials was for a Cabinet paper setting out the possibilities of increasing colonial production of the foodstuffs and raw materials that Britain needed, and of re-routing colonial exports 'so that more of their existing production comes to this country instead of going to other less laudable destinations' (359). CO research established that except for a few commodities such as copper, cotton, manganese and sugar, the chances of increasing colonial supply to Britain in the short to medium term were in fact very limited. Much depended on the reciprocal willingness of British public authorities and private firms to invest in colonial production (360, 368). But the attracting of private investment would depend in turn on a more generous Treasury attitude towards double taxation arrangements and depreciation allowances; and the Treasury was distinctly reluctant to yield. It was a familiar dilemma. Lyttelton believed that 'development of the productive capacity of the Colonies could in the long term transform the economic position of the United Kingdom' (360), but, as will be shown, he and his officials were to be much frustrated by the enormous difficulty of mustering the requisite financial and capital goods inputs.

Secondly, the colonies were members of the sterling area. Some of them earned significant non-sterling revenues; in the early 1950s, while Britain, the Commonwealth countries and the sterling area as a whole were running up increasing deficits in their current accounts with the dollar area, the colonies were maintaining a substantial surplus, partly because of the high commodity prices of the time. They were also in surplus on their transactions within the sterling area, especially with Britain. Colonial 'sterling reserves' held in London—technically, debts owed by Britain to the colonies—amounted to around £1000 million in 1952. These were free balances, meaning that the colonies were in principle entitled to draw upon them. That the colonies were not in general applying for the release of these reserves was partly because the import goods on which they might have wished to spend them, especially capital goods needed for development, were in very short supply. Some key United Kingdom goods, such as steel and tinplate, were subject to export quotas and colonial allocations were small indeed. Lyttelton told Cabinet in November 1951 that although it was a sound principle to set aside reserves in prosperous times, 'any further substantial deliberate withholding of purchasing power from the Colonial producer seems to me to be unjustified'. He argued for giving the colonies a higher priority in the allocation of goods under quota; he also proposed that the restrictions on colonial imports from Japan and the USA might be eased (361; cf 363).

No doubt the CO was delighted that the new minister went in to bat so strongly for colonial interests. But Lyttelton's attitude had very soon to be revised. The Commonwealth finance ministers' conference of January 1952 resolved that urgent measures must be taken to halt the deterioration of the sterling area's balance of payments with non-sterling areas. The colonies might be in overall surplus, but they were in increasing deficit with Western Europe and this was contributing to a drain on the gold reserves. Hence Lyttelton was obliged to ask all colonies to reduce the value of their imports from non-sterling sources, especially but not only Europe, by some fifteen per cent (364–366). This measure, in the opinion of Sir Hilton Poynton, deputy under-secretary of state at the CO, was quite inappropriate for territories 'still in a primitive state of development' (370), and it seems likely that Lyttelton privately agreed. More than that: he evidently felt 'that there was a good deal of substance' in accusations that Britain's practice of holding on to the colonial sterling reserves, and making various short-term uses of them, amounted to exploitation (373, note).

In 1953 a Treasury-CO-Bank of England working party met to consider all aspects of the question of the colonial sterling balances. It concluded that the holding of these assets in London 'is in present circumstances inevitable', and of benefit to both Britain and the colonies, but did tend to weaken international confidence in sterling in that it was a component of British indebtedness. So long as the balances were not drawn down 'beyond a certain level', it was probably a good idea that some should now be released for development expenditures while Britain still had sovereignty in colonial territories—for there was no guarantee that successor regimes would spend as wisely (373–375).

These concerns over the use of the colonies' earnings tied in with wider concerns about multilateral trade. As of 1952 the Conservative government remained rhetorically committed to imperial preference (372). But with all Commonwealth countries seeking trade deals wherever they could find them, it was a doctrine much diluted since the time of the Ottawa agreements. Poynton openly doubted its value to colonies (376). In late 1953, with the pressure on the balance of payments somewhat relieved, the Treasury was prepared to argue for the continuation of colonial importing from Japan ('unless we provide Japan with this trade we can hardly hope to induce her not to switch trade to the dollar area') (377). In 1954 Cabinet contemplated a general relaxation of United Kingdom import restrictions, in the knowledge that this would probably hurt West Indian and other colonial producers who had hitherto enjoyed preferential access to the British market for their commodities (378; cf 380). Such measures indicated an increasing distancing of British policy from traditional notions of imperial preference.

The underlying reality for Britain was that the development of industrial export production carried with it the need for markets with technologically advanced needs and high purchasing power, higher than the empire and Commonwealth countries could generally manage to provide. A steady expansion of trade with Europe seemed the natural course to follow. And indeed, by 1956 the volume of British trade with Europe was on the way to overtaking the volume of trade with the United States and the old Commonwealth combined. This was the context in which Macmillan and Thorneycroft launched their initiative for a European free trade area, described earlier. But it needs to be emphasised that the growth of European trade was not meant to preclude the maintenance of empire trade; Macmillan's confederal scheme was essentially intended to give Britain the best of both worlds. Colonial trade was still seen as important, and there was still a concern to provide various kinds of assistance to colonial exporters. In its extended discussions of the review of the General Agreement on Tariffs and Trade in 1955, Cabinet had resolved that Britain should seek a 'colonial waiver' from the treaty's no-new-preference rule—and even that Britain should refuse to accept other treaty revisions unless satisfaction on this point was obtained. It was (382, 383). By the same token, the implications of Plan G for colonial trade were carefully thought through. Existing arrangements were not to be jeopardised. In any case, it would be unthinkable for Britain to cease protecting its colonial trade so long as France refused to do likewise (391, 393–395).

The management of colonial commerce was closely linked with another issue area, colonial economic development. Each was seen as in some degree a function of the other. Trade, especially the import of producer goods, enhanced development. In turn, the government intended that various development projects should generate exports that would serve the wider purposes of the sterling area; Lyttelton more than once stressed this point in circular despatches (411, 413). But the primary rationale of economic development was that it should promote growth and rising living standards *within* the colonial territories. This was, of course, one of the major 'settled' objectives of colonial policy.

It was also, as every government knew, formidably difficult. Selection and implementation of projects were always beset with hazards—political, economic, geographical, climatic, technical. Success was never guaranteed. The groundnuts scheme in particular provided a chastening recent example of development as *débâcle*.[53] Few in the Conservative Cabinet would have put much faith in large-scale public corporations as agents of development anyway. The Overseas Food Corporation was wound up in 1954. Labour's other creation, the Colonial Development Corporation, was critically scrutinised and enjoined to concentrate on potentially profitable ventures (452–456).

CO officials nevertheless had reasonably firm ideas of what colonial development was about. Two main emphases emerge from the documents of the time. Firstly there were large infrastructural projects such as the Owen Falls hydro-electric scheme, the Kariba dam and the Volta River dam. It was intended that these would generate energy for local economies and revenue for local exchequers, and by facilitating the production of commodities (copper and aluminium in the latter two cases), be of value to Britain and the sterling area (409, 430, 435, 436). Secondly there was the broad range of slow, patient and smaller scale work in agronomic research, water control, soil improvement, disease control, technical education, transport and communication development and a host of related matters, whose ultimate general objective was the improvement of agriculture and the conditions of rural life (398; cf 407, 427). It was not then the nature of colonial development that was in dispute. What most preoccupied policy makers was the logically prior and perennially difficult problem of finding the necessary money.

The major financial instrument for colonial development was the Colonial Development and Welfare Act, under which Parliament voted some £10 to £20 million annually in the early 1950s. The current Act was due to expire in 1955. Only too well aware of Treasury views on 'overseas commitments', the CO and its ministers lobbied actively from mid 1953 in order to put the Act's renewal beyond doubt, while also accumulating from the territories a lengthy shopping list of projects in need of funding (412, 413, 417, 419–424). Possibly they were lucky in their timing. In the temporarily less stringent economic climate of the winter of 1954–1955, Butler agreed, after spending 'a fructuous recess' going into the matter, to make £115 million available for 1955–1960 (424). This was not very far short of what Lennox-Boyd had sought.

Nevertheless, it fell far short of the vast sums that colonial development could in principle absorb. All colonial secretaries understood that public money would never be sufficient for the task, and all sought accordingly to attract private capital. Lyttelton, with his City background and connections, gave this effort very high priority. He pressed hard for tax relief schemes for colonial investors; advocated increased local equity in mining firms to make them less vulnerable to 'anti-British' measures, and so more attractive to investors (he had Iranian oil in mind); and unlike some of his colleagues, had few qualms about trying to attract American money into British territories (399–404, 406; cf 360).

The market, however, proved notably unenthusiastic. No matter how great the colonies' need for capital, what counted with private investors was the potential for a good rate of return. There seemed little prospect of that in colonial development in the 1950s. American investors, who would in any case have been interested only in strategic mineral projects, proved all but impervious to persuasion and prospectuses from the CO (402, 404). The only major American investment of the period took the form of outright purchase by the Texas Oil Company of an established enterprise, the Trinidad Oil Company, a transaction which Macmillan advised Cabinet to accept (437). And there was the further factor of political uncertainty. Knowing that the days of British sovereignty were numbered, investors worried about the long term security of colonial investments. By the very nature of colonial policy, this problem had to be expected to increase as time went on. Colonial loans floated on the London money market were seriously undersubscribed in 1953, 1954 and 1955. The Crown Agents asked for a public statement that the British government would guarantee loans to colonies, but this the government felt unable to provide if only because it might seem to indicate a lack of faith in post-colonial stability by the government itself (415, 416, 425, 429).

Rejected by the market, the CO turned back to the Exchequer. Between 1954 and 1956 plans for direct Exchequer loans, withdrawals from the National Debt Fund and colonial savings certificates were tried on the Treasury. They were resisted (418, 426, 428, 432–434, 449). CO officials noted cynically that the Exchequer seemed quite capable of funding new overseas loans if *Realpolitik* required it; apparently Yugoslavia was more important than British colonies (431). At the very end of Eden's premiership, however, the Treasury finally relented on the question of direct Exchequer loans to colonies, offering qualified support for this 'lesser evil' and so opening a path towards the incorporation of this new provision in the next CD(&)W legislation, eventually enacted in 1959 (450, 451).

Settled policy had it that political advance should go hand in hand with economic development. The actuality was that the devolutionary measures of the mid-1950s went virtually unaccompanied by major new development commitments. The idea of a 'Colombo Plan' for West Africa, where political advance was fastest, was explicitly rejected (440, 446, 448). Treasury logic had it that progress towards independence should entail increased efforts by colonies to find their own development finance, whether from international sources such as the World Bank (414) or from their domestic savings (379, note 8). By the same token, metropolitan funding should be tapered off in territories nearing independence (194). Thus CD(&)W assistance, the Treasury argued in 1956 against some demurral from both CO and CRO, should be phased out in the Gold Coast (439, 441–445, 447). Equally, the CDC should undertake no new operations in either the Gold Coast or Malaya. On this matter CO and Treasury were more or less united against the CDC, whose chairman, Lord Reith, they saw as a prima donna who harboured unacceptably grandiose ambitions for his organisation. Reith for his part hated dealing with the 'blasted Treasury' and the 'wretched Colonial Office',[54] and chafed against the bureaucratic constraints on his vision of Commonwealth development (457–467).

For the CO, the struggle for development finance was unremitting and deeply disillusioning. 'We now know', wrote R J Vile in 1956, 'that at some time in the next six to nine months we shall under present conditions come to a grinding halt in the raising of London market loans for Colonial Governments. . . . This is a fantastic situation'.[55] There were those in the Office who felt that development funding had become so squeezed that the very sustainability of colonial policy was in doubt. 'I know that there is a school of thought', Poynton minuted to his minister in July 1956, 'which holds that, if the available resources are too small to go round, we may have to begin to have a deliberate policy of shedding some of our colonial burdens' (438).

Social policies
A standard motif of settled colonial policy was that the advancement of colonies was to be achieved in three interlinked domains: political, economic and social. The last was the province of the CO's social service departments, whose brief was to plan and provide for indigenous populations in such areas as health, education, welfare, labour, training, and community development generally. Although largely based on ethnocentric notions of what was required—Western-style schools, community organisations, vocational associations and so on—their work was well-intentioned, reflecting that strain of humane paternalism which had always been integral to the ideology of trusteeship.

From the point of view of higher level policy makers, however, social development was by the 1950s the lagging priority. Colonial policy was driven hardly at all by welfarist considerations, a great deal by considerations of political and economic gain and loss. Although some colonial problem or other appeared on the agenda for almost every Cabinet meeting in the years 1951–1957, questions of colonial social development never surfaced at Cabinet level except in the most incidental way, and then only because of their connection with economic or political issues.

Part of the difficulty experienced by the social services departments lay in the way the relationship between economic development and social development was in fact perceived by policy makers. In his circular despatch of July 1953, written in anticipation of the new CD(&)W Act, Lyttelton called on colonial governments to give priority to projects which would generate an economic return, out of which social developments schemes might then be financed (413). In effect, D took precedence over W. Within the CO, Poynton argued similarly that the economic development chicken should precede the social development egg (486). Social services department officials such as J K Thompson (community development) and R J Harvey (education) took exception to this view, not least because they saw education, for example, as a necessary condition of successful economic development. The issue of economism versus welfarism was argued out in many a well-reasoned Office minute (486, 487, 492). But for the most part it was the welfarists who felt themselves on the defensive.

'Community development', or 'mass education', had been put on the policy agenda by Mr Creech Jones in a 1948 circular despatch.[56] The essential idea was to socialise apathetic or ignorant people into 'modern' attitudes and work-styles as a basis for progressive social and economic change. In 1952 Lyttelton issued a follow-up despatch to see what progress had been made (480). Little had. Many officials, it seemed, remained unsure about the very meaning of community development. In operational terms it seemed to boil down to training selected individuals for community leadership. But even this was taking place hardly at all outside the Gold Coast and Kenya (479). Much of the trouble lay in the fact that emergent colonial leaders were typically more interested in politics at the centre than in local community leadership programmes—a problem analogous to that which hampered the local government programmes also initiated in Creech Jones's time (cf 484).

Politics was steadily taking command in colonies, and as it did so the CO was experiencing diminishing demand for its services as adviser on colonial social and educational policies. Colonial politicans and civil servants in search of help on such matters were increasingly inclined to engage specialist consultants on an *ad hoc* basis rather than turn to the CO as had long been the practice (483, 489, 494). 'It is possible to look forward to a time, probably not far off, when advice from the Colonial Office ... will not be sought and, indeed, may be unwelcome' (494). One consequence of this trend was that some of the non-official committees set up to advise the secretary of state in these fields were beginning to run out of useful things to do. In 1953, senior officials decided to begin 'rationalising' these advisory structures. Not altogether without resistance from a few of what Jeffries described as 'the home-based starry-eyed' (483), three bodies—the Social Welfare Advisory Committee, the Community Development Committee and the Adult Education Sub-Committee of the Advisory Committee on Education in the Colonies—were merged into one, the Advisory Committee on Social Development. But this became demoralised and by 1956 was barely functioning (481–485, 488–489). The Advisory Committee on Education in the Colonies, once a body of some dynamism, was also experiencing doubts about it own future relevance (490, 494). Educational expertise was still urgently needed, as Sir Christopher Cox stressed (495); but perhaps it would become appropriate to deliver it through different channels. What further complicated the education debate (along with a good many other debates) was the rising of the political temperature in the more advanced territories. Problems such as the establishment of a university in the Central African Federation or the maintenance of educational standards in the Gold Coast and elsewhere had increasingly to be addressed with an eye to political considerations: the fear that new political elites might seek to control educational institutions for their own political purposes; the need to preserve British influence wherever possible (491, 493, 496, 497).

In another area of CO concern, labour, policy debates similarly reflected the increasing salience of political factors. The goal of 'non-political' colonial trade unions, which would concern themselves primarily with industrial relations, was still officially espoused. Yet in many colonies it was clear that trade unions, even those in the most rudimentary stages of development, were already prey to politics. Accordingly a good deal of the discussion in London between the CO's Labour Department, the Trades Union Congress and the Overseas Employers Federation dwelt on political problems. How could the British protect colonial unionism against communist influence? And for that matter, American influence (503–505, 507–510)? The International Confederation of Free Trade Unions was at once anti-communist and anti-colonial; how could British policy exploit the former quality and neutralise the latter (499, 501–502)? And what of the International Labour Organisation? It did much good work but it too had an anti-colonial streak, and it was seeking to extend its influence in African colonies. It seemed on collision course with the International Labour Institute, a body created by British and other colonial powers as an offshoot of their Commission for Technical Co-operation in Africa. But if Britain were to try to defend the ILI against the ILO, it might find itself cast in the undesired public role of partner to South Africa and Portugal, with their inflexible resistance to African political change. By what diplomacy could this issue be resolved (498, 500, 506)? 'Settled' policy provided no ready answers to these new kinds of problems.

Nor was there any obvious way of dealing with a problem as old as imperialism itself and indeed inherent in it: that of race relations. Once again, the new politics was heightening the sensitivity of the issue. For one thing, the emerging indigenous political class was becoming vocal on questions of racial discrimination. For another, there were fears that poor race relations might provide openings for communist subversion (511). The reality was that racial distinctions of various kinds were part of the colonial order. Communal electoral rolls were a standard device. Asians in East Africa could not buy land. Policy in settler colonies looked forward to 'multi-racial' politics, not 'non-racial' politics. Opposition backbenchers at Westminster might urge the abolition of institutionalised discrimination through sweeping changes to the law; the government rejected such ideas as impracticable (512), and was prepared to defend existing practices on a variety of political, administrative and social grounds, including the ground that they were generally in the best interests of the indigenous peoples for whom Britain was trustee.

Overtly racist behaviour, however, was another matter, and much to be deplored. In the early 1950s some in the CO worried a good deal about potentially racist attitudes among the numerous British contract workers and their wives who were going out to Africa as part of the second colonial occupation. W L Gorell Barnes, an assistant under-secretary of state, proposed the compilation of 'a "bible" of guidance on the way to behave in Africa'. This did not eventuate. But the Office, with assistance from the Church of England, did institute a series of instructional courses and seminars through which, by 1956, some 400 Africa-bound Britons had passed—though with what social consequences it is impossible to say (511, 513–515).

Racial issues were not confined to the colonies. Within the metropolitan power itself, nothing brought home the latter-day consequences of imperialism so sharply as did the phenomenon of reverse migration, especially from the Caribbean and South Asia. Transient colonial students, of whom Britain had long experience, were one thing; permanent settlers in quest of work and social services, quite another. The Labour Cabinet had considered the issue, but inconclusively.[57] In 1952 Churchill called for a report, and thereafter 'coloured workers' and 'colonial immigrants' became recurrent items on the Conservative Cabinet's agenda. Especially in the years 1954–1956, Cabinet was the scene of many a struggle between conscience and pragmatism; between liberal principles and worries about electoral backlash; between the belief that colonial immigration was of economic value to Britain and the view that major economic and social problems were being stored up for the future; between the argument that a liberal race policy at home was essential if multi-racial policies were to be pursued abroad, and the argument that if Britain were to enact racially restrictive immigration laws it would only be doing what almost every Commonwealth country and colony already did. Various ministerial and official committees came up with legislative formulae. None proved acceptable. On one hand, Cabinet was unwilling to go public with restrictions based on patently racial criteria. On the other, it felt unable to approve comprehensive restrictions that would have caught immigrants from Ireland and the old Commonwealth in the same net as the South Asians and West Indians (516–526).

Not until 1962, by which time non-white immigration was running at more than 130,000 a year, compared with fewer than 10,000 a year a decade earlier, would a British government manage to settle upon a formula for immigration control. Ironically, the minister whose responsibility it was to announce the voucher system was R A Butler, who in the early 1950s had been a liberal voice in Cabinet on the issue (517, note 2). It was one of the less dignified moments in Britain's retreat from empire.

*   *   *   *

Many thousands of the documents held at the Public Record Office were scrutinised during the preparation of this volume. Each document was assessed against one very broad criterion: did it help to illuminate imperial or colonial policy in the period under review? There were several ways in which a document might do this, and thereby qualify for inclusion. First, even if it did not deal directly with imperial or colonial policy as literally defined, it might provide a sense of the relevant high policy context. Second, it might aid comprehension of a specific issue, by explicating its nature or by setting out arguments or opinions about it. Third, it might throw light on the process of policy-making. Fourth, it might capture the moment at which an official or ministerial decision was made. A single document might well fulfil more than one of these purposes; but in a collection such as this, it was felt, every document should justify its presence by fulfilling at least one of them.

The aim of all the 'A series' volumes in this project is to provide a wide conspectus on events rather than to focus on a single country or group of countries. Selection of material becomes correspondingly problematical: for it is a matter of choosing not just among documents but among the many possible themes, emphases and issues which might be held to be relevant. Somehow a balance must also be struck between trying to illuminate grand policy and trying to convey the substance of everyday concerns. The main emphases of this volume are, it is hoped, sufficiently obvious; they are broadly indicated by the headings to the three parts, the seven chapters, and the numerous sub-sections. The high policy context—international relations, strategy and international economic policy—receives considerable coverage. So does metropolitan thinking on the political, administrative and economic aspects of current and future colonial policy. There is selective coverage of developments in policy for certain territories which were of wide imperial significance; in the period 1951–1957 this means, in particular, the Gold Coast, Malaya, Cyprus and Malta. Less fully documented are issues of social, educational and labour policy; while some areas of colonial policy, such as local government, legislative drafting, personnel matters, research, science, technology and public health, are barely touched at all, notwithstanding the extraordinary volume of official paper they generated at the time. This pattern of choice reflects, in the first instance, the stated purposes of the project. But there are some aspects of the pattern which primarily reflect the interests and preferences of the volume editor, a point which is here freely acknowledged.

A further general principle of selection was to document an issue at the highest level at which it was treated. This means that Cabinet and Cabinet committee memoranda and minutes have been heavily mined; so too have letters and notes between ministers, documents written at the top three or four levels of the bureaucratic hierarchy, and the proceedings of high level intra-departmental and inter-departmental committees, especially (in the latter case) committees at which Treasury, Defence, Foreign Office and/or Commonwealth Relations Office were represented along with the Colonial Office.

But such is the quantity of material at the PRO that even within these delimited categories, only a very small fraction of what was sighted could be included in the volume. In general, the most difficult editorial decisions were about what to leave out. And of course there were also omissions of an involuntary kind. In the first place, many official files are still withheld from public scrutiny. Included in this category, naturally enough, are files containing intelligence material. It is simply not possible to determine how large a quantity of material this lacuna represents, since the titles of intelligence files are not listed in the PRO's indices. More tantalising for the researcher are cases where the titles of retained files are indeed listed; a number of such cases are indicated in the link passages and footnotes of this volume. In the second place, there are the omissions which result from the sheer impossibility of scanning all the thousands upon thousands of arguably relevant files. Every researcher knows this frustration. But in a project such as this, to become obsessed with the 'undone vast' is to court paralysis. One can but proceed, on an eclectic basis of knowledge, suggestions from fellow editors, deduction, guesswork and instinct about where the good materials might be found. It feels very like prospecting for lode. One seam after another is uncovered and worked. But it is a search that must eventually be wound up, with such valuables as have been discovered being then tallied and put on display.

There is finally one aspect of the organisation of the volume, as distinct from the criteria for the selection of documents, that needs to be highlighted. In assembling a collection which deals for the most part with broad policy issues, it seemed appropriate to follow thematic principles. Thus, documents relating principally to matters of international strategy are grouped together in one chapter; documents dealing with economic policy in another; those dealing with constitutional questions in another; and so on. But this pattern of organisation, it has to be said, harbours a potential problem. It runs the risk of seeming to separate out aspects of policy which were in reality tightly linked, and which the policy makers themselves no doubt perceived as a totality. In the arena of imperial affairs, political, administrative, economic and strategic issues were often so closely interconnected that none could be fully understood, or coped with by policy makers, without reference to the others. Cyprus, Malta, Somaliland and Malaya, for example, regularly confronted Cabinet with the need to deal with problems of military strategy and problems of constitutional change in relation to each other. Thus to separate (say) a document on plans for Somali self-government (297) from documents discussing Somaliland's strategic significance (88, 89, 90, 94, 97, 98) might seem to compartmentalise the 'Somaliland problem' in a way that the policy makers themselves, and in particular Cabinet ministers, would not have done.

Could this problem have been avoided? This is really a question about possible alternative methods of organising the collection. The documents could, for example, have been arranged in a single chronological sequence; and this might well have helped convey the day-to-day reality as the policy makers experienced it—a host of disparate problems crowding upon their attention, and all demanding decisions. Or an attempt might have been made to group the documents on a region-by-region basis. But the larger question is whether either of these approaches would have better served the purposes of the volume as a whole. The first would have necessitated a dense thicket of editorial interpolation, voracious in its consumption of space and surely a trial to the reader. And the second would have quickly come up against the considerable problem that a great many of the documents in the collection do not refer to any regions or countries in particular.

And so the principle of thematic organisation prevailed. In consequence, documents about different aspects of certain problems—the affairs of the four territories mentioned, for example—will indeed be found distributed between different chapters. Readers who wish to peruse in sequence all the documents referring to a given territory may of course do so; the cross-referencing is intended to facilitate precisely that. More broadly, it is hoped that this essay will have sufficiently conveyed a sense of interconnections. For that has been a large part of its purpose.

* * * *

To the extent that this volume succeeds in meeting the objectives of the British Documents on the End of Empire Project, as set out in the general editor's foreword, it is to a substantial degree because I have been the beneficiary of so much guidance, encouragement and good advice from the general editors and the members of the project team. I thank them all. I am grateful also to Monash University, which made the research possible by granting me a period of study leave and subsequently an award to fund a return visit to the PRO. I thank Pauline Bakker, Marion Merkel, Eleni Naoumidis and Cecilia Thorei for wordprocessing. I thank Jo, Patrick and Daniel Goldsworthy for support and understanding. Finally I thank those people who gave me such welcoming homes away from home for long periods: my mother-in-law Helen Wolff and my friends Ted and Julia Whybrew.

D Goldsworthy

Notes to Introduction

1 Diary, 10 Apr 1952, quoted in H Macmillan, *Tides of fortune 1945–1955* (London, 1969) p 384.

2 Diary, 7 Jan 1953, quoted in E Shuckburgh, *Descent to Suez: diaries 1951–1956* (London, 1986) p 71.

3 CAB 131/12, D(52)41, 29 Sept 1952.

4 DEFE 4/87, COS(56)56, 5 June 1956.

5 BDEEP series A, R Hyam, ed, *The Labour government and the end of empire 1945–1951* (London, 1992) part II, 161.

6   Diary, 3 Sept 1954, quoted in Macmillan, *op cit*, p 480.

7   On the events leading to this agreement, see Hyam, ed, *op cit*, part III, 310, 312–315.

8   Sir Pierson Dixon, deputy under-secretary of state at the Foreign Office, put rather plaintive questions to the Americans. 'In the case of Persia we had received support from the United States, and the result had been that we had got the resumption of diplomatic relations, which we had wanted. Why could the Americans not give us the same full support in the case of Egypt? Was there not a chance that we might be right there as we had been in the case of Persia?' (CAB 129/64, C(53)360, 'Persia', memo by Eden, 24 Dec 1953). The Americans remained unmoved.

9   See BDEEP series B, J Kent, ed, *Egypt and the defence of the Middle East*.

10   Diary, 8 Nov 1955, quoted in Shuckburgh, *op cit*, p 298.

11   Diary, 3 Mar 1956, quoted in *ibid*, p 341.

12   Diary, 15 Aug 1956, quoted in W Clark, *From three worlds* (London, 1986) p 174.

13   Indeed extensive documentation of the crisis itself—ie the operational phase from July to November, when discussion of the options preoccupied senior ministers and officials more or less continuously—has not been attempted here. Key documents drawn from the Cabinet minutes, the Cabinet Egypt Committee papers and the Eden–Eisenhower correspondence have been published in D Carlton, *Britain and the Suez crisis* (London, 1988) pp 113–158, and comprehensive documentation is anticipated in the FO series of *Documents on British Policy Overseas*.

14   In 1951 when the ANZUS treaty was being planned, the Foreign Office and the Chiefs of Staff had both expressed alarm. In their view, a security treaty between the United States, Australia and New Zealand would be interpreted 'as evidence of rift in policy between UK and United States'; while 'grave repercussions' could be expected in Hong Kong and Malaya, since the exclusion of these mainland territories might be seen as evidence that in an emergency they would be abandoned to communism. These views were conveyed to the Americans; see *Foreign Relations of the United States 1951* vol VI *Asia and the Pacific* (Washington, 1977) pp 139–144. In fact the initiative for this treaty stemmed from Australia, not the United States, with the primary aim of guaranteeing security in the South-West Pacific, not in Asia.

15   CAB 131/14, D(54)7, 20 Dec 1954.

16   See BDEEP series B, A J Stockwell, ed, *Malaya*.

17   Hyam, ed, *op cit*, part IV, 442, 443.

18   Until the mid-fifties there was an understanding between London, Canberra and Wellington that in the event of global war Australia and New Zealand would despatch land and air forces to the Middle East. But events in Asia—especially the Malayan insurgency, the Korean war and the conflict in Vietnam—forced a reconsideration by all three parties. In 1953 Britain began pressing Australia to provide ground support (in addition to the air support already provided) for the British military effort in Malaya. By 1955, Britain had accepted that Australian and New Zealand forces should focus on their own strategic zone. The creation of the Commonwealth Strategic Reserve based in Malaya, with British, Australian and New Zealand troops serving side by side as from 1955, formalised this understanding.

19   See Hyam, ed, *op cit*, part III, 288, 289, 292, 293.

20   See CAB 129/85, C(57)38, 15 Feb 1957.

21   FO 371/123714, 17 July 1956. See also part I of this volume, 96, note 5, for a similar expression of FO opinion.

22   See BDEEP series B, R Rathbone, ed, *Ghana* (London, 1992) part II, 135, 145–149.

23   The records of this committee have yet to be made available at the PRO. The committee is mentioned in an internal Foreign Office minute in FO 371/18677, no 39. See also part I of this volume, 99, note 6.

24   CAB 131/16, DC 3(55)1, 10 June 1955.

25   CAB 128/25, CC 93(52)3, 6 Nov 1952.

E

26   *H of C Debs*, vol 531, col 508, 28 July 1954.

27   FO 800/764, R Scott (British embassy, Washington) to FO, 8 Sept 1954.

28   CAB 129/74, C(55)93, 5 Apr 1955.

29   Eden was 'bitter' about this, and his press adviser 'spoke to *The Times* which wrote a sharp leader'. W Clark's diary, 2 Oct 1956, quoted in Clark, *op cit*, p 194.

30   FO 371/95757, no 13, 16 Nov 1951.

31   eg FO 371/101394, no 4, 6 June 1952.

32   Hyam, ed, *op cit*, part IV, 432.

33   See also PREM 11/1367, 19 Feb 1952.

34   FO 371/90114, early Dec 1951.

35   CO 537/6696, 10 Dec 1951.

36   CAB 128/25, CC 75(52)7, 31 July 1952; cf Hyam, ed, *op cit*, part II, 183, 188, 190.

37   FO 371/123715, no 29, Sept 1956.

38   BDEEP series B, D Johnson, ed, *Sudan*.

39   PREM 11/1367, 12 Feb 1952.

40   For detailed documentation, see Rathbone, ed, *op cit*.

41   CAB 134/1201, CA 5(55)2, 10 Nov 1955.

42   Though not of the internal governance of Northern Rhodesia and Nyasaland, which remained a Colonial Office responsibility.

43   CO 554/254, no 10, Lloyd to Macpherson, 5 Mar 1953, reproduced in Rathbone, ed, *op cit*, part II, 123.

44   Hyam, ed, *op cit*, part IV, chapter 8(1).

45   CAB 128/26/2, CM 26(53)5, 14 Apr 1953.

46   CAB 130/111, GEN 501/3, 15 Aug 1955.

47   Australia, New Zealand and Canada, which were parties to the UK–USA intelligence-sharing agreement of 1948, were regularly taken into confidence on military intelligence matters; South Africa only sometimes; India, Pakistan and Ceylon, seldom.

48   See Hyam, ed, *op cit*, part I, chapter 2.

49   CO 554/254, no 10, Lloyd to Macpherson, 5 Mar 1953, reproduced in Rathbone, ed, *op cit*, part II, 123.

50   Lennox-Boyd's phrase 'bloody and disastrous consequences' anticipated by several years Iain Macleod's oft-quoted remark 'any other policy would have led to terrible bloodshed'. *The Spectator*, 31 Jan 1964, p 127.

51   DO 35/6177, no 122, 29 Jan 1957.

52   CAB 129/76, CP(55)65, 9 July 1955; CAB 129/78, CP(55)184, 29 Nov 1955; CAB 128/29, CM 22(55)3, 12 July 1955.

53   Hyam, ed, *op cit*, part II, 132–134, 136, 137.

54   Diary entries, 18 and 26 Oct 1956, C Stuart, ed, *The Reith diaries* (London, 1975) pp 400, 401.

55   CO 1025/76, Vile to Poynton, 23 Aug 1956.

56   Hyam, ed, *op cit*, part IV, 365.

57   *Ibid*, 351–355.

Summary of Documents: Part I

Chapter 1 The international and strategic environment: high policy considerations

(1) International relations, strategy and the empire: general

(3) East and South East-Asia

(4) Africa

Chapter 2   Colonial policy in Britain's
international relationships

(1) The United States

CHAPTER 1

The International and Strategic Environment: High Policy Considerations

Document numbers 1–99

1   DEFE 7/415, no 5a   24 Oct 1951

'The share of the colonies in defence': memorandum by Trafford Smith[1]

[In a covering letter to F Wood (assistant secretary, Ministry of Defence, 1947–1955), Trafford Smith noted that this memo had been written 'on the assumption that its purpose is to have the arguments marshalled in readiness for a new Minister who may ask why it is that we don't make more use of Colonial manpower and Colonial forces' (Trafford Smith to Wood, DEFE, 7/415, no 5, 24 Oct 1951). See also BDEEP series A, R Hyam, ed, *The Labour government and the end of empire 1945–51*, part III, 336–340.]

1. The Colonies play their part in defence in two ways:—

(1) By raising and maintaining forces from their local manpower. These forces have the primary role of safeguarding internal security in their territories, thereby preserving the usefulness of the territories as bases and sources of manpower, raw materials, etc., and also to a large extent relieving United Kingdom forces of their obligation to intervene for the preservation of law and order – an obligation inherent in the status of the Colonial Dependencies *vis-à-vis* the United Kingdom. Colonial forces are also available for local defence, and in special circumstances can be expanded so as to provide troops for service in other theatres: cf. the plans for sending two East African battalions and one Fijian battalion to Malaya. There are, however, the limitations on the expansion of Colonial forces referred to below.

(2) By maintaining or increasing their contribution to the pool of economic resources available for the Commonwealth war effort. It is not proposed to enlarge on the economic contribution made by the Colonies in this paper.

2. It must be borne in mind that a balance must be maintained between the demands on the Colonial Dependencies under (1) and (2) above. The potential size of Colonial forces is limited by the following factors:—

(a) The manpower position in the Colonial Dependencies. In many territories it is not in fact possible to recruit large bodies of men for defence purposes without prejudicing the supply of labour to local industrial and agricultural projects whose

---

[1] Trafford Smith, assistant secretary, CO, 1945–1953; seconded to Imperial Defence College, 1950–1951; lt-gov, Malta, 1953–1959.

F

output is important to the Commonwealth war effort in the economic sphere.

(b) Finance. In practice many Colonial territories are unable to maintain the scale of forces laid down by the Chiefs of Staff (C.O.S.(49)44) as the minimum necessary to maintain internal security, without financial assistance from the United Kingdom. In each case in which financial assistance has been granted in this way, a thorough investigation has first been made to ensure that the Colonial territory receiving it is contributing to defence the maximum it can afford consistent with the maintenance of its development and welfare programme. All the major territories either have been or are being approached with a view to ensuring that they make their maximum contribution to defence either in cash or in kind. Financial assistance granted by the United Kingdom towards the maintenance of internal security in the Colonial territories has been provided from the Colonial and Middle Eastern Services Vote. United Kingdom Service Departments have no surplus funds available to devote to Colonial forces.

(c) Supplies of equipment are inadequate for forces already in existence, and would be rendered even more difficult by the necessity to equip Colonial forces additional to those already in existence.

(d) Similarly, there is a scarcity of trained officers and N.C.Os. for forces already in existence. In certain advanced territories, however (notably West Africa, Malaya and Fiji), a beginning is being made with the creation of an officer cadre from local material and candidates from these territories are already under training at Sandhurst under the same conditions as British cadets. It will thus be seen that any further increase in the size of Colonial forces is primarily dependent on the provision of finance, equipment and training staff from the United Kingdom. A table is attached[2] showing the present Colonial forces in being or contemplated. It will be noted that an important contribution is made by certain dependencies in the provision of pioneer units, and that, in addition to internal security forces, a number of Colonial local forces (such as the East African and Mauritius naval forces and the R.A.F. (Malaya)) have been raised, with assistance from United Kingdom Service Departments, for the purpose of local defence.

3. *Colonial manpower in the United Kingdom forces*. The present position is that Colonials must enlist in United Kingdom forces, subject to their reaching the required standards, if they present themselves for enlistment in the United Kingdom itself. The Service Departments have hitherto set themselves against schemes for the recruitment of Colonials in the Colonies for United Kingdom forces, principally on the grounds of the differences of habit and custom which make a mixed force (and especially a mixed ship) of Englishmen and Colonials difficult to handle. No doubt a wider use of Colonial manpower could be made in this way, especially of West Indians, if a solution could be found for this problem.

---

[2] Not printed.

2   CAB 129/48, C(51)32   29 Nov 1951
'United Europe': Cabinet note by Mr Churchill

It may simplify discussion if I set forth briefly my own view and the line I have followed so far.

1. At Zürich in 1946 I appealed to France to take the lead in Europe by making friends with the Germans, "burying the thousand-year quarrel," &c. This caused a shock at the time but progress has been continual. I always recognised that, as Germany is potentially so much stronger than France, militarily and economically, Britain and if possible the United States should be associated with United Europe, to make an even balance and to promote the United Europe Movement.

2. As year by year the project advanced, the Federal Movement in many European countries who participated became prominent. It has in the last two years lost much of its original force. The American mind jumps much too lightly over its many difficulties. I am not opposed to a European Federation including (eventually) the countries behind the Iron Curtain, provided that this comes about naturally and gradually. But I never thought that Britain or the British Commonwealths should, either individually or collectively, become an integral part of a European Federation, and have never given the slightest support to the idea. We should not, however, obstruct but rather favour the movement to closer European unity and try to get the United States' support in this work.

3. There can be no effective defence of Western Europe without the Germans. As things developed my idea has always been as follows: There is the N.A.T.O. Army. Inside the N.A.T.O. Army there is the European Army, and inside the European Army there is the German Army. The European Army should be formed by all the European parties to N.A.T.O. *plus* Germany, "dedicating" from their own national armies their quota of divisions to the Army now under General Eisenhower's[1] command. Originally at Strasbourg in 1950 the Germans did not press for a national army. On the contrary they declared themselves ready to join a European Army without having a national army. The opportunity was lost and there seems very little doubt that Germany will have to have a certain limited national army from which to "dedicate." The size and strength of this army, and its manufacture of weapons, would have to be agreed with the victorious Powers of the late war. In any case the recruiting arrangements for covering the German quota would have involved a considerable machinery.

4. In the European Army all dedicated quotas of participating nations would be treated with strict honourable military equality. The national characteristics should be preserved up to the divisional level, special arrangements being made about the "tail," heavy weapons, &c. I should doubt very much the military spirit of a "sludgy amalgam" of volunteers or conscripts to defend the E.D.C.[2] or other similar organisations. The national spirit must animate all troops up to and including the

---

[1] General D D Eisenhower, supreme allied commander, Europe, 1950–1952; president of the United States, 1953–1961.

[2] European Defence Community. Negotiations between Belgium, France, Italy, Luxembourg, the Netherlands and West Germany (subsequently the Common Market 'Six') led in May 1952 to a draft treaty providing for a supra-national community with common armed forces. But the plan was effectively vetoed by French politicians fearful of German military resurgence.

divisional level. On this basis and within these limits national pride may be made to promote and serve international strength.

5. France does not seem to be playing her proper part in these arrangements. France is not France without "L'Armée Française." I warned MM. Pleven[3] and Monnet[4] several times that "a Pleven Army" would not go down in France. The French seem to be trying to get France defended by Europe. Their proposed contribution for 1952 of five, rising to ten, divisions is pitiful, even making allowances for the fact that they are still trying to hold their Oriental Empire. They have no grounds of complaint against us who have already dedicated four divisions to General Eisenhower's Command. We must not lose all consciousness of our insular position. I noticed some time ago the faulty structure of the present French arrangements, and in particular how the few combatant divisional formations they have will be deprived of all training efficiency by the vast mass of recruits annually flowing in upon them.

6. On the economic side, I welcome the Schuman Coal and Steel Plan[5] as a step in the reconciliation of France and Germany, and as probably rendering another Franco-German war physically impossible. I never contemplated Britain joining in this plan on the same terms as Continental partners. We should, however, have joined in all the discussions, and had we done so not only a better plan would probably have emerged, but our own interests would have been watched at every stage. Our attitude towards further economic developments on the Schuman lines resembles that which we adopt about the European Army. We help, we dedicate, we play a part, but we are not merged and do not forfeit our insular or Commonwealth-wide character. I should resist any American pressure to treat Britain as on the same footing as the European States, none of whom have the advantages of the Channel and who were consequently conquered.

7. Our first object is the unity and the consolidation of the British Common-wealths [sic] and what is left of the former British Empire. Our second, the "fraternal association" of the European-speaking world; and third, United Europe, to which we are a separate closely- and specially-related ally and friend.

---

[3] R Pleven, prime minister of France, 1950–1951, 1951–1952; minister of defence, 1949–1950, 1952–1954.

[4] J Monnet, creator of the Monnet Plan 1947; president, preparatory conference on Schuman Plan 1950; president, European Coal and Steel Community, 1952–1955.

[5] A plan for the integration of the French and German coal and steel industries; see BDEEP series A, R Hyam, ed, *The Labour government and the end of empire 1945–1951*, part II, 157–159.

3   CAB 129/53, C(52)202   18 June 1952
'British overseas obligations': Cabinet memorandum by Mr Eden.
Annex

The object of this paper is to consider the tasks to which the United Kingdom is committed overseas and to examine where if anywhere our responsibilities can be reduced so as to bring them more into line with our available resources.

2. An attempt has been made to estimate the cost of our overseas commitments. Certain limited figures are available which give an indication of the order of

magnitude involved, and these are attached as an Annex. But it is impossible to give precise figures of the real cost of maintaining any individual commitment, or to quantify the many intangible factors in the problem.

Basic factors

3. The foreign policy of Her Majesty's Government in the United Kingdom is determined by certain fundamental factors:—

(a) The United Kingdom has world responsibilities inherited from several hundred years as a great Power.

(b) The United Kingdom is not a self-sufficient economic unit.

(c) No world security system exists, and the United Kingdom with the rest of the non-Communist world, is faced with an external threat.

4. The essence of a sound foreign policy is to ensure that a country's strength is equal to its obligations. If this is not the case, then either the obligations must be reduced to the level at which resources are available to maintain them, or a greater share of the country's resources must be devoted to their support. It is becoming clear that rigorous maintenance of the presently-accepted policies of Her Majesty's Government at home and abroad is placing a burden on the country's economy which it is beyond the resources of the country to meet. A position has already been reached where there is no reserve and therefore no margin for unforeseen additional obligations.

5. The first task must be to determine how far the external obligations of the country can be reduced or shared with others, or transferred to other shoulders, without impairing too seriously the world position of the United Kingdom and sacrificing the vital advantages which flow from it. But if, after careful review, it is shown that the total effort required is still beyond the capacity of existing national resources, a choice of the utmost difficulty lies before the British people, for they must either give up, for a time, some of the advantages which a high standard of living confers upon them, or, by relaxing their grip in the outside world, see their country sink to the level of a second-class Power, with injury to their essential interests and way of life of which they can have little conception. Faced with this choice, the British people might be rallied to a greater productive effort which would enable a greater volume of external commitments to be borne.

Withdrawal from obligations

6. There are very strong arguments against a complete abandonment of a major commitment. First, in the present state of world tension, unless arrangements have been made for the burden to be transferred to friendly shoulders, the Russians would be only too ready to fill any vacuum created by a British withdrawal, with a consequent shifting of the balance of power against the West. It is further obvious that when an area falls into Communist hands its economic and trading value to the Western world becomes greatly reduced while Western capital assets are liquidated with little or no compensation.

7. Secondly, withdrawal from a major commitment would affect the international status of the United Kingdom. By reducing the value of the United Kingdom as a partner and ally, it would undermine the cohesion of the Commonwealth and the special relationship of the United Kingdom with the United States and its European

partners and other allies. Their attitude towards us will depend largely upon our status as a world Power and upon their belief that we are ready and willing to support them. It is evident that in so far as we reduce our commitments and our power declines, our claim to the leadership of the Commonwealth, to a position of influence in Europe, and to a special relationship with the United States will be, *pro tanto*, diminished.

8. Thirdly, the British world position brings with it concurrent and beneficial results of an economic and financial nature. The abandonment of our position in any area of the world may well have similar concurrent and adverse effects on our economic and trading interests.

9. Finally, there is the general effect of loss of prestige. It is impossible to assess in concrete terms the consequences to ourselves and the Commonwealth of our drastically and unilaterally reducing our responsibilities; the effects of a failure of will and relaxation of grip in our overseas commitments are incalculable. But once the prestige of a country has started to slide there is no knowing where it will stop.

Classification of obligations

10. The same reasoning applies to a lesser extent to a policy of reduction and sharing of obligations. It is, therefore, essential that this policy should be contrived in such a manner and applied in such areas as to do the least harm to the world position of the United Kingdom. In order to determine where, if anywhere, our responsibilities could be diminished, it is now necessary to survey our existing obligations.

11. These fall broadly into three categories:—

(a) Obligations arising from the geographical position of the British Isles.
(b) Obligations arising from our imperial heritage.
(c) Obligations arising from our international position.

12. (a) *Obligations arising from the geographical position of the British Isles*
Defence of the United Kingdom and Western Europe.
Preservation of sea and air communications.
Membership of N.A.T.O.
Maintenance of forces on the Continent.

(b) *Obligations arising from our imperial heritage*
Maintenance of security and economic and social development in British Colonial territories.
General support for other Commonwealth countries.
Defence of the British position in Egypt and responsibility for security in the Middle East generally.
Restoration of order in Malaya.
Maintenance of a world-wide system of garrisons and bases, *e.g.*, Gibraltar, Malta, Persian Gulf, Singapore, Hong Kong, Falkland Islands and Caribbean.

(c) *Obligations arising from our international position*
Share of international action in resisting aggression; e.g., Korea.
Share of economic assistance to other countries, e.g., Yugoslavia, Korea.
Obligations arising from participation in International Organisations, e.g., U.N.O., G.A.T.T., O.E.E.C., E.P.U.

Other external commitments, e.g., Iraq, Jordan, Arab refugees.

13. There is the further category of purely financial obligations which fall partly under (b) and partly under (c). These obligations arise from the position of the United Kingdom as the holder of the central reserves of the Sterling Area and the liabilities arising from the Sterling balances. Apart from a reference to the Sterling balances in paragraph 27 below, the problems of the Sterling Area are not discussed in this paper. But it should be emphasised that the existence of the Sterling Area and the functions of the United Kingdom within it are important factors in the world position of the United Kingdom. If the Sterling Area were to be weakened or broken up, this would be regarded in other countries as a heavy blow to the influence and prestige of the United Kingdom; it would undermine the cohesion of the Commonwealth; and would thus further weaken British authority in world affairs.

14. It is evident from this classification that theoretically, it would be open to us in some cases to cut out a commitment altogether, since we are alone in holding the commitment (e.g., the surrender of Hong Kong to the Chinese). In other cases, where we are co-operating with other countries in assuming international commitments, we could only contract out of them or reduce them by negotiation (e.g., our general contribution to the defence effort through N.A.T.O., including our specific allocation of 4⅓ British divisions and the Second Tactical Air Force to Western Germany). It is also evident that some measure of relief might be obtained by reducing the scale of our contributions to International Organisations. But wherever we decide to reduce, the result would be a greater or less diminution of our influence as a world Power. We come back therefore to the problem of finding those areas in which reduction could be effected with the least harm to our position.

Possible methods of relief

15. If total withdrawal from any major obligations is ruled out, there are three ways in which we can effect reductions in our obligations: by reducing the scale; by sharing the burden with other friendly Powers; or by transferring a *minor* obligation to friendly shoulders. These methods could also be used in combination.

Category A obligations

(i) *Defence of the United Kingdom and Western Europe*

16. Western Europe is, within the Atlantic Pact, the heart of the defence of the British Isles and the nucleus of any Western system of defence. Any relaxation of our effort here is bound to have a direct effect on our own security. It could only be justified by the greater danger of over-straining our economy or in the light of the most careful calculation of the risk of Soviet aggression. Broadly speaking, our obligations here must have the first priority.

(ii) *N.A.T.O.*

17. N.A.T.O. is a chosen instrument of United Kingdom policy: through it we obtain not only greater security, but also prestige and influence with the United States and our European allies. Any unilateral decision to reduce our agreed share in the defence programme would react adversely on our position as a world Power, depress the Europeans and hearten the Russians. Any substantial slowing up of N.A.T.O. defence production in general (from which the United Kingdom benefits

equally with others) would seriously compromise the Western policy of seeking peace from strength. The course we should seek to follow is to persuade the United States to bear a share in the programme more commensurate with their economic strength.

Maintenance of forces in Europe
(iii) *Germany*

18. Any reduction of our forces in Germany in the relatively near future would carry very serious implications. Partial withdrawal at once or in the immediate future would have a most disturbing effect in Germany and elsewhere. It would endanger ratification of the E.D.C. Treaty and thereby the strength of the united effort on which the security of Western Europe depends. In due course, but certainly not before the beginning of 1954, German units will begin to be available for Western defence. At that stage a progressive reduction in our own forces in Germany might perhaps be contemplated. The German contribution to Western defence will, however, be based, like our own, on the normal N.A.T.O. screening machinery. If, therefore, there were a general reduction in our defence effort, the Germans, and probably also the French, might similarly wish to reduce their own defence effort. The French, in addition, might seek economy by withdrawal from Indo-China in order to maintain superiority *vis-à-vis* the Germans in Europe. Psychologically the reduction and still more the complete withdrawal of United Kingdom forces from the Continent, even if kept in being in the United Kingdom, would have a serious effect on the will of all our European allies to resist aggression. A special factor which may, however, compel us to consider some reduction in our forces in Germany is the fact that after June, 1953, we must be prepared to pay in addition to our present expenditure a sum probably amounting to about £100 million a year in foreign exchange in respect of the local costs hitherto borne on the German occupation budget. These should be fully covered by Germany as part of her defence contribution only until June, 1953.

(iv) *Austria and Trieste*

19. These by comparison with Germany are lesser commitments:—

(a) It is our aim to conclude an Austrian Peace Treaty as soon as possible, followed by the withdrawal of all foreign troops from the country. But until this is achieved, there can be no question of a unilateral withdrawal on our part. The commitment both in men and money is at present relatively small, though the question of occupation costs might become more acute next year (possibly of the order of £2 million in foreign currency).

(b) Provided that a settlement can be reached between Italy and Yugoslavia, or be imposed on them by Her Majesty's Government and the United States Government, the British (and United States) forces could be withdrawn from Trieste. It is the aim of Her Majesty's Government to achieve this as soon as possible. This would represent a saving of the order of £1¾ million in foreign currency.

Category B obligations

(i) *Maintenance of security and economic and social development in colonial territories*

20. The question whether any reduction could be made in the United Kingdom

contribution to colonial development is outside the scope of this paper. Possibly some alleviation of this burden might be found:—

(i) Through greater use of colonial troops to back our major commitments;
(ii) Through allocation by the United States of larger funds for investment in the colonial Empire.

(ii) *Commonwealth*

21. This is another aspect of the problem which is outside the scope of this paper. Generally speaking, however, members of the Commonwealth enjoy the fruits of the rearmament efforts of the free world without making commensurate contributions. An effort might be made to persuade other Commonwealth countries to agree to relieve the United Kingdom of some of the burden.

(iii) *Egypt and the Middle East*

22. In time of war, the Middle East will have priority second only to Western Europe. Its oil is essential to the United Kingdom in peace-time and a proportion of it might well be essential in war. But it is clearly beyond the resources of the United Kingdom to continue to assume the responsibility alone for the security of the Middle East. Our aim should be to make the whole of this area and in particular the Canal Zone an international responsibility. Hence every step should be taken to speed up the establishment of an Allied Middle East Defence Organisation. It should, however, be recognised that the setting up of such a defence organisation will not result in any immediate alleviation of the burden for the United Kingdom. The United States have refused to enter into any precise commitments in the Middle East or to allocate forces, and it should be the constant object of Her Majesty's Government to persuade them to do so. In addition, every possibility should be explored of committing the United State military, e.g., to the building of bases, the provision of material, the sharing and reconstruction of airfields. During the present crisis any reduction in the British forces in Egypt is a military problem in which the need for safeguarding British lives and property in case of an emergency must be the first consideration. The dilemma is that until we can come to an agreement with Egypt no effective international defence organisation for the Middle East can be established; and so long as there is no settlement with Egypt and no international defence organisation we are obliged to hold the fort alone.

(iv) *Malaya and South-East Asia*

23. The security and defence of South-East Asia is of very great importance. In conditions short of general war any sign of weakness, involving even a partial reduction of effort there, would be most damaging to ourselves and an immense encouragement to the Communists. The remedy here lies in committing the United States and Australia and New Zealand to the defence of Malaya and Indo-China, perhaps by the establishment of a Far Eastern Regional Security Pact on N.A.T.O. lines. In the meantime, possibly greater use could be made of locally raised forces, in addition to British and Gurkha troops as available.

(v) *World-wide garrisons and bases*

24. Theoretically it might be possible to obtain relief by sharing upkeep with one

or more friendly countries, on the same principle as the Canal Zone might become an international command headquarters. Thus Malta and Gibraltar could be made charges on N.A.T.O., Cyprus on the Middle East Command, Hong Kong and Singapore on a Far Eastern Regional Security Pact. Depending on the method and timing adopted, such a policy might be carried through successfully. A very minor commitment which we could endeavour to dispose of to the United States is the Falkland Islands Dependencies. I do not, however, advise such action, for public admission of our inability to maintain these traditional possessions would cause a loss of prestige wholly out of proportion to the saving in money obtained. It might precipitate a scramble by the numerous claimants to various parts of British territory.

Category C obligations

(i) *Share in international action in Korea*

25. There are strong objections to a reduction of British Forces. Through our contribution we have acquired not only prestige throughout the free world, but a right to American consideration in matters affecting both Korea and the Far East generally.

(ii) *Economic assistance to other countries and subscriptions to international bodies*

26. The main items here are the grants in aid to Jordan, Yugoslavia, Palestine Refugees and Korean Reconstruction. The first of these is primarily a military commitment: while we could consider a reduction here, this might, in effect, be a false economy in that Jordan and the Arab Legion contribute to Middle East defence and stability at relatively low cost to ourselves. We are already tapering off our aid to Yugoslavia. We could consider reducing our contribution to rehabilitation in Korea. But we could only reduce our help for Palestine refugees at the cost of arousing ill-feeling with the Americans. We could also in theory reduce the scale of our contributions to international bodies generally. But this could only be done by international agreement and the saving in money might well be quite out of proportion to the ill-will which is likely to be engendered towards the United Kingdom.

Sterling liabilities

27. Finally there is a possibility of reducing United Kingdom sterling liabilities. The total of United Kingdom sterling liabilities (i.e., including Sterling Area and non-Sterling Area countries) was £4,373 million at 31st December, 1951. The biggest individual holders of sterling at that time were members of the Commonwealth, Japan, Egypt, and the Colonies. Theoretically it would be possible to reduce these liabilities by scaling them down or reducing the rate of release of sterling allowed for in individual financial agreements. But from the standpoint of foreign policy this process must be one brought about by negotiation and agreement. The prospect for success of such negotiations will vary according to the country and the type of obligations.

Conclusions

28.   It is apparent from this review that there are few ways to effect any reductions in our overseas commitments which would provide immediate relief to our economic difficulties. Some immediate relief could be afforded by a reduction in our economic assistance to certain foreign countries (paragraph 26), though it is very questionable whether the relatively small economic gain would be worth the loss of prestige and hence influence: we might obtain some alleviation by arrangements within the Colonial Empire (paragraph 20) and with the Commonwealth (paragraph 21), and we may be able to save the expense of the maintenance of British forces in Trieste (paragraph 19 (b)). But these would be matters for negotiation and persuasion, with no certain prospect of substantial alleviation of the burden on the United Kingdom.

29.   If, on a longer view, it must be assumed that the maintenance of the present scale of overseas commitments will permanently overstrain our economy, clearly we ought to recognise that the United Kingdom is over-committed and must reduce the commitment. The only practical way of removing this permanent strain would be for the United Kingdom to shed or share the load of one or two major obligations, e.g., the defence of the Middle East, for which at present we bear the responsibility alone (paragraph 22), or the defence of South-East Asia, where we share responsibility with the French (paragraph 23). Our present policy is in fact directed towards the construction of international defence organisations for the Middle East and South-East Asia in which the United States and other Commonwealth countries would participate. Our aim should be to persuade the United States to assume the real burdens in such organisations, while retaining for ourselves as much political control — and hence prestige and world influence — as we can. As regards the defence of Western Europe, we should seek to induce the United States to assume a larger share of the common burden. A further substantial alleviation might be possible in 1954 and subsequent years if the build up of German contingents enables us to reduce British forces in Germany without endangering the common Western defence effort (paragraph 18).

30.   The success of this policy will depend on a number of factors, some favourable, some unfavourable. The United States is the only single country in the free world capable of assuming new and world-wide obligations; being heavily committed to the East–West struggle they would not readily leave a power-vacuum in any part of the globe but would be disposed, however reluctantly, to fill it themselves if it was clear that the United Kingdom could no longer hold the position (as they did, for example, in Greece). On the other hand, the history of the Middle East command negotiations and the unwillingness of the United States Chiefs of Staff to commit forces to it illustrates the American reluctance to enter into new commitments in peacetime. In South-East Asia only the sketchiest form of cooperation exists. Moreover, distrust of the British and fear of becoming an instrument to prop up a declining British Empire are still strong. (This is truer among Republicans than Democrats, but we must clearly prepare ourselves to deal with either Government.) As regards the United Kingdom part, a policy of this kind will only be successful with the United States in so far as we are able to demonstrate that we are making the maximum possible effort ourselves, and the more gradually and inconspicuously we can transfer the real burdens from our own to American shoulders, the less damage we shall do to our position and influence in the world.

Annex to 3

1. The cost of our overseas commitments cannot be readily calculated. But certain figures have been supplied to me which give an indication of the scale of certain elements in this cost. These fall under three heads:—

(a) The total expenditure in local currencies which is estimated to be incurred on our forces overseas in 1952 is approximately £125.9 million. The main items in this are Malaya and Singapore, £31.7 million, O.E.E.C. countries (excluding Germany and Austria, where we continue, for the time being, to received [sic] occupation costs) £24.7 million, Malta and Gozo £11.8 million and Hong Kong £10.7 million.

To the figure of £125.9 million should be added £14.7 million for oil for forces overseas giving a grand total of *£140.6 million*. This includes the cost of the United Kingdom share of the common infrastructure programme and of colonial forces to the extent that they are financed from the United Kingdom exchequer. It does not include Korea, where payment for local currency issues and United States logistical support has yet to be made and, for different reasons, contains exceptionally low figures for Egypt and Japan.

(b) A further figure of *£100.9 million* for the year 1952 is estimated to cover our expenditures in foreign currencies on behalf of forces in the United Kingdom or the forces generally in the following items:—

   (i)   Machinery and Production for defence purposes (£45.3 million).
   (ii) Manufacture for defence (£33.6 million).
   (iii) Oil for forces in the United Kingdom (£22 million).

It is not possible to estimate what part of this sum is attributable to forces overseas.

(c) There are also certain figures of overseas expenditure on commitments of the type covered by the Vote for Foreign Office Grants and Services. This Vote amounts to £21.9 million out of a total of £92.7 million in various votes included in Civil Estimates Class II — 1952–53 — Commonwealth and Foreign. It includes Jordan (£8.7 million), Yugoslavia (£5.6 million), Palestine Refugees (£2.5 million), Libya ([£]2.2 million), Reconstruction in Korea (£2 million).

2. As regards military expenditure, the total of (a) and (b) above does not represent the full cost of United Kingdom military commitments. Full cost would include not merely the foreign currency expenditure but also all those costs which are met in sterling, such as expenditure on stores and food, that part of the pay and allowances of troops and civilians which is not converted into local currencies, transportation costs of men and stores, &c.

3. The extent to which the liquidation of a particular commitment would produce savings either in overseas expenditure or in the total defence budget, cannot be worked out unless information is available on the manner and extent to which a reduction in a particular area is envisaged. In particular it would be necessary to know whether forces were to be disbanded or merely moved elsewhere and also to determine the extent of the terminal charges which would arise if a commitment were to be liquidated.

4 CO 936/217, no 1   21 June 1952
[The problem of nationalism]: letter from Sir W Strang to Sir T Lloyd.
Enclosure: FO Permanent Under-Secretary's Committee paper

I enclose herewith a copy of a paper prepared by the Permanent Under-Secretary's Committee here, entitled "The Problem of Nationalism".

This paper deals with nationalism in general terms as a global problem and does not attempt an analysis by regions. Its aim is to assess the significance and strength of present day nationalism and the threat which it presents to British interests, and to suggest possible measures to maintain our position in the face of this threat. The concluding section of the paper contains recommendations for policy.

The paper has been generally approved by the Foreign Secretary who has agreed that we should now seek the views of the Colonial Office. I should therefore be grateful for any comment you may care to make both as regards the general approach of the paper to this very complex problem and, in particular, on paragraph 24(i), which trespasses to some extent on your province.

I am writing similarly to Liesching.

Enclosure to 4

A. *Aim*
The general aim of this paper is to suggest means by which we can safe-guard our position as a world power, particularly in the economic and strategic fields, against the dangers inherent in the present upsurge of nationalism. On the economic side we have to maintain specific British interests on which our existence as a trading country depends. In the field of strategy we have to ensure our own and Commonwealth security within the larger framework of our obligations as a leader of the free world.

2. In more detail the aims of this paper are:—

(i)   To assess the significance and strength of present day nationalism;
(ii) To note certain manifestations of nationalism in action;
(iii) To calculate the risks to British interests;
(iv) To suggest possible measures to maintain our position and hence
(v)   To propose recommendations for policy.

B. *Nationalism – significance and strength*
3. The war has greatly increased Great Britain's vulnerability as a world power. On the one hand our economic weakness has led to a marked decline in our power to control the activities and policies of other Governments and to a lesser extent in our prestige in world affairs. On the other, the creation of new states and the widespread diffusion of the ideals of a world democracy as expressed, e.g. in the U.N. Charter, and including the condemnation of the use or threat of force, have severely limited the ability of the great Powers to enforce their points of view.

4. This has affected our relations with all countries, particularly the backward and "new" nations in Asia and Africa, including the peoples of our own Colonial territories. The practical results are broadly to increase the pressure:–

(i) in our own (and other countries') dependent territories for a speeding up of the process of granting sovereign independence;

(ii) in independent countries for the elimination of real or imaginary British interference in their internal affairs and the enforcement of real or imaginary claims against the United Kingdom.

The forces by which this pressure is directed and intensified may be loosely termed the forces of nationalism.

5. For the purposes of this paper nationalism is defined as the emotions of a people or group of people primarily in backward or "new" countries seeking to assert their national aspirations. These can often but by no means invariably be fulfilled only at the expense of the older Western Powers.

6. Nationalism is dynamic. It can be a great force for good where it is based on sober pride and patriotism, leading to the establishment of strong and effective governments. Intelligent and satisfied nationalism is an essential factor for the stability of any modern state. National states of this sort provide a firm bulwark against Communism and offer corresponding possibilities of genuine and trustworthy cooperation in international affairs.

7. But nationalism may also run, or be driven, out of control. Exploited or dissatisfied nationalism produces a state of mind in which any sense of grievance, injustice or inferiority is magnified out of all proportion. This can lead to a state of unbalance amounting in the worst cases to hysteria. This state of mind is highly infectious.

8. Virulent nationalism may lead states already independent to disregard of the normal rights and obligations owed by one sovereign state to another, or to its fellow sovereign states collectively. At this stage the only remedy lies in collective international counter-action.

9. There is nothing new in nationalism. The present state of affairs is a logical stage in the continuing historical process by which the nations of the world have been formed, and in which Britain has played a leading role, e.g. in Greece, Latin America, the Commonwealth, etc. This process cannot be stopped.

10. Some of the factors contributing to the present extreme nature of the problem of nationalism have already been noted. Others are:–

(i) The general impetus given to nationalist independence movements by the events of the war and the subsequent withdrawal of the Western Powers from territories such as India, Syria, or Indonesia;

(ii) The emergence as the world's greatest and richest power of the U.S.A., whose own origins were in successful revolution against Great Britain, and whose attitude towards "colonialism" is, to say the least of it, equivocal;

(iii) Misinterpretation of the British policy of encouraging healthy nationalism and promoting the independence of dependent territories as a sign of the decline of the former greatest world Power and mercantile Empire which can now, it is supposed, be attacked with impunity;

(iv) The moral and sometimes physical support lent by International Communism in encouraging revolt against the Western Powers;

(v) General suspicion of foreign economic and financial influence;

(vi) Reaction to the intrusion of the West and Western ideas on the traditional way of life of indigenous societies;

and in the Middle East particularly

(vii) The resentment felt in the oil-producing countries at the exploitation of their main and highly valuable source of wealth by Western powers;

(viii) The suspicion of the new bourgeoisie that the old landowner class and the régimes they represent enjoy the favour of the Western powers.

11. The task of this paper is to discover how Britain can guide the forces of nationalism in areas where we can still exert some control over events into channels of fruitful cooperation. This means adopting policies to meet existing or anticipated nationalist aspirations which will at the same time safeguard our own vital interests and those of the free world.

C. *Manifestations of nationalism*

12. While the general trend is clear and simple, the resulting manifestations are widely different. Considering purely the practical problem of risks to British interests, the principal actions which have been or may be taken to our detriment by nationalist leaders or Governments appear to include any of the following:—

(i)   insistence on managing their own affairs without the means or ability to do so, including the dismissal of British advisers;

(ii) expropiation of British assets;

(iii) unilateral denunciation of treaties with the U.K.;

(iv) claims on British possessions;

(v)   ganging up against the U.K. (and the Western Powers) in the United Nations.

13. Such actions are not mutually exclusive; they may and do occur individually, in series, or in parallel. Nor is there any clear pattern of evolution through which countries or peoples arrive at a stage of nationalism in which these actions occur.

14. Once the forces of nationalism have been allowed to get out of control it is impossible to anticipate what action may not follow. The immediate motives are usually a compound of:–

(i)   opposition to paternal restraint, or kicking over the traces;

(ii) internal discontent and the need to find a scapegoat or distraction;

(iii) opportunism and desire to cut a figure in international affairs.

15. The timing may be closely related to (ii) above or to a manifestation of weakness by the paternal Power, sometimes both. Given that the ground is prepared, timing may be more directly related to personalities, e.g. to the peculiar brand of patriotism, fanaticism or unscrupulousness with which a nationalist leader or group of leaders may be imbued.

D. *Risks to British interests*

16. The risks to British interests may be divided into:–

(i)   politico-economic

(ii) politico-strategic

(iii) purely political.

17. Obviously no clear-cut line can be drawn between these variations. The following are examples corresponding to the above categories:–

(i) Persia: seizure of oil and refinery.
   Argentina: British owned public utilities driven out of business and
                 sold up.
(ii) Egypt: denunciation of Treaty.
    Spain: claim to Gibraltar.
(iii) Guatemala: claim to British Honduras.
     Argentina: setting up of Antarctic bases on British territory.

18. These are examples of the steady attempted sapping at our position as a world power by less developed nations. While some actions hurt us more in the economic and others in the strategic field, the net result is to undermine us politically.

19. Each attempt cuts at our prestige, which is a factor common to our relations with all countries, e.g. the loss of Persian oil directly affects our balance of payments, and hence contributes to world uneasiness as to our financial and economic position: but the general effect is to encourage world-wide speculation as to our ability and readiness to maintain our position as a world power.

20. As long as this process continues, there is always the danger that a particular blow may set off a chain reaction with incalculable results, affecting not only Great Britain but other Western powers and thus the stability and strength of the free world.

E. *Measures to maintain our position*

21. There are a number of methods open to us to deal with nationalist behaviour. They are by no means mutually exclusive. On the contrary, they are and should be in most cases complementary.

(i) Domination by occupation. This applies only to territories where we are already established, either by right of conquest or by treaty.
   Provided we have the forces necessary, we can always maintain our position, but we must bear in mind

   (a) the danger of prolonging occupation by force to the point where it may cast doubt on our real desire to lead dependent peoples to independence.
   (b) the resources open to our opponents, e.g. appeals to outside assistance, particularly international organisations.
   (c) the drain that may result on our own resources.

(ii) Domination by intervention (and thence possibly occupation). Use of force to save British lives and in certain circumstances to protect vital British interests or property is often a practical possibility, but it also has practical limits set by world opinion and international law. In special circumstances, it may be possible to justify intervention, to prevent the establishment of a Communist régime.

(iii) Threat of intervention. This is a dangerous method which should only be adopted after the most careful consideration. A bluff which can be called may cost more than throwing in the hand right away. In the case of the United Kingdom, where doubts exist in many countries as to our readiness and ability to use force, the results could be very serious indeed.

(iv) By trying, where we are losing our influence in the political field, to increase it in the cultural, social and economic fields. This can be done in a general way by spreading Western education and by inculcating the virtues of responsible democracy.

(v) By guiding the energies and abilities of nationalist leaders towards cooperation with British interests in the economic field. Particularly in the oil-producing countries of the Middle East we should encourage the use of revenues accruing from oil for the welfare and development of the countries concerned with the help of British technical skill, thus, at the same time, providing an increase of opportunities for the educated and the semi-educated.

Other general lines of approach might be:—

(a) To enlist nationalist support for development schemes to which the U.K. might contribute aid. Success here will depend first on our ability to give i.e. to pay for or find technicians, advisers, material etc. and secondly, on the willingness of the other country to receive. Without material aid we are unlikely to be successful in many cases, particularly in view of the vastly greater benefits to be obtained from the U.S.A.

(b) To encourage local participation in British commercial enterprises in foreign countries. This would not only help to satisfy local ambitions, but might to some extent safeguard our own interests by ensuring that the risk-capital involved and higher business posts available are shared with natives of the country concerned. In general this suggests the creation of a vested interest which would be bound to us politically and/or economically.

(c) To promote cooperation through international solutions: e.g. association in advisory commissions under the authority of a world international organisation, industrial consortia, waterways and land development boards etc.

22. The above measures are listed roughly in the order in which they might be applicable to the various stages of political development reached in territories or states where risks of nationalist action must be faced. But the guiding principles as far as we are concerned must always be:—

(i) To anticipate and, as far as possible, to forestall by adaptation of existing policies nationalist demands which may threaten our vital interests;

(ii) To induce greater maturity of thought in nationalist peoples and leaders, without which any form of cooperation may prove temporary and illusory.

F. *Recommendations for policy*

23. In framing our policies we should accept the following conclusions:—

(i) Progress towards sovereign independence is in our view both inevitable and desirable. We are bound to swim with the tide but we can hope to exert influence on the speed at which the tide runs, both in general and in specific cases.

(ii) Since on the one hand nationalism almost invariably contains an actual or potential element of xenophobia, while on the other Great Britain has wider interests in the world than any other nation, we are bound to be the worst sufferers from nationalist activities.

(iii) Conversely, it is for us to give a lead in dealing with the problem of nationalism. In our highly vulnerable position our aim must be to minimise loss to ourselves and to establish new and fruitful relationships at all stages.

G

(iv) While the trend of nationalism is clear, there is no other common thread or pattern of nationalist action; hence there is no common pattern of counteraction.

(v) Encouragement of healthy nationalism both in dependent territories and sovereign states is a traditional British policy, continuation of which is essential to our efforts to safeguard our position as a world of Power and to the maintenance of a firm front against Communist infiltration. In pursuing this policy we must pay close attention to the possible repercussions of our actions on the interests of other Western Powers, and hence on our relations with these Powers.

(vi) We can always hope to deal with satisfied nationalism as e.g. in India. On the other hand, while it should be our policy to meet nationalist aspirations to the best of our ability, and within the limits imposed by the need to safeguard our own vital interests, we must take care to avoid giving any impression of weakness.

(vii) In adopting attitudes towards nationalist behaviour we shall have to take into account United States opinion, world (e.g. U.N.) opinion, and our own public opinion, probably in that order. On our side we must take care that our behaviour to the people of the countries concerned is free from a detectable assumption of superiority.

(viii) In the present state of world affairs no country or territory is likely to be satisfied for any length of period with any solution that appears to fall short of full sovereignty, not excluding control by an international body or group of nations.

(ix) We are dealing with both Governments and peoples: Governments cannot, even if they wish to, hold out for long against public opinion.

24. If these conclusions are correct, steps to be taken by H.M.G. appear to be as follows:—

(i) To examine every point of the world, including our own colonial territories, at which our strategic or economic interests are being or might be threatened by nationalist agitation: to analyse carefully and with a long term view actual or potential nationalist aspirations in each case, and to consider the best means of drawing the forces of nationalism on to our side: to determine whether an implied threat of force can still be used; which if any of the measures or combination of measures outlined in section E can be used effectively to ensure the continued cooperation of the country concerned; whether overt or covert measures can be taken to prevent nationalism getting out of control, e.g. by creating a class with a vested interest in cooperation.

(ii) So to educate the United States Government and public in our ideas of colonial and national development (particularly by emphasizing the contribution made by it to combating the spread of Communism) that we can rely on obtaining a sympathetic hearing for our interests and requirements and obtain an assurance of their cooperation *vis-à-vis* the country concerned with the United Nations and world opinion. The combination of the two great English-speaking Powers could be effective in many instances in checking the more dangerous manifestations of nationalism. Generally speaking, we cannot hope to deal effectively with nationalism where we can be played off against the U.S.A. On the other hand, wherever

U.S. influence is introduced, our own is likely to decline, with consequent danger to the maintenance of our own interests.

(iii) To enlist the active support and sympathy in our problems of other members of the Commonwealth, particularly those of non-Anglo-Saxon origin who have advanced from purely colonial status to part or full independence. Pakistan's influence in the Moslem world should be particularly borne in mind.

(iv) To seek by consultation with the other Western Powers an agreed policy as far as possible both in regard to nationalism in general and for dealing with specific manifestations.

(v) To attempt to direct the emotions and aspirations of nationalist leaders towards the creation of the sort of healthy nationalism which is of advantage to the peoples of the countries concerned and with which we can hope to deal: by showing sympathy for their desires for social reforms: by interesting them in social welfare and economic development projects: and by inculcating in them a sense of responsibility by every means and at every opportunity, e.g. through Her Majesty's Representatives abroad, by cooperation in the United Nations, through consultation on international commissions, etc.

5 CAB 129/54, C(52)253   22 July 1952
'The defence programme': Cabinet memorandum by Lord Alexander

As the Cabinet will be called upon to take final decisions this week which will greatly affect the Defence Programme, I feel that my colleagues should be clearly informed of the questions at issue.

2. In August, 1950, the late Government launched a 3-year rearmament programme, the total size of which was increased in January, 1951. The financial year 1951/52 was the first effective year of this programme, and the plan then approved allowed for the following expenditure:—

1951/52	1952/53 £m	1953/54
1,250 (actual)	1,531	1,694

The above figures total £4,475 millions. The plan amounted to £4,700 millions, the difference being accounted for by expenditure on civil defence and stockpiling.

3. The programme was delayed in the first year with the result that the actual expenditure in 1951/52 was £1,132 millions. In December, 1951, a defence budget for the three years 1952/53 to 1954/55 was prepared. This revised the original plan to allow for increase in prices, and carried it on for a further year. The figures in this four year budget were as follows:—

1951/52	1952/53 £m	1953/54	1954/55
1,132	1,666	1,838	1,916

4. During the course of the winter, the estimate for 1952/53 was examined and a

number of cuts were imposed which reduced the figure for the current financial year to £1,462 millions. The £200 millions taken off the estimate was largely for items which would have to be postponed to subsequent years. At the same time it was announced in Parliament that the three-year rearmament programme was being rolled forward to cover a longer period.

5.   In March, of this year, I asked the Chiefs of Staff Committee to re-examine the strategic basis of our defence plans, so as to provide for the next two or three years a policy upon which rearmament could proceed. It had become evident that the rapid development of atomic weapons and the build-up of United States strategic air power were changing the strategic picture which had been formed two years previously. In addition, the strain on our economy called for a re-examination of the scope of our rearmament, to bring it into line with what we could afford to maintain for a long period. The outcome of this study by the Chiefs of Staff is the memorandum on Defence Policy and Global Strategy (D.(52) 26)[1] which my colleagues have now seen. It should be read in conjunction with the Foreign Secretary's memorandum (C.(52) 202) on British Overseas Obligations.[2]

6.   The Chiefs of Staff's memorandum has been before the Defence Committee and has been generally approved as a sound strategic policy. Decisions have not yet been taken, however, on the actual size and build-up of the forces required to give effect to the policy, as set out in Section XIV of the memorandum. It was first necessary to ascertain the cost of what was proposed and to see whether this cost was acceptable. It is not only a financial question. It is also a question of whether the industrial resources required for the rearmament programme can be spared from other vital uses.

7.   The costing has now been done, admittedly rather hastily, and has been carried to the year 1955/56. The resulting figures at present prices which are in excess of the prices ruling in previous calculations, are as follows:—

1952/53	1953/54	1954/55	1955/56
		£m	
1,462 (actual)	1,759	1,857	1,867

It will be seen that the figures for the years 1953/54 and 1954/55 are somewhat smaller than the figures of the December 1951 defence budget, which are given in paragraph 3 above. They would be smaller still, to the tune of about £200 millions each year, if there had not been a number of new items to include, namely the rise in prices (£50 millions per annum), the probable cost of maintaining our forces in Germany (£70 millions to £90 millions per annum), additional duty on oil products (a book-keeping transaction which throws £35 millions per annum on to the Defence Vote), and a number of other smaller items including £15 millions per annum for cancelled contracts. On a strictly comparable basis, therefore, the costing of the Chiefs of Staff memorandum shows a saving of nearly £300 millions per annum in each of the next two financial years on the previous figures.

8.   There are two further elements in the rearmament programme which have to be looked at separately. They are:—

---

[1] Dated 17 June 1952 and retained in department (CAB 131/12).   [2] See 3.

(a) the cost of overseas commitments in foreign exchange; and

(b) the load on the metal-using industries.

It is clear from the Foreign Secretary's memorandum that there is little hope of any reduction in our overseas commitments. The whole of the Regular Army, amounting to 11 Divisions, is committed abroad in Germany, the Middle East, Malaya and Korea. We are under obligation to our Allies in N.A.T.O. to maintain the present land forces in Germany, to build up the Tactical Air Force, and to increase the anti-U boat and anti-mine resources of the Royal Navy. Reductions in all these commitments can only be made at the risk of grave repercussions on the general strength and morale of the Western World, to whom our example is of great importance.

9. The permissible load on the metal-using industries is the chief limitation on the speed and scale of the re-equipment of the Forces with modern weapons. It should be realised that during the five years following the end of the war forces had to be maintained all over the world of a size large by peacetime standards. But during that period little or nothing could be done to re-equip them with new weapons. This was a serious matter when it is realised what strides have been made since the war, particularly in the field of aircraft, of electronics, and in all the many items of equipment on which scientific skill has been concentrated. When the rearmament plan was started therefore a tremendous leeway had to be made up. Under the Chiefs of Staff's plan, which has now been costed and which considerably modifies the ultimate size of the forces previously planned, re-equipment with new weapons will not be complete until April 1958. Any substantial reduction of this plan will mean either a reduction in the size of the forces, or a still further delay in the process of re-equipment, or both.

10. The load on the metal-using industries of the Chiefs of Staff's plan has been calculated as follows:—

1952	1953	1954	1955
£500M	£500M	£570M	Cannot yet be calculated, but would not be less than £570M.

11. In the discussions that have been proceeding over the last two or three weeks, the Chancellor of the Exchequer has asked first that the total figure for expenditure on defence in each of the next three years should be kept down to the current figure of £1,462 millions; secondly that the load on the metal-using industries through the same three years should be kept down to £450 millions per annum. I have agreed to re-examine the programmes and to do everything possible to reduce the load on the metal using industries for 1953 from £500 millions to a lower figure by accepting reductions where it can reasonably be shown that these will benefit the export industry. No decisions have yet been proposed for the load on the metal using industries for future years, nor upon the size of the defence budget as a whole. I only wish, at this moment, to warn my colleagues that if the level of expenditure and resources devoted to the defence programme is cut much below the level now proposed by the Chiefs of Staff, the rearmament programme will be largely abandoned. We are now in the second year since the start of the original plan, and the great bulk of orders for the programme, amounting to some £1,500 millions, have already been placed. As everyone knows, it is in the third and fourth years of a

plan that the full flow of material takes place. A rearmament plan cannot avoid a rising curve of expenditure over the first three or four years, though thereafter the curve may flatten out and possibly descend. Drastic reductions in the second and third years, and the stopping of all rise in the future, merely dislocates the whole programme and ensures that the results will be inefficient and dangerously incomplete. I am prepared to do all I can to meet the wishes of the Chancellor of the Exchequer, and it may well be that financial considerations must override others. The Cabinet should be under no illusion, however. They cannot have it both ways. Severe cuts cannot be made without industry, the Armed Forces, and, before long, our Allies, realising that our rearmament programme is being emasculated and is taking second place to housing, consumer goods, and social services, which are remaining virtually unaffected.

6 CO 936/217, no 4/5   9 Sept 1952
[The problem of nationalism]: letter (reply) from Sir T Lloyd to Sir W Strang

I regret that it has taken so long to let you have our views on the paper "The Problem of Nationalism" enclosed in your letter of the 21st June.[1]

2. As you say in your letter, the aim of the paper in its present form is to "assess the significance and strength of present-day nationalism and the threat which it presents to *British* interests". Given this object, we think the paper deals convincingly with nationalism as a global problem and as viewed from a purely British angle. But (and this is our difficulty) the global approach tends to obscure the fact that nationalism takes two forms—destructive when based on xenophobia and fear of alien domination, and constructive when motivated by legitimate aspiration to self-government and a place in the comity of nations. It is the former type with which the paper is chiefly concerned, but it is the latter which is more important in the Colonies even though it may be marred by feelings of race. Its existence both arises from and underlies our basic Colonial policy, namely the guidance of the Colonial peoples to self-government within the Commonwealth. We would feel inclined to suggest therefore that, if the paper is to take account of the special brand of nationalism which appears in the Colonies, it should also suggest means by which we can convert the present upsurge of nationalism into a force which will be helpful to the economic and strategic position of the Commonwealth.

3. The most noticeable type of nationalism in the Colonial territories involves agitation for political "freedom" and power. Such demands are made because the peoples concerned feel that political power is the only means of obtaining greater material prosperity, expanding social services and freedom from differentiation between races in the provision of such services and in opportunities for employment, as well as from the social manifestations of colour prejudice. In dealing with this situation it is necessary to realize that the outlook of settled European groups in the Colonies is not the same as the outlook of the U.K. public. These groups are themselves potentially nationalist and their nationalism necessarily conflicts with

---

[1] See 4.

that of other racial groups in the territories concerned. The problem which faces us here is that of fusing the different nationalist elements into one. Although the attitude of the public in the U.K. to the colour question is for the most part healthy, very often our compatriots in direct contact with coloured races have strong and deeply-rooted prejudices which, if allowed to develop, may become dangerous to ourselves and the Commonwealth. This danger is increased by our having to maintain solidarity with other nations who are less liberal in outlook than ourselves, so that we often have to tolerate or at least refrain from objecting to policies which we and the world know are reactionary. This is at the root of the numerous and growing embarrassments which face us in Africa as a result of our failure, for reasons of general Commonwealth strategy, to say what we think in public, and particularly in Africa, about the native policies of the Union of South Africa.

4. Subject to the general reservation expressed above, I hope you will find useful the following observations on particular paragraphs of your paper:—

(a) *Paragraph 21(i), (ii), (iii):*
Provided that we have the necessary forces it is possible that circumstances may arise in which we should use them, but by and large it is inconceivable in the circumstances of the world today that we could use force actually to retain a large Colony under British administration against the wishes of a majority of its people.

(b) *Paragraph 21 (iv):*
This is, in our view, unquestionably one of the most valuable steps which we could take but its implementation will require a change in present financial policy towards information services, the activities of the British Council, the overseas Services of the B.B.C., etc., etc.

(c) *Paragraph 21 (v):*
This is a line of action which has long been reflected in our Colonial activities. The Secretary of State attaches very great importance to getting Colonial Governments and peoples to take a closer interest in the prosperity of overseas enterprises operating in their territories and has emphasized the desirability of them having some share in the equity capital of such enterprises. But economic development can never be a substitute for political development, and since, given the climatic and other conditions in most Colonies, wholly satisfactory economic conditions are probably unattainable, the demand for political progress will doubtless continue.

5. As to the recommendations for policy, the somewhat different approach to the problem of nationalism which, as I have suggested above, is more appropriate in the case of the Colonies, necessarily modifies to some extent the conclusions in paragraph 23 of the paper, though it does not invalidate them. It seems to us that it is becoming increasingly impracticable to maintain "Imperialism" (i.e. U.K. hegemony) even if disguised. Nevertheless the U.K. and the Colonies have a common and indivisible interest (which can be presented quite openly to Colonies and their cooperation sought) and this can probably best be put across if we pursue the line (which also has its value so far as nationalism outside the Colonies is concerned) that any idea of complete independence which nationalists may hold is unrealistic in the world of today. Total independence is as much an illusion for the U.K. as for any Colony or any sovereign state and insistence on complete independence and self-sufficiency is dangerous to world peace. By taking such a standpoint, it becomes

much more respectable for us to attack the more objectionable manifestations of nationalism whether in the Colonies or elsewhere, and this is what, in our view, requires to be done.

(a) *Paragraph 23 (vii):*
What has first to be taken into account (so far as Colonial nationalism is concerned) is the broad trend of public opinion in the Colonies concerned. British public opinion is in the main largely in sympathy with nationalist trends in the Colonies and our primary object must therefore be to keep Colonial and British opinion in sympathy. If we do that any dificulty that might still persist with United States or other world opinion would clearly be of much less account.

(b) *Paragraph 24 (i):*
The question of nationalist agitation in each of our territories is, of course, a constant preoccupation in the Colonial Office, as I think the observations I have made above will show.

(c) *Paragraph 24 (ii):*
The need for educating United States opinion referred to in this paragraph has long been recognized and consistently advocated by the Colonial Office and we have, I think, on many occasions in the past expressed our views on this subject quite forcibly, most recently in a personal and confidential letter which Martin sent Mason on the 13th June.[2]

6. Broadly speaking the conclusions in paragraph 23 and the proposals in paragraph 24 of the paper are acceptable to the Colonial Office, but since the problems arising from nationalism in the Colonies are a primary daily concern in the Office we are not convinced that any new and comprehensive examination of the subject is necessary: we are, of course, ready and willing at any time to make our contribution to the study envisaged in paragraph 24 (i).

7. I hope the foregoing will prove to be of some value to you. We should have no objection to the circulation of your paper in the Foreign Office and Whitehall distribution but hope that it will first be reconsidered in the light of our comments and views.

8. I am sending a copy of this letter to Liesching.[3]

---

[2] P Mason, assistant under-secretary of state, FO, 1951–1954. Sir J Martin's letter to Mason is at FO 371/101383, no 2411/8, June 1952.

[3] An FO print of the paper, taking into account CO and CRO comments, was circulated to all Cabinet ministers and major diplomatic posts in Dec 1952. The CO restricted its circulation to seventeen of the colonial governors. This was not because of the paper's confidential character but because it was thought that even the revised version took insufficient account of the CO point of view. Some officials also thought it of low quality, minuting for example 'Not to Mediterranean territories. . . . a jejune, misguided and in places slightly horrific document' (J S Bennett (assistant secretary, CO, 1946–1966), 26 Dec 1952); 'I would not trouble S.E.A. Governors with this Sixth Form essay' (J E Marnham (assistant secretary, CO, 1948–1964), 31 Dec 1952) (both CO 936/217).

7   CO 968/353, no 37   24 Sept 1952
'Communist literature in the colonies': minutes of the Official
Committee on Communism   [Extract]

... it had previously been decided that it was not practicable to prevent Communist literature from leaving the United Kingdom; any action to exclude it from the Colonies would therefore have to be taken by Colonial Governments themselves. The Committee would wish to know how this matter now stood in the Colonies.

Mr. Trafford Smith said that the Colonial Office had some time ago sent out to all Colonial Governments a model Ordinance for dealing with undesirable literature, which would give the Governments full powers but also a discretion as to how far they should use them. Most Colonies had now passed such ordinances, but the extent to which they were used in any particular Colony depended on the Governor or the Governor-in-Council. Colonial Governments had been advised not to impose a blanket ban, e.g. on the publications of any particular form, but rather to judge each item on its own demerits.[1] Though each Colonial Government must necessarily act on its own authority, they had been asked to try to secure a broad regional co-ordination in their actions. The Colonial Office held a list of all the publications banned in the Colonies, from which it appeared that there was still a considerable difference in the practice of the various Colonies. Some Colonies, of course, such as the Falkland Islands, had no need to ban Communist literature. The West African Governments were acting on the whole on the right lines, though here there were practical difficulties in keeping out Communist literature, in spite of the ban.

Mr. Ingrams[2] said that, as regards West Africa, by far the most important thing was the provision of "positive" literature describing the western way of life, British institutions etc. for general use. The briefing of officials came next, and definitely anti-Communist literature for general use was last. There was already a big supply of Communist literature in the Colonies, cheap and attractively produced, which was eagerly bought up because of the general thirst for reading matter of any kind. It was for this reason that it was so important to provide the Colonies with suitable reading matter, and a number of steps had been taken to this end. The Colonial Development and Welfare Fund had provided £30,000 for library vans to be used by Missions etc. The C.D.W.F. was also financing literary bureaux in East and West Africa which produced literature, both in English and the vernaculars, at low prices. These bureaux were flourishing and expanding. The Colonial Office also gave as much help as possible to publishers (e.g. Penguins) who contemplated operating in Africa. There was also a certain amount of official literature provided free through the Public Relations Departments in the Colonies. The fact that this was Government-issued did not make it objectionable to the population, as long as the information contained in it was of a "positive" kind, and the illustrated magazine "To-day" had become very popular.

---

[1] This advice had been given by Mr J Griffiths (S of S for the colonies 1950–1951) in a confidential circular despatch of 25 May 1950. In Feb 1953 Mr Lyttelton modified the policy, advising governors that a blanket banning of the publications of the World Federation of Trade Unions, 'which, as you know, is a major instrument of Communist penetration of Colonial territories', would have his support (circular savingram no 207/53, 28 Feb 1953, CO 968/353, no 42).

[2] W H Ingrams, adviser on overseas information services, CO, 1950–1954; author of *Communist prospects in East and Central Africa*, confidential print no 1180, Apr 1953 (copy in CO 879/157).

Generally speaking, the provision of literature for the African Colonies was going well, but, owing to the Information cuts, was not on a sufficiently large scale. This, it was suggested, was a point which might be put by the Colonial Office to the Committee of Enquiry into the Information Services . . . .[3]

---

[3] For extracts from this committee's report, see 12.

8   CAB 129/55, C(52)316   3 Oct 1952
'The defence programme': Cabinet memorandum by Lord Alexander

On 22nd July, 1952, I circulated a memorandum to the Cabinet (C. (52) 253)[1] in which I set out the estimated expenditure over the next three financial years required to give effect to the policy set out in the Chiefs of Staff Review of Defence Policy and Global Strategy (D. (52) 26). On 23rd July, the Cabinet asked me to examine the effects of adopting lower figures both for annual expenditure and for the load thrown by the rearmament programme on the metal-using industry (C.C. (52) 72nd Conclusions, Minute 5). In subsequent discussion with the Chancellor of the Exchequer he and I agreed on certain alternative figures as a basis for this further examination, which has now been carried out. The results, with the comments of the Chiefs of Staff, have been circulated in D. (52) 41. The Annex to that paper contains a careful and detailed analysis of the ways in which the programme devised to give effect to the Chiefs of Staff's Strategic Review would have to be modified if either of the alternative lower figures (Exercises I and II—see Table I of the Report) had to be accepted. A defence programme is a highly complex affair and it is not easy from a study of a mass of detail to derive a clear picture of the general effect of different levels of expenditure. I want in this paper to help my colleagues to realise clearly what is at stake, and to state my own conclusions on the proper size of the programme for the next three years.

2.   In my previous memorandum (C. (52) 253) I drew the attention of the Cabinet to the importance of the Chiefs of Staff's Review, which they completed in July of this year. For the first time since the beginning of the rearmament programme we had a full and careful assessment of our world-wide tasks and obligations made in the light of the rapid development of atomic weapons and of the United States' strategic air power, and taking account of the economic situation of the country. That Review and the Foreign Secretary's memorandum on British Overseas Obligations (C. (52) 202),[2] both of which were generally endorsed by the Defence Committee, set before us a coherent basis for our defence planning. The Chiefs of Staff, in their new report, once more emphasise that any marked departure from the programme worked out from their Strategic Review would be attended by unacceptable military risks. They point out that they did everything they could to confine their rearmament proposals within the limits imposed by economic necessity. The resultant programme did not by any means build up completely equipped forces in three or four years. Far from it. Re-equipment with new weapons under that programme would have reached a

---

[1] See 5.   [2] See 3.

reasonably satisfactory level by 1958, but much would have remained to be done even after that date in all three Services if they were to be fully prepared for war. This must be borne in mind in considering any further reduction of the programme.

3. Our defence plans have to cover the current needs of forces of a certain size, the build-up of the forces where they are clearly insufficient, and a re-equipment programme for providing them with modern equipment where this is necessary, and for building up war reserves to a minimum level. With regard to the size of the forces and the build-up that is planned, the position is quite simple. No increase or decrease is planned in the size of the active Army, the whole of which is committed in the Cold War, and only four of our reserve divisions are to be equipped for war. There will be some decline in the active strength of the Navy, though it is intended to build up the number of anti-submarine craft and minesweepers—the additional ships would be mainly in reserve—in which our deficiencies are most serious, and to proceed with the modernisation of old ships to fit them for the conditions of modern warfare. The whole of the programme will be carried out at a slower pace than previously intended. The Royal Air Force is to be expanded from its present dangerously low level in order to strengthen the defences of this country against air attack and to contribute to the deterrent forces of the Atlantic Alliance. The expansion is, however, much smaller than that to which we have been working since January 1951. Our contributions to N.A.T.O. will generally fall far below those which we accepted at Lisbon; this applies especially to bomber and tactical air forces.

4. The main issue on the re-equipment programme is how rapidly we should introduce modern equipment to replace the old, and how quickly we should build up the small war reserves for which the new strategic concept calls. The programme recommended by the Chiefs of Staff already moves uncomfortably slowly. To reduce it much further would increase the danger that should war come the forces we should have to commit would be gravely underequipped and outmatched by the enemy. If we are to have a rearmament programme at all, we must spend enough on it to make it effective; nothing would be more uneconomical than to spend considerable sums over many years without increasing the effectiveness of our armed power.

5. Given our strategic commitments, our obligations to our Allies, and our general tasks in the Cold War, our right course would be to accept the programme which the Chiefs of Staff have recommended. However, in assessing what is needed to carry out a given policy, there is room for argument about the precise composition of the programme, and about how far we should go in discounting the possibility of war in the next three or four years. There is also room for discussion about the degree of obsolescence that can be accepted in some types of equipment.

6. I have, therefore, in accordance with the policy which I have consistently followed since I took up office, and in full consciousness of our grave economic problems, felt it my duty to examine most carefully the programmes of the three Services to see whether expenditure could be reduced without irreparable damage to the main structure of the rearmament plan. In consultation with the Service Ministers and the Chiefs of Staff, I have personally scrutinised in detail the programme of each Service.

7. The result has been to confirm the validity of the recommendations made by the Chiefs of Staff and to demonstrate that they are not making any excessive demands.

8. I have, nevertheless, investigated certain further economies, which while they would be most undesirable and extremely painful, would not destroy the whole basis of the programme, though they would materially set back our readiness for war.

9. These further economies cover a wide range, but the following brief account will, I hope, serve to indicate their general nature. In the Army's programme, the main change would be a cut of more than three-quarters in the number of tanks with the 120-mm. gun to be delivered in the three-year period. This would severely reduce the fighting power of our divisions on the Continent, but the number of tanks left in the programme would be sufficient to keep the production line going at minimum level and to put enough tanks into the front line to act as a wholesome deterrent. In the Royal Air Force, the completion of the build-up of the night fighter force in Fighter Command would be delayed from the end of 1953 to the end of 1954; the creation of the mobile reserve of fighters would be slowed down; and expansion of Bomber Command planned to take place by the end of 1955 would be greatly reduced. This would mean taking the Washingtons (B.29s) completely out of service. In the Navy, our own programme of minesweepers would be reduced by 40, and the ships would be offered to the United States as an off-shore purchase for allocation to N.A.T.O. countries, so that they would still go to reduce the general deficiencies of minesweepers. For all three Services, the vehicle programmes would be cut, the accumulation of war reserves of warlike stores in several important categories, as well as of general stores and clothing, would be delayed; all further stockpiling of oil fuel would cease, except for aviation fuels, our stocks of which are far too low, and stocks would be run down to some extent. Further reductions would be made in works programmes and staffs would be reduced wherever possible. The numbers of Z reservists called up for training would be substantially cut, and there would be some reduction in the refresher training of reserve pilots.

10. If all these economies were forced upon us, the saving during the three years would be about £250 million.

11. I can summarise the position as follows. The original costing of the Chiefs of Staff Review gave the following figures:—

1952–53 £M.	1953–54 £M.	1954–55 £M.	1955–56 £M.	Total, 1943–54– 1955–56 £M.
1,462 (actual)	1,759	1,857	1,867	5,483

A revised and more accurate costing of the programme has since been worked out, making better allowances for shortfalls in production, giving the following figures:—

1952–53 £M.	1953–54 £M.	1954–55 £M.	1955–56 £M.	Total, 1943–54– 1955–56 £M.
1,462 (actual)	1,719	1,777	1,790	5,286

The figures that would result from the Chiefs of Staff Review, if the savings mentioned in paragraphs 9 and 10 were made in full, would be:—

1952–53 £M.	1953–54 £M.	1954–55 £M.	1955–56 £M.	Total, 1943–54– 1955–56 £M.
1,462 (actual)	1,645	1,688	1,698	5,301

12. In comparing the figures of future expenditure with the provision for the current year, it should be remembered that they include, as pointed out in paragraphs 5 and 6 of the Annex to D. (52) 41, substantial amounts for services for which either no provision, or much smaller provision, had to be made this year. In considering these amounts, the following factors should be borne in mind:—

(a) *Germany*

It has been assumed that from July 1953 the local costs of United Kingdom forces in Germany will be met in full by the United Kingdom Exchequer. We have maintained that we cannot accept this additional burden on our balance of payments. The Americans are well aware of this. There is also likely to be some delay in raising the first German forces. Against this background I suggest that it would be reasonable to assume that our local costs after July 1953 will not have to be borne in full by the United Kingdom Exchequer, but that they will be offset from Germany or from American aid in a substantial degree, which I should estimate at possibly £30 million in 1953–54 and £35 million in each of the two succeeding years.

(b) *G.P.O. charges*

Under a recent Cabinet ruling the cost of G.P.O. expenditure on defence account is now being recovered from defence votes, and thus forms part of the defence budget though *not* an additional charge on the Exchequer.

(c) *Expenditure in Malaya*

Again under a recent Cabinet ruling the extra cost of preserving internal security in Malaya has been transferred from the Colonial and Middle Eastern Services Vote to Defence Votes, with *no* extra charge to the Exchequer.

(d) *Petrol duty*

The figures include about £40 million a year for petrol duty, which returns immediately to the Exchequer. This amount has been greatly increased, to the extent of no less than £35 million a year in comparison with previous years, by increased duty and because jet aircraft now use dutiable fuel. Clearly this expenditure is *no* burden on the Exchequer.

13. The sums concerned in these four items are:—

		1953–54 £M.	1954–55 £M.	1955–56 £M.	Total £M.
Germany ...	...	30	35	35	100
G.P.O. Services	...	10	11	12	33
Malaya ...	...	8	8	9	25
Petrol Duty	...	39	38	40	117
		87	92	96	275

Full allowance must be made for this additional burden on the defence budget in any comparison between current and future estimates.

Metal-using industries

14. If the further economies mentioned in paragraphs 9 and 10 above were made in full, the load imposed on the metal-using industries by the defence programme would be reduced:—

					1953 £M	1954 £M.	1955 £M.
From	...	...	...	...	515	580	590
To ...	...	...	...	...	485	540	550

These figures are admittedly somewhat higher than the figures which I had suggested to the Chancellor as a basis for examination, and a good deal higher than the flat level of £450 million, which the Chancellor suggested. Metal-using production is, however, the heart and core of the rearmament programme and I am fully satisfied:—

(a) that, after making every effort, all possible economies in this sphere, which are consistent with the maintenance of the rearmament programme at an adequate level, have been made;

(b) that to impose further reductions on the figures now suggested would create very serious risks;

(c) that to impose a flat level of metal-using production over the next three years at this stage of the rearmament programme is not practicable without destroying the whole basis of the programme and causing far more serious dislocation and inefficiency than that with which we are already faced.

15. I would ask my colleagues to bear in mind, too, that these calculations on metal-using production are not by any means precise and that the whole matter must be considered against the background of a total metal-using production in the country of somewhere between £3,500 million and £4,000 million annually. It does not seem to me that for the sake of £30 million or £40 million annually we should be justified in inflicting the serious damage to the rearmament programme which would result from further reductions of this kind.

Investment programmes

16. The investment programmes (new works and building in the United Kingdom only) corresponding to the financial estimates under Global Strategy require £118 million in the calendar year 1953. The economies which I have mentioned in paragraphs 9 and 10 would reduce this figure slightly and generally I am prepared to keep the 1953 programme within the limit of £114 million upon which the Cabinet agreed in principle at their meeting on 24th July (C.C. (52) 73rd Conclusions, Minute 8). In the years 1954 and 1955 the figures fall to £102.5 million and £98.5 million respectively, a significant reduction which should be of considerable assistance to the economy.

Prices

17. When I undertook my further study of the programme, I agreed with the Chancellor of the Exchequer that this should be in terms of real resources and not simply of money. All the figures in this memorandum and in D. (52) 41 are based on

the level of costs, prices and wages prevailing in June 1952 and no allowance has been made for any increases during the next three years. The programme would thus not be susceptible of reduction to offset rises in costs. Neither, of course, could any reductions be made to accommodate any further items such as those mentioned in paragraph 12 which it may be decided in future to transfer from other votes to defence votes.

Conclusion
18.   It is essential for domestic and international reasons that a broad decision on the size of our future defence programme should be reached as soon as possible, and that this decision should cover the next three years. We cannot delay any longer in deciding what figures we are to use for the N.A.T.O. Annual Review, our reply to which is already a month overdue. The further examination I have made has confirmed my view that to carry out our agreed policy we need a defence budget of the size which I recommended in my earlier paper C. (52) 253 of 22nd July, as adjusted in Table III of the Annex to D. (52) 41, *i.e.*, £5,286 million for the three years. If, however, our economic difficulties compel us to reduce all forms of Government expenditure and use of economic resources, I should be prepared, though with great reluctance, to make further economies in order to come down to £5,031 million. I could not possibly recommend going any further than this. I recognise that we are living in times when risks must be run—political, economic and military. But the balance of risk must be evenly borne. I could not subscribe to a policy which, in a manner so familiar in the past, threw all the risks on to defence and the armed forces.

9   CAB 129/55, C(52)320   3 Oct 1952
'Defence and economic policy': Cabinet memorandum by Mr Butler.
Appendix: 'Load of defence on the balance of payments'

Introduction
We were all agreed when we took office that the defence programme which we inherited was beyond the nation's means. It was based on assumptions about American aid and the strength of our economy which have since been proved false. The programme would have involved a defence budget of £1,650 million in 1952–53. We cut this back to £1,462 million, and within this total we limited expenditure on metal goods to £460 million.
2.   These reductions were not enough. In the Spring we directed Departments to adjust the programme, so as to contribute £40 million to the balance of payments in 1952–53, by liberating steel and diverting armaments to export. As long ago as May we decided to review the further stages of the defence programme, both to make more metal goods available for export and to reduce overseas expenditure.
3.   These efforts to deal with the situation this year have necessarily been piecemeal. They have not produced the results which we hoped for:—

(a)   Some Defence Departments are finding it difficult to keep within their voted provision: we may be asked to consider at least one substantial Supplementary.
(b)   Defence production of metal goods has increased by rather more than total

metal-goods production: the load is now likely to reach an annual rate of £500 million towards the end of the year.

(c) Service Departments estimates of military expenditure overseas in 1953–54 show an increase of roughly £50 million (about 40 per cent.). This includes £30 million for Germany.

4.   In the Economic Debate at the end of July, the Prime Minister and I, with the agreement of the Cabinet, assured the House that it would be possible to limit the demands made by defence on the engineering industry so as to set free a valuable part of its capacity for the expansion of our civil exports. I have framed my conclusions in paragraphs 14–16 below after re-reading the speeches we made on that occasion.

Minister of defence's proposals

5.   The Minister of Defence was good enough to discuss his Paper (C (52) 316)[1] with me before he put forward his proposals. I recognise the very thorough and careful examination which he has given to the subject, and the grounds on which he feels compelled to propose a Defence Budget of no less than £1,645 million in 1953–54 rising to £1,688 million in 1954–55, and rising yet again to £1,698 million in 1955–56. The corresponding metal-using loads are £485 million, £540 million and £550 million.

6.   These figures *do not* include the defence efforts of the Civil Departments. These will add a further £65 million to £70 million a year (including £20 million further load on the metal-using industries) or £200 million over the three years. There is nothing included here for shelters. Most of the items are of great direct importance to the defence effort, *e.g.*, the communications network for "ROTOR" (the Control and Reporting System), emergency port and oil installations, measures to safeguard essential services, fire-fighting equipments, emergency hospital services, &c. The Minister of Defence's figures also exclude Ministry of Supply assistance to industry and expenditure on nuclear research and stockpiling.

The budgetary problem

7.   It is my duty to look at defence expenditure not in isolation but in relation to our whole economic position. Already in the first half-year the Exchequer Account shows a larger deficit than usual. We are spending more than we expected this year, and, with rising expenditure, we shall start next year with a considerable risk of inflation. The indications so far for next year are unfavourable, with debt interest rising, capital for local authorities outrunning the estimates, and further large rises in social service expenditure threatened in departmental forecasts. This will in itself present a serious problem and if in addition there is a substantial increase in defence expenditure we shall only be able to avoid inflation by making substantial reductions, involving major decisions of policy over the field of public expenditure as a whole. The alternative of a heavy increase of taxation, the bulk of which would have to be found from income tax, would be a reversal of policy which we ought not to contemplate. To find the extra money asked for by the Minister of Defence even in 1953 would mean, if it were wholly by way of income tax, another 1*s*. in the £. I need

---

[1] See 8.

not dwell upon the atrophying effects of taxation even at its present level. It stifles the very virtues—enterprise, initiative, thrift—on which we must rely for rescue from our perils.

8. I am again forced to the conclusion which I have repeated consistently to my colleagues since we took office, and particularly in the papers which I circulated last May (C (52) 166, 172 and 173),[2] that in total we are trying to do far more than our resources permit. If my colleagues are convinced that we must carry on the defence programme at its present level, then there must be adequate reductions in our efforts in other directions. If, to go further, they are convinced that nothing less than the Minister of Defence's proposals will meet the situation, then, of course, the reductions in other directions must be so much the more severe. In other words, if, as regards defence, we go partly over to a war effort, then, on the rest of the field, we must go partly over to a war economy.

Balance of payments

9. The gravity of the aggregate defence load on the balance of payments (over £700 million a year) is described in the Appendix.

10. In the last twelve months there has been a marked improvement in our balance of payments. This is mainly due to the vigorous measures we have taken, such as the import cuts, but it is also thanks to the improvement in the terms of trade and to the aid which we have received from America. These helpful factors cannot be relied on indefinitely. In particular, unless there is some change in the American outlook under the new administration, we are unlikely to receive aid from that quarter on the same scale and in the same form as has benefited our economy hitherto. It is, moreover, only in the last half of 1952 that we expect to be in balance with the non-sterling world on current account and it is only from this point we can start building our reserves. Failure to maintain a strong exchange position will jeopardise the whole economy. Our defence efforts will then be undermined. Moreover, we shall be unable to fulfil our commitments to the Commonwealth and we shall thus forfeit the opportunity to give them the moral leadership for which they are entitled to look to us.

11. An expensive solution of our balance of payments problem depends upon increasing our exports. That means, more than anything else, increased exports by the metal-using industry. Although, as the Minister of Defence points out in paragraph 15 of his paper, total metal goods output is £3,500 to £4,000 million a year, over £1,600 million of this consists of spare parts and consumer goods. A defence load of £485 million in 1953–54 will be about one-quarter of the residue. This residue is the heavier sectors of the engineering industry which provide our best exports and essential home investment requirements. I concluded in C. (52) 173 that we could not safely devote to defence in 1953 and 1954 more than about £400 million worth of metal goods at the prices then ruling. I then made certain assumptions about production and exports which subsequent events have shown to be in general by no means too pessimistic. Certain adverse developments such as a lower export performance by some non-metal goods, and even by some classes of metal consumer goods, look like making us even more dependent on the heavier sectors of the engineering industry for our exports.

---

[2] C(52)166 and 172 are reproduced in part III of this volume, 367, 368.

H

12.　I can therefore find no ground for altering the broad conclusion that any rising level of defence production would impede exports by that sector of engineering with the best continuing export prospects. We cannot abandon our export target at the first sign of sales difficulties, particularly at a time when the Commonwealth Conference is considering proposals which would increase our commitments to finance development in the Commonwealth. Apart from any new commitments, it is necessary for us to pay our way by consistently exporting more than we import, so that a balance on current account is available to meet our existing liabilities.

Germany

13.　As the Minister of Defence points out, we have maintained and continue to maintain publicly that the United Kingdom Budget and Balance of Payments are in no condition to accept any additional load in respect of Germany: and there is certainly no authority from the Cabinet to accept it, or any part of it. I agree, however, that it is realistic in our defence planning to make some provision against the contingency of our not succeeding in getting the whole of our costs in Germany met from outside sources. I agree to take £30 million in 1953–54 and £35 million in each of the two subsequent years as planning figures for this purpose. I feel that this course is justified by the consideration that Germany, though it may constitute a fresh financial commitment, is not a fresh military one. Any additional expenditure on Germany which we may be forced to accept over and above these figures must not only be covered within the total of the defence budget but balanced either by further savings in other overseas military expenditure or by further limitation of the load of defence on the metal-using industries.

Conclusions

14.　As I have indicated in paragraph 8 above it will be necessary, if the defence effort is to be sustained at its present level, let alone increased, to secure retrenchment in other sectors of Government expenditure. Provided my colleagues are prepared to accept the implications of this, I consider that we could face the financial consequences of allowing defence expenditure in 1953–54 to continue at the present level. But planning must clearly proceed on the basis that this is the maximum, not only for 1953–54, but for the two subsequent financial years of the period now under review. I refer to costs in the next paragraph. I agree that the figure should be adjusted upwards to take account of the new impositions on Service Votes which the Minister of Defence mentions and which do not involve any real increase in the defence burden. These additions amount to £57 million in 1953–54. With the additional £30 million for Germany mentioned in paragraph 13 above I reach a total figure for 1953–54 of £1,549 million, say £1,550 million.

15.　I recognise that a defence total of £1,550 million in 1953–54 and the two subsequent years might have to be adjusted to take account of variations in costs, upwards and downwards, as time goes on. But such adjustments cannot be automatic and should be considered on their merits in the circumstances at the time and having regard to the causes underlying the variations. I can go thus far as regards possible adjustments of the total, but I cannot entertain the suggestion made in the Working Party's Report (not, however, repeated in the Minister's covering Paper) that the Defence Budget should be increased to take account of expenditure by the Services on equipment which will not now be completed or will be surplus to requirements.

16. As regards the metal-using load, I consider that £400 million is the most we ought to afford. I am prepared to risk £450 million (£470 million with the inclusion of civil defence requirements), though this must hamper the export drive. To the extent that we go above this level, it will be necessary to make compensating adjustments elsewhere in the economy—particularly in the import programme—to off-set the loss of exports of engineering goods.

Summary

17. (a) Decisions are overdue. The right ones must be taken immediately if they are not to be too late.

(b) We are attempting to do too much. If the Defence Programme is to be sustained at its present level, there must be retrenchment in other expenditure of national resources.

(c) One the understanding that the neesary [sic] compensatory adjustments are made, the Defence Budget can remain at its present level, with certain book-keeping additions and an extra £30 million to take account of Germany. That is, £1,550 million in all.

(d) Within a Defence Budget of £1,550 million, defence claims on the metal-using industries must be limited to £450 million (£470 million including civil defence); and every effort must be made to reduce military expenditure abroad.

(e) We must not plan now for any greater burden of defence in 1954–55 and in 1955–56.

(f) The most that can be allowed, even as a planning assumption, for Germany is about £30 million. Any excess over this must be covered, within the Defence Budget, by savings on other expenditure directly affecting the balance of payments.

(g) Anything more than the current level of expenditure means moving towards a war economy, with radical revision of our social and economic policies.

Appendix to 9

1. My colleagues should be aware of how much of the Defence Budget impacts on our balance of payments. This may be seen from the following Table.

2.

	1951	Estimate 1952	Estimate 1953
		(£ million)	
Metal goods for Defence ...	300	450	450*
Imports of machinery and manufactures	28	82	33
Direct overseas military expen- ditures	122	143	178[†]
	450	675	661
Defence Budget financial years	1,132 1951–52	1,426 1952–53	1,550 1953–54

* At March 1952 prices.

[†] Includes £20 million only for Germany in calendar year 1953.

This does not represent the full cost of defence to our balance of payments. There are other items, such as, strategic stockpiling, oil for Forces in the United Kingdom and imports of raw materials for manufacture of defence non-metal goods.

3. Even on the foregoing figures (which are based on the lower levels of expenditure indicated in paragraphs 14–16 of the Paper and not the full amounts for which the Minister of Defence asks) the load of defence on our balance of payments would be in the region of £700 million in 1953. This would be roughly the equivalent of 70 per cent. of the total imports by the Ministry of Food or about 25 per cent. of our total visible exports.

4. Even on these reduced fiures we will be taking serious risks with our economic policy objective of paying our way in the world.

10   CAB 131/12, D(52)45   31 Oct 1952
'Defence programme': report by COS for Cabinet Defence Committee

Her Majesty's Government are pursuing a policy in the field of Imperial and foreign affairs which they have constantly reaffirmed in public, and which can be summarised as follows:—

(a) To maintain our vital interests in various parts of the world, which are threatened by the Cold War tactics of Russia and China. These vital interests are set out in the Foreign Secretary's paper C (52) 202,[1] of which the Cabinet took note on 9th July.

(b) To build up, together with our Allies and friends, defence forces of a nature and size effectively to deter aggression, and to equip these forces to modern standards.

(c) To make reasonable provision for the security of the United Kingdom and our other interests throughout the world, in case war should come.

2. We were asked to review the general strategic situation and to make recommendations for a defence programme which would enable this policy to be carried out with due regard to the economic difficulties of the country. This we did in our Review of Defence Policy and Global Strategy (D. (52) 26), which was generally endorsed by the Defence Committee and by the Cabinet last July. Since then there has been increasing pressure on us to reduce the cost of the Defence Programme that we recommended in our Review. We accepted with reluctance and misgiving a number of reductions suggested by the Minister of Defence, in an effort to meet the views of the Chancellor of the Exchequer. We have now been told to examine the consequences of figures for defence expenditure far below the "Minister of Defence's compromise." (C. (52) 316.)[2] These new figures are such as to provide in real resources less in 1953 than in 1952; and it has been indicated to us that there must be no rise above this level of expenditure in subsequent years. It will at once be seen that the rearmament programme, launched two years ago, is to take a downward turn in its third year, instead of rising to its peak as previously planned.

3. We are, of course, prepared loyally to carry out any decision that the

---

Government may impose upon us, but we must make it unmistakably clear that the Chancellor's latest proposals[3] represent such a complete departure from the programme to which we have been working, and would produce results falling so far short of what we recommended in our Global Strategy Review, that they cannot be accepted without a marked change in the policy of Her Majesty's Government, as summarised in paragraph 1 above. In our view, either Her Majesty's Government must change their policy, or they must provide the military resources required to carry it out.

4. We attach at Annex I[4] a summary of the main effects on the three Services of reductions in the Defence Budget to meet the Chancellor's latest proposals. This is merely a broad indication on the basis of straight percentage cuts; we have made no attempt to re-apportion the overall cut between the Services, because we cannot see any reasonable strategic policy to which any reallocation could be geared.

5. At Annex II we have set out a comparison of the forces available to-day and those which would be available in 1955 under the Chancellor's latest proposals. This comparison has been made both in a global setting and in the N.A.T.O. setting.

6. We cannot over-emphasise that the description at Annex I of the military consequences of the Chancellor's proposals is not exaggerated. Our detailed examination of the defence programme has continued since last April, to say nothing of the process that led to the reductions in the 1952–53 Estimates. Throughout this period the Service Departments and the Ministry of Supply have overhauled every element of their expenditure, in the knowledge that a considerable reduction in the planned totals was inevitable. It was clear to us that the more that could be found by reductions in standards, by administrative economies, and by taking calculated risks in the level of our preparedness, the smaller would be the reduction in our fighting strength. We have also critically examined each other's proposals from every standpoint. The results are incorporated in the figures which Her Majesty's Ministers have before them. We are fully satisfied that no opportunity for finding economies has been overlooked, and that, within the limits proposed by the Chancellor, the effects outlined at Annex I would be inevitable.

7. We submit that there are now only two alternatives open to Her Majesty's Government:—

either

(a) To provide the resources which we affirm are the minimum required to carry out the policy of Her Majesty's Government and to support our commitments and status as a.Great Power;

or

(b) To reduce our national commitments—and hence our status—to a level which can be supported by the resources for which Her Majesty's Government are prepared to pay.

8. We are convinced that there is no possibility of continuing to meet our present commitments with the resources to which we should be reduced under the Chancellor's latest proposals.

---

[3] See 9.   [4] Annexes not printed.

9. In point of fact paragraph 7(b)—the reduction of our national commitments and status—is not an alternative at all. The Foreign Secretary's paper (C (52) 202) makes it clear that, whether we like it or not, we are a Great Power with world-wide responsibilities. British commitments cannot be cast aside like an outworn coat: they are a world-wide agglomeration of political, economic and commercial interests and obligations involving not merely British prestige but the livelihood—indeed the actual lives—of millions of British subjects.

10. Considering the Middle East, we are not yet in a position to withdraw the 3rd Division and 16th Parachute Brigade to the United Kingdom. We may not even be able to withdraw any forces next year. If the Neguib régime were to break down and Egypt be cast into disorder, we might even have to reinforce the Middle East, unless we were prepared to leave British nationals to be massacred as our people were in Cairo last January.

11. If and when we have achieved a settlement with Egypt and come down to the Global Strategy garrison, we cannot contemplate yet further reductions. The Foreign Secretary has recently been assuring the Turkish Prime Minister and Foreign Minister of our permanent and effective interest in the Eastern Mediterranean and in the Middle East. It will be patently impossible to support that policy if we cut our Middle East garrisons to a token force which even the Arab States will know would be completely useless in war.

12. Similarly, in the Far East, it is unthinkable that we should throw away the fruits of all our toil, effort, and sacrifice in Malaya over the past five years—and with them abandon our greatest dollar-earner—on what may be the brink of success. Nor can we contemplate handing over to the Chinese Communists our interests in Hong Kong, and the lives of all who have sought our protection there. Equally, we cannot default on our United Nations' commitment in Korea by withdrawing the Commonwealth Division.

13. All over the world we are under the greatest pressure to hand over our responsibilities and our possessions. Any evidence of readiness to quit will start a landslide which we shall be quite unable to control. Are we, for instance, to cancel our Treaty and pull out of Iraq just as we embark on a Middle East Defence Organisation? Or are we prepared to deprive ourselves of the ability to intervene quickly to protect British lives in circumstances such as those prevailing in Kenya? What is the good of even discussing a Federation of British Central Africa, if we are to begin by proving to Her Majesty's subjects in Africa that we are quite powerless to protect them in trouble?

14. All this goes to prove that the second alternative (paragraph 7(b) above) is quite impossible, and that we must be given the resources which are necessary for fulfilling the commitments and for carrying out the declared policy of Her Majesty's Government.

15. Finally, turning to N.A.T.O., our contribution to the Alliance is not an act of altruism; nor is this an old-fashioned alliance like the *Entente Cordiale*. On the contrary, N.A.T.O. is vital to the survival of the United Kingdom. Three years ago we faced the stark reality that this island could not possibly be defended in isolation. To-day our very existence depends on the unity and strength of N.A.T.O. and on American support—the two are irretrievably entwined.

16. We, after the United States, are the main pillar of N.A.T.O. We are anxious enough already of the effect on the Alliance of the reductions in our contribution

proposed even under "Global Strategy." It is no exaggeration to say that default on the scale involved under the Chancellor's proposals might well shake the whole N.A.T.O. structure: it might even result in the United States falling back on a Taft-Hoover policy of isolation behind a vast Navy and Atomic Air Force.

17. The Foreign Secretary's paper (C. (52) 202) concludes that we should endeavour to get the United States to bear a greater share of the burden. It points out, however, that such a policy could be successful only "in so far as we are able to demonstrate that we are making the maximum possible effort ourselves." Even now the Americans are far from convinced that this is so. If we accept the implications of the Chancellor's latest proposals, and particularly if we default too flagrantly on our N.A.T.O. obligations, the Americans will be convinced that it is not so. The reactions not only on our military but also on our economic position might well be catastrophic.

18. Our estimate of the forces required to provide a reasonable security for the United Kingdom, and to meet our N.A.T.O. and world-wide commitments, was based on our belief that the likelihood of war had receded. However, the United States Joint Chiefs of Staff rate higher than we do the likelihood of war in the near future; in particular they regard 1954 as a dangerous year. The re-equipment of our forces which we proposed in "Global Strategy" was steady, though slower than originally conceived under the £4,700 million programme; but under the Chancellor's latest proposals our re-equipment will be so retarded that preparations for war in the reasonably foreseeable future will virtually have ceased.

19. Finally, we submit that the Foreign Secretary has said the last word in C. (52) 202.

"The British people ... must either give up for a time some of the advantages which a high standard of living confers upon them, or by relaxing in the outside world see their Country sink to the level of a second-class power with injury to their essential interests and way of life of which they can have little conception."[5]

In our considered opinion, to go beyond the "Minister's compromise" (C. (52) 316) means, sooner rather than later, the acceptance of the Foreign Secretary's second alternative.[6]

---

[5] Emphasis in original.
[6] The report was signed: W J Slim, J C Slessor, R McGrigor.

11   CAB 129/56, C(52)393   5 Nov 1952
'Defence programme': Cabinet memorandum by Mr Butler

To remain a great power we must first of all have economic strength, since it is only on this basis that military strength can be supported. The next three years are the crucial ones in our efforts to re-build our economic defences. World and domestic opinion will judge us in 1956 on the job we have done by then.

2. Our external position is better than it was when we came into office, but it is still far from secure. Our exports are dangerously down on my Budget Estimates. They must have first claim on any additional resources we may have available. Only

by doing this can we get away from the succession of balance of payments crises, and dependence on United States Aid, which have marked the British economy since the end of the war. Moreover, investment in industry in recent years has been kept far below the level which is necessary to modernize our industry and keep up with our main competitors. Already we are losing contracts to Germany and Japan. Unless we can keep down the burdens on the economy I see little prospect of being able to do anything in this field. The claims of defence and industrial investment and of our best exports are directly and inescapably competitive; they all depend on the same sections of the engineering industry.

3.   I have never singled out defence as the only object for economy. My anxiety has been that we are attempting to carry a large and rising housing programme, and a defence programme of a size unknown in peace time. We are in danger of continuing the practice of the previous Government of adopting policies which inevitably commit the Exchequer to carry increasing burdens in the years ahead. In this way our resources are mortgaged in advance, and all prospect of escaping from our economic difficulties and developing our own line is inexorably denied to us.

4.   Let us look at the prospect which faces us. Expenditure next year looks certain to be much higher than this year's Budget Estimates. Increased civil expenditure, higher interest on the floating debt and loans to local authorities (mainly for housing and schools) look like involving us in an extra £175 millions compared with this year's figure. If we take the defence budget at the Minister's figure of £1,645 millions there is, even allowing for transfers between Votes, a further £150 millions of increase here. On the revenue side, I shall get an extra £170 millions from the first year of Excess Profits Levy and the stopping of initial depreciation allowances (i.e. extra income from what would be mainly savings of companies) but against this there will be falls of revenue due partly to the deflation which we ourselves have encouraged and partly to the full effects of the tax concessions made in the last Budget. Overall, the net worsening between this year and next is well over £300 millions. I am prepared to propose to my colleagues economies to cover about half this sum, but these will involve sacrifices in social policy.

5.   We have continually urged, and are still being strongly urged by our supporters, to hold down and reduce public expenditure of all kinds, primarily with the objective of making a start on the intolerable tax burden on industry. A resolution to reduce expenditure was carried at Scarborough despite my plea for understanding of the difficulties. So long as we accept the present level of taxation and are ready to incur additional commitments up to that limit, we shall be denying a cardinal article of our economic and political faith and shall have lost an opportunity to serve the country's best interests.

6.   So far as concerns 1953/54 I am prepared, if my colleagues agree, to make the cuts mentioned in paragraph 4 above amounting to £180 millions or so on the understanding that defence expenditure makes some contribution. We have already cut social and food subsidy expenditure last session. It would surely be difficult to defend further social cuts in Parliament if, after criticising the Socialist Government's defence plans for being too big, we come forward with proposals involving a considerable increase in defence expenditure. I hope we shall bear this in mind when we settle the defence estimates for 1953/54.

7.   Thereafter I would hope that we could plan a pattern of defence expenditure to which we can work during the precarious years in front of us without chopping and

changing with every shift in economic circumstances. This should be based on a considered view of the probable cost, over a long period ahead, of the forces we are proposing to build, maintain and keep equipped with the best weapons; but if it becomes plain, as I think it must, that we can only maintain the highest possible standard of equipment for our forces if their numbers are somewhat less than now planned, we should at once review the situation and take the necessary steps to reduce numbers.

8. I do not myself see how we can go on planning for armed forces of over 850,000 men and women, with well over one million civilians employed in administering, maintaining and equipping them. It would mean devoting indefinitely something like 10 per cent of the total working population to defence.

9. It must be remembered that in addition to our enormous defence budget we have to provide for £60 millions to £70 millions a year (and that on a programme cut by over 40 per cent) for defence efforts of the Civil Departments, together with further sums for stockpiling, atomic energy and Ministry of Supply assistance to industry. *In all, the sums required by the needs of defence come to over one-third of our total budgetary expenditure above and below the line.*[1]

10. Surely such a review, which should of course include the overseas commitments to which our defence expenditure is related, could be conducted without causing any offence or difficulty with other North Atlantic Treaty Powers and with the U.S.A. We know that the American programme is to level off next year. There are signs that we should not surprise the Continent if we actually reduced our defence effort from its present level. There can surely be no just cause for complaint abroad if we do not go on increasing it. At home we can hardly defend a continually increasing burden, calling for yet further sacrifices, when the largest and most prosperous of the N.A.T.O. partners will have stopped increasing its effort.

---

[1] Emphasis in original.

12 CAB 129/64, C(53)305	13 Nov 1953

'Report of the Independent Committee of Inquiry into the Overseas Information Services' (chairman, Lord Drogheda);[1] recommendations for maintaining ties with the colonies	[Extract]

Our Committee was appointed in October 1952 with the following terms of reference:—

> To assess the value, actual and potential, of the overseas information work of the Foreign Office, Commonwealth Relations Office, Colonial Office, Board of Trade and Central Office of Information; the External Services of the British Broadcasting Corporation; and the work of the British Council; to advise upon the relative importance of different methods and services in different areas and circumstances and to make recommendations for future policy.

---

[1] The report was submitted to Cabinet under cover of a note by Mr Eden. A summary of the report was published as Cmnd 9318, Apr 1954.

2. We have had sixty-seven meetings and have heard the evidence of fifty-nine witnesses. We have also had before us a large number of written statements submitted both by Departments and by non-official persons and organisations. In addition, we have inspected the work in various countries in Asia, Africa, Europe and America. We have come to the following general conclusions:—

First. The Overseas Information Services play an important and indeed essential rôle in support of our Foreign, Commonwealth and Colonial policies.
Second. This work should be done well, continuously and on an adequate scale.
Third. If all these requirements are to be met more money must be spent on the Overseas Information Services.
Fourth. Changes are required in the pattern of the work in order to bring it into line with our political, strategic and commercial needs.

3. These conclusions have been forced upon us by sheer weight of evidence. At first we were inclined to be sceptical about the value of activities which are still comparatively new and have been the subject of much criticism. Moreover, we could not but feel suspicious of this invasion by Government of a field which in the not very distant past could be left to non-official agencies. Nevertheless, we have found it impossible to avoid the conclusion that a modern Government has to concern itself with public opinion abroad and be properly equipped to deal with it. This is not just our own view. It is the unanimous view of all the Heads of Mission, Colonial Governors and Military Commanders with whom we spoke. It is the view of the Foreign Office, the Commonwealth Relations Office, the Colonial Office and the Board of Trade. It is the view both of the Federation of British Industries and of the Trades Union Congress. And the same view is held by the Chiefs of Staff who regard the Overseas Information Services as a weapon no less essential than those employed by the fighting forces. Moreover, unlike all others, it is a weapon which does not become obsolescent and which will be needed however and whenever the cold war ends.

4. In the following sections of this report we have endeavoured to show how our conclusions have been reached by going over the ground step by step in much the same way that we ourselves had to do. First it was necessary to find out how and why these services had come into being; next we had to know of what they consisted and how they worked. Finally, we had to assess the need for information work in relation to the political, strategic and commercial requirements of this country overseas and the best methods to apply in different parts of the world. . . .

35. The Colonies too are advancing with challenging rapidity towards self-government. As political control from London is progressively being loosened by constitutional advances it becomes more and more necessary to take steps to strengthen the bonds of sentiment and enlightened self-interest between the United Kingdom and these Dependencies. In addition there is a growing need to counter Communist·machinations in the Colonies. This can best be done by emphasising the democratic alternative to Communism, but a certain amount of direct counter-propaganda is also necessary. Finally, as was noted above, world opinion is becoming increasingly concerned with Colonial affairs and our relations with the Colonies are increasingly affected by world opinion. . . .

48. It is vitally important to maintain our ties with the Colonies at a time when they are advancing so rapidly towards self-government and are becoming increasing-

ly threatened by Communism. All three instruments are required: Information Services to explain the policies of Her Majesty's Government; the British Council to assist in adult education in the broadest sense; the British Broadcasting Corporation to supply Colonial broadcasting systems (which they have helped to build up on the British Broadcasting Corporation pattern) with news and transcriptions. . . .

59. The Colonial Office do not at the moment maintain an organisation for United Kingdom information work in the Colonies. Their Information Service consists only of a small head office in London which, drawing its supplies from the Central Office of Information, provides material for distribution by the Information Departments of the Colonial Governments. This system is no longer satisfactory in those Colonies which have advanced far along the path towards self-government and particularly in those cases where native-born Ministers are now responsible for the work of the Colonial Governments' Information Departments. It is the function of these Departments to serve the interests of the Colonial Government, not of Her Majesty's Government, and after a certain stage of development has been reached it becomes difficult and even embarrassing for them to act also as the main channel for information and publicity about the United Kingdom. Apart from this, the Colonies are increasingly becoming a target for Communist propaganda and there is a need for counter-propaganda designed both to expose the dangers of Communism and expound the virtues of the democratic way of life as an alternative to Communism. We therefore believe that in certain Colonies, United Kingdom Information Offices should be set up to ensure that there is effective representation of the British point of view, effective distribution of British material and effective anti-Communist propaganda.

60. As a beginning, we recommend that four of these offices should be established in Nigeria, the Gold Coast, East Africa and the West Indies. As other Colonies get nearer to self-government such offices may well be required elsewhere; they should be regarded as being, as it were, the advance guard of the High Commissions which will eventually be required when these territories achieve independence within the Commonwealth. The estimated annual cost of the four United Kingdom offices proposed is approximately £60,000. Approximately £30,000 more is required on the Central Office of Information budget in order to provide these new offices with material and also to supply suitable material to Colonial Government Information Departments in the remaining territories. . . .[2]

---

[2] Mr Butler proposed to Cabinet that £150,000 should be shared between FO, CO and CRO to meet the rising cost of existing information services, and that £82,000 should be made available for new services; of this latter sum, the FO should receive £40,000, the CO £35,000, and the CRO £7,000. Cabinet 'approved in principle' (CAB 128/27/1, CC 7(54)5, 3 Feb 1954).

13 PREM 11/702   21 June 1954

[Anglo-American defence relations]: private and personal telegram from Sir W Churchill to President Eisenhower

My dear Friend,
I have always thought that if the French meant to fight for their empire in

Indo-China instead of clearing out as we did of our far greater inheritance in India they should at least have introduced two years' service which would have made it possible for them to use the military power of their nation. They did not do this but fought on for eight years with untrustworthy local troops, with French cadre elements important to the structure of their home army and with the Foreign Legion, a very large proportion of whom were Germans. The result has thus been inevitable and personally I think Mendes-France [sic],[1] whom I do not know, has made up his mind to clear out on the best terms available. If that is so, I think he is right.

2. I have thought continuously about what we ought to do in the circumstances. Here it is. There is all the more need to discuss ways and means of establishing a firm front against Communism in the Pacific sphere. We should certainly have a SEATO corresponding to NATO in the Atlantic and European sphere. In this it is important to have the support of the Asian countries. This raises the question of timing in relation to Geneva.[2]

3. In no foreseeable circumstances except possibly a local rescue could British troops be used in Indo-China and if we were asked our opinion we should advise against United States local intervention except for rescue.

4. The SEATO front should be considered as a whole and also in relation to our world front against Communist aggression. As the sectors of the SEATO front are so widely divided and different in conditions, it is better, so far as possible, to operate nationally. We garrison Hong Kong and the British Commonwealth contributes a division to Korea. But our main sector must be Malaya. Here we have twenty-three battalions formed into five brigades. You are no doubt aware of the operation contemplated in the event of a Communist invasion from Siam. I will bring the detailed plan with me. Alex,[3] who I understand is coming over in July, will discuss it with your Generals. The question is whence are we to draw reinforcements. There are none at home; our last regular reserves are deployed. It would be a pity to take troops from Germany. On the other hand we have what are called 80,000 men in the Egyptian Canal Zone, which mean 40,000 well-mounted fighting troops. Here is the obvious reserve.

5. Now is the time the Middle East front should be considered together by the United States and Britain. I had hoped more than a year ago that the United States would act jointly with us in negotiating an agreement with the Egyptian military dictatorship in accordance with the terms already agreed between the British and American staffs. It was however felt at Washington that America could not go unless invited. The negotations therefore broke down. Since then there has been a deadlock though the area of dispute is limited.

6. As time has passed the strategic aspect of the Canal Zone and Base has been continually and fundamentally altered by thermo-nuclear developments and by a Tito–Greeko–Turco front coming into being and giving its hand to Iraq and by America carrying NATO's finger-tips to Pakistan. I like all this improvement in which you and the power and resources of the United States have played so vital a part.

---

[1] P Mendès-France, prime minister and foreign minister of France, 1954–1955.
[2] A reference to the Geneva conference of Apr–July 1954, convened to discuss the problems of Korea and Indo-China. See also 61, 62.
[3] Lord Alexander.

7. These events greatly diminish the strategic importance of the Canal Zone and Base, and what is left of it no longer justifies the expense and diversion of our troops, discharging since the war, not British but international purposes. As far as Egypt is concerned we shall not ask you for a dollar or a marine. I am greatly obliged by the way you have so far withheld arms and money from the Egyptian dictatorship.

8. The general theme of completing and perfecting in a coherent structure the world front against Communist aggression, which I suppose might in current practice be described as NATO, MEATO and SEATO, is of course one, but only one of the topics I am looking forward to talking over with you.

9. The other two have long been in my mind. One is the better sharing of information and also perhaps of resources in the thermo-nuclear sphere. I am sure that you will not overlook the fact that by the Anglo–American base in East Anglia we have made ourselves for the next year or two the nearest and perhaps the only bull's eye of the target. And finally I seek as you know to convince Russia that there is a thoroughly friendly and easy way out for her in which all her hard-driven peoples may gain a broader, fuller and happier life.

10. You know my views, already expressed in October 1953, about Germany. If E.D.C. fails we ought to get her into NATO or a revised form of NATO under the best terms possible.

11. I would not have tried to put all this on paper but for your direct request. So if there is anything in it which you do not like, let it wait till we are together for our weekend meeting, to which I am so keenly looking forward.

With kindest regards,
WINSTON

14   CAB 129/69, C(54)250   24 July 1954
'Report by the Committee on Defence Policy': Cabinet memorandum by Lord Salisbury

While the Prime Minister was in Washington I presided over the concluding meetings of the Committee; and, as the Minister of Defence is now abroad, it falls to me to present the Committee's report.

2. We were instructed to review, in the light of recent developments in atomic weapons, the strategic assumptions underlying current defence policy and the scale and pattern of defence programmes, military and civil. In doing so, we have sought to secure all practicable economies in defence expenditure in 1955 and subsequent years.

Strategic policy

3. A new strategic appreciation by the Chiefs of Staff has been circulated separately to the Cabinet (C. (54) 249). The Committee invite the Cabinet to endorse the following statement, based on that paper, of the aims and objectives of our defence policy.

Our primary aim must be to prevent a major war. To that end we must strengthen our position and influence as a world Power and maintain and consolidate our alliance with the United States. If we do so, it is reasonable to hope that major war may be averted, at any rate during the next four or five years, during which the United States will retain their superiority in atomic weapons and will themselves be comparatively immune from atomic attack. Therefore, during that period, the military means to exert our influence as a world Power and to meet our "cold-war" commitments should have priority over preparations for major war, wherever there is conflict or competing demand on limited resources. Such resources as we can devote to preparations for major war should be concentrated on measures which would be effective immediately on the outbreak of war.

Thus, the main objectives of our defence policy should be:—

(i) To possess the most modern means of waging war, so that we may hold our place in world councils on the issue of peace or war and play our part in deterring aggression.

(ii) To continue to play our part throughout the world in checking the spread of Communism.

(iii) To preserve security and develop stable government in our Colonial territories and to support our world-wide trading interests.

Revision of military programmes

4. The programmes of the Service Departments have been revised in the light of this strategic concept and with the object of achieving the maximum practicable economy. The changes proposed are summarised in Annex I.[1] In the following paragraphs I mention the main proposals, including those which present political difficulties.

(a) The strength and composition of the fleet

5. New building and modernisation will be confined to those ships which can play a valuable rôle in both war and peace. Nearly all the future building of the mine-sweeping fleet will be suspended and the conversion of escort vessels will be curtailed. The remaining programme will be spread over a longer period.

The man-power of the Navy will be reduced over the next two and a half years by one-eighth to a strength of 120,000. The active fleet will be reduced to the minimum required for peace-time commitments.

The reserve fleet will be drastically reduced. 4 carriers, 7 cruisers and about 30 destroyers and frigates now in the lowest category of reserve will be scrapped.

(b) The size of the army

6. Owing to shortage of man-power, the strength of the Regular Army must fall by April, 1956, from 435,000 to 400,000. This will involve the early disbandment of a number of units, including 8 infantry battalions.

The production programme will be reduced, so as to provide for the equipment of 8 (instead of 10) Regular divisions, 2 (instead of 4) Territorial divisions, and a much-reduced Anti-Aircraft Command (see paragraph 9). The pace of the programme will also be retarded.

Only 2 Territorial divisions will be equipped and trained for service overseas.

---

[1] Annexes not printed.

(c) The medium bomber force

7. No reduction is at present proposed in the programme for the development of the Medium Bomber Force. This is an essential part of our contribution to the deterrent. In any event, a reduction in the ultimate planned size of the Force (*viz.*, a front-line strength of 240) would yield no financial saving in 1955.

(d) Air defence of the United Kingdom

8. The Chiefs of Staff have revised our air defence plans in the light of the new strategic concept and the threat of attack by nuclear weapons of enormously increased power. They believe that, if a nuclear attack were made on this country, it would be delivered by manned aircraft flying at heights over 40,000 ft., probably at night—and, after 1960, possibly by ballistic rockets as well. Against the latter no defence is yet in sight: against the former the Swifts and Hunters will only be partially effective as they cannot operate effectively at night or, except for a few aircraft, carry air-to-air guided weapons. The Chiefs of Staff consider that, in order to provide an effective deterrent during the next few years, we must maintain a fighter force which, though smaller in size than that planned hitherto, will have at least 50 per cent. of night/all-weather aircraft and be re-equipped as soon as possible with the newest types of aircraft now under development carrying improved radar aids and guided weapons. It is therefore proposed that:—

(i) The number of aircraft in each squadron should be reduced from 22, as now planned, to 16. This will reduce the planned size of the force from 792 aircraft to 576, of which half will be night/all-weather fighters.

(ii) We should slow down the programme for replacing the obsolescent Meteor aircraft by Hunters and Swifts and reduce the supply of the latter types to the R.A.F. This will mean that Hunters and Swifts will be sold abroad during the next two years while the Air Force still have a proportion of Meteors in front-line squadrons, and this will certainly involve some political difficulty. But it will enable us to reduce by rather more than 400 the number of Swifts and Hunters to be purchased to replace the Meteors.

In the long run, these measures will produce a relatively small but effective fighter force.

9. Anti-aircraft gun defences cannot make any real contribution to defence against aircraft flying at heights over 40,000 feet or against ballistic rockets. It is therefore recommended that Anti-Aircraft Command should be disbanded, except for about 10 regiments of light A.A. guns for the close protection of radar stations on the coast. The small size and isolation of these targets make it more likely that they would be attacked by low-flying aircraft armed with conventional weapons than by high-flying aircraft armed with nuclear weapons.

This step will certainly give rise to public discussion and anxiety. It can be justified only on the basis that anti-aircraft artillery affords no effective defence against the form of attack to which we are likely to be exposed. This argument can best be deployed in the context of a general explanation of our revised defence policy as a whole (see paragraph 18 below).

Economies in expenditure

10. If the Cabinet approve the changes which we recommend in Service

programmes, expenditure on the Armed Forces in 1955 will total £1,630 millions. This represents a reduction of £120 millions on the large total expenditure which would have been required if present plans had remained unaltered.

Revision of civil programmes

11. The development of nuclear weapons calls for a new approach to the problem of civil preparations for war. Plans must be directed to ensuring national survival during the initial phase of a future war. The rôle of the Civil Defence Services will be concerned largely with the after-effects of raids—emergency feeding, treatment of casualties, providing for the homeless and restoring order. A new importance will attach to the mobile columns and, to the extent that it is practicable, dispersal will be a better safeguard than shelter. All the war preparations of Civil Departments are now being overhauled in the light of the new strategic concept.

12. Meanwhile, we have considered what should be the level of expenditure on these preparations in 1955. We have advised Civil Departments to revise their defence programmes in accordance with the following principles:—

(i) During the next four or five years the resources available for defence will be directed primarily to the discharge of our commitments in the "cold war" and to the building up of deterrent strength to prevent the outbreak of major war. Existing plans should be revised on the basis that, wherever there is conflict or competing demand on limited resources, these objectives will take priority over preparations for major war.

(ii) We should, however, take some measures of insurance against the risk that we may fail to achieve our primary aim of preventing major war. We should therefore continue to devote a modest proportion of available resources to those measures which are indispensable to national survival in the initial phase of a major war.

(iii) In general, we should not devote resources to making preparations or providing protection which, though adequate against attack by high explosive or other conventional weapons, would be ineffective against thermo-nuclear weapons.

(iv) Civil Defence programmes should be concentrated upon the measures essential to building up public confidence in Civil Defence and sustaining the efficiency and morale of the Civil Defence Services.

(v) Subject to these qualifications, expenditure by Civil Departments on war preparations should be reduced as rapidly as possible, though all "paper plans" should be revised in the light of the foregoing principles and kept up to date.

We invite the Cabinet to endorse these principles. We set out in Annex II some of the main changes in the policies and plans of Civil Departments which would follow from their adoption.

13. We are not in a position to submit a detailed statement of the savings to be secured in 1955 as a result of the application of the foregoing principles. Under existing plans defence expenditure by Civil Departments would have amounted in 1955 to £45.6 millions, with an additional £18 millions on Post Office communications to be financed by loan. A preliminary survey by the Departments suggests that the application of the policy proposed in this report would make it possible to reduce the figure of £45.6 millions by about one-third, viz., a cut of the order of £15 millions. In addition, there would be a reduction of about £4 millions in the Post

Office expenditure which is financed by loan.

(It should be noted that this figure of £15 millions includes a cut of £1.6 millions in expenditure on defence preparations at ports, for which credit has already been taken in the report of the Committee on Civil Expenditure (C. (54) 232).)

If the principles which we have formulated are strictly applied in the detailed examination of the Departmental estimates, the Treasury should be able to secure still further reductions in the defence expenditure proposed by Civil Departments for 1955.

Stockpiling

14. Departments were planning to spend in 1955 a total of £47 millions on increasing our strategic reserves of food, oil and materials.

A working party of officials is now reviewing this programme in the light of the new strategic concept. It has been instructed to frame a five-year programme, in which stocks required for national survival will have priority over those needed for maintaining industrial production. Food, oil and materials needed for the emergency repair of air-raid damage will now be more important than raw materials needed by industry. Special attention will be given to the need to store strategic stocks outside the target areas.

This review will not be completed until September and its financial results cannot yet be forecast. Though the new strategic concept gives an added importance to stockpiling, it would be idle to accumulate stocks which cannot be stored outside the target areas and this consideration may at first impose a limit on expenditure. There may therefore be scope for some savings under this head in 1955.

Defence expenditure in 1955

16. The Minister of Defence is satisfied that, even if the Cabinet approve all the changes proposed in this report, expenditure on the Armed Forces in 1955 cannot be less than £1,630 millions. The Chancellor of the Exchequer cannot see his way to provide for this purpose more than £1,500 millions. There thus remains a gap of £130 millions.

The Cabinet should, however, realise that the figure of £1,630 millions includes a provision of £80 millions against the possibility that the whole cost of the British forces stationed in Germany may have to be met in 1955 from the Exchequer. No provision for this was included in the Estimates for 1954. No firm forecast can yet be made of the date on which the German Federal Government will cease to bear this cost. There is general agreement that it is most unlikely that the whole of the cost in 1955 will fall on the Exchequer. If the Estimates contained no provision for meeting any part of this cost in 1955 the gap would be one of £50 millions.

17. The Minister of Defence is convinced that greater economies in the expenditure of the Service Departments can only be secured by changes in policy even more drastic than those recommended in this report, including the further abandonment of existing military commitments. Even so, it is doubtful how far the effects of such further changes could show themselves in financial savings in 1955. The problem of closing the gap, which would stand at £50 millions if no provision were made for meeting the cost of British troops in Germany, is one of major policy which calls for decision by the Cabinet.

18. From the point of view of presentation, some advantage could be obtained by

I

presenting together in the next Statement on Defence the whole of our defence expenditure, military and civil. There is a strong case on the merits for putting forward, in the Defence White Paper, a comprehensive picture of our defence effort as a whole. Indeed, as stated in paragraph 19 below, we have little prospect of gaining public acceptance for our revised plans for Civil Defence unless they can be presented as an integral part of a new policy for defence as a whole. From the financial angle, this would have the advantage that we should be able to bring into account in a Statement on Defence a saving of some £15 millions on the defence preparations of Civil Departments.

Presentation of new defence policy

19.   The policy outlined in this report will clearly need most careful presentation to the public. Many people are preoccupied with the destructive power of the latest atomic weapons. Fewer perhaps have yet recognised that the development of these weapons may have made major war less likely. The public as a whole will therefore find it difficult to understand why, as the destructive power of air attack increases, we propose to cut down our fighter and anti-aircraft defences and reduce the scale of our expenditure on Civil Defence. These and other changes recommended in this report certainly could not be defended in isolation. Public acceptance of them can only be secured if they are presented as parts of a coherent plan based on the recognition that no purely defensive policy could ensure the safety of these islands and those who live in them and that the main weight of our defence effort must now be concentrated on building up the deterrent strength which will prevent the outbreak of a major war.

If therefore the Cabinet approve the changes in policy and programmes which are recommended in this report, we suggest that we should on this occasion anticipate the annual Statement on Defence, which is normally published in February, by presenting in the autumn a special White Paper on Defence containing a full statement of our new defence policy as a whole. This could be followed in February, when the Estimates are presented, by a White Paper confined to a statement and explanation of the details of defence expenditure of all kinds proposed for 1955.

15   CAB 129/71, C(54)329 (annex)   3 Nov 1954
'Defence policy': report for Cabinet by Lord Swinton   [Extract]

[Cabinet discussed the report by the Committee on Defence Policy (see 14) on 27 July 1954. Swinton then undertook, at Churchill's request and in the absence of Alexander, a further review of defence programmes to determine whether any additional adjustments were called for, beyond those recommended by the Committee on Defence Policy, and also to consider what further reductions might be secured in expenditure on defence during 1955. Swinton was assisted by Mr Duncan-Sandys (minister of supply, 1951–1954; minister of housing and local government, 1954–1957) and Mr N Birch (parliamentary secretary, Ministry of Defence, 1952–1954). The service ministers and Chiefs of Staff were consulted, Alexander was associated with the inquiry in its later stages and Churchill presided over the final meetings. Swinton's report was submitted to Cabinet by Churchill who endorsed the recommendations in a covering note.]

. . .

The army

The strategic reserve

19. The army programme provides for building up in the United Kingdom a strategic reserve equivalent to 2⅓ divisions. Apart from its military advantages, this will bring with it financial savings because the cost of maintaining these forces will be lower at home than abroad. For both these reasons, there must be no avoidable delay in lightening the overseas commitments of the Army on which the withdrawal of their troops to the United Kingdom depends. Now that our relations with Egypt have improved, it may well be found possible to complete the evacuation of our bases in the Canal Zone more rapidly than has hitherto been considered practicable, with possible further savings under this head. A new study should be made at once aiming at halving the time of withdrawal. The earliest possible start should be made in reducing our forces in Korea and Hong Kong. The battalion which was recently sent to British Guiana is, on present plans, not due to be withdrawn until it can be replaced by a West Indian battalion, which it is hoped to form by the end of 1956. We are satisfied that it must remain there for the time being but the possibility of withdrawing it earlier should be kept under review.

Colonial forces

20. Everything possible should be done to build up local Colonial forces in order to reduce the demands on our own Army. We shall not get quick relief in this way, but the point is of such importance that we consider this question should now be studied by Ministers and pursued as a deliberate policy. In this study we suggest that special attention should be given to the possibility of strengthening Colonial police and security services. These are the front line of defence against subversion and we are informed that recent experience has revealed defects in their organisation. Efficient police forces and Intelligence Services are the best way of smelling out and suppressing subversive movements at an early stage, and may save heavy expenditure on military reinforcements. They are an insurance we cannot afford to neglect. . . .[1]

---

[1] In Cabinet 'there was general support for the proposal . . . that local Colonial forces and, in particular, Colonial police and security services, should be enlarged and improved' (CAB 128/27/2, CC 73(54)1, 5 Nov 1954).

16   DEFE 7/415, no 40   27 Nov 1954
[Colonial armed forces]: brief by Sir H Parker for Mr Macmillan

I attach a note for your meeting with the Colonial Secretary and S. of S. for War[1] on Colonial Forces.

The S. of S. for War has strong views on this and it might be a good plan to ask him to open up.

There are two facets to this problem. From time to time suggestions are made that we should create a great Colonial Army to replace the old Indian Army, something on the lines of what the French do in Northern and Equatorial Africa.

The trouble about this idea is that the U.K. would have to meet virtually the whole

---

[1] Mr A Head, S of S for war, 1951–1956.

cost. The Colonial Forces if they were raised would probably have to be at the expense of existing white forces and notwithstanding the excellent service which Colonial forces have rendered, expert opinion holds that on balance we should not benefit. The advocates of the Colonial Army forget that certainly until shortly before the war the greater part of the cost of the Indian Army was met from Indian and not U.K. revenues.

The second point is quite a different one. We have drifted into trouble in many Colonial territories—Malaya, Kenya, British Guiana. The S. of S. for War and the Chiefs of Staff feel that had our local intelligence and our local security forces been better organised, we might never have got into the mess, or, alternatively, if help had to be given by the Army it might have been given earlier in the day.

To put it in other words, the Army argues that the Colonial Office gets into a mess and then asks the Army to help it out. Experience shows that this is a long and expensive business.

The Colonial Secretary will probably not accept this view. He has his difficulties. Personally, I have always felt that the share of the budgets of the various Colonies devoted to law and order may well be inadequate.

Social uplift is popular and most people do not mind how much money you spend on it, but a proposal to increase your Police Force by 25% or to set up a competent Criminal Investigation Department is subjected to microscopical examination.

17   CAB 131/14, D(54)43   **23 Dec 1954**
'United Kingdom defence policy': memorandum by COS for Cabinet Defence Committee

Introduction
1.   The revolution in weapons of war over the last two years, which has resulted from the application of new scientific knowledge, has completely altered the world situation. This has necessitated a review of our strategic policy.

World-wide threat
2.   The Free World continues to be menaced everywhere by the threat of Communist subversion and expansion which has world domination as its ultimate aim. The aim of Russia is supported and extended by her Satellites and by Communist China and Communist sympathisers throughout the world: and, whether or not the policy of Communist China is controlled by Russia, the threat to South-East Asia is very serious. The conflict with the Free World which arises from this threat and from the plight of the Satellites, even if it does not lead to global war, is likely to last for a long time with periods of greater or less tension.

Likelihood of war
3.   Under cover of an ostensible policy of peaceful co-existence Soviet Russia and Communist China are at present employing the technique of subversion, backed by supply of arms and financial aid, as opposed to overt attack or invasion. They are being successful in this and we believe that they are likely to continue to aim at extending the Communist sphere of influence by infiltration and disruption of the

existing Governments of Free Countries. The danger of war remains, however, because the fundamental aims of both sides are in conflict.

4. After examination of the intelligence material available, we have reached the following conclusions:—

(a) Russia is most unlikely to provoke war deliberately, particularly during the next three or four years when she will be vulnerable to nuclear attack by the Allies and unable effectively to strike against the United States.

(b) Even when Russia is able effectively to attack the United States, the deterrent will remain, since global war would probably result in mutual annihilation.

(c) Careful judgment and restraint on the part of the Allies on a united basis will be needed to avoid the outbreak of a global war through accident or miscalculation resulting from an incident which precipitated or extended local war.

(d) A possible danger is that differences between the United States and Communist China may tempt the Communists to use force; this use of force might lead to global war. The conventional military strength of China must not be overestimated (see Appendix)[1] but their provocative power is nonetheless a serious danger.

(e) It is most probable that the present state of "cold war", under even graver conditions, will continue for a long time with periods of greater or less tension.

5. Our general conclusion is that, provided the Allies maintain their unity and continue to increase their military strength and preparedness, global war is unlikely and should be avoidable. But this proviso is of crucial importance. The Free World cannot afford to relax. It must as a matter of urgency revise its plans and production programmes to meet the changed strategic needs of global warfare with nuclear weapons. The greater the deterrent, the less the risk. Allied policy should therefore be to build up this deterrent in two ways:—

(a) The accumulation of nuclear weapons, strategic and tactical, and the establishment of Allied airfields widely dispersed round the periphery of the Communist *bloc*, from all of which the attack can be concentrated on pre-selected targets.

(b) Holding forces ready for action in the key positions which we must defend, with supplies for them dispersed and promptly available.

The deterrent to global war

The main deterrent—nuclear capability

6. The nuclear threat is the main deterrent to war. Moreover, an immediate and overwhelming counter-offensive with the most powerful nuclear weapons offers the only hope of defeating the enemy's attempt to destroy us and bring the war to an early halt. We must therefore produce the required stockpile of nuclear weapons and perfect the means of delivering them.

The complementary deterrents

7. *N.A.T.O.* The maintenance of the political unity of the North Atlantic Treaty Organisation (N.A.T.O.) and the provision of a shield of land and air forces in Western Europe and of naval and air forces for the protection of Allied sea

---

[1] Not printed.

communications is an essential complement to the main deterrent. The Russians must be made to realise that quick territorial gains at little cost are no longer possible. This element of the deterrent must be provided by a sufficiency of land and air forces at a high state of readiness on the Continent. A German contribution is a most important factor in achieving this sufficiency of forces. For our part we have given an undertaking to retain the equivalent fighting strength of four divisions and a Tactical Air Force on the Continent indefinitely and we have also assigned naval and air forces to the Supreme Allied Commanders Europe and Atlantic and to the Channel Command.

8. *Action in the cold war.* As part of the deterrent the successful waging of the cold war is of very great importance. All Free Countries should continue to build up their political and military strength and to stop the further spread of Communism.

Cold war

9. *Allied Aims in the cold war.* We must try to forestall Communist intentions; if we fail to do so, we must counter Communist pressure wherever it occurs. Russia and China working on internal lines and with the initiative can strike at a place and a time of their own choosing. Allied political aims in the Cold War are to stimulate and fortify the will and strength to resist Communist aggression or subversion. We, with our world-wide commitments, must build up a highly mobile force in the United Kingdom which can be switched to counter the Cold War threat wherever it may occur. In overseas theatres we must build up resistance to Communist expansion by a strong policy the outlines of which are given below.

10. *Europe.* Our policy will be to play our part in welding together the forces of N.A.T.O. into an effective fighting machine. To this end we must accept those measures of integration which add to efficiency without placing upon us undue economic burdens.

11. *Middle East.* Our ability to resist Soviet aggression in the Middle East in war will depend on the degree to which we can maintain in peace the stability of Middle East countries and build up their resistance to Communism. We aim at drawing together, as soon as the circumstances are favourable, the countries concerned in this theatre, particularly South Africa, Pakistan, Turkey and the Arab States. Israel, too, could play an important part in the Middle East defence and, even if co-operation in peace is impracticable, we hope to enlist her support in global war. In the meantime, we must maintain small highly efficient land/air forces in the area and demonstrate our ability to reinforce them rapidly so as to show not only our power to fulfil our treaty obligations but also our continuing interest in the Middle East as a whole and our determination to take vigorous action to defend it.

12. *Far East.* The Far East is the present focus of Communist aggression and every effort should be made to drive a wedge between Russia and Communist China. To ensure an effective defence of the area a South-East Asia Collective Defence Treaty (S.E.A.C.D.T.) has been signed and we shall do all in our power to make it an effective instrument. The defence of Malaya is indispensable to our strategic position in the Far East and vital to the security of Australia and New Zealand. Our firm resolve to defend Malaya and our ability to do so must be made apparent to all nations of South-East Asia as well as to the United States. Knowledge of these facts plays an essential part in preventing the spread of Communism towards Australia and New Zealand. We are already making a major contribution in Malaya, and we hope

that a Commonwealth strategic reserve will be established there as a surety of our firm resolve to maintain our position in South-East Asia.

13. *Security in colonial territories and dependencies.* The United Kingdom is at present ultimately responsible for maintaining the territorial integrity of and internal security within our Colonial territories and dependencies overseas. It is our aim that Colonial Governments should progressively accept responsibility for their own internal security. But in the meantime we cannot afford to relax our security arrangements in the Colonies: indeed, we may have to strengthen them.

Effect of nuclear weapon developments on the nature of future war

14. The progress made in the development of nuclear weapons is such that:—

(a) the measure of military power in the future will be the ability to wage war with up-to-date nuclear weapons;

(b) their use will lead to widespread devastation.

Possible restrictions on nuclear warfare

15. We have given much thought to the highly speculative question whether, if global warfare should break out, there might initially be mutually acceptable restrictions on the use of nuclear weapons. We have come to the conclusion that, if war came in the next few years, the Allies would have to make immediate use of the full armoury of nuclear weapons with the object of countering Russia's overwhelming superiority of man-power. We must therefore plan on the assumption that, if war becomes global, nuclear bombardment will become general.

The position of the United Kingdom and the United States

16. Should the deterrent fail in its purpose and the Russians decide to launch a surprise attack, they will, we believe, appreciate that, apart from its importance as a strategic base, the United Kingdom is the major political target in Western Europe. The more they can devastate and immobilise the United Kingdom, the weaker the resistance in Europe owing to our temporary inability to reinforce with men and materials. We therefore consider that, whatever the Russian ability to attack the United States, the United Kingdom will be a primary military target for the enemy's nuclear attack. We also believe it possible that the Russians are capable even now of delivering one-way air attacks on the United States, and that in the course of the next few years, as they develop a stock-pile of nuclear bombs and the means to deliver them, they should be able progressively to increase the effectiveness of their attacks against United States centres of government and production.

17. No foreseeable air defence system can provide the scale of protection necessary against attack by a determined enemy using the latest nuclear weapons. We can count on the Allied strategic and tactical air forces being able to strike an immediate crippling blow at the sources of attack and centres of control since the counter-offensive can be mounted from a multiplicity of sources, both land and sea based, widely dispersed. In making our plans, however, it must be borne in mind that the main production centres of Western Europe, of the United Kingdom and, in the not so distant future, of the North American Continent must be expected to receive severe damage. Therefore, although the Russian power to continue "unconventional" or even modernised conventional war may be ended in the opening phase, ordinary prudence requires the ceaseless building up of an ample and dispersed stock-pile.

Other theatres and sea communications

18. Besides deploying a vast army and possessing a very large and modern air force Russia has now emerged as a first-class naval Power. We can expect that, concurrently with strategic air operations, major attacks will be made by Soviet naval, land and amphibious forces, supported by part of the Soviet nuclear potential, against Western Europe and our sea communications. We must also expect the Soviet to launch an offensive campaign in the Middle East, and Communist China to launch attacks in the Far East designed to expand Communist influence and Communist-controlled territory. The scale and progress of these offensive operations will depend on the extent of the preparedness of the forces situated in and readily available for reinforcement of these areas and on how quickly the Allied strategic air offensive can take effect.

Warning period

19. Because of the reluctance of either side to resort to nuclear war there may be a period of increasing tension before general hostilities break out. But we cannot count on this. There may well be a "bolt from the blue." In no event can we hope for a period of warning which would enable us to complete preparations for war.

Progress of the war

20. The opening phase for global war is likely to be characterised by intense air attacks with nuclear weapons being used by both sides. The outcome will be determined by the success of these initial bombardments. The results of the first phase are bound to limit considerably the capabilities of the contestants and the scale of their operations, but the war is likely to go on. The loss of centralised control will require local Commanders to act on their own initiative to a greater extent than ever before. The outcome of their campaigns can be greatly influenced by the vigorous prosecution of the war, making the best use of local resources.

Biological and chemical warfare

21. While the Soviet Union may well be capable of initiating biological and chemical warfare, it seems very unlikely that they will do so as long as they have nuclear weapons at their disposal.

Summary

22. We summarise our conclusions as to the likely form of a future war if it should become global:—

(a) The employment of nuclear weapons will at once become general. It is of vital importance that the Allied strategic and tactical air forces should be capable of hitting back immediately without any limitation on targets or weapons.

(b) The destructive power of modern nuclear weapons is so great that we must be prepared for the main production centres of western Europe, the United Kingdom and in the not so distant future, the North American continent to receive severe damage in the opening days.

(c) It is of the utmost importance for the Allies to hold the front in Western Europe and, in view of Russia's emergence as a first-class sea power, to gain command of the sea from the outset by destroying her fleet, her mercantile marine and her bases.

(d) In spite of the devastating effect of the initial bombardments on both sides, the war is likely to go on. The loss of centralised control means that local Commanders will have to act on their own initiative to a greater extent than ever before.

Conclusions

23. From the foregoing review we have reached the overriding conclusion that, short of sacrificing our vital interests or principles, our first aim must continue to be to prevent global war. We believe it to be most probable that the present state of cold war, under even graver conditions, will continue for a long time with periods of greater or less tension and that global war should be avoidable, provided the Allies use careful judgment and restraint and maintain their unity, military strength and preparedness. The objectives of our strategic policy should therefore be:—

(a) to contribute to the deterrent by possessing the means of waging successful war with the most up-to-date nuclear weapons;

(b) to play our part with the Commonwealth and our Allies in stopping the spread of Communism;

(c) to preserve security and develop stable government in our Colonial territories and overseas dependencies and to support our world-wide trade and cultural interests.

24. We have reached the following additional conclusions which bear upon our defence policy in the event of global war:—

(a) The measure of military power in the future will be the ability to wage war from the moment of attack with up-to-date nuclear weapons.

(b) It is vital that the Allied strategic and tactical air forces should be capable of an immediate and overwhelming counter-offensive, as the course of the war will be largely determined by the result of the initial nuclear bombardment.

(c) It is of major importance for the Allies to hold the front in Western Europe and to gain command of the sea from the outset by destroying the Russian fleet, mercantile marine and bases.

(d) Although there may be a period of increasing tension before general hostilities break out we cannot count on this. There may well be a "bolt from the blue." In no event can we hope for a period of warning which would enable us to complete our preparations for war.

(e) It is only prudent to plan on the assumption that the main production centres of Western Europe, the United Kingdom and, in the not so distant future, the North American continent will receive severe damage in the opening days of war. It follows that, as far as is operationally and economicaly practicable, our forces and reserve stocks should be dispersed; and Commanders-in-Chief overseas must be prepared for some time to conduct their operations without reinforcement and supplies from the major allied centres of production. Stockpiles should be built up in all overseas theatres.

18 CAB 129/72, C(54)402   29 Dec 1954

'Internal security in the colonies': Cabinet memorandum by Mr Macmillan

On 5th November the Cabinet endorsed the view expressed in C.(54)329 that local Colonial forces and, in particular, Colonial police and security services, should be enlarged and improved (C.C.(54) 73rd Conclusions, Minute 1).[1]

2. The risk of a major war will probably continue to recede as its character grows more devastating. But the corollary to this is that the cold or warm war will continue for a long time at its present tempo and may indeed be intensified.

3. During the next few years our Colonial Empire in its varying stages of development is likely to be a vital "cold war" battleground. If we are defeated here much of our effort in Western Europe will be wasted. Trouble in the Colonial Empire may be directly inspired by the Communists. Alternatively, they may exploit troubles basically of a nationalist or other character.

4. As Minister of Defence, my particular interest in the problem arises from the fact that, when trouble breaks out, heavy demands are made on the Armed Forces. Malaya, Kenya and British Guiana are a large drain upon United Kingdom money and manpower.

5. Our objective must be to prevent trouble arising. It will pay us to spend some money if we can achieve this end. Moreover, in so far as troubles are Communist inspired, they are centrally directed. Our preventive action is more likely to succeed if it is centrally co-ordinated.

6. We need good security intelligence, efficient and well-trained police forces and properly organised Colonial armed forces.

7. It may well be that we may need a new type of central organisation to assist local effort.

8. These are, of course, matters which are primarily the responsibility of the Colonial Secretary, with whom I have had some preliminary discussions.[2] I am, however, concerned whether as a Government we are giving sufficient thought to the overall problem. If we are to win the struggle our plans must be well-founded and we must have the means to implement them. I therefore suggest that the matter should be examined by a small Committee of Ministers who would draw attention to the weaknesses, if any, in existing arrangements and recommend how best these could be overcome.[3]

---

[1] See 15 and 15 note 4.   [2] See 16.

[3] A Ministerial Committee on Colonial Security was set up in Jan 1955 under Lord Swinton's chairmanship. On 12 Jan Eden requested, and received, Churchill's approval for FO representation on the committee 'since . . . our foreign relations are liable to be seriously affected in a number of ways (for instance Malaya and Cyprus) by developments in the colonial territories and since the activities of world Communism are peculiarly a Foreign Office concern' (minute by Eden to Churchill, FO 800/757, p 45, 12 Jan 1955). On 25 Jan the committee asked General Sir G Templer (high commissioner and director of operations, Malaya, 1952–1954; chief of imperial general staff 1955–1958) to enquire into the causes of the emergencies in Malaya, Cyprus, Kenya, British Guiana and elsewhere. Templer's report on colonial security was submitted in Apr. Both the committee's papers and Templer's report have been retained by department, although passages from the report may be found in other PRO files; eg the section on 'The duty of the British overseas' (paras 378–390) may be found in CO 859/890 along with a brief on this section prepared by CO officials for their S of S. See also 82. The report is generally regarded as having had little impact on policy.

19   CAB 128/28, CC 3(55)2   13 Jan 1955

'Afro-Asian conference': Cabinet conclusions on the Afro-Asian conference at Bandoeng

[This issue came before Cabinet because CO and FO disagreed on whether or not countries within the British sphere of influence, especially in Africa, should be 'discouraged' from attending the Bandoeng conference. The CO advocated discouragement since attendance by such states as the Gold Coast, the Central African Federation and the Sudan could associate them with unfortunate conference resolutions and impair Britain's relations with them. A conference 'engineered by certain Asian Prime Ministers' should not be seen as 'competent to pronounce on the affairs and destinies of Africa' (letter from Lennox-Boyd to Eden, CO 936/347, no 124/5, 11 Jan 1955). The FO argued that Britain should not be seen to be dissuading countries from attending but should rather advise friendly countries which did attend to try to exercise a moderating influence at the conference.]

The Foreign Secretary said that, at the initiative of the Indonesian Government, the Prime Ministers of the Colombo Powers[1] had invited the Governments of a number of countries in Africa and Asia to send representatives to an Afro-Asian Conference to be held at Bandoeng towards the end of April. This was an unfortunate initiative and seemed likely to result in resolutions deprecating Colonialism and urging the prohibition of all further development of thermo-nuclear weapons. It was now clear, however, that the Conference could not be prevented, and he had been considering what guidance could be given to those of the Governments invited to it who were likely to accept advice from us. It would, he thought, be unwise to encourage such Governments to send representatives to the Conference if they were reluctant to do so. He proposed that we should content ourselves with offering information, help and advice to those Governments who were proposing to be represented at the Conference.

In discussion there was general agreement that this Asian intervention in African affairs was not to be welcomed. It would be preferable on this account that Governments of British territories in Africa should not be represented at the Conference. The Cabinet were informed that the Prime Minister of the Gold Coast had shown no special wish to send a representative and was likely to accept such advice as the Governor might give him on this point. The Government of the Central African Federation, who had also been invited, were showing no enthusiasm for the Conference.

The Cabinet:—

(1) Endorsed the Foreign Secretary's proposal that, as regards foreign Governments which might accept guidance from us, we should do nothing to encourage attendance at the Afro-Asian Conference but should be ready to give information, help and advice to Governments wishing to be represented at the Conference.

(2) Invited the Commonwealth Secretary and Colonial Secretary to take discreet steps to discourage the Governments of the Central African Federation and the Gold Coast from sending representatives to this Conference.[2]

---

[1] India, Pakistan, Ceylon, Burma and Indonesia. These countries collaborated for some purposes as the 'Colombo powers' from 1954 to 1956.

[2] The CO felt that the Cabinet's second conclusion was 'the right one', and noted that the FO was 'apparently not too happy' about it (minute by E M West, principal, CO, CO 936/348, 28 Jan 1955). The

Bandoeng conference of Apr 1955 marked the emergence of the non-aligned movement, with India as its leading power. For the British government's assessment of the conference, see 108.

20   CAB 134/1315, PR(56)2   20 Mar 1956
'Defence policy': joint memorandum by Mr Macmillan and Sir W Monckton to Sir A Eden

As you know, we and our predecessors have been struggling to produce a new long-term defence policy.

2. We have an uneasy feeling that at present we are spending a great deal of money to provide defences which are not effective, and in some important respects are little more than a facade. To do this we are placing so heavy a burden on our economy that defence may well be a cause of weakness rather than of strength.

3. We do not think that we should obtain the right answer by simply pursuing our previous studies, and believe that there must now be a reappraisal at the highest level of the whole basis on which our defence policy should rest. We suggest that the essential first step in such a reappraisal would be for Senior Ministers to have a general discussion covering such matters as the following:—

(i) Is the defence of the United Kingdom in global war a feasible proposition?
(ii) If the answer to (i) is no, what changes ought logically to be made in our present arrangements for defence?
(iii) What are the impediments to a statement by Her Majesty's Government of their intention to make these changes? What would be the effect on opinion at home and abroad, with special regard to our allies?
(iv) Assuming that the answer to (i) is in the negative, and that our paramount interest is therefore to prevent global war, on what scale and in what form should we contribute to the Deterrent? For what reasons? (The nature of the Deterrent should itself be defined, with special reference to our present commitments to N.A.T.O.)
(v) What are our vital interests in peacetime and by what means can they best be safeguarded (e.g. Middle East oil)?
(vi) For what situations short of global war should we be prepared?
(vii) What economic advantages would be gained by recasting our defence policy?

4. In the light of the general discussion of these matters, we could then consider what resources should be provided for defence and how they would best be used to execute policy. Here we shall have to consider our policy on National Service (the present legislation expires at the end of 1958). We shall also have to consider what provision we make in future for Home Defence.

5. In our view, the matters listed above must be discussed by Ministers in the first place; officials could then be instructed to carry out more detailed studies. But it is very difficult to find adequate time for discussion, even of such crucial issues of policy. We wonder, therefore, whether you would be prepared to set aside in the near future two or three days (perhaps at a weekend) during which, under your chairmanship, the appropriate Ministers could concentrate on these problems.

21   CAB 134/1315, PR(56)3   1 June 1956

'The future of the United Kingdom in world affairs': memorandum by officials of the Treasury, Foreign Office and Ministry of Defence for Cabinet Policy Review Committee. *Appendix* A

[Sir N Brook explained in a prefatory note that this memo had been prepared 'as an initial basis for the review of national policy which Ministers are to undertake in the light of recent changes in the international situation'. No doubt it was originally inspired as a response to the questions posed by Macmillan and Monckton in their joint memo to Eden (see 20). With this assessment by officials available, Eden appointed a Cabinet Policy Review Committee. Members of the Committee were Eden (chair), Salisbury, Macmillan, Selwyn Lloyd and Monckton. Sir N Brook defined the Committee's functions: 'In the course of the next few weeks the Prime Minister proposes to consider, with the Ministers immediately concerned, what adjustments should be made in Government policy in view of changes in the methods, if not the objectives, of the Soviet Union. This review, which will take account of our economic and financial circumstances, will cover changes in domestic and overseas policy and adjustments in our defence programmes. . . . [The] Committee will lay down the broad lines on which the review of policy and programmes should be undertaken, and will receive and consider reports on progress made with the review. Other Ministers will be brought into consultation, as required, as the review proceeds' (CAB 134/1315, PR(56)1, note by Brook, 4 June 1956). The Macmillan-Monckton memo to Eden and this memo by the officials were the first two papers submitted to the Committee.]

I. The problem

Two main factors call for a review of United Kingdom policy:—

(a) The external situation confronting us has changed. The hydrogen bomb has transformed the military situation. It has made full-scale war with Russia or China unlikely. And conventional forces, though still of great importance in some situations, have become a relatively less important factor in world affairs. The Russians have recognised this change, and they are adapting their actions to it. While their objectives may remain unaltered, their methods of attaining them are changing. We must modify our own tactics accordingly.

(b) It is clear that ever since the end of the war we have tried to do too much—with the result that we have only rarely been free from the danger of economic crisis. This provides no stable basis for policy in any field. Unless we make substantial reductions in the Government's claims on the national economy we shall endanger our capacity to play an effective role in world affairs. We must therefore concentrate on essentials and reduce other commitments. Only thus shall we be able to find the means to place our economy on a stable basis and to counter the new forms of attack with which we are being confronted.

2.   This paper therefore begins with an examination of our economic development since the war and an assessment of our prospects for the future. In the light of this it examines the whole field of our policies—internal and external, civil and military—seeks to establish our essential objectives, and suggests studies on the results of which Ministers can base their decisions on future policy. To deal effectively with these problems major decisions will be needed in all areas of policy, and especially of defence policy. Finally it emphasises the need to negotiate some of these changes of policy and commitments with our Allies, especially the United States, and empha-

sises the importance of an early completion of the studies on which policy decisions can be based.

II. Economic objectives

3.   In Appendix A we attach a summary review of our economic achievement since the end of the war and a forecast of our economic prospects. This shows that throughout the post-war period:—

(a) we have been able to succeed in our policies only with the aid of £3,000 million of help from abroad; and
(b) despite this aid (i) we have had constant anxiety about our balance of payments and the gold reserves which even now are lower than at the end of the war; and (ii) home investment has been inadequate.

But we have maintained sterling, and the sterling system, as the major instrument of world trade and finance.

4.   As regards the future it shows that, on the basis of present policies and commitments actual and potential, we have no prospect of being any more free from strain and crisis than we have been since 1945. For the foreseeable future, we shall be dependent on external supplies of vital foods and raw materials, in particular of oil from the Middle East. It would not be wise to count, in advance at any rate, on such an expansion of our economic strength as would transform the prospects and make us comfortable if not safe. If we are to get away from the constant threat of crisis, we must make the maximum internal effort and seek to reduce our commitments— internal and external. This means that we must:—

(a) establish where our vital interests lie and what we must do to secure them;
(b) avoid mortgaging our future increase in wealth in advance and seek through strict internal policies to put more resources into home investment and building up our reserves and less into consumption; and
(c) to the extent that we have to shed external burdens or commitments, shed them in an orderly way and seek wherever necessary to ensure that other friendly countries assume them.

5.   The main aim of United Kingdom economic policy can be defined as to ensure a sound, prosperous and dynamic economy on which to base an increasing standard of living and our democratic way of life. To this end, it is essential for us to promote expanding world trade and to follow internal and external policies which will enable us to maintain our full share of it.

6.   If we are to secure this aim we must:—

(a) ensure that we do not undertake too much, either at home or abroad, so that we are in continuous danger of crisis or weakness; and
(b) employ the utmost skill in getting the best value out of the limited potentialities which we have available.

7.   There are many areas or aspects of policy in which a failure could make it more difficult for us to attain these aims. But there is one, success in which is a matter of life or death to us as a country. This is the maintenance of the international value of sterling.

The maintenance of the international value of sterling

8. Sterling has three separate characteristics:—

First, it is the national or international currency of the United Kingdom alone and not of the sterling area. Its maintenance is therefore our own responsibility, though its position and value can be affected greatly by actions by other countries. But if we fail as a country to maintain its value, then it will soon cease to have the other two characteristics mentioned below.

Second, it is the reserve currency of all sterling area countries. It is this which constitutes the peculiar quality of our relation with the rest of the sterling area. This is a source of strength in many ways; but as shown in paragraph 10(b) of Appendix A our liabilities have now grown up to dangerous levels.

Third, it is the major trading or international currency in the world. It finances half the world's trade and payments.

9. These facts show why a real failure to maintain the value of sterling would be fatal to our interests and aims.

(a) *At home* our own currency would lose its value and would endanger our political and social stability and all the policies which we are pursuing.

(b) *In the sterling area*, which comprises some 600 million people, it would have both economic and political consequences. First, it would mean a great material loss to these countries; their reserves would diminish or vanish. Our devaluation of 1949 caused great strains within the sterling area: the cohesion of the sterling area would not withstand another devaluation. But there would be political consequences as well. Sterling has been an important Commonwealth link. If it were removed, and especially if it were removed because it had lost its value by our actions, the effect on the political cohesion of the Commonwealth would be disastrous. Commonwealth countries would look to more dependable currencies and countries with which to ally themselves.

(c) *In the free world* such a collapse would remove one of the main foundations of world trade and finance. Instead of steadily expanding world trade, there would be a period of great confusion and depression, with all the effects on the free world's social, political and military policies. This would be a major victory for the Communist view that the capitalist system contains the seeds of its own destruction.

10. Thus, our own national interests combine with the interests of the Commonwealth and the free world to make it vital to maintain sterling as a stable, trusted and effective instrument of national, Commonwealth and world trade and finance.

11. Success in this is the greatest single contribution we can make to the maintenance of our own position in world affairs and to the success of the policies which the free world is seeking to pursue. Yet it is a fact that in the ten years since the end of the war we have run sterling on most inadequate reserves and thus taken terrible risks.

12. At present our reserves amount to £800 millions. Their smallness can be gauged in two ways:—

First in relation to our short-term liabilities, which at present amount to £3,742 millions. We just could not meet a major run on sterling—and hope to maintain sterling at any real value.

Second in relation to our trade. The following table shows how our position compares with that of other areas:—

	Reserves as percentage of visible trade	
	1951	1955
United Kingdom	12½	11
United States (gold only)	85	78
Continental E.P.U. countries (including dependencies	15	21
Latin America	21½	25

13. Whatever risks we may have taken since the war in other areas of policy, they are nothing compared with the risks we have taken, are taking and must for some time to come continue to take, in this vital sector.

The essential policies to maintain sterling's value
14. The basic need is to follow internal policies which will make room in the economy for:—

(a) an adequate level of home investment;
(b) an adequate degree of flexibility in industry and labour;
(c) an adequate balance of payments surplus.

15. Unless we succeed in this we shall, sooner or later, be faced with three developments which would be fatal:—

(a) continued inability of the United Kingdom "to pay her way externally" a term which is defined later;
(b) withdrawal (in the sense of ceasing to trade in or hold reserves in sterling) from the sterling area of two countries—which are major dollar earners and hold large sterling balances—the Federation of Malaya and the Gold Coast; or of one or more countries whose withdrawal would start a run in the sense both of other, sterling area, countries following suit and of action to convert their reserve holdings of sterling into dollars;
(c) fatal weakening of sterling by similar and simultaneous failures by other major members of the sterling area.

The size of the problem
16. Considerably more study would be needed in order to get anything like an accurate estimate of the changes which would be required in order to ensure that our economy was really viable, as distinct from being in a position merely to avoid crises. But it is clear that very large resources are needed if we are to increase our home investment in productive industry to the level needed to enable us to maintain our place in world trade. A substantial, but again at present undefined, addition would be needed to give our economy the flexibility it needs.

17. The additional resources required to meet the third requirement, namely, an adequate balance of payments surplus, is clear. Last year we had a deficit of £100 millions on our external account, whereas we need, if we are to make reasonable provision for building up the reserves, a surplus of £300 millions. The additional resources required, therefore, are £400 millions. This would make some provision

for building up the gold and dollar reserves from their present precarious level. If we were to build them up to twice their present figure—*i.e.*, to £1,600 millions—in the course of the next few years, we should not at the end be more than comfortable; and in the meantime we should still be at great risk—first, because of demands to use existing sterling balances for perfectly legitimate purposes such as development; and second, because an adverse movement in the terms of trade can have a major effect upon us. For example, an adverse movement of as little as one point adds something like £30 millions to the extra burden we have to bear on the economy to achieve the same current balance. It is therefore most important that we should not regard ourselves as "paying our way" unless we have a current surplus of £300 millions year in, year out.

We recommend, therefore, that there should be a detailed analysis of the additional resources which we would require if we are to make room in the economy for the three essential elements set out in paragraph 9 above.

How can the problem be solved?

18. The resources needed for this can be found, even with an increasing national product, only by a combination of resolute action in the fields of both internal and external commitments.

Internal commitments

Consumption

19. At present, two-thirds of any increase in the national product goes to increase in consumption. We must take a major cut here. This is a matter for Budget and wages policy, and

We recommend that a major objective of policy should be to reduce substantially over a period of years the percentage of the increase in the national product which goes with consumption.

Social investment

20. Here, housing must provide the main target; and

We recommend a radical review of Government and local authority policies in the field of social investment.

External commitments

21. While the main saving must come under internal commitments, a comprehensive review of the whole area of Government *external* commitments is needed.

Capital commitments

22. These are set out in paragraph 10 (b) of Appendix A. First is inter-Government lending, and net repayment of debt (*i.e.*, our repayments to other people, less other people's repayments to us). The latter averaged between £5 millions and £6 millions over the years 1952 to 1955. The main element in these payments to overseas countries has been about £20 millions per year on the North American loans. The capital element in the load service is, however, much smaller (at present) than the interest element, and the issues raised by the very heavy and

continuing burden of the load service are dealt with under commitments on current account below.

23. *Net* inter-Government lending abroad has averaged just under £15 millions a year since 1952, and the greater part of it consists of assistance to Colonial Governments in the form of loans (grant assistance comes into current commitments). It is a legitimate addition to other long-term investment which, though mainly private in character, contains some lending by the United Kingdom Government for commercial purposes and a good deal of borrowing by other Governments in the London market. By far the largest part of this investment is in the sterling Commonwealth, but there is also investment in the United States and Canada, and to a lesser degree in other countries. This covers, not only investment in programmes carried out by Commonwealth countries, but also investment by our own United Kingdom companies overseas—especially in oil. The sum, though variable from year to year, is large—always well over £100 millions and sometimes just over £200 millions a year. It therefore contributes a heavy direct addition to our balance of payments problem.

24. We are committed, as in the 1952 Prime Minister's Economic Conference Declaration (Cmd. 8717, paragraph 12), to making a special effort for Commonwealth development. This is important—both for itself and as a bond within the sterling area and with Canada. But we cannot say that this item in its *entirety* is vital. Nor can we say that we are not lending to countries who are not making sufficient effort themselves.

We recommend that our policies on external investment should be re-examined radically, bearing in mind the absolute need for adequate home investment (paragraphs 14–16 above).

Current commitments

25. External expenditure on defence (average £150 millions per annum) and on relief and other grants (average £20 millions per annum) is dealt with in Part III. Colonial grants (average £30 millions per annum) are referred to in Part IV.

26. £40 millions of our commitments on current account consist of the interest on the North American loans. While we cannot default on the capital element in the loan repayments—that would damage sterling very greatly and, of course, our whole relationship with the United States—we *may* legitimately be able to get some relief on these interest payments.

27. There is no doubt, however, that the remission by the United States (and Canada) of these debt repayments, which hang over our economy for the years up to 2000, would be a major contribution to the strength of sterling, the sterling system and the whole free world. The repayments mean *nothing* in a material sense to the United States (capital and interest amount to $140 millions) against an annual budget running at $60,000 millions and a foreign aid programme of $4,000 millions. The repayment—$140 millions—is equivalent to one-third of 1 per cent. of the United States receipts from income tax. In Canada, the amount involved—$40 millions—is more important.

28. We are bound to say, however, that we have failed to get the United States Government to take a reasonable view of provisions in the 1945 Agreement under which, if sensibly interpreted, we could be entitled to the waiver of interest—currently about two-thirds of the total. It is pretty clear that we cannot hope to make

any real progress on this matter as an isolated issue. It may be that we cannot make any progress on it in any context. But we consider the matter again in paragraphs 68–75 below.

Summary of recommendations, Part II

29. The maintenance of the international value of sterling should be our prime aim (paragraphs 8–13). In order to achieve this we recommend:—

(a) A detailed analysis of the additional resources required to achieve in our economy:—

    (i)   an adequate level of home investment;
    (ii) an adequate degree of flexibility in industry and labour;
    (iii) an adequate balance of payments surplus (paragraphs 14–17).

(b) The substantial reduction of the percentage by which the value of any increase in national production is offset in consumption (paragraph 19).
(c) A review of Government and local authority policies for social investment (paragraph 20).
(d) A review of our policies on external investment (paragraphs 21–24).

III. Political and military objectives

30. Our political and military objectives are:—

(a) to avoid global war;
(b) to protect our vital interests overseas, particularly access to oil.

Attempts to secure these objectives are likely to fail unless we:—

(a) maintain North American involvement in Europe;
(b) maintain a large measure of identity between the interests of America and Canada and our own and develop closer co-operation with those countries;
(c) maintain the cohesion of the Commonwealth.

31. Our means of pursuing these objectives must reflect the fact that there has been a major change in the political situation.

32. The Joint Intelligence Committee recently stated their views on the likelihood of global war up to 1965, and the paper was approved by the Chiefs of Staff on 15th May. These views were as follows:—

"We have appreciated over the last few years that the Soviet leaders do not want war. We believe that their views will remain unchanged certainly over the next few years, and probably over the whole period under review unless the political situation changes in some completely unexpected fashion (such as through the emergence of more aggressive Soviet leaders) and provided the West maintains its strength and cohesion and continues to act with restraint. We therefore believe that war is unlikely during the period."

This report (J.I.C. (56) 21 (Final) of 1st May) is reproduced in Appendix B.[1]

---

[1] Not printed.

33. Our problem is to decide how best we can take advantage of this situation in order to reduce the great strain and risk to which our present military burdens are subjecting the United Kingdom, and to release resources in order to counter the new form which the Soviet threat is taking; and to do so without weakening those factors which have made war unlikely, namely, the deterrent and the cohesion of the West.

34. The problem is not easy. However, reductions in our commitments have been achieved in the past. In 1952, the Cabinet approved a paper (C. (52) 202 of 18th June, 1952), in which it was recommended that in order to reduce our commitments overseas we should aim at terminating the Suez Canal base and the garrisons in Austria and Trieste. At that time the prospects of achieving these reductions did not look good, but it has since been done.

35. In many areas of the world the crucial question will probably be found to be how far we can substitute political, economic and information measures, which can be taken at comparatively low cost, for some at least of our present expensive military commitments. In an era of competitive co-existence we must examine how in the various areas of the world we can compete most effectively with the political and material challenge of Russian Communism. Our military means of defence should be regarded wherever possible as an essential adjunct and backing to these non-military measures rather than as a first line of defence.

36. The problem is examined below under the following heads:—

(a) Possession of nuclear and thermo-nuclear weapons and the means of their delivery.
(b) Military measures in the United Kingdom and Europe.
(c) Political, financial and military measures in other areas.

Nuclear and thermo-nuclear weapons
37. These weapons are in a different category from other military power.
38. The objectives over which these weapons can help us are:—

(a) Contributing to the deterrent against global war. The Russians are only redirecting their efforts because the deterrent is working. We should do what we can to help the Americans to ensure that it continues to work, and in particular to prevent a situation developing, even temporarily, in which the Russians believe that they have sufficient technical advantage to enable them to risk a war.
(b) Developing our community of interest with the Americans. If we have a worthwhile contribution to make to the deterrent, the Americans will be more likely to help defend our interests generally. If they alone provide the deterrent, we could not expect them to defend our interests where their own are not involved, or where a conflict of interest arises.
(c) Maintaining our prestige in the world. If we possess these weapons the Americans will be prepared to pay attention to our opinions in a way they would otherwise not. The same applies to our standing in the eyes of other countries, such as Germany. And our lesser potential enemies, such as Egypt, will feel that we might, if pushed too far, use nuclear weapons against them.

39. These are great advantages, which these weapons can secure more cheaply than we could get them otherwise. An illustration of them is seen in the succeeding section: our contribution to the deterrent puts us in a much stronger position than

we should otherwise be to negotiate with our Allies the reshaping of NATO policy which the new situation has made essential.

40. The question is how large our nuclear and thermo-nuclear capacity needs to be in order to secure them.

We recommend that this should once again be studied.

Military measures in the United Kingdom and Europe

41. Our military expenditure at present amounts to £1,500 millions a year out of a total Supply expenditure of £3,980 millions. The most striking point about this expenditure is the very large proportion that is tied up in conventional forces and weapons maintained against the threat of a Russian attack on the United Kingdom and the Continent. The proportion allotted to the defence of our interests elsewhere is small. If we are to make reductions of the size that the new situation demands, they must be found largely in our expenditure on our defence in Europe. It is there that the greatest scope exists for reducing demands on our engineering industry, our military manpower, our technical and scientific resources and our foreign exchange, in the interests of re-establishing our economic strength.

42. Looking at the problem purely through United Kingdom eyes, we may conclude that in the new circumstances there is a strong case for making large reductions in these forces in the United Kingdom and on the Continent, and in home defence expenditure. Provided we guard against the risk of the Russians' thinking that the deterrent can be neutralised, we can attach much less importance than we have in the past to "contributory deterrents," in an era when no country is likely to look further, in deciding for peace or war, than the nuclear or thermo-nuclear threat. Nor can it now be worth making heavy sacrifices in order to improve our chances of "survival" in a war which would in any event mean the destruction of nearly everything worth preserving.

43. However, virtually the whole of these forces are assigned to NATO. In addition, we have undertaken a solemn treaty obligation under the Paris Agreements to maintain our forces on the Continent at their present level and not to withdraw them except with the consent of the majority of the W.E.U. Powers. Our present force plans are already well below the "force goals" we have declared to NATO; we certainly cannot claim that any further reductions would be justified on the grounds that we were still maintaining equivalent fighting capacity. Even our home defence preparations are now the subject of NATO scrutiny.

44. Accordingly the solution, if we are to make the reductions that are essential and at the same time to maintain the cohesion of the West and North American involvement in Europe, is to work for the adoption of a new strategic concept by NATO as a whole. We must avoid unilateral reductions unrelated to any common strategic concept, which would be liable to set off a general landslide that would end in the disintegration of NATO and North American withdrawal from Europe. And we need more than a general agreement that the present scale of conventional forces can be reduced. We must not allow the feeling to develop that everything but the deterrent is now merely a facade. The new strategic concept must be one that can be interpreted in terms of lower but militarily definable force levels, and a planned and coherent Allied effort. The form which this new concept might take is a matter for consideration by the Chiefs of Staff in the first place. It might perhaps be based mainly on the idea of the "plate-glass window" or "trip-wire."

45. We cannot hope to achieve results quickly, and the new strategy will have to be most carefully presented. We should be wise to enter into advance consultation with the United States and Canadian Governments. We shall also need to take account of the psychological impact on European opinion, particularly in Germany and France.

46. *We recommend* that studies should be made of:—

(a) the development of a new NATO strategic concept designed to adjust the level of NATO forces to the new political situation;
(b) the method by which adoption of this new concept can best be achieved;
(c) present expenditure on the defence of the United Kingdom, including home defence.

The Middle East

47. The uninterrupted supply of oil from the Middle East is vital to the economy of the United Kingdom and of Western Europe. It now depends more upon our being able to obtain the friendly co-operation of the producing and transit countries than upon the physical strength we can deploy in the area. This means not only ensuring their defence against external threat but also providing economic and technical assistance in the rapid development of their economies and countering hostile influence and propaganda within the countries themselves. It is increasingly a political rather than a military problem.

48. The physical means at our disposal for protecting this vital interest are two-fold [sic]:—

(a) the forces we maintain in the Persian Gulf area and in Aden for the defence of the Sheikhdoms under our protection;
(b) the arrangements we have made through the Bagdad [sic] Pact for the security of Iran and Iraq;
(c) the bases serving these areas (Cyprus, Libya, Jordan, Suez).

49. There can be no question of reducing the (very limited) amount of force we maintain in the Persian Gulf, nor of jeopardising the stability of Iraq and Iran by failing in our support for the Bagdad [sic] Pact. Subject, however, to these two conditions, we should review the British commitments and positions in the Middle East in order to see what alleviation is possible. They are as follows:—

(i)   the headquarters and forces in Cyprus;
(ii)   British forces and air bases in Jordan; and the Arab Legion;
(iii) right to use air bases in Iraq;
(iv)   the civilian-operated base in Egypt;
(v)   British forces in Libya;
(vi)   Aden and the Protectorate;
(vii) the Gulf.

Our military expenditure in the area amounts, from the balance of payments point of view, to about £25 millions a year. In addition Her Majesty's Government are spending about £15 millions a year of Exchequer money on grants to Jordan and Libya and the United Kingdom contribution to Palestine relief; and about £5 millions on other Government services, such as a loan to Jordan, grants to Aden and the Middle East information services.

50. The scope for reductions in military expenditure in this area, on account of a recession of the threat of war, is in no way comparable to that in Europe. We are spending relatively little on global war preparations in the Middle East, apart from the Canal Zone base. And under the Bagdad [sic] Pact, which is one of our main instruments for preserving our interests, we shall certainly be pressed to undertake new military expenditure, for example, contributions to infrastructure projects such as airfields in Iraq. Other adverse factors are that the military strength of trouble-makers like Egypt and Saudi Arabia is likely to increase and that the potential air barrier between the United Kingdom and parts of the Middle East is likely increasingly to limit our flexibility in the use of forces.

51. The main lines of policy we should pursue are these:—

(a) We should not allow the Bagdad [sic] Pact to be treated simply as a military association. We should work out with the Americans definite plans to build up the political, economic and social side of the Pact, and to transform it from a purely military alliance into an association which is demonstrably to the political, economic and social advantage of its members. It should be our policy to make it plain that such aid as is given to member States is the consequence of their membership of the Pact and is given in furtherance of its objectives. Military assistance can also be channelled through the Pact, but the Middle East States should be encouraged to look to the United States for the provision of any equipment and to the United States and ourselves for training facilities.

(b) We should endeavour to ensure that our military contribution to the Bagdad [sic] Pact takes, as far as possible, forms other than the stationing of large conventional forces in Middle East countries. We should examine whether, at the expense of taking some risks, for example with the implementation of our undertakings under the Tripartite Declaration, we cannot plan a substantial run-down over the next few years of our forces in Libya, Jordan and Cyprus, starting with the first. We shall need facilities in these places and we must be seen to be in a position, if necessary, to exercise military power if our interests are threatened; but it should not be necessary for us in the long run to station there permanently forces on anything like the present scale.

(c) We should examine how soon the Canal Zone base can be liquidated.

(d) We should recognise that the Middle East is now the most critical theatre politically and must have a corresponding priority of attention. We should develop non-military methods of maintaining and extending our influence, including technical assistance and information services; and we should improve our Intelligence services. In our own dependent territories, we should do all we can to promote education on the right lines; to improve the police and local security forces; and to improve counter-subversion.

(e) We should continue to give economic assistance, so far as our resources permit, and where we can foresee a substantial return in the form of economic progress and resistance to Communism and to co-operation on the part of the countries we help. We should recognise, however, that our capacity for economic assistance is severely limited. Our grants to Libya and Jordan should be kept under review with an eye to their reduction if and when that can be done without disastrous consequences.

(f) We should continue our efforts to improve the harmony of American policy with our own.

We recommend that studies be made of these points.

Eastern Asia

52. The United Kingdom's most important direct interest in this region is to preserve for the sterling area the dollar earnings of Malaya and Singapore. We must also maintain our position in Hong Kong, chiefly for reasons affecting our prestige. Throughout the region the immediate threat is primarily political and not military. The Joint Intelligence Committee believe that the Chinese leaders wish to avoid war. Our policy should be to promote stability and to help the small neighbouring countries, as well as our own territories, to improve their administration and security and to acquire a vested interest in their own freedom and the desire and ability to resist Communism. In peacetime we thus have an important role to play in South-East Asia: in North-East Asia we must leave the main effort to the Americans, while not neglecting the opportunities that offer, especially in Japan, for maintaining our own influence.

53. In carrying out our policy of promoting stability and improving standards in the smaller countries of Eastern Asia we should make the fullest use of existing international organisations such as the United Nations agencies, the Colombo Plan and SEATO. We should co-operate with the Americans in developing the non-military aspects of SEATO and in seeking to build it up in the eyes of the States of Eastern Asia as an organisation which gives all its members a vested interest in good administration, security and economic progress.

We recommend that the means of bringing about this change of emphasis in SEATO should be studied.

54. The principal military threat in Eastern Asia is from China (and her Communist satellites in North Korea and North Vietnam). The nuclear deterrent is in American hands. Through SEATO the United States, as well as Australia and New Zealand, are committed to the joint defence of the Treaty area, whereas we have no corresponding obligations in respect of Formosa or Japan. In war against China our own contribution must of necessity be a minor one and ancillary to the main American effort directed from the North-East. We should have great difficulty in bringing substantial reinforcements into the area.

55. In this situation our aim should be to reduce and limit our commitments and expenditure and to concentrate our available resources on a more vigorous and effective peacetime policy rather than on preparation for war.

56. *We recommend* that, in the light of a survey of all existing expenditure of the United Kingdom Government in Eastern Asia, studies should made of the following:—

(i) The possibility of a substantial reduction of our military forces in Malaya and Singapore and their possible replacement by local forces as soon as the requirements of internal security permit.

(ii) The policy of maintaining large bases in territories where the political conditions are uncertain.

(iii) The situation in Ceylon.

(iv) The possibility of withdrawing all remaining Commonwealth forces from Korea.

(v) Means by which more resources could be devoted to the development of our own territories, especially Borneo and Sarawak, and to more vigorous peacetime measures, *e.g.*, publicity, technical aid, trade promotion, English teaching, visits, training courses, &c., designed to strengthen the independent countries of South-East Asia, to increase our influence there and to counter the Communist trade and cultural drive.

(vi) Methods of inducing Australia and New Zealand to take the lead in promoting the stability and security of this area and of carrying India with us as far as possible.

Africa

57. Africa is an area of great potential danger. Not only is extreme nationalism already at work against our interests in East and North Africa, but we know that the Communist *bloc* have plans for subversion throughout the Continent. But if we take prompt and resolute action we should be able to nip trouble in the bud.

58. The action needed is:—

(a) assistance in economic development;

(b) the supply of competent administrators and technicians;

(c) added attention to education on the right lines, and improvements in propaganda;

(d) improvements in police, intelligence and counter-subversion.

59. For (a) our capacity is limited. We must seek to promote investment and technical assistance by the United States and other countries of the free world. For (b), the Colonial Secretary has recently announced proposals designed to ensure that British administrators and technicians remain in the employment of the Government of Nigeria after Nigeria reaches independence; and similar arrangements will be considered elsewhere as occasion arises. Certain action in respect of (c) and (d) is already in hand. *We recommend*, however, that a study should be made to confirm that everything possible is being done in these respects by way either of action in dependent territories or of assistance elsewhere, bearing in mind that it is much more expensive to deal with disasters like Mau Mau than to prevent them happening.

Other territories

60. Various minor miscellaneous commitments constitute a drain on our resources and should be re-examined in the light of modern conditions. For example, there may now be scope for savings in the garrison forces in the West Indies. Even in Bermuda we are still incurring some military expenditure. We should also endeavour to curtail our expenditure in the Antarctic region.

We recommend study of these points.

61. *We also recommend* a review of relief grants, such as grants for Korean reconstruction and other United Nations relief.

Summary of recommendations, Part III

62. In the light of the changed political situation, we should seek means of reducing our present military burden and of developing non-military measures for the protection of our interests. We recommend studies of the following:—

(a) The size of our nuclear and thermo-nuclear capacity (paragraph 40).

(b)   The development of a new NATO strategic concept designed to adjust the level of NATO forces to the new political situation (paragraph 46).

(c)   The method by which adoption of this new concept can best be achieved (paragraph 46).

(d)   Plans for building up, in association with the United States, the political, economic and social side of the Bagdad [sic] Pact and for channelling United States military assistance through that Pact (paragraph 51 (a)).

(e)   Plans for the gradual reduction of forces stationed in the Middle East (paragraph 51 (b)).

(f)   The liquidation of the Canal Zone base (paragraph 51 (c)).

(g)   The development of non-military methods of exercising our influence in the Middle East (paragraph 51 (d)).

(h)   Economic and financial assistance to Middle East countries (paragraph 51 (e)).

(i)   Improving the harmony of United States policy in the Middle East with our own (paragraph 51 (f)).

(j)   Developing, in co-operation with the United States, the non-military aspects of SEATO (paragraph 53).

(k)   The reduction of present commitments in Eastern Asia and the development of new political and economic measures (paragraph 56).

(l)   Measures needed in connection with education, propaganda, police, intelligence and counter-subversion in African territories (paragraph 58).

(m) The possibility of eliminating or reducing military commitments in other areas (paragraph 60).

(n)   Expenditure on external relief grants (paragraph 61).

IV. Presentation and timing

63.   We conclude by examining:—

(a) how to present any major changes in external policy and commitments to our Allies—particularly the United States and Canada, and the rest of the Commonwealth;

(b) how to ensure that others assume any burdens we may shed;

(c) timing.

64.   The presentation of our case will be of the greatest importance. The worst possible impression would be given if we failed to convince others that the changes we were making were designed, and would be used, not merely to safeguard our own living standards but to help us play an effective role in world affairs and in particular to meet the Russian threat—a redirection of effort that is called for not only on the part of the United Kingdom but of other countries in the free world, particularly NATO countries. Presentation of our case in that light will not be easy, as there will certainly be those who will argue that we are taking these actions merely to avoid difficult decisions on our internal policies. It will therefore be essential that our "package" should contain recognisably firm action on the internal front. If the only area in which any real saving is made is defence, it will be impossible to argue our case convincingly, and we shall have little or no chance of getting others, such as the United States, to come in to share the burden.

65.   Of the military commitments discussed in Part III, by far the most onerous is the contribution made by our defence spending in the United Kingdom and in Europe in defence of the NATO area. It is still the credo of American policy that the determination of European countries to play their part in resistance to communism is best judged by their maintenance of such contributions; and in consequence any reduction of these contributions carries with it the risk of an "agonising reappraisal" of American policies and an American withdrawal from Europe. We must do what we can to accelerate American recognition of the fact that the Russian threat, while as formidable as ever, is changing its character; and that some transfer of effort by European countries is in the best interests of the free world.

66.   It is not possible to set out a case on all this in detail until the nature of the decisions are known; but we feel it right at this stage to emphasise the importance of this aspect and to make these general comments.

67.   There are two major sources to which we can look to assume some of the burden—the United States, and the Rest of the Commonwealth.

The United States

68.   We should continue to try to secure direct United States help in defence, particularly where this would enable duplication of effort between the two countries to be avoided. It would be wrong, however, to count on being able to do so.

69.   If properly presented, the following course might result in considerable help in the development of the Commonwealth (and possibly under-developed areas generally).

70.   We have paid out an average of £30 millions a year over the last five years in Colonial grants, partly on grants under the Colonial Development and Welfare Act, under which we are committed to an expenditure of £120 millions between 1955–56 and 1959–60, and partly on grants on the Colonial Services Vote. We do not make grants to the independent Commonwealth, but of course we make loans and there is a large volume of investment each year.

71.   We have referred above to the difficulties we have had with the problem of the waiver on the United States loan. We known that the United States is very interested in and concerned about the development of under-developed countries, and there is evidence that at any rate some important elements in the United States now recognise that what they term our "new" colonialism is good, not self-seeking, and above all vital to the security of the free world. Could we bring these together? Could we make a deal with the United States, whereby in return for our giving up the right to the waiver under the loan agreement they would agree that sums equal to the annual payments should be set aside for additional Commonwealth development—or, if they so preferred, as they probably would, for development of under-developed countries generally, including the Commonwealth?

72.   The problem of negotiating such a settlement would be great; but, if it could be brought off, the prizes would also be very great. For example:—

(a) The vexed question of the waiver would have been removed from the field of Anglo-American differences.

(b) The United States would be seen to be encouraging— not criticising—our colonial policies.

(c) Development in the under-developed areas could go ahead faster.   .

(d) We should have a large sum available over the next 40 years or so in relation to the development (but a sum which is totally insignificant in relation to the United States Budget).

73. If the United States seemed likely to agree, we should also bring Canada in very early.

74. Another possibility which might be explored is an approach to the Ford Foundation for a really large Colonial programme.

75. *We recommend* that a study be made of these possibilities of American assistance and that definite proposals be drawn up for Ministers to consider.

The rest of the Commonwealth

Economic

76. On the whole, we cannot at present complain of the policies of the rest of the sterling area. Last year, the deterioration in our payments with the rest of the world was almost wholly on United Kingdom account. Australia is a notable exception. On the other hand, we must expect—and cannot complain about—greater use of sterling balances by, *e.g.*, India and West Africa, for development. In any case, the main responsibility for sterling is ours in the United Kingdom.

77. We therefore do not recommend any special action in respect of the rest of the sterling area other than that they should be informed of any new decisions and asked to consider their policies in the light of them.

Military

78. We shall need to consider, in the light of the decisions taken, what extra effort we can ask for from Commonwealth countries, for example, from Australia and New Zealand in South-East Asia and, possibly, from Canada in the West Indies.

79. *We recommend* that any approach to Commonwealth countries, on the economic or military side, should be considered again in the light of the decisions taken.

80. Finally, on timing, we recommend that the studies of long-term issues we have suggested should not in any way hold up more immediate—or medium-term—issues already under discussion. But if any major changes are to be made, and negotiated in an orderly fashion, great urgency attaches to the studies we have recommended. The very latest date for the completion of *all* the studies is set by the conjunction of three events in November and December of this year:—

The Presidential Election at the beginning of November,
The NATO meeting in mid-December,
The consideration of Service Estimates during December.

This major review of our policies would call for discussions at the highest level with the United States and other Governments. We should *not* defer these until after the Presidential Election, as that may leave too little time for decisions to be taken by the vital date—mid-December. We may find that we cannot settle everything, or indeed anything, *finally* until after the Presidential Election. But the sooner we can start talks the better.

81. *We recommend* that the studies we have proposed should be given the highest urgency, and reports be made as soon as each is finished.

Summary of recommendations, Part IV
   82. *We recommend*

(a) a study of methods of securing United States participation in the burden of economic development of under-developed countries and the Colonies (paragraphs 68–75);
(b) consideration be given later to an approach to the Commonwealth on their contribution in the economic and military fields (paragraph 79);
(c) highest priority be given to the studies proposed and reports be made as each one is completed (paragraph 81).

Appendix A to 21

Assessment of our economic capacity since the war to support our policies
Since the end of the war, the United Kingdom has many achievements to its credit; for instance:—

At home
(a) we have established a Welfare State and accomplished a major social revolution;
(b) we have made a great advance in the reconstruction of industry and expansion of agriculture; we have greatly increased our exports and our record of industrial peace has been good;
(c) we have borne a major defence burden, especially since 1950, and have yet more than doubled gross investment at home in real terms from £925 millions to £2,000 millions between 1946 and 1954.

Abroad
(d) we have granted full independence to India, Pakistan, Ceylon, and are about to do so to the Gold Coast and Malaya, and at the same time have kept them with us in the Commonwealth.

2. In addition we have, in conjunction with our Allies:—

(a) faced Sino-Soviet aggression and brought it to a halt;
(b) forced the Sino-Soviet *bloc* to re-assess its behaviour and tactics;
(c) consolidated much of the free world in NATO, SEATO, the Bagdad [sic] Pact, &c.

3. But we have not managed at home to master inflation; and thus, though we have done well, we have not done well enough. This is shown clearly by the most sensitive guide to our success in supporting our own policies—namely, our balance of payments on external account. Both post-war and pre-war, the totality of our policies—economic, social, political and military—must have their impact in the end upon our external balance of payments. The great and vital difference now is that our external balance of payments is so much more important because we have never had adequate gold and dollar reserves to meet adverse movements of trade between the sterling area as a whole and the rest of the world, and rapid calls upon our debts or sterling balances.

4. We have now virtually reached the end of the post-war period of external aid

(loans or grants) and are started on the half-century of repayment. The picture of the past is this. We have, since the war, received a great deal of external help which is now at an end. This has amounted to upwards of £3,000 million over the ten years. At the end of this period, our gold and dollar reserves, at about £800 million, are lower than they were at the end of the war; and quite apart from other external commitments we face the prospect of repaying our borrowing from the United States and Canada at the rate of £80 million per annum until the year 2000. We have, of course, made considerable *long*-term investments abroad; but, excluding the United States and Canadian loans, which are long-term, our position on *short*-term debts—or sterling balances—is as follows:—

				£ million 31st December	
				1945	1955
Sterling Area ...	...	...	...	2,452	2,972
Non-sterling Area	...	...	...	1,224	770
Total ...	...	...	...	3,676	3,742

It will be seen that the total outstanding has not fallen and is still vast, though the composition has changed for the better, and of course their *real* value (and thus the real demand on our resources) has diminished greatly.

5. Despite this vast borrowing and free aid under the Marshall Plan, we have in point of fact—despite the increase referred to above—not had a satisfactory rate of home investment since the end of the war. This was made very clear in a recent report by E.C.E. We have totally neglected our railways and our roads, whose efficient working is very important to our efficiency and competitive power, and we have had three economic crises and one devaluation. In fact, since the end of the war, the position of sterling, of our balance of payments and of our reserves has been a constant source of anxiety, despite all the aid we have received. These anxieties have arisen first because we had to build up our trade so fast before external aid ended, and then because we had to take on rearming before we were strong enough. The main trouble has been that we have always mortgaged future increases in production and never had anything over to build up the reserves. So our position, though it has got stronger, has always been precarious—we are like a man with an increasing income who is always living beyond it.

6. But one of our most notable post-war achievements has been that, despite all, we have managed to maintain sterling and the sterling system as the major instrument of world trade and finance.

The outlook for the future

7. It is difficult too look into the future with certainty. The best we can do is to draw lessons from the past, attempt to gauge the nature of our commitments, and see what chances there are of making substantial improvements in our economic capabilities by any *new* policies—internal or external.

8. In assessing the future—and, indeed, our role in world affairs—there is one major new factor which has emerged more clearly, and more widely, since the war. It is that the United Kingdom has ceased to be a first-class Power in material terms. The United States and Russia already far outstrip us in population and material

wealth, and both have vast untapped resources. Canada, India and China, to name only three, are at the beginning of their development and in time will certainly outstrip us. Nearer home, Germany has re-established her economic position and currently has gold and dollar reserves 50 per cent. greater than the central reserves of the whole sterling area. She is only beginning her defence effort, has no internal debt and is almost certainly a large *net* creditor on external account. All this will not be altered by the advent of atomic energy. This will help us, but it will also help others. We have, of course, a great potential for expansion in our skill, industry and inventiveness. But the vital point is that we do *not* have in the material sphere, in comparison with the other countries named, apart from Germany, the great untapped sources of wealth.

9.   Thus we cannot hope that, on the basis of material strength alone, we shall be able to play a major or dominant role in world affairs. We shall always be competing with countries whose population or wealth or command of essential food and raw materials is much greater than ours. Even our present material strength—in fact our whole livelihood—is at risk, because among our raw materials one, namely oil, *which is absolutely vital to us*, already comes largely, and in future will have to come still more, from the Middle East, and we have not absolute control over what happens there. (This also applies to many other countries, *e.g.*, Germany.)

10.   No precise assessment of the size of our future burdens can be made. We can only look at our certain and probable commitments and make a judgment as best we can. The following factors are relevant:—

(a) There is no doubt that to maintain our place in world trade we must spend a larger proportion of our total effort on investment at home in productive industry. This means comparatively less for consumption—or other commitments—or an increased burden on our external balance of payments.

(b) Our external payments are already too big; we should be reducing them. But, so far as can be judged, they seem likely to be greater in future years than in the recent past. The following table shows what we have had to spend on capital and current external commitments in recent years:—

	Average in £ millions for 1952–55
Obligations on Capital Account	
(i) Net Government lending repayment of debt ...	20
(ii) Net long-term investment	160
Total of obligations on capital account (i.e., *minimum charge on surplus without allowing for drawing on sterling balances or rebuilding reserves*)	*180*
Government Obligations on Current Account	
(iii) Military expenditure	150
(iv) Colonial grants	30
(v) Relief and other grants	20
(iv) Net interest on Government loans	40
Total of obligations on current account	240
Grand Total	420

These figures do not take account of any change in German support costs. If we bear these in full and no change is made in our military disposition, then we must add £80 million per annum to the total. It should be noted that even this very large total of £500 million per annum does *not* make any provision for *net* drawing down of sterling balances or the rebuilding of the reserves. We cannot guarantee that with the growing tempo of development in, for example, India and the Colonies, we may not have to face some *net* drawing down of the sterling area's sterling balances in certain years.

In addition, new claims are constantly arising—the Soviet economic offensive, the Indus Waters, Bagdad [sic] Pact and so on. The total commitment, unless we alter our policies, is likely to increase rather than decrease.

(c) If we are to meet even minor changes in the economic situation—quite apart from any major changes, such as real trouble with the Middle East or a substantial change in the terms of trade—we must build up the central gold and dollar reserves quickly and substantially. A figure of £1,500 million—or about twice the present figure—would be no more than comfortable.

(d) There is added strain on the balance of payments which will necessarily follow if we carry out our *international* commitments under G.A.T.T., and I.M.F. and O.E.E.C., especially the removal of discrimination against the dollar, which is also part of our agreed Commonwealth policy of making sterling fully convertible as soon as we can safely do so.

11. How far can we expect to improve our capacity to meet this increasing commitment through changes in our policies—internal or international?

12. We should consider first whether we can really hope for such a change in the total attitude of this country—people, employers or trade unions—to our problems that they will recognise the full scope and range of our responsibilities and also be ready to forgo the increases in personal consumption and leisure which we must forgo if we are to produce the savings and exports which we need. In the light of past experience it would be unwise to count on this—at any rate in advance. Our post-war history has in the main been one of mortgaging well in advance the gains which we hope to make. The result has been that we have rarely if ever had anything in reserve; and that when those gains have not been made, or some external factor such as the terms of trade have gone against us, we have had a crisis. Only when the terms of trade have been favourable or we have been in receipt of massive external aid have we really had any comfort or latitude. But, even if our best hopes are realised and the country is prepared to forgo increases in leisure and personal consumption and our economic effort is directed towards the right kind of production, the analysis made above shows that we shall need the minimum external commitments, for the next few years at any rate, if we are not to be under constant strain or crisis. Quite apart from any reduction in commitments, increasing competition, especially from Germany, Japan and United States, will of itself require the maximum internal efforts here.

13. The second question is whether we can hope for any moves in international economic organisation, with whatever political consequences that may have, of a kind that will free us from our constant post-war anxieties about our external balance and our reserves.

14. Under this head, two studies are at the moment in progress, one about

possible arrangements with Europe and the other about the future of the sterling area. Both these will be coming forward fairly soon; and, whatever may be decided, they certainly will not lift a great burden from our shoulders. But some developments of policy could help more than others to get others to help us to carry these burdens.

22   CAB 134/1315, PR(56)6   6 June 1956
[Defence expenditure]: memorandum by Sir W Monckton for Cabinet Policy Review Committee

[A meeting of ministers was called on 16 May 1956 to discuss ways of reducing government expenditure by some £100 million in 1956–1957 (CAB 130/115, GEN 527/1). The chancellor, Mr Macmillan, hoped that a substantial part of this total could be found in the areas of defence and home defence. Because of the implications for defence policy this matter was taken up by the Policy Review Committee.]

When we last discussed the savings of £100 millions in 1956/7 (GEN.527/1st Meeting), the Chancellor of the Exchequer suggested that we should try to find £25 millions in 1956/7 from measures other than major changes in policy.

2. The Service Ministers have done better. They believe that they can see their way to savings totalling about £34 millions. More than half of this has been found by the War Office.

3. This does not include any allowance for short-falls in production. In accordance with what the Chancellor of the Exchequer said in the House of Commons on 23rd April, I am assuming that we should not at this stage take account either of these production short-falls or of unforeseen items on the other side of the ledger.

4. In this study, the Service Ministers and I have taken into account the suggestions made by the Treasury, and those discussed at our last meeting, so far as they affect expenditure in 1956/7.

5. I must emphasise that although these savings have been referred to as "house-keeping" economies,[1] they are in many cases things that involve some risk.

6. I have received from the Minister of Supply a list of savings which might be sought by selling equipment to other countries at the expense of deliveries to our own forces, by slowing down deliveries and by cancelling orders. The Service Ministers and I hope that it may be possible to find a few millions more in these ways. However, before the issues of policy that would be involved can be presented for decision, there is some more factual work to be done by officials, for example in examining whether Hunters could be sold without our losing dollars on American orders, and how far the list overlaps with the proposals the Service Ministers have made already.

7. For further savings we must look to the basic changes of policy we are now starting to consider in this Committee; although the major changes can only to a small extent affect expenditure in 1956/7.

---

[1] In a memo to the Policy Review Committee Macmillan described the money saved by the service departments as 'entirely composed of "housekeeping economies".' He hoped that the service departments could save a further £10 million 'as the immediate result of [defence] policy changes' (memo by Macmillan, CAB 134/1315, PR(56)4, 6 June 1956).

K

8. The Chancellor of the Exchequer speaks in his paper (P.R.(56) 7) of a saving of about £7 millions in the defence expenditure of civil departments in addition to the £5 millions already secured. I could not pledge the departments to such a figure without discussing it fully with them. However, taking this figure for the sake of argument with the £34 millions from the Services we should have a total of £46 millions on defence. I suggest that it would be inconsistent with the thought behind the paper by officials (P.R.(56) 3)[2] to look for appreciably more than half of the £100 million saving from the defence element of Government expenditure. As this paper points out (paragraph 64) it is essential that the measures we take to put our economy on a sound footing should be a "package" containing retrenchment both in non-defence as well as defence expenditure; and to find too much from defence, in advance of any consultation with the Americans or other N.A.T.O. countries about a change in the N.A.T.O. strategic concept might look as if we were merely trying to reduce our burdens at our Allies' expense, and would increase the difficulties of bringing about the early change of N.A.T.O. policy which is so important to us in the longer term.

9. I suggest that we should set ourselves the aim of saving on defence about £50 millions—a few millions more than the £46 millions mentioned above. We shall not find this remaining sum easily.

---

[2] See 21.

23   CAB 134/1315, PR 2(56)   8 June 1956[1]
'Reductions in government [defence] expenditure in 1956–57':
Cabinet Policy Review Committee minutes

The Committee had before them two memoranda by the Chancellor of the Exchequer (P.R.(56) 4 and 5) and a memorandum by the Minister of Defence (P.R.(56) 6).[2]

The Chancellor of the Exchequer said that he had been considering the timetable for the presentation of the Government's proposals to Parliament. He had in mind the following:—

14th June – decision by the Cabinet
18th June – last day for receipt by the Treasury of draft Revised Estimates from Departments
22nd June – proofs of Revised Estimates sent to Stationary Office
26th June – statement by the Chancellor of the Exchequer
5th July – publication of the Revised Estimates.

In discussion, it was suggested that the Government's proposals might be presented to Parliament in two instalments. The Government were not at present in a position—in advance for example, of further study of the effect on military expenditure of the changes in defence policy now under discussion—to take final decisions about how the total reduction in expenditure should be secured. This indicated that the Chancellor of the Exchequer might inform Parliament in July of

---

[1] The meeting was held on 7 June 1956; the minutes are dated 8 June.
[2] See 22.

those reductions on which a decision was already possible and explain that he would announce later in the year such further measures as were necessary to complete the rest of the saving.

The Committee:—

(1) Agreed with the timetable proposed by the Chancellor of the Exchequer.

(2) Took note that it might prove impossible for the Chancellor of the Exchequer to announce to Parliament in July all the measures by which the total saving in 1956/7 was to be secured.

The Chancellor of the Exchequer then explained how matters at present stood about the composition of the saving.

On defence, the Service Ministers were aiming to save £34 millions on what he might term "house-keeping" economies. He was very grateful for their efforts. He still thought, however, that a little more—say £2 millions—might be found from this range of measures. The Treasury would discuss with the Ministry of Defence and the Service Departments some suggestions about such additional savings.

He hoped that some £10 millions savings might also accrue in 1956/7 from the major changes of defence policy which the Committee were now examining.

On the defence expenditure of Civil Departments, it was already agreed that savings of £5 millions could be found. He now believed that it should be possible to increase this sum to £16½ millions. Of this additional £11½ millions, £4 millions might be found by running down the strategic stockpile of materials, £6 millions by reductions in purchases of food for turning over the food stockpile and £1½ millions from elsewhere in the defence spending of Civil Departments.

On non-defence expenditure, it was already agreed that administrative and other economies should yield £11 millions. He hoped that he might find an additional £1 million from Colonial Office expenditure, £1 million from Foreign Office expenditure and £½ million from economies by the Ministry of Labour and the Ministry of National Insurance.

There remained those measures which had been discussed by the Social Services Committee, namely measures affecting school meals, prescription charges and milk. These measures were capable of yielding a total of £15¼ millions. A further saving of £1½ millions could be made if the October price increase of ½d. were applied to welfare milk as well as to ordinary milk.

The Ministry of Defence said that he must emphasise that the saving of £34 millions which the Service Ministers had in mind should not be thought of as "house-keeping" economies. A substantial proportion of it represented anticipation of the changes in defence policy now under consideration. The Service Ministers had made a very searching review, as was shown by the size of the figure they had produced. The Committee would now be proceeding to elaborate the changes in defence policy which had been adumbrated at their last meeting and to consider their effects on the programmes of the Services. Those effects were likely to be far-reaching, but he must warn the Committee that it was unlikely, considering the contractual and other commitments of Departments and the fact that the Service Ministers had already utilised so much of the scope for immediate savings, that substantial further savings would be found in 1956/7. He suggested that it might be explained to Parliament in due course that only a small part of the changes in defence policy proposed by the Government would be reflected in savings in 1956/7, and that these changes would produce substantial savings in later years.

He thought it particularly important to our relations with our Allies that the reductions in Government expenditure in 1956/7 should include an appreciable element in respect of social expenditure. Our Allies were inclined to believe that the United Kingdom could not at the same time discharge her obligations as a world power and maintain her high level of social security. It was important that we should not give the impression that, in order to preserve all our social expenditure, we were seeking to transfer our military burdens to our Allies.

In discussion of defence expenditure, it was urged that the major changes in defence policy which the Committee contemplated ought to yield substantial savings in 1956/7. For example, it would be wrong to exclude the possibility of slowing down the production of medium bombers this year, even though the present strength of the Medium Bomber Force amounted to only twenty-four Valiants, if only because hydrogen bombs of United Kingdom manufacture were not available to match this Force. Again, it was true that all the aircraft for Fighter Command allowed for in the Estimates were to be paid for by the United States, but it was open to us to reduce the size of the Command and thus to save operating costs, which were substantial. However, there was much to be said for the suggestion that it should be explained to Parliament that the bulk of the savings that were being made in defence expenditure would not accrue until after 1956/7.

The Prime Minister said that he had had an opportunity of informal discussion with Lord Ismay[3] about the changes in defence policy which the Government had in mind. Lord Ismay had welcomed these proposals, which were in line with his own views. He hoped that we should lose no time in presenting them to the North Atlantic Council. Such an initiative by the United Kingdom was the most promising way of obtaining the change in N.A.T.O. policy which was required. Lord Ismay had added that General Norstad[4] was thinking on similar lines: he recognised that the day of large armies was over.

The Committee then discussed briefly the measures affecting the social services.

The Prime Minister said that it was desirable that the reductions in Government expenditure should include one of the measures in the field of social expenditure. He hoped, however, that it would be unnecessary to include more than one.

The following points were made in discussion:—

(a) It was especially undesirable to find savings at the expense of children's health. On the other hand, it need not be assumed that a moderate increase in the cost of school meals would necessarily mean that fewer parents took advantage of the service. To increase the charge to 1/- would do no more than cover the real cost of the meals (which was 10d.) and the cost of administration.

(b) The Committee were informed that the Secretary of State for Scotland and the Minister of Agriculture preferred not to reach an immediate decision about a seasonal increase of a further ½d. a pint being imposed on milk in October, but would wish to wait for experience of the effect of the ½d. a pint increase already authorised to start on 1st July.

---

[3] Baron Ismay, S of S for Commonwealth relations, 1951–1952; secretary-general of NATO, 1952–1957; vice-chairman of North Atlantic Council, 1952–1956.

[4] General L Norstad, deputy (air) to supreme allied commander, Europe, 1953–1956; c-in-c, US European command, 1956–1962.

(c) All three measures in the social field were proposals for increasing the charges on personal incomes and were therefore liable to be used in support of demands for higher wages.

(d) The Ministers concerned with these measures had only been prepared to accept them on the understanding that they were indispensable to honouring the Government's undertakings about reductions in expenditure.

(e) The memorandum by the Chancellor of the Exchequer (P.R.(56) 5) on the possibility of making arbitrary cuts in grants to local authorities showed that the difficulties of such a course were extremely formidable.

The Committee:—

(3) Agreed that the propoosal to make arbitrary reductions in grants to local authorities need not be further examined.

(4) Invited the Chancellor of the Exchequer to consider, in the light of their discussion, which of the measures under consideration should be presented to Parliament in July; and to bring proposals before the Cabinet in the following week.

(5) Invited the Chancellor of the Exchequer to continue his discussions with the Ministers concerned about ways in which further savings in 1956/7 might be secured otherwise than by major decisions.

24   CAB 134/1315, PR 3(56)2, 4 & 5   9 June 1956
[Defence policy]: Cabinet Policy Review Committee minutes[1]

2. *United Kingdom contribution to N.A.T.O. forces*
The Committee proceeded to consider paragraphs 41–46 of the memorandum by officials (P.R.(56) 3) dealing with military measures in the United Kingdom and Europe.[2] They also had before them a note by the Foreign Office and Ministry of Defence (P.R.(56) 9) dealing with the way in which the withdrawal of an armoured division from Germany could best be discussed with our Allies and the timing of such discussions.

The Prime Minister said that what was required was a new military policy for N.A.T.O. He hoped that the Chiefs of Staff might be able to assist in the formulation of United Kingdom proposals for such a revision of policy. These proposals would be discussed initially with the United States and Canadian Governments and thereafter by the North Atlantic Council. They might be based on the concept of the "trip wire". He had discussed this concept informally with Lord Ismay, who had told him that it was in accordance with his own views. Lord Ismay believed that both General Gruenther[3] and General Norstad agreed that a revision of N.A.T.O. policy on these

---

[1] The meeting was attended by Eden (chair), Salisbury, Macmillan and Monckton. Also present: Lord Cilcennin (J P L Thomas (Viscount Cilennin 1955), first lord of the Admiralty, 1951–1956), Mr Head (secretary of state for war), Mr R Maudling (economic secretary, Treasury, 1952–1955; minister of supply, 1955–1957), Sir I Kirkpatrick (FO), General Sir G Templer (chief of the imperial general staff), Air Chief Marshall Sir D Boyle (chief of air staff) and Vice-Admiral Sir W Davis (vice-chief of naval staff, 1954–1957), with Sir N Brook and R C Chilver as secretaries.
[2] See 21.
[3] General A M Gruenther, supreme allied commander, Europe, 1953–1956.

lines was required and would welcome an initiative from Her Majesty's Government on the point. Without such an initiative the machinery of N.A.T.O. could not be expected to produce a revision of policy with the necessary speed.

The Prime Minister added that the new N.A.T.O. policy he had in mind would be one which would permit substantial reductions, not only in the United Kingdom Forces stationed on the Continent but in Naval Forces maintained for global war purposes.

The Chief of the Imperial General Staff said that he did not believe that the United Kingdom Chiefs of Staff had sufficient information on which to evolve detailed proposals for a revision of N.A.T.O. military policy and force requirements. This was a task for N.A.T.O. military staffs who had the necessary information and were indeed already engaged in studies on these lines in preparation for the next major staff exercise, CPX.7, which was to be held next year.

The Committee's discussion showed agreement with the view that the initiative taken by Her Majesty's Government for the review of N.A.T.O. policy should deal essentially with the broad directions in which military policy should be reviewed in the light of the changed situation and should not set out detailed proposals for the changes which this new policy would imply in N.A.T.O. strategy and in the forces of all member countries. However, Her Majesty's Government need not feel precluded from setting out at a fairly early stage the kind of changes which they visualised might result in the forces contributed by the United Kingdom. It was already recognised in N.A.T.O. procedure that the "force goals" approved by N.A.T.O. were based on proposals made unilaterally by member countries, having regard not only to requirements but to their military and economic capabilities.

The Chancellor of the Exchequer said that our handling of the review of N.A.T.O. policy must have regard to the urgency of our need to reduce our forces on the continent. In respect of land forces, our objective was to ensure that ultimately our contribution did not exceed two divisions and that we were enabled to withdraw one division at an early date.

It was open to us to justify our proposals to our Allies both on our difficulties about foreign exchange and on the new strategic situation. He thought it wise, however, to concentrate on one justification; and it seemed best that our case should rest primarily on the fact that our commitment had become out of date. Our present force contribution was related to a strategic situation which no longer existed. Moreover, insofar as our commitments were related to providing the French with safeguards against German aggression, it was to be noted that the French had now withdrawn the greater part of their Forces from Europe and that the Germans still had virtually no Forces in being. We could go on to make the point that in the new situation which had arisen in which the most immediate threat was economic, it was unrealistic that the United Kingdom should maintain a N.A.T.O. contribution of its present size.

Our method of discussion with our Allies must ensure speed while avoiding the appearance of unilateral action. We should try to ensure that the changes we wished to make flowed from a reappraisal of N.A.T.O. strategy. We should therefore propose an early meeting of the North Atlantic Council to set this reappraisal in train.

It would be necessary during the next few days to reach a decision about an offer from the German Government about Support Costs, which was unlikely to amount to more than £30 millions compared with actual costs of about £70 millions. He thought it most important that if we accepted this offer we should do so in a way which avoided any legal or moral commitment to continue maintaining four divisions on the Continent. In this connection, it was to be noted that the United States Government had recently concluded an agreement with the German Government about Support Costs unilaterally.

The Committee's discussion showed general agreement with the proposals of the Chancellor of the Exchequer. Points made in discussion were:—

(a) Account must be taken, in connection both with the reduction of our Forces on the Continent and with the handling of wider questions of N.A.T.O. policy, of the letter dated 6th June which the Prime Minister had received from Mr. Bulganin[4] on the subject of disarmament. This letter raised big issues and early consultation would be required with our Allies about the way in which it should be handled. An important point to be noted was that for the first time the Russian Government were prepared to discuss proposals for the reduction of Forces in Germany as distinct from proposals for their complete withdrawal.

It would be most important, in handling this letter, to keep the subject of reductions of Forces in Europe wholly separate from the question of German reunification and of thermo-nuclear disarmament.

(b) Proposals for reducing our Forces in Germany were likely to be welcome to the German Government because they would release barracks. Otherwise, the Germans would have to build new barracks at a time when their building industry was under strain.

(c) Use might be made of the argument that our reduced Forces would not necessarily have a reduced fighting capacity. It was on these grounds that SACEUR did not appear unduly disturbed about the numerical reductions we were already proposing to make in the 2nd Tactical Air Force.

The Committee agreed that the next step must be to prepare a cogent memorandum setting out the factors on which a reappraisal of the requirement for N.A.T.O. forces could be based. The memorandum should explain that the need for this reappraisal arose from two factors:—

(i) the changed strategic situation produced by the development of megaton bombs;

'X'   (ii) the fact that the immediate Russian threat was now economic rather than military.

Mention might perhaps be made, in connection with these factors, of the latest Russian communication on the subject of disarmament. The memorandum should urge that a Ministerial meeting of the North Atlantic Council should be held at an early date, so that instructions for the reappraisal could be given to the N.A.T.O. military authorities.

The memorandum would be discussed in the first place with the United States and Canadian Governments.

It would be for consideration whether, immediately after the meeting of the North Atlantic Council, a meeting of members of the Western European Union should be arranged, at which Her Majesty's Government would set out their proposals for the early withdrawal of an armoured division from Germany.

---

[4] N Bulganin, chairman of Council of Ministers, USSR, 1955–1958.

The Committee:—

(1) Invited the Permanent Under-Secretary of State for Foreign Affairs, in consultation with the Ministry of Defence, to prepare, as a matter of urgency, a memorandum as described at 'X' above, for discussion initially with Governments of the United States and Canada.

(2) Invited the Permanent Under-Secretary of State for Foreign Affairs to instruct H.M. Ambassador in Washington to inform the United States Government that Her Majesty's Government would welcome an early opportunity of discussing with them the replies to be made to the Russian Government's communication of 6th June on disarmament.

In the light of the proceeding [sic] discussion it was suggested that in addition to preparing a memorandum for presentation to our Allies, we should need to formulate our own ideas about the effect on N.A.T.O. Forces, and particularly our own contribution to which the new N.A.T.O. policy might apply, and about the reasons which might be advanced for particular reductions in our own contributions. What was needed was a military brief to guide our representatives when these matters were discussed. It would be a mistake to leave it wholly to the N.A.T.O. military authorities to work out what N.A.T.O. Forces the new concept implies. This brief should set up the level of the United Kingdom contribution which might be appropriate under the new concept (including a reduction of Rhine Army to not more than two divisions, a reduction in the 2nd Tactical Air Force and a substantial reduction in our Naval contribution to N.A.T.O.), and should explain why in our view contributions of this order would be appropriate to the new circumstances.

The Committee agreed with this proposal. In discussion the point was made that the forces at present in existence fell a long way short of requirements as at present stated—for example, the French had withdrawn five divisions and none of the additional twelve German divisions had been formed. The total land forces we proposed under the new concept might well be nearly as large as those which actually existed at present.

The Committee:—

(3) Invited the Minister of Defence to arrange for the preparation of a brief on the above lines for the use of United Kingdom representatives at discussions within N.A.T.O. about the reappraisal of N.A.T.O. Force requirements.

4. *United Kingdom contribution to the deterrent*

The Chancellor of the Exchequer recalled that at their meeting on 6th June, the Committee had discussed the United Kingdom contribution to the deterrent and had invited the Minister of Defence to arrange for a study to be made in the light of their discussion. He would like to put forward some suggestions on the subject.

The present plan provided for the Medium Bomber Force to be built up to a front line of 200 aircraft. With this in view, the following aircraft had been or were to be produced:—

    67 Valiants at a cost of £29 millions
    107 Victors "   "   £70   "
    152 Vulcans "   "   £92   "

The Committee had agreed that there should be a review both of the size of the Force and of its phasing; the latter taking account of the rate of British production of nuclear weapons and of the date when medium range guided missiles would be available.

Production of Valiants was already far advanced and he saw no advantage in slowing down the rate of delivery unless it appeared that to do so would assist the production of Viscounts. As regards Vulcans, he understood that the Air Staff considered that the Victor had more potentiality for development, and he suggested that a decision might be taken not to place any further orders for the Vulcan (and indeed possibly to cancel some of the existing orders) and to reduce the rate of production to the lowest economic rate. The rate of production of the Victor might similarly be reduced to the lowest economical rate. Under these proposals, there would still be a steady increase in the size of the Medium Bomber Force until it reached its final figure, but the date at which it reached any particular figure would be one or two years later. There was no strategic reason why the Force should reach a particular size by a given date; and the slowing down which he proposed would be economically advantageous, because it would prevent the firms concerned from seeking to increase their labour force at the expense of other firms.

Points made in discussion were:—

(a) The basis of the new defence policy which was now contemplated was that war had become less likely and conventional weapons less important because of the existence of the thermo-nuclear and nuclear deterrent. In these circumstances, was it wise to reduce our contribution to the deterrent?

(b) It was proposed that we should recommend to N.A.T.O. a new concept which flowed from the existence of the new weapons. Might it not militate against our success if we were at the same time deliberately to reduce and slow down our own programme for these new weapons, particularly in the initial stages of the programme, when our Medium Bomber Force was still extremely small? The present plan for the Force already provided for a slower expansion than we had led our Allies to expect.

(c) The Government had hitherto emphasised publicly that the early production of medium bombers was of the highest importance. Their production had been given "super-priority", and the utmost pressure had been placed on the firms. There might be a loss of confidence if the Government's attitude were now to be reversed. On the other hand, it could be pointed out that the situation had changed.

(d) It was true that United Kingdom production of nuclear and thermo-nuclear bombs would be behind the production of bombers. However, this did not affect the argument about the deterrent power of our Force, because the Russians would assume that United States bombs would be available to us.

(e) It was at present planned that production of the supersonic bomber should be undertaken by A.V. Roe Ltd. after the production of the Vulcan. To terminate production of the latter earlier than at present planned might leave a gap.

The Committee considered that the decision ultimately to be taken on the production of medium bombers would turn largely on a balance between strategic and economic factors. It was, therefore, important to have information about the industrial consequences of measures such as those the Chancellor had suggested. It was most important, however, that the enquiries made on this subject should not become known, since they might do great harm to the negotiations we were about to have with our Allies.

The Committee:—

Invited the Minister of Supply to make confidential enquiries about the industrial implications of reducing or delaying production of Valiant, Vulcan and Victor medium bombers.

5. *Future of the Suez Canel zone base*

The Secretary of State for War said that some preliminary consideration had been given, in accordance with the Committee's instructions, to the question of the future of the base in the Suez Canal Zone. His opinion was that if a decision were given now that the base would not be required after 1961, it should be possible to work out an economical plan to meet the Army's requirements in the Middle East meanwhile. If the base had to be closed down earlier and improvised arrangements made for dealing with its tasks, more expenditure would be involved. For example, it was proposed that the maintenance of soft-skinned vehicles should be carried out in the Canal Zone after 1958, by which date we were under obligations to the Libyan Government to vacate Benghazi, where the work was being done at present. In the longer term, it was proposed to arrange for the work to be done in Malta. If it could not be done in the Canal Zone in the interim, the vehicles would have to be sent back to the United Kingdom, which would be expensive. Again, if perishable stores had to be moved out of the Canal Zone before accommodation was ready for them elsewhere, there would be losses through deterioration.

The following points were made in discussion:—

(a) The proposal to carry out maintenance at Malta was attractive, since there was unemployment there.

(b) It was possible that the Libyan Government could be induced to prolong our tenure of Benghazi.

(c) Careful thought should be given to the way in which the matter should be handled with the Egyptian Government. It would be unfortunate if we were seen to leave the Canal Zone as a result of pressure from the Egyptian Government. Such pressure was more probable if the Egyptian Government believed us to be anxious to stay; whereas, if they believed we had no desire to stay, they might press us to do so, particularly since we might be able to do certain maintenance work for them at the base.

The general view of the Committee was that it could be assumed that the base could be vacated by 1961, provided that this could be arranged without provoking trouble with the Egyptian Government.

The Committee:—

Invited the Permanent Under-Secretary of State for Foreign Affairs to consider, in consultation with the War Office, what tactics should be followed with the Egyptian Government in connection with the Suez Canal Zone base, on the assumption that it would be our objective to vacate the base by 1961.

25   CAB 134/1315, PR(56)11   15 June 1956

'Assumptions for future planning': note by Sir A Eden for Cabinet Policy Review Committee

The Committee have approved the following as a basis for our military and political planning:—

1. Our political and military objectives are:—

(a) to avoid global war;
(b) to protect our vital interests overseas, particularly access to oil.

Attempts to secure these objectives are likely to fail unless we:—

(a) maintain North American involvement in Europe;
(b) maintain a large measure of identity between the interests of the United States and Canada and our own and develop closer co-operation with those countries;
(c) maintain the cohesion of the Commonwealth.

2. In our studies of future policy we must bear in mind that:—

(a) The main threat to our position and influence in the world is now political and economic rather than military: and our policies should be adapted to meet that changed situation. Effort must be transferred from military preparations to the maintenance and improvement of our political and economic position.

(b) The period of foreign aid is ending and we must now cut our coat according to our cloth. There is not much cloth. We have to find means of increasing by £400 millions a year the credit side of our balance of payments.

(c) In our defence programmes generally we are doing too much to guard against the least likely risk, *viz.*, the risk of major war; and we are spending too much on forces of types which are no longer of primary importance.[1]

---

[1] In a note of 10 July 1956 (CAB 134/1315, PR(56)16), Eden listed the policy areas he intended the committee to review in the next four weeks. Week 1: national service; home defence. Week 2: new strategy for NATO (COS appreciation); bombers; fighters. Week 3: Royal Navy; forces for limited war and internal security; military facilities in Middle East and Far East; non-military measures in Middle East; non-military measures in South-East Asia; Antarctica; relief grants; Treasury reports on Part I of PR(56)3, 'The future of the United Kingdom in world affairs'. Week 4: research and development; medium-range ballistic missiles; Africa; review of NATO reappraisal; round up and conclusion. This programme was not carried out in full; see 27, note.

26 CO 1032/51, no 112   June 1956
[The Commonwealth and international relations]: CRO paper on the
probable development of the Commonwealth over the next ten or
fifteen years   [Extract]¹

The setting of the problem
It is difficult to give a satisfactory answer to this question without some assessment
over the period in question of:–

(a) the changes to be expected in Europe;
(b) developments in Soviet policy;
(c) developments in China and Japan;
(d) possible changes in U.S. policy;
(e) developments in defence and in the atomic energy field.

2. For the purpose of this paper the following assumptions are made on the
points above:–

(a) Germany and the Soviet (including the satellites) politically and economically
the dominating powers *inside Europe*. German military resurgence likely, but
counterbalanced by the Soviet. France increasingly in decline.

(b) A strongly organised and developing *Soviet*, likely to maintain, whatever its
professions, and subject to minor or temporary tactical variations, its present
policy of spreading the Communist ideal of world domination through penetration, and of the undermining in Asia and Africa of the influence of the West and of
America.

(c) Progressive population pressure and nationalistic resurgence in *China and
Japan*. Active economic competition by Japan based on lower standards of living.
Penetration by China particularly in the military and subversion fields of the
surrounding areas (Malaya, Singapore, the former Indo-China, perhaps the
Philippines) assisted by the expansion of the Chinese element in the populations of
thoese territories but without a clash with India or Russia. Pressure, more
particularly from Japan, for modification of Australian racial policy and the
admission of non-Europeans to her open spaces.

(d) The increasing wealth, population, and technical devélopment of the *U.S.A.*
will make her less responsive to persuasion in the economic and political fields by
the United Kingdom and the Commonwealth, but the existence of the Soviet
threat, particularly if accompanied by a close understanding between the Soviet
and China or Japan (though unless Japan goes Communist an understanding
between her and the Communist bloc is perhaps unlikely), will act as a
counterbalance: and if only to preserve overseas markets and offset or reduce the
dangers of Communism, extensive aid, military and economic, to the countries of
the free world and the under-developed countries, will continue. A close understanding, but one in which the United States' view will tend to carry progressively
increasing weight, will continue with the United Kingdom and the Common-

---

¹ This paper was prepared in the CRO for circulation by Lord Home to Cabinet ministers. The sections
dealing with Australia, New Zealand, Canada, India, Pakistan and Ceylon are not printed here.

wealth. The effect on United States' thinking and policy of the solidarity of the Commonwealth, if that can be maintained, is likely on the other hand to remain substantial. Some danger, if not likelihood, of United States' influence increasing and consolidating itself in certain Commonwealth countries because of military and economic threats which the United Kingdom will be unable to help to counter, and because of United States overseas investment. Notably in Australia: possibly also in Pakistan and the Middle East: possibly in S.E. Asia.

(e) *Defence*.

No war, but little if any decline in the cold war. No satisfactory agreement about disarmament. A reduction in expenditure in conventional weapons and in non-technical armed forces of all services. The A and H bombs and their developments, the effective restraint on war.

(f) *Atomic power*.

Over ten years, it should be possible to gauge more accurately the future civil uses to which atomic energy can be turned, and the further developments possible in its use in aspects of the defence field. But no very decisive development in a practical way in the field of civil energy within say 15 years.

The present pattern of the Commonwealth

The Commonwealth links

(a) *General*

3. A group, of which the United Kingdom is the keystone, and which but for the existence of the United Kingdom would disintegrate regionally, of independent sovereign States with varying constitutional structures, races, religions, historical and economic backgrounds, linked by allegiance to, or the common headship of, the Sovereign; and held together by ties of

(i) Sentiment;
(ii) Tradition;
(iii) Interest.

4. *Sentiment* is of particular importance in the case of the "old" Commonwealth countries other than South Africa, and of small significance in the case of the "new".

Tradition and cultural background are of great importance in all cases. The "new" dominions have been shaped by British political thought. They have inherited, to a greater degree than they realise, British cultural and governmental standards. The significance of the Monarchy is of primary importance principally in Australia, New Zealand, and, to a lesser extent, Canada, where, however, it is material to the politically important French element. But while the Monarchy does not hold so deeply rooted a place in India, Pakistan and Ceylon, it may well be that it can retain a special position in emerging African territories, where there is so strong a tradition of tribal loyalty.

5. *Interest*, reinforced to some extent by sentiment, is increasingly the decisive link.

(b) *Specific links*

6. But in considering the links that hold the Commonwealth together weight must be given also to the facts that:—

(i) in recent years we have actually been drawing closer in understanding with the old Commonwealth countries. It is true that they are becoming stronger and are hence physically better able to pursue their own line where they wish. But, as they increasingly understand the reality of their independence they have fewer inhibitions in co-operating with us: there is less temptation for them to strike an independent line merely in order to demonstrate their independence. Our physical means of maintaining close consultation with them on all matters have greatly increased. Consequently they have an increased understanding of our problems, as we have of theirs. We may expect this tendency to increase during the next few years;

(ii) the economies of all Commonwealth countries which are members of the Sterling Area are very closely tied up with our economy. They are accustomed to trade with us, as we are with them. That is why it is in their interest that their currencies are tied to sterling and the fact that their currencies are tied to sterling increases the tendency for us to trade with each other. These bonds should continue independently whether some Commonwealth countries (particularly the emergent ones) become Republics or even leave the Commonwealth. These economic bonds with us inevitably affect the policies of the countries concerned, and will tend to keep them in the Commonwealth.

Practical signifiance of the Commonwealth links

7. The Commonwealth association, informal, flexible, and adaptable, a dynamic and developing organism, based as it is on the elements described above, is of value to its members, not only because of their substantial overall identity of interest, but because of its very informality. Foreign nations find it difficult to understand why it holds together, when it embraces so many different and conflicting interests; why it works, when it has no apparent set of rules or constitution; how close the links are that bind it, or how seriously internal dissensions in it should be taken; and, most important of all, how it will react as a whole to any particular situation and in particular to any threat to its individual members.

8. In practice, while each member is sovereign, and takes its own decision on any issue, there is, broadly speaking, a degree of common outlook, common thinking, interests, and understanding, that is likely to produce a *broadly* common reaction. The knowledge of this, and the uncertainty how strong that reaction may be, are, it is suggested, in practice, a deterrent to possible aggressors. Even within the Commonwealth, the significance of common opinion may help to keep internal dissensions from going to extremes (India and the Tamils of Ceylon: India and Pakistan: India and South Africa) and to protect the weaker parties from pressure that might otherwise be applied to them.

The importance of the United Kingdom in the Commonwealth structure

9. It has to be accepted that the United Kingdom is the keystone of the Commonwealth arch. Without it it is impossible to conceive the Commonwealth holding together for long. Nor it is easy to conceive any other Commonwealth country, however greatly its wealth and population might increase, taking its place, even if the Sovereign were to move to it.

10. The United Kingdom:

(i) is the headquarters and normal residence of the Sovereign, who is the sole formal link between the Commonwealth countries;

(ii) is responsible for the Colonial Empire which is world wide and which constitutes a series of links, geographical, military and economic, between the Commonwealth countries. The major units in the Colonial Empire are moving forward to Commonwealth Membership. But the process is very gradual;

(iii) has closer links, political, economic, sentimental, traditional, with each individual Commonwealth country than any of them have with any other Commonwealth (or indeed foreign) country, save perhaps for the U.S.: Canadian relation;

(iv) is closely tied in with Europe, the traditional source of world conflict; a bridge between free Europe and the U.S.A.; and a halfway house between the U.S.A. and Soviet Russia.

(v) is economically a great world centre of industry, commerce, and finance, and the headquarters of the sterling area. Economic self interest binds the Commonwealth countries and the United Kingdom together;

(vi) is still in its own right a very great power, and incomparably more important internationally than even the most important of the Commonwealth countries.

(vii) is a major contributor to Commonwealth defence.

What changes are likely over the next 10 to 15 years in the position of the U.K. and the Commonwealth?

The United Kingdom

11. Particularly if the burden of defence expenditure can be eased, there seems no reason why, despite the increasing weight of an ageing population, the United Kingdom should not continue, unless there is general recession, to expand production and to develop economically.

12. Relatively to the Commonwealth countries and particularly to Canada, its *economic and financial* position will be progressively less dominant as theirs develop. But over 10 to 15 years no decisive change in the balance need perhaps be anticipated. Our industrial and financial "know-how", and our financial and economic adaptability, are not likely to dissipate. If the conception of the sterling area and the value of the £ can be maintained, that will be of critical importance.

13. *Politically*, subject again to the rise of Germany and to Soviet policy, and to the maintenance, as may be anticipated, of a close relation with the U.S.A., the United Kingdom should maintain its general world position. As in the economic field that position may be less dominant as the Commonwealth countries develop. But, with the maintenance of the Commonwealth structure, it should remain very substantial.

14. Over the period the larger countries of *the Colonial Empire* may progressively be expected to move into the category of independent Commonwealth members. That will reduce the area under direct United Kingdom control, and will necessitate still greater concentration by the United Kingdom on maintaining its political influence and its markets throughout the Commonwealth. Nor can it be overlooked that certain Commonwealth countries may, because of internal dissensions or over-ambitious planning, prove unable to stand the pace, with the result that they either move into other associations, or will need support on a major scale, even if

only temporarily, from the United Kingdom. . . .

South Africa

28. The uncertainties of the native problems and the internal strains arising from it, make it very difficult to estimate the course of events.

29. *Constitutionally* the Union is likely sooner or later to become a Republic. Her relations with India are likely to continue strained, but there is no present reason to expect that she will leave the Commonwealth. Her Government's reaction to the admission to Commonwealth Membership of African States, such as the Gold Coast or Nigeria, shows signs of mellowing.

30. But these States, when admitted, are reasonably certain to be active supporters of Indian criticism of South African native policy, and might join India in public denunciation of that policy in the United Nations and other international gatherings. The emergence within the Commonwealth of two groups with con-flicting views on so important a matter (particularly as our sympathies are opposed to South African policy) would place an increasing strain on the United Kingdom and possibly on other "old" Members in trying to hold the balance, and might result in a situation in which the Union would leave the Commonwealth.

31. *Internally* there is little likelihood of the present dominant position of the Nationalist Afrikaners being shaken. They are, however, unlikely to attempt to put into operation any of the more extreme theories of racial separation which are sometimes advocated and, as the demand for African labour in industries and the mines rises, the extent to which the Africans are integrated into the economy of the country will increase. The real danger lies less in what the South African Government do, than in the strongly racial character of their public statements, and the discussions which they encourage of proposals for racial separation which would administratively be quite impracticable.

32. There will be a gradually growing risk of the feeling between the White and Black races in South Africa in due course leading to serious disorder. The danger of a major collapse once the African throws up leaders, and realises the sanctions which organised withdrawal of labour would place in his hands, is great and might materially affect this assessment. But at the present time the Union Government are fairly strongly placed to deal with this and would be ruthless in doing so; the Africans are still unorganised; and though serious trouble may not arise within the next ten years, the possibility of its doing so cannot be entirely discounted.

33. *Economically* the Union has every prospect of marked industrial and economic development. At present the economy of the country is mainly in the hands of the English-speaking element and many British firms have established manufacturing subsidiaries in South Africa. To an increasing extent the Afrikaners are developing their share in industry. But we may expect the existing good business relationship with the United Kingdom to be maintained and consolidated on a basis of mutual self-interest. As the economy further develops, and given the discouraging attitude of the Union Government towards European immigration, Africans are bound to obtain semi-skilled and skilled jobs to an increasing extent and this improvement in their economic position may help to reduce racial strains.

34. Neither politically nor in business will sentiment count for anything: but economic development is likely to provide substantial scope for United Kingdom exports. . . .

The Central African Federation

50. *Economically* the Federation, with its great mineral and industrial potential, and its abundant supply of labour, has every prospect of a marked and progressive advance. Kariba will bring immense development: the Copperbelt is a stable and expanding source of revenue: coal and other minerals in Southern Rhodesia are likely to be exploited. Increasing employment for Africans, and the wages that will accompany it, are likely to lead to a high level of demand.

51. Everything will depend first on the working out of the policy of partnership between European and African, and secondly upon a co-operative understanding between the Federation and the three territories of Northern Rhodesia, Southern Rhodesia, and Nyasaaland. The Africans of the two Northern territories are suspicious of the Europeans of Southern Rhodesia and of the Federal Government whom the Europeans inevitably dominate at the present time.

52. The fact that race relations in Southern Rhodesia have in fact been more peaceful during the last 50 years than in almost any other terrtitory in Africa where Europeans have settled affords some hope that a sensible system of race relations can be worked out by the people on the spot, and once this has happened the way will be open in the political field for the Federation to become a full member of the Commonwealth. It is, however, of the utmost importance to the political future and the economic development of the Federation that (in accordance with the settled policy of Her Majesty's Government) a good understanding in this matter should be reached, and everything possible done to convince the African of the advantages he will secure from Federation.

53. On the assumption that this can be achieved, a prosperous and strong new Commonwealth country, with close links with the United Kingdom, and offering a substantial and an assured market for British goods, can be looked for in Central Africa over the period now under review. Failure to secure it might not only set back the political advancement of the Federation, but might imperil the stability of the Federal structure.

Territories now forming part of the colonial empire

Probable constitutional developments

54. The Gold Coast, if all goes well, may be ripe for Commonwealth Membership in the Spring of 1957; Malaya "if possible" by August 1957, but perhaps more probably early in 1958; the Caribbean Federation perhaps by 1960 or 1961; Nigeria, if local difficulties can be overcome, perhaps by about the same date. Singapore, Borneo and Sarawak may come in as part of a Malayan Federation.

55. The Central African Federation is likely to move on to Commonwealth Membership in the period covered by this paper, and may be followed later by some of the larger territories in East Africa.

56. It is perhaps unnecessary to consider in detail from the standpoint of Commonwealth Membership the constitutional developments that may be expected over that period in the smaller Colonial territories, and in particular the possibility of their federation with larger Commonwealth units in their neighbourhood (e.g. Sarawak and Borneo, and possibly Singapore, with a Malayan Federation: British Guiana and British Honduras with the Caribbean Federation).

L

Future relations with the U.K. and the Commonwealth as a whole

57. It is impossible to lay down a precise timetable for the developments referred to above.

58. But in the political field it can be assumed that it will continue to be the policy of the U.K. Government of the day to do all in its power, once any of the larger Colonies, or any Colonial Federation has become self-governing, to encourage it to remain in the Commonwealth, and to support it in seeking Commonwealth Membership. Nor, on experience hitherto, does there seem any reason to fear that such a policy will not be successful.

59. It may well be, however, that nationalistic urges, and an anxiety not to be left behind in the race, will mean that certain areas will press for, and may have to be conceded, internal self-government, and possibly full self-government with Commonwealth Membership, before they are ripe for it. That is a risk that must be faced, and balanced against the risk of causing still greater harm internationally and to the Commonwealth structure if such ambitions are repressed. But the danger of resultant instabilities, economic, financial, political, defence, cannot in such circumstances be overlooked.

60. As is pointed out elsewhere, the addition of this substantial group of areas of races and colours different from those of the older Commonwealth countries must affect the balance inside the Commonwealth and may give rise to strains where racial issues are involved. So far the Commonwealth structure has shown itself capable of digesting and absorbing very widely differing elements. It is to be hoped that, as the process of expansion now under consideration will be gradual, and will be spread over a number of years, it will continue to be able to do so.

61. In population, and in economic development, all the territories now under consideration (save possibly in the economic field the West Indies) can expect marked progress over the next ten to fifteen years. They are all of them closely tied to the United Kingdom economically by past history, and it is to be hoped that they will continue to afford a reliable and substantial market for the United Kingdom, and to export their products to her on a major scale.

62. Politically and economically it will remain of the utmost importance to keep the territories now under consideration within the Commonwealth orbit. That may present new and difficult problems of handling, and the technique for dealing with these areas may need adaptation in the light of experience. But there seems no reason to think that it will be impossible to achieve the objective.

What changes are likely in the position of the Commonwealth as a whole?

63. The membership of the Commonwealth is likely to expand at the expense of the Colonial Empire (the Gold Coast, Nigeria, Malaya and adjacent territories, the Caribbean Colonies, the Central Africa Federation, and possibly some of the larger East African territories, are likely to become Commonwealth countries over the next 15 years: and other Colonies may enter as members of Federal groups).

64. The expanded Commonwealth will be increasingly non-European and tropical. Constitutionally many of the new States may incline to a Republican status, though not necessarily immediately upon obtaining Commonwealth membership.

65. There seems no reason why, with careful handling, any of the new States should wish to leave the Commonwealth. But they will in the aggregate represent a background and an outlook which may differ radically from those of the older

Commonwealth countries, and this cannot but affect general Commonwealth policy and the conduct of Commonwealth relations and discussions.

66. Certain of the new States may secure their full independence before they are ready for it. They may well be sensitive about accepting from us guidance that would be greatly in their interest until such time as they have found their feet. The possibility of internal instabilities or economic mismanagement leading to break-down which will not do credit to the Commonwealth, cannot be ignored. But the risk is one that has to be taken.

67. It seems inevitable that our relationship with the "old" Commonwealth countries is likely to develop somewhat differently from our relations with the new ones. Our common interests in the fields of foreign policy and defence are not unlikely increasingly to consolidate relations between the old Commonwealth countries and ourselves. The same could be true in the economic field. In foreign policy and defence our common interests with "new" Commonwealth countries are likely to be less marked.

68. Broadly speaking there seems no reason why the Commonwealth as it expands further should not hold together, always with the United Kingdom as the nexus and keystone. The considerable progressive development of its constituent parts is likely to be reflected in the growing importance of the association as a whole. Its greater diversity, as new members are added to it, will be balanced by correspondingly great opportunities in a vast and increasingly significant trading area possibly unified (save for Canada) by a common or an interchangeable currency system. Its looseness and flexibility as a political grouping should add to rather than detract from its international importance.

U.K. policy over the next 10 to 15 years

69. The United Kingdom will, on any reasonable expectation, continue itself to develop.

70. It will become progressively less a dominating feature in the *Commonwealth* as the "old" Commonwealth countries expand industrially and in population, and with the emergence of large Afro-Asian groups of Commonwealth countries; and in the *world* as the U.S.A., the Soviet and Germany expand.

71. The Commonwealth can hardly remain in being without the uniting bond of the United Kingdom and the Monarchy.

72. While it does so remain, the United Kingdom as its oldest member, occupies a world position far more important than she could claim solely in her own right; though that will increasingly cease to be the case as the major elements in the Colonial Empire become self-governing.

73. Were the United Kingdom to stand by herself, her importance would still be great, but immensely less than it is while she remains the centre of the Common-wealth.

74. If that is so, it will be vital in decisions of policy to give the fullest weight to the necessity to keep the Commonwealth together, and to Commonwealth reactions.

Conclusion

75. The present study is directed primarily to the probable evolution of the Commonwealth over the next 10 to 15 years. It suggests that subject to the movement of affairs in the outside world, and particularly to Soviet policy and to

developments in the Far East, there is no reason to anticipate that the Commonwealth cannot be held together under United Kingdom leadership, and that it will not remain, on its present general basis, an international association of the first importance.

76. Our history does not, in experience, change dramatically. Our pattern is, and has been evolution. Over the next ten to fifteen years there will be progressively changes in the Commonwealth of great significance. But we can expect that Commonwealth organisation will be able to adapt itself to new situations and to take advantage of them.

77. But the increase, over that period, in the size of the Commonwealth, and the growing diversity of its composition, will make it more essential than ever that the United Kingdom, as the focus and keystone of the Commonwealth, should be at pains:–

(i) to intensify consultation, liaison, the existing processes of supplying information and comment (admittedly, as at present, there will be differences in practice in the technique employed, and in the degree of consultation etc., which will reflect the varying position and conditions of the Commonwealth countries concerned);

(ii) to attach greater weight even than at present to taking the Commonwealth countries with her and to watching the effect of action whether in or by the United Kingdom or elsewhere on the Commonwealth association: bearing in mind;

(iii) that while for a long period to come the United Kingdom can, in its own right, exercise great influence as a Power in the world, its authority and influence will continue, in an increasing degree as its rivals grow in strength and power, to derive from its headship of, or association with, the world-wide group of States that compose the Commonwealth.

78. The future will, in a word, depend on two things:–

(a) outside events;
(b) U.K. leadership

79. We cannot control the former. The latter is in our gift and our responsibility. If we seize our chances boldly; if, while doing so, we have in mind in framing policy its reaction on the Commonwealth, and the importance of holding the Commonwealth together, there seems every reason to hope that it will be possible to preserve the best, to maintain the high principles which have historically governed our conduct in increasing areas of the world, and still to secure for the United Kingdom the advantages that flow from the existence of the Commonwealth and our leadership of it.

27 CAB 134/1315, PR 9(56)1   25 July 1956
'Non-military measures in the Middle East and Eastern Asia': Cabinet Policy Review Committee minutes

[On the day after this meeting Egypt nationalised the Suez Canal. The policy review programme, as originally mapped out by Eden, was effectively suspended as senior ministers became embroiled in the Suez crisis. The general review of defence policy was nevertheless completed by early 1957; see *Defence: Outline of Future Policy* (Cmnd 124, Feb 1957). Very broadly, this White Paper consummated the tradition of thought on defence problems which had characterised British policy since the end of the Korean war (see 14, 17, 20, 22–24), stressing the need to cope with cold rather than hot war conditions, the importance of the nuclear deterrent, the need for redeployment of and reductions in personnel (especially the reduction of overseas garrisons), and the continuing need for economy.]

The Committee had before them memoranda by the Foreign Secretary (P.R.(56) 29 and 26) to which were attached reports drawn up by official committees under the chairmanship of Mr. Dodds-Parker and Lord Reading on the political, economic and information measures necessary to maintain and promote United Kingdom interests in the Middle East and in Eastern Asia.[1] They also had before them a memorandum by the Chancellor of the Exchequer (P.R.(56) 31) in which he proposed that a standing committee of Ministers should be set up under the chairmanship of the Financial Secretary, Treasury, to scrutinise proposals for overseas expenditure under these heads.

The Prime Minister said that it would be convenient to have a standing committee of Ministers, as proposed by the Chancellor of the Exchequer, to consider detailed proposals for such expenditure. Such a committee would not, however, be able to get to work in August. He therefore suggested that in the first instance the Secretary of the Cabinet might convene a small group of officials who could carry out during August a preliminary survey of the suggestions made in P.R.(56) 26 and 29, taking into account views expressed by Ministers on the reports now before them and on the question of military expenditure in the Middle East and Eastern Asia which they were to discuss later in the week. The results of this survey could be made available for consideration by Ministers in September.

The Committee approved this proposal. It was suggested that the Working Party of officials should also take account of the memorandum on the teaching of English which had been circulated to the Cabinet by the Minister of Education (C.O.(55) 175).

The Committee's further discussion was mainly directed to the question of the medium that should be used for broadcast propaganda.

It was pointed out that the Government had at present insufficient control over the content of the overseas broadcasts of the British Broadcasting Corporation (B.B.C.). It was suggested that it would be possible to justify a difference in treatment between home and overseas broadcasts. At home the revenue of the B.B.C. was derived from licences, and the Government rightly abstained from interference with the content of broadcasts. Overseas broadcasts, on the other hand, were paid for by the Government and it was reasonable that they should reflect Government policy. Too much importance was at present being attached to the argument that the reputation of the B.B.C. for impartiality and trustworthiness must be maintained. In particular, the argument that this would be important for broadcasts to Europe in another war was now made out of date by strategic developments.

Two courses were possible. One was to arrange with the B.B.C. that its overseas broadcasts should be used as an instrument of Government policy: the other was to make use of a different organisation and reduce Government expenditure on B.B.C.

---

[1] For the reports by Dodds-Parker and Reading, see 53 & 66.

overseas broadcasts. The former would be preferable if the B.B.C. would agree to it, since use could be made of the facilities and *expertise* of the Corporation. The B.B.C. were about to put their overseas services under the charge of a new Director with great experience of the Middle East. An arrangement might perhaps be made under which a separate organisation for overseas broadcasts was established within the B.B.C. and it was made clear publicly that the Government and not the Corporation were responsible for the content of these broadcasts. In considering such an arrangement, advantage should be taken of the information possessed by the Foreign Office of the methods which had been used during the war. It might be found, however, that the B.B.C. were unwilling to agree to any such arrangement. It might in fact be held to be contrary to their Charter.

The Prime Minister also suggested that consideration should be given to the appointment in the Foreign Office of a senior official, with experience of propaganda, to relieve Ministers in the over-sight of propaganda activities generally.

The Committee agreed that it was important to press forward the establishment of a medium-wave relay station in the Middle East on the assumption that means would be found of exercising more effective control over the content of the broadcasts to be relayed by it. *The Foreign Secretary* said that this station would be powerful enough to cover the Persian Gulf.

The Committee:—

(1) Instructed the Secretary of the Cabinet to convene a working party of officials which would submit comprehensive proposals, for their consideration in September, about non-military measures in the Middle East and Eastern Asia.

(2) Invited the Foreign Secretary to consider by what means the Government could best secure a larger measure of control over the content of broadcasts to the Middle East and Eastern Asia.

(3) Invited the Foreign Secretary to arrange for the early development of a broadcast relay station in the Middle East.

(4) Invited the Foreign Secretary to consider the appointment in the Foreign Office of an officer charged with the over-sight of propaganda activities.

28   CAB 129/84, CP(57)6   5 Jan 1957
' "The grand design" (co-operation with Western Europe)': Cabinet memorandum by Mr Selwyn Lloyd

Background
Two great Powers, America and Russia, now immeasurably outstrip all the others.

2. In 1914 great Powers were comparatively numerous. Nor was there the present gulf between great Powers and other Powers. When the chief armament of war was the rifle, the machine-gun and the field-gun, Serbia could fight Austria and Turkey hold her own with Britain.

3. Twenty years later, in 1939, no Power of much less than 50 millions, backed by a well-developed industrial system, could make effective war. Neither Italy nor France, still less Yugoslavia or Turkey, qualified. The only effective combatants were America, Russia, Britain, Germany and Japan.

4. By 1957 the process has gone further; and it will go further yet. An

industrialised country with 50 million inhabitants is no longer large enough or powerful enough to produce and man the weapons required for modern war, nuclear or conventional. A country which wishes to play the role of a great Power must not only possess certain conventional forces. It must also make and have the power to use the whole range of thermo-nuclear weapons, including the megaton bomb. Although, if all goes well, Britain will shortly have the know-how of the megaton bomb and the possession of some kiloton weapons, Britain cannot by herself go the whole distance. If we try to do so we shall bankrupt ourselves. The choice is therefore clear. We must stop short with an insufficient stockpile and inadequate means of delivery or we must seek to achieve our end by other means.

Part I   A Western European military and political association

5. If we are to be a first-class Power with full thermo-nuclear capacity, it can only be done in association with other countries. Britain and the other six Western European Union (W.E.U.)[1] Powers have a combined population of over 210 millions, together with very considerable industrial capacity, resources and skill. If these were pooled, the resultant association could afford to possess full thermo-nuclear capacity. It could be the third great Power.

6. Such an association would not be a "Third Force" between America and Russia. Its object would rather be to develop into one powerful group within the North Atlantic Treaty Organisation (N.A.T.O.), almost as powerful as America and perhaps in friendly rivalry with her. The high political and strategic direction would remain in N.A.T.O. as long as the Americans remained there.

7. The most important step in the development of the Western European association on these lines would be a joint research and development programme for atomic and thermo-nuclear weapons, including all the means of delivery. There would also have to be arrangements for the common financing of this programme, for integrated production and for the use in the joint interest of the end-products.

8. This military association of the seven Powers would in practice entail a closer political association between them. Once the association had thermo-nuclear capacity, it would have to have the machinery for deciding about the use of that capacity. There need be no supranational machinery not responsible to Governments. Nor need we ever come to a complete merging of forces. The machinery of W.E.U. could serve, developed in due course as was necessary for closer co-operation both in the nuclear and conventional fields.

Advantages and disadvantages of the above

9. In making proposals on the above lines to our European allies, we should be offering them a great deal. In thermo-nuclear matters, we are vastly ahead of them in knowledge, manufacturing capacity, testing facilities, etc. Therefore we should be in a strong position to see that the arrangements were made on our terms.

10. The political advantages would be solid. Germany, Italy, Benelux and probably the present French Government would welcome the proposal. They have always wanted us to "go into Europe". We should do much to correct French and German tendencies to neutralism. In particular, we would bind Germany more

---

[1] The WEU was established in 1955 following the abandonment of the EDC project (see 2, note 2).

tightly into the Western family at a time when such binding is vital. We might win next summer's election for Dr. Adenauer.[2] The arrangements could be made to fit in with our plans for force reductions. We should facilitate the financial arrangements for maintaining our forces on the Continent and for continuing our research and development programme.

11.   It would be logical to accompany the military arrangements by arrangements for civil nuclear co-operation; and we should have to reconsider our relationship with EURATOM. The result might be to modify the present views of the other six Powers about EURATOM.

12.   As part of a larger confederation we could hope to make Western European influence stronger, e.g. in Africa and the Middle East. While we should not set up as rivals to America, we should nevertheless attain to some degree of reinsurance against an eventual American withdrawal from Europe, either partial or total. We should take our place where we now most belong, i.e. in Europe with our immediate neighbours, and thereby give greater cohesion and strength to Europe. Nor need these arrangements lead to any weakening of Commonwealth ties. Finally, the financial contributions of our W.E.U. partners would help us considerably in our balance of payments.

13.   There are, however, grave risks unless our proposals are handled right. We should risk our special arrangements with America and Canada, particularly in the nuclear and intelligence fields.

14.   The close relationship between the three Anglo-Saxon Powers is based on mutual confidence. Unless we retain the present links in substantially their present form, the production of thermo-nuclear weapons, etc. might be delayed for years owing to the change in the system, and the need for the necessary planning, construction and training of scientists in conjunction with our new associates.

15.   Our nuclear arrangements with America are governed by two agreements, covering the military and civil fields respectively and representing actual and potential benefits which would be a most serious loss. We should have to proceed circumspectly with the Americans. But we are not without bargaining counters. The Anglo–American Agreement of 15th June, 1955, for military co-operation can only be terminated by the mutual agreement of both Parties. It forbids either Government to communicate information made available to it under the Agreement to third parties without the consent of the originator. But it does contain a provision that "nothing herein shall be interpreted or operate as a bar or restriction to consultation and co-operation by the United Kingdom or the United States with other nations or regional organisations in any fields of defence".

16.   The first and most difficult problem with the Americans will be that of security. They are sensitive about this, as Mr. Charles Wilson's[3] remarks in the N.A.T.O. meeting in Paris showed. German and French security is bad; it would have to be improved and this would take time. Meanwhile, we should have to make it clear to our European allies that, unless we were to risk losing American co-operation, they might have to leave to us in the United Kingdom responsibility for certain parts of the thermo-nuclear programme, at any rate in the initial stages. In reverse, this progress could be used as a bargaining counter with the Americans. But arrange-

---

[2] K Adenauer, chancellor of West Germany, 1949–1963.
[3] C E Wilson, US secretary of defence, 1953–1957.

ments of this kind might only be a temporary phase. What would be in question would be security *vis-à-vis* Russia. Russia would in any case be technically well in advance of Western Europe, at any rate at the beginning. In any case if, as the Americans say, it will not be many years before almost every country has the possibility of thermo-nuclear weapons, then security becomes of diminishing importance.

17. To sum up, the choices are either:—

(a) to go on alone by ourselves at the risk of bankruptcy; or
(b) to stop short at a point where we would be a nuclear Power only in name; or
(c) to pool research and development and the end-products along the above lines.

18. I prefer the last choice. We should thereby enlist not only the resources and skill of our European neighbours, particularly the Germans, but also their finance. If we had to pay, say, 25 per cent of the cost, our economic burden would be enormously lightened; and we should in due course free a large number of scientific personnel who are urgently required elsewhere than in the field of defence.

19. On the other hand, it must be realised that this choice would involve the risk of a hostile Soviet reaction, and the weakening of our links with America.

20. The possibility of Dr. Adenauer losing the next election need not affect our choice because that would occur at so early a stage in our programme.

21. The negotiations would be complicated but there is a favourable atmosphere in Europe at present.

Part II   Other elements in the "grand design"

22. Unless W.E.U. co-operates on this nuclear basis I do not think there is much scope for co-operation between the W.E.U. Powers except on normal N.A.T.O. lines. That, however, does not mean that there are no other fields in which we can draw closer to Europe.

23. In Paris when I sketched out at the North Atlantic Council in December this idea of a "Grand Design" for the rationalisation of the proliferation of the Atlantic and European organisations, I covered also the economic and Parliamentary aspects.

Economic

24. In the economic field the idea, very briefly, is to continue to look to the Organisation for European Economic Co-operation (O.E.E.C.) as the main instrument for co-operative effort and to try to consolidate under its aegis the other European economic organisations. The Six-Power communities need not be dissolved but the association of other European States with those communities should be effected within the frame-work of the O.E.E.C. Thus the machinery required to regulate the European Free Trade Area[4] should be set up as part of the O.E.E.C.

Parliamentary

25. Another element in the Grand Design might be a General Assembly for Europe which would replace the separate assemblies which have been or are liable to be set up for each organisation, e.g. Council of Europe, W.E.U., EURATOM, N.A.T.O.

---

[4] See part III of this volume, 387, 389–395.

This General Assembly could divide its work as is done in the United Nations Assembly between Committees, each discussing a different category of subjects, e.g.—

(a) *First Committee* (Political)—to hold general debates;
(b) *Second Committee* (Economic)—to discuss problems of European economic co-operation and the activities of O.E.E.C.;
(c) *Third Committee* (Social and Cultural)—to carry on the work already done in this field by the Council of Europe and W.E.U. Assemblies;
(d) *Fourth Committee* (Defence)—to discuss problems of European defence, including the W.E.U. Arms Control activities.

26. Thus we might get away from the competition and overlapping between the existing assemblies and establish instead one centre, serviced by one Secretariat where Parliamentarians of the Western nations could meet to discuss any aspect of Western co-operation. When [the] subjct of discussion was defence, certain countries, e.g. Sweden and Switzerland, would probably not wish to be present but for the rest the wider the attendance the better and I would hope that American and Canadian Parliamentarians would participate on the strength of their associate membership of N.A.T.O. and their associate membership of O.E.E.C.

27. Arrangements on these lines would permit the neutral European countries and even eventually the Eastern European States to participate in economic and Parliamentary institutions without having to join N.A.T.O. or W.E.U.

Part III

Procedure
28. If the foregoing is generally agreed, the procedure might be as follows:—

(i) I would float these ideas, in confidence and in general terms, with M. Spaak[5] when he comes to London on Sunday, 13th January. I would then discuss them with the Italians, Germans and French (leaving it to M. Spaak to inform his Benelux colleagues). I would propose to visit Bonn and Paris this month on my way to or from Rome. If all went well, a meeting of the W.E.U. Foreign Ministers would then be required, perhaps at the end of January; this to be followed by a working party of officials to work out the details.

(ii) The timing of the approach to the Americans and Canadians is important. It might be in two stages:—

(a) Just before I talk to M. Spaak on 13th January, the Americans and Canadians would be told that we were exploring the possibilities of the United Kingdom drawing closer to Europe over and above our plan for a Free Trade Area. It is for consideration whether we should also explain to them that we were becoming ever more conscious of the weight of our defence programme and that we were exploring the possibilities of relieving ourselves possibly by some sharing with our W.E.U. allies of the burden of our research and development. The Americans and Canadians would likewise be told of our general thinking on the lines of Part

---

[5] P-H Spaak, foreign minister of Belgium, 1954–1957, secretary-general of NATO, 1957–1961.

II of this paper in amplification of my remarks at the N.A.T.O. meeting in Paris about the "Grand Design".
(b) Immediately after my talks in Rome, Bonn and Paris, and before the meeting of W.E.U. Foreign Ministers, our scheme (possibly modified by my talks in Rome, Bonn, etc.) would be laid before the American and Canadian Governments who would be informed that we proposed to raise it at the W.E.U. Ministerial meeting.

29. We should at all stages emphasize to the Americans and the Canadians that our ideas were within the ambit of the Atlantic Alliance and designed to strengthen it. We should also make it clear that we relied on their encouragement and regarded their continued co-operation as essential.

29   CAB 128/30/2, CM 3 (57)   9 Jan 1957[1]
'Europe': Cabinet conclusions on political and military association

The Cabinet considered a memorandum by the Foreign Secretary (C.P. (57) 6)[1] of [sic] outlining a plan for closer military and political association between the United Kingdom and Western Europe.

The Foreign Secretary said that there was in Europe a propitious atmosphere for a fresh initiative towards closer co-operation. On the economic side we had already taken the lead; and good progress was being made with the proposals for a common market and a free trade area. On the Parliamentary side, there would be no difficulty in putting forward a plan for a General Assembly of Europe on the lines indicated in paragraph 25 of his memorandum. There would be some value in replacing the various existing assemblies by a single General Assembly with a number of functional committees; and the unifying influence of the existing organisations would be enhanced if they could be brought together at a single headquarters with a single secretariat.

The more significant, and possibly more controversial, part of his memorandum was that which proposed a closer military association between the United Kingdom and Western Europe. It seemed clear that we could not for long sustain the defence burden which we were now carrying; but our international standing would suffer if we sought relief by a unilateral reduction in defence expenditure. He had therefore outlined in his memorandum a possible method of sharing our defence burden with our friends in Western Europe. For this purpose he would prefer to work through Western European Union (W.E.U.); for past experience suggested that in the North Atlantic Treaty Organisation (N.A.T.O.), with its large military bureaucracy, we should find less sympathy with our need to reduce defence expenditure. We could not hope to develop a strength in nuclear weapons comparable to that of the United States or the Soviet Union; and there seemed little advantage in continuing alone with the development of the megaton bomb if we had not the resources to manufacture thereafter an adequate stockpile of these weapons. Might it not be

---

[1] The meeting was held on 8 Jan 1957; the minutes are dated 9 Jan.
[2] See 28.

better, in these circumstances, to pool our resources with our European allies so that Western Europe as a whole might become a third nuclear power comparable with the United States and the Soviet Union? By this means we might be able both to reduce our own defence burden and to develop within N.A.T.O. a group almost as powerful as the United States. A policy on these lines need not imply antagonism towards the United States; it might well be developed in co-operation with them.

The Lord President said that he had been disturbed by the proposals outlined in the Foreign Secretary's memorandum. He doubted whether a policy on these lines could be pursued consistently with the maintenance of the Anglo-American alliance which, in his view, offered the best hope of securing the free world from Soviet aggression. It would be specially unfortunate if an approach towards a closer military association with Europe were based on proposals for the common development of nuclear weapons. For it was a main aim of United States policy to ensure that the capacity to manufacture nuclear weapons was limited to those countries which already possessed it. This indeed was the primary purpose of the new disarmament proposals recently put forward by the United States Government; and the policy outlined in the Foreign Secretary's memorandum would run counter to those proposals. For himself he could not accept the Foreign Secretary's assumption (paragraph 4 of C.P. (57) 6) that it was the nuclear element in our defence programme that would drive us into bankruptcy. But it was certain that the United States, if their hostility was aroused by our adoption of a policy on the lines now suggested, could seriously damage our programme of nuclear development, both civil and military. They had the means of preventing us from drawing supplies of uranium from Canada, and they could probably secure two-thirds of what we hoped to obtain from South Africa.

In paragraph 17 of C.P. (57) 6 the Foreign Secretary had suggested that the choices open to us were to go on alone at the risk of bankruptcy; to stop short at a point where we should be a nuclear power only in name; or to pool research, development and manufacture of nuclear weapons with our allies in Western Europe. The Lord President said that there was a fourth course—namely, to continue our co-operation with the United States. This, in his judgment, was the better course and one which was more in accordance with the fundamental basis of our foreign policy. Our main aim at the present time should be to repair the breach which had been made in Anglo-American relations by the Suez dispute.

Finally, the Lord President said that he was even more disturbed by the suggestions on procedure which were outlined in paragraphs 28 and 29 of C.P. (57) 6. If, in the light of recent experience over Suez, a plan of this kind were discussed in Europe without prior consultation with the United States Government, there would be grave risk that the Anglo-American alliance would be finally undermined. If we were to proceed at all with a policy on these lines, we ought surely to discuss it in the first instance with the United States as part of a full and frank review of our defence policy.

The Commonwealth Secretary, in supporting the views expressed by the Lord President, said that a policy of the kind outlined in C.P. (57) 6 could not safely be launched without the fullest prior consultation, not only with the United States, but with the older members of the Commonwealth. Even then, it would involve great risks; and he would himself prefer to seek closer co-operation with the United States and Canada in the development of nuclear power for civil and military purposes.

The Minister of Defence said that, in general, his sympathies lay with the views expressed by the Lord President. He also saw great practical difficulties in the proposals put forward by the Foreign Secretary. It would be between seven and ten years before we were able to supply our European allies with nuclear weapons. The United States, on the other hand, could supply their needs, if they so desired, within a year or so. They were therefore in a position to frustrate this plan if we put it forward without their prior approval. They were unlikely to approve it, since it was their policy that Western Europe should remain dependent on the United States for the supply of nuclear warheads. So long as they held the monopoly of supply, they would be able to keep the issue of these warheads within their control. If, however, European countries were invited to contribute towards the development of these weapons on the lines contemplated by the Foreign Secretary, they would surely expect to own and control their share of the product. To this the United States would presumably be opposed. And were we ourselves prepared to contemplate German possession of nuclear weapons? Finally the Minister of Defence said that he agreed with the Lord President that the cost of the nuclear element of our defence programme should not be exaggerated. It amounted to little more than 10 per cent. of the total and was not in itself a crushing burden.

In discussion there was general agreement that a fresh initiative towards closer European co-operation should not be based on proposals for co-operation in the development of nuclear weapons. Such an approach would tend to array the rest of the world against our efforts for European unity. It would in particular arouse the antagonism of the United States. And in present circumstances the whole economy of Europe could be undermined unless the United States was ready to help to protect the sources of its oil supplies in the Middle East.

On the other hand, strong support was expressed for the general concept of a closer association between the United Kingdom and Western Europe. On this the following arguments were put forward:—

(a) The Anglo-American alliance was vital to the security of the free world: but the Suez crisis had made it plain that there must be some change in the basis of Anglo-American relations. It was doubtful whether the United States would now be willing to accord to us alone the special position which we had held as their principal ally during the war. We might therefore be better able to influence them if we were part of an association of Powers which had greater political, economic and military strength than we alone could command. We ought to be in a position to deal with the United States Government on equal terms; and, if that position had now to be founded on economic strength and military power, we must seek it through a new association with other countries.

(b) In external, as well as domestic policy, the Government needed new themes with which to rally their supporters throughout the country. The public evidently felt the need for positive policies which held out greater hope for the future. There was already a substantial body of support in the Conservative Party for the concept of closer association with Europe, and this would be a favourable moment at which to make it a central theme of foreign policy.

(c) This theme could be developed consistently with the maintenance of the Anglo-American alliance and the cohesion of the Commonwealth. For some time past the United States Government had favoured the idea of European unity. The proposals for a common market and a free trade area in Europe already had the sympathetic interest of the United States Government and of the older Common-wealth Governments.

(d) If we took the initiative in pressing this concept and putting forward practical proposals for giving effect to it, we had the opportunity to seize the political leadership in Europe. This opportunity should not be missed.

(e) It would be useful if the W.E.U. Powers could operate more cohesively as a group within N.A.T.O. It would certainly be valuable if a European *bloc* could emerge within the United Nations. This development might even be welcomed by the United States Government, who were concerned at the growing influence of the Afro-Asian *bloc* in the Assembly.

(f) While there was certainly scope for rationalising the numerous international organisations in Europe, it might be inexpedient to take an initiative on this without regard to the progress of the negotiations for a free trade area in Europe. Those negotiations were now entering a more difficult phase, and any bargaining cards which we held should be kept in our hands for the time being.

The Foreign Secretary, summing up the discussion, said that there seemed to be general agreement in the Cabinet that the time was ripe for a fresh initiative towards closer association between the United Kingdom and Europe. A good start had been made, on the economic side, with the proposals for a common market and for a free trade area in Europe. These might now be supplemented by proposals for a closer political association and, possibly at a later stage, a military association between the W.E.U. Powers within N.A.T.O. It was evident, however, that the Cabinet would prefer that no such approach should be made to any European country without full prior consultation with the United States Government and with the Governments of the older Commonwealth countries; and that, in those consultations, no suggestion should be made that military co-operation between the European Powers should be based on the common development of nuclear weapons. The Cabinet would evidently wish to consider at a later stage the extent to which our political association with Europe could safely be carried: they would certainly wish that it should stop short of federation. On procedure, the first step would be to open full and frank discussions of this whole question with the United States Government and thereafter with the Governments of the older Commonwealth countries. Any detailed plans for develop-ing new military associations in Europe would, however, be concerted with the Minister of Defence before any communication was made to other Governments.

The Cabinet:—

(1) Invited the Foreign Secretary to report to the Prime Minister the broad conclusions which had emerged from the Cabinet's discussion.

(2) Agreed to resume their consideration of these questions at a later meeting.

30 PREM 11/208   8 Nov 1951
[Middle East policy]: minute by Lord Cherwell[1] to Mr Churchill

In considering whether we should accept large commitments in the Middle East the following points seem relevant.

Now that we have lost India and Burma the freedom of the Suez Canal is an

---

[1] Baron Cherwell, paymaster-general, 1951–1953.

international rather than a specifically British interest. In any event to sail through the Mediterranean will be difficult with enemy aircraft operating from Bulgaria unless fighter cover is provided. This would mean bases in Africa, Crete and Cyprus all of which would have to be defended against air-borne landings and bombing. It is doubtful whether this would be worth while merely in order to shorten the voyage from Britain to Australia by a couple of weeks.

Middle East oil is an immensely valuable asset. But we have already abandoned our Persian oil and the remainder is largely in American hands. Is it not for America rather than for Britain to defend it?

The only other reason for holding the Middle East is to prevent another large accession of territory and manpower to the Communists. This falls under the Truman doctrine and as such is more an American than a British responsibility.

For these reasons it would seem that the U.S. should undertake the defence of the Middle East. With such grave dangers nearer home the U.K. in my view should not accept such a strain on its resources of manpower and shipping.[2]

---

[2] Churchill minuted in reply: 'I am keeping your paper about the Middle East which contains many unpleasant truths. I have had to agree to Anthony's [Eden's] proposals. They will probably lead to a deadlock. It is of the utmost importance to get the Americans in' (PREM 11/208, 10 Nov 1951).

31   CAB 129/54, C(52)267   28 July 1952
'Suez Canal': Cabinet memorandum by Mr Eden

The basic assumption of this paper, which I am circulating for the consideration of my colleagues, is that steps must be taken to safeguard the free transit of the Suez Canal irrespective of whether or not current bilateral discussions with Egypt make headway and irrespective of the decision taken in regard to a Middle East Defence Organisation. The measures suggested here will have to be related to both these projects, and it is desirable to leave some flexibility in the timing.

Present position
2. An ill-disposed Egyptian Government might at any time try to restrict or stop traffic going through the Suez Canal. It could do this either by direct obstruction or by applying pressure to the Suez Canal Company. The Suez Canal Company could also be rendered so inefficient through pressure upon its technicians as to restrict the Canal's operation.

3. Recent evidence that Egypt might abuse her geographical position in this way is as follows:—

(a) In 1948, in connexion with the Palestine conflict, the Egyptian Government imposed contraband control on cargoes passing through the Canal for Israel, thereby causing heavy losses to British Insurance interests and shipping. They invoked Articles 9 and 10 of the Suez Canal Convention of 1888 which gave Egypt the right to take the necessary measures for ensuring the execution of the Convention and the defence of Egypt, including the maintenance of public order by their own forces. The Egyptian Government defied the Resolution of the

Security Council of 1st September, 1951, calling upon them to remove these restrictions.

(b) In January of this year the then Egyptian Prime Minister, Nahas Pasha, threatened the Suez Canal Company. The Company fear that although their concession does not expire until 1968, the fact that the Company is foreign owned and makes large profits for Her Majesty's Government and other foreign shareholders makes it an attractive target for nationalist Egyptian politicians in much the same way as the Anglo-Iranian Oil Company was to nationalist Iranian politicians up to 1951.

(c) In June of this year the Egyptian authorities requested the Suez Canal Company to pay in Egyptian pounds the dividend payments due to Her Majesty's Government in sterling on 1st July. This request fortunately came too late to hold up this payment in sterling. In July the Egyptians further requested the Company to place at the disposal of the Bank of Egypt the Company's sterling earnings until the end of this year. The Company, whose position is weakened by the fact that they are an Egyptian company, felt obliged to fob the Egyptians off with an offer to transfer £3 million from the sterling currently at their disposal. In return the Company have obtained only oral assurances against renewed demands and there is a danger that their weakness on this occasion, coupled with Egyptian sterling shortage, may encourage further Egyptian demands on the Company's sterling.

4. The purported Egyptian abrogation in October 1951 of the Anglo-Egyptian Treaty (together with the Immunities Convention concerning the immunities and privileges to be enjoyed by the British forces in Egypt) has led to Egyptian interference with the free working of the Canal:—

(a) The Wafd Government did not actually prevent shipping passing through the Canal but some disorganisation was caused by the withdrawal of stevedores and other Egyptian labour and by the imposition of unreasonable customs and other formalities. In order to keep ships moving the Royal Navy had to step in and assist in such tasks as berthing, loading and unloading and marshalling of convoys.

(b) The purported Egyptian abrogation of the Immunities Convention also implied the renunciation of the 1921 Customs Agreement by which the British forces were permitted to import various goods into the Canal Zone free of charge. The agents of the shipping companies have therefore been subjected to numerous Egyptian fines for handling black-listed cargo conveyed to the military ports and for other "illegal" acts and may also receive demands for the payment of considerable arrears of customs duty on such goods.

Legal position

5. In regard to freedom of Transit, Article 1 of the Suez Canal Convention of 1888 says that "The Suez Maritime Canal shall always be free and open in time of war as in time of peace to every vessel of commerce or of war without distinction of flag." The signatories of this Convention were Great Britain, Germany, Austria-Hungary, Spain, France, Italy, the Netherlands, Russia and Turkey. The original Article 8, which provided that the agents in Egypt of the signatory Powers should watch over the execution of the Convention, was never put into effect and the responsibility for safeguarding freedom of transit has devolved mainly upon Egypt. In regard to the wording of Article 9 of the Convention, "In case the Egyptian Government should not

have sufficient means at its disposal it shall call upon the Imperial Ottoman Government," we hold that Her Majesty's Government in the United Kingdom have inherited the responsibility of the Imperial Ottoman Government (see legal notes attached to this paper—Annex 1).[1]

6. The instrument by which the Canal is operated is the 99-year Concession granted to the Suez Canal Company by the Ottoman Government. It expires in 1968, by which time new arrangements will have to be made. Although the Canal Company is an Egyptian Company, the management is in Paris and the technical personnel are French. In 1949 a new Convention was negotiated by the Company and the Egyptian Government which increased the latter's royalty to 7 per cent. of the gross profits and accelerated the rate of Egyptianisation of the Company's services in Egypt. The Wafd resisted the passing of the 1949 Convention although in general they did not infringe its terms during their period of office.

Presence of British land forces

7. Legal position apart, there is no doubt that the presence of British Land Forces in the Canal Zone in accordance with the provision of the 1936 Treaty is a deterrent to precipitate action by the Egyptians although the object of the Treaty was joint Anglo-Egyptian defence against outside attacks. In modification of this generalisation one may add (a) that the presence of troops in the Canal Zone has been built up by Egyptian propaganda to be the main obstacle to friendly Anglo-Egyptian relations and (b) that if the Egyptians really made up their mind to interfere with the Canal the presence of British troops in the Treaty area alone would, because of the very length of the Canal, be ineffective in stopping them. Nevertheless so long as it is impossible to rely on a comparatively responsible Government remaining in power, the withdrawal of troops would facilitate Egyptian action and would render far more difficult a repetition of emergency operations such as the Royal Navy undertook at the end of 1951.

British interests involved

8. A stoppage of free transit through the Canal would have a disastrous effect upon British trade with all countries East of Suez including members of the Commonwealth. The Canal is of more importance to the world to-day than ever before. The net tonnage passing through last year was nearly double that passing in 1939. British ships constitute about one-third—being at least double that under any other flag—and in addition a proportion of the tonnage of other flags passing through, particularly tankers, is chartered to British interests. Even a temporary reversion to the Cape route would have most damaging consequences, with increased costs and disruption of trade. This is particularly true in the case of oil, which in 1951 represented 72 per cent. in weight of all northbound traffic through the Canal. The refineries which have been built in the United Kingdom since the war, at a cost of £165 million, rely on shipments from the Persian Gulf for 60 per cent. of their crude oil. Since the world tanker fleets are already fully occupied, this volume of imports could not be maintained over the longer Cape route, even with dollar chartering. A shortage of petroleum products in this country would therefore follow almost immediately on any interruption of Canal traffic.

---

[1] Annexes not printed.

M

9. The consequences of delays in Canal passages, without a complete stoppage, would also be serious. Delays could arise not only through deliberate Egyptian interference but also through inefficient operation if inexperienced Egyptian personnel took charge of Canal operations. The anxiety of the British shipping industry about the future both of the Canal and of the Canal Company was expressed by a delegation which met the Secretary of State for the Co-ordination of Transport, Fuel and Power, and the Minister of Transport, in March this year. If the Canal Company were interfered with, reduced efficiency of operation or Egyptian attempts to use it for revenue purposes would probably result in the raising of transit dues and Her Majesty's Government, along with other users of the Canal, would suffer from the increased freight charges. This would impair our ability to meet growing Japanese competition in Middle Eastern and Far Eastern markets.

10. If the Canal Company's concessions were terminated by Egypt, the Exchequer would be deprived of revenue amounting to £3 million a year which Her Majesty's Government might reasonably expect to continue until 1968 as revenue on its holding in the Suez Canal Company. Without going as far as this the Egyptian Government might attempt (as they have already done) to prevent the payment of this revenue in sterling.

Interests of other powers

11. The annexed memorandum (Annex 2) shows the nationality of the shipping passing through the Suez Canal in 1951. After the United Kingdom, the main shipping countries involved are the Scandinavian countries (especially Norway), France, the United States, the Netherlands and Italy. The same countries were the main countries of destination of goods passing through the Canal in a northerly direction. Australia, New Zealand, India and Pakistan are, in terms of goods sent and received, big users of the Canal. Japan is also likely to resume its place among the principal users. Western Europe relies on shipments from the Persian Gulf for approximately 50 per cent. of its oil requirements and supplies could not be maintained if the Canal were closed. Moreover, storage capacity is limited and even a temporary interruption of traffic would entail serious oil shortages.

12. While many other countries share our interest in maintaining sea transport, there has in fact been little response to overtures by Her Majesty's Government and the French Government to obtain the support of other countries in keeping the Canal open. On the other hand, fresh diplomatic action has been pressed upon us by the Government of Israel. On 6th June the Israel representative at the United Nations proposed to Sir Gladwyn Jebb and his United States and French colleagues that:—

(a) If there were an early settlement of Anglo-Egyptian negotiations and the settlement did not include the lifting of the blockade, the three Governments should at once take up this point with the Egyptians;
(b) That if the settlement were long delayed the three Governments should take it up anyway as a separate issue.

The Scandinavian countries have also shown interest in the possibilities of fresh diplomatic action, but have confined their attention to the situation which would occur after the expiry of the Suez Canal Company's concession. The Scandinavian Shipowners' Association recently recommended the internationalisation of the Canal under the United Nations with Great Britain as the political mandatory Power and with the Suez Canal Company as economic administrator. We have not encouraged this approach any more than we have encouraged the Israel Government to press for action on the Security Council resolution since we hoped to make progress in bilateral negotiations with the Egyptians on defence.

13. Distinct from their interest in the freedom of transit, the French Government have a strong interest in the position of the Canal Company. Most of the shares are held by private French investors. They have therefore been more forthcoming than any of the other Governments approached during our difficulties with the Egyptians last winter. In reply to the invitation from Her Majesty's Government to consider providing a warship to be stationed alongside the Royal Navy vessels in Suez or Port Said, the French Government proposed a meeting between representatives of the United Kingdom, France, the United States, Norway, the Netherlands and Italy to concert a plan of action. Her Majesty's Government were willing to accept this suggestion, but in fact it was not followed up because the fall of the Wafd Government put an end to the immediate emergency.

14. The United States Government, because of their interest in the Panama Canal, would not wish to encourage any general demand for the international safeguarding of all international waterways.

15. The Arab States might well regard any attempts to obtain further safeguards for the free transit of the Canal as primarily designed to further the interests of Israel by removing Egyptian restrictions on the passage through the Suez Canal of goods bound for that country.

Necessary action

16. In view of the large British interests involved and the extent to which they are shared by other countries, it is incumbent upon Her Majesty's Government to take steps to consult the main maritime powers in order to forestall action by an ill-disposed Egyptian Government. These steps may be divided into two phases:—

(a) consultation with the main maritime Powers, which should take place as soon as possible;
(b) an approach by the maritime Powers to the Egyptian Government, the timing of which should be decided at a later stage, bearing in mind, *inter alia* the state of Anglo-Egyptian relations at the time.

17. While, to preserve our rights under it, we wish the 1888 Convention to remain in force, there is no advantage in revising it. Russia was a signatory and the Soviet Union would never agree to co-operate over the Canal. Moreover, of the other signatory Powers, Austria-Hungary has ceased to exist and Germany, Spain and Turkey are not now leading maritime countries. Ideally, we should wish to see the present leading maritime Powers take up the struggle for freedom of transit where the signatories of the 1888 Convention left off. We would have to keep the friendly ex-signatories of the Convention informed of what we were proposing to do, but there would be no necessity to invite them to a Conference.

18. The French Government suggested that in addition to the United States, France and ourselves an approach should be made to Norway, the Netherlands and Italy. Sweden and Denmark, who have shown a strong interest in this question, might also be approached. No wider representation would be necessary at the outset and the consortium which it is hoped will emerge from the meeting should be on a

narrow basis, in order that any necessary action may be concerted with ease and promptitude. The old Commonwealth countries, however, should also be kept informed.

19. If a conference were held, Her Majesty's Government might propose that the main maritime Powers should approach the present Egyptian Government jointly and request:—

(a) A reaffirmation by Egypt of the principle of free transit of the Canal and a clarification of what Egypt understands by this term.
(b) Recognition of the special interests of the main maritime Powers in the safeguarding of freedom of transit and in the position of the Canal Company.
(c) An undertaking to refer any complaints of violation of the free use of the Canal to the International Court of Justice at The Hague, to abide by its judgment and to refrain from repeating the act complained of until its judgment had been given.
(d) An assurance that the unhampered operation of the Canal Company would be maintained at any rate until the expiry of its concession in 1968.

20. In addition to this joint *démarche* to the Egyptian Government we might explore how far the other maritime Powers would undertake to intervene if the Egyptian Government refused to give or broke any of these undertakings or otherwise interfered with the freedom of transit or failed to protect international shipping. We might also discuss whether we could do any more to protect the status of the Suez Canal Company from being altered or the servants of the Canal Company from being intimidated in such a way as to render it incapable of running the Canal efficiently.

21. Such possible joint measures would be:—

(a) Joint diplomatic action.
(b) Prompt joint use of such international machinery as may be considered approprite.
(c) If these measures were ineffective, agreement by France, Italy and the Netherlands (in accordance with Article VII of the 1888 Convention) to join with Her Majesty's Government in placing warships at the entrance to the Canal and in general to act as the Royal Navy were obliged to act last October.
(d) Agreement to take ships through the Canal without Customs clearance if restrictions were applied by means of arbitrary Customs and other regulations over and above what Egypt is entitled to apply under Article XV of the Convention.
(e) If these measures still proved ineffective, to consider what further action could be jointly taken to bring pressure to bear upon the Egyptian Government.

22. No guarantees that might be obtained from the Egyptian Government nor measures adopted by the maritime Powers could be regarded as effective unless they led to the removal of Egyptian contraband control or cargoes passing through the Canal for Israel. Indeed this would be among the first issues to be considered by the consortium if it were set up, although we should be reluctant to be further implicated in the dispute between Israel and the Arab States. Not only Egypt, but also all other Arab States would be strongly opposed to any measures designed to break their blockade against Israel; and before a decision was taken to adopt those foreshadowed in paragraph 21 above it would be necessary to give further considera-

tion to the possible adverse effect of such Arab opposition on United Kingdom and other Western interests.

Conclusion and recommendation

23.—(a) An ill-disposed Egyptian Government might at any time restrict or stop traffic going through the Suez Canal either by direct obstruction or by applying pressure on the Suez Canal Company.

(b) In view of the heavy British interests involved and the extent to which they are shared by other countries, I recommend to my colleagues that Her Majesty's Government should suggest to the French Government that they should, in conjunction with Her Majesty's Government, review their proposal for a confidential exchange of views between the maritime Powers:—

(i) to consider a joint approach to the present Egyptian Government in order to obtain firmer guarantees; and

(ii) to explore the possibilities of joint action in the event of failure by the Egyptian Government to give such guarantees or to maintain freedom of transport and to safeguard the Canal Company.

(c) I consider that this consultation with the maritime Powers should take place as soon as possible. The timing of any approach by the maritime Powers to the Egyptian Government should be decided later, bearing in mind *inter alia* the state of Anglo-Egyptian relations at the time.

24. I annex draft despatches to Paris and to the other countries concerned.

32 DO 35/6950, no 21 [Aug 1952]
'Colonial questions in the United Nations, 1952': memorandum from UK government to US government; strategic importance of Cyprus
[Extract]

. . . 44. Our attitude is based on the fact that strategic considerations require the maintenance of complete sovereignty over Cyprus and that no end can be seen to this requirement. This view is believed to be shared by the U.S. Military Authorities, and the State Department, in an Aide-Mémoire submitted to H.B.M.'s Embassy in Washington on 1st October 1951, stated that the surrender of British sovereignty over Cyprus would have a most serious effect on the Allied strategic position in the Middle East. The continued disturbed state of the Middle East underlines the necessity of maintaining complete control over an alternative base to the Suez Canal Zone, quite apart from the intrinsic strategic value of Cyprus, and it is clearly desirable that the base should be capable of immediate and efficient development and operation without regard to Balkan politics. Moreover, any transfer of sovereignty could not fail to have the most serious repercussions on our relations with Turkey, in view of the historical links between Turkey and Cyprus and the presence of a large Turkish minority in the Island.

45. The possibility which has from time to time been raised of surrendering sovereignty and concluding a bases agreement with the Greek Government is unacceptable for a number of reasons. H.M.G. could not take the risk in view of the

possibility that the present Greek Government might be replaced by one of a very different complexion. A partial surrender of sovereignty would almost certainly lead to renewed Enosis agitation which it might prove impossible to resist and the purely administrative problems which it would cause would in any case seriously diminish the usefulness of the base.

46.   It has also been suggested that a statement about the possibility of Enosis at some future time might be made in one form or another. The arguments against such a step are numerous and, in the view of the U.K. Government, conclusive, especially since the U.S. Government, in its Aide Mémoire of the 1st October, 1951, agreed that there was no step which could be taken and no statement which could be made which would appease the proponents of Enosis for the immediate future. . . .[1]

[1] For subsequent British policy on the question of a change of sovereignty in Cyprus, see part II of this volume, 321–333.

33   CAB 129/56, C(52)269   27 Oct 1952
'Egypt: defence negotiations': Cabinet memorandum by Mr Eden

Since his *coup d'Etat* on 23rd July, 1952, General Neguib,[1] the Egyptian Prime Minister, has been consolidating his position by a number of measures, including further purges and the reduction of the Egyptian political parties to impotence, and it seems likely that the present Egyptian Government will succeed in maintaining its position, perhaps on increasingly dictatorial lines.

2.   General Neguib's record, and that of his associates, contains a number of disquieting features and there is a real danger that extremist anti-foreign elements in the new régime may gain the upper hand. Nevertheless, General Neguib himself has shown a certain degree of moderation and a greater sense of reality than previous Egyptian Prime Ministers. It would probably be wrong to expect the new Egyptian Government to show any friendliness towards us, but they may approach Anglo-Egyptian problems in a more practical way. H.M. Embassy and the United States Embassy in Cairo, in a joint appreciation forwarded to me on 20th September, concluded that General Neguib's Government merited our support. H.M. Ambassador in a recent despatch to me (No. 213 of 25th September) expressed the view that we have now an opportunity to lay the foundations of a sound understanding with the Egyptian Government, but he does not think that the opportunity will last indefinitely.

3.   I suggest therefore that it may be useful now to consider whether any fresh instructions should be sent to H.M. Ambassador at Cairo, with special reference to our defence problems, and if so, on what lines these instructions can be drafted.

4.   Hitherto the basis of our policy towards Egypt has been the advice which we have received that it is essential to maintain in peace-time the Egypt base if the Middle East is to be successfully defended in war. The maintenance of the base did not however preclude the withdrawal from Egypt of British combatant land forces, provided that Egypt was prepared to agree to certain conditions. These considerations underlay the instructions which were sent to H.M. Ambassador at Cairo last

[1] Major-General M Neguib, prime minister of Egypt, 1952–1954.

spring; I attach at Annex[2] a recapitulation of these instructions.

5.   Since last spring, however, we have to take into account certain factors which are new or which have lately come into greater prominence. I would list these as follows:—

(a) The entry of Turkey into the Middle East as a firm ally.

(b) Financial considerations may well necessitate the reduction of the forces which we are able to maintain in the Middle East in peace-time. Furthermore, forces deployed in the Middle East in the first six months of war may be smaller than previously envisaged.

(c) We are making some progress towards the setting up of the Middle East Defence Organisation. This is now designed in the first instance as a planning organisation, and references in our earlier instructions to H.M. Ambassador to a Supreme Allied Commander and a Middle East Command are therefore now inappropriate. If, however, further progress is to be made with the establishment of the proposed organisation, we should try to ensure that any solution of Anglo-Egyptian problems should fit in with the form of that organisation.

(d) The emergence of the new régime in Egypt may offer us a better chance of coming to terms than we have had in the past.

6.   General Neguib has not displayed any haste to enter into discussions with us on defence, and indeed has hitherto indicated that he would prefer to deal with internal Egyptian problems first. H.M. Ambassador at Cairo, however, is anxious not to miss any opportunity which may offer, and meanwhile to create an atmosphere of confidence which might improve the chances of success in any negotiations. Moreover, any discussion with the Egyptians of the Middle East Defence Organisation is bound to precipitate an Egyptian request that Her Majesty's Government define their attitude towards the continued presence of British forces in the Canal Zone.

7.   I think, therefore, that it would be desirable to send some instructions at an early date to H.M. Ambassador at Cairo. The difficulty is that any instructions which we can send now may be invalidated by the new factors which have arisen, particularly (a) and (b) in paragraph 5 above. These two considerations have, I understand, made it necessary to review in detail our whole strategy in the Middle East. This review is now proceeding, and it may emerge that a base in Egypt, although desirable, is no longer absolutely essential. We should not in my view embark upon negotiations in which, by insisting upon requirements for ourselves which are unacceptable to the Egyptians, we risk a major breach with Egypt and the Arab world, only to discover that those requirements are no longer essential to the defence of the Middle East. The most important thing therefore is to complete as soon as possible the necessary studies of our strategic and financial needs, in order that in the light of them we may reconsider our whole policy towards Egypt.

8.   Meanwhile, however, since we must proceed on the assumption that the Egypt base is a desirable asset until we have reconsidered our position as I have suggested, I think that the principles which should *for the present* continue to guide us should be as follows:—

[2] Not printed, cf BDEEP series A, R Hyam, ed, *The Labour government and the end of empire 1945–1951*, part I, 33–35.

(i) We should not for the moment withdraw any troops from the Canal Zone. But, if at some future date we do start discussions with Egypt on defence, we should start withdrawing the reinforcements over and above the normal garrison as soon as these discussions make real progress and when we are satisfied that RODEO[3] will no longer be required. Moreover, we should be prepared, as we were last spring, to withdraw the mobile land forces constituting the normal garrison in return for a satisfactory agreement with Egypt on the lines set out in pargraphs (ii), (iii), (iv) and (v) below. It would probably be necessary to withdraw these forces within one year from the conclusion of an agreement with Egypt (I understand that it would in any case take eighteen months to move the Headquarters, calculated from the date of any decision to do so; I recommend therefore that this decision should be taken as soon as possible).

(ii) We should seek to maintain the base installations and stores in existence. As part of a general settlement, and once we were assured of genuine Egyptian co-operation, we could agree to place responsibility for guarding the base on the Egyptian authorities. A joint Anglo-Egyptian Board could be set up as a co-ordinating authority to resolve many problems of administrative control. The installations and stores which are an essential part of the maintenance of British forces should remain in the ownership of and under the control of the British.

(iii) We should agree to set up an Anglo-Egyptian air defence organisation. This should, if possible, include British units. It must be recognised that if we are to keep British fighter squadrons in Egypt we must be allowed to retain the necessary British personnel for their maintenance.

(iv) Egypt should agree to give us and our allies associated with us in the Middle East Defence Organisation full military facilities in time of war or imminent menace of war.

(v) Any new agreement with Egypt should be regarded as superseding the 1936 Treaty.

9. We may also have to be prepared, at some stage, to make available to Egypt the arms and equipment for which she is asking, including jet aircraft and Centurion tanks. The Cabinet has recently authorized the release of up to 15 Meteor aircraft to Egypt as a gesture of confidence.

10. These principles should be used only as guidance by H.M. Ambassador at Cairo if he finds it impossible to avoid some preliminary discussion with the Egyptians before our own further studies to which I have referred are ready. He should of course be warned that these studies are on the way.

Recommendations

11. I therefore recommend—

(a) That the further studies referred to should be carried out as a matter of urgency and that our policy should then be reconsidered in the light of them;
(b) that H.M. Ambassador at Cairo should be warned that these studies are being carried out and that meanwhile he should so far as possible avoid discussions with the Egyptian Government on the possibility of the withdrawal of British troops from the Canal Zone and the future of the base there;

---

[3] Code name for a military operation to evacuate British subjects from the delta region.

(c) that if it proves impossible to avoid all discussions, without arousing Egyptian resentment, H.M. Ambassador should meanwhile be guided by the principles laid down in paragraph 8 above;

(d) that he should in any case do his utmost to keep the Egyptians in play pending the reconsideration of our policy which I have recommended.

34   CAB 128/25, CC 101(52)9   3 Dec 1952

'Middle East headquarters': Cabinet conclusions on the proposed transfer of military headquarters to Cyprus

The Cabinet had before them a memorandum by the Minister of Defence (C. (52) 382) inviting them:—

(a) to approve in principle the transfer of Joint Headquarters, Middle East, to Cyprus;

(b) to authorise expenditure on certain preparatory work up to a limit of £500,000.

This would leave open the question of the exact composition of the Headquarters, but it was desirable that preparatory work on the site should begin without further delay.

The Foreign Secretary said that a move to Cyprus offered certain definite political advantages. Thus, it would be very acceptable to Turkey and should help to convince the Greeks that we intended to stay in the island.

The Prime Minister suggested that the Cabinet might approve in principle the proposed move to Cyprus but should reserve for detailed examination the numbers of Service personnel and civilians whom it was proposed to accommodate in the new Headquarters and the details of the expenditure proposed.

The Cabinet:—

(1) Agreed in principle that the Joint Headquarters, Middle East, should be transferred from Egypt to Cyprus.

(2) Agreed that preliminary work on the preparation of the Headquarters in Cyprus could be commenced, subject to the normal Treasury sanction of detailed proposals for expenditure.

(3) Invited the Minister of Defence to re-examine the proposed establishment of the Joint Headquarters and to submit to the Cabinet revised estimates of the Service personnel and civilians for whom accommodation would be required.

35   FO 800/827, p 2   15 Jan 1953

[Policy towards Egypt]: inward personal telegram no 12 from Mr Churchill to Mr Eden[1]

Thank you so much for all your telegrams, and I congratulate you on the progress in the Persian Oil. We seem to have been ill served by our agents in the Sudan. Money has evidently been freely used by the Egyptians. Surely we should now confront

---

[1] This telegram was sent from Jamaica and it was dispatched 'Emergency, Top Secret'.

Neguib resolutely and insist on execution of the treaty till 1956 failing a satisfactory agreement. It should also be made clear that, if we should be forced to evacuate before the expiry of the treaty, all sterling balances will be cancelled to indemnify us for the act of violence. Of course, what happens here will set the pace for us all over Africa and the Middle East. I trust that no final decision need be taken before my return. I can easily fly from New York.

36   FO 800/827, pp 7–8   4 Feb 1953
[Policy towards Egypt]: record of Anglo-American meeting in the Foreign Office[1]

Sudan
The Secretary of State said that the Cabinet had yesterday approved an offer to General Neguib which went 95 per cent. of the way to meet him.[2] On the position of safeguards for the South we were prepared either to make the whole matter *ad referendum* to the Sudanese Parliament, or to make the exercise by the Governor-General of his special responsibility for the South subject to the advice of his commission. On Sudanisation we were prepared to accept the Egyptian terms subject to the establishment of an international commission to supervise the whole process of self-determination including Sudanisation. He hoped that, on this basis, Mr. Dulles might feel able to instruct the United States Ambassador in Cairo to tell General Neguib that the United States Government thought this a reasonable offer which the Egyptians ought to accept. We were extremely anxious to reach an agreement and should spare no effort to this end.

Mr. Dulles wondered whether it would be possible to combine an instruction in these terms to Mr. Caffery[3] with a solution of the difference between us on supplying arms to Egypt. He had it in mind that Mr. Caffery might say that he took it for granted that the Egyptians would accept this offer by the British Government and that it was on that understanding that the United States would be prepared to sell equipment to the Egyptians. If, of course, the offer were not accepted, then the matter of equipment would have to be reconsidered.

The Secretary of State pointed out that some of the equipment which the United States Government proposed to sell to Egypt could very easily be used against British troops in Egypt in the event of trouble. If Mr. Dulles's plan were followed it would be desirable to go through the list of equipment with this in mind. *Mr. Dulles* said that it might be possible to take the line that, if the Sudan agreement went through, the United States Government would in fact allow the Egyptians to purchase some of the non-lethal equipment, but that a delay should be imposed on the provision of equipment to which the British Chiefs of Staff raised objection. In any case he doubted whether any of the equipment could in fact be delivered within forty-five days.

---

[1] The ministerial leaders of the UK delegation were Mr Eden, Lord Alexander and Mr Selwyn Lloyd. The US delegation was led by J F Dulles (secretary of state, 1953–1959) and H Stassen (director, Foreign Operations Administration, 1953–1955).

[2] In negotiations on the Anglo-Egyptian condominium of the Sudan.

[3] J Caffery, US ambassador to Egypt, 1949–1954.

It was agreed that the list of equipment should be reconsidered in the light of this discussion, and that meanwhile the State Department might suggest to Mr. Caffery that he should support the British offer to General Neguib.

Egypt
Mr. Dulles enquired the British view on the stability of the Neguib régime. *The Secretary of State* said that there were doubts about its stability. For example, the Sudanese were anxious to reach an agreement with Egypt because they thought that the present régime might not last.

Mr. Dulles said that it was because of such doubts that the United States Government wished to allow the Egyptian Government to purchase equipment.

The Minister of Defence doubted whether the present was the moment to offer the carrot to the donkey.

The Secretary of State thought that we might allow the Egyptians to have equipment for training purposes, but that other equipment should not be made available until the defence negotiations were under way.

Mr. Dulles said that it was the policy of the new Administration to take a more favourable attitude towards the Arabs than their predecessors. For this reason the President was unwilling to go back upon an agreement with an Arab State which the previous Administration had made. He believed that the previous Administration had in fact signed an agreement which made Egypt eligible to purchase arms, and it was therefore open to her to make cash purchases in the United States. Nevertheless, some administrative delays might be possible.

37   FO 800/827, pp 9–10   13 Feb 1953
[Egypt, the Sudan and Middle East defence]: record of Anglo-French meeting in the Foreign Office[1]

Egypt and the Sudan
The Secretary of State, after recalling that our very difficult negotiations with the Egyptian Government about the Sudan had been concluded the previous day in an agreement with Egypt, mentioned that this agreement had been possible because General Neguib had decided to forego the Egyptian claim to sovereignty over the Sudan. This decision had been one of great importance to the Sudanese, who were consequently extremely anxious that an agreement should be concluded embodying Egyptian recognition of their right to self-determination. We had therefore had to decide broadly whether to accept the present agreement, which was in fact better than that concluded between the Egyptian emissary in Khartoum and the Sudanese politicians, or to refuse it, in which case the Egyptians would have gone back to the Sudanese with their previous offer and the Sudanese would probably have accepted it. The Sudanese for their part thought that they could arrange matters with the Egyptians to their own satisfaction. However that might be, we had decided to make the best of the agreement which we had secured after such protracted negotiations.

---

[1] The ministerial leaders of the UK delegation were Mr Eden, Lord Alexander, Lord Reading and Mr Nutting. The French delegation was led by G Bidault (foreign minister, Jan–June 1953) and R Massigli (ambassador to Britain, 1944–1955).

The Secretary of State said that he did not know when it would be possible to open negotiations with Egypt on the other outstanding matter, namely, defence. He thought that we should have to see whether the atmosphere improved. He thought that Neguib's remarks so far about the Sudan agreement were reasonable, and he would like now to be able to go on to the question of defence, but if the Egyptians re-started their campaign of abuse against us, it would be very difficult.

On the whole, he thought that this régime in Egypt was a better one than any that had been there before. He promised that the French should be kept informed of our progress.

M. Bidault thanked the Secretary of State for his explanations and recalled that there was in fact more than one Sudan. There was also a French Sudan. It was important for France that the French Government should be kept in touch with developments in the Anglo-Egyptian Sudan, since these must affect territories in the French Union. The rapid advance which was now taking place in the Anglo-Egyptian Sudan, and in particular the move towards independence, must have repercussions in the French Union.

The Secretary of State agreed, but pointed out that the Anglo-Egyptian Sudan was in some respects a case on its own, since it was a Condominium. Its problems differed therefore from those of a colonial territory.

M. Bidault, in answer to a question from the Secretary of State, confirmed that there was the closest liaison on an official level between the French Ministère d'Outre Mer and the Colonial Office.

The Secretary of State then referred briefly to the Anglo-French approach in Washington to the Americans regarding the Suez Canal. He thought this was a good example of co-operation, and hoped that the United States Government would be willing to discuss the position with us.

M. Bidault confirmed that, according to his information, they would do so.

Middle East Defence Organisation

M. Bidault asked for information about the present position on the organisation of defence in the Middle East.

The Secretary of State said that everything depended on whether we could get anywhere in our negotiations with the Egyptians. So far the Egyptian attitude had been that we must get out of the Canal Zone before we could start talks about Middle East defence with Egypt. This was of course unsatisfactory.

There followed a discussion on the nature of the proposed Middle East Defence Organisation and the possibility of a liaison between it and N.A.T.O. The question of the site of the Headquarters was also raised. In the course of discussion the *Minister of Defence* informed the French delegation that the decision to move our own Middle East Headquarters from the Canal Zone to Cyprus had already been taken in principle. We should, however, wish a base in the Canal Zone to be maintained.

M. Bidault drew attention to the French view that the Standing Group must ultimately be responsible for strategic planning in the Middle East, and asked for our support. It was recalled that the Americans did not share the French view, but it was thought that the problem would be resolved in due course when a clearer picture could be obtained of the nature of the Middle East Defence Organisation.

38   CAB 129/59, C(53)65   16 Feb 1953
'Egypt: the alternatives': Cabinet memorandum by Mr Eden

I have been giving continuous thought to our Egyptian conundrum and I thought it might be of some help to my colleagues if I set down my broad reflections, even if [sic] the somewhat inconclusive form which follows.

2.   In the second half of the 20th century we cannot hope to maintain our position in the Middle East by the methods of the last century. However little we like it, we must face that fact. Commercial concessions whose local benefit appears to redound mainly to the Shahs and Pashas no longer serve in the same way to strengthen our influence in these countries, and they come increasingly under attack by local nationalist opinion. Military occupation could be maintained by force, but in the case of Egypt the base upon which it depends is of little use if there is no local labour to man it. We have learned the first lesson in Persia: we are learning the second in Egypt.

3.   In most of the countries of the Middle East the social and economic aspirations of the common people are quickening and the tide of nationalism is rising fast. If we are to maintain our influence in this area, future policy must be designed to harness these movements rather than to struggle against them.

4.   Our strategic purposes in the Middle East can no longer be served by arrangements which local nationalism will regard as military occupation by foreign troops. It is immaterial from what country those troops come. It would be a delusion to suppose that, in Egypt or elsewhere in the Middle East, local opinion would tolerate occupation by American or French forces any more readily than the Egyptians tolerate the British garrison on the Canal.

5.   Our strategic interests in this area must in future be served by arrangements designed to enable its peoples to play a significant, if not a principal, part in its defence. They must at least appear to have a determining voice in the disposition of the defence forces for the area. But, if that principle is conceded, they may accept the assistance of ourselves, the Americans and the leading Powers of Western Europe in organising and equipping their own forces; and they may also be willing that the defence of the whole area shall be organised in association with those Powers.

6.   This was the basis of the Four-Power approach to Egypt. That was not a plan to substitute for the British occupation a military occupation by an international force. It was a plan for establishing a Middle East Defence Organisation (M.E.D.O.) in which Egypt and the other countries of the Middle East would be associated with ourselves, the Americans, the French, the Turks and the Commonwealth countries concerned in planning and organising the defence of the Middle East as a whole. In the early stages the Middle East Command was to be no more than a planning organisation. The Supreme Allied Commander would not have-power to station forces in any Middle Eastern country without its consent.

7.   In the defence negotiations with the Egyptians, our main aim has been to secure their agreement to entering into a Middle East Defence Organisaation on that basis. Our offer to withdraw British troops from the Canal Zone has been conditional upon their agreeing to enter into such an Organisation. And we have throughout intended that our withdrawal should keep in step with the development of this new international defence organisation.

8. We have at no time contemplated withdrawal under duress. Nor have we been willing to promise withdrawal unconditionally. It has been our position throughout that we will withdraw our troops only when there is a reasonable prospect that other satisfactory arrangements will be made, on an international basis for securing the free use of the Suez Canal, planning the defence of the Middle East, and ensuring the use of the military base in Egypt in a future war.

9. What other course could we follow? Could we stand on our rights under the 1936 Treaty? We may reproach Egypt for her unilateral renunciation of the Treaty. But let us not forget that we are ourselves in serious breach of it. It allows us to maintain not more than 10,000 troops in Egypt in time of peace: since 1936 we have rarely had so few there, and we now have nearer 80,000. Moreover, the Treaty expires at the end of 1956, and it will take at least 18 months to complete the withdrawal of our troops. Even if we decide to hang on until the Treaty expires, withdrawal will have to begin in two years' time. Thus, a policy of standing on the Treaty would be shaky in the present and barren for the future.

10. We could undoubtedly deal effectively with any immediate attempt by the Egyptians to eject us by force from the Canal Zone. But the situation which this would create would almost certainly compel us to re-occupy Egypt, with all the consequences which this would entail. We should be likely to have world opinion against us and would find it difficult to make a case if Egypt took us to the United Nations. It is hard to see what future there is for such a policy. We cannot afford to keep 80,000 men indefinitely in the Canal Zone. Already our overseas current expenditure—mainly military—has risen from £160 millions in 1950 to £222 millions (provisional estimate) in 1952. This does not include the local cost of our troops in Germany which, as the Cabinet know, may bring us an additional liability of up to £80 millions in coming years.

11. With our limited resources, it is essential that we should concentrate on the points where our vital strategic needs or the necessities of our economic life are at stake and that we should utilise our strength in the most economical way. It is not possible for our present forces in the Canal Zone to support our peace-time interests elsewhere in the Middle East. If we leave them there in defiance of the Egyptians they will be wholly absorbed in coping with the situation which their very presence creates.

12. For these reasons I believe that the defence of our strategic and commercial interests in the Middle East can best be served through an agreement with the Egyptian Government on the lines proposed in my paper (C. (53) 17 Revise).[1]

---

[1] Eden's proposal in this memo was for phased British withdrawal on condition that Egypt committed itself to the MEDO plan and permitted a residual British technical presence in Egypt capable of reactivating the Suez base if necessary. This plan had American support ('Egypt: defence negotiations', Cabinet memo by Eden, CAB 129/58, C(53)17, 14 Jan 1953).

39   CAB 129/68, C(54)187   3 June 1954
'Egypt': Cabinet memorandum by Mr Selwyn Lloyd

A decision on the future of the Canal Zone is urgently needed. We must redeploy our troops. Commitments elsewhere (and the general need for drastic economies) make a rapid and large reduction of expenditure in the Canal Zone essential.

2.   The Egyptian Government appear to have their domestic situation in hand and to be anxious to reach agreement with us. They are probably as satisfactory from our view as any possible alternative. But, if we wait too long before reopening discussions, the Egyptian Government may be unable to prevent such a deterioration in the situation in the Canal Zone as would make a resumption of negotiations impossible. The situation had considerably improved until the incidents of 29th and 30th May. The Egyptian Government have been told that the future will be governed by the extent to which they co-operate in tracing and punishing the criminals.

3.   At our request the United States Government are withholding economic and military aid.[1] They will probably be unwilling to go on doing so much longer, particularly as the funds earmarked for Egypt will disappear on 30th June, the end of the United States financial year, unless Congress renews them.

4.   There appear to be two ways in which negotiations might be resumed with some prospect of progress.

The first would be to continue discussions on the existing scheme for using service technicians to maintain the base, but to agree that they shall not wear uniform in exchange for the Egyptians agreeing to include Turkey in the availability clause and provided that satisfactory arrangements are made regarding the status of the technicians.

The second would be to suggest the maintenance of the base by a civilian organisation, with American participation in some form, in return for the grant by the Egyptians of a longer period for the withdrawal of our troops and a longer period of availability. This was the suggestion which the Cabinet invited Foreign Office to explore, in consultation with the Americans, on 22nd March (C.C.(54) 21st Conclusions, Minute 2).

5.   The advantage of the first course is that some progress has already been made with the Egyptians and that we have good reason to believe that they are prepared to include Turkey in the availability clause, if we will not insist on uniforms. The disadvantages are that, although we might agree Heads of Agreement, we would probably have considerable trouble in working out the details and, in particular, in securing satisfactory immunities for our technicians. We might be held in this country to have given away under Egyptian pressure the right of The Queen's soldiers to wear The Queen's uniform.

6.   As regards the second course, proposals were worked out in some detail and submitted to the Americans, who replied that they regarded the plan favourably and would be willing to participate in working out a solution of this kind if invited by the Egyptians. They cannot, however, guarantee the participation of American firms. The Secretary of State for War has also had some consultations with British industrialists. Their reply showed that they consider the scheme to be on the whole practicable, though full of difficulties. They made it clear that they would only participate if appealed to at the highest level. The scheme would be very expensive if the installations were to be maintained on any considerable scale. But it has considerable merits, in that it avoids the deadlock on uniforms and the need to use military personnel whose status may be insufficiently protected.

7.   In my view the question of what is actually maintained in the base is no longer of the first importance. The essential thing is to ensure that when we leave Egypt we

---

[1] See 36.

do so with an agreement which gives us the right for an adequate period to return in war. Our prestige throughout the Middle East would be seriously affected if we failed to secure this right. A civilian contract scheme on a large scale would be very expensive. In the light of the above considerations I therefore think that our aim should be to maintain, for as long as possible, by civilian labour, a minimum form of nucleus base and to secure a satisfactory agreement on availability in war. On that basis we could secure a very considerable saving in money.

8. The main points of such an agreement would be as follows:—

(i) Complete removal of our troops from Egypt within about two years.

(ii) The right to return if an attack is made on the Arab States or Turkey. It would be good if Persia could be included in the formula as well, but we should not insist on this. We should try to secure this right for as long as possible, and certainly for considerably longer than seven years.

(iii) The removal or sale of the stores in the base within about two years (except what may be required under (iv) below).

(iv) Maintenance by civilian contractors (of British or any other nationality), subject to British inspection of certain minimum facilities such as:—

(a) one or more airfields (to include Abu Sueir), where we must also secure the staying [? staging] rights in peace-time which we need;

(b) some road and port facilities;

(c) a few essential installations on a care-and-maintenance basis.

The contractors would be under contract to the Egyptian or British Governments, and maintenance would be paid for wholly, or in part, by Her Majesty's Government.

(v) We should still desire the association of the United States Government in some way with the arrangement. For instance, the acceptance of an arrangement on the above lines by the Egyptians might be made a condition precedent to the grant of United States aid to Egypt.

9. On his return the Foreign Secretary will want to raise these matters urgently. I am therefore submitting this paper now for consideration by members of the Cabinet.

40 PREM 11/702   21 June 1954

[Anglo-American relations and Middle East policy]: minute by Mr Eden to Sir W Churchill

I have been thinking over your suggestion that we should ask the Americans to join us in negotiating a settlement with Egypt.[1] I see the advantages which it might have politically. But I think I should warn you it may raise some serious difficulties.

First, it would make an agreement much more difficult for the Egyptians. The Americans are not more popular in the Middle East than we are—maybe less so. If

---

[1] See 13, para 5.

Nasser[2] were to accept an arrangement of this kind, he would be open to the charge of having allowed two Great Powers into the Canal Zone instead of one. Moreover, as I mentioned to you, I have some doubts whether admitting the Americans to a share in the supervision of our base installations would make the arrangements more popular at home.

Secondly, there is surely value in keeping control (as we should under the agreement which I propose) over the important staging facilities in the Canal Zone. The Americans will want to make use of these as they did recently in connexion with Indo-China. We should of course let them do so, but it would give us something to gain credit for.

Thirdly, I am apprehensive of the effect in other Middle East countries (especially Iraq and the Persian Gulf) if we appear unable to settle this business for ourselves and have to ask help from the Americans. You will have seen Dulles' recent disagreeable remarks (Washington telegram No. 1217).[3] This makes me anxious that our approach to the Egyptians should not seem to be dictated by the Americans.

On the other hand, we do want support from the United States. I suggest that it should take three forms:—

(i) Strong public approval of our new basis for agreement, possibly as an outcome of the Washington talks.

(ii) Some link to be made between American economic and financial aid to Egypt and the agreement reached by us.

(iii) A special public endorsement at the appropriate time of the passage relating to freedom of navigation through the Canal.

I really think that this is simpler than trying to bring the Americans into the negotiations. I cannot believe that the Egyptians would accept the other method and the result might be a setback to the prospect of reaching an agreement.

Finally, I believe it is most important that we should give the Egyptians, before we leave for Washington, some indication that we hope shortly to renew negotiations and an outline of the plan we now have in mind. This would also help us to get American support agreed while in Washington and publicly expressed at the end of your talks there.

---

[2] G A Nasser, prime minister of Egypt, 1954–1956; president, 1956–1970.

[3] In tel 1217, 19 June 1954, to the FO Sir R Makins (the UK ambassador in Washington) enclosed what was described as a 'fairly accurate' report from the *Washington Post*, 19 June: 'Secretary of State, John Foster Dulles, was reported yesterday to be ready to notify Britain and France that the United States intends to pursue a more independent policy in the strategic Middle East and Africa. . . . Dulles has told friends in the past few days of his determination to talk bluntly about the Middle East and of his aim to shift policies. Dulles believes . . . that American policy in the oil-rich Middle East as well as Asia has been badly handicapped by a tendency to support British and French "colonial" views . . .' (PREM 11/702).

41   CAB 128/27/2, CC45(54)2   1 July 1954

'Aden': Cabinet conclusions on the security of the protectorate

The Cabinet had before them a memorandum by the Colonial Secretary (C. (54) 212) reporting that the security of the Aden Protectorate was threatened by an increasing number of frontier incidents and seeking the Cabinet's approval for measures to deter raiders from Yemen territory.

The Colonial Secretary said that the Imam of the Yemen had long maintained an ill-founded claim to the whole territory of the Colony and Protectorate of Aden. In recent months he had intensified his efforts to stir up trouble in the western area of the Protectorate by supporting the activities of rebels against loyal Chiefs. The number of incidents was increasing and these were clearly a part of a sustained campaign to undermine our authority. The ground forces available to the Governor were insufficient to deal with the situation, and plans were already under consideration to raise additional local levies and to provide them with more arms and equipment. It would, however, be several months before these measures could contribute to improving the frontier situation. Meanwhile, friendly tribes in the Protectorate were becoming increasingly concerned that we should take more vigorous measures for their protection, and the local situation was deteriorating. He therefore sought the Cabinet's authority to warn the Yemen Government that any further acts of aggression would be met by air action against the bases within Yemen territory from which the raiders came.

The Minister of Defence said that he supported firm and prompt action to prevent further deterioration of the situation. Bombing operations after due warning were likely to be effective without causing loss of life and, unless vigorous steps were now taken, we might later on find ourselves obliged to maintain a greater military effort over a long period. He was particularly concerned that we should avoid any further commitment of British ground forces in this area.

The Minister of State[1] reminded the Cabinet that Yemen was a member of the United Nations and that any military action taken across the frontier could be held to be an act of aggression of which the Security Council would be bound to take cognizance. It would be open to us to claim that such action had been taken in self-defence, but in that event we ought to report the matter to the Security Council and it would be expedient that we should prepare the way for this by giving due warning to the Yemen Government and by securing full publicity for the incursions which were taking place from Yemen territory. It must be assumed that, if we did not report the situation to the Security Council, the Yemen would lodge a complaint with the Council if we took the military action proposed. In either event there would be serious repercussions on our relations with Egypt and the Arab States. He had already asked the Yemen Minister in London to convey a protest to his Government and had asked for a reply by the end of the week.

The Cabinet:—

(1) Invited the Minister of State to arrange for a strongly-worded note of protest to be sent to the Yemen Government regarding the raids which had been taking place

---

[1] Mr Selwyn Lloyd.

from Yemen territory into the frontier areas of the Aden Protectorate, and to consider whether the terms of this note should not be made public.

(2) Invited the Colonial Secretary and the Minister of State to take steps to ensure that full publicity was given to the incursions which were being made into the Aden Protectorate from Yemen territory.

(3) Invited the Minister of State to circulate a memorandum on the probable international effects of the course of action proposed in C. (54) 212.

(4) Invited the Chancellor of the Exchequer to inform the Prime Minister of the substance of the Cabinet's discussion on this question; and agreed to resume their discussion at a meeting in the following week.

42   CAB 129/69, C(54)248   23 July 1954

'Egypt: defence negotiations': Cabinet memorandum by Mr Eden

Advantages of an agreement with Egypt

We can re-deploy our troops and release our Army from a commitment which is becoming intolerable.

2. We shall secure an immediate financial saving.

3. Nuclear weapons have changed the whole picture of warfare. Smaller bases, re-deployment and dispersal are a more efficient way of employing our strength.

4. We now need a smaller base, workshop facilities for our Middle East forces in peace and storage for war reserves, at least for the next few years. We also need air transit facilities. We have them now, and we can keep them by agreement with the Egyptians.

5. An agreement will give us a clause on the Suez Canal which will underline Egypt's obligations to maintain free navigation.

6. We hope that an agreement will lead to an improvement in our relations with the Arab world.

Disadvantages of having no agreement

7. We secure none of the above advantages, except such military facilities as we are at present maintaining at great cost and effort.

8. We relapse into a vicious circle of incidents and counter-measures, leading probably to intervention in Egypt by British troops.

9. The Treaty to all intents and purposes expires in 1956. We could not then, in the face of world opinion, refuse abitration. As that time approaches, we have less and less to negotiate with, and our chances of securing our essential needs diminish.

10. We lose the chance of better relations with Egypt, and other Arab States.

11. A fighting withdrawal would either cause us a great loss of prestige or else involve us in the same commitments as the policy of standing our ground. We should of course lose the facilities, and the Suez Canal declaration, which we would get under an agreement.[1]

---

[1] The Anglo-Egyptian agreement was concluded in Cairo on 19 Oct 1954, and was published as *Agreement between the Government of the United Kingdom and Northern Ireland and the Egyptian Government regarding the Suez Canal* (Cmd 9298, 1954). For detailed documentation, see BDEEP series B, J Kent, ed, *Egypt and the defence of the Middle East*.

With this agreement concluded, Britain renewed its efforts to involve the US in a wider Middle East defence organisation. The US did take part in talks but in the event held itself aloof from the Baghdad Pact. This organisation was established by treaty between Iraq and Turkey in Feb 1955, with Britain acceding in Apr 1955 and Iran and Pakistan acceding later. As of June 1955 the FO was still hoping that the US might join, see 81. Instead, the US preserved its independence of action by signing bilateral agreements and by promulgating, in 1957, the 'Eisenhower doctrine' under which the US would give assistance, in consultation with the UN, to any Middle Eastern countries requesting it, especially against communist aggression.

43   CAB 134/801, COS(54)303, annex   13 Sept 1954
'Strategic importance of Cyprus': report by COS[1]

Introduction
1.   To arrive at a sound conclusion on the importance of Cyprus to our strategy it is necessary first to consider our global defence policy and the importance of the Middle East as a whole.

Global defence policy
2.   In view of the recent developments in nuclear weapons our policy must be, more than ever before, to prevent war. To this end we must maintain the economic strength of the Free World and by rendering aid to backward countries lessen their vulnerability to Communism. We must create a stable and self-confident spirit in the world, and by building up alliances against aggression, and military strength by rearmament, ensure that aggression is halted and Communism contained. Above all we must strengthen our position as a major power and thus maintain our influence in the councils of the world.

The importance of the Middle East
3.   *To the free world*. The Middle East is of great importance to the Free World for the following reasons:—

(a) It is the land bridge between Europe, Asia and Africa and is the keystone of the defence against Communist infiltration into Africa.
(b) Now that Turkey is a full partner in NATO it is important that a power-vacuum is not allowed to build up on her southern flank. The defence of this area in war is vital in order that the flank should not be turned.
(c) The value of its oil resources.
(d) The Middle East is the centre of the Moslem world which it is important to retain in the Western Orbit.
(e) The Middle East is an essential link in the chain of air and military bases containing Russia.

4.   *To the United Kingdom in particular*. The United Kingdom has a particular concern and responsibility in the Middle East because of our long-established

---

[1] The COS forwarded this report to the Ministry of Defence 'as an expression of their views' (note by H Lovegrove, secretary, COS Committee, CAB 134/801, 13 Sept 1954). It then went to the Cabinet Committee on Cyprus which Cabinet had recently established (CAB 128/27/2, CC 57(54)6, 27 Aug 1954); this committee comprised junior ministers from the CO, FO, CRO and Ministry of Defence, with the CO's minister of state, Mr Hopkinson, in the chair.

economic interests, our treaty obligations to certain states such as Iraq, Jordan and Libya, and our Commonwealth sea and air communications.

Her Majesty's government's policy in the Middle East

5. The policy of Her Majesty's Government, therefore, must be to maintain our ability to fulfil our treaty obligations and to defend the Middle East in war. In peace, we must also retain sufficient forces in the theatre to promote stability and cohesion and to convince the Middle East states of our ability and resolve to defend the area in war. These forces must have secure stations from which to operate.

6. Cyprus is the only remaining British territory in the Middle East. Its cession to Greece would undoubtedly weaken United Kingdom influence in the area and would be a grave setback in the Cold War. Indeed following on our evacuation of the Canal Zone it might well be regarded as a further indication of our weakening resolve to honour our treaty obligations and defend the Middle East in war.

Strategic requirements in the Middle East

7. It is the intention to continue to station in the Middle East in peace land and air forces supported by the units of the Mediterranean fleet. Politically these forces must be located where they can exercise the greatest influence. Militarily they must be located in areas which provide security of tenure and give us freedom to come and go as we please. At the present time the only country which satifies these conditions is Cyprus. In these circumstances it is essential that we retain the freedom to station there such part of the Middle East forces which may be considered necessary at any time to meet our strategic and peacetime requirements. It is not considered that this would be practicable under any arrangements which Greece might be prepared to make should the island be ceded to her. Greece is a member of N.A.T.O. and our interests will coincide in global war. In peace however, British interests and obligations in the Middle East are far wider and may conflict with those of Greece.

Strategic importance of Cyprus

8. *Peace and cold war*. Cyprus lies in the Eastern basin of the Mediterranean and is regarded by the countries of the Middle East as part of it. It is the only British Territory in the Middle East where our combined headquarters and centre of intelligence can be located, and where we can keep troops in peace to exert British influence and to meet sudden emergencies of any kind. It is geographically convenient for this purpose and also has airfield facilities which could receive reinforcements from the U.K. Strategic reserve and operate reinforcing aircraft in case of need. It is becoming an increasingly important link in our imperial air routes. Its chief defect is lack of port facilities.

9. *War*. In war, if the forward strategy now being planned is a practical operation, the use of the Cyprus airfields will prove an important adjunct to those in Turkey, Jordan and Iraq. In addition they will give added flexibility to the strategic bomber force. Furthermore Cyprus lies athwart our sea route through the Eastern Mediterranean and is capable of supporting to a limited extent small numbers of light naval forces.

Retention of sovereignty

10. A most important strategic consideration in regard to Cyprus is that the

island should not come under Communist control in peace. There is already a strong Communist element in Cyprus. The possibility, however remote, of a Communist controlled Cyprus is quite unacceptable.

11. It is essential that our combined Headquarters should be in a country over which we have responsibility for administration and internal security. Otherwise a situation may arise such as obtained in Egypt.

12. We consider that, in the long term, any arrangement by which Greece was given sovereignty over Cyprus, and the United Kingdom only retained military rights by Treaty, would never be satisfactory. As time went by more and more pressure might be applied to whittle down the rights and facilities available in the island. The United Kingdom might in the end be forced to relinquish her military facilities in Cyprus, and with them her status in the eyes of the Middle East countries as a military force of any consequence. The liklihood [sic] of any real cohesion in the defence of the Middle East would then become remote.

44 CAB 131/14, D(54)37   10 Nov 1954
'Cyprus': minute by Mr Macmillan to Sir W Churchill on the proposed Middle East headquarters in Cyprus

In reply to your minute of 28th October, I attach a paper[1] prepared by the Chiefs of Staff, setting out the main functions of the combined Middle East Headquarters which it is proposed to set up in Cyprus. I have discussed this paper with the Chiefs of Staff.

2. We hope in time to see the Middle East States built up and welded together into some form of defence organisation. But this will not come about if, on leaving Egypt (with all that this implies), we cease to maintain in the Middle East any organisation which can exercise military influence with the Middle East States. I do not believe that this can be done by a Major General and an Air Vice Marshal who will be fully occupied with the day-to-day tasks of commanding, training and administering their scattered forces. Such officers have not, in any case, the status to deal with Ministers and Chiefs of Staff of foreign states. In my opinion a higher command organisation with Commanders-in-Chief of rank, experience, and prestige must be maintained to perform the functions stated in paragraph 5 of the Chiefs of Staff memorandum.

3. I hope that you will accept this view. In the meantime I have given instructions to the Chiefs of Staff to review immediately the size of the staffs required. I am confident that large reductions can be made on the numbers of Staff Officers originally proposed.

4. I am sending a copy of this minute to the Foreign Secretary, who is naturally much concerned in this question.

---

[1] Not printed.

45   CAB 129/78, CP(55)152   14 Oct 1955

'Middle East oil': Cabinet note by Mr Macmillan. *Annex*: report by the Middle East Oil (Official) Committee

The attached report by officials shows that, if United Kingdom fuel needs during the next twenty years are to be met, our imports of oil must be trebled. The Middle East is the only source. British oil companies own investments there valued at £600 millions, and by their sales of oil abroad earn enough foreign exchange to cover the total cost of our oil transactions, including imports.

2. There is a serious danger that the Middle East will slip away from us. The Egyptians, the Saudi Arabians and now the Russians are making great efforts to undermine our position, and spending large sums of money.

3. Apart from the sums spent to fulfil our treaty obligations to Jordan and our contribution to United Nations Works and Relief Agency (Palestine refugees), Her Majesty's Government's total expenditure in the area is at present less than £2½ millions a year.

4. Although the defence of our position depends primarily on the solution of major political problems, our prospects could be considerably improved by an increase in Government expenditure. A great deal could be done even within the range of £1 million a year.

5. I therefore ask my colleagues to endorse the principle in the conclusion of this report that our position in the Middle East is vital to the economy of the United Kingdom and that Her Majesty's Government should be prepared to spend in the area on a scale more closely related to our essential interests there. The report recommends that a working party should be set up to make urgent recommendations for action in the light of this general principle.

Annex to 45

The need

Within the next 20 years the United Kingdom's annual fuel requirements seem likely to increase by over 100 million tons (coal equivalent). Coal production cannot be increased to meet this. The present atomic energy programme will be supplying 40 million tons a year by the end of the period and this may be increased to 60 million tons a year. The remainder must come from oil. This means that within the next 20 years our present annual consumption of 26 million tons of oil must be roughly trebled. This increase will be required if our consumption of oil rises by just under 6 per cent. a year. The increase so far this year over 1954 is 14 per cent.

2. Our sales of oil abroad are likely to increase at a rate not far behind the rise in our own requirements. At present our oil companies play a considerable part in the international trade in oil, with corresponding advantage to our balance of payments. Very much more oil is sold in this way than is supplied to the United Kingdom, and the increase to be expected in this business will therefore require an enormous increase in production, mainly from the Middle East. Even to-day, sales abroad by British companies earn enough foreign exchange to cover the total cost of all our oil transactions, including imports.

3.   Although some of the extra oil required will come from the Caribbean area, the greater part must come from the Middle East, where the major proved reserves of the world are situated and where our companies have their greatest interests. There is no alternative source, as the only other large producing area, the United States and Canada, has become a net importer. Therefore supplies of Middle East oil are essential to the economy of this country. If they were cut off or seriously interrupted irrevocable harm would be done to our economic position, and a British investment now valued at some £600 millions would be lost. Western Europe as a whole is similarly dependent on the Middle East for its oil supplies, 75 per cent. of which came from that area last year.

4.   The massive growth to be expected in production will bring even more wealth than at present to the Middle East. This will make more urgent than ever the need to increase our exports to that area in order to "mop up" the sterling which it will receive. Various means of stepping up our exports to this valuable market are being actively pursued by the Board of Trade. This problem will be the subject of a separate report by the Overseas Negotiations Committee, whose recommendations will have to be taken into account in considering action on this report.

The danger

5.   The Middle East oil producing countries receive payment for their oil by taxing profits on crude oil production, under the various "50/50" agreements. They regard this payment as no more than their due. Indeed they still question the right of the oil companies to retain large profits on oil produced from their soil, and the right of Western Governments to derive large revenues from taxing the refined products. Pressure can therefore be expected from time to time to increase their share of the profits, *i.e.*, the price at which they allow us to have the oil, and since they have a virtual monopoly they are well placed to extract more from us. New agreements, however, have recently been made between the oil companies and most of the Middle East States, and there would be a fair prospect of these enduring were it not for the unwillingness of the Saudi Arabian Government to come to terms with the American oil company (Aramco) holding their concession. It is important to maintain the principle of equal profit-sharing. If it were breached, there is no knowing where the rapacity of the Middle East States would end, and there would be an increased cost to our balance of payments, including an increase in the net cost of our oil imports.

6.   Experience in Persia shows that mere increase in payments is not enough to ensure stability of supply. We need to promote internal political stability and in particular to influence individuals so that public opinion does not become so hostile to our oil companies that their commercial operation becomes impossible. The companies have themselves done much in this direction by their welfare services, education schemes, and "good employer" policies. They could do more, in particular by encouraging local industry and commerce, and by other indirect methods. They are in a better position to do so now that they can obtain relief from United Kingdom income tax in respect of their tax payments to the Middle East Governments. But the scope for oil company action is limited because they are suspect as interested parties. This is a field for Government action. Her Majesty's Ambassador at Beirut has reported as follows:—

". . . we are not doing nearly enough to protect our long-term interests in these countries. We should plough back a much greater proportion of our profits on oil, in our own interests, and build up for ourselves a position of greater strength, not only in the British protected territories and in countries where we have treaty commitments, not only in the sterling-area oil-producing lands, but, as opportunities offer, in every single country in the region, in the region as a whole. One rotten apple can spoil a barrel. We should concentrate particularly on Iraq; on the Sheikhdoms in the Gulf and on the 'transit' countries." (Syria and Lebanon.)

7. The danger is that our enemies may play on the indigenous forces of nationalism and cupidity in order to disrupt the commercial operation of our oil companies. What are our enemies doing?

(a) *The Russians* have recently increased their effort in the Middle East. Apart from the supply of arms to Egypt, they maintain bigger missions than we do in many Arab States, they have taken part in the Damascus trade fair for purely political purposes, and they have organised visits of many hundreds of young Arabs to Russia and to the Iron Curtain countries. They broadcast in Arabic, Persian and Kurdish. They use their own Muslim population to emphasise their link with the Middle East. Finally, they organise and pay for a nucleus of support in each country in the shape of the Communist Party.

(b) *The Egyptians* are exercising their influence against us. They claim the cultural leadership of the Arab world and their main weapons are press, radio and education. They subsidise the salaries of Egyptian teachers throughout the area (as the Greeks have done in Cyprus). The result is that, even where our influence is strongest, *e.g.*, in Iraq and Kuwait, the majority of the teachers are Egyptian. They are also talking of sending a "trade mission" to the Persian Gulf.

(c) *The Saudi Arabians* use a large proportion of the oil revenues for buying individuals abroad. By this method they are often able to neutralise our influence, even in Jordan. There are also signs of a drive for economic penetration of the Persian Gulf States.

What can Her Majesty's Government do?

8. A major improvement in the area must depend on the solution of political problems. The effectiveness of any action taken must also depend on the degree of co-ordination with the Americans (who now own two-thirds of Middle East oil concessions), and on the extent to which the producing countries themselves can be induced to follow social and economic policies designed to promote stability. But there is no doubt that an increase in Government expenditure, modest as compared with the value of the investment and of the fuel supplies which are at stake, would improve the atmosphere.

9. Her Majesty's Government's expenditure in the Middle East excluding Aden, at present amounts to £15,350,000 a year, of which some £10·7 millions a year goes to the subsidy for the Jordan Government and the Arab Legion. This expenditure of £10·7 millions, which is a direct consequence of our Palestine policy (and which provides us with a division in the Middle East at very low cost), is not directly relevant to the protection of our oil interests. The same is true of our contribution of £2,500,000 to U.N.W.R.A. for relief of Palestine refugees.

10. The remainder is spent as follows:—

		£
(a) Her Majesty's Missions (Diplomatic and Commercial)		1,210,000
(b) British Council		330,000
(c) Technical Assistance (including Development Division and various subventions)		120,000
(d) Information work		150,000
(e) Various (largely Security Forces in Persian Gulf)		310,000
Total		2,120,000

Her Majesty's Government receives some £8 millions in direct taxation on the profits of our oil companies' operations in the Middle East and a further £8 millions in British Petroleum dividends.

11.   Further action by Her Majesty's Government might include the following:—

(a) *The British Council* is perhaps the most effective instrument for spreading our influence. It is not able to meet the active demand for the facilities which it offers, still less to go out and make converts. It has only this year been possible to open British Council offices in Tehran and Kuwait and these are under-staffed. An extra £250,000 would more than double the impact upon the educated and half-educated population of the area and go far to counter Russian and Egyptian influence in the cultural field.

(b) A similar increase in our *information* effort should help to increase our influence, though its results are more limited by the general political atmosphere than are those of the British Council. There is the new opportunity offered by television. The Iraq Government have bought a station, perhaps prematurely. But it would be highly desirable to help them to operate it. We could also provide the means for the B.B.C. to increase its transmissions to the Middle East and its help to local stations in the form of material for their own use. The number of visits to this country by important people might usefully be stepped up; and the range of visitors increased beyond the scope of those normally handled by the information departments. Finally, our supply of films to the area could usefully be increased.

(c) *Technical assistance* in the mass form in which the Americans have used it, is largely discredited in the Middle East. But a discreet increase in the activities of the Middle East Development Division, and establishment of a fund to enable Her Majesty's Government to provide or subsidise experts in fields where local governments are unwilling to pay adequately for them, would not only increase our influence but help the economic development of the area. Not more than £25,000 a year is required for this.

(d) *In education*, the provision of teachers and if necessary the subsidising of their salaries would enable the Middle East Governments to recruit the British teachers whom they are already willing to employ, although in technical subjects the demand will still exceed the supply. The establishment of British schools, particularly that projected in the Lebanon, for the training of future leaders of the Northern Arab States, could not fail to have an important influence within 10 or 15 years. The initial cost of the Lebanon school to Her Majesty's Government would be £100,000 and there might be a further contribution of £10,000 a year towards running expenses.

(e) The possibility of supplying *arms* on credit should be further examined in the light of the latest Soviet moves;

(f) In order to maintain the standard of staff in Her Majesty's Missions in the area, steps should be taken to make service there more attractive. At present members of Her Majesty's Foreign Service serving in the Middle East enjoy no advantages over their colleagues in other pleasanter areas, although it is intended that there should be some advantage for Arabists from the point of view of early promotion. There are other ways in which their conditions of service could be improved.

Conclusion

12. Middle Esat oil is vital to our economy. This is not a matter of priorities as between one area of the world and another in the cold war, but an essential need. We are vulnerable in this area, which is at present slipping away from us because of the indigenous forces of nationalism, and because our enemies are making a greater effort than we are.

Recommendation

13. Ministers are therefore recommended to endorse the principle that our position in the Middle East, and in particular in the oil bearing states of Iraq and the Persian Gulf, is vital to the economy of the United Kingdom; and that Her Majesty's Government should be prepared to spend in the area, in furtherance of their objectives, on a scale more closely related to our essential interests there.

It is therefore recommended that Ministers should authorise the establishment of a Working Party under Foreign Office chairmanship consisting of representatives of the Foreign Office, Treasury, Board of Trade and Ministry of Fuel and Power, with the following terms of reference:—

"With a view to safeguarding the free flow of oil supplies from the Middle East, to consider urgently—

(a) what further action Her Majesty's Government should take; including action which involves increased expenditure:
(b) what action the oil companies concerned should be urged to take:

and to make early recommendations if necesary in the form of interim reports."

46   CAB 128/30/1, CM 22(56)13   13 Mar 1956
'Aden Protectorate': Cabinet conclusions on federation in South Arabia

The Cabinet were informed that, at a meeting on the previous day, the Colonial Policy Committee had discussed a proposal by the Colonial Secretary that the Governor of Aden should be authorised to open collective discussions with the Rulers of the various States in the Protectorate with a view to promoting constitutional development in the direction of a Federation or Federations. The Committee had agreed on the terms in which the possibility of federation should be broached to the Rulers, if any approach to them was to be made. The Minister of State for Foreign Affairs had, however, argued that no suggestion should be made at the present time of constitutional development in the Protectorate. He feared that such a move would give offence to the Yemen and to Saudi Arabia, and might cause those countries to increase their efforts to stir up trouble in the Protectorate. In view of the many problems which were engaging our attention in other parts of the Middle East, it would be a mistake to take any step which might precipitate further trouble. The Colonial Secretary, on the other hand, thought that this step, far from increasing the risk of trouble, might have the effect of reducing it. Both the Yemen and Saudi Arabia were already trying to detach States in the Protectorate from the British allegiance, and the plan for federation was designed to encourage the States to resist those advances. The Governor had already had some preliminary talks with the Sultan of Lahej, and was due to hold a conference with all the Rulers on 17th March. If this meeting were now postponed at the last moment, we should give an impression of indecision which our enemies would be quick to exploit. The other members of the Committee had supported the Colonial Secretary's view.

The Prime Minister said that this matter had been reported to him because of the failure to reach agreement at the Colonial Policy Committee. On balance he favoured the view taken by the majority of the Committee.

The Cabinet accepted this view.

The Cabinet:—

Invited the Colonial Secretary to authorise the Governor of Aden to open discussions with the local Rulers on future constitutional development in the Protectorate, on the basis approved by the Colonial Policy Committee.

47   CAB 131/17, DC 5(56)1 & 2   1 May 1956
[Defence of the Persian Gulf and Jordan]: Cabinet Defence Committee minutes   [Extract]

1. *Persian Gulf*

The Prime Minister said he was concerned about the arrangements for protecting vital British oil interests in the Persian Gulf Area. At a meeting on 13th April (14/31/88—1st Meeting) it had been agreed that the plans for the movement of British troops to Kuwait in the event of trouble should be reviewed in the light of the doubts that had been expressed about the airfields in Kuwait, that a cruiser should be stationed in the Persian Gulf and that the question of retaining an additional battalion in Kenya as a strategic reserve should be examined. What progress had been made in the preparation of these plans?

The Chief of the Air Staff[1] said that from 18th May the main runway at Kuwait would be operational. Before that date, the subsidiary runway could be used in an emergency, though at the expense of the payload that could be carried.

The Chief of the Imperial General Staff[2] said that it was planned to fly in a battalion at short notice from Cyprus. According to the political circumstances at the time, other troops could be flown in from the United Kingdom or from Cyprus. The time factor in their arrival would depend mainly on the amount of warning which could be received so that troops and aircraft could be alerted and prepared.

The First Sea Lord[3] explained that the Loch class frigates were air conditioned so that they could operate for a considerable time in the Persian Gulf. There were

---

[1] Sir D Boyle.   [2] Sir G Templer.   [3] Lord Mountbatten.

disadvantages in using a cruiser in the Persian Gulf since a cruiser had to anchor twelve miles out and could not therefore be seen from the shore. Moreover, cruisers were not air conditioned. He suggested that if a cruiser was at a week's notice to reach the Persian Gulf, the political requirements could be met. A third frigate could also be made available provided other arrangements were made for weather reporting at the Montebello trials.[4]

The Committee:—

(1) Invited the Chiefs of Staff to submit to the Minister of Defence a further report on the plans for the movement of British troops to Kuwait in the event of trouble.

(2) Invited the First Lord of the Admiralty to arrange—

  (a) for two air conditioned frigates to be stationed in the Persian Gulf; and

  (b) for a third air conditioned frigate and a cruiser to be available at a week's notice to reinforce the Persian Gulf.

The Committee then considered the question of keeping a second battalion in Kenya as a strategic reserve.

The Secretary of State for War[5] said that it was quite possible to keep a second battalion in Kenya, but there would be no great saving in the time taken to provide reinforcements in the Persian Gulf area unless the aircraft to move the troops were also stationed in Kenya. If the aircraft had to come from this country it would be much quicker to send the troops direct from the United Kingdom to the Persian Gulf.

The Chief of the Air Staff said that it was very much quicker to fly troops from Cyprus to the Persian Gulf than from Kenya, even if this included flying via Turkey. It could be extravagant to station small numbers of the limited transport aircraft available permanently in distant parts of the world. There were difficulties at present in maintaining the ten aircraft at short notice in Cyprus.

The Prime Minister said that he was concerned that we only had one battalion south of the potential air barrier, which mean [sic] that the movement of reinforcements was dependent not only on over-flying Turkey, but also on the free use of Iraqi facilities.

The Chief of the Imperial General Staff said that the War Office were examining as a long term project the possibility of keeping two battalions in Kenya for use to meet Colonial requirements in East and Central Africa. These two battalions would need barracks which would be costly to provide.

The Committee:—

(3) Invited the Chiefs of Staff to submit a report to the Minister of Defence on the Army and Air Force aspects of keeping part of the strategic reserve in Kenya.

2. *Jordan*

(Previous references: D.C.(55) 15th Meeting, Minute 1; D.C.(56) 4th Meeting, Minute 4)

The Committee had before them two memoranda by the Chiefs of Staff (D.C. (56) 10 and 11) dealing, respectively, with the implications of the Anglo-Jordan Defence Treaty and with the plans for possible contingencies in the event of trouble in Jordan.

---

[4] ie, the British nuclear tests at Montebello Island, Western Australia.

[5] Mr Head.

The Committee first considered the proposals in paragraph 4 of D.C. (56) 10 for aid to Jordan in the event of Israeli aggression and in discussion the following points were made:—

(a) It was unlikely that Israel would attack Jordan, but the Jordan Government were at present obsessed with this possibility and it was politically important to prevent their aligning themselves more closely with Egypt. It would be necessary therefore to convince the Jordan Government that we intended to honour our obligations under the Anglo-Jordan Defence Treaty.

(b) In view of the deterioration of the Arab Legion as a fighting force as a result of the recent changes in command,[6] it was doubtful whether the airfields at Amman and Mafraq could be held by the Jordanian Forces for sufficient time to enable British reinforcements to be flown in. In the event of hostilities it would be inadvisable therefore to move to these airfields the three fighter squadrons as originally proposed. The squadrons would now have to operate from Cyprus, which would make it more difficult to neutralise the Israeli Air Force and establish the necessary acceptable air situation which was an essential pre-requisite to the movement of British troops by air to Jordan.

(c) *The Chancellor of the Exchequer* said that as the military value of the Arab Legion had declined, there appeared to be less justification for the present substantial subsidies that were being paid to Jordan. A review should be made of the strategic importance of Jordan in the event of global war, and in the meantime any long-term commitments, relating purely to global war, should be avoided.

(d) In this context, reference was made to certain improvements to the airfields at Amman and Mafraq on which work had temporarily been suspended. The complete abandonment of these projects would be likely to create an unfavourable impresssion on the Jordan Government and work on improvements required in the short term should continue.

The Committee went on to consider what should be said to the Jordanian authorities at the forthcoming meeting of the Anglo-Jordan Joint Defence Board. In discussion the following points were made:—

(e) In the past the plans for aid to Jordan had only been discussed informally with General Glubb and certain British officers; no details had been revealed to the Jordan military authorities. If the object of convincing the Jordan Government of our intention to honour our Treaty obligations was to be achieved, it would be necessary on this occasion to put forward detailed plans.

(f) In submitting any proposals, it should be made clear that they were based on the assumption that Jordan had been the victim of a deliberate aggression by Israel and that the dispatch of British reinforcements would depend on the Jordanian Forces being able to hold the airfields at Amman and Mafraq. With these qualifications there would be little risk in revealing some details of our proposals since in the event of hostilities the implementation of any plans would depend on the circumstances existing at the time.

The Committee finally considered the plans outlined in D.C. (56) 11 for possible contingencies in the event of trouble in Jordan.

In discussion it was recognised that any British intervention in the event of

---

[6] The Jordanian government had dismissed General J B Glubb from his position as commander of the Arab Legion in Mar 1956.

internal disorders in Jordan, particularly if this involved conflict with the Arab Legion, would be likely to alienate the other Arab States, with possible serious consequences for our oil supplies from the Persian Gulf. . . .

48   CAB 128/30/1, CM 36(56)8   15 May 1956
'Aden': Cabinet conclusions on future policy

The Cabinet considered two telegrams from Aden (Nos. 300 and 302) suggesting that an early public statement should be made on the political future of the Colony.

The Colonial Secretary said that this proposal was made as a result of consultations in Aden between the Parliamentary Under-Secretary of State for Colonial Affairs, the Governor, the Air Officer Commanding and the Commander-in-Chief, Middle East Air Forces. The purpose of such a statement would be to check the demands of certain local political parties for further constitutional advance, to strengthen the hands of the moderate party, and to counter the propaganda which was being conducted by Egypt, Saudi Arabia and Yemen against the British position in the Aden Protectorate. It would be made clear in the statement that in view of Aden's strategic and economic importance within the Commonwealth, the United Kingdom Government could not foresee the possibility of any fundamental relaxation of their responsibility for the Colony. It would also be made plain that, while further advance might come in due course, the degree and pace of constitutional development must depend on the sense of responsibility displayed by the people and their leaders.

The Cabinet:—

(1) Approved, subject to certain drafting amendments suggested in the discussion, the proposed statement on the political future of Aden.

(2) Invited the Colonial Secretary to authorise the Parliamentary Under-Secretary of State for Colonial Affairs to make a statement in these terms in the course of his present visit to Aden.

49   DEFE 4/87, COS 55(56)2, annex   28 May 1956
'Facilities required by HM forces in Cyprus in peace and war': report by JPS to COS (JP(56)54(Final))

Introduction

1. In July 1955, the Chiefs of Staff expressed their views in a report[1] to the Ministry of Defence on the strategic importance of Cyprus to the United Kingdom. They were of the opinion that British influence and prestige in the Middle East as a whole could not be maintained without the retention of our present military position in Cyprus, which was therefore strategically essential; moreover, our military requirements within the island could only be met if the control of its administration in matters of defence, external affairs and internal security remained in British

[1] COS(55)159.

hands. Against this background the Chiefs of Staff Directive[2] to the Commanders-in-Chief, Middle East, was written in August 1955.

2. The BDCC(ME) have recently examined[3] the military facilities which they consider should be retained in Cyprus, to enable them to carry out this Directive. Their purpose was to emphasize these requirements and to ensure that they should not be lost sight of while talks, which might lead to a change in the form of Government, were in progress.

3. The Governor of Cyprus has also examined British military requirements in Cyprus in his appreciation[4] on the future of the Island. He suggests that pending the outcome of a re-examination of the United Kingdom strategic interests in Cyprus, the only sound course is to assume that in the present international context we must retain control of the Island.

Aim

4. The aim of this paper is to examine the strategic importance of Cyprus taking into account the BDCC(ME)'s report on the military facilities needed to carry out their Directive and the Governor's appreciation regarding the degree of political control which it would be feasible and necessary to retain in order to meet our various strategic needs.

BDCC(ME)'s views

5. The BDCC(ME) list a variety of requirements under peacetime, limited and global war conditions, which impinge on every aspect of government. They state that these requirements would be the same whatever the form of government in Cyprus.

6. They further point out the difficulty of conducting a limited war if Cyprus were under Greek control or independent. Such a limited war would presumably be in furtherance of British policy in the Middle East and might well be at variance with Greek policy. An additional complication was whether Cyprus or Greece would accept the risk of bombing attacks on Nicosia or Athens as a retaliation against the British use of Cypriot airfields.

Views of the governor of Cyprus

7. The Governor affirms his view that, in the present international context, the full use of the whole island for military purposes is indispensable to the fulfilment of British strategy and to the maintenance of British influence in the Middle East. He considers that present strategic requirements cannot be met by the provision of leased bases in a Cyprus under Greek sovereignty.

8. On the other hand he points out that with the rapid development of new weapons and equipment, the whole concept of warfare and strategy in the Middle East, as elsewhere, is changing. The value of Cyprus as a peacetime air staging post is being steadily reduced by the curtailment of overflying rights in the Middle East, and the increasing speed and range of transport aircraft will reduce its value still further. The Governor has queried[5] whether the BDCC(ME) in their proposals look far enough ahead or take sufficient account of the rapidly changing political situation in

---

[2] COS(55)216.   [3] COS(56)85.
[4] The Future of Cyprus, Appreciation by the Governor [Sir J Harding] on 4th April, 1956.
[5] Cyprus to Colonial Office telegram 611.

the Middle East. He suggests that unless the military aspects are clarified there is the risk that military requirements may unnecessarily prejudice political negotiations. It is, moreover, possible to foresee a time—the Governor suggests fifteen to twenty years from now—when, except for prestige, Cyprus will have little positive strategic value.

9. The Governor also suggests that a new approach to a political settlement should include a firm promise to the Greek Government that self-determination would be applied to Cyprus in our time and on our conditions. He visualises that strategic considerations may require a minimum period of fifteen years before self-determination can be allowed, the precise period to depend on re-examination of the strategic requirements by the Chiefs of Staff.

Our comments
10. We do not intend to comment on the BDCC(ME) requirements individually but to consider for what purposes and to what extent the use of Cyprus is essential. We examine this question under the headings of global, limited and cold war.

Global war
11. The military facilities required in Cyprus in global war should be viewed against the background of the nuclear counter-offensive, the development of long range weapons and United Kingdom obligations under NATO and the Baghdad-Pact.

Strategic air counter-offensive
12. Should global war break out it is probable that the initial Soviet air offensive will be against the combined United States/United Kingdom nuclear strike forces. Akrotiri is at present planned to be an advanced base for the V-bomber force. Although by about 1960 Cyprus will be within range of both the Soviet medium bomber force and their medium range ballistic missiles, its use as an air base will still be necessary owing to the need for alternative bases for the dispersal of the bomber force. The use of as many dispersal bases as possible will increase the chance that the counter-offensive will succeed.

Baghdad Pact
13. *Land forces.* At present the planned United Kingdom land force contribution to the Baghdad Pact is part of the division located in the Middle East. Cyprus is unsuitable for stationing the armoured element of this force. Under present circumstances Cyprus provides the nearest base to the Baghdad Pact area in which the United Kingdom contribution of land forces can be located in peacetime.

14. *Air forces.* The main United Kingdom contribution to the military effectiveness of the Baghdad Pact will be nuclear interdiction, on the effectiveness of which depends the concept of the defence of the Baghdad Pact area. For this task bases in Cyprus could play an importance [sic] role. So long as short range strike aircraft are to be used in support of Baghdad Pact operations, bases in Cyprus will be essential.

Bases in Cyprus
15. British global war requirements in Cyprus would be met without retaining full British sovereignty over the island, provided that Cyprus is in the hands of a

o

Power or Powers which could be absolutely relied upon to permit, in all circumstances, the use of bases for both NATO and Baghdad Pact purposes.

Limited war

Arab-Israel dispute

16. So long as danger of an Arab-Israel war exists, there is likely to be a United Kingdom commitment to intervene under the terms of the Tripartite Declaration of 1950 or under a UNO declaration carrying similar responsibilities. Anglo-United States air operations could be undertaken from aircraft carriers and bases other than Cyprus. The unimpeded use of the latter for this purpose is not therefore essential. Cyprus would also under present circumstances be used as a mounting and support area for United Kingdom land forces partaking in these operations.

Suez Canal

17. The economic existence of the United Kingdom will for many years depend upon Middle East oil and the ability to transport it through the Suez Canal. Since it is in the power of Egyypt to deny this latter facility to us, it is essential to retain some means by which British military power could, in the last resort, be brought to bear on this state. Cyprus would be a valuable asset for this purpose.

Anglo-Jordan treaty

18. A commitment at present exists to go to the assistance of Jordan in the event of that country being attacked. Under present plans Cyprus is the base from which air transport operations would be conducted for the rapid support of Jordan by land forces. It is also essential for land-based offensive air operations.

Cold war

19. In the present fluid and dangerous political situation in the Middle East the retention of our land and air forces in Cyprus is an outward and visible sign that the United Kingdom means to retain her influence in the area and to honour her treaty commitments. The purposes for which these forces may be required are discussed below.

Oil

20. Oil remains our main long term interest in the Middle East. We must therefore be able to honour our obligations to the local rulers in the Persian Gulf and the Arabian Peninsula and be able to maintain stability in the area. Because of the possibility of overflying rights being denied, Cyprus is not the ideal location for forces required for these tasks.

Suez Canal

21. The ability to use and reinforce Cyprus as a base for limited war operations augments other deterrents against Egyptian adventures, including closure of the Suez Canal.

Jordan

22. There are at present a number of operations planned for Jordan which range

from evacuation of nationals to the restoration of law and order. Forces required for these operations cannot be moved in quickly without the use of Cyprus.

Staging

23. At present Cyprus is an important staging point on the air route for trooping to Africa and the Far East. When long range aircraft are in commission the importance of Cyprus as a staging point will decrease.

Baghdad Pact and NATO

24. Although the Baghdad Pact and NATO originated as the means of guaranteeing the integrity of the land frontiers of certain of the Member States, these Pacts are also of value in the Cold War in that they provide the confidence on which political and economic wellbeing and stability depend. Our position in Cyprus, therefore, in so far as it provides potential support in Global War, also has an important part to play in the Cold War. The withdrawal or weakening of this potential would have an adverse effect on the confidence of our Allies. The Governor of Cyprus states in his appreciation that the one interest unifying the three nations in dispute over Cyprus is the defence of the free world against Communist pressure and aggression. We consider therefore, that in the context of the Baghdad Pact and NATO our Cold War purposes could be served without our necessarily retaining sole sovereignty in Cyprus.

Conclusions

25. We conclude that:—

(a) There are no Global War commitments which would not be met by a treaty agreement with a Cyprus in the hands of a Power or Powers which could be absolutely relied upon to permit, in all circumstances, the use of bases for both NATO and Baghdad Pact purposes.

(b) In the Cold War it is essential that the reliability of arrangements made for the fulfilment of our Global War obligations should be evident to our NATO and Baghdad Pact allies. We consider that this would also be achieved without our retaining sole sovereignty in Cyprus, as could our other Cold War activities, apart from those directly connected with the prosecution of purely British interests.

(c) Our requirements for Limited War under the auspices of the United Nations could be met by the same facilities and with the same political safeguards as for our Global War requirements.

(d) Our requirements in Cyprus for any Limited War in furtherance of purely British policy in the Middle East, which might well be at variance with either Greece and/or Turkey could not be guaranteed except under sole British sovereignty. The disadvantages which would follow from a denial to us of the full use of these facilities must be weighed against the possibility of replacing them by other means and the advantage of reaching a political settlement in Cyprus.

26. We further conclude that there are no overriding strategic requirements which preclude an attempt to reach a settlement in Cyprus, involving a partial transfer of sovereignty.

50   DEFE 4/87, COS 55(56)2   31 May 1956
'Facilities required by HM forces in Cyprus in peace and war': COS Committee minutes

The Committee considered a report[1] by the Joint Planning Staff which examined the strategic importance of Cyprus and took into account the report by the B.D.C.C.(M.E.) on the military facilities needed to carry out their Directive and the recent appreciation on Cyprus by Sir John Harding.

Mr. Morris[2] (Colonial Office) stressed the importance that was attached to the views of the Chiefs of Staff on the strategic value of Cyprus and the degree of control they wished to retain there in conditions of global, limited and cold war, since U.K. policy towards the island would be largely based on their requirements.

Sir William Davis[3] said that from the purely Naval point of view, the Royal Navy had no requirements for facilities in Cyprus in global or limited war.

Sir Ronald Ivelaw-Chapman[4] said that the paper provided no real answer to the question put by Sir John Harding in his telegram. It was important that the Committee should try to assess our requirements in Cyprus against a time factor, bearing in mind that our interests in the Middle East states might still apply in say five to seven years time, but in ten years a whole number of new factors might have arisen which would change or even reverse any views they might hold today.

In discussion *The Committee* agreed:—

(a) Certain amendments to the report.

(b) That paragraph 15, which should be the conclusion to the global war section of the paper, required expanding to stress the fact that global war requirements would impinge on every aspect of government, but that our requirements there could be met, provided the same relationship existed between the United Kingdom and any Government of Cyprus as between NATO occupiers of bases in this country and the British Government. It would be exceedingly dangerous to transfer our sovereignty over the island as at present this relationship could not be guaranteed.

(c) That a new paragraph should be inserted after paragraph 18 as a conclusion to the limited war section of the paper. This should stress that in the present concept of limited war, as we understood it, full military rights must always be guaranteed. It was doubtful whether this requirement would be satisfied if sovereignty over the island was granted to Greece. At the same time the value of Cyprus was liable to change with the political condition of neighbouring states. Its present military value in limited war might have radically altered in the not too far distant future.[5]

(d) That in paragraph 24 references to NATO were only confusing and should be deleted. We had a double interest in retaining our position in Cyprus. The fact that it was British territory and held substantial British forces was a stabilizing

---

[1] See 49.
[2] W A Morris, assistant secretary, CO, 1948–1963 (cf part II of this volume, 327, note 3).
[3] See 24, note 1.
[4] Air Chief Marshal Sir R Ivelaw-Chapman, vice-chief of air staff, 1953–1957.
[5] The phrase 'the not too far distant future' was inserted in the minutes by hand, replacing the phrase 'ten years time'.

influence on the Middle East and in particular on the Baghdad Pact countries. Secondly, the transfer of control of Cyprus to Greece when it was so close to Turkey might cause that country to withdraw from the Baghdad Pact which would probably collapse without her support.

(e) That a new paragraph should be inserted after paragraph 24 as a conclusion to the cold war section. This could well be on similar lines to the conclusion to the limited war section and should stress the imponderables of the time factor.

(f) That the report should be re-drafted on the lines of their views agreed above, for consideration by the Chiefs of Staff on Tuesday, 5th June, 1956.

(g) That a summary of their views should be forwarded to the Colonial Office for despatch to Sir John Harding.

The Committee:—

(1) Invited the Foreign Office and Colonial Office to take note of their views as agreed in discussion above.

(2) Instructed the Joint Planning Staff to take the necessary action as agreed at (f) above.

(3) Instructed the Secretary to take the necessary action as agreed at (g) above.[6]

---

[6] At two subsequent meetings of the committee (COS(56) 56th and 58th meetings, 5 June and 12 June 1956), several further amendments were made to the JPS report. The report as amended was then submitted to the Cabinet Defence Committee but was not considered until the committee's meeting of 29 Nov 1956, a delay presumably caused by the Suez crisis. The minute of the committee's discussion of the report has been retained by department. The final version of the report has also been withheld; however, its contents can be constructed from a scanning of the amendments adopted at the COS Committee meetings of 31 May, 5 June and 12 June. The amendments included the following:—

(1) 'We have certain British commitments in cold war which can at present be met most efficiently and expeditiously from Cyprus, although it is not the ideal location. . . . We could only dispense with full British sovereignty if two conditions were fulfilled—first that our existing base facilities were guaranteed by international agreement and secondly that Turkey was not antagonised thereby weakening our whole position in the Middle East. As in the case of limited war, political developments may result in a revised assessment of the cold war importance of Cyprus in the not too distant future' (new para 26, preceding conclusions). DEFE 4/87, COS 56(56)2, annex, 5 June 1956.

(2) 'Unless any significant development takes place, it is difficult to see how we could contemplate relinquishing sovereignty over Cyprus for at least ten to fifteen years' (replacing final sentence of conclusion (d)). DEFE 4/87, COS 58(56)2, annex, 12 June 1956.

51　CAB 131/17, DC(56)17　　　　　　　　3 July 1956
'United Kingdom requirements in the Middle East': report by COS for Cabinet Defence Committee. *Annex*

Introduction

Up to 1945 the United Kingdom enjoyed great influence in the Middle East. This rested on our physical control of many of the key countries in the area, our economic strength and the absence of any serious competition by other great Powers. Since the war, however, a number of changes of great and lasting significance have affected our ability to influence events in the Middle East. These changes are set out at Annex.

2. On balance these changes have been greatly to our disadvantage and have

produced a vicious circle in which a reduction in our ability to influence events leads to a loss of prestige. This in turn creates both the incentive and the opportunity for countries hostile to us to take action harmful to our interests. This will continue unless we determine our long-term essential requirements in the area and shape our policy accordingly.

Aim

3. The aim of this paper is to:—

(a) Define essential United Kingdom requirements in the Middle East and to examine how best to obtain and maintain them.
(b) Consider the deployment of our forces.

United Kingdom defence policy

4. The defence policy of Her Majesty's Government is to:—

(a) Prevent global war, short of sacrificing our vital interests.
(b) Maintain and improve our position in the cold war.
(c) Win any limited war should it break out.
(d) Survive global war should it occur.

While this policy serves as a general guide, mainly in relation to priorities, it does not give a sufficiently clear indication of the ultimate political objectives of Her Majesty's Government on which all plans for the Middle East depend for their validity. We have assumed for the purposes of this paper that our policy must not run counter to that in (a) to (d) above, must also take into account our increasing dependence on Middle East oil, the security of which, Ministers have recently stated, remains the principal object of our Middle East policy.

5. We consider that in assessing the absolute importance of any issue in the Middle East the criterion which should be applied to it is whether Her Majesty's Government would be prepared to regard it as a warrantable risk of war. We believe that in the Middle East Her Majesty's Government would, in the last analysis, only risk war:—

(a) To support a NATO or Baghdad Pact ally attacked by the Soviet *bloc*.
(b) To secure our supplies of Middle East oil.
(c) To secure the continued use of the Suez Canal.
(d) In accord with a United Nations resolution.

United Kingdom aims in the Middle East

6. Whilst it may sometimes be necessary to follow short-term expedients and commitments, we must guard against their prejudicing our long-term aim in the Middle East, the requirements for which we discuss below.

Global war

7. So long as there is no radical change in Soviet policy and the United Kingdom and United States retain the ability to carry out effective nuclear retaliation, we consider global war to be unlikely. Although global war might start as a result of a miscalculation, we think this is unlikely to occur in the Middle East. Further, should there be a global war, the Middle East would be a subsidiary theatre and events there

would not significantly affect its result. Nevertheless, as members of the Baghdad Pact and North Atlantic Treaty Organisation, we cannot ignore the attitude of our allies who measure the value of these pacts not only from the political and economic standpoints but also as guarantees of the integrity of their land frontiers. Our aim must therefore be to give our allies the necessary confidence which will improve our position in the cold war.

Cold war

8. We live in an age of rising nationalism which is often used by the Soviets to foster subversion to our disadvantage. Subversion is not easily countered by military forces which tend to become involved only when political policies have failed and armed rebellion or rioting has broken out. The British serviceman on foreign soil is often repugnant to the local inhabitants.

9. We must therefore increase the effectiveness of our political cold war measures. Certain steps are already being taken, but it is essential that we should intensify our efforts in all possible ways. In particular, we consider that there is an immediate need to expand and improve local police forces and intelligence, thereby reducing the need for military intervention. Furthermore we see great advantages in offering training facilities in this country to the military and police forces of the appropriate Middle East States. We also consider that every encouragement and assistance should be given to indigenous forces under British control. We must do everything possible to prevent further Middle East States from turning to the Communist *bloc* for military equipment and techniques. Measures should also cover the diplomatic, economic and cultural fields; and we should seek to make effective use of psychological and clandestine operation. In addition, in colonial territories and protectorates, we must improve and control educational facilities. However vigorous our political measures may be, military forces may eventually have to be called in and our cold war requirements attained by their use. The location of our forces in peace-time must take this into account.

10. A component of our cold war aim must be to remove the causes of limited war.

Limited war

11. Russian interference in the Middle East has increased the instability of the area. There are a number of sources from which limited war might arise in which the United Kingdom might be involved. The most effective deterrent to such a war would be the knowledge that the United Kingdom and the United States had combined military plans for immediate action against the aggressor and the belief that they would be put into effect.

12. In order to prevent limited war breaking out or, if it does, to be able to intervene quickly and effectively we need:—

(a) Air strike forces, whether land or carrier based.
(b) Adequate ground forces, with air transport readily available, so located that they can be speedily moved to their likely objectives.
(c) Naval forces for blockade and coastal operations.

13. However necessary it may be in the short term to take strong action in the

Middle East, a war, whatever its result, would further Communist aims. The prevention of a limited war is therefore of the utmost importance.

Deployment policy

14. The guide to the composition and disposition of our forces should be the degree to which they contribute towards the winning of the cold war and thus prevention of limited war. In considering our future deployment policy in the Middle East there are three major factors:—

(a) The stationing of our armed forces in certain Middle East countries provides a potential focus of irritation and enables the Russians to use nationalism to further Communist aims.

(b) The implications of nuclear strategy have outmoded a concept embracing large conventional forces dependent on major administrative bases.

(c) A potential air barrier from Syria to the Sudan which in certain circumstances could greatly complicate the movement of forces by air from West to East, combined with the loss of our control over the Suez Canal, divides the Middle East.

15. In planning any redeployment the following additional factors must be taken into consideration:—

(a) The use of air tranpsort makes possible a new pattern in the deployment of our forces within the limits imposed by political factors.

(b) Our forces should, as far as possible, be stationed in those places where they would not be under constant pressure to evacuate.

(c) Account must be taken of our obligations to particular States in the Middle East. We must avoid the impression of either failing to fulfil our commitments to these States, or of evacuating under pressure.

(d) The advantages and disadvantages of the withdrawal of one Service in relation to the others should be considered.

(e) Better living conditions must be provided than have been available in recent years, if the morale of our forces overseas is to be maintained.

16. The above factors necessitate, and should govern, a reappraisal of our long-term deployment policy in the Middle East. The implementation of this policy will take time and will be dependent upon the speed with which a favourable political atmosphere can be created. In the following paragraphs we discuss the deployment of our forces.

Cyprus

17. While the present emergency lasts, Cyprus is a military commitment. It is well placed and equipped as a base for the air support of the Baghdad Pact and for the strategic air offensive. As a base for substantial land forces it suffers from the lack of adequate port capacity and poor armoured training facilities. It is, however, the only possible location for land forces in the Eastern Mediterranean. In the present dangerous and fluid political situation in the Middle East the retention of our land and air forces in Cyprus is an outward and visible sign that the United Kingdom means to retain her influence in the area, to honour her treaty commitments and to ensure her essential oil supplies.

18. Our military requirements in Cyprus impinge on all aspects of Government. This factor, combined with the desirability of carrying Turkey with us as an important member of the Baghdad Pact in any changes of Government in the island indicate that we should certainly not relinquish our sovereignty over the island for the present.

19. Political developments in the area are unpredictable but could cause a radical change in our assessment of the importance of Cyprus at any time. Unless any significant development takes place, it is difficult to see how we could contemplate relinquishing sovereignty over Cyprus for at least ten to fifteen years.

Malta

20. Malta offers certain possibilities as a location for British forces. Though Malta would not be so effective as Cyprus in this respect as a location from which to exercise British military influence in the Middle East, it would provide a good measure of permanence, particularly if politically integrated with the United Kingdom. There is little possibility of requisitioning land for new construction, and in any event the provision of adequate training areas for ground forces is not possible. The present facilities in Gozo are even more limited. The stationing of an infantry brigade in Malta could therefore only be done at the expense of the Royal Marine Commando Brigade and the Anti-Aircraft Regiments now stationed there.

21. We consider that the maximum use should be made of Malta as a location for building up war reserves and for repair workshops. The removal of these installations from politically vulnerable areas such as the Suez Base and Libya to a place of more assured tenure, would add considerably to the flexibility of our military policy in the Middle East, besides providing useful and needed employment for local labour.

Jordan

22. The overriding consideration must be the political necessity of preventing Jordan from aligning herself more closely with Egypt since this would so isolate Iraq that she would be unlikely to be able to withstand the combined hostility of the remainder of the Arab world. The Arab Legion can now no longer be regarded as an effective or reliable force in war. Militarily the Anglo-Jordan treaty is now an embarrassment and is of little further value to us. Although desirable for the time being, to assist our political aim, the stationing of British forces in Jordan is not strategically necessary. Our main requirements are for overflying rights and the ability to use Mafraq as a bomber base for the strategic air offensive and for the support of the Baghdad Pact. We are examining the possibility of surrendering our rights to the use of Amman airfield and the withdrawal of the Royal Air Force Squadron from there. Land forces should be retained at Aqaba for as long as their presence is deemed necessary to support our political aims in that area, namely the psychological support of our Baghdad Pact allies and the maintenance of our influence in Jordan.

23. From a military point of view any future commitment to aid Jordan in the event of Israeli aggression should be confined to action under the Tripartite Declaration of 1950 or, better still, under a United Nations declaration.

Libya

24. Military facilities and accommodation have been provided for our land and air

forces in Libya at considerable expense. This country provides a good station and satisfactory training facilities particularly for armoured forces. Our present relationship with the Libyan Government is good, and the presence of our forces is a counter to Egyptian and Russian penetration. Such penetration would alter the whole position along the Southern Mediterranean littoral and gravely embarrass France. Furthermore, our position on Egypt's Western flank provides Nasser with a salutary pre-occupation which may be a curb to his ambition. Although the Baghdad Pact Powers are aware that our land forces in Libya could not be moved instantly to their aid in war, their removal would weaken the confidence which our allies in the Pact have in our intentions. We should not abandon our position in Libya as long as Egypt adopts her present attitude and Russian-attempted penetration of North Africa continues. For the foreseeable future therefore, land forces will be needed. Nevertheless it is quite possible that before the expiry of the Libyan Treaty in 1973,[1] political and/or military conditions may change so drastically that it would no longer be expedient or possible to retain any forces in Libya. We should in any case retain our naval and air facilities under treaty. The latter are particularly important for peacetime staging, operational training and as limited war bases against Israel and emergency bomber bases in the event of global war.

Egypt

25.   The Canal Zone base could play no useful part at the start of a global war in support of operations in the Baghdad Pact area on account of the remoteness both of its geographical position and its chances of survival in nuclear warfare. In limited war against the Arab States it would be a useless embarrassment. In a war against Israel its stocks and repair facilities might be of some use. The relatively small functions which it fulfils in the cold war could be met by other arrangements, albeit at some expense. We should therefore plan on the assumption that we will not retain the base on the expiry of the Canal Zone Agreement in 1961.

Iraq

26.   We consider that every possible military, political and economic measure should be taken to strengthen the power and stability of Iraq. As regards the Baghdad Pact, it should be our aim, by agreement, to ensure that airfields in North-East Iraq and at Habbaniya are maintained to a standard suitable for light jet bombers and fighters. We should maintain staging facilities at Habbaniya, together with *the right to stockpile and* the maintenance, training and other facilities required in accordance with the Anglo-Iraq Agreement.

Aden and the Protectorates

27.   The need to deploy forces in the Colony of Aden and the Aden Protectorate will continue for as far as we can see. The air barrier complicates the move of any reinforcements from the United Kingdom or the Levant. We do not recommend any change in the planned garrison, including an infantry battalion and a small air transport force, which could be reinforced if necessary from elsewhere. Air staging

---

[1] In 1953 Britain and Libya had signed a 20-year treaty of alliance which secured British air and military bases in Cyrenaica.

facilities will still be required there for the additional aircraft which may be needed to lift reinforcements rapidly from Kenya or elsewhere.

The Persian Gulf

28. The oil resources of the Persian Gulf territories are vital to our interests and we cannot therefore allow our position to be weakened. These territories are in a different category from other Middle East areas because they still rely on British patronage to give them continued stability and an independent existence. We must therefore be able to intervene by force if necessary, although we hope that we will not have to station forces in these territories. We consider that there will be a continuous requirement for frigates to be stationed in the Persian Gulf, and that, in normal circumstances, these are more suitable than cruisers. We must be prepared to fly in troops from elsewhere.

29. As in the case of Aden, the air barrier may complicate rapid reinforcement from the United Kingdom or the Levant. Under these circumstances reinforcements from Aden, Kenya or elsewhere in that area may be quicker and easier. This would necessitate locating land forces in the area with sufficient air staging facilities to ensure that the necessary transport aircraft could take up troops and convey them to the disturbed area without delay. It would be financially unacceptable to tie up highly expensive transport forces permanently in the area as a local reserve.

Somaliland

30. We have recently given our opinion[2] that:—

(a) In view of recent events in the Middle East, the strategic importance of the Somaliland Protectorate has increased.
(b) If self-government were granted to the Protectorate, it would be essential to retain the following minimum strategic rights:—
   (i) Overflying and staging rights.
   (ii) The right to station forces.
   (iii) Concessions in respect of possible oil and mineral production and pipeline facilities.
   (iv) Use and development of ports and anchorages.

31. We do not consider that there should be any need to station forces permanently in Somaliland, but we must be able to send forces there if required.

Africa

32. Our immediate requirement both now and in the future is to maintain law and order. Although Mau Mau has been virtually eliminated, further trouble might arise there or elsewhere in East Africa. As long as a Central African battalion remains in Malaya we are committed to sending a battalion to Central Africa should it be needed. On present plans, it is hoped that local forces will be capable of dealing with these situations. If, in the event, they are not, reinforcements would be required. Once again, the possible obstacle of the air barrier to reinforcement from the United Kingdom must be taken into account.

---

[2] See 90.

33. If a land force was stationed in Kenya it would be conveniently located for action to protect vital British interests in the Arabian Peninsula and East Africa. The capital cost of providing permanent accommodation for a force of some two British battalions would be in the order of £8½ million. To ensure the rapid lifting of these troops by air to disturbed areas it would be necessary to maintain suitable airfields and loading facilities near the location of Army garrisons. It is probable that Nairobi airfield would satisfy these requirements with little if any additional expense. There would be no need to locate transport aircraft permanently there. Even when the advent of very long-range transport aircraft make it easier to meet emergency commitments direct from the United Kingdom, there would remain military advantages in having a force near its area of operation.

Conclusions

34. We conclude that:—

(a) Our essential aims in the Middle East are to safeguard our vital oil supplies, prevent war and support the Baghdad Pact (paragraphs 4–7 above).

(b) We can no longer rely solely on the threat of military force to attain political stability and we must therefore devote much more of our non-military resources to this end (paragraphs 8 and 9).

(c) Political developments could at any time radically alter the strategic importance of Cyprus thereby changing completely our current assessment of its value. In the absence of any such developments it is difficult to see how we could contemplate relinquishing sovereignty over Cyprus for at least ten to fifteen years (paragraphs 17–19).

(d) Malta would provide a suitable location for building up war reserves and for repair workshops, but it would not provide a suitable alternative to Cyprus as a base in the Eastern Mediterranean (paragraphs 20 and 21).

(e) Although desirable for the time being to assist our political aim—namely the psychological support of our Baghdad Pact allies and the maintenance of our influence in Jordan—the stationing of British forces in Jordan is not strategically necessary, although we require to retain the use of Mafraq as a bomber base for the strategic air offensive and for the support of the Baghdad Pact (paragraphs 22 and 23).

(f) Libya provides good training facilities for our armoured forces and air forces. They provide support for the Baghdad Pact and act as a deterrent to Egyptian and Russian ambitions in North Africa. We should therefore retain our land forces there for the foreseeable future unless, before the expiry of the Libyan Treaty in 1973, conditions change so drastically as no longer to make it expedient or possible to retain any forces there; in the long term we should retain our naval and air facilities under the Treaty (paragraph 24).

(g) We should plan on the assumption that we will not retain the Canal Base after 1961 (paragraph 25).

(h) We should take every measure to strengthen the power and stability of Iraq and the Baghdad Pact. We should retain our present facilities under the Anglo-Iraq agreement (paragraph 26).

(j) We should retain our planned garrison in Aden, including an infantry battalion and a small air transport force (paragraph 27).

(k)   We should locate reinforcements for the Persian Gulf in an area from which they can be rapidly transported by air to any disturbed area (paragraphs 28 and 29).

(l)   We should retain our present strategic rights in Somaliland (paragraphs 30 and 31).

(m) A land force permanently stationed in Kenya would be conveniently located to protect vital British interests in the Arabian Peninsula and East Africa. Permanent accommodation for this force will involve considerable initial capital expenditure. To ensure the rapid lifting of these troops by air to disturbed areas it will be necessary to maintain suitable airfields and loading facilities near the location of army garrisons. There would be no need to locate additional transport aircraft permanently in the area (paragraphs 32 and 33).[3]

Annex to 51: Factors affecting United Kingdom ability to influence events in the Middle East

The major factors of an unfavourable nature are:—

(a)   The rise of nationalism in the Middle East states.

(b)   The increasing degree to which the United Kingdom economy is dependent on oil supplies from the Middle East.

(c)   Our withdrawal from Palestine and the creation of the State of Israel.

(d)   Our withdrawal from the Indian sub-continent and thus the loss of the "Indian Army."

(e)   Our failure to take a strong line in the Abadan crisis.

(f)   The withdrawal of our forces from Egypt following the Canal Zone agreement, which has greatly enhanced the prestige and ambitions of the Nasser régime and has given Egypt the physical ability to close the Suez Canal.

(g)   Our withdrawal from the Sudan.

(h)   The worsening situation in Cyprus, which is tying down large forces and which has exacerbated British and Turkish relations with Greece.

(j)   The ability of the Middle East states, being members of the United Nations, to influence world opinion.

(k)   The provision by the Soviet *bloc* of arms to Egypt, and now Syria, concurrently with an intensive drive by the Soviet Union for economic and political influence in the Middle East.

(l)   The virulent and highly effective Egyptian propaganda campaign against the Western powers, and particularly the United Kingdom, throughout the Middle East.

(m) The decline in the effectiveness and reliability of the Arab Legion following General Glubb's dismissal which has undermined our policy in Jordan.

(n)   The enormous flow of money into the Middle East through oil royalties and its misuse by Saudi Arabia for wholesale bribery and corruption.

(o)   Our straitened economic circumstances.

In addition, potential causes of friction have arisen between ourselves and the

---

[3] The report was signed: Mountbatten of Burma, G W R Templer, D A Boyle.

Americans due to the strong Zionist influence in the United States and to competitive commercial interests, particularly with regard to oil.

2. Major factors of a favourable nature are:—

(a) The extension of N.A.T.O. to include Greece and Turkey.
(b) The creation of the Baghdad Pact and increasing United States support for it.
(c) The emergence of Turkey as a staunch ally.
(d) The committing of Iraq and Iran to a policy of collaboration with the West.

52   CAB 131/17, DC 6(56)2   10 July 1956
'United Kingdom requirements in the Middle East': Cabinet Defence Committee minutes

The Committee had before them a note by the Minister of Defence (D.C. (56) 17) circulating a report[1] by the Chiefs of Staff submitted as an interim expression of their views on United Kingdom requirements in the Middle East.

The Minister of Defence said that there was little he need add to the report by the Chiefs of Staff, the conclusions of which were summarised in paragraph 34.

In connection with what was said in the report about Jordan, the Committee should be aware that it appeared from recent telegrams that the Government of Jordan did not now contemplate calling on the help of British troops if they became involved in hostilities.

The Prime Minister said that he agreed generally with the analysis which the Chiefs of Staff had made of our requirements in the Middle East. It did not appear, however, that this analysis pointed to any substantial reduction in the size of the forces maintained in the area. It was important therefore that demands for the construction of additional facilities should be kept to a minimum, and that no opportunity should be lost of making savings in other directions. In particular, it seemed to him that the reserve of land forces which was being built up in the United Kingdom was unduly large in relation to any calls that might be made on it for reinforcing overseas theatres. There were certain advantages in maintaining forces on the spot, where they would have a moral effect, rather than tying them up in the United Kingdom. For example, the Governor of Hong Kong was pressing strongly that the size of the garrison in Hong Kong should not be reduced, because of the adverse moral effect which that would entail.

The Secretary of State for War said that the War Office was carrying out a major examination of the optimum deployment of an Army of some 200,000 men. Among other things, this would probably provide for a smaller strategic reserve in the United Kingdom. He would prefer to avoid committing himself about the details of deployment until that review was complete. Meanwhile, the size of the Army was being reduced at the rate of 30,000 men a year; to accelerate this reduction in advance of the formulation of a new plan would be liable to lead to confusion.

If all the fighting units of the Army were stationed overseas, a large proportion of the personnel of the Army would have little opportunity of service at home, which would militate against recruiting. He suggested that the policy should be to maintain

---

[1] See 51.

overseas such forces as were necessary for the defence of the particular territories in which they were stationed and for purposes of moral effect, but to station at home those forces which were required as reinforcements if trouble developed. Assuming that adequate air transport existed, little was gained, if troops had to be sent to the Persian Gulf, for example, from transporting them from Kenya rather than from the United Kingdom. If they were located overseas permanent accommodation and suitable amenities had to be provided for them. *The Vice-Chief of the Imperial General Staff*[2] added that the Chiefs of Staff had recently discussed the representations made by the Governor of Hong Kong. They were inclined to think that his objects could be met by arranging for the retention in Hong Kong of an armoured regiment and by allowing other reductions to proceed as planned. And this would not mean the retention of additional manpower, since the armoured regiment would otherwise have been brought home and retained in the United Kingdom.

There was general agreement in the Committee that while the size of the strategic reserve to be maintained in the United Kingdom needed careful examination, it was sound in principle to rely on this reserve for reinforcement of threatened areas rather than on forces maintained overseas. In particular, Ministers were not inclined to favour the provision of permanent accommodation in Kenya for a force of some two battalions at a cost of about £8½ millions. *The Minister of Defence* explained that a memorandum on the question of accommodation in Kenya was in preparation, and he would prefer that a decision on this subject should be deferred until the memorandum had been circulated.

In further discussion, it was suggested that it would make for efficiency and economy if responsibility for the control of the Persian Gulf were entrusted to the Royal Navy and if any necessary operations to restore order in that area were carried out by H.M. Ships and by Royal Marines; or at least if the operations involving all three Services in that area could be avoided. *The Chief of Staff* explained that they had this subject under consideration.

The Committee:—

(1) Took note of D.C.(56)17.

(2) Invited the Minister of Defence to bring before the Policy Review Committee, in the light of D.C.(56)17 and of their discussion, proposals with regard to the maintenance of forces in the Middle East.

(3) Took note that the Minister of Defence would shortly circulate a memorandum on the question of the construction of army accommodation in Kenya.

---

[2] Sir W Oliver.

53   CAB 134/1315, PR(56)29   23 July 1956

'Political, economic and information methods necessary to maintain and promote United Kingdom interests in the Middle East': report by the Official Committee on Middle East Policy[1] for Cabinet Policy Review Committee

Introduction

This Committee was appointed to study and report to the Policy Review Committee through the Foreign Secretary on political, economic and information measures to maintain and promote United Kingdom interests in the Middle East.

2. We have regarded our study as covering an area stretching from Libya to Pakistan and including not only Aden and the Aden Protectorates and Somaliland but also Malta and Cyprus. We recognise the importance of both the latter two territories to our position in the Middle East. Since, however, the problems of both territories are already continuously under review we have not attempted to formulate proposals in connection with either.

3. We have regarded the exact extent by which our military potential may be reduced and the distribution of expenditure as between military and non-military measures in the Middle East as falling outside our terms of reference. We have confined ourselves, therefore, to recommending such non-military measures as we believe to be most conducive to the interests of the United Kingdom.

4. We consider that the immediate aims of our non-military measures in the Middle East should be:—

(a) To make clear our intention to maintain and secure our position in the British and British protected territories in the region (including the States in the Persian Gulf).

(b) To secure the continued development of Middle East oil supplies.

(c) To secure and develop the most economic communications, especially through the Suez Canal.

(d) To convince the countries of the Middle East that their best chance of political freedom and stability, and of economic prosperity, lies in co-operation with the United Kingdom.

(e) To continue to work for the greatest possible United States support for United Kingdom policies, and, in particular, to enlist United States aid (and that of the International Bank) whenever possible in countering Soviet economic penetration.

(f) To increase our direct efforts to counter Russian and Egyptian influence.

(g) To strengthen those forces which favour co-operation with the United Kingdom as opposed to Russian and Egyptian influence.

Political measures

5. We would draw attention first to the following considerations in the political field which we think important in themselves, but which (with the exception of a settlement of the Palestine problem) need not directly involve expenditure:—

---

[1] The committee was chaired by Mr Dodds-Parker, parliamentary under-secretary of state, FO.

(a) We should recognise the extent to which Israel is regarded by the Arabs as the creation of the United Kingdom, and consequently as an instrument of our policy, and, while continuing to give the highest priority to the settlement of the Palestine problem, we should not, therefore, let it appear that our policies coincide with those of Israel.

(b) We should recognise the fact even when the protection afforded by our military forces is welcome, and in spite of the economic advantage which this brings to the country in question, the actual presence of foreign forces can be a powerful psychological and political irritant. We should, therefore try as far as possible to keep any United Kingdom forces in the area to the bare minimum necessary for strategic purposes and to keep them away from the centres of political activity.

(c) We should recognise the special importance of a satisfactory settlement of the problem of the Haud to the maintenance of our position among the Somali peoples.[2]

(d) We should show sympathy with and unostentatiously establish contact with non-Communist groups favouring constructive ideas for political change to the greatest extent compatible with the mainenance [sic] of our influence with the Governments in power. Co-ordination between the Foreign Office and the Colonial Office will be important so that developments in the Gulf States can, where appropriate, be kept in step with those in our dependent territories.

Present United Kingdom expenditure in the Middle East

6. Total military expenditure in the area in respect of Imperial forces is difficult to assess but, on a balance of payments basis alone, will amount to £56.7 millions in 1956/7.

7. Her Majesty's Government's expenditure in other directions in this area for 1956/7 is set out at Annex A[3] and is of the order of £31½ millions. A substantial proportion of this expenditure is devoted to support of *local* military and other security forces; it includes in particular £9½ millions in respect of the Arab Legion and other Jordan Forces.

8. These figures take no account of a number of additional commitments either already accepted or which we may well have to undertake in whole or in part, and which are set out in Annex B. These amount to capital expenditure of the order of perhaps £8¾ millions and recurrent expenditure of some £3 millions, but even so take no account of the cost of expansion of the Libyan armed forces or of the Jordan air force, nor of the possibility of a Palestine settlement which would cost us £15 millions. Thus, even as matters stand, in a year or two's time expenditure in the area might be running at the rate of £34¼ millions a year. This is a very substantial total comparing with the present figure of £9 millions in the Far East and £18 millions for all Colonial Welfare and Development, and excluding representational costs is not far short of half of Her Majesty's Government's current budgetary expenditure on non-military items overseas. It is therefore of great importance to ensure that sums of this order of magnitude are spent to the best advantage and to establish priorities for expenditure within the area. There is at present a serious lack of balance in this

---

[2] See part II of this volume, 297.   [3] Annexes not printed.

P

expenditure, the most glaring example being Jordan where large sums are being spent on budgetary and economic aid without commensurate return. On the other hand expenditure on the Bagdad [sic] Pact—one of the main instruments of British policy in the Middle East, and on the information services, is at present extremely small. Present expenditure on development in the Trucial States also falls considerably short of what H.M. Political Resident in the Persian Gulf considers to be the minimum necessary to maintain our position there. We should endeavour to secure a more sensible balance and in particular to reduce our commitments in Jordan while retaining our essential bases there.

Need for increased non-military expenditures

9. We now consider in broad terms the measures on which we believe further expenditure to be necessary if our position in the Middle East is to be satisfactorily maintained. Some further expenditure will be necessary for internal security (as in the Aden Protectorates). The remaining measures fall under the general headings of economic aid, and development of trade, information, and technical assistance.

Economic aid

10. We have in mind here not only assistance with the development of British dependent territories and Protectorates, with particular reference to the Aden Protectorate, Somaliland and the Gulf States, but aid to other countries, the chief instrument for which should be the Bagdad [sic] Pact. The scale of financial effort here need not be very great because of the resources already available to some of the Pact members through their oil revenues, but our contribution should be significantly larger than the £50,000 a year now approved. Moreover in the case of the Somaliland and Aden Protectorates, and of certain of the Gulf States, the rate of development may be kept below what is politically desirable by the inability of the local administrations to plan and carry out larger development programmes. This can only be remedied by the increased provision of administrative and/or technical staff, which may involve increases in grants-in-aid of administration. In Libya we have recently agreed to increase our budget subsidy and to expand the local armed forces. In addition it has been suggested that we might study with the United States Government the possibility of markedly stepping up the rate of development in Libya where in view of the low population an impressive political effect, notably on Egypt, might be produced at relatively little cost.

11. In general we need on the one hand to demonstrate that on our side co-operation is given willingly, generously, and effectively, thus weakening the psychological attraction of Russian and Egyptian offers, and on the other to take such steps as we can to counter Soviet economic penetration in the area. There is no way of preventing some offers from the Soviet *bloc* being accepted, but there will be occasions when it will be particularly important to prevent the Soviets from achieving a dominant role in financing or carrying out a particular project. In such cases our own resources are likely to be used more effectively in combination with those of other Western Powers. The necessary machinery to this end is being discussed with the Americans.

Trade

12. The Middle East (Official) Committee have been examining the possibility of

increasing our share of trade with the Middle East and have recommended in particular that the possibility of cover by the Export Credits Guarantee Department for the capital risks of British firms in establishing selling or servicing organisations, or investing in local industries should be explored. We are agreed that every effort must be made to interest British firms in the possibilities of this area, both for the political reasons and because of the large sterling balances now available to the oil producing countries. While recognising the objections to subsidising United Kingdom exports, we consider that a study should be made of the possibilities of ensuring at least that British consulting engineers are able to compete successfully for important surveys and projects in the area.

Information

13. This aspect is of special significance in the Middle East because of the importance of the spoken word in this area with its single language, the effective propaganda services already established by Egypt, and the evident increase in Russian attention to the region as a whole, both in itself and as a base for infiltration into Africa further south. Our efforts should not only be intensified but should be sustained long enough for them to produce their effect. We note that it has so far only been possible to increase the British Council's expenditure in the area by £150,000—half the figure recommended by the Middle East Oil Committee last year.[4] Further expenditure is urgently necessary on broadcasting (both by way of relaying B.B.C. programmes and the establishment of new transmitting stations, e.g. in the Gulf and North Africa) and on the production of broadcasting and television material. Further resources should also be devoted to magazine production and to the issue of Arabic translations of English books.

Technical assistance

14. We attach great importance to the provision of training facilities by the Services for the armed forces of the Middle Eastern countries, including the loan of British instructors and professional advisers. Much could be done in an unspectacular way by allowing Service personnel to give instruction to local forces, e.g. in Libya. Greater efforts should also be made to provide British professors and lecturers for Middle East universities and technical schools; more places should be provided in British educational institutions for Middle East students; and we should help Middle East countries to set up their own training courses for school teachers in order to avoid the employment of Egyptians. The difficulty here is the availability of British staff for such purposes. We consider that the new central pool contemplated in paragraphs 3 and 4 of Cmd. 9768[5] would ease this situation by offering prospects of steady employment to people who are prepared to serve permanently abroad.

Programme of additional expenditure

15. Annex C contains a list of projects which the political considerations render necessary and urgent though we have not been able to go into the details in all cases. These provide for the following additional annual expenditure on:—

---

[4] See Annex to 45, paras 10 and 11(b).
[5] See part II of this volume, 242.

Broadcasting	£59,000	(plus £330,000 capital expenditure)
Information	£254,000	
Development	£255,000	
	£568,000	(plus £330,000 capital expenditure)

16. We have expressed recurrent costs in terms of annual expenditure, but it must be realised that in practice the incidence of these costs will vary from year to year. It has not yet been possible to provide an estimate of the further costs which might be incurred on technical training and education: we understand that the Minister of Defence has put forward separately proposals for financing the provision of training facilities by the Services, which might cost £300,000 for the Middle East area.

17. We regard the total additional expenditure contemplated as by no means large by comparison with existing expenditures, more particularly if any savings are to be found from these, e.g. from the present Jordan subsidies. We should, however, draw attention to two directions in which further expenditure might have to be incurred. In the first place the Chiefs of Staff consider that the Bagdad [sic] Pact military organisation will inevitably engender military plans which will go beyond what the United Kingdom would regard as militarily necessary, but which it will be impossible entirely to discount if confidence in the Pact is to be maintained among its Middle East members. For example, there may be pressure for a skeleton Command organisation, and for a modest programme of military infrastructure. The United Kingdom financial contribution is hard to assess in the present early stage of planning; it might mean an initial capital cost of about £500,000 and an annually recurring cost of about £600,000. In the second place we have made no estimate of such further commitments as it may be considered necessary from time to time to incur in countering particular drives in the Soviet economic offensive. There can be no doubt that a very large field of aid will remain in the Middle East into which it will not be possible to prevent the Soviet bloc from entering should they so desire. Fortunately, however, large portions of the area are already well served with large oil revenues. For this reason we would attach the highest importance to improvement in our information services and the spreading of British influence by the services which our own people can give as teachers and technical experts.

Recommendations

18. We therefore recommend that the Policy Review Committee:—

(i) should approve that any additional expenditure which may be authorised should be incurred in the general directions set out in this report;
(ii) should indicate, if need be on a provisional basis, the annual increase which is likely to be available in non-military expenditure in the Middle East.

54   CAB 128/30/2, CM 54(56)   27 July 1956
'Suez Canal': Cabinet conclusions on future policy

[President Nasser nationalised the Suez Canal on 26 July 1956.]

The Cabinet considered the situation created by the decision of the Egyptian Government to nationalise the Suez Canal Company.

The Prime Minister said that, with some of his senior colleagues, he had seen the French Ambassador and the United States Chargé d'Affaires on the previous evening and had informed them of the facts as we knew them. He had told them that Her Majesty's Government would take a most serious view of this situation and that any failure on the part of the Western Powers to take the necessary steps to regain control over the Canal would have disastrous consequences for the economic life of the Western Powers and for their standing and influence in the Middle East. The Cabinet should now consider what courses of action were open to us to safeguard our interests. Our first aim must be to reach a common understanding on the matter with the French, as our partners in the Canal enterprise, and with the United States Government. The French Foreign Minister, M. Pineau, was due to arrive in London on 29th July; and he proposed that he should send an urgent message to the President of the United States inviting him to send a representative to take part in discussions early in the following week.

The Cabinet were given the following information of the importance of the Suez Canal to trade and the flow of supplies, and of Egypt's financial position:—

(i) *Oil.* Of a total of some 70 million tons of oil which passed annually from the Persian Gulf through the Suez Canal, 60 million tons were destined for Western Europe and represented two-thirds of Western European oil supplies. To move this volume of oil by the alternative route round the Cape would require twice the tonnage of tankers. If the Egyptian Government decided to interfere with the passage of oil through the Canal, it would be necessary for Western Europe to turn to the western hemisphere for supplies; as much as 10 million tons might be involved, and it would be necessary to ask the Americans to divert to Western Europe the supplies they now recieved from the Persian Gulf. We ourselves had supplies sufficient to last for about six weeks. In order to conserve these it would be necessary at an early date to introduce some arrangement for the restriction of deliveries to industry and to garages.

(ii) *Trade.* Interference with traffic passing through the Suez Canal would not seriously affect the flow of imports other than oil into this country, but it would seriously hamper the export trade, particularly to India. Our exports costs would also rise, as freight charges would go up.

(iii) *Egypt's sterling balances.* Egypt had £102 millions in her blocked account, of which no more was due to be released until January 1957. In addition she probably had about £14 millions available on current account, of which £7 millions was held by the blocking of the current balances would probably not seriously incommode Egypt at the present time. Her cotton crop, of which about one-third went to Soviet countries and little was purchased by us, would be coming on to the market shortly and the proceeds from this would tend to put her in funds.

The Cabinet next considered the legal position and the basis on which we could sustain, and justify to international opinion, a refusal to accept the decision of the Egyptian Prime Minister, Colonel Nasser, to nationalise the Canal.

The Cabinet agreed that we should be on weak ground in basing our resistance on the narrow argument that Colonel Nasser had acted illegally. The Suez Canal Company was registered as an Egyptian company under Egyptian law; and Colonel Nasser had indicated that he intended to compensate the shareholders at ruling market prices. From a narrow legal point of view, his action amounted to no more than a decision to buy out the shareholders. Our case must be presented on wider international grounds. Our argument must be that the Canal was an important international asset and facility, and that Egypt could not be allowed to exploit it for a purely internal purpose. The Egyptians had not the technical ability to manage it effectively; and their recent behaviour gave no confidence that they would recognise their international obligations in respect of it. Moreover, they would not be able to provide the resources needed for the capital development needed, in widening and deepening the Canal, to enable it to carry the increased volume of traffic which it should carry in the years ahead. The Canal was a vital link between the East and the West and its importance as an international waterway, recognised in the Convention signed in 1888, had increased with the development of the oil industry and the dependence of the world on oil supplies. It was not a piece of Egyptian property but an international asset of the highest importance and it should be managed as an international trust.

The Cabinet agreed that for these reasons every effort must be made to restore effective international control over the Canal. It was evident that the Egyptians would not yield to economic pressures alone. They must be subjected to the maximum political pressure which could be applied by the maritime and trading nations whose interests were most directly affected. And, in the last resort, this political pressure must be backed by the threat—and, if need be, the use—of force.

The Cabinet then considered the factors to be taken into account in preparing a plan of military operations against Egypt. In this part of the discussion the following points were made:—

(a) Egypt's military forces consisted mainly of three infantry divisions and one armoured division. She had about 500 tanks, and a great deal of armoured and wheeled equipment which was of doubtful efficiency. There were some 600–800 Polish and Czech technicians at present employed in the Egyptian Army, but it could not be predicted whether they would be willing to help the Egyptians in active operations. If they were, the Egyptian Army would be a more dangerous force. About two-thirds of the Egyptian forces were in the Sinai area; the armoured division, however, straddled the Canal.

(b) A military operation against Egypt, including consequential responsibilities for keeping the Canal in operation and controlling the area, would require the equivalent of three divisions. The necessary forces could be made available for this purpose; but, as a great quantity of vehicles and other heavy armoured equipment would have to be transported to the area by sea, the necessary preparations for mounting the operation would take several weeks. It would be necessary, moreover, to requisition ships and, possibly, to direct labour.

(c) While the military plan was being worked out, preparations would be made to build up a ring of bomber forces at points around Egypt. Fighter squadrons would also be sent to Cyprus. It would be a week before the full resources of Transport Command could be mobilised. The size of the air forces needed would depend on the type of bombing to be carried out.

(d) The naval forces available in the Mediterranean consisted of a carrier, a cruiser of the New Zealand Navy, 3 Daring Class destroyers, 7 destroyers and an amphibious warfare squadron. Another cruiser was approaching the Canal from the Red Sea; and, after discussion, it was agreed that she should be diverted to Aden. Summer leave in the Home Fleet was due to begin in the following week: it would be necessary to consider whether this should be stopped.

(e) In preparing any plan for military operations account must be taken of the possible effects on our Arab allies in the Middle East and the Persian Gulf if force were used against Egypt. It was important that the operations should be so planned as to reduce to the minimum the risk that other Arab States would be drawn into supporting Egypt.

(f) Consideration should be given to the possibility of cutting the oil pipeline from the Canal to Cairo, which was vital to the economic life of Egypt's capital.

The Prime Minister said that against this background the Cabinet must decide what our policy must be. He fully agreed that the question was not a legal issue but must be treated as a matter of the widest international importance. It must now be our aim to place the Suez Canal under the control of the Powers interested in international shipping and trade by means of a new international Commission on which Egypt would be given suitable representation. Colonel Nasser's action had presented us with an opportunity to find a lasting settlement of this problem, and we should not hesitate to take advantage of it. An interim note of protest against the decision to nationalise the Canal should be sent forthwith to the Egyptian Government and this should be followed up, as soon as possible, by more considered representations concerted with the Americans and the French. We should also consider inviting other maritime and trading countries to support this diplomatic pressure. Commonwealth Governments might suggest that the matter should be referred to the Security Council. He did not favour this course, which would expose us to the risk of a Soviet veto. It would be necessary, however, to consider denouncing the Canal Base Agreement of 1954 in view of the fact that Egypt had given an undertaking in this Agreement not to interfere with the Canal. The fundamental question before the Cabinet, however, was whether they were prepared in the last resort to pursue their objective by the threat or even the use of force, and whether they were ready, in default of assistance from the United States and France, to take military action alone.

The Cabinet agreed that our essential interests in this area must, if necessary, be safeguarded by military action and that the necessary preparations to this end must be made. Failure to hold the Suez Canal would lead inevitably to the loss one by one of all our interests and assets in the Middle East and, even if we had to act alone, we could not stop short of using force to protect our position if all other means of protecting it proved unavailable.

The Cabinet finally discussed a number of consequential matters on which decisions were needed:—

(g) The British cruiser which was at present paying a goodwill visit to Alexandria should be withdrawn immediately. Steps should be taken, short of physical interference with the vessels, to delay for as long as possible the departure of the four Egyptian ships which were at present in the United Kingdom or in Malta.

(h) The export of arms and military materials to Egypt should be discontinued forthwith.

(i) No action need be taken in regard to Egyptians who were on training courses in military and other establishments in this country or who were due to come here for that purpose.

(j) It could be decided on 30th July whether leave in the Home Fleet should be cancelled. Meanwhile, Commanding Officers could be warned privately that this was a possibility.

(k) The Bank of England and the commercial banks would need formal authority to block the current Egyptian balances held in London. It would be difficult to justify the release of such balances in present circumstances and there was support for the view that these balances should be blocked if the French Government decided to take similar action in regard to balances in France. Efforts should also be made to prevent the Egyptian authorities from securing control of the funds and negotiable assets of the Suez Canal Company which were held in London. *The Chancellor of the Exchequer* undertook to give further consideration to these points in the light of the Cabinet's discussion.

(l) Between 10,000 and 15,000 British subjects were understood to be resident in Egypt at the present time. These included some 8,000 Maltese and about 800 contractors' employees in the Canal Zone. It would not be possible to arrange for the evacuation of the whole number. The Foreign Office should, however, consider urgently whether some of them should not be warned to leave.

The Cabinet:—

(1) Agreed that Her Majesty's Government should seek to secure, by the use of force if necessary, the reversal of the decision of the Egyptian Government to nationalise the Suez Canal Company.

(2) Invited the Prime Minister to inform Commonwealth High Commissioners in London of this decision later that day.

(3) Invited the Prime Minister to send a personal messasge to the President of the United States asking him to send a representative to London to discuss the situation with representatives of the Governments of the United Kingdom and France.

(4) Appointed a Committee of Ministers consisting of:—
　　Prime Minister (*In the Chair*)
　　Lord President
　　Chancellor of the Exchequer
　　Foreign Secretary
　　Commonwealth Secretary
　　Minister of Defence
to formulate further plans for putting our policy into effect.

(5) Instructed the Chiefs of Staff to prepare a plan and time-table for military operations against Egypt should they prove unavoidable.

(6) Invited the President of the Board of Trade to arrange for the further export of arms and military supplies to Egypt to be stopped.

(7) Instructed the First Sea Lord to take the action noted in paragraphs (d) and (g) above.

(8) Invited the President of the Board of Trade, in consultation with the Minister of Fuel and Power, to consider what arrangements might need to be made for the restriction of oil deliveries.

(9) Invited the President of the Board of Trade to consider, in consultation with the Minister of Transport, what action might need to be taken to ensure an adequate supply of shipping for any military operations that might become necessary.

(10) Agreed that we should act in concert with the French Government in blocking Egyptian current financial balances held by the central banks of the two countries.

(11) Invited the Foreign Secretary to consider what warnings of the situation could and should be given to British nationals resident in Egypt.

55   CAB 129/83, CP(56)205   5 Sept 1956
'The strategic importance of Malta': Cabinet memorandum by Sir W Monckton. *Annex*: report by COS

At their meeting on 20th July, 1956, the Cabinet took note (C.M. (56) 51st Conclusions, Item 7) of a Memorandum by the Colonial Secretary (C.P. (56) 169)[1] which discussed the possible constitutional alternatives to integration for Malta. I was invited to ask the Chiefs of Staff whether in the light of the Colonial Secretary's Memorandum they had anything to add to their previous appreciations of Malta's strategic value to the United Kingdom. Their reply is annexed. I endorse their conclusion that the strategic value of Malta has increased during the past year and in the foreseeable future is likely to increase rather than decrease.

2.   I invite my colleagues to take note of this paper.

Annex to 55

Introduction

1.   British strategic interests in the Mediterranean are centred on ensuring the security of vital Commonwealth sea and air communications. We have obligations to support N.A.T.O., the Baghdad Pact, Jordan, Libya and the Tripartite Declaration of 1950, all of which contribute to the stability of the area. To meet these commitments it is necessary to station British forces in the Mediterranean.

Bases in the Mediterranean

2.   No one base in the Mediterranean can meet all the requirements of the three Services. Libya and Cyprus between them accommodate the land and the majority of the air forces normally required in peace. Gibraltar can accommodate the maritime forces but it is badly placed for exerting influence in the Middle East. Malta is, however, well placed and equipped as a base for naval forces; it has good airfields, but

---

[1] CP(56)169 is reproduced in part II of this volume, 320.

can only accommodate limited land forces. If the three Services are to play their part in the Mediterranean then the retention of Malta as a maritime base is essential.

Malta as a base in peace

3.   The strategic importance of Malta has been relatively increased by the loss of facilities in Egypt and the Levant. It is also a most important link in the British air routes to the Middle East and Far East. There exist in Malta extensive facilities for command, supply, repair, training and recreation which cannot readily be found elsewhere in the Mediterranean. There is, in addition, a supply of technically-trained labour. The British contribution to N.A.T.O. in the Mediterranean is centred on the organisation of CINCAFMED, whose Headquarters, together with the comprehensive communications, is strategically well sited in Malta.

Malta as a base in global war

4.   If global war occurs Malta might well be the target for nuclear or conventional air attack. However, as it is not planned to use it as a strategic bomber base the probability of nuclear attack is reduced. The possibility could be further reduced by dispersing the N.A.T.O. maritime forces, but in view of the effort being expended in strengthening the facilities for command Malta will remain the first choice for the centre of maritime command in the Mediterranean.

5.   The acceptance by N.A.T.O. of the new strategy which is being proposed by the United Kingdom would not, we consider, reduce the importance of Malta, since CINCAFMED's command is a visible sign of N.A.T.O.'s preparedness to resist aggression.

Malta as a base in limited war

6.   The unsettled political climate in the Mediterranean and Middle East may force us to relinquish our treaty rights to station forces in Libya. It is already clear that we cannot use our Libyan bases for mounting operations against any other Arab State. In addition, political developments could at any time radically alter the strategic value of Cyprus. Should these two eventualitites occur we would be left with Malta and Gibraltar as our only Mediterranean bases.

7.   The present situation over the Suez Canal emphasises the importance of Malta in the mounting and launching of any limited war operations in the Mediterranean and Middle East. The success of any limited war operation in the Far East will depend to a large extent on the use which the United Kingdom can make of the Mediterranean sea and air routes. If we are denied the free use of Malta, the lack of the excellent facilities for the command and support of military operations would gravely prejudice the prosecution of a limited war in the Middle East and, to a lesser extent, the Far East.

Conclusion

8.   We conclude that the strategic value of Malta has increased during the past year and, in the foreseeable future, is likely to increase rather than decrease.

56   CAB 134/1217, EC(56)67   8 Nov 1956

'Review of the Middle East situation arising out of the Anglo-French occupation of Port Said': memorandum by COS for Cabinet Egypt Committee

[On 5 and 6 Nov Britain and France invaded Egypt. Coming under extreme international pressure, especially from the United States, they ordered a ceasfire at midnight on 6 Nov. On 15 Nov the Cabinet Egypt Committee was informed that there would be no American financial support for the embattled pound until an Anglo-French withdrawal from Egypt had begun. Fifteen days later Cabinet agreed to an unconditional withdrawal. Evacuation of British troops was completed on 22 Dec. On 9 Jan 1957 Eden resigned. The Suez Canal, which Egypt had blocked on 4 Nov 1956, was reopened on 24 Apr 1957, with all parties accepting a settlement to the dispute based on 'six principles' for the Canal's management which had been agreed by Britain, France and Egypt on 10 Oct 1956.]

The situation

1. Our forces hold Port Said and the causeway as far south as Kantara. The Egyptian forces, particularly their Air Force, have suffered a severe defeat, but Nasser is still in power supported by that considerable part of the Egyptian Army which remains intact. The war has not been brought home to the ordinary Egyptian and he has therefore had no reason to lessen his allegiance to Nasser.

2. There are no immediate military factors to prevent us from exploiting our success, but for political reasons we have accepted a cease fire. This has been forced on us by:—

(a) UNO pressure.

(b) The possibility of Russian intervention and the consequent necessity for realigning ourselves alongside the United States from whom our previous actions have estranged us.

(c) The political climate in the United Kingdom.

3. The attitude of the other Arab States has so far been conditioned by the violence and success of the Israeli and Anglo-French operations. Whilst the Arab States are likely to retain a healthy respect for the Israelis after their overwhelming defeat of the Egyptians, and hence are unlikely to take overt unsupported action against them, the premature suspension of Anglo-French operations is likely to make it increasingly difficult for our Arab friends to hold the position unless we are also associated with action against Israel. This will be particularly true if we appear to give way before Russian pressure.

4. The possibility of setting up a UNO Force to separate the contestants and to secure a peaceful solution is now the subject of a UNO resolution. The UNO Force covered by this resolution will be designed solely for the purpose of stopping hostilities and restoring the status quo on frontiers. There has been no suggestion that it should in any way seek to impose a settlement of the Suez Canal dispute. Permanent Members of the Security Council will be ruled out from contributing to this force. It will, therefore, not include British or French contingents.

United Kingdom aims

5. Her Majesty's Government have expressed the British aims for the current operation as being to separate Egyptian and Israeli forces, to ensure the security of

the Suez Canal and to obtain the withdrawal of Israeli forces to the Gaza Area. Tacit aims have been to impose a satisfactory settlement of the Suez Canal dispute with Egypt and to effect the downfall of Nasser.

Likely developments

6. It is clear that we can no longer achieve our tacit aims of securing a Suez Canal settlement satisfactory to us and of overthrowing Nasser except by renewing fighting and thus flouting the United Nations resolutions with the added danger of bringing about Russian intervention. Our avowed aims would be achieved however provided either our own forces or those of UNO could keep peace and reopen the Suez Canal. The withdrawal of Israeli forces can only be achieved by United Nations action.

7. We consider that events may now follow two possible courses. If we press on with military operations, or even if we remain in occupation of Egyptian territory without fighting, it seems likely that Russia will intervene either covertly in the shape of volunteers, or overtly as the so called agent of the United Nations. Whatever the course of events Russia is likely to re-constitute the Egyptian air force and thereby pose a serious threat to all our forces in the area.

Alternative courses of action

8. There are three courses of action open to us:—

(a) To proceed with our original plan and occupy the Canal Zone, accepting the risks involved, with no restriction on air operations.

(b) To withdraw unconditionally in compliance with the United Nations resolutions.

(c) To remain in our present positions until we can hand over to a UNO force.

9. From the military point of view there are no immediate factors which rule out course (a), but if this course were politically acceptable we should presumably not already have agreed to a cease fire. We therefore do not consider this course further (but see para. 13 below).

10. In the absence of wholehearted United States support both inside and outside UNO, course (b) may be forced on us. It would, however, represent a major success for Russia (and Nasser) and a major defeat not only for Britain and France, but for the West, and its repercussions throughout the Middle East would be disastrous. We must therefore seek to contrive a means of avoiding this course.

11. Course (c) entails only slightly less risk of Russian intervention than does course (a), but there is a possibility that the United States could be persuaded to underwrite it as the least harmful to Western interests of the alternatives now open to us. Time is the crux of the matter, and we consider that our chances of being able to follow this course are in direct ratio to the speed with which at least a token United Nations Force can be flown in to replace our own. We do not consider that an offer to put our own forces under the United Nations Commander would be accepted by UNO.

Canal clearance

12. The clearance of the Canal is now Her Majesty's Government's first priority in the area. Until it has been seen how UNO reacts to our proposal that Anglo-French clearance teams should undertake the task it is not possible to relate it to the three

possible courses of action discussed above.

Conclusions

13. We conclude that the least damaging course to follow is course (c). In view of the highly inflammable situation in the Middle East and the unpredictable Russian reactions, however, we consider that we should be prepared in the worst case for a Russian sponsored war in the Middle East involving major threats to:

(a) Our position in Port Said;
(b) All sources of oil in the Middle East;
(c) Our Meditteranean bases.

This would undoubtedly involve fighting, initially, a defensive battle followed by the adoption of course (a).

14. We have put in hand the preparation of a report covering the implications of (including those affecting UNO and NATO) and requirements for a war on the scale envisaged in paragraph 13 above. This study will include an estimate of the force requirements and dispositions on the assumption that:—

(a) Some or all of the other Arab States ally themselves to Egypt;
(b) Russia will provide equipment and possibly 'volunteers'.

15. Pending the outcome of this examination we show at Annex[1] a suggested deployment of forces to meet the requirements of paragraph 13 above. In arriving at this deployment we have given full weight to the need for maximum economy.

Recommendations

16. We recommend that the ministers approve the deployment suggested at Annex so the action may be taken to impoement it without delay.[2]

---

[1] Not printed.   [2] The report was signed: Dickson, Mountbatten, Templer, Boyle.

57   CAB 131/17, DC(56)29   4 Dec 1956
'Middle East deployment up to April, 1957': memorandum by COS for Cabinet Defence Committee   [Extract]

. . . 11. *Jordan.* The future of Anglo-Jordan relations is obscure. However, so long as United Kingdom forces remain in Jordan, which we consider they should unless and until Jordan is irrevocably lost to the Egyptian-Syrian bloc, a United Kingdom military commitment will remain. Although we must now be prepared for the early abrogation of the Anglo-Jordan Treaty we have assumed in this paper that it is still in force.

12. *Libya.* Although the long term need for the continued presence of United Kingdom forces in Libya is open to doubt, we consider that it would be inopportune to make any major withdrawal at a moment when any such withdrawal would be interpreted as a sign of weakness. Unless the United States were prepared to take our place, any vacuum created by our departure would be filled by Russian and/or Egyptian influence.

Factors affecting the disposition of forces

Maintenance of internal security

13. *Cyprus.* The situation in Cyrprus has deteriorated during the operations against Egypt, particularly due to the removal of the Parachute brigade. The Governor has stated his requirements for the internal security forces which he considers necessary to prosecute the campaign against the EOKA terrorists. He considers that it is essential that the terrorist organisation should be broken with the least possible delay. If this is not achieved the continuation of repressive measures over a prolonged period might make it impossible to regain the goodwill of the public.

14. *Persian Gulf and Aden.* At present there are four battalions and one field squadron Royal Engineers in the area together with the numerical equivalent of four rifle companies provided by H.M. ships. We consider that we should plan to retain the ground forces at their present approximate strength until the overall situation in the Middle East becomes clearer and particularly as it effects the 'air barrier' and the Suez Canal. Because of the lack of hot weather accommodation it would be necessary for the Army to withdraw two of the four battalions not later than April, 1957. While it is reasonable under present circumstances to plan to withdraw these battalions, it may well be that at the time there will still be a requirement for one of them. Plans must therefore be made as a matter of urgency to provide hot weather accommodation for a full battalion at lower establishment in the Persian Gulf area in addition to that for two battalions at lower establishment in Aden.

15. *Libya.* For the reasons given in paragraph 12 above, we assume that, during the period under review, we shall retain forces in Libya, although the composition of the garrison may be adjusted. So long as these forces remain, there will be an internal security commitment. . . .

Proposed dispositions—army forces

Positioning of reserves

22. *Strategic reserve in the United Kingdom.* We consider that the sooner 2 Infantry Division, 16 Independent Parachute Brigade and 24 Infantry Brigade are concentrated in the United Kingdom as a world-wide strategic reserve the better.

23. *Reserves in the Middle East*

(a) We consider that the primary reserve for the Middle East should be a nominated Brigage Group of 3 Infantry Division in the United Kingdom. This Brigade Group should have its equipment and vehicles stockpiled in Cyprus. It can be properly trained in the United Kingdom and move to the Middle East by sea or air as circumstances permit.

(b) An Infantry Brigade could be provided from Cyprus but this should only be done if the general situation made this absolutely necessary.

(c) In addition to these two courses there remains the Royal Marine Commando Brigade less one Commando in Malta, which could be used for an immediate task prior to the arrival of a stronger force, and the Parachute Brigade Group in the United Kingdom.

24. *Armour.* We consider that the Brigade Group from the United Kingdom

should have an Armoured Regiment in support. It would however take at least three weeks to move this regiment with its tanks from the United Kingdom to the Eastern Meditteranean. If tanks could be stockpiled in *Malta* or *Cyprus* this time might be reduced, but there are a number of difficulties in this proposal which are being investigated further.

25. *Impression of strength*. In spite of the proposal to withdraw the forces in paragraph 22 above, twenty-three major army units would be retained in Cyprus. Details are in Appendix.[1] This in fact is the maximum that existing accommodation will allow and we consider that this force, whilst meeting the requirements of the Governor of Cyprus, would also give a very adequate impression of strength.

26. *Kenya*. Although there is now no internal security need to station a battalion in Kenya, we consider that, in view of the closure of the Suez Canal and the possible restriction of overflying rights, it will be necessary to continue to station one battalion in Kenya for some time. In any event it has been agreed with the Colonial Office that a battalion will remain there until April, 1958. One of the battalions now in the Persian Gulf should therefore be withdrawn to Kenya when the internal situation in the Persian Gulf shows that it is prudent to do so. . . .

---

[1] Not printed.

---

58   CAB 134/897, FE(0) 1(52)3   8 Jan 1952
'Review of the situation in the Far East': Official Far East Committee minutes   [Extract]

At the request of the Chairman,[1] *Sir John Sterndale Bennett*[2] gave a general review of the situation in South-East Asia.

Sir John Sterndale Bennett said that events in South-East Asia were increasingly determined by the events outside the area. It followed that although the Commission-General, Singapore, dealt directly only with South-East Asia, their interest ranged over the whole Far East. They had for example a lively concern with the changing scene in China and were watching carefully the implications of the re-emergency [sic] of Japan. In general, the countries of South-East Asia treated with some reserve the prospect of increased Japanese influence and there was some fear of Japanese infiltration.

The situation in the whole of South-East Asia was precarious. Indeed many regarded it as a miracle that the four foreign territories—Burma, Siam, Indo-China, and Indonesia—had maintained their independence even till now. In Burma there were seven distinct civil wars, and there was a growing Chinese threat to the North-Eastern frontier. Siam lay under the uneasy dictatorship of Marshal Phibul. In Indo-China the military action against the Viet Minh forces dominated the scene, and although the Viet Namese politicians had a hearty dislike for the French they were dependent on them. In Indonesia a handful of capable administrators were at present

---

[1] R H Scott (KCMG 1954), assistant under-secretary of state, Far East Dept, FO, 1950–1953; minister, British embassy, Washington, 1953–1955; commissioner-general, South-East Asia, 1955–1959.

[2] Sir J S Bennett, deputy commissioner-general in South-East Asia, 1950–1953.

in control and were adopting a realistic approach to their many problems. But the teeming population of Indonesia was very susceptible to the activities of agitators and there were great economic difficulties. It was by no means certain that the present administrators could retain power.

There was a growing, but still insufficient, general recognition of the importance of South-East Asia to the Commonwealth. One way of measuring this importance was to consider the economic and strategic implications of Communist control, and in particular the implications for our own territories. The danger of Communism lay, not in its appeal to the peoples of the area, nor primarily, perhaps, in the possibilities of armed aggression, but in the number of issues—racial, religious and political—which were ripe for exploitation by troublemakers and seekers after power. But the dangers of further armed aggression should not be under-estimated and precautionary plans must be made.

The area possessed considerable economic resources which could provide a substantial access of strength to world Communism. The rice of Siam and Burma was of the greatest importance to our own territories, and for this and other reasons, Communist control of Indo-China, Siam, and Burma, would make the situation in Malaya incomparably more difficult. Such a Communist success would, moreover, have important political and psychological effects throughout the whole Far East.

The Communist threat must be met with military, economic, and political weapons: our aim must be to promote stability, confidence, and prosperity, throughout the area.

There was a growing regional consciousness in South-East Asia which had been fostered by improved transport facilities. It followed that the relation between our Foreign and Colonial policy in the area was becoming increasingly intimate; this was exemplified in the composition and responsibilities of the Commission-General.[3]

The countries of South-East Asia recognised that they were dependent on foreign aid, but they were, nevertheless, suspicious of the implications of receiving it. In particular they feared United States economic domination.

There had been a great revival of interest in the United Nations since the United Nations action in Korea which had been [sic] proved, against all expectation, that collective measures of defence might succeed. In general, confidence throughout the area had fluctuated with the degree to which the United States and the United Kingdom had followed a common line in the United Nations.

It was difficult to give any precise definition of the role of the Commission-General, but its functions were mainly to smooth the relationship between our own territories and the foreign territories of the area; to provide early reports of regional trends; and to provide a point at which the various aspects of our policy could be integrated. The Commission-General had provided a central briefing point for Australian and United States missions to the area, as well as United Kingdom missions; and the Commissioner-General's house had become a recognised meeting place for politicians from all over the area.

The Commission-General were very conscious of the urgency of the matters with which they dealt. They recognised that the problems with which they were faced were so complex that it would impossible for them to receive immediate replies from

---

[3] The commissioner-general in South-East Asia reported to both the foreign secretary and the colonial secretary.

London to many of their requests for guidance. But there were very great dangers in any delay in giving effect to our policies. For example, there had been much disappointment that the Colombo Plan, although launched in January 1950, had not come into operation until July, 1951.

The immediate objectives for South-East Asia must be:—to gain more information about China which could be of use for propaganda and other purposes; to secure a closer co-ordination of policy with the United States on China and Japan, and indeed on Far Eastern matters generally; to ensure that there was no relaxation of our effort in South-East Asia, despite the general cry for retrenchment; to ensure that the United Kingdom, United States, France, Australia, and New Zealand, concerted plans against any further aggression; and to secure a clear policy towards Malaya so that no doubts would remain among the public there about our ultimate intentions.

Summing up, Sir John again drew attention to the extremely precarious nature of the situation in South-East Asia; the importance of the area to the Commonwealth; and the necessity for precautionary action so that we should not again, as in 1941, find ourselves insufficiently prepared for an emergency. . . .

59   PREM 11/645   30 Apr–2 May 1953
[Security situation in Indo-China]: minutes by Mr Head and Sir W Churchill

Prime Minister
As a member of the Defence Committee I feel bound to express my very grave concern at the present situation in Indo-China and our decision that nothing whatsoever can be done to help. I am very well aware of French weakness in forces, leadership and strategy; of their touchiness where suggestions about policy are concerned. I also realise that we are at present stretched to the full and that the Americans will be extremely reluctant to enter into new commitments. Nevertheless, the consequences of French defeat in Indo-China are so far reaching that I do not feel that even a remote chance of avoiding it should be neglected.

I think it is generally agreed that if Indo-China falls Burma and Siam will soon go Communist. We should then find ourselves defending Malaya in what is geographically a strong position; but what will be going on behind our line in the waist? All those who have been sitting on the fence will see clearly which way the wind is blowing; the Communists in Malaya will become far more active and the internal security problem will be acute. We shall be further embarrassed by the difficulties and expense of feeding the country when the rice growing countries are against us. Under these circumstances I doubt whether the Communists would bother to attack our position. They would be more likely to concentrate on dominating Indonesia, a course which, if successful, would make the fall of Malaya almost inevitable.

All this would take time but I cannot escape the conviction that a Communist triumph in Indo-China will in the long term lead to the loss of the whole of South-East Asia. I asked some time ago if there was an appreciation of the economic consequences to the West if this happened. It had not then been made but if there is one today I think it will inevitably show the extremely serious effect not only on our British economy but on Western Europe.

Q

In the Global Strategy paper which was approved by the Defence Committee the then Chiefs of Staff wrote: "Malaya is of the greatest economic value to the United Kingdom and its strategic importance in a war lies largely in its position as an outer defence of Australasia. French Indo-China is the key to the defence of Malaya. If the Communists were to gain control of Indo-China, the will and ability of other countries in South-East Asia to resist the spread of Communism would be seriously weakened and, with the inevitable fall of Siam, a Communist country would be established on the borders of Malaya. It is therefore a Commonwealth strategic interest of major importance in the Cold War to do everything practicable to bolster up French and Viet-Namese resistance in Indo-China".

Is it certain beyond doubt that the military situation in Indo-China is beyond salvation? Is it absolutely certain that a high level approach by yourself to the President followed by a joint offer of maximim help within our capacity in exchange for some guidance and say in the conduct of the war would be abortive?

I am more than aware of the intense difficulties with which we are confronted but the longer term consequences seem to be so serious as to justify the most strenuous efforts to avoid them even if events do confirm that the situation is beyond reprieve.

I have sent a copy of this minute to the Minister of Defence.

A.H.
30.4.53

Secretary of State for War
There are a lot of things happening which we rightly view with anxiety. I do not think these anxieties would be diminished by our becoming involved in the immense regions concerned. I am glad the Americans are sending some transport aircraft to the French, but I think we were quite right not to dissipate further our own limited and over-strained resources. It is not much use setting forth vague but natural desires without having some practical plans for giving effect to them. I doubt very much whether a direct communication by me to the President at this juncture would produce effective results. He would probably reply: "We, like you, are greatly concerned at the whole situation, and have already sent some aircraft. We should be very glad to know what you feel able to do." The root of the evil in Europe and in Indo-China is the French refusal to adopt two years' national service, and send conscripts abroad as we do. Their political infirmities have prevented them from doing this and they have so weak an army that they can neither defend their own country nor their Empire overseas. They have however been successful in delaying the formation of a German army for three or four years, thus weakening NATO and all that it stands for.

I am sending a copy of this Minute to the Minister of Defence.

W.S.C.
2.5.53

60 CAB 128/27/1, CC 29(54)1 15 Apr 1954

'Hong Kong: reduction of garrison': Cabinet conclusions

The Foreign Secretary drew attention to the decision taken by the Defence Committee, at their meeting on the previous day, that after the end of the Geneva Conference[1] the Hong Kong garrison should be reduced by gradual and unobtrusive stages to the level required for internal security purposes. If this decision became known to the United States authorities, it would prejudice the prospects of establishing a system of collective defence in South-East Asia and the Western Pacific. And if the Chinese got to know of it, negotiation at Geneva would be made even more difficult. He hoped, therefore, that nothing would be said to indicate to the Governor of Hong Kong, or to the military commanders in the Far East, that a decision had already been taken to reduce the garrison after the Geneva Conference.

The Prime Minister agreed that the decision taken by the Defence Committee must be kept most secret. For the time being the Governor of Hong Kong should be told that no action was being taken on the proposal to reduce the garrison and that the matter would be reviewed after the Geneva Conference. In the meantime, no hint of any kind should be given that a reduction of the garrison was contemplated.

The Cabinet:—

Invited the Colonial Secretary to inform the Governor of Hong Kong that no immediate action would be taken to reduce the garrison, that the matter would be reviewed after the Geneva Conference, and that in the meantime no hint should be given that any reduction was contemplated.

---

[1] The Geneva conference of Apr–July 1954 was convened to discuss political arrangements in Indo-China and Korea. It was attended by representatives of the USA, the UK, France, the USSR, the People's Republic of China, the Indo-Chinese countries and both Koreas. Its most notable outcome was the effective division of Vietnam into north and south along the cease-fire line that marked the formal ending of the Franco-Vietnamese war. See also 61.

61 CAB 129/68, C(54)155 27 Apr 1954

'Indo-China': Cabinet note by Sir N Brook of two emergency meetings of ministers held on 25 Apr 1954 to discuss an American proposal for Anglo-American military intervention in Indo-China

[Churchill presided over both meetings. The first, held at 11 am, was attended by Eden (FO), Alexander (Defence), Lyttelton (CO), Head (War), Lord De L'Isle (S of S for air, 1951–1955), Selwyn Lloyd (minister of state, FO), Sir R McGrigor (first sea lord), Sir J Harding (chief of imperial general staff) and Sir W Dickson (chief of air staff). The second, held at 4 pm, was attended by Eden, Alexander, Lyttelton, Macmillan (minister of housing), Selwyn Lloyd, McGrigor and Harding.]

Record of first meeting

The Foreign Secretary said that, while he had been in Paris for the meeting of the North Atlantic Council, the United States Secretary of State, Mr. Dulles, had initiated a number of conversations about the military situation in Indo-China. He had reported the gist of the conversations in Paris telegrams No. 257, No. 262 and No.

267; but the proposals which Mr. Dulles was putting forward were of such importance that he had thought it right to return to London for personal consultations before going on to the Geneva Conference. He had discussed the position with the Prime Minister immediately on his return, and they had both felt that such of their colleagues as were immediately available should be brought together at this emergency meeting so that they might have an opportunity of expressing their views before the Foreign Secretary went to Geneva.

The Foreign Secretary said that the military situation in Indo-China was extremely grave. It now seemed inevitable that the French garrison at Dien Bien Phu would be overwhelmed, or compelled to surrender. Mr. Dulles evidently feared that this would be promptly followed by the collapse of all French resistance throughout Indo-China; and, in order to avert this, he favoured some dramatic gesture of Anglo-American intervention in Indo-China. He had originally been thinking in terms of action by United States air forces for the relief of Dien Bien Phu; but he had now been persuaded that this could not in fact save the garrison there. Though he still favoured early air action he now envisaged it as a means of rallying French and Viet Namese morale elsewhere in Indo-China with a view to preventing a general collapse. Military intervention in Indo-China could not be authorised by the United States Administration without the approval of Congress; and Mr. Dulles believed that Congress would be more likely to accord this approval if the intervention were undertaken on a joint Anglo-American basis. His specific proposal was, therefore, that the United States and United Kingdom Governments should jointly give an assurance to the French that they would join in the defence of Indo-China against Communist aggression; and that, as an earnest of their intention to carry out this assurance, there should be some immediate military assistance, including participation by token British forces.

Mr. Dulles believed that an Anglo-American initiative of this kind would have a powerful moral effect in rallying the anti-Communist forces in Indo-China. He also seemed to believe that military intervention by air forces alone could make an effective contribution towards retrieving the local military situation. The Foreign Secretary said that he could not share either of these beliefs, and had done his best to make this plain in his conversations with Mr. Dulles. He was doubtful whether such intervention would have any substantial effect in rallying public opinion in Indo-China. He was certain that it would not be welcomed by nationalist opinion in South-East Asia generally. As for the military results, the limited measures which the Americans were contemplating would not, in his opinion, achieve any substantial results. Admiral Radford, the Chairman of the United States Joint Chiefs of Staff, who was with Mr. Dulles in Paris, was thinking solely in terms of attack by land-based or carrier-borne aircraft. This would have to be limited in the main to attacks on the supply columns and lines of communication of the Viet-minh troops, and was not likely to have any appreciable effect on their efficiency. Admiral Radford had not contemplated the possibility of sending ground forces into Indo-China. In fact, however, the "war" in Indo-China was a widespread insurrection, comparable to the situation with which we had originally been confronted in Malaya; and no military aid to the French could be fully effective unless it included the provision of ground troops.

The Foreign Secretary said that the French had at first showed [sic] little enthusiasm for Mr. Dulles' proposals. In particular, they had not asked us for any military help—though they had said that they would be grateful for any that we might feel able to provide. This had strengthened his view that the Americans should be discouraged from taking precipitate action on the lines envisaged by Mr. Dulles; and he had done his best to point out the dangers of this course and the limited advantage which it seemed likely to bring to the French. Finally, he had indicated that it was most unlikely that the United Kingdom Government would feel able to associate themselves with such an American initiative, and that he would certainly need to consult his colleagues in London before he could express any final view on Mr. Dulles' proposal.

The Foreign Secretary said that, after reflecting further on the matter and discussing it with the Prime Minister, his recommendation to his colleagues was that they should decline to give any immediate undertaking to afford military assistance to the French in Indo-China. It now seemed inevitable that large parts of Indo-China should fall under Communist control, and the best hope of a lasting solution lay in some form of partition. Our object should therefore be to strengthen the negotiating position of the French at the Geneva Conference. Their position would not be strengthened by a premature military intervention which would soon be seen to have been ineffective. On the contrary, he thought that France's Allies could at the moment make a better impression on the Chinese if they left them to guess what action they might subsequently take to help the French in Indo-China. He therefore suggested that, in his further discussions on this subject at Geneva, he should be guided by the following principles which he submitted for the approval of his colleagues:—

"1. We do not regard the London communiqué as committing us to join in immediate discussions on the possibility of Allied intervention in the Indo-China war.

"2. We are not prepared to give any undertakings now, in advance of Geneva, concerning United Kingdom military action in Indo-China.

"3. But we shall give all possible diplomatic support to the French delegation at Geneva in efforts to reach an honourable settlement.

"4. We can give an assurance now that if a settlement is reached at Geneva we shall join in guaranteeing that settlement and in setting up a collective defence in South-East Asia, as foreshadowed in the London communiqué, to make that joint guarantee effective.

"5. We hope that any Geneva settlement will make it possible for the joint guarantee to apply to at least the greater part of Indo-China.

"6. If no such settlement is reached we shall be prepared at that time to consider with our Allies the action to be taken jointly in the situation then existing.

"7. But we cannot give any assurance now about possible action on the part of the United Kingdom in the event of failure to reach agreement at Geneva for a cessation of hostilities in Indo-China.

"8. We shall be ready to join with the United States Government now in studying measures to ensure the defence of Siam and the rest of South-East Asia including Malaya in the event of all or part of Indo-China being lost."

In discussion the following points were made:—

(a) French morale was undoubtedly at a low ebb. If the garrison at Dien Bien Phu were overwhelmed or compelled to surrender, it was very likely that the French Government would fall. It might be succeeded by a neutralist Government. And, if after the fall of Dien Bien Phu the French abandoned the struggle in Indo-China, their position in Africa might well be undermined and their prestige as a world Power would be seriously impaired.

(b) These considerations should not, however, lead us into an unjustifiable military adventure in Indo-China. If we could have assisted in rescuing Europeans from Dien Bien Phu, this would have been an operation which could have been justified to British public opinion. This, however, was not a feasible operation. Indeed, the consensus of military opinion was that the fall of Dien Bien Phu could not be prevented by an Anglo-American air attack which could be mounted within the next few days. *The Chiefs of Staff* agreed that air operations could not now have any appreciable effect on the outcome of the battle for Dien Bien Phu.

(c) A general assurance of Anglo-American military assistance in the defence of Indo-China was bound to lead to our committing ground forces in this theatre. And, in view of the history of the campaign, it seemed likely that very substantial forces might be required over a long period. *The Chiefs of Staff* expressed the view that it was quite unrealistic to suppose that effective assistance could be given to the French in Indo-China by naval and air forces alone. It was recalled that, at the outset of their intervention in Korea, the American military authorities had similarly believed that the South Koreans could be effectively supported by naval and air action alone.

(d) It seemed likely that the air action which Admiral Radford had in mind would not be confined to Indo-China. It was known that Admiral Radford had for some time held the view that Chinese support of Communist insurrections in other countries of Asia should be checked by vigorous military action against the Chinese mainland, *e.g.*, blockade of the Chinese coast and air attack on military targets in China. He believed that direct military action could be taken against China without drawing the Soviet Union into the conflict. *The Foreign Secretary* said that he rated very much more highly the risks of such a course of military action. He considered that anything like open war with China might well involve the Soviet Union and lead to a third world war.

(e) *The Foreign Secretary* said that while he was in Paris he had taken the opportunity of discussing Mr. Dulles' proposals with the Canadian and Australian Ministers for External Affairs. Mr. Pearson[1] fully shared his view that immediate military intervention in Indo-China would be ineffective locally and would be ill received by world opinion. Mr. Casey[2] was less clear in his views: the spread of Communism throughout South-East Asia concerned Australia more nearly than Canada: but there seemed to be a good prospect that the Australian Government would support the response which we were proposing to make to Mr. Dulles' initiative.

The Prime Minister, summing up this part of the discussion, said that we should clearly be ill-advised to encourage the Americans to take precipitate military action in Indo-China. The effects of a Communist triumph at Dien Bien Phu would be grave and far-reaching. It would be greeted throughout Asia as a notable triumph of Communism over capitalism, and of Asians over Europeans. Within Indo-China opinion among the Viet Namese would at once become more unsympathetic towards

---

[1] Mr L B Pearson, Canadian minister for external affairs, 1948–1957.
[2] Mr R G Casey, Australian minister for external affairs, 1951–1960.

the French, and the local situation would certainly become much more grave. At a later stage serious threats of Communist encroachment would develop in Siam and Burma and ultimately in Malaya. But, grave though these consequences were, it did not follow that they could be averted by precipitate military action on the lines envisaged by the Americans. Therefore, he strongly recommended that the policy of the United Kingdom Government should be founded on paragraphs 4, 6 and 8 of the draft directive which the Foreign Secretary had put before his colleagues.

In discussion of this draft directive, the following further points were made:—

(f) In the measures for the defence of South-East Asia, which were contemplated in paragraph 8 of the draft directive, our primary rôle would be the defence of Malaya. It should be made clear to the Americans that we could not be expected to carry this out effectively if we were compelled to dissipate our resources in other parts of the area, *e.g.*, Siam. It was desirable that the Americans should make themselves responsible for any military assistance which might have to be given to Siam.

(g) Communist control of Indo-China would reduce the rice supplies available for the free countries of South-East Asia. *The Colonial Secretary* undertook to put in hand an immediate study of this problem, including the possibility of acquiring some of the surplus supplies of rice which were now available.

(h) If Communist encroachment spread from Indo-China to Siam, Burma and Indonesia, it would in the long run become much more difficult for us to maintain our position in Malaya. That situation was not, however, likely to arise for some time to come.

(i) The Americans were, however, disposed to exaggerate the immediate difficulties which we should encounter in Malaya. *The Colonial Secretary* and *The Minister of Defence* undertook to supply the Foreign Secretary with up-to-date information on the political and military situation in Malaya, for use in his further discussions at Geneva.

(j) If Indo-China passed under Communist control and Siam were threatened, increasing importance would attach to our military plans for sealing off Malaya against infiltration from the north. The Foreign Secretary and the Chiefs of Staff were authorised to disclose these plans in confidence to the United States authorities, in the course of their further conversations on Indo-China, and to enlist their support for them.

The Meeting:—

Agreed that the United Kingdom Government should not associate themselves with any immediate declaration of intention to afford military assistance to the French in Indo-China; and invited the Foreign Secretary, in his further discussions on this question at Geneva, to be guided by the principles embodied in paragraphs 1–8 of the draft directive set out above.

Record of second meeting
Later in the day, a further meeting was held to review the situation in the light of a communication which the French Ambassador in London had made to the Foreign Secretary after the end of the morning meeting.

At the morning meeting the Foreign Secretary had referred to a letter which Mr.

Dulles was thinking of sending to the French Foreign Minister in reply to a suggestion by the French military commander in Indo-China that nothing but an attack by American air forces could save the garrison at Dien Bien Phu. Mr. Dulles had been proposing to reply that, according to his military advice, such air intervention could not at this juncture save the garrison. He had intended, however, to add that there was no military reason why the fall of Dien Bien Phu should materially and vitally alter the military situation in Indo-China; and that, if early action were taken to establish a system of collective defence for South-East Asia, the position in Indo-China could be held by the collective action of the free nations having vital interests in the area. The letter would conclude with an offer of closer and more vigorous combination with France and a call to the French to show the resolution and the will required to enable them to overcome their present difficulties.

The Foreign Secretary said that soon after the end of the morning meeting he had learned that this letter had been delivered to the French Foreign Minister: its text was reproduced in Paris telegram No. 274. The French Ambassador in London had handed him copies of the letter and of M. Bidault's reply (Paris telegram No. 275). The reply dealt solely with the question of immediate military intervention at Dien Bien Phu. It repeated the view of the French military advisers that the garrison could still be saved by a massive intervention by American aircraft. In addition, however, M. Massigli[3] had informed the Foreign Secretary of an oral communication made to the French Ambassador in Washington on behalf of the United States Government. In this it was suggested that an immediate declaration should be made, on behalf of the Governments of the United States, the United Kingdom, France, the Philippines and the Associated States in Indo-China, proclaiming the common will of the signatories to check the expansion of Communism in South-East Asia and to use "eventual military means" for this purpose. The French Government had been urged to do everything in their power to persuade the United Kingdom Government to join in such a declaration and to co-operate forthwith in Washington in the preparation of a draft of the proposed declaration. They had been informed that, once he was assured that the United Kingdom Government would associate themselves with such a declaration, President Eisenhower would be prepared to seek Congressional approval for military intervention in Indo-China, and that it was possible that United States naval aircraft might be able to launch an attack by 28th April on the forces now besieging Dien Bien Phu. M. Massigli had strongly urged that the United Kingdom Government should at once indicate that their willingness to join in making a declaration on the lines proposed.

The Foreign Secretary said that he was disturbed by the tactics followed by the Americans in making this indirect approach to the United Kingdom Government through the French. Though a long conversation had been held with the French Ambassador in Washington, no corresponding communication had been made to Her Majesty's Ambassador there. We were being pressed to join in a general declaration of readiness to fight Communism in South-East Asia in order to support a request to Congress for authority to employ naval air forces of the United States in an air strike against the besiegers of Dien Bien Phu. The proposal for this air strike was evidently based on Admiral Radford's conviction that the time was ripe for the

---

[3] See 37, note 1.

Western Powers to show that they were ready to take direct military action to check the ambitions of Communist China in South-East Asia. Admiral Radford had admitted that naval aircraft could not intervene effectively in the actual battle at Dien Bien Phu, as the forces on either side were now so closely interlocked that direct air attack on the besiegers was no longer feasible, and he had recognised that the air strike could be made only against "second-line targets." It was evident that in this phrase he included, not only supply lines to the beseiging [sic] forces, but also airfields in China.

The Foreign Secretary said that Ministers had no authority from Parliament to support such a direct military intervention in Indo-China. Nor would the action proposed have the approval of the United Nations. Action on the lines contemplated by Admiral Radford would mean that United States air forces would become engaged in direct hostilities with China. If the United States began to wage open war against China, there was a grave risk that the Soviet Union would feel obliged to intervene. This action might therefore be the first step towards a third world war.

In discussion the *Chiefs of Staff* confirmed the view that the proposed intervention by American naval air forces could not be effective in saving the garrison at Dien Bien Phu.

The *Prime Minister* said that what we were being asked to do was in effect to aid in misleading Congress into approving a military operation which would itself be ineffective and might well bring the world to the verge of a major war. He had no doubt that this request must be rejected. He considered that the Foreign Secretary should proceed to Geneva, as planned, and should tell Mr. Dulles and M. Bidault that our military advice gave us no confidence that the fortress of Dien Bien Phu could be effectively relieved by air intervention of the kind now proposed. In any event we ourselves had no air forces which could assist in such an operation. In his further conversations the Foreign Secretary should be guided by the directive which Ministers had approved at their first meeting earlier in the day.

The Meeting:—

Reaffirmed the decision taken at the meeting earlier that day, and authorised the Foreign Secretary to reject the specific request that the United Kingdom Government should associate themselves with an immediate declaration of intention to check the expansion of Communism in South-East Asia and to use "eventual military means" for that purpose.

62   PREM 11/645   30 Apr 1954

[Colonial powers' dilemma in South-East Asia]: minute by Lord Salisbury to Lord Alexander

This[1] is an extremely interesting but most depressing assessment of the situation in Indo-China. I had no idea that the degree of Viet Minh infiltration was so great. Nor is it apparent how the French can start their recovery. The difficulty here is the same as in other parts of Asia, but more acute. There appears to be no real will on the part of the Asiatics to *fight* Communism. They don't like it; but they wont [sic] do

---

[1] Paper by Sir C Loewen (c-in-c, Far East Land Forces, 1953–1956), not printed.

anything to save themselves from it. As a result, the so-called Colonial Powers are put in the dilemma: if they don't grant a high measure of self-government, they are told that they are alienating the whole indiginous [sic] population. If they do grant a high measure of self-government, not only do they no longer control the situation themselves, but they have handed over to people who have not the will to fight for anything. That seems very much the position of the French in Indo-China now. We ought therefore I am sure to be prepared for an anti-Communist collapse in that country, and be ready to move, with the Americans, in Siam. That seems to be the clear lesson of Sir Charles Loewen's paper. But we may have to face the same difficulties with regard to Siam.

63 FO 371/111852, no 5   8 Aug 1954

'Relations with the United States, China and the Colombo powers': note by M J MacDonald (Singapore)

Our relations in Asian affairs with the (i) United States, (ii) the People's Republic of China and (iii) the "Colombo Powers" are three factors which can affect profoundly the issue whether there will be peace or war in Asia. The following are a few brief comments on these matters, made almost wholly from the point of view of an observer in South-East Asia.

(i) *The United States*

2. The conduct of American foreign policy towards Asia during recent months has left the United States with few friends, many enemies and almost universal critics amongst Asian Governments and peoples. It has done America's reputation shattering harm, appears sometimes to Asians to support the Communist contention that the United States are the real "war-mongers" in the world, and has left the United States virtually isolated here except for the support of some of the least influential Asian nations, like Siam and Chinese Nationalist Formosa. Yet fundamentally the Americans believe in and are striving for similar political ideas to those which most Asian Governments support. It is appalling that American statements and actions have caused such gigantic misunderstandings, and that the vast influence which America could exert for good has been turned to grave disadvantage to us all.

3. For the United States are not the only sufferers. In spite of the United Kingdom Government's remarkable success in pursuing a different policy at the Geneva Conference—which has distinctly increased our reputation and influence throughout Asia—we are regarded as being either too much under American influence or else too incapable of countering it to achieve adequate independence in international affairs. American policy is generally regarded as dominating all Western policy towards Asia, and the Asians are inclining to feel increasingly pessimistic about the chances of fruitful understanding and co-operation between them and "the West."

4. If we are to maintain a reasonable measure of sympathy and ultimately, agreement by the majority of Asian countries with "Western" policy, the United Kingdom must:–

(a) continue to pursue, as far as the overriding necessity for co-operation with the United States permits, its own unfettered foreign policy towards Asian affairs, and

(b) seek by every possible means to influence American policy—and the statement and conduct of that policy (for often these are more at fault than the policy itself)—in the same direction.

5. Unless the misunderstanding and hostility which is growing between America and Asia is checked, enmity between the two may become for a period irreconcilable—with grave results.

(ii) *Communist China*

6. The contacts between the British and Chinese representatives at Geneva have clearly led to some (at least) slight improvement in political and diplomatic relations between their two countries. If we can take advantage of this situation to achieve gradually a further improvement—without it causing a serious deterioration in Anglo-American relations (which is admittedly difficult in present circumstances)—the result might be a real relaxing of international tension in Southern Asia. We must be careful of course, not to fall into any Chinese Communist "traps".

7. There is one aspect of this which has particular importance to us in South-East Asia. One of our major problems, and dangers, is the existence of considerable populations of "Overseas" Chinese in several countries in the region. The difficulty is that the great majority of them still owe their primary loyalty to China, are liable to yield to pressure from the existing Government in Peking (whatever its political complexion), and are therefore now a potential "fifth column" for further Communist advances in South-East Asia.

8. This tendency has been supported in the past by:—

(a) the policy of successive Chinese Governments that all "Overseas" Chinese remain Chinese nationals debarred from becoming nationals of the countries of their adoption; and,
(b) the complementary policy of the local Governments in treating their Chinese residents as foreigners, and refusing them citizenship rights.

9. It appears that during their recent conversations with Mr. Chou En-lai,[1] Mr. Nehru[2] in Delhi and U Nu[3] in Rangoon both urged the Chinese Prime Minister to change the traditional Chinese policy, and that Mr. Chou said something to the effect that his Government might make a declaration that "Overseas" Chinese should become nationals of their country of adoption or else cease to interfere in local politics. Such a declaration would have a great effect for good amongst the Chinese in South-East Asia and in particular would help us in Malaya to realise our policy of turning the primary loyalty of the local Chinese from China to Malaya. Admittedly Mr. Chou may be at least partly insincere in his professions, and may have some ulterior Communist motive in suggesting a declaration of the kind; nevertheless whatever his purposes, we could exploit such a statement greatly to our advantage.

10. I urge therefore that we should:—

(a) encourage Mr. Nehru, U Nu (and Indonesian leaders also) to continue to put judicious pressure on Mr. Chou to confirm and publicise the suggested new policy;

---

[1] Chou En-lai, premier of the People's Republic of China, 1949–1976.

[2] J Nehru, prime minister of India, 1947–1964.

[3] U Nu, prime minister of Burma, 1947–1956, 1957–1962.

(b) use our own increased influence with the Government in Peking—if Mr. Trevelyan[4] judges that prudent—towards the same purpose.

(iii) The "Colombo Powers"

11. The success of our policy in South-East Asia depends partly on general sympathy and, if possible, active support for it by the Governments and peoples in the region, and by those of India, Pakistan and Ceylon. If these are estranged from us and oppose our policy, it has comparatively little chance of success; but if they approve and support us, it has a good prospect. This is one direction in which the Americans have taken a wrong turn, for they seem to underestimate the importance of securing the understanding of public opinion in Southern Asia. Nothing in United Kingdom policy has been more admirable than our close contact throughout the Geneva and subsequent negotiations with the "Colombo Powers." It has made a most friendly impression in Asia, given many Asian leaders a clear understanding of our motives and aims, increased our influence throughout Asia, and prevented a much worse division of opinion than now exists between "the West" and Asia from arising.

12. The Governments of the "Colombo Powers," as a whole, are irresolute and weak in their recognition of the Communist threat to their countries and the world, and their belief in "neutrality" makes our task of averting that threat exceedingly difficult. Nevertheless, they are slowly but surely learning the facts of international life, and are moving gradually towards the adoption of more positive and helpful foreign policies. I have had unique opportunities, during periodic visits to some of their capitals over the last six years, to watch this evolution in their thinking. In Rangoon, for example, the development has been continuous and marked, if slow, and the change in thought exists not only amongst responsible Ministers, but also amongst many prominent local journalists, and other fashioners of public opinion. I believe that in most of the "Colombo" countries these processes will continue, if we remain patient and understanding in our relations with them, and especially if the United Kingdom Government keeps in close, friendly, influential touch with their Government—and can prevent the Americans from taking drastic actions which will disastrously alienate them.

---

[4] H Trevelyan (KCMG 1955, Baron 1968), British chargé d'affaires in Peking, 1953–1955.

64   CAB 131/14, D(54)41   3 Dec 1954
'Defence in South-East Asia': memorandum by COS for Cabinet Defence Committee

[Macmillan circulated this memo to the Defence Committee on 16 Dec 1954. He suggested that it should be despatched to the prime ministers of Australia and New Zealand as background for the discussions at the Commonwealth Prime Ministers' Conference. He also explained that the memo did not represent the final views of the COS who were awaiting the outcome of the current ANZAM planning talks in Singapore and those of the Manila Treaty Working Party in Washington.[1]]

---

[1] ANZAM, denoting Australia, New Zealand and the Malayan area, was a planning mechanism for the co-ordination of the defence of air and sea communications in the region. It operated from 1948 until shortly after Malaya's independence in 1957 (see 65, note). The Manila Treaty of 8 Sept 1954 established

The purpose of this memorandum is to review the present problems of defence in South-East Asia, with particular reference to Malaya, and the measures necessary to meet the increased potential threat to that region.

Importance of South-East Asia
2. It is necessary to block the spread of Communism in South-East Asia. Politically the area is unstable and positive action is needed if the peoples and countries are to be retained in the Free World. Their loss to Communism would be a major defeat. Economically it is of great importance to retain the resources of South-East Asia and to deny them to the Communists. Strategically, control of the area with its sea and air communications prevents a direct threat to Australia and New Zealand. The focus of the communications through the area lies in Singapore. It is essential therefore that the surrounding territories remain in the Free World.

The threat
3. The threat to South-East Asia comes from the inherent weakness of the Governments of the area, coupled with the expansionist policy of Communism backed by the massive armed forces of China and her satellites. The Communists are unlikely to employ open aggression at present to further their expansion in South-East Asia; but political pressure and subversion are more effective if employed with the knowledge of massive armed support in the background. The degree to which vulnerable countries of South-East Asia are threatened is outlined in the following paragraphs.

General situation in South-East Asia
4. It seems probable that Southern Viet Nam will come increasingly under Communist influence within the next two years (a state of affairs which is likely to be reflected in the results of the 1956 election). If so, Laos and Cambodia may well follow suit. In this event the threat to Siam would crystallize sooner than expected at present.
5. In Siam the situation is at present stable and Western influence in the country is increasing; but the Siamese Government has insufficient popular support to be sure of weathering an economic crisis which might well create a situation beyond its control. If the Communists gain control of the whole of Indo-China, the Siamese Government would be subjected to great pressure in the hope of discouraging them from their association with the Western powers and inducing them to be more co-operative towards Communism.
6. In Burma the political situation is reasonably firm. If there is no major deterioration in the country's economy, Communism is unlikely to make any headway without active outside support.
7. In Indonesia the present unstable conditions are likely to continue and may well deteriorate in the near future owing to the increasing propaganda and activity of the Communist Party and the instability of the present Government. The country is therefore liable to be used by the Communists as a base for subversive activities in neighbouring countries.

---

the South-East Asia Treaty Organisation (SEATO), which brought three Asian countries—Pakistan, the Philippines and Thailand—into a collective defence alliance with the USA, the UK, France, Australia and New Zealand.

8. The internal situation in Malaya has improved but the end of the emergency is likely to be a matter of years rather than of months. It will continue as long as there is hope by some, and fear by others, of further Communist expansion towards and into Malaya.

9. We have previously stated that should control of the Tongking Delta be lost, the threat to South-East Asia generally would increase. This has now occurred, and in spite of the Geneva settlement there is every indication that the spread of Communism has not been halted. Hence the threat to South-East Asia is likely to continue to increase.

Measures to meet the threat

10. The method of combatting subversion is to aid countries to build up a sound administration and security forces and to assist them to stand on their own feet economically. Neither of these are in themselves sufficient unless the Free World makes it clear that it is able and determined to defend the area against open aggression. The solution of this problem depends largely on our ability to enlist speedily the determined support of the leaders and people of the free South-East Asian countries in the struggle against Communism.

11. From the military viewpoint, an essential factor in the maintenance of internal security is the existence of strong reliable, well trained and well equipped forces including police. The establishment of such forces would contribute not only to internal security but also to the general defence of South-East Asia.

12. The free nations cannot match the Communists in the numerical strength of field forces, nor should they attempt to do so. In building up the defence of the area against open aggression therefore, the free nations should establish sufficient forces both to convince the Asian countries of their determination to defend South-East Asia and to act as a deterrent, backed by superiority of weapons.

The Manila Treaty

13. The South-East Asia Collective Defence Treaty (SEACDT)[2] has laid the foundation for achieving a measure of stability in certain countries but as yet it has no military machinery. It is therefore not yet effective in providing the military solution to the problems discussed above. The United States attitude at the Manila Conference favoured a loosely knit organisation, while the United Kingdom, Australia and New Zealand would have preferred military planning machinery for co-ordinating defence in the area. It would be dangerous for the Free World to await the next crisis in South-East Asia before taking the necessary steps to set up this military machinery.

The Melbourne proposals

14. The aim of the Melbourne Proposals was to strengthen the defence of South-East Asia, including Malaya. Australia has now accepted in principle the main recommendations of the Melbourne Report. She has also initiated individual discussions between the Australian Chiefs of Staff and United Kingdom Commanders-in-Chief, Far East. Australia has, however, emphasised that before any of her forces can be firmly committed to the defence of Malaya, effective co-

---

[2] ie, the Manila Treaty.

ordination with United States strategic planning and assurance of support from United States forces in the defence of South-East Asia are ultimately essential. New Zealand has not yet endorsed the Melbourne Proposals, but has, nevertheless, agreed to be represented at the combined planning meeting in Singapore.

Defence of Malaya

15. It is of the greatest importance that the Commonwealth countries should press on with constructive plans for the defence of Malaya and thus demonstrate to the Americans our determination to help ourselves. In this lies the greatest hope of securing United States co-operation in the long run.

16. Malaya is economically and strategically of the greatest importance to the United Kingdom and is the first line of defence for Australia and New Zealand. The United Kingdom is determined to hold in Malaya and to make the maximum military contribution to its defence that we can afford. The United Kingdom, Australia and New Zealand should be capable of jointly providing sufficient forces for the defence of Malaya against all but a full scale Communist attack, and in such an event we could almost certainly count on American assistance on the sea and in the air.

17. The defence of Malaya must be considered in the light of the situation in Siam. Militarily the only position from which the United Kingdom or Common-wealth forces can defend Malaya against an over land attack is Songkhla in the Kra Isthmus in Southern Siam. With the forces immediately available the operation to occupy this position could only be carried out against virtually no opposition and must therefore be completed before the Communists could forestall us.

18. Apart from open aggression, the Communists might establish themselves in Siam either by a *coup d'état* or as a result of a gradual swing to Communism. We consider the latter to be more probable. In both these eventualities, however, we appreciate that the launching of the operation might have grave political implica-tions, especially if it could be construed as unilateral action without the agreement of a fellow member of the United Nations and a co-signatory of the Manila Treaty. In the case of a gradual swing to Communism, the timing of a decision to occupy the Songkhla position might be most difficult from the standpoint of justifying it to the world, as the threat to Malaya might not be openly apparent. However, it is considered that such a deterioration in the situation in South-East Asia would be the subject of consultations under the framework of the Manila Treaty with the object of reducing this difficulty.

19. A United Kingdom plan has been prepared for the initial occupation of the Songkhla position but the forces in Malaya are inadequate to hold it against a sustained or heavy Communist attack. Once the operation was launched Malaya would have to be reinforced from the United Kingdom, unless global war was imminent, but we would also require Australian and New Zealand reinforcements. We hope that the military need for executing this plan will become progressively less as the SEACDT organisation gains in strength.

20. The immediate consequences of launching the operation would be certain to include an increase in terrorist activity in Malaya and, at the least, increased tension between the Western Powers and China.

Commonwealth Far East Strategic Reserve

21. The early formation of the Commonwealth Far East Strategic Reserve, as

agreed at the Melbourne Conference, would be the first step to strengthen the position in Malaya. The presence in Malaya of Australian and New Zealand forces would increase the deterrent and would make a deep impression on neighbouring countries. At the same time this reserve could be available to support SEACDT. The planned composition of the reserve agreed at Melbourne is outlined at Appendix.[3]

22. We appreciate that care would be required in the presentation to the Malayan rulers and people of the increased share in their defence to be undertaken by Australia and New Zealand. It is essential to avoid giving them any impression that this represents an attempt on the part of the United Kingdom to escape from its obligations towards them.

---

[3] Not printed.

---

65   FO 371/116915, no 12   11 Aug 1955
[Defence policy in South-East Asia]: letter from A G Gilchrist[1]
(Singapore) to W D Allen[2]   [Extract]

[When the COS memo (see 64) was discussed in the Cabinet Defence Committee, the point was made that 'our declared policy of bringing about the independence of Malaya in due course was regarded in Malaya and also in Australia as being to some extent inconsistent with our strategic aim of building up the strength of Commonwealth forces in Malaya as a focal point for the defence of South-East Asia'. It was therefore very important to think about 'future measures' for the regions's defence (CAB 134/14, D 7(54)2, 20 Dec 1954). In the knowledge that doubts existed about the strength of Britain's commitment to the defence of the region after independence, Lennox-Boyd in Feb 1955 wrote a paper 'United Kingdom aims in Malaya' (see part II of this volume, 347) in which he listed, as one of four essential preconditions for independence, 'agreement upon measures which would at once afford the country security against external aggression and provide the free world with . . . [a] firm base for defence against Communist attack'.]

. . . [T]he Secretary of State for the Colonies' paper on "U.K. aims in Malaya" provided just the right assurances about H.M.G.'s policy for the Commanders in Chief and enabled us to carry them with us. Astonishing as it might seem to you, none of them was previously aware of the fact that it was Her Majesty's Government's policy to safeguard the future of the base [Singapore] by the negotiation of a defence agreement or that H.M.G. were determined to link the questions of a Defence Agreement and Independence in the way which is so clearly set out in the paper. . . .

3. Considerable stress has been laid in the SEACOS telegrams to which I have referred on the question of reassuring both our ANZAM and SEACDT allies about the aims of H.M.G.'s policy in South East Asia and the Far East. That there is anxiety, or at least doubt, about our policy in the minds of these people is certain. Air Marshal Fressanges[3] brought back this impression from his recent trip to Australia and New Zealand. General Loewen came back from this month's meeting of the Military Advisers at Bangkok with the same feeling. I myself have noticed it in conversation with our American friends here and a Royal Navy officer serving on the staff of

---

[1] A G Gilchrist, FO counsellor on staff of commissioner-general in South-East Asia, 1954–1956.
[2] W D Allen, Far Eastern Dept, FO; deputy commissioner-general in South-East Asia, 1959–1962.
[3] Air Marshal Sir F Fressanges, c-in-c, Far East Air Forces, 1954–1957.

CINCPAC at Pearl Harbour made exactly the same point to me the other day. I do not think therefore that we can afford to ignore it. What positive action we can take to counter it is more difficult to determine. We have however tried to make some recommendations in SEACOS 21. As we see it, the people who must at all costs be reassured and made to feel that they are fully in our confidence are the governments of Australia, New Zealand and the United States. Without confidence between us joint planning can never become a reality. Therefore, I should greatly hope that the U.K. High Commissioners at Wellington and Canberra and our Embassy in Washington could be authorised to show the paper on U.K. aims to the three governments, emphasising of course its highly secret nature. We would also like to show it to Watt[4] and Shanahan[5] here. I am sure that it would impress them as no reiteration of past statements would.

4. Clearly we cannot go so far in regard to our other SEACDT allies.[6] It is for consideration, however, whether at the next full meeting of the Council an occasion might not be made for a statement on Malaya by our representative on much the same lines as we make statements in the NATO Council about events of current interest. This would provide a suitable framework for the necessary phrases.

5. Apart from educating our Allies, there is also the question of making clear to the general public and above all to the politicians in Malaya that Her Majesty's Government's long term intention is to link the granting of independence to the conclusion of a satisfactory Defence Agreement. This is a point which for obvious reasons has never previously been made in public and which I well understand cannot be made in public even now in so many words. We must, nevertheless, try to get the idea across to the public by every possible means and we should all always have it in mind when statements about the future of Malaya are made, whether in the United Kingdom or here or in third countries, so that at least a glancing reference to it can be worked in. . . .[7]

---

[4] Sir A Watt, Australian commissioner in South-East Asia, 1954–1956.

[5] F Shanahan, New Zealand commissioner in South-East Asia, 1955–1958.

[6] ie, France, Pakistan, the Philippines and Thailand.

[7] An Anglo-Malayan defence agreement was subsequently negotiated in tandem with the negotiations for Malaya's independence. The defence agreement was concluded in Oct 1957, superseding ANZAM. See BDEEP series B, A J Stockwell, ed, *Malaya*.

---

66   CAB 134/1315, PR(56)26   23 July 1956

'Report on political, economic and information measures in East Asia': report by the Official Committee on East Asia Policy[1] for Cabinet Policy Review Committee

Part I: Introduction
The Committee was set up by the Policy Review Committee with the following terms of reference—

---

[1] This was an inter-departmental committee of officials chaired by Lord Reading, minister of state at the FO.

R

"To examine political, economic and information measures for the maintenance and promotion of United Kingdom interests in Eastern Asia, bearing in mind that it is the objective of Her Majesty's Government to reduce military commitments in that area; and to report to the Policy Review Committee through the Foreign Secretary."

2.   Since no estimates of possible savings in military expenditure were or at this stage could be available to the Committee, we decided that our first task should be to examine our current expenditure in the area, which we defined as the whole of South and South-East Asia and the Far East from Afghanistan to Japan inclusive. This showed how small a proportion of our total expenditure in the area we devote at present to developing our dependent territories and to assisting the Commonwealth and foreign countries with technical and other aid.

3.   There is no doubt that during the past five or six years we have lost many opportunities for maintaining and extending our influence in the area. Not only have we been obliged to reject a substantial number of requests made to us for assistance of all kinds but we have been unable ourselves to take the initiative in offering help. It is not surprising therefore that some of the countries of the area are beginning to look for help to the Soviet Union and China.

4.   There are still opportunities open to us. If we fail to seize them now while at the same time we reduce our military strength, our influence throughout the area will begin to decline rapidly. But there is this in our favour, that even modest increases in the sums spent at present on non-military methods of maintaining our influence have a disproportionately great effect on our efforts to achieve that object.

5.   Other Commonwealth countries Canada, Australia and New Zealand are also closely concerned in the problems of Eastern Asia, particularly in the sphere of defence and development. We should aim at concerting any new plans for development closely with the above Governments, whose financial assistance would also be valuable.

Part II: Current United Kingdom expenditure in the area

6.   In 1956/57 non-military expenditure will be about £9.5 millions, of which in round figures £4.5 millions will fall to the Colonial territories, £1.6 millions to Commonwealth countries and £1.8 millions to other countries, the balance going to International Organisations in the area and other miscellaneous items.

7.   This non-military expenditure will be broadly divided as follows:—

	£
Colonial Service Vote	625,000
Colonial Development Corporation	2,400,000
Colonial Development and Welfare	1,407,000
Colombo Plan	931,000
Representation Costs	1,846,000
Information Services	382,000
British Council	331,000
British Broadcasting Corporation	120,000
International Bodies	557,000
Miscellaneous	867,000
	£9,466,000

8.   In addition to the annual expenditure tabulated certain Government loans or

credits for special purposes have been and are in future likely to be extended to countries in the area. Other similar commitments may also have to be contemplated. The problems involved, however, are of a substantially different kind from those concerned directly with the presentation of the British standpoint or the development of British territories.

9. Total military expenditure in the area is difficult to assess. But on a balance of payments basis alone it will amount to £51 millions in 1956/57.

10. It is evident that at present the emphasis in our expenditure is very heavily on the military side, though the non-military expenditure is subject to marked variations from year to year and the figure of £9.5 millions cannot be taken as necessarily representative of our past and future commitments in the area. The basic question for consideration is whether this deployment of our resources is best suited to promote and protect our interests in view of the changed nature of the threat to them and the present state of our economy.

Part III: Future needs

11. The Colonial Office, Commonwealth Relations Office and Foreign Office have for the purposes of this Committee drawn up their own tentative programmes for projects which in their view are the most urgently needed in the territories with which they deal. The extent to which these projects can be carried out must depend upon the money available. But certain general conclusions may be drawn from the Departments' statements about the form which any increased non-military expenditure might most usefully take in the event of a reduction of our military commitments.

(i) Much needs doing in order to improve the security and welfare of our dependent territories, especially in regard to the problems of Chinese schools in Singapore, Malaya and Borneo, housing in Hong Kong and the development of the Borneo territories.

(ii) The Colombo Plan must remain the chief instrument of United Kingdom economic aid to the independent Commonwealth and foreign countries. The funds we can supply are so small in relation to the development needs of the area that they must continue to be devoted primarily to the Technical Co-operation Scheme. But there is a strong case for increasing our contribution to that scheme (at present £1 million a year) and especially the amount of aid given to foreign member countries (at present only one-fifth of the total). With more money to spend we could also aim to accept a limited number of requests for small-scale capital aid. This would be of particular political advantage in those countries which are not yet sufficiently developed to benefit adequately from the Technical Co-operation Scheme. In order to prevent misunderstanding and to scotch any idea that capital aid on a large scale was being made available we should need to make at an appropriate moment a carefully worded statement of the exact amount of money involved and of the ways in which we proposed to spend it.

(iii) Both within S.E.A.T.O. and outside it we need to intensify the efforts already being made, especially through training courses in Malaya and the United Kingdom, to strengthen the administration and internal security of the independent countries of South-East Asia.

(iv) There are also measures of assistance to the armed forces of Asian countries which, although their military value may be small, nevertheless offer opportunities for the exertion of political influence which we cannot afford to ignore. These measures would include assistance in the expansion, development, equipment and training of the armed forces of certain countries in the area.

(v) Any reduction in our military strength will make it all the more necessary to intensify our information and cultural activities. There is still, for example, an unsatisfied demand for the teaching of English. Increased activity in this field by the British Council and by our information services and the British Council in related fields could be a highly important means of maintaining our influence, especially in non-S.E.A.T.O. countries such as Burma, Ceylon, India, the Indo-China States, Indonesia and Japan.

Part IV: Illustrative programmes for additional expenditure

12. We have set out below three programmes based on additional annual expenditure of £1 million, £2 millions and £3 millions respectively.

Items	Estimated cost (£'000) Programmes		
	I	II	III
Colonial Office			
1. Chinese education and contributions to general development in N. Borneo and Sarawak	250	500	800
2. Hong Kong—housing, social services, development and University.	150	400	600
3. Expanding United Kingdom Information Services in Malaya and Singapore and British Council activities there and in N. Borneo and Sarawak.	100	100	100
Foreign Office			
4. Colombo Plan	150	250	500
5. Security measures	25	75	125
6. Information	10	110	110
7. Cultural activities	65	65	65
Commonwealth Relations Office			
8. Colombo Plan	125	250	350
9. Service items, e.g., training, military equipment	35	65	135
10. Information and British Council	55	125	155
11. Staff (non-information)	35	60	60
TOTAL (£'000)	1,000	2,000	3,000

13. These programmes are designed simply to illustrate what might be done with certain sums. Even the largest of them would be no more than a beginning towards meeting some of the more urgent problems confronting us in our own dependent territories and towards taking advantage of some of the opportunities still open to us in Commonwealth and foreign countries. They have inevitably been prepared in London without consultations with our various overseas representatives and with the Colonial Governments concerned.

14. Increased expenditure in South-East Asia even at the rate of £3 millions a year would not make certain of matching everywhere the Russian and Chinese effort. But that cannot be our aim. We should rather concentrate on certain key fields, developing tried policies rather than initiating new ones.

15. In many fields shortage of man-power and facilities is a limiting factor as well as shortage of money. In drawing up these illustrative programmes account has been taken of these shortages. They are therefore of necessity modest in relation to the needs of the area. In some fields the expansion of our activities might have to be gradual over the years. The essential thing is that the effort, once begun, should be sustained and where possible intensified as opportunities present themselves.

Part V: Recommendations
16. We recommend that the Policy Review Committee should:—

(i) indicate, if necessary on a provisional basis, the annual increase to be aimed at in non-military expenditure in the area, in the light both of whatever reductions in military expenditure may be decided upon and of other financial commitments in the rest of the world;
(ii) approve the general lines of such additional expenditure, as set out in this report;
(iii) authorise the Departments concerned, in consultation with United Kingdom representatives and Colonial Governments in the area, to formulate detailed schemes within the general framework of the illustrative programmes set out in Part IV of this report.

67 CAB 131/17, DC 7(56)2   2 Oct 1956
'Malaya: reduction of the army garrison': Cabinet Defence Committee minutes

The Committee had before them a report by the Chiefs of Staff (D.C. (56) 22) proposing reductions in the Army garrison in Malaya and a memorandum by the Commonwealth Secretary (D.C. (56) 24) about the likely reactions of the Australian and New Zealand Governments to these proposals.

The Chief of the Imperial General Staff[1] said the agreed Army garrison in Malaya after the country had achieved independence was one and one-third divisions. In view of the improvement in the emergency situation in Malaya, the Chiefs of Staff considered that certain major units which were surplus to the long-term order of battle could be withdrawn when they had completed their present tours of duty. There would be political advantages in carrying out these reductions in the Army garrison before Malaya achieved independence. The proposals would involve the withdrawal of two British infantry battalions in December 1956 and June 1957 respectively and one British armoured car regiment in May 1957. An African infantry battalion would not complete its tour until February 1958, but the Government of Malaya should be consulted about the possibility of withdrawing it earlier. The Malayan Government might also wish to retain the Special Air Service Regiment,

---
[1] Sir G Templer.

since there was likely to be a continuing operation requirement for this unit after independence. He suggested that in accordance with the undertaking given at the Malayan Constitutional Conference earlier this year, the Federation Government should be consulted about all these reductions.

The Commonwealth Secretary said that the Australian Government would be likely to regard these reductions as inconsistent with the numerous assurances they had been given about our determination to defend Malaya in the event of war. There had been considerable difficulty in persuading both the Australian and New Zealand Governments to contribute forces to the Commonwealth Strategic Reserve in Malaya and if United Kingdom units were now to be withdrawn the other two Governments would probably take the opportunity of reducing their own contributions. Moreover, the Policy Review might involve reductions in naval and air forces in the Malayan area and possibly, further reductions in the Army garrison. The confidence of the Australian and New Zealand Governments in our defence plans for Malaya would be seriously undermined if a series of force reductions were to be announced piece-meal. It would be preferable, therefore, not to make any reductions, with the possible exception of withdrawing the infantry battalion in December 1956, until the Australian and New Zealand Governments could be given a comprehensive picture of our future intentions with regard to all three Services in the whole area. At least, the two Governments should not be notified of any decision to withdraw the second battalion and the armoured car regiment until such reductions could be related to a full re-appraisal of global defence strategy as a result of the Policy Review.

The Colonial Secretary emphasised the importance of honouring the undertaking to consult the Malayan Government before making any substantial changes in the size of the United Kingdom and Commonwealth forces in Malaya. The Suez crisis and the need to re-route troop ships round the Cape had increased the difficulties of reinforcing Malaya in the event of a sudden emergency. The Malayan Government would not wish to retain any forces in Malaya unnecessarily. They were, however, relying on the United Kingdom forces to make a major effort to eradicate the remaining Communist terrorists before the country achieved independence, and there might well be suspicions that these withdrawals constituted an attempt to delay the grant of independence unless all the circumstances were fully explained to them in advance.

In further discussion the following points were made:—

(a) The main object in obtaining force contributions from Australia and New Zealand to the Commonwealth Strategic Reserve in Malaya had been to reduce the relative burden on the United Kingdom in providing for the defence of an area which was of vital importance also to these two countries.

(b) The proposed reductions could be fully justified, both to the Malayan Government and to the Governments of Australia and New Zealand on the ground that there were at present in Malaya more units than at the height of the emergency in 1951. Since then, the overt threat from Communist terrorists had been considerably reduced and the efficiency of the anti-terrorist operations had been increased by greater use of helicopters and the provision of better equipment, weapons and vehicles.

(c) Any delays in reducing the number of units in Malaya would aggravate the problem of providing permanent accommodation for the troops. Considerable additional capital expenditure would already be required for this purpose.

(d) It was proposed to retain an additional battalion in the garrison at Hong Kong as a strategic reserve for the Far East. This battalion would be available to reinforce Malaya in an emergency.

(e) It would be inadvisable at this stage to inform the military authorities in the South East Asia Treaty Organisation about these proposed reductions in Malaya. The Commissioner General for South-East Asia would be made aware of these reductions through the British Defence Co-ordinating Committee, Far East.

(f) *The Chancellor of the Exchequer* said that the future strength of the Army garrison in Malaya would necessarily be considered further in the course of the Policy Review.

The Committee:—

(1) Approved the proposals in D.C. (56) 22 for reducing the Army garrison in Malaya.

(2) Invited the Colonial Secretary to arrange for the Government of Malaya to be consulted about these proposals.

(3) Invited the Commonwealth Secretary to consider, in the light of the discussion, how and when the Australian and New Zealand Governments should be informed of these proposals.

68 CAB 131/17, DC 1(57)3 3 Jan 1957
'Garrison in Hong Kong': Cabinet Defence Committee minutes

The Minister of Defence said that the recent riots in Hong Kong had caused the Governor to reassess the troops required for internal security. He had asked for seven battalions for this role which would involve a heavy commitment for this limited purpose. It might be better to make a greater effort to expand the police force in Hong Kong in order to reduce the number of troops required. The Services were now working out what forces would be available for deployment to meet overseas commitments in accordance with the new long-term defence policy. Later in the month he would be in a better position to see to what extent the Governor's wishes could be met. It was almost certain that we should not be able to meet his full requirements.

The Prime Minister said that it would be desirable to have a jet aircraft squadron based on Hong Kong. This might be provided by redeploying one of the squadrons at present in Malaya, while retaining its present commitment in support of the South-East Asia Treaty Organisation.

In the discussion on the internal security aspect it was pointed out that Hong Kong was the only British territory which was contiguous with the Iron Curtain and internal security was therefore a difficult problem, particularly in view of the large population. On the other hand, the Colony was wealthy and should be able to afford the cost of providing a larger police force.

The Committee:—

(1) Took note that the Minister of Defence would submit a paper later in the month showing what forces could be provided for the garrison at Hong Kong, taking into account the world-wide deployment of the forces.

(2) Invited the Colonial Secretary to examine the possibility of strengthening the police forces in Hong Kong.

69 FO 371/96672, no 44   24 Dec 1952

[International defence co-operation in West Africa]: letter from A Rumbold[1] (Paris) to R Allen[2]

[In Aug 1951 Britain and South Africa jointly convened an African Defence Facilities Conference in Nairobi. The other participants were Belgium, Ethiopia, France, Italy, Portugal and Southern Rhodesia; the US sent observers. The conference dealt with the logistical problems of moving troops and supplies between Southern Africa and the Middle East in the event of war or emergency, and was generally regarded as successful. Shortly afterwards France proposed a conference in Dakar to deal with similar problems in West Africa. Britain found itself embarrassed by this proposal. Rumbold wrote to S A Lockhart (African Dept, FO) on 4 Feb 1952: 'We could not very well exclude the South Africans in view of their earnest interest in these problems, nor could we exclude the West African Ministers; yet, for reasons which the French would understand, we could not have both at the same table. Moreover it was highly unlikely that the West African Ministers would be able at their present stage of political development to restrain themselves from raising controversial political issues at the conference and thereby wrecking it completely' (FO 371/96672, no 8).]

I wrote to Lockhart on the 4th February (1192/3/52) about the French desire to hold a second African defence facilities conference at Dakar. We heard nothing further from them about this proposal until the 23rd December when Wilford[3] was asked to call at the Quai d'Orsay to see Jurgensen[4] and Blanchard.

2. After giving him the French Government's reply about the communication of the report of the Nairobi Conference to the N.A.T.O. Standing Group (about which we have reported separately by despatch) Jurgensen went on to say that the French Government remained exceedingly anxious to hold a second conference, which would be complementary to that held at Nairobi and would deal with that part of Africa south of the Sahara which had not been covered at Nairobi. He went on to explain that no approach had so far been made to any other Governments since it was the wish of the French Government that Her Majesty's Government should first of all be invited not only to participate, but if they so wished to be co-hosts with the French. (See however paragraph 6 below.)

3. Jurgensen then said that, so far as other participants were concerned, the French Government were of the opinion that Belgium, Portugal and Liberia should be invited to attend. He then raised the question of Spain. The French Government would be glad to know whether Her Majesty's Government considers that Spain should also be invited to attend in view of her interest in West Africa. Wilford said that he personally thought that Her Majesty's Government would not be in favour of her participation and Jurgensen replied that the French Government leaned towards that view, but would like our opinion.

4. The object of the conference would be to consider virtually the same questions in connexion with West Africa as had been covered at Nairobi in relation to East Africa. The main purpose would be to consider the strategic position of West Africa with particular reference to its importance as the base from which lines of

---

[1] A Rumbold, counsellor, British embassy, Paris, 1951–1954.

[2] R Allen, head of African Dept, FO, 1950–1953; assistant under-secretary of state, 1953–1954.

[3] K M Wilford, British embassy, Paris.

[4] J D Jurgensen, sous-directeur d'Afrique-Levant, Quai d'Orsay, 1951–1955. Blanchard was Jurgensen's assistant.

communication lead northward to Tunisia and Morocco and north-eastward to the Middle East. Jurgensen handed to Wilford the attached proposals[5] for the agenda of the Conference which is largely based on the Nairobi agenda.

5. So far as timing was concerned, the French Government were of the opinion that the preparations for the conference would take about two or three months and they therefore thought that it might be held in March or April 1953. They would be very happy if it were decided to hold the conference at Dakar, but were not in any way wedded to this venue and would like Her Majesty's Government's views on this also if they were to decide to participate.

6. Finally Jurgensen said that the United States Government had been informed in confidence of the fact that the French were considering holding such a conference and had reacted very favourably to the idea. He thought that they would again ask to be represented by observers as they had been at Nairobi.

7. It was clear from the conversation which followed that the French have devised their plan in such a way as to make it as difficult as possible for us to quote our desire to avoid seating West and South Africans at the same table as an excuse for not attending such a conference. They stressed that by pointing out the complementary nature of the proposed conference with that at Nairobi (which the South Africans attended) there would be no need—unless we so wished—to invite the South Africans again. Thus they feel that they have met the points which we made to them as reported in my letter under reference.

8. They are obviously extremely anxious that such a conference should be held and Wilford got the definite impression that a refusal by Her Majesty's Government to attend, while it would be deplored, would not necessarily dissuade the French Government from holding a conference with the other interested parties.

9. So far as representation of the British territories in the area was concerned, Jurgensen said that it was entirely a matter for Her Majesty's Government to settle and that any solution proposed by them would be accepted. Thus he did not know whether the Gold Coast would be represented by a national delegation or not, and there was also the question of South Africa to which I have referred above.

10. I well understand the difficulties which face the Colonial Office and the Commonwealth Relations Office as regards this problem, but I feel bound to say that from the point of view of this post there seems every advantage in getting together as the French propose and planning together for all eventualities. I hope therefore that the matter will be given favourable consideration since it is obvious that the French have done their best to meet the preoccupations which we have previously expressed to them.

11. I attach three spare copies of this letter, but am not sending it direct to anyone else.[6]

---

[5] Not printed.

[6] The second African Defence Facilities Conference was eventually held in Dakar in Mar 1954. It was convened jointly by France and Britain, and was attended by Belgium, the Gambia, the Gold Coast, Liberia, Nigeria, Portugal, Sierra Leone and South Africa. The US and the Central African Federation were represented by observers. Discussion remained at a technical level and there were no political clashes between the West African representatives and the South Africans. For a British evaluation of the conference, see 80.

70 PREM 11/581   29 July 1954

[Defence of East Africa]: letter from C J M Alport[1] to Sir W Churchill

I write as Chairman of the Joint East and Central African Board,[2] to place before you our views regarding the possible effects on Eastern Africa of the withdrawal of British military forces from the Suez Canal Zone.

In asking you to consider our views, may I assure you that we do not feel that it would be proper for us to pronounce upon the wider strategic, political and economic implications of such a move. We are merely concerned to ensure that the interests of the territories of Eastern Africa, which fall within the scope of the Board's charter, suffer no adverse effects.

There is no doubt that the withdrawal of British troops from the Suez area will be viewed with deep concern in Eastern Africa, unless Her Majesty's Government finds it possible to redeploy the forces which will then become available in such a way as to provide a permanent European element in the formations at the disposal of the General Officer Commanding-in-Chief, East Africa Command. Although military operations in Kenya have achieved notable successes against Mau Mau terrorism, it is unlikely that the internal security situation in the Colony will improve so rapidly that it will be possible to withdraw all European units for many months to come. In Uganda unrest continues despite the declaration of an emergency by the Uganda Government. While the situation in Tanganyika appears at present tranquil, it would be unwise to assume that the influences which are affecting adversely the progress of Kenya and Uganda are not operating in the trusteeship territory, and may not at some future date face the Tanganyika Government with an anxious security situation. The fact that after the withdrawal of our forces from the Suez area, no United Kingdom formation, other than a small force based on Libya, will be stationed at any point in the African continent, must increase the sense of insecurity which at present afflicts law-abiding communities of all races throughout the territories of Kenya, Uganda and Tanganyika.

In addition to the internal security considerations outlined above, my Board hope that Her Majesty's Government will not overlook certain important military and political advantages which would result from stationing a formation of the size of, let us say, a brigade group in Kenya Colony or in Tanganyika. These are:—

Military
(i) Her Majesty's Government would have a valuable reserve fully acclimatised to operations in tropical countries and trained in both desert or jungle conditions.

(ii) Admirable facilities would be available for the families of married officers and other ranks, thus the long separation at present inevitable in overseas service would be avoided.

(iii) Kenya could be developed as a secondary base for the area lying between Eastern Mediterranean and Pakistan. Kilindini is a potential fleet base and good airfields are in being.

---

[1] C J M Alport (Baron cr 1961), Con MP for Colchester, 1950–1961; high commissioner to Central African Federation, 1961–1963.

[2] This body's main function was to represent the views and interests of business concerns operating in East and Central Africa.

(iv) Air transport would enable any formation based on East Africa to be moved to Persia or the Middle East at very short notice.

(v) The presence of European units in the East Africa Command would undoubtedly increase the efficiency of the African colonial forces and would eventually make considerable economies in European manpower possible.

Political

(i) The presence of several thousand European troops together with their families would be a valuable economic asset to the territories during the period of recovery from the set-back of the Mau Mau outbreak.

(ii) A number of officers and other ranks would find permanent homes in East Africa and thus provide a welcome addition to the strength and stability of the European community.

(iii) The declared intention of Her Majesty's Government to maintain a permanent garrison in Kenya would counteract the tendency among certain groups within the Colony with South African connections to look to the Union for future political support.

(iv) Such a decision would also set at rest the fear of many people both in the U.K. and in Africa, who are at present strongly opposed to an agreement with Egypt.

I apologise for setting out these considerations at such length. At the same time my Board feels that insufficient attention has so far been given to this aspect of the problem of redeployment of British forces in Africa and the Middle East.

71   FO 371/108148, no 8   25 Aug 1954
[Simonstown naval base]: personal minute (M148/54) by Sir W Churchill to ministers[1]

[In 1951 the Labour government had begun negotiations with South Africa on the future of the Simsonstown naval base. The broad intention was to transfer control of the base from Britain to South Africa in exchange for a South African guarantee of British naval access. The negotiations were inconclusive (see BDEEP series A, R Hyam ed, *The Labour government and the end of empire 1945–1951*, part IV, 423, 438, 442, 443). In 1954 the Conservative government began planning for a resumption of negotiations.]

To weaken our rights over Simonstown as settled in treaty by me and Smuts in 1921, and in 1930, is a very serious step. To do it at the same time as we are giving up the Suez Canal in fact is cutting off the remaining link between Britain and Australia and New Zealand.

Let me have a report upon Durban harbour and the facilities that could be made available there. If as is quite possible Malan[2] repudiates British Sovereignty,[3] Natal will be our only hope.

---

[1] Mr Thomas (Admiralty), Mr Eden (FO), Lord Alexander (Defence) and Lord Swinton (CRO).

[2] D F Malan, prime minister of South Africa, 1948–1954.

[3] ie, over Simonstown. Durban harbour was not in fact suitable for naval use.

72   FO 371/108148, no 3   6 Sept 1954

[Defence co-operation with South Africa]: minute by Lord Swinton to Mr Eden

Lord Alexander has sent you a copy of Erasmus's[1] letter to him of the 6th September proposing a Regional Defence Organisation in South Africa. This idea is not new; the South Africans have tentatively made the suggestion before. I think there is a good deal to be said for encouraging this idea.

2. The most important thing is to get South Africa away from the Hertzog idea of neutrality, which was still in their minds in 1951, when they refused unconditional availability of Simonstown in war; and to get them firmly committed to fight in the Grand Alliance. In this connection the Regional Defence Organisation has the following advantages:—

(a) South Africa would be committed to France, Portugal and Belgium as well as to the United Kingdom.

(b) There would be less risk of South Africa pulling out of the commitment if they got at loggerheads with a Socialist Government here later on.

(c) South Africa is not alone among the Commonwealth countries in finding it easier in defence to accept an international obligation rather than a Commonwealth one.

(d) It would bring the Colonial Powers in Africa together.

3. It is important that a Regional Organisation should not imply that South Africa is to be defended south of the Equator. Lord Alexander and the Chiefs of Staff think the South Africans have abandoned this notion. That is my impression too; and I think a Regional Organisation would strengthen rather than weaken them in a right disposition of their forces in war.

4. What other objects have they in this proposal? In addition to the considerations I have set out in paragraph 2, I would guess the South Africans are thinking on these lines. They fear Communist infiltration as much as, and perhaps even more than, Communist aggression. They fear it in adjacent territories as well as in their own land. If they were associated with other Colonial Powers in Central and South Africa, they could pool intelligence and concert common action against subversion.

5. In all our dealings with South Africa, there is a new factor which may be of the utmost importance. The belief is growing that Malan will soon retire and that Havenga[2] will succeed him. One member of the South African delegation has told me that he thinks this is probable. If it should prove true, nothing could be better.

6. For all these reasons I hope we may encourage the suggestion of a Regional Defence Organisation.[3]

---

[1] F C Erasmus, South African minister of defence, 1948–1959.

[2] N C Havenga, South African minister of finance, 1948–1954.

[3] In addition to writing to Eden, Swinton minuted some 'thoughts' to Alexander: 'Vital in our interest to have South Africa as a full co-operating partner in war. . . . Even if we stand on letter of Simonstown agreement, it is very doubtful if we should have legal right, if South Africa was neutral. It is therefore supremely important to get a new agreement on availability. . . . We need the S.A. Division and S.A. Squadrons in Middle East. We shall only get this as part of a new agreement. . . . In the global structure we need the Commander in Chief Gibraltar to Mombasa in the Cape' ('South African defence', minute by Swinton to Alexander, FO 371/108148, no 3A [ca 6 Sept 1954]).

73   FO 371/108148, no 3   7 Sept 1954

'South African proposal for regional defence': FO brief for Mr Eden

Mr. Erasmus the South African Minister of Defence has proposed in a letter to Lord Alexander the establishment of an African Regional Defence Organisation composed of countries with territorial interests in Africa south of the Sahara against possible Communist aggression in that part of the world. Mr. Erasmus quotes the Nairobi Conference of 1951 and the Dakar Conference of 1954 as laying the foundations for mutual defence in Africa.

2. In his letter of September 6 the Secretary of State for Commonwealth Relations points out that the South African proposal would have the advantage of commiting South Africa to the defence of the West so that her defence obligation would thus be an international one rather than purely Commonwealth. Lord Swinton also thinks that another advantage in the proposal would be that it would bring together the Colonial Powers in Africa.

3. The South African Government have hinted at the possibility of setting up a Regional Defence Organisation before—particularly at the time of the Conference of Commonwealth Defence Ministers in June 1951.[1] It was then made clear to them that they could give much more effective help to the defence of the West if they were to contribute military and air forces to the defence of the Middle East. At that time the possibility of a Middle East Defence Organisation was under consideration and the South Africans dropped the idea of any Regional Defence Organisation in South Africa in favour of a contribution to the Middle East.

4. Despite the advantages which the South African proposal might have in binding South Africa more closely to the defence of the West it is suggested that the proposal has a considerable number of disadvantages, as follows:—

(a) The Nairobi and Dakar Conferences underlined the reluctance of Belgium and Portugal to do more than exchange information about defence facilities through the ordinary diplomatic channels. They did not look with any favour on the setting up of even a modest follow-up organisation such as the South Africans—and to some extent the French—have contemplated. There does not seem the faintest possibility of either country agreeing to be associated with the South Africans in a proposed Regional Defence Organisation.

(b) Even if the doubts of the Portuguese and Belgians were overcome we should not perhaps encourage the idea of a Regional Organisation for Africa in which South Africa would clearly be the predominant partner. Any such development would be likely to have serious repercussions in our own territories in Africa.

(c) Lord Swinton has suggested that the South African proposal would not affect South African participation in the defence of the Middle East and it is understood that the Chiefs of Staff have broadly accepted this view. On the other hand, there would be a danger of South African forces which might otherwise be free for Middle Eastern defence purposes being retained in South Africa as the defence forces of the new Regional Defence Organisation.

(d) It is better to avoid making any additions to the great number of international

---

[1] See BDEEP series A, B Hyam, ed, *The Labour government and the end of the empire 1945–1951*, part IV, 437.

organisations that exist already if that is possible—particularly at a moment when a defence organisation is being established in South East Asia.[2]

5. Before reaching a final decision on the proposal however it really seems essential that the South Africans should come forward with some more details of what they have in mind. Do they contemplate a defence organisation on the NATO model? What other countries would they propose to invite as members? Are they thinking in terms of a Russian attack from without or are they more concerned about Communist infiltration from within?

Recommendation

6. It is suggested that when the matter is discussed in tomorrow's Cabinet the Secretary of State should point out some of the considerations referred to in paragraph 4 above. He might then go on to say that the proposal is an important and ambitious one. Before reaching a final decision on it the South African Government might perhaps be invited to come forward with rather more precise details of what they have in mind.[3]

---

[2] The Manila Treaty, establishing SEATO, was signed on 8 Sept 1954; see 64, note 1.
[3] Eden initialled his acceptance of this brief on 8 Sept.

74   FO 371/108148, no 5   9 Sept 1954

'Defence discussions with South Africans, with particular reference to their proposal for an African regional pact': note by W A W Clark[1] of an inter-departmental meeting

A meeting of officials was held in Sir S Garner's room this morning.

2. The following points were made in regard to the South African proposal for an African regional defence organisation (Mr. Erasmus' letter of 6th September to Lord Alexander):—

(1) The Colonial Office strongly emphasised the unfortunate repercussions in our colonial territories, particularly in West Africa, of United Kingdom entry into a South African sponsored pact aimed primarily at combatting Communist and subversive activities.
(2) The Foreign Office pointed out that on present form the Belgians and Portuguese would not be much enamoured of such a proposal and Middle East countries would be critical.
(3) The Ministry of Defence suggested that, particularly if the pact was limited to countries in Africa south of the equator, it would have little or no military value; indeed because of its probable untoward effects in colonial territories it might almost have positive military disadvantage.

It was agreed that for these reasons it would be unwise to encourage the South African idea at the present stage and it would be bad tactics to invite the South

---

[1] W A W Clark, assistant under-secretary of State, CRO, 1945–1956. The meeting was attended by officials of the CRO, Ministry of Defence, FO, CO, Admiralty and the COS secretariat.

Africans themselves to develop their rather vague proposal. Nevertheless it should not be rejected out of hand. Provided it was clearly subsidiary to Middle East defence (the sound organisation of which must come first), a lot could be said for a supporting organisation in Africa concerned with communications, logistics, etc. This could be a logical corollary to the Nairobi and Dakar Conferences and would not be open to the same objections as an anti-Communist military alliance, with South Africa playing the lead.

3. Officials therefore suggested that Ministers might speak to Mr. Erasmus on the lines set out in the first annexure (A) to this note.[2]

4. It was also agreed to recommend to Ministers a draft communiqué, for issue on the conclusion of the talks, on the lines set out in the second annexure (B).

5. Subject to Ministerial approval, the C.R.O. agreed to suggest to the South Africans that the final meeting should be between Ministers only (and the South African High Commissioner) with one official to take a note.[3]

---

[2] Annexures not printed.

[3] Alexander and Swinton followed the line recommended in this note in their meeting with Erasmus on 10 Sept. Subsequently the British dragged their feet; on 25 Nov it was reported to Eden that the CRO and the Ministry of Defence 'have made very little progress in considering the [South African] proposals'. Some other initiatives were followed up, however. It was agreed that a joint Anglo-South African working party would be set up in Pretoria to carry out the recommendations of the African Defence Facilities Conference in Nairobi, which was 'very welcome to the South Africans'; and an Admiralty party 'has just returned from Simonstown after preparing in collaboration with the South Africans a plan for handing over the base to South Africa if and when a decision in principle on the subject is taken' (brief by T E Bromley, head of African Dept, FO, 1954–1956, for Eden, FO 371/108148, no 17, 25 Nov 1954).

75   PREM 11/581   [Sept] 1954
[Defence of East Africa]: joint memorandum by CO and War Office

[Acknowledging Alport's letter of 29 July 1954 (see 70), Churchill replied with a brief letter which enclosed a copy of this memo and which suggested that Alport might wish to convey in confidence the points mentioned to members of his board (PREM 11/581, Churchill to Alport, 15 Sept 1954).]

The importance of East Africa and the military and political advantages of stationing a permanent garrison of British troops there have not been overlooked.

2. Several years ago the Chiefs of Staff considered the desirability of using East Africa as a main base.[1] The climate, communications and lack of technical manpower made it unsuitable as a base, and it was found to be uneconomical as a store-holding area.

3. This decision in no way precluded further study of the advantages of stationing a British garrison in East Africa, and this proposal has in fact been carefully re-examined in recent months.

4. Owing to limitations of manpower and money, we are bound to reduce the number of our permanent garrisons overseas. It is intended however that rapid and

---

[1] See BDEEP series A, R Hyam, ed, *The Labour government and the end of empire 1945–1951*, part III, 319, 320 and 324.

effective support should be despatched to our Colonies, when needed, from reserve forces, rendered highly mobile by air transport, located at strategic centres.

5. The main centre must be the United Kingdom—for reasons of economy and mobility as well as for the general well-being of the Army. Other centres of strategic garrisons will be in the Middle East and in Malaya. We simply have not got the resources to add East Africa as a fourth centre.

6. Forces to deal with the present emergency in East Africa will be kept there as long as they are necessary. Thereafter, the situation will be carefully watched and forces from the strategic reserve could be made available at very short notice.

7. It is an important feature of our policy to encourage each Colony to build up the local forces needed for its own security and defence, and thus to reduce to a minimum the potential calls on the United Kingdom for support. Seven infantry battalions, one armoured car squadron and one heavy anti-aircraft battery are contributed by three East African territories. (Naturally these territories need to spend much of their resources on economic development.)

8. Political and financial considerations govern the extent to which Colonial forces can be used outside their own territories. The battalion from East Africa which is now operating in Malaya is giving a good account of itself. It is shortly to be relieved by another battalion from the Central African Federation.[2]

---

[2] Evidently this reply did not entirely satisfy Alport and his colleagues on the Joint East and Central African Board. A few weeks later another member of the Board, F M Bennett (Con MP for Reading North, 1951–1955), aired the issue in Parliament (*H of C Debs*, vol 532, cols 263–264, 2 Nov 1954). But a letter in reply to Bennett from R Turton (parliamentary under-secretary of state, FO, 1954–1955) scotched the idea of a base in Kenya even more firmly than the CO-War Office memo had done (letter from Turton to Bennett, FO 371/108149, no 2, 1 Dec 1954).

---

76 FO 371/113479, no 6   18 Feb 1955

[South African proposals for regional defence]: letter from K M Wilford (Paris)[1] to W N Hillier-Fry[2]

Thank you for your letter of February 12 (J 1192/5) about the meeting of our Anglo/French working party here. I attach a further copy of the French record of the meeting for which you asked.[3]

You inquired also whether the French had communicated a copy of this record to the South Africans here. I asked Lavéry at the Quai whether they had done so. He said that they had been wondering whether to do so and asked whether we would have any objections if they did. I gave it as my personal opinion that we would not. I hope this is right.

This brings me to the fact that Sole of the South African Embassy has called to see me to ask about the meeting. I gave him a full account of what passed and he had no comment of substance except on the question of an African regional defence organisation. He said quite openly that Mr. Erasmus' proposals for such an African organisation were made for purely political reasons. The South African Government had to keep before their electors the idea that the danger to the Union might come

---

[1] See 69, note 4.   [2] W N Hillier-Fry, African Dept, FO.   [3] Not printed.

not only from the Soviet Union, but also from India. This point of view was not shared, Sole said, by permanent officials who agreed with our policy of defending the Union as far to the North as was possible. Since some compromise between these two points of view was essential if the South African Government were not to find themselves out on a limb, Sole said that, in the view of officials, some progress towards an African defence organisation might be necessary. In the official view this should take the form of preparing some kind of infrastructure for such an organisation. This could flow logically from the recommendations of the Dakar Conference. As Sole saw it, once the information, for the exchange of which provision had been made at Dakar, was available to all concerned, it would be possible to see what facilities were in existence and what more remained to be done. Deficiencies might become apparent for example in fuel storage facilities, in signal links or in early warning radar equipment. Such deficiencies could then be met by a common programme commonly financed by all the countries involved, as in the N.A.T.O. infrastructure programme. It seems to be that such ideas are much more sensible and a better basis for progress than setting up some strategic planning organisation which in present circumstances at any rate could have little reality. I told Sole that, speaking quite personally, I thought some such method of progress would be more acceptable to us than would the more grandoise conception. If these ideas commend themselves to you, you may feel that we should espouse them ourselves on the grounds that it will provide us with a not altogether negative approach to the problem of African defence which might upset the South African Government and that we have the knowledge that such ideas will have a ready welcome at least in official quarters in Pretoria.

I attach four spare copies of this letter for you to distribute as you think fit.[4]

---

[4] P Hayman of the FO minuted on this letter on 22 Feb: 'Commonly financed infrastructure programmes were only approved with great difficulty by the 14 N.A.T.O. Powers. I cannot imagine that the Nairobi and Dakar Powers would come within a million miles of reaching agreement upon them!!'

77 FO 371/113481, no 8   21 Mar 1955

[Defence co-operation with South Africa]: letter from Lord Swinton to Mr Macmillan

My dear Harold,
I send you a note[1] of an interview I have had today with South African High Commissioner. You will also have recieved Liesching's despatch of the 17th March and his note of his interview with Erasmus. I think both these are pretty satisfactory. Both throw a new light on the proposal for an African Defence Organisation. I believe that Jooste[2] and Erasmus are sincere in what they say about this, and I think it is clear that the Defence Pact is not intended as a means of suppressing black men. I said frankly to Jooste that when this had been proposed before, I thought it was aimed at the suppression of subversive activities in the Union. He assured me that this was not so, and that the need and purpose was that described to us by Erasmus and himself.

---

[1] Not printed.   [2] G P Jooste, South African high commissioner to Britain, 1954–1956.

S

This is borne out of some information we have now received about the activities of Mr. Louw,[3] who is a bad man. Louw has proposed to the French, Belgian and Portuguese Ambassadors and the High Commissioner of the Rhodesian Federation that there should be a Pan-African Conference which would discuss, among other things:—

1. Common measures against Communism.
2. A common line on United Nations interference on matters of domestic policy.
3. A common policy on stopping Indian immigration and infiltration into Africa.
4. Defence.

I am afraid we shall be asked to join this awful party; and I am sure we could do no such thing.[4] But if we are to scotch this project of Louw's, I think we shall have to be more forthcoming on the Erasmus African Defence Organisation provided it has a different and much less objectionable purpose and can be made a counterpart of the scheme for the defence of Africa as a whole in the Middle East.

I am sending a copy of this letter and of the note to the Foreign Secretary, the Colonial Secretary and the First Lord.

Yours ever,
Philip

---

[3] E H Louw, South African minister for finance, 1955–1956, minister for foreign affairs, 1955–1963.
[4] Swinton's view of Louw's proposed conference was widely shared in Whitehall. Sir R Powell (deputy secretary, Ministry of Defence, 1950–1956, permanent secretary, 1956–1959) thought it 'so horrifying that it looks as though we may be forced to give some backing to Mr Erasmus's plan as very much the lesser of two evils' (letter from Powell to W A W Clark, FO 371/113481, no 89, 1 Apr 1955). But the colonial secretary, with his different perspective on Africa, remained suspicious even of the Erasmus plan: 'I am still not altogether sure that Erasmus's defence pact, whether intended to do so or not, would not give the South African Government a very convenient platform for trying to interfere in our African policies' (letter from Lennox-Boyd to Swinton, FO 371/113481, no 8, 5 Apr 1955). See also, 145, 148.

---

78   FO 371/113481, no 9,   30 Mar 1955
[Middle East policy and South Africa]: minute by C A E Shuckburgh[1]

I am not at all happy about this telegram[2] which Lord Swinton wants to send to South Africa. I am afraid that if Mr. Erasmus is encouraged to come here in June to talk about the whole range of Middle East topics, described in paragraph 4 of the telegram, we shall have on our hands a great embarrassment. In the first place there is no certainty that we shall by then have worked out with the Americans a common political and strategic plan for the Middle East, though I would hope that we would have. But even if we have done that, South Africa is certainly not the next country that ought to be taken into our confidence over Middle East defence plans. There is France, clamouring to be consulted; there is Turkey, with whom, so far, we have had staff talks but no serious politico/military planning; there are our allies in the Middle East itself viz: Iraq and Jordan who, with all their weaknesses, play much more of a

---

[1] C A E Shuckburgh, assistant under-secretary of state, FO, 1954–1956.
[2] Not printed.

part in the area than South Africa in peacetime. Finally, we have to see what is going to happen about new accessions to the Turco/Iraqi Pact.[3] I should think Pakistan will be the next to join, and then, perhaps, Persia; and then, possibly Jordan. I see great difficulty about discussing all these things with Mr. Erasmus when they are half cooked.

2. I should also like to know what is meant by "peacetime co-operation by South Africa in the Middle East" (see paragraph 4(iii)). I do not know of any plans for such co-operation in peace.

3. The exercise to be done with Mr. Erasmus is, by inducing him to take an interest in the forward Middle East defence strategy, to discourage him from building up an African defence organisation. It seems to me, however, that the Commonwealth Relations Office have got rather carried away by this and are bringing South Africa very much more fully into Middle East problems than is necessary for this purpose.

4. In short, I would like to suggest the elimination of paragraph 4(iii) and (iv) and the last two sentences of paragraph 5.

5. I think it would have been much better if Mr. Erasmus could have been persuaded to wait until September before coming but Lord Swinton seems to have committed himself to June.[4]

---

[3] The Baghdad Pact; see 42, note 1.

[4] Lord Swinton and the CRO were persuaded to agree with the views expressed in this minute.

79 FO 371/113481, no 12   29 Apr 1955

'Defence talks with South Africa': joint minute by Lord Home and Mr Selwyn Lloyd to Sir A Eden

With the approval of their colleagues—Defence Committee Minutes D.(55)3rd Meeting Item 5—our predecessors agreed to further defence talks with the South African Minister of Defence in London in June. Mr. Erasmus has now asked us to fix a date, since he has to be in Washington in the last week of the month for an engagement he cannot break.

2. We have asked Mr. Erasmus to make it as late as possible in June and certainly not earlier than the 15th.

3. Postponement until later in the summer would have suited us better. It is inconvenient to be faced with these talks so soon after the Election and the reassembly of the new House. Later in the summer we might also have a clearer picture of United States intentions in the Middle East. But we consider that postponement would be impolitic. The main item on the agenda from the South African point of view is Simonstown. Our predecessors deliberately spun this out and a further, and probably final, round cannot be put off longer than June without incurring South African suspicions and a loss of goodwill. Over the Middle East the balance of advantage probably lies in trying to screw Mr. Erasmus up, before he goes to Washington, to acceptance of a commitment, even if it is contingent on United States support in this theatre being forthcoming. If he were to go to Washington first, he might give the Americans a poor impression of Commonwealth resolution to

defend this gateway to Africa as far forward as possible; he has parochial ideas about hedgehogs along the Limpopo. Lastly we want the South Africans to buy British and we should get in our say before he becomes the target of American sales talk.

4. We therefore plan to conduct talks with him in London about the middle of June. The range of subjects to be covered includes:—

(1) A settlement over Simonstown in its widest context of naval co-operation;
(2) South Africa's contribution to Middle East defence in peace and war;
(3) Suggestions which Mr. Erasmus has made regarding the establishment of an African Defence Organisation, and
(4) South Africa's equipment programme, including purchases in this country.

5. A copy of this minute is being sent to the Foreign Secretary, the Colonial Secretary and also to the First Lord of the Admiralty who has concurred in its terms.

80 CAB 131/16, DC(55)10   7 June 1955
'Defence co-operation with South Africa—talks with Mr Erasmus': joint memorandum by Lord Home, Mr Selwyn Lloyd and Mr Thomas for Cabinet Defence Committee

We begin another round of talks with Mr. Erasmus on the 15th June.

2. The agenda is:—

(1) A comprehensive plan for naval co-operation in African waters and the South Atlantic, including a settlement over the future of Simonstown;
(2) The South African proposal to establish an African Defence Organisation;
(3) The rôle of the South African forces in war;
(4) Peacetime co-operation by the South African forces in the Middle East.

3. Mr. Erasmus will expect to reach a settlement over Simonstown, providing for ultimate South African control. It has been made clear to him that we expect also to determine conclusively the part South Africa is prepared to play in Middle East defence. In other words we seek a "package deal."

4. We do not anticipate much difficulty about the terms and conditiions of a Simonstown settlement. Mr. Erasmus is so keen to secure South African control that he is unlikely to jib over the very reasonable provisions upon which we insist (see D. (55) 14).

5. But we fear that he may not be so ready to bind South Africa to the despatch of troops and air force units to the Middle East promptly in the event of war. His advisers are not wholly convinced that the Middle East can be held with the forces available or that the line of communications to the Zagros Mountain passes would be secure. They are obsessed with the dangers to internal security in the Union and neighbouring territories in the event of war. They may urge that the Union should keep its forces uncommitted at home until the course of events is seen. In any case Union forces are in no fit state at present to fight a modern battle. So far the South African Government has shown no disposition to embark on the expensive programme of re-equipment and training necessary to bring their forces to efficiency. They may also need additional legislation.

6. But we consider that we should put the utmost pressure on the South Africans to live up to their protestations about being in the struggle against Communism. We must convince them that

(1) strategically the Middle East is the key to the defence of Africa; there can be no effective defence of the continent if the Middle East falls; and
(2) the Middle East is defensible, if all concerned, including the South Africans, do their bit.

We should do our best to secure from Mr. Erasmus a firm and binding commitment for the despatch of an armoured brigade and a wing of three fighter squadrons to the Middle East on D-day, to be followed by the remainder of their armoured division and two more fighter wings as soon as possible.* The Chiefs of Staff consider that the timely arrival of such a contribution would be invaluable to the defence of the area. To be effective and for us to be able to rely on it, the promise would however have to be backed by a programme of re-equipment and training to match, *i.e.*, calculated to bring the South African forces up to efficiency and make them fit to fight a modern battle. Further tangible evidence of the seriousness of South African intentions would be the stockpiling of equipment for their forces in the Middle East; this too would be essential if they were to honour a commitment of the kind we seek.

7. A very awkward question arises, if Mr. Erasmus proves reluctant or is unable to accept such a commitment and all its implications. Should we abandon hopes of a "package deal" and settle nevertheless over Simonstown?

The Admiralty, we understand, consider a secure base in South Africa essential. They would not therefore want to see a complete break made over the Simonstown negotiations. (As our predecessors emphasised, Simonstown would be virtually useless to us without South African goodwill and co-operation; only a new agreement, freely negotiated, can assure its use, and the use of other South African ports, to us in war. This the proposed agreement does, besides giving the Royal Naval Supreme Commander control of the South African Navy in war.) But the Simonstown settlement could be used as a bargaining counter to put pressure on the South Africans over the Middle East. We feel therefore that, if Mr. Erasmus will not or cannot enter into a firm, prompt and worthwhile commitment over the Middle East, we should suggest to him that he should go back to his Cabinet again. He could report to them that the United Kingdom Government is prepared to subscribe to a settlement over Simonstown but wishes it to be part of a comprehensive defence agreement of which a firm contribution to Middle East defence is an important feature in United Kingdom eyes. Mr. Erasmus's disappointment would of course be great; this is the third or fourth time he has discussed Simonstown with the United Kingdom Government and all the signs are that in the naval field he is prepared to meet all our main desiderata. But we could argue that the Middle East commitment would be a token of their determination to play an active part, along with other Western nations, in the defence of the free world against communism—a determination which South African Ministers have consistently reaffirmed since 1951, *e.g.*, Mr.

---

* Their existing (1951) commitment was for the despatch of one division to be ready for battle in D+10 months and three air wings in D+3, 6 and 12 months respectively, but Mr. Erasmus has recently talked of the commitment being to an organisation, *i.e.*, a Middle East Command or Organisation "that has since lapsed."

Swart's[1] statement at the Prime Ministers' Meeting in February. We can remind him too that we have our problem of presentation to Parliament and public who would take more kindly to the Simonstown transfer, if it were seen to be part of a comprehensive understanding that is clearly of benefit to the United Kingdom. We can also point out that it has been implicit in all the discussions over Simonstown that South Africa had a commitment in the Middle East, which she was prepared to honour and, we hoped, improve.

8. In the last resort, if Mr. Erasmus came back later still empty handed over the Middle East, we should probably have to settle over Simonstown. But we feel that, if he is not prepared to enter into a Middle East commitment now, it is worth insisting on another round of talks, both because of the intrinsic military value of a South African contribution to Middle East defence and because public presentation here of the Simonstown settlement would be easier if it was part of a comprehensive defence agreement.

9. There is also the question of an African Defence Organisation, which Mr. Erasmus contends is essential if the South African public is to be reconciled to a commitment to fight overseas. He argues that this would fill an obvious gap in the pattern of world alliances and he would no doubt like to make it a mutual defence pact, guaranteeing the security of South Africa's "hinterland." The United Kingdom High Commissioner reports that he may table proposals modelled on the lines of South-East Asia Treaty Organisation, membership being confined to countries in "Southern Africa," which would exclude our West African Colonies.

There are obvious dangers in the United Kingdom becoming involved in a defence organisation that the South Africans may seek to dominate and might mis-represent as giving them a say in the conduct of affairs outside their boundaries. The Colonial Secretary has, we understand, the gravest fears about the effect on the African populations of our African territories. We admit the dangers and would not urge that we should embark unnecessarily on the establishment of an organisation that would cause us political embarrassment or worse. Certainly we could not contemplate anything that included internal security among its functions.

But it is a very valid point for the South Africans to make that, if their forces are to be engaged in the Middle East in war, the line of communications should be secured. We consider that in view of the importance attached by the Chiefs of Staff to a timely South African contribution in the Middle East, we should be prepared to go as far as we can, without serious political embarrassment, to meet the point, if they display a readiness to co-operate over the Middle East.

Two international conferences have already been held on African defence facilities—one in Nairobi in August, 1951, in which the United Kingdom, the Union of South Africa, Belgium, Ethiopa, France, Italy, Portugal and Southern Rhodesia took part and the other in Dakar in March 1954, attended by the United Kingdom, France, Belgium, the British West African territories, Liberia, Portugal and the Union of South Africa. These conferences did not take things very far, except to agree about the exchange of information concerning existing facilities. But they caused no awkward political repercussions and we see no reason why we should not offer to pursue a further conference or conferences along these lines to continue this work and even to indulge in paper planning for the development and use of such facilities

---

[1] C R Swart, deputy prime minister of South Africa, 1954–1959.

in the event of war. Nor do we see any reason why we should not offer to support the South Africans in pressing at the reconvened conference or conferences for a small combined secretariat and/or planning staff to be set up. (The Portuguese and Belgians were previously opposed to this, but mainly on the grounds of finance.) We could emphasise to the South Africans that in our experience it is always best to let things grow and take shape from such practical beginnings.

A note on the Nairobi and Dakar Conferences is attached at Annex A.[2]

10. If it seemed desirable to go a little further to secure a commitment in the Middle East, we might offer an extension of the Naval Command Organisation to include France, Belgium and Porgugal, provided these countries were willing and that the Supreme Command remained in British hands.

11. To summarise, we seek our colleagues' consideration of the following tactics:—

(1) to seek a comprehensive understanding over defence co-operation with South Africa including:

(a) a satisfactory plan of United Kingdom-South African naval co-operation, including a British Supreme Command in war, and leading to transfer of control of Simonstown to South Africa on conditions which would assure to us and our allies the facilities we need;

(b) a binding commitment by South Africa to despatch land and air forces to the Middle East promptly in the event of war, and the undertaking of a programme of training, re-equipment and stock-piling to match;

(c) to agree, if the South Africans are prepared to enter into a binding commitment to fight in the Middle East, to pursue the possibility of holding a further conference or conferences on the lines of the conferences on African defence facilities at Nairobi in 1951 and Dakar in 1954 with a view to giving more substance and formality (e.g., a permanent Secretariat or planning staff) to the recommendations of these conferences;[3]

(d) if need be some extension of the Naval Command Organisation as suggested in paragraph 8 above.

(2) if Mr. Erasmus will not or is unable to accept (b) above to defer final decisions over (a), (c) and (d) while he pursues further with his colleagues the question of a Middle East commitment.

---

[2] Not printed.

[3] The FO, sharing Lennox-Boyd's dislike of the African Regional Defence Organisation proposal, felt that 'it would be preferable not to offer even the small concessions to Mr Erasmus proposed in paragraph 11(c)' ('Defence co-operation with South Africa', brief by T E Bromley for Mr Macmillan, FO 371/113482, no 18, 9 June 1955). On the following day the Cabinet Defence Committee was persuaded to agree that concessions should be kept to the absolute minimum; specifically, they should not go beyond an offer to hold further talks on communications and logistics following the lead of the Nairobi and Dakar conferences (CAB 131/16, DC 55(3), 10 June 1955). It may be noted that the main advocate of defence co-operation with South Africa, Lord Swinton, was no longer in the government. Eden, on becoming prime minister on 6 Apr, had replaced him at the CRO with Lord Home.

81 FO 371/113482, no 26 20 June 1955

[Defence co-operation with South Africa]: minutes by C O I Ramsden[1] and C A E Shuckburgh

A meeting of the United Kingdom Ministers concerned in the discussions with Mr. Erasmus is to be held at 4.30 this afternoon in the Ministry of Defence. The Minister of Defence, I am told, intends at this meeting to report on the position reached in the discussions. No minutes have of course yet appeared of this morning's meeting with Mr. Erasmus, but I understand from Sir Richard Powell that the following is the position reached.

2. The paper which had been prepared by the Ministry of Defence and C.R.O. on the proposal to hold further conferences of the Nairobi and Dakar type was handed to Mr. Erasmus this morning. It was made clear to him that these proposals were conditional upon a satisfactory South African commitment to the defence of the Middle East.

3. Mr. Erasmus did not produce the expected counter-draft to the draft U.K. formula on Middle East Defence. The South Africans have however undertaken to produce three papers at the meeting which is to take place tommorrow afternoon, June 21, at 3 p.m. These papers will consist of:—

(a) A document regarding understandings between the South African Government and H.M.G. about the South African commitment to the defence of the Middle East, which is to be suitable for publication.

(b) A document containing secret assurances about South African commitments in the Middle East which will go beyond the terms of (a).

(c) A document containing South African undertakings about the purchase of arms in the U.K.

4. The South African delegation have however indicated that any commitment by South Africa to take part in the defence of the Middle East must be conditional on the creation of a Middle East Defence organization, or at the very least upon the holding of a conference to discuss Middle East defence; this conference to be attended by all powers interested in the defence of the Middle East and particularly by the Americans.

5. The U.K. Ministers who have been concerned in the talks up till now, have expressed the view that they may need to give more information to the South Africans about what has passed between H.M.G. and the U.S. Government concerning Middle East defence. So far all that has been said to the South Africans has been the statement by the C.I.G.S. at the first meeting with Mr. Erasmus on June 15. The preliminary view of officials in the Ministry of Defence is that, while they would have preferred to say no more than this to the South Africans, they think that there may be a case for taking them into our confidence a little more than we have done up till now.

C.O.I.R
20.6.55

---

[1] African Department, FO.

I have all along been very much opposed to telling Mr. Erasmus more than was absolutely necessary about our proposed talks with the Americans. In the first place, we have had great difficulty in getting these talks at all and the Americans have shown the utmost sensitiveness to any leakage, even of the fact that they are taking place. (They are very sensitive to the fact that the Turks are not taking part.) Secondly, it seems to me still very likely that the talks will not give us very much comfort and that we shall not emerge from them with a much clearer idea of American policy and intentions. If we play them up with the South Africans before we know how they are going to work out, we may arouse false expectations.

2. I am sure the thing to remember is that the elaboration of a joint US/UK policy for the Middle East is an essential; whereas the achievement of a promise of South African reinforcements in war is a desirable but secondary objective. We must not endanger the first for the second.

3. We have already agreed that Mr. Erasmus may be told that we are trying to get talks going with the Americans. I think the Minister of State should resist going any further than this, perhaps with the following exception.

4. It might be thought desirable to hint to Mr. Erasmus that we are encountering some difficulty in bringing the Americans along to play their full part in the preparation of Middle East defence plans; and that any indication the South Africans might be prepared to give in Washington that their contribution is dependent on American participation might be useful. Such a hint in Washington, combined with evidence that Pakistan is awaiting a more forward American policy and that the Turco/Iraqi Pact is going to sleep because the Americans are holding back on it, may result in a more forthcoming American attitude.

5. If the South Africans make a commitment conditional on "the creation of a Middle East Defence Organisation or at the very least upon the holding of a conference to discuss Middle East defence" (paragraph 4 above), then I hope it may be possible to avoid making them any promises. It should be explained to them that the creation of a Middle East Defence Organisation is a very delicate operation on which we have been engaged for several years, with several false starts, and that we are only now (through the Turco/Iraqi Pact) beginning to see something emerge which may result in a wider organisation. It would be fatal to try to run ahead of Arab opinion, since any defence of the area depends in the first place upon willing co-operation of the countries in the forward positions. The calling of a conference on Middle East defence at the present juncture would require very careful thought from this point of view, having regard particuarly to the sensitivity of Egypt, Syria, etc: and the present excited and divided state of Arab opinion (not to mention Israel and the fuss they would make if we called such a conference without their participation).[2]

C.A.E.S.
20.6.55

---

[2] The outcome of the talks was that the Simonstown transfer was agreed; South Africa agreed to organise a task force for use outside the Union, but without making a firm commitment to participate in the defence of the Middle East; and the two governments agreed to sponsor a logistics and communications conference in succession to Nairobi and Dakar. In a [draft] circular telegram, Lennox-Boyd assured African governors that the agreement to sponsor a conference 'does not, repeat not, in any way involve concern in internal security of British Colonial territories and hence in local racial or political matters. The importance of refraining from any suggestions inconsistent with the above has been impressed upon Erasmus' ([draft] telegram from Lennox-Boyd to African governors, FO 371/113483, no 38, 1 July 1955).

82   CAB 130/111, GEN 501/3 (final)   15 Aug 1955

'Interim report of the Official Committee on the Military Implications of General Templer's Report': note by Sir H Parker (chairman) on military planning in East and West Africa

[Following General Templer's submission in Apr 1955 of his report on colonial security (see 18, note 3), the Ministerial Committee on Colonial Security invited the Ministry of Defence to set up an official committee with the terms of reference: 'to examine the military implications of General Templer's Report on Colonial Security with special regard to the system of command and administration necessary to achieve zonal systems of defence in East and West Africa' (CAB 130/108, GEN 485/3, 27 June 1955, minutes of meeting retained by department). At the same meeting the ministerial committee endorsed a new statement of roles for the colonial forces which was subsequently approved by Cabinet (see para 2 of this document). The official committee was chaired by Sir H Parker (Ministry of Defence) and included A M Allen (Treasury), Maj-Gen W H A Bishop (CRO), H H Hobbs and Maj-Gen J H N Poett (War Office), and C Y Carstairs[1] and J S Bennett (CO).]

In accordance with the instructions of the Committee (GEN. 485/3rd Meeting, Conclusion (1)) a Committee of Officials has, as requested by Ministers, begun its examination of the military implications of General Templer's Report on Colonial Security by considering the system of command and administration necessary to achieve zonal systems of defence in East and West Africa.

2. The Cabinet have accepted the role of the Colonies in War as:—

(a) to provide for their internal security;

(b) to provide, as far as possible, for their own local defence;

(c) to provide for Commonwealth land, sea and air forces such installations as are necessary to facilitate their strategic employment;

(d) to provide reserves of man-power on which we can draw after the first phase of nuclear war to sustain whatever operations are necessary;

(e) to provide such industrial and material resources as can be developed;

and have agreed that the role might well be described as providing for local and regional defence requirements.

They have also agreed:—

'in principle that the system of administration of Colonial forces by the War Office should be replaced by administration by Colonial Governments, who would thereafter become primarily responsible for the financing of their own forces. This principle is not intended to be applied simultaneously over the whole field, but would be carried into effect in individual territories or regions at a pace dictated by local circumstances and after consultation with the Colonial Governments concerned'.[2]

East Africa

3. The existing command structure in East Africa is satisfactory, and must be retained at least as long as the emergency in Kenya lasts. The nucleus of a regional

---

[1] C Y Carstairs, director of information services, CO, 1951–1953; assistant under-secretary of state, 1953–1962.

[2] CAB 128/29, CM 26(55)6, retained by department.

civil counterpart exists in the East Africa High Commission, which has Defence as one of the subjects allocated to it, and in the East Africa Defence Committee, whose composition and terms of reference however require review to bring them up to date. None of the territories is as yet on the verge of independence; they are all contiguous; and a unified military command is therefore calculated to offer practical advantages and attractions even after administrative responsibility for the forces is transferred (whenever that occurs) to the Colonial Governments. It is by no means certain that the ultimate political future of East African is as one unit, but this need not affect plans for the co-ordination of the local forces in the nearer future. We therefore recommend that no change should be made in the command structure at the present time, but that this should be periodically reviewed in the light of constitutional developments, particularly in relation to Uganda.

West Africa

4. Owing to the rapid rate of political development in West Africa, the position there is somwhat different. The Gold Coast is to assume full responsibility for its own forces from 1st July, 1956, and it seems reasonable to expect Nigeria to do likewise within the next two or three years. The existing command structure in West Africa cannot survive the transfer of responsibility for the forces in the Gold Coast, and will, as from 1st July, 1956, be replaced by three separate territorial commands covering respectively the Federation of Nigeria and Sierra Leone and Gambia combined (both of which will be for the time being under War Office control) and the Gold Coast (which will be responsible to the Governor). The Committee have accordingly sought to make recommendations which will be suitable both for the interim period when the territories are at differing stages of development, and which could be adapted as successive territories become independent.

5. At present there is in West Africa a West African Armny Advisory Council, which was set up last year as a form of civil counterpart to West African Command. The functions of this Council are to advise the West African Governments on matters affecting their military forces, and to keep under review measures to further West African military co-operation. The Council consists of not more than two representatives, usually of Ministerial rank, from each West African territory, who provide the Chairman in rotation; the General Officer Commanding-in-Chief, West African Command, and the Chief Secretary, West African Inter-Territorial Secretariat. As the Council was set up for the specific purpose of providing a means of contact between the four Governments and West African Command, the disappearance of the latter would bring the future of the Council into question.

6. After 1st July, 1956, it will still be desirable for an inter-territorial organisation in the defence field to exist in West Africa to perform the following functions:—

(a) To maintain uniformity of training in the four territories, and in particular to supervise the running of the existing Combined Training School which trains both officers and other ranks, including technicians. This has recently been completed at a cost of £700,000 and it is suggested might well continue to serve all West African Territories on the grounds of economy, continuity and efficiency.

(b) To co-ordinate within West Africa arrangements for the despatch of a brigade and supporting arms from West Africa to the Middle East after the first phase of a war.

(c) To co-ordinate as far as political considerations permit the regional defence policy of the territories.

(d) To act as a West African link for war planning with the rest of the Commonwealth.

(e) To co-ordinate the equipment requirements of the territories.

(f) To co-ordinate and arrange for the supply of officers and other ranks from the United Kingdom to meet the needs of West Africa.

7. It is hoped that the West African Army Advisory Council will continue in some form or another in order to perform the above function. To do so, the Council would need military advice on matters outside the province of the local commanders in the participating territories, and there would consequently be many advantages in associating with it, as part of the Council, a small military advisory and co-ordinating element under a Military Adviser. Furthermore, if West Africa Command is abolished next year and nothing then replaces it, the chances of introducing some co-ordinating machinery at a later date would be remote.

8. On the other hand, it is recognised that there may be political difficulties in appointing a Military Adviser whose responsibilities extend beyond the Gold Coast. Any arrangement which seemed to carry with it "interference from Whitehall" would not be brooked, and it is for consideration whether satisfactory co-ordination could not be achieved by the Commander, Gold Coast Forces, or whatever title may be approved, working in closely with the military authorities of the other territories in the area. It should be made clear from the outset that there is no intention of imposing a permanent organisation which might be found later to be politically undesirable.[3]

9. Before reaching a final conclusion we think it very desirable to have informal consultation with the Governors concerned and the General Officer Commanding-in-Chief, West Africa, both as to the merits of the proposal and as to the way in which it should be presented, which may be vital to its acceptance. From the political point of view it is very desirable that the request for a Military Adviser should come from the Colonial Governments themselves, with the full approval of African Ministers and that he and his staff should be paid by the territories. It should be explained to the Governments concerned that, in these suggestions, we were wishing to observe both the constitutional proprieties and the realities of the situation. It was not a question of the United Kingdom attempting to evade financial responsibility. Nevertheless, the United Kingdom would be willing to consider alternative methods of meeting the cost of the Military Adviser and his staff, if the territories saw difficulty in accepting

---

[3] The official committee was much concerned with the political sensitivity of these matters. Bishop referred to the 'likely' relevance of the Ceylon precedent, under which a British officer had been invited to command the Ceylonese forces for several years after independence, but stressed that 'there must be no appearance that we doubted in any way the competence or willingness of African Ministers to conduct their own affairs efficiently' (CAB 130/111, GEN 501/1, 15 July 1955). Parker noted that the history of defence advisers 'had been unsatisfactory in other territories, such as Burma, when for political reasons goodwill had disappeared', and felt that it would be better to accept the recommendations of the Gold Coast and Nigerian governments 'even if these failed to give us all we required' (ibid, GEN 501/2, 8 Aug 1955).

the charge. Any arrangement reached could be subject to review after, say, two years, that is about a year before the first adviser and his staff completed their term of office.

10. There is one related, though longer-term, issue. We should hope that the West African territories on achieving independence would agree to undertake some external defence commitment, on the lines of the present commitment to provide a Brigade for use in a major war, as part of the obligations arising from Commonwealth membership; in this the attitude of the Gold Coast may well be crucial. We propose informally to consult the Governor of that territory how best this issue can be raised.

11. The Governors of Territories and their military advisers are being informed forthwith of the role and system of administration of Colonial forces as approved by Ministers. The Governor of the Gold Coast has already been informed of the proposal to hand over control of the armed forces with effect from 1st July, 1956, and has confirmed that this is acceptable to him and his Ministers.

Recommendations

12. We recommend that:—

(a) As soon as Governors have received the background in paragraph 11 above they should be asked their views (i) on the acceptability of a Military Adviser with a small staff within the West African Advisory Council on the lines set out above, and (ii) on how best to raise the matter with Ministers or other appropriate bodies in the territories concerned.

(b) Governors should be asked to reply by 30th September. On receipt of their replies, my Committee will make further recommendations as to the nature and method of presentation of the formal proposals to be put to the West African territories.[4]

---

[4] This chairman's note was endorsed by the committee as its report to ministers. Within a few days the report had been approved by the minister of defence and the minister of state for colonial affairs.

83   CO 822/1195, nos 2 & 3   23–28 Nov 1955

'The Sudan': minutes by Mr Lennox-Boyd and Mr Macmillan on the implications of Sudanese independence for East African security

Foreign Secretary

I have been following events in the Sudan these last few months with much concern.

As you know, the chief interest from my point of view springs from the close affinity of the Africans of the Southern Sudan with those in the north of Uganda. There is a good deal of commerce backwards and forwards and events in the Southern Sudan have their immediate repercussions in Uganda, as they did, for example, at the time of the recent "mutiny".[1]

I wonder, however, whether we ought not to take a fresh look at the wider implications of what might develop in the Sudan. I understand there is a lot of

---

[1] A reference to the mutiny in Aug 1955 of the Equatoria Corps, the all-southern section of the Sudanese army.

feeling amongst the Africans in the Southern Sudan that we have betrayed them. This feeling, combined with the extension of northern domination over the Southern Sudan, may well as things develop mean an extension of Egyptian influence (and of whatever influence accompanies the arms Egypt is now getting from behind the Iron Curtain) to the northern frontiers of Uganda and Kenya.

I do not know how you at present assess the likelihood of an effective Egyptian extension southward. But if this is a serious possibility, I wonder whether we should not now ask the Chiefs of Staff to give us a new assessment of the strategic importance of the East African territories in these circumstances and of the measures necessary to secure their defence. If the situation developed along the lines of which I am apprehensive, it might equally be valuable to compare notes with the French and Belgians and possibly even the Ethiopians. I feel myself that we must plan to maintain firm control for many years over the whole of East Africa. Of the East African territories Uganda is our potential Achilles' heel, both politically and geographically. At the same time it is also of great importance, since in any showdown with Egypt the control Uganda gives us of the source of the White Nile must clearly be of paramount importance.

These are only general thoughts on a large topic and one which I know must have been occupying a great deal of attention in the Foreign Office. I should be grateful for any views you may have on what I have said above.

I am sending copies of this minute to the Prime Minister and the minister of Defence.

A.L.B.
23.11.55

Secretary of State for the Colonies
I quite understand the interest and concern expressed in your minute of November 23 about the course of events in the Sudan.

2.   It is difficult to assess the real feelings of the Southerners in the Sudan as there are so few who are capable of giving expression to any views. Experience has shown that the politicians elected by the South cannot be relied on to support us in resisting Egyptian malpractices. Their publicly expressed view is that the British are imperialists and that the Sudan should be purged of both Britons and Egyptians. On the other hand it is doubtless true that many Southerners do in their hearts regret the departure of our administrators on whom they relied in the past for fair treatment. And it is also true that past history and the differences of race, religion, culture and development between North and South have made for the lack of Southern confidence in Northern intentions which lay at the bottom of the recent mutiny.

3.   That need not in itself lead to an extension of Egyptian influence in the Southern Sudan; some Southerners might rather hope to obtain some degree of local autonomy later on within a Sudanese state. As far as the Sudan as a whole is concerned, it seems likely, despite past Egyptian pressure, that the choice which is now to be made about the Sudan's future by means of a plebiscite will be in favour of independence. Any immediate extension of Egyptian influence over the country does not seem therefore to be likely.

4.   But it cannot be ruled out that Egyptian influence over the Sudan may grow

later on, particularly since the two countries have certain inescapable common concerns such as Nile Waters. In view of this and of the importance of knowing exactly what our interests are in what happens in the Sudan I agree with you that a new assessment of the strategic importance of the East African territories would be useful.

5. It might at a later stage be valuable to compare notes with the French and Belgians. The latter showed some anxiety during the recent mutiny. I am not sure how useful a contribution we could get from the Ethiopians but we do know that they would view an extension of Egyptian influence in the Sudan with considerable apprehension.

6. I am sending copies of this minute to the Prime Minister and to the Minister of Defence.

H.M.
28.11.55

84 CO 882/1195, no 8/E   28 Dec 1955
[Strategic importance of East Africa]: letter from T E Bromley[1] to H Lovegrove[2]

It has been agreed between the Foreign Secretary, the Minister of Defence and the Colonial Secretary that it would be useful if the Chiefs of Staff could be asked to carry out a new assessment of the strategic importance of the East African territories.

2. It is suggested that this assessment should be based on the following two alternative assumptions:—

(a) that the Sudan maintains its independence and continues in friendly and reasonably co-operative relations with Her Majesty's Government and the United Kingdom, or.
(b) that the Sudan either goes into some form of political association with Egypt or comes increasingly under Egyptian domination or influence.

3. It would be appreciated if the Chiefs of Staff could state what in their view would be the strategic requirements of the United Kingdom in East Africa, on these two alternative assumptions,

(i) for the defence of East Africa in a global war;
(ii) for the defence of East Africa in the case of a limited war and, in particular, if we make assumption (b), of local aggression by Egypt.

4. I realise that political penetration and propaganda may well represent a greater danger than military aggression. I think, however, that plans for dealing with the former could be made more satisfactorily in the light of the answers to the questions on which the Chiefs of Staff are being asked to advise.

5 I am sending a copy of this letter to Kisch[3] at the Colonial Office.[4]

---

[1] See 74, note 3.   [2] Commodore H Lovegrove, secretary, COS Committee.
[3] J M Kisch, principal, CO, 1946–1956.
[4] This assessment was deferred pending further consideration of policy towards the Somaliland protectorate (CO 822/1195).

85   FO 371/118676, no 1   30 Jan 1956

[Soviet influence in Africa]: letter from R L D Jasper[1] to J H A Watson[2]

Since our conversation the other day I have sent you a copy of my letter to Ronald Belcher[3] in Capetown about South African foreign policy questions. I have also noted, and explained to the other heads of Departments concerned here, the range of problems on which you would like to be kept closely informed.[4] We will do our best.

There are a number of problems on which we from our side should like to be kept closely in the picture. We are giving rather more consideration to this, and I will let you have a general note later. But one in which my Secretary of State is at present taking a close personal interest is the question of Soviet influence in North and mid-Africa, and its effect upon South Africa, Rhodesia, and those Colonial territories which are approaching the stage of independence.

Your third room were good enough some weeks ago to get for my Secretary of State a report from Capper[5] in Monrovia about the visit of a Russian Delegation to the Liberian Government. Capper's report was useful but not very full. And I understand that you will be asking him to keep you in close touch. It may perhaps be a help if I indicate the points which particularly interest us in this at the moment:—

(a) The possible effects of Soviet presence in Liberia on the political attitudes of the Gold Coast and Nigerian Governments to matters arising out of their progress towards independence. One must remember that Nkrumah[6] was once a member of the Party.

(b) The effect of Soviet penetration on the attitudes of South Africa and Rhodesia to this area. Paradoxically we may gain some advantage from this if South Africa's interest in West Africa grows as a result.

(c) The need for close consultation between you, the Colonial Office and ourselves on these aspects of Soviet penetration.

I should be most grateful for any further material you can let us have on this question, and if you think it useful we might have a talk one day soon with the Colonial Office, with your Northern Department, and with Constitutional Department and Central African Department here.

I am sending copies of this letter to John Marnham[7] in the Colonial Office. . . .[8]

---

[1] R L D Jasper, CRO 1955–1960; member of UK delegation to UN, 1955 and 1956.

[2] J H A Watson, British embassy, Washington, 1950–1956; head of Africa Dept, FO, 1956–1959.

[3] R H Belcher, assistant secretary, CRO, 1954–1956; deputy high commissioner in South Africa, 1956–1959.

[4] Watson had just taken over as head of the FO's African Dept.

[5] Maj C F Capper, UK ambassador to Republic of Liberia, 1952–1956.

[6] Dr Kwame Nkrumah, leader of government business, Gold Coast, 1951–1952; prime minister, 1952–1957; prime minister of Ghana, 1957–1960; president, 1960–1966.

[7] See 6, note 3. Marnham was head of the International Relations Dept, CO, in 1956.

[8] The FO was receiving reports from its own intelligence sources about increasing Soviet interest in Africa. On 8 Feb, Watson, 'disturbed by the evidence' but 'not sure just what the evidence is', called for a report assessing the evidence that 'the priority given to African matters by Communist parties, subversive organisations, Front organisations, Communist broadcasting stations, etc., has increased in the last few months . . . It would be useful to have this in time for the drafting of the Russia Committee's monthly paper for February' (minute by Watson, FO 371/118676, no 4, 8 Feb 1956). See 87.

86 FO 371/118676, no 7 9 Feb 1956

[US concern at Soviet activities in Africa]: letter from A Campbell (Washington)[1] to R J Vile[2]

With reference to my letter Ca.35/56 of the 24th January, it will not have escaped you that in the "Times" of the 2nd February there is a Reuter report from Moscow to the effect that when Mr. Volkov was asked whether the Russians had it in mind to establish diplomatic relations with the Gold coast, he replied: "Why not establish diplomatic relations? I assume the establishment of normal relations is not excluded, provided there is good will on the part of both sides."

I was asked to go down to the State Department yesterday to see the Head of the African Division, and Donald Dumont, who looks after East and West Africa. They read me an excerpt from a despatch which Lamm, their Consul-General in Accra, had sent to them about another matter which is, in their minds, because of the Liberian experience, linked up with this question of exchanging diplomatic representation. Lamm's despatch reported the desire of Botsio,[3] who was at the Liberian celebrations, to invite Russia to the Gold Coast independence celebrations.[4] According to Lamm, although Botsio had not in fact come out into the open and said Russia must be invited, he had persistently turned down lists of countries to be invited on the grounds that the range was not wide enough, and Lamm seems to have got it into his mind that he is determined that Russia should get an invitation. The Americans fear that this may lead to an exchange of diplomatic representation. Although they would not be so clumsy as to try to persuade the Gold Coast to avoid this, they are deeply disturbed at the resultant opportunities for trouble if such an exchange of representation did in fact take place.

It is somewhat unusual for the African Division of the State Department to ask me to go down and see them: generally I have to take the initiative, and in the past Communism in West Africa has not been one of the subjects which has got under their skin. Now, however, they seem to be seeing a Communist behind every chair, so I asked them what was the reason for this. They said that the proposed exchange of diplomatic representation with Liberia—which they are fairly confident that Tubman[5] will scotch—and also Russian activities in Libya had made them very apprehensive. The Russians have a mission of 17 people in Libya, and the calibre of their Ambassador is such that they do not regard his parish as being confined to Libya at all. They have also offered Libya technical assistance, and every time the Libyans get an offer from Russia they come round to the State Department in order to raise the wind a little stronger with them. In any case it is, of course, perfectly true that the Russians are bound by their revolutionary philosophy to take an interest in the Gold Coast and Nigeria, and despite past rebuffs they may feel that they are now

---

[1] A Campbell, colonial attaché, British embassy, Washington, 1953–1956.

[2] R J Vile, principal, CO, 1947–1953, assistant secretary, West Africa Department 'B', 1954–1961 (deceased).

[3] Kojo Botsio was a close associate of Nkrumah and minister of state in the Gold Coast Cabinet, 1954, and leader of the Legislative Assembly, 1956.

[4] The US State Department was equally concerned that a Chinese delegation had been invited to attend the independence celebrations in Accra. See correspondence in PREM 11/1859; also, BDEEP series B, R Rathbone, ed, *Ghana*, part II, 292.

[5] President of Liberia.

T

technically well enough equipped to offer these two countries something which they need.

I should be grateful therefore if you would let me know what truth there is in Lamm's reports about an invitation to the independence celebrations, as well as any information which you may have on exchange of diplomatic representation.[6] I would require to know whether I could pass any of it on to the Americans.

---

[6] Sir G Hadow, deputy governor, Gold Coast, wrote to Vile on 2 Mar that Gold Coast ministers would indeed invite Soviet representatives to their independence celebrations in order to 'demonstrate their freedom of action', but that an exchange of diplomatic representation was 'very doubtful so far as we can at present foresee' (FO 371/118676, no 7).

87   FO 371/118676, no 9   [Feb 1956]
'Soviet penetration of Africa': report by Information Research
Department, FO   [Extract]

Summary
Recent Soviet moves in Africa, such as the establishment of diplomatic relations with Libya and the visit of a Soviet delegation to Liberia, are part of a concerted plan to follow up the Soviet thrust into the Middle East. Using Egypt as a "bridge", the Communists hope to gain more direct contact with the rebel movement and Communist networks in French North Africa and to use this territory for penetration southwards at a later stage.

I. *Recent developments*
Overtures by the Communist bloc to Egypt, Syria and Saudi Arabia began to increase sharply after the Bandung Conference in April, 1955. At this gathering Colonel Nasser, the Egyptian Prime Minister, played a prominent part in smoothing out the rift between countries prepared to accept the advances of Communist China and those who attacked Communist imperialism: Iraq, Persia, Pakistan and Ceylon. After advocating the formation of a Middle neutralist block in July and August, Soviet propaganda in Arabic hardened in September, 1955, calling on the Arab countries to develop closer links with the Communist bloc. Simultaneous diplomatic overtures reinforced this appeal.

Egypt
In August Colonel Nasser agreed to visit the Soviet Union. In September a Cultural Bureau operated by the Soviet VOKS organisation was opened in Cairo, following arrangements with Egypt hastily concluded in June. On September 27, the Czech-Egyptian arms deal was announced; on October 10 Solod, then Soviet Ambassador in Cairo, offered Egypt economic aid with the High Dam project, and proposed the exchange of agricultural, educational and other missions. . . .

The Sudan
Evidence of Communist intentions to penetrate further South, taking advantage of imminent Sudanese independence, was also forthcoming. Czech and Russian trade delegations visited the Sudan in February and June, 1955. On October 20 *Reuter*

reported Sudanese Cabinet approval for the opening of Czech and Soviet "Liaison Offices" in Khartoum, and the same month the Sudanese Minister of Transport visisted Prague. Following the declaration of Sudanese independence, the Soviet bloc hastened to recognise the new Government and offered to establish diplomatic relations. Additional offers and expressions of interest and recognition were noted from Communist China, Hungary, Roumania and Bulgaria.

Ethiopia

During 1955, Czechoslovakia first sent a trade mission to Addis Ababa and later established a Legation there. This was followed by Czech offers of sugar-factory machinery and cotton-spinning equipment, including complete buildings and technical staffs.

Polish, Bulgarian, East German and Hungarian missions also visited Addis Ababa during the year, while Czechoslovakia participated in the Ethiopian Jubilee Trade Fair in the Autumn.

II. *Axis of new communist drive in Africa*

Apart from a number of small rival Communist groups in Egypt and two similar organisations in the Sudan, there is at present little scope for developing a mass political movement capable of assisting a Communist rise to power in these countries. Nevertheless, considerable scope for the training of agents is implicit in offers of complete factories with "technical" staffs. Such offers have been a feature of recent Soviet bloc overtures. A notorious example of the use of these methods was the Caspian Fisheries Concession in Persia, closed down early in 1954.

For penetration into Africa, the importance of French North Africa as chief bridgehead has long been recognized by Soviet students and tacticians. Among Soviet approaches to African countries, those to Libya and Liberia, which adjoin French territory, seem particularly significant.

Libya

Soviet propaganda has hitherto presented Libya as a "terror-police régime" imposed by the "imperialists". King Idris was denounced as a "feudalist" and a "creature of the English" in an official publication of the Soviet Academy of Sciences issued in Moscow in 1954 under the title *The Imperialist Struggle for Africa*.

In the United Nations the U.S.S.R. at first sought to convert Libya from an Italian colony into a Trusteeship territory, with Soviet representation on its Governing Council; Soviet recognition of Libya was later refused when the country's independence was proclaimed in December, 1951. This, however did not prevent the Soviet Union from seeking to establish diplomatic relations with Libya at short notice in September, 1955.

Three months later, in January, 1956, a Soviet diplomatic mission headed by a trained Orientalist, N I Generalov, was established in Tripoli. . . .

IV. *Controversy in Moscow*

After the failure of the main Communist effort to penetrate North African between 1950 and 1954 through political channels, a trades union approach was attempted which was likewise unsuccessful. The Communists then resorted to new but vain attempts to exploit nationalist groups.

In the large number of expert studies on Africa written in Moscow in recent years, several important facts stand out. The strategic significance of French North Africa for Soviet penetration of the continent as a whole is consistently recognised, as also is the importance of the area to Western defence plans. Previous failures to establish well-defined channels for political or trade union penetration, however, have given rise to a good deal of uncertainty and academic debate. . . .

Examples of discimination [sic] between nationalist movements regarded as capable of exploitation and those that are genuine are seen in recent Communist attacks on the nationalist parties in Tunisia and Algeria, and on the Muslim nationalist movement *Masjumi*, in Indonesia. In Iran, it will be remembered, Dr. Mussadeqh was supported by the Tudeh Party only when his policies were thought to suit Communist purposes. Today, for the same reason, the Soviet Union adopts a flattering attitude to the Egyptian Government, although not long ago the same régime was frequently and contemptuously described as a "Fascist military dictatorship".

Role of communist organisations
The Soviet campaign to penetrate Africa is part of the grand strategy of the Kremlin leaders, the latest stage in their struggle for world domination. . . .

88 CAB 129/80, CP(56)84   24 Mar 1956
'The Horn of Africa': joint Cabinet memorandum by Mr Selwyn Lloyd and Mr Lennox-Boyd on security problems

Our colleagues should be aware of certain developments in this area, which can be defined as that lying to the East of Longitude 43° on the accompanying map.[1] It is inhabited almost exclusively by Somalis and includes British Somaliland, the Trusteeship territory of Somalia (ex-Italian Somaliland) under Italian administration, and a portion of Ethiopia.

2. The Somali population, although in many respects backward, is increasing rapidly and is also becoming increasingly nationalist-minded. Somalia is due to achieve independence by 1960, and may do so before. The effect of this development on the Somalis of the Somaliland Protectorate is considered in the paper on future policy in the Protectorate by the Colonial Secretary (C.P.(56) 89).[2] The purpose of this paper is to invite consideration of the policy which we should adopt towards an independent Somalia.

3. The natural resources of Somalia are insufficient to make her economy viable without outside help. At present the Italians subsidise it to the extent of £2–3 millions a year; they get nothing in return for this and there are reports that they wish to withdraw. We have asked them what their intentions are.

4. The Egyptians are showing an increasing interest in Somalia and also in the Protectorate. Because of the lack of Arabic teachers elsewhere the Italians have imported large numbers of Egyptians and Egypt is also represented on the United Nations Advisory Council for Somalia. Nasser is therefore in a good position to carry

---

[1] Not printed (see 97, note 1).   [2] See part II of this volume, 297.

on intensive propaganda among the Somalis. An independent Somalia under Egyptian influence, which must now be reckoned to carry with it the probability of Russian infiltration, would be a direct threat to Kenya, which has a considerable Somali population. If the Sudan were also under Egyptian influence, we should be faced with a pincer movement threatening all our East African territories.

5. If independent Somalia is to be prevented from coming under the influence of Egypt or the Russians, the West will need to subsidise her and provide advisers and technical help. One possibility would be for us to do this alone. But this might alienate the Italians and the Ethiopians; it would also be expensive. An alternative would be to form a consortium of Powers (which would have to be acceptable to the Somalis of the Protectorate as well as of Somalia); not to administer the country, but to provide the necessary financial and technical help. The Powers who might be invited to joint the consortium would be the four who have responsibility for Somali population (ourselves, France, Italy and Ethiopia—but see paragraph 6), the United States as the major financial power of the West, and perhaps Pakistan as a respectable and nearby Moslem power. We do not know the views of any of these Powers; but the Italians are also apparently thinking in terms of a consortium; and the Americans and the French are also aware of the problem posed by expanding Somali nationalism.

6. Logically Ethiopia should certainly take part in the scheme. But there is a long standing hostility between the Ethiopians and the Somalis both of the Protectorate and Somalia. This has been exacerbated recently by Ethiopian behaviour over the Haud[3] and the Reserved Areas. Such indeed is the resentment of all Somalis, and particularly our own Somalis, that unless the Ethiopians were prepared to make a major concession over these territories (free access to and control of which is a vital need for our Somalis) any attempt to include Ethiopia in a consortium against the wishes of the Somalis would founder, might well drive all Somalis into the arms of the Egyptians, and would create serious disturbances in Somali territories. But to exclude Ethiopia would ensure her opposition to any progressive policy for the Somalis. It might even drive her to seek the support of the Soviet *bloc*, who are making increasing efforts to penetrate the country. This would open up an equally serious threat to our East African territories. This question is considered further in paragraph 10 below.

7. The Ethiopians are themselves alive to the danger of becoming surrounded by aggressively nationalist Moslem states. They already see the Egyptians aiming to dominate the Sudan on their Western border and they must be aware of Egyptian activities in Somalia. We therefore suggest that the delegation which goes to Addis Ababa next month should draw their attention to the danger of Egyptian penetration with the object of persuading the Ethiopian Government that it is in their own interests to co-operate with Her Majesty's Government in a more sympathetic policy towards the Somalis.

---

[3] The Haud was an area of Ethiopian territory traditionally used by pastoralists from British Somaliland for seasonal grazing. By agreement with Ethiopia Britain had maintained a military administration there for many years. In an Anglo-Ethiopian agreement of 1954 Britain had confirmed its recognition of Ethiopian sovereignty over the Haud and had withdrawn its personnel in exchange for an Ethiopian guarantee of Somali access to the grazing lands. By 1956 there were signs that Ethiopia was failing to honour this agreement. For earlier background, see BDEEP series A, R Hyam, ed, *The Labour government and the end of empire 1945–1951*, part III, chapter 6(2).

8. The central question is that of the Haud and there are various ways in which the present resentment of the Somalis might be mitigated. The minimum would be a radical change in the attitude of the Ethiopian authorities towards the Somali tribes in the territories covered by the Agreement of 1954. The recent conversations in Harar were designed to achieve this but failed in their purpose. We have considered the possibility of a lease of the territories. We do not consider that in the long run this would be satisfactory, and in any case the Ethiopians refused the idea three years ago. If they should raise it of their own accord we would however want to examine it again. But the only entirely satisfactory solution from our point of view would be outright cession of the territories by the Ethiopians to the Protectorate. From what we know of the Ethiopian attitude to their own territory there is little chance of our achieving this. But we recommend that the attempt should be made and that Her Majesty's Government should be willing to offer a substantial payment to that end: even if this is rejected by the Ethiopians, the Somalis will see that we have been willing to make a sacrifice in order to secure their essential grazing rights. We understand that the Treasury, with whom our Departments have been in consultation, feel that the kind of sum which would have to be offered (probably a minimum of £5 millions) should not be paid and therefore that no firm offer of a money payment should be made to the Ethiopians. We still feel, however, that a firm offer of this kind should be made and therefore ask that our colleagues should consider the proposal.

9. In return for the *cession* of the territories we should be prepared to offer the Ethiopians not only a substantial cash payment (if our colleagues agree), supplemented if necessary by a gift of military and naval equipment; but also the following undertakings:—

(i) to ensure in the Agreement registering the cession that the traditional grazing rights of Ethiopian Somali tribes in the territories and in the Protectorate were guaranteed, and would be entrenched in any instrument conferring self-government on the Somalis of the Protectorate;

(ii) to facilitate the opening of an Ethiopian Consultate in Hargeisa as soon as practicable;

(iii) to press to an early conclusion the Treaty of Friendship and Commerce with Ethiopia already being considered;

(iv) to discuss the possibility of a further Treaty of Alliance.

10. The question arises whether we should also be prepared to tell the Ethiopians that, if they will agree to the cession of the Haud, we will support, with the other parties concerned, the idea of their participation in any international arrangements which may be made in relation to Somalia after the Italian withdrawal. The Governor of the Protectorate has advised in the strongest terms that, even if we concluded a cession of the Haud, any attempt on our part to bring the Ethiopians into a consortium would have a devastating and irrevocable effect on Somali opinion and bring about just [sic] all those consequences in the Horn of Africa which it is our main object to avoid. Accordingly his view, which is supported by the Colonial Office, is that this offer cannot be made to the Ethiopians, even in return for a cession of the Haud. The Foreign Office, on the other hand, consider that, if this offer is not made, such prospect as there might otherwise be of a cession of the Haud will disappear; and also that for us to sponsor any international arrangements for Somalia from

which Somalia's closest neighbour is excluded, would have a disastrous effect on our relations with Ethiopia, push her towards our enemies, and make her more intransigent towards Somalia. This issue is therefore one on which we cannot make an agreed recommendation and would like to discuss with our colleagues. If the Ethiopians are not prepared to agree to cession, the delegation should endeavour to secure from them a satisfactory change in their interpretation and operation of the 1954 Agreement. If necessary, they should explore what inducements the Ethiopians might require for this purpose, such as, for example, an offer of co-operation for the improvement of land-usage in Ethiopia. Our colleagues should know however that the Protectorate Government foresees great difficulty in conceding any of points (ii), (iii) and (iv).

11.   In the meantime we propose that we should examine with the United States, French, and Italian Governments the question of the future of Somalia after the Italian withdrawal. Although we would not commit Her Majesty's Government to any particular solution we might try out with them the idea of an international consortium.

89   CAB 128/30/1, CM 26(56)1   29 Mar 1956
'Somalia and British Somaliland': Cabinet conclusions on future policy   [Extract]

The Cabinet had before them a joint memorandum by the Foreign Secretary and Colonial Secretary (C.P. (56) 84)[1] on future policy towards an independent Somalia, and a memorandum by the Colonial Secretary (C.P. (56) 89) on the future of British Somaliland.[2]

The Cabinet first discussed the proposals in C.P. (56) 84 on the future of an independent Somalia. They were informed that the Egyptians were showing increased interest in this area and that large numbers of Egyptian teachers had recently been brought into it. If, after attaining independence, Somalia fell under Egyptian influence, this would represent a direct threat to the security of Kenya; and, if Egyptian influence also extended to the Sudan, the security of all British territories in East Africa would be threatened. If Somalia was to be kept under Western indluence, she would need financial assistance and technical help from the West. The Cabinet agreed that this could not be provided by the United Kingdom alone. If we accept any fresh commitments in this area, we must do so in association with other Powers. If a consortium of Western Powers could be established for this purpose, Ethiopia should logically be associated with it. This, however, would be unacceptable to the Somalis. With a view to improving relations between Ethiopia and the Somalis and, more immediately, for the benefit of British Somaliland, our first aim should be to seek a solution of the problem of Somali grazing rights in the Haud. For this purpose it was suggested that Ethiopia might be asked to cede the Haud to British Somaliland in return for a cash payment of not less than £5 millions and certain other concessions set out in paragraph 9 of C.P. (56) 84.

---

[1] See 88.
[2] Only the conclusions on Somalia are reproduced here; for Lennox-Boyd's memo on British Somaliland (CP(56)89) and Cabinet discussion thereon, see part II of this volume, 297.

In discussion the following points were made:—

(a) *The Foreign Secretary* said that he was making enquiries about the reported increase in the numbers of Egyptians who were being brought into Somalia, as teachers and in other positions. If the facts justified such an approach, he would make representations about this to the Italian Government.

(b) It was doubtful whether the Ethiopian Government would be willing to entertain the suggestion that they should voluntarily cede a portion of their territory. On the other hand, if the offer were made and refused, we should at least be able to inform the Somalis that we had made this effort on their behalf.

(c) *The Chancellor of the Exchequer* said that he was far from satisfied that we should be justified in making any cash payment for the cession of this territory. Even if the Ethiopians were willing to consider the possibility, they were likely to ask for substantially more than the minimum figure of £5 millions which was mentioned in C.P. (56) 84. Whatever the sum, we should have to pay it in gold or dollars; and in present circumstances he would be most reluctant to accept such a commitment.

In discussion it was argued that, if the whole of this area fell under the influence of hostile Powers, we should face a much heavier commitment in safeguarding the security of other British possessions in East Africa. It was, however, suggested that the Ethiopians might be willing to accept compensation in kind, instead of cash. They were beginning to show interest in sea power; and they might be willing to accept, at least in part payment, some of the warships which we were now keeping in the lowest class of reserve.

The Prime Minister, summing up this part of the discussion, said that this memorandum unfolded large possibilities, which could only be approached by stages. The Parliamentary Under-Secretary of State for Foreign Affairs (Mr. Dodds-Parker) was shortly undertaking a mission to Ethiopia during which he would be discussing the question of Somalia-Ethiopia relations. In the course of his negotiations he might tentatively explore the possibility of a cession of territory to British Somaliland. He could not be authorised at this stage to offer any cash payment; but he might, if opportunity offered, canvass the possibility that the Ethiopians might accept some warships in return for a cession of territory. The Prime Minister added that he would himself send a personal message to the Emperor of Ethiopia seeking his co-operation.

The Cabinet:—

(1) Invited the Foreign Secretary to give instructions to the Parliamentary Under-Secretary of State of Foreign Affairs (Mr. Dodds-Parker) along the lines indicated by the Prime Minister in summing up the discussion.

(2) Took note that the Prime Minister would send, through Mr. Dodds-Parker, a personal message to the Emperor of Ethiopia inviting his co-operation. . . .[3]

---

[3] For the outcome of the Dodds-Parker mission, see 97.

90   CAB 129/81, CP(56)109   1 May 1956

'Strategic importance of the Somaliland Protectorate': Cabinet
memorandum by COS

[In discussing Lennox-Boyd's memo on British Somaliland at its meeting on 29 March
(see 89, note 2 and part II of this volume, 297), Cabinet had invited Monckton to 'arrange
for the Chiefs of Staff to submit an appreciation of the strategic value of British
Somaliland to the British position in this area'.]

Introduction

1.   Our recent agreement with Ethiopia providing for the withdrawal of our
Military Administration from the Haud, and the approach of the grant of independence to the Trust Territory of Somalia in 1960, has made it necessary to reconsider
our future policy in the Protectorate.

2.   This reconsideration of future policy is being carried out by the Colonial Office
and, in this connection, the Minister of Defence has asked us:—

(a) To reaffirm our assessment of the strategic importance of the Somaliland
Protectorate and of the minimum strategic rights which we should retain there if
British control were relinquished.
(b) To state the degree of importance which we attach to the achievement of these
rights.
(c) To state whether we regard the rights as so important that a formal agreement
embodying them is an essential pre-requisite to self-government.

Strategic considerations

General

3.   The Somaliland Protectorate offers strategic advantages somewhat similar to
those of Aden, except that its port facilities are not sufficiently developed to be of any
value to the Royal Navy. As our influence in the Suez Canal area diminishes, so will
the Southern Red Sea area assume for us an ever-increasing importance.

4.   There are, however, reasons why too great a degree of dependence upon our
existing facilities in Aden may prove unwise in the future. These are:—

(a) The Russians are at present attempting to undermine our Northern Tier
system of defence in the Middle East by subverting the Arab States in its rear.
(b) In face of subversion by Saudi Arabia and the Yemen, possibly Soviet
encouraged, coupled with internal disorders in the Aden Protectorate, we may
eventually find that the Aden base would be less secure than it appears at present.
(c) The grant of independence to Somalia in 1960 is bound to have an unsettling
effect in Aden.

5.   We therefore feel that, in considering our possible requirements in Somaliland, we should not assume that Aden facilities will necessarily be adequate or secure
for all purposes in the future.

6.   The situation would be worsened if, after gaining independence in 1960,
Somalia fell under Egyptian or Russian influence. This would represent a direct
threat to the security of Kenya and if this influence were also extended to the Sudan,

the security of all the British territories in East Africa would be threatened. We consider that retention of the airfields and other facilities in British Somaliland may well play a vital part in maintaining stability in North-East Africa. The relinquishment of British control of the Protectorate would make the effective use of these facilities more difficult and there would be a positive military advantage in retaining our control as long as possible. If self-government is eventually granted, it is essential that our minimum strategic rights are safeguarded.

Minimum strategic rights

7.   *The overflying and air staging rights*. As a result of the loss of our unrestricted overflying rights in Egypt, the movement of aircraft through the Middle East will, after April 1956, depend not only on the goodwill of those countries which we wish to overfly, but also on their tacit approval for the operation on which we are engaged. In addition the situation in the Sudan is uncertain, and it is possible that we may lose our overflying rights in this area. If this happens, and in addition we lose the northern route through Syria or Turkey, our route, United Kingdom–Far East, would have to be redirected through central Africa. Therefore the retention of overflying rights and air staging rights in Somaliland might be important. In addition, should Egypt and the Sudan deny us overflying rights, it would be desirable to be able to overfly Somaliland on the Middle East–East Africa route.

8.   *Stationing of forces*. We should retain the right to station forces in British Somaliland if the need arises. This would enable us to maintain stability in the area and would ensure our ability to make use of the staging facilities.

9.   *Other rights*. It is desirable to have such rights of use and development in the ports as are required to support any forces which it may be necessary to station in the Protectorate.

10.   *Oil*. Oil prospecting is being carried out, and if this is successful, the strategic value of the Protectorate would be enhanced. We must therefore ensure that we would have the right to develop any oil resources in the territory.

The necessity of a formal agreement

11.   Although the Somalis are at present well disposed towards us, we cannot be certain that their attitude may not change, after self-government has been granted, to one of aggressive nationalism.

12.   We therefore consider that these rights should be embodied in a formal agreement as an essential prerequisite to self-government.

Conclusions

13.   We conclude that:—

(a) In view of recent events in the Middle East the strategic importance of the Somaliland Protectorate has increased.

(b) If self-government were granted to the Protectorate it would be essential to retain the following minimum strategic rights:—

   (i) Overflying and air staging rights.
   (ii) The right to station forces.
   (iii) Concessions in respect of possible oil and mineral production and pipeline facilities.

(iv) Use and development of ports and anchorages.

(c) The embodiment of the strategic rights in paragraph 13(b) above is an essential prerequisite to self-government.[1]

---

[1] During Cabinet discussion of this memo 'it was suggested that . . . it would be preferable that Italy should not withdraw from Somalia in 1960' since 'there were powerful arguments for preserving the *status quo* in this area'. The foreign secretary, Selwyn Lloyd, was invited 'to consider what prospect there might be of securing an extension of Italian trusteeship for Somalia' (CAB 128/30/1, CM 36(56)3, 15 May 1956). See 94.

---

91 FO 371/118676, no 11   2 May 1956

[Egyptian and Soviet policy in Africa]: brief by African Dept, FO, for Lord Lloyd's[1] discussions in Rome

H.M.G. must regard with suspicion present Egyptian attempts to expand their influence in the Horn of Africa. For despite attempts on our part to improve Anglo-Egyptian relations (withdrawal from the Suez Canal, High Aswan Dam, etc.) the Egyptians have maintained a steady stream of abusive propaganda against us. They have beamed critical and inflammatory broadcasts (extolling Mau-Mau etc.) towards our East African territories. They abuse our attempts in the Horn of Africa and East Africa to maintain law and order and develop our territories on sound principles.

2. In regard to Somalia itself, we are concerned by the questionable activities of the representative of Egypt on the Advisory Council. (The Somali Democratic Party have already complained about this to the United Nations.) We are also disturbed by the large influx of Egyptian teachers. We fully realise that Education is a fundamental requirement if Somalia is to be a stable modern state. (H.M.G. is giving serious consideration to this problem, not only in regard to British Somaliland, but as regards the whole Horn of Africa.) A cadre of educated citizens will obviously have to be formed to take over the administration of the country. We appreciate the Italian arguments that at present Egypt alone can provide teachers that they require. However, we should point out to the Italians the obvious dangers of recruiting all teachers from this one source.

3. Egyptian infiltration is the more dangerous, in that it may be exploited by the Soviet and satellite powers. Egyptian offers of financial and technical help could well provide good cover for Communist infiltration.

4. Present Soviet policy is clearly to extend Communist influence in under-developed and uncommitted countries. A Sino-Soviet economic drive in the Middle East and South and South-East Asia is already under way, and takes the form of extremely favourable offers of capital equipment and assistance over development projects, and also of arms deals. In the Middle East, the main objectives include Egypt and the Sudan.

5. In Egypt there have been the Soviet offer of assistance over the High Dam and the Czech arms deal. A Soviet trade mission and other satellite missions are likely to be established in Khartoum; and a Sudan Defence Force mission has visited Prague.

---

[1] Lord Lloyd, parliamentary under-secretary of state, CO, 1954–1957.

There are also signs that the Soviet bloc is trying to penetrate Ethiopia; the principal method used is the granting of very favourable commercial terms (e.g. by Czech and East German trade missions) to Arab and Indian merchants in the provinces.

6. Although this economic drive is unlikely to lead to severe competition with the West within the next five years, it has great long-term dangers and carries with it a more immediate political threat in the form of the encouragement of neutralism; the use of economic links as blackmail; and the fostering of Communist and fellow-travelling activities. The penetration of the armed forces of the under-developed countries through the provision of Soviet weapons and technical facilities is particularly dangerous.

7. There are in addition signs that a Communist drive on "black" Africa has begun which, while not a serious danger at present, is likely to face the West with a serious threat within the next two years. A Soviet publication at the end of 1954 reached the conclusion that the necessary social forces now exist in Africa to organise the struggle on a regional and national basis. An African section was formed last year in the Soviet Academy of Sciences to study the history, economy, language and literature of the peoples of South and Central Africa and to compile Hausa and Swahili dictionaries. Soviet Scientific missions seem likely to play their part in this African campaign and international "front" organisations like the I.U.S., W.F.T.U., and W.F.D.Y. have been instructed to pay more attention to African affairs.

92   FO 371/118676, no 14   14 May 1956
[NATO concern at Soviet policy in Africa]: letter from N J A Cheetham (Paris)[1] to J H A Watson

Thank you for sending us a copy of your very interesting despatch J 1023/6 G of April 21 to Paris and other posts about long term Russian policy in Africa.

2. As you know, NATO has for the last year or so been taking a much greater interest in the world wide Communist threat. At the last three Ministerial meetings, for example, a good deal of time has been spent in discussing the current situation in the Middle East and Far East. And at the Ministerial meeting a year ago, Dr. Cunha, the Portuguese Foreign Minister, pointed out that in this connexion Africa also would in time be as important as the Middle East and Far East.

3. This broadening of NATO interest has of course corresponded to the development of the international situation in the last few years. It was owing to the immediate threat of Russian military aggression in Europe that NATO was set up in the first place. It was no doubt largely because of NATO's success in meeting this threat that the Russians probed deeply and energetically in Asia and the Middle East. As the Russian intentions became clearer there was a fairly general awareness that NATO had a responsibility to meet the Communist threat throughout the whole world. If NATO's flank were turned all that NATO stood for might be lost. And the flank could be turned not merely in a military sense. There was also the danger, in some ways greater, that Russia would acquire a dominant political influence in certain key countries of the East.

4. It is also worth bearing in mind that the four great colonial powers in

---

[1] N J A Cheetham, UK deputy permanent representative on North Atlantic Council, 1954–1959.

Africa—ourselves, Belgium, France and Portugal, are all members of NATO. From certain points of view Italy might be added to this list. All of these countries have particular interests in Africa. It is only because of their African possessions that Belgium and Portugal—and, one might even say, France—are anything more than medium sized European Powers. And we ourselves and the sterling area depend vitally on Africa for raw materials e.g. gold, uranium and copper.

5. This combination of wider and narrower, shorter and longer term interests shows that the Russian initiatives directed towards Africa affect NATO closely.

6. You might therefore wish to consider whether the North Atlantic Council could not play a useful part in discussing an issue which, in the long term, is a matter of vital importance to us all. It might be over ambitious to hope that NATO could function as an efficient coordinating machine. Regular discussions, however, and exchanges of information might well have useful practical results and moreover serve to keep in the forefront a threat which is not impressed on NATO by, for example, the newspapers.

7. Could you please let us know what you think of these suggestions and in the meanwhile keep us informed of the replies from posts to your despatch? In the light of such replies, we can consider at what stage to sound our colleagues in the more interested Delegations.

8. I am sending copies of this letter to Paris, Brussels, Lisbon, Washington, Bonn, Rome and Moscow.

93   CO 936/336/3D   15 May 1956

'Arab influence on other African Moslems': note by J H A Watson for UK delegation to Anglo-French official talks on colonial problems, May 1956

The Arab world has a natural attraction for all Moslems, since it is the cradle and fountain of Islam. The improvement in means of travel, of disseminating news and the spread of literacy has considerably increased the attraction of the Arab world.

2. The principal attraction for the Moslem intelligentsia of Africa is Egypt. Egypt is an important African power. It is the cultural centre of the Arab world. Its well-produced broadcasts have a considerable and growing appeal, theological students are trained in the Azar and other students go to lay Egyptian universities; they often return impressed. Egyptian teachers and preachers are also to be found in Moslem Africa.

3. The second greatest Arab attraction for Moslem Africans are the holy places in Saudi Arabia. The Pilgrimage is becoming increasingly easy owning to air travel. These visits do not necessarily make pilgrims pro-Saudi; but they do bring them into contact with Nationalist and other ideas which are assiduously disseminated among pilgrims.

4. The influence of the Arab world, and especially that of Egypt, is increasingly political and increasingly hostile to western influence and leadership. It paints the white man as an enemy and an oppressor. It advocates neutralism and extreme nationalism; and is in many ways a forerunner of Communist ideas which it does nothing to combat.

5. The strategic importance of the Sudan in this context is considerable. It is the only important land gateway from Egypt and the Middle East into Black Africa. The efforts of the Russians, Chinese and Satellites in the Sudan emphasise the importance attached by the Communists to the use of this gateway for the offensive against Black Africa which they are now visibly preparing.

6. It is too early to say what the effects of the independence of the Sudan and the new North African states, (Libya, Tunisia and Morocco) will have [sic] on Moslems to the south. If these new African countries come to resist and resent Egyptian dominance and adopt a policy of alliance and interdependence with the West, while enjoying full sovereignty at home, other African Moslems may draw the conclusion that this is also the right policy for them. But if these countries come to adopt a neutralist policy, or (worse still) become actively hostile to the West and align themselves with Egypt, the effect on other African Moslems will obviously be very serious.

94   CAB 129/81, CP(56)130   29 May 1956
'Somalia': Cabinet memorandum by Mr Selwyn Lloyd on the prospects of extending Italian trusteeship

The Cabinet on 15th May invited me to consider what prospect there might be of securing an extension of Italian trusteeship for Somalia (C.M. (56) 36th Conclusions, Minute 3).[1]

2. It is clear that the attempt to secure such an extension would be fraught with difficulty.

3. The United Nations decided, by a resolution passed in 1949, that Somalia should become independent by 1960. Any extension of Italian trusteeship would require the rescinding of this resolution by a two-thirds majority. This would involve a full-dress debate in the United Nations and our Permanent Representative reports that a majority of members would undoubtedly oppose any attempt to repeal the 1949 resolution. Without succeeding, we should provoke accusations of suppression of national aspirations.

4. Moreover, the Italians do not appear to want their trusteeship extended. They have made it clear in official discussions that they do not intend to remain in Somalia after 1960 (although they may be prepared to continue some sort of financial assistance). They would only consider continuing their responsibilities if persuaded to do so by a majority of Powers, and even then would be bound to take into account the wishes of the inhabitants of Somalia. They would be very unlikely to accept any postponent of their promised independence.

5. I recommend therefore that this proposal should not be further pursued.[2]

---

[1] See 90, note 1.
[2] Cabinet accepted this recommendation (CAB 128/30/1, CM 39(56)2, 5 June 1956).

95 FO 371/118677, no 24   11 June 1956

[US concern at Soviet policy in Africa]: letter from B Salt (Washington)[1] to J H A Watson

In his letter 10663/3/2/56 of May 14 Ronald Bailey[2] referred to the action taken by the Embassy in leaving with the State Department a copy of a paper based on Foreign Office despatch No. 307 to Paris (J 1023/6G) of April 21 about the possible extension of Soviet subversive activities in Africa.

2. Ronald is away at the moment and the Office of African Affairs have now given us informally a copy of the enclosed paper,[3] which represents the recommendations they have put up to a higher level in the State Department. It should therefore be regarded merely as the tentative thinking of the Department at desk level. You will see that the paper agrees generally with your assessment of the Communist threat and proposes the establishment of a Committee of officials from the Governments of the United Kingdom, France and the United States (and possibly Belgium) which would meet regularly to make joint recommendations for ways and means of combatting the Soviet campaign of subversion in this area. While it would not, of course, be correct for us at this stage to make any formal reply to this suggestion, which has not yet been put to us officially, there might be advantage in our letting the State Department know informally as soon as possible what you think about it. No doubt George Allen[4] will be considering the matter in connection with his recent African tour.

3. From the point of view of this post there seems at first sight to be some merit in the idea. It is to our advantage that the Americans should be encouraged to take an interest in the Colonial territories in Africa, provided of course they do not seek to interfere with matters which we regard as solely our concern. The main reason why the United States Administration, and the State Department in particular, have more sympathy for our Colonial policy than do the majority of the American press and people is their realisation that premature abdication of our Colonial responsibilities would leave a void, of which the Communists would not be slow to take advantage. It is therefore in our interest that they should get used to discussing with us means of repelling Communism in the Colonial territories. The Committee would presumably meet in private and would therefore not have the advantage of committing the United States publicly to the support of the Administering Powers. But its discussions might usefully colour the United States Government's thinking and hence affect the tone of their public pronouncements.

4. The idea of a confidential anti-Communist Committee is, of course, quite different from John Ford's proposal for cooperative political planning in the field of constitutional development, about which Willie Morris[5] was discouraging in his letter to him 1048/26/56G of May 28, which was copied to you. To begin with, the anti-Soviet Committee would work in private and would therefore not be exposed to interference by other non-Administering Powers. Another material difference seems

---

[1] Miss B Salt, counsellor, British embassy, Washington.

[2] R W Bailey, 1st secretary, British embassy, Washington.

[3] Not printed.

[4] G Allen, assistant under-secretary of state, US State Dept, in charge of Middle East and African affairs.

[5] W Morris, 1st secretary, British embassy, Washington.

to be that on the subject of Communism our aims and those of the United States are identical, whereas they tend to think differently from us about the rate of constitutional development.

5. I am copying this letter to John Beith at Paris, Mr. Curle at Brussels and Christopher Gandy at Lisbon.

96 FO 371/118677, no 26   4 July 1956

[Inclusion of Portugal in discussions on Soviet policy in Africa]: letter from Sir C Stirling (Lisbon)[1] to I T M Pink[2]

I notice from Miss Salt's letter to Watson of June 11 (Washington reference 10663/3/9/56)[3] that once again it is proposed to exclude Portugal from international consultations about Africa, this time in connection with Soviet subversion.

You will have seen from my despatch No. 117 of June 21 (and my letter No. 2222/15/56 of the same date to you alone) that I deprecate in general the omission of Portugal from such consultations. Apart from the effect on the feelings of the Portuguese Government, it seems to me that anything which associates them with our way of thinking on colonial questions has a useful educative effect. From the point of view of Portuguese feelings there is obviously much less objection to the exclusion of Portugal from a body which is clearly sponsored by the Americans. (I assume that the proposed committee would sit in Washington). On the other hand, if Belgium is included, I do not see why Portugal should be left out. On the question of Communist subversion in Africa we could not have a more reliable ally; and contact between the Portuguese and the Americans on colonial questions might be enlightening to both.

If the Embassy in Washington felt able to put the arguments in the preceeding paragraph discreetly to the State Department, I should be grateful. I can quite see that it might not do for us to push the Portuguese down American throats especially after the trouble Mr. Dulles got into with his statement on Portuguese India; and of course we should not want Portuguese colonial policy to be associated in American minds with our own.

If the Committee is not to sit in Washington the best solution might be for it to be set up discreetly within the framework of N.A.T.O. I see that Cheetham suggested something of the kind in his letter of May 14th to Watson.[4] This would make it easy to include Belgian and Portugal but not Spain and South Africa.

I am having this letter copied to Washington, Paris and Brussels.[5]

---

[1] Sir C Stirling, UK ambassador to Portugal, 1955–1960.
[2] I T M Pink, assistant under-secretary of state, FO, 1954–1958.   [3] See 95.
[4] See 92.
[5] Pink replied to Stirling that for the time being the FO would not take up either the American proposal of an official committee or Cheetham's proposal of talks within the NATO framework. The main reason was that 'we are having a lot of difficulty in convincing the Colonial Office, and also the C.R.O., that the Communist threat to Africa is as serious as we believe it to be.' Only when Whitehall achieved a unified view could there be any discussions with other governments. But if and when this came about, 'I am sure that we shall want the Portuguese to take part' (letter from Pink to Stirling, FO 371/118677, no 26, 27 July 1956).

97   CAB 129/82, CP(56)180   25 July 1956

'Somaliland Protectorate and the Horn of Africa': Cabinet memorandum by Mr Lennox-Boyd advocating the creation of a Greater Somalia.
Appendices: A & B

On 29th March the Cabinet considered the difficulties created for us by the
resumption of Ethiopian administration over the Haud and Reserved Area—called
"the Territories." A map of the area is attached (Appendix D).[1] They authorised the
Parliamentary Under-Secretary of State for Foreign Affairs (Mr. Dodds-Parker),
leader of the United Kingdom delegation to Ethiopia in April, to explore the
possibility of a cession of the territories by Ethiopia to the Protectorate and they
agreed that the policy statement for the Protectorate should be made (Appendix B
(C.M. (56) 26th Conclusions, Minute 1).[2]

2. Mr. Dodds-Parker tried to persuade the Ethiopian Government to cede the
Territories but was met with so vehement a refusal that one must conclude that no
attempt on our part to obtain the Territories by lease, barter or purchase at any price
which would be considered possible is ever likely to succeed. The United Kingdom
delegation then discussed with the Ethiopian Government the practical methods of
an harmonious working of the 1954 Agreement and received some assurances that
appeared to be satisfactory.

3. Recent events in the Territories and in particular the interference by the
Ethiopians with the internal tribal organisation of British Somali tribes (Appendix C)
indicate that the Ethiopian Government have no real intention of keeping the 1954
Agreement. A strong protest has been delivered regarding the incident but the
Ethiopian Government are already contesting the facts. It seems clear that the
deliberate policy of the Ethiopians is to try to absorb the Somali tribes in the
Territories with a view to the later incorporation of the whole Protectorate and
ultimately of all Somalis in the Horn of Africa within the boundaries of the Ethiopian
Empire.

4. When, last May, Lord Lloyd made the policy statement authorised by the
Cabinet, there was bitter disappointment amongst Somali leaders at the lack of any
reference to the Territories. In his Report (Appendix A) Lord Lloyd has confirmed
that the Somalis in the Protectorate will not rest until they have recovered the
Territories which they, regardless of the 1897 Treaty, regard as rightly theirs. Indeed
the National United Front has once more asked Her Majesty's Government to
facilitate their approach to the International Court of Justice for an advisory opinion
on their petition to the United Nations which they first made in 1955. No reply to this
request has yet been given, but the reply cannot be favourable for the same reasons
which led us to reject their appeal for support for their petition in 1955.

5. In the meantime as a result of recent Ethiopian behaviour in the Territories
the Somalis are becoming increasingly bitter and less confident of the ability of Her
Majesty's Government to assist them. If no new initiative is taken there is likely to be
serious trouble in the Protectorate itself and we cannot rule out the possibility that

---

[1] Appendices C and D not printed. A map of the area in question is reproduced in BDEEP series A, R Hyam,
ed, *The Labour government and the end of empire 1945–1951*, part III, p 282.
[2] See 89.

U

senior officers of the Government might ask to be relieved of their posts in a situation which they might regard as hopeless. It has become urgently necessary to reconsider our future policy in the Protectorate and in the Horn of Africa generally. The courses of action open to us would appear to be as follows.

6. *We could allow an approach by the Somalis to the International Court.* This would call in question our domestic jurisdiction in respect of all our Protectorate Treaties and might even concede to the United Nations the right of interference in a wide range of Colonial issues. The result of such an approach could only be embarrassing to Her Majesty's Government and would not in fact help the Somalis.

7. *We could repudiate the 1954 Agreement.* This would leave the Somalis with only their rights under the 1897 Treaty which are very vague and less satisfactory than those under the 1954 Agreement.

8. *We could repudiate the 1897 Treaty.* For this to be effective we should have to occupy the Territories which would be an act of war against Ethiopia. This course can scarcely be considered except as a last resort after all other measures have been tried.

9. *We could withdraw from the Somaliland Protectorate.* This would involve abandoning our responsibilities towards the Somalis and, apart from what might be considered over-riding moral considerations, is open to the following further serious objectives:—

(a) we should lose the confidence of all those who look to us for protection throughout the Commonwealth;

(b) even if we were to continue to subsidise the new State there would not be the indigenous technical, or administrative, talent, or material to enable it to stand on its own feet. We should therefore, both politically and economically, create a vacuum which the Russians and the Egyptians would be quick to exploit;

(c) there are strategic arguments against withdrawal, particularly in relation to Aden;

(d) an independent Somaliland Protectorate whether or not associated with Somalia would inherit our obligations under the 1897 Treaty. We could not therefore support the new State in any attempt forcibly or through an international tribunal to repudiate that Treaty. Any guarantee of the frontiers of the new State (which would be expected by the Somalis) would only extend to the present frontiers of the Protectorate and would not include the Territories.

10. *We might encourage an Ethiopian/Somali rapprochement.* Ethiopia is in the strong position of being in possession of the Territories. Any rapprochement therefore would inevitably be upon Ethiopian terms. Some qualified observers regard some form of federation between the Somalis and the Ethiopians, whereby the Somalis would regain the Territories, as the only logical solution. The fact must nevertheless be faced that the Ethiopians are hated and distrusted by the Somalis, and that the Somali leaders are publicly committed to precisely the opposite policy. There is therefore no chance at the present moment that they could be persuaded to adopt this line and any attempt on our part to encourage them to do so would merely bring additional odium upon our heads.

11. *We could arraign Ethiopia before the United Nations for breach of the 1954 Agreement.* We have clear evidence of such a breach. Under the 1954 Agreement the position of the Protectorate tribes in the Territories is more favourable than their

position simply under the 1897 Treaty. In particular the Agreement allows the Protectorate tribes to have their own tribal organisation, supervised by liaison staff of the Protectorate Government. For various reasons, however, it has been found almost impossible to compel the Ethiopians in practice to observe the terms of the Agreement, and although we now have clear evidence that the Ethiopains have broken the Agreement, this difficulty still remains.

Even if we were to take the case to the United Nations the most we could hope to achieve would be an admonition to the Ethiopians to observe the Agreement followed by an assurance as valueless as that given to Mr. Dodds-Parker in Addis Ababa. The difficulty of enforcement would still remain.

Admittedly there is a certain publicity value in such a course, but on the other hand there is still a considerable danger—since the United Nations may be swayed less by concern for Somali welfare than by a wish to score off a "Colonial Power"—that the debate might become enlarged into an examination of the 1897 Treaty or that it would take some other undesirable turn embarrassing to Great Britain and perhaps other Colonial Powers, such as the French or Belgians.

Finally even if successful it would fail completely to satisfy the Somalis who have, with justice, no confidence in Ethiopian promises and whose object in any case is to recover the Territories.

12. *We might try yet again to persuade the Ethiopians to cede the Territories.* For many years before 1954 attempts were made to persuade the Ethiopians to cede the Territories, *e.g.*, by an exchange of the Zeia Corridor, but all failed. In view of the present expansionist policy of the Ethiopians in Somali areas, in addition to the traditional reluctance of the Emperor of Ethiopia to let go any part of his Imperial heritage, it seems quite clear that the Ethiopians will not give up the Territories unless the strongest possible pressure is brought to bear upon them. The Governor of Kenya has recently suggested that an area, the Mandera Quadrilateral, in the Northern Province of Kenya might be offered to the Ethiopians in return for the Territories. This suggestion is being studied and it is too early to say whether it is possible to offer the Ethiopians this area. Even if it should prove possible, and even if we managed to persuade the French and Americans to bring pressure upon the Ethiopians to cede the Territories in exchange for it and a sum of money, which would undoubtedly have to be very large, it is doubtful whether the Ethiopians would agree to do so. To reopen the possibility of cession at this stage is likely simply to result in delay, delay which will be dangerous at a time when the situation is so rapidly deteriorating.

The Kenya Government's offer will of course be borne in mind as a possible make-weight in some other solution to the problem.

In considering any solution involving cession of the Territories, careful thought will have to be given to Ethiopian suspicions that these areas are coveted because they are believed to contain oil. Ethiopia's interests in any such oil might have to be safeguarded to her satisfaction, which would require very skilful negotiations so as not to offend the Somalis unnecessarily.

13. *Finally, we can try to create a Greater Somalia which would include the Territories.* Logically and objectively the best policy for the Horn of Africa would be the creation of a Greater Somalia, which would include from the outset the Italian Trust Territory (due to become independent in 1960), the Somaliland Protectorate and the Ogaden. (There are also parts of Northern Kenya which are inhabited by a

predominantly Somali population, but the inclusion of these, as well as Djibuti, in Greater Somalia need not be considered immediately.) The creation of a new Muslim State in the Horn of Africa is admittedly not without dangers from our own point of view, but the risk of the area falling under Egyptian and Russian influence through such a scheme seems less than the extreme likelihood of the same thing happening under any alternative course. Moreover an early initiative in this direction by Her Majesty's Government would succeed, as nothing else would, in convincing the Somalis of the Protectorate, at the present crucial time, that we really had their interests at heart.

The revival of the Greater Somalia idea, which came to nothing when advanced by Mr. Bevin in 1946,[3] none the less confronts us with formidable difficulties. First, we shall have to face the obvious prospect of Ethiopian opposition. Secondly, the scheme is likely to antagonise the French, who will probably regard it as a threat to Djibuti and who in any case have a profound suspicion of British policy in the Horn of Africa. Thirdly, even the Italians, though they may be easier to persuade than the French, may suspect that we intend to bring the new State within the Commonwealth.

I do not regard these difficulties as fatal, but they undoubtedly make it necessary for us to prepare the ground with extreme care. The first essential would be to persuade the French and the Italians (particularly the former) that the present situation is as inimical to their interests as to our own and that our aim in the Horn of Africa is to maintain not *British* influence as such but *joint Western* influence. Once we can convey to our Western allies that our aim is to pursue a combined policy with them (as indeed it must be if there is to be any hope of success) and not to increase our influence at their expense, I feel that the dangers of resurrecting the Greater Somalia idea will be much reduced. We may then, moreover, be able to bring the French in particular to understand, as they do not seem to do at present, the full dangers of the present position. They tend to regard us as having wilfully created Somali nationalism. Nothing could be further from the truth. Somali nationalism has created itself, and the problem will in any case come to a head in 1960. All that we are trying to do is to contend with the facts as we find them, and to keep the situation under control. The present Ethiopian attitude in the Territories which the French seem almost inclined to encourage, is the one thing which above all else will drive the Somalis into the hands of the Egyptians and make them bitterly and permanently hostile to the West.

If this line of thought is accepted by my colleagues, a positive course of action begins to emerge. The stages would be as follows. First, we should enter into close and confidential consultations with the French and the Italians on the lines of the preceding sub-paragraph. I would like once again to stress the importance of this stage, since I regard the achievement of a mutual understanding with our Western allies as one of the most vital factors in this whole problem. At the same time it would be equally important, perhaps even more important, to explain our ideas and plans to the Americans, if only because of their decisive influence in Ethiopian foreign policy. If we were able to secure American, French and Italian support, a joint approach would be made to the Ethiopians. It would be brought home to them with renewed force that their present policies towards the Somalis are likely to have a

---

[3] See Hyam, *op cit*, part III, 288, 289, 292, 293.

disastrous effect on themselves by exposing their eastern flank to Egyptian and probably Russian influence. Some more positive bait than this would, however, be needed; and I suggest that the Ethiopians should be told that Greater Somalia, once created, could federate with Ethiopia if, of its own free will, it decided to do so. This prospect would provide the Ethiopians with some incentive to behave decently towards the Somalis in the future.

The above suggestion admittedly leaves some points unanswered. First, how would the Greater Somalia scheme be launched? The details of this could be worked out with our allies, but it may be necessary to propose at an early stage the convening of an international conference. Secondly, what would be the status of Greater Somalia after it had come into being? Here again, discussion with our allies would be required. The objective would presumably be that Greater Somalia should from the outset form an independent State but it would almost certainly have to be supported by financial and other assistance from the Western Powers concerned. This would in fact amount to an unofficial "consortium," with which Ethiopia might be offered the prospect of participation, dependent upon good behaviour towards the Somalis from now on. (This condition would not be an idle threat, since in the present state of Somali feeling any association of Ethiopia with the control of Somali affairs, however, unofficial, would be out of the question.) It might be necessary, however, to envisage some more formal type of consortium, under the aegis of the United Nations. This would present dangers and difficulties, and if we were to embark on any such course it would be doubly essential that the Americans, the French, and the Italians and ourselves should first be in full agreement on the whole policy. Otherwise there would be no guarantee whatever that a United Nations sponsored consortium would not simply let in the Russians and the Egyptians through the back door.

14. *Conclusions.* Despite the difficulties it involves, I believe after serious consideration that renewed sponsorship of a Greater Somalia project is the best course for Her Majesty's Government to take in the present situation in which all the possible courses of action appear to involve great risks. I therefore invite my colleagues to agree that we should initiate confidential discussions with the French, American and Italian Governments on the lines outlined in the preceding paragraph. I must stress that in view of the present deteriorating circumstances speed is of vital importance. In the meantime there is no alternative but for the Protectorate Government, aided by the firm action now being taken by our Ambassador at Addis Ababa, to persist in trying to make the 1954 Agreement work.

Appendix A to 97: Report by Lord Lloyd on his visit to Somaliland, 20–31 May 1956

General
I spent ten days in the Protectorate during which time I was able to see a fair amount of the country and to meet a large number of Somalis from different sections of the community. Details of my programme are in the Appendix (not printed) to this Report. At the end of my visit I made a statement on the radio regarding Her Majesty's Government's future policy for the Protectorate.

2. There was inevitably a large number of detailed matters which I discussed with the Governor and his officials and on which I was able to form a view. These matters

will be pursued in the Department but for the sake of brevity are not covered by this report, the object of which is to endeavour to give a general picture of the political situation and prospects in the Protectorate as they appeared to me.

Political situation

3. Two factors appear to dominate political thought in the Protectorate. First and most fundamental, the bitterness which is felt generally over the loss of the Haud and the Reserved Area and, secondly, political development in Somalia.

4. It will be a great mistake I think to under-estimate the feeling that exists regarding the Haud and the Reserved Area. Everywhere I went it was the first—and in some cases the only—topic that was raised, and in the minds of the majority of people at the present time it occupies a much more prominent place than even political and economic advance. The reasons are not far to see. One has only to travel through the barren and water-less land of the Protectorate and subsequently to visit the country adjacent to the Haud and Reserved Area to realise the infinitely superior grazing value of these latter Areas and it is clear that no agricultural development that could be economically undertaken within the Protectorate could possibly compensate for the loss of the best grazing land in the whole area.

5. The loss of the Haud and the Reserved Area is therefore a mortal economic blow to the Somalis. It may be said that they still enjoy the use of both the Haud and the Reserved Area and with qualifications that is certainly true. It must be remembered nevertheless that they only do so in constant fear of being molested and persecuted by the Ethiopians and the public execution of 7 Somalis (not it is true British Somalis, but Somalis nevertheless) in Jigjigga some months ago has undoubtedly made a profound impression, as also did the case of Mohamed Bogorreh. I will deal with the present situation in the Haud and Reserved Area at a later stage in this report.

6. Apart from the economic aspect, the Somalis feel a real sense of injustice over this matter. Rightly or wrongly they have always regarded these territories as an integral part of the Protectorate. The fact that Her Majesty's Government has allowed the Ethiopians to resume the administration there, they regard as a grievous betrayal of trust.

7. Whilst there is a demand for political and economic advance amongst all sections of the community, it is, as one might expect, most vociferous amongst the small number of professional politicians. There is one main political party in the Protectorate at the present time, namely the National United Front which has for the time being more or less absorbed the Somali Youth League and Somali National League, though how long this alliance will last is a matter for conjecture. Its chief spokesman is Mr. Michael Mariano. Its official policy is first and foremost the return of the Haud and the Reserved Area; secondly, independence for British Somaliland and, thirdly, association with Somalia.

8. The demand for independence is conditioned by two particular factors. First, there is a strong feeling that if Somaliland were an independent State the dispute with Ethiopia over the Haud and Reserved Area could be taken to international arbitration with a good chance of success. The fact that this view is over-optimistic does not affect the strength of Somali feeling on this point. Next there is the feeling that they must not be left behind Somalia and that when Somalia becomes independent they should be in as strong a position as their neighbours, both

politically and economically, in any negotiations that may take place regarding association. It is the same basic feeling which is behind the demand for a timetable for self-government and more definite financial commitments in respect of development by Her Majesty's Government.

9. The party, like all political parties, has its different sections. There are the tribal rulers whose main concern is the restoration of the Haud and the Reserved Area and to whom political advance is on the whole subsidiary. There are the extremists whose main preoccupation like that of the Somali Youth League is the earliest possible independence regardless of their readiness for it and, finally, there are the moderates of whom Mariano is leader, who although just as anxious for independence as the extremists, would probably if left to themselves be rather more reasonable about the method of achieving it and the pace at which it can be achieved.

10. In any assessment of the political situation mention must be made of the Somali Officials's Union. In the Somali Officials' Union, as one would naturally expect at this stage of the Protectorate's development, is found a large proportion of the most intelligent and level-headed Somalis. It is significant, leaving aside their direct personal interest in achieving a speedy acceleration of the entry of Somalis into the higher posts of Government, that they are widely regarded as taking a no less advanced line than the political parties on the burning questions of the Haud and Reserved Area, and of the future pace of constitutional and economic development vis-à-vis Somalia. After talking informally with various Somalia officials, I have little doubt that they do in fact feel very strongly on these points. It was indeed reported to me that one or two of the more promiment Somalia officials were considering whether to resign or not in order to enter the political fray.

11. Generally, although there is much talk of independence there is I believe amongst the ordinary people little realisation of its implications, and in practice I believe at the present time most of them are not really looking much further ahead than internal self-government and would be much distressed and shocked if our protection and, above all, our financial assistance, were suddenly removed.

12. In the economic and social field, there is a quite genuine demand amongst all sections of the community that more should be done for them. There is no doubt that the money which we have spent in the Protectorate compares very unfavourably with what the Italians have spent in Somalia although much of the Italian expenditure has been for the shop window. For example, I was frequently told about the 200 primary schools built by the Italians compared with the number built by us in the Protectorate. This view exaggerates both the number and quality of the Italian primary schools, and ignores the fact that Italian numbers are, as compared with Somaliland, out of balance with their single intermediate and single secondary schools. It is probably true therefore to say that what money we have spent we have spent more wisely than the Italians. Nor do the Somalis take into account the superior natural advantages of Somalia which has two rivers. Nor again do they remember that education in the Protectorate was held up for many years by the violent campaign against it waged by their own religious leaders or that agriculture was similarly handicapped by the prejudices of the graziers. Nevertheless the fact remains that insufficient development, either social or economic, has in point of fact taken place and in any case the Somalis are very conscious of this.

13. Finally in this connection it should be noted that Mr. Mariano has been very imprudent over the question of development. When he returned from London,

although no specific financial promises were made to him by the Secretary of State, he told everybody that he had got £5 million out of Her Majesty's Government over the next 5 years. It is conceivable that he misunderstood the next 5 years and took it to mean £1 million a year for the next 5 years. It is also possible that he deliberately misrepresented the fact in order to maintain his prestige with the extremists.

The policy statement

14. Towards the end of my visit I was authorised by Her Majesty's Government to make a statement of future policy and this I did over Hargeisa Radio on Tuesday, 29th May. I had had one meeting with the Elders and National United Front leaders in Hargiesa the day after my arrival and had met them on various social occasions in the interval. They had asked, however, for a further meeting after the making of the policy statement in order that they might have an opportunity of discussing it with me, and I had arranged to set aside the whole of Wednesday morning for this purpose. Half an hour before this meeting was due to take place I received a letter from the National United Front expressing their bitter disappointment with the statement and informing me that in the circumstances they felt that no useful purpose could be served in having the meeting. As a result Mr. Stebbing, the Chief Secretary, and Mr. Morgan of the Colonial Office, met the leaders of the National United Front and expressed to them my disappointment at the discourtesy and also the irresponsibility of their action. As a result they later asked if they might see me after all, and I ultimately met them for half an hour during the afternoon.

15. The sharp reaction of the National United Front was a considerable surprise to the Governor and all of his officials. They had none of them expected that the statement would be acclaimed, not because the offers which it made were unreasonable, but because no politician dared express unqualified approval of any statement which did not offer immediate independence and an annual grant of £10 million a year. They had not, however, expected that the National United Front would take so extreme a line and the cause of this reaction was not immediately apparently to any of us. In the course of their conversations with the leaders of the National United Front, the Chief Secretary and Mr. Morgan elicited that although there were a number of subsidiary causes for their disappointment with the statement—notably the absence of any timetable for progress towards self-government and absence of any figures relating to the aid which Her Majesty's Government were prepared to give—the main reason for their boycott of the meeting had been in order to demonstrate their bitter disappointment at the lack of any reference to the return of the Haud and the Reserved Area in the statement, and that since they had avoided any other demonstrations during my visit they felt that they must make this protest before I left. They indicated incidentally that the protest was not aimed at me personally, but at Her Majesty's Government as a whole.

16. During the brief meeting in the afternoon the question of the Haud was not further discussed and they contented themselves with asking for certain assurances regarding the statement itself. They asked in the first place that the statement should be published as a White Paper. I pointed out that this was not usual where a statement had been made personally by a Minister, but they attached such importance to it, that, whilst fully safeguarding my position, I promised them that I would give it further consideration. They asked, secondly, that the statement should be repeated in Parliament and I gave them an assurance that this would be done.

They next asked for early publication of details of the development plan and the amount of money that is to be spent. In view of his very imprudent promises in this respect to which I have already referred, Mariano is under heavy pressure on this point, and it was agreed that as soon as ever the plans were finalised they should be announced either by the Governor or in the new Legislative Council, whichever was most agreeable to the National United Front leaders. They asked that a Development Board with Somali members upon it should be set up and this the Governor expressed his willingness to do, probably as a sort of sub-committee of the Legislative Council. After I left Mr. Morgan also gave them certain explanations regarding development finance and the methods of constitutional development, which he says they appeared to receive with satisfaction: he has reported separately on this.

Economic development

17. In the course of my visit I was able to see a certain amount of the country and, although I did not go into either the Haud or the Reserved Area, I was able to see the country adjoining, which is fairly similar. The greater part of the Protectorate is arid and waterless and water is the key to any agricultural development that we can do there. The Somalis have an idea that there is water over wide areas which could be used if we were prepared to spend sufficient money on drilling wells, &c. Something can be done, and must be done, on these lines, but the Somalis' own ideas of what can be achieved are greatly exaggerated.

18. There is however a great deal I believe that could be done by making the maximum use of the rainfall through dams and bunds. Near Borama I saw a valley which had been bunded in this way and where excellent crops of sorghum were being grown, and I have no doubt that a great deal more on these lines could be done. Indeed the District Commissioner, Borama, believes that in this way the Protectorate could be made completely self-sufficient in sorghum within a comparatively short space of time.

19. Similarly there is probably a reasonable future for date gardens which equally might make the Protectorate self-sufficient in dates. I am sure that these agricultural development schemes should now be pursued with vigour not only because economically they are most important to the Protectorate, but also because they would be widespread and a large number of people could see with their own eyes the work that was going on. From the propaganda point of view this is most important, and I was interested to see the effect that even a few tractors had on the minds of the local people.

20. There is a rather expensive scheme for the development of the Port of Berbera. Certain aspects of this may need further investigation but benefits will certainly come from it although they will only be apparent to a limited, though important, section of the population.

Education

21. There is a growing demand for education which I am sure we have got to try to satisfy. The publication of a target of 200 scholarships was very well received. Whilst I do not propose here to discuss the problems of education in any detail, it is fair to say that, whilst there is a need for more schools everywhere, the chief need is for more intermediate and secondary schools.

22. There is also a serious problem over the question of teachers. Owing to the

shortage of schools there are not at present sufficient Somali teachers for even the existing, let alone an expanded, educational programme. Since there is no written Somali language and since some Arabic is needed for religious purposes, there is a tendency to look to Egypt for teachers. This is a danger which somehow or other we have got to overcome. It is a real problem since the sources of obtaining properly qualified Arab teachers are very limited, but somehow or other the gap between the present time and the time when the flow of Somali teachers begins to make itself felt must be bridged. It is, moreover, most important that the education programme should go ahead quickly.

23. In this connection it is worth considering again the whole question of the introduction of a written Somali language. This is an old problem and the difficulty has always been that the Somalis, both in British Somaliland and Somalia, are quite unable to agree whether Arabic or Roman script should be used and, if the latter, which of the three possible varieties. If we wait for the Somalis to agree we shall never get a written Somali language. On the other hand, if we take the plunge and introduce in the Protectorate a written language with a Roman script, it is possible that, despite a good deal of initial criticism, the idea would appeal to Somali national pride and be followed in Somalia. And if it came off it would have the great advantage of making the use of Arabic unnecessary in the schools, though, of course, Arabic would continue to be taught in the Koranic schools for religious purposes.

The problem in the Protectorate

24. We are undoubtedly in an extremely difficult position in the Protectorate at the present time. It would I believe be quite unrealistic to think that you can tell the Somalis that they must face the facts of life and forget about the Haud and the Reserved Area. They are not prepared to do so and are determined if possible to take their case to the United Nations and to take any other steps which are open to them to regain the lost territories. One of the greatest disasters of this whole business is the loss of confidence in Great Britain that has resulted from this event. They are now very doubtful about our ability to protect them against the Ethiopians and are sceptical of any promises unless they are given so precisely that there is no chance of our wriggling out of them.

25. Our only hope is therefore to divert their thoughts as far as possible into other fields, such as political advance and development, and it is of the first importance that we should really get moving with the promises made in the policy statement. Financial assistance from Her Majesty's Government will of course be essential. It was clear during my visit that recent assistance to Cyprus, Jordan and the High Aswan Dam has not gone unnoticed by the Somalis, and if they do not themselves receive reasonably generous treatment there is clearly a danger that they will draw their own conclusions. Even so there is one great difficulty, namely, their renewed demand to be allowed to take their case to the International Court. When I was in Hargeisa, I deliberately held up the proposed reply to this demand since to have made that reply at that particular moment would have been completely disastrous from the point of view of the policy statement. Nevertheless, a reply cannot now be long delayed, and if it is unfavourable there is the real danger that at the present moment they may refuse co-operation with the Government—including possibly a boycott of the new Legislative Council—and it is almost certain that they

will turn a much more attentive ear to hostile propaganda. This will also have a damaging effect upon our prestige in Somalia.

Present situation in the Haud and Reserved Area

26. During my visit, although I did not go into the Haud or the Reserved Area, I went out to the frontier adjacent to both and at Tug Wajale I met Mohamed Bogorreh, who has now been safely returned to the bosom of his people. I also had the opportunity of having discussions with Mr. Drysdale and Mr. Hilliard, the Liaison Officers concerned. In the Haud at the present moment things are tolerably peaceful, not I think because of any change of heart by the Ethiopians, but because they have realised that it is impossible to stop the people crossing the frontier and that it is much more difficult in the Haud to establish a case that tribes are sedentary. Finally, the Ethiopian police, which is more or less synonymous with the Army, is concentrated on the Somalia border owing to the frontier dispute with Somalia and there are comparatively few police in the Haud at the present time.

27. In the Reserved Area things are very different. Here it has become increasingly clear that the Ethiopians have not the slightest intention of observing the spirit of the 1954 Agreement. I understand from Mr. Drysdale that none of the minor Ethiopian officials have even heard of what went on during the conversations at Addis Ababa, that Colonel Kifle has not been near the area since those conversations and that in the meantime the Ethiopians are encouraging the Gadabursi, one of our tribes, to plough up land. This breaks the clause of the Agreement which prohibits the restriction of grazing, and the object of this manoeuvre is fairly simple. If the land is ploughed up it is easy to say that the people who have ploughed it up are sedentary and do not come under the Agreement. The eventual object no doubt is to get the whole of the Reserved Area ploughed up, whereupon the Ethiopians will claim all those living there as Ethiopian subjects and say that the 1954 Agreement is no longer applicable to any part of the area. Nor is it easy for us to do a great deal about it. Although we know that the Gadabursi tribe are being actively encouraged by the Ethiopians to plough up land by a combination of threats and blandishments, it is very difficult to get positive proof. If, as we should like to do, we were to go in and arrest our own tribesmen who are ploughing up traditional grazing lands, the Ethiopians would immediately claim them as Ethiopian subjects, and there is evidence that many of these people in return for being allowed to plough up the land are being obliged to make their mark on a document certifying that they are of Ethiopian nationality.

28. For these reasons, although there is a strong demand in the Protectorate that the Protectorate Government should be allowed to take more positive action to stop what is going on, such action presents real problems. However, I have no doubt that we must consider what can be done and that we probably have enough evidence to enter an early protest with the Ethiopian Government at their failure to implement any of the promises which they gave in Addis Ababa.

Ethiopian policy

29. Even so, I very much doubt whether any amount of diplomatic activity by Great Britain alone will have much effect. It is difficult to be certain about Ethiopian policy, but the impression one gets is that the Ethiopians are determined to cling to the Haud and the Reserved Area as a bargaining counter to be used to persuade the

Somalis to some sort of association with Ethiopia after 1960. Although this is purely conjecture it is fair to say that the absorption of the Somalis has always been an Ethiopian dream ever since the days of Menelik. Moreover, when I was in Rome the Italians told me that the Ethiopians were deliberately more forthcoming to the Somalis when the Italians were not present than when they were and that the Ethiopian delegates deliberately indicated to the Somalis that they would be prepared to be much more accommodating once the Somalis were independent.

Future policy in the Horn of Africa

30. At the present moment we do not appear to have any very definite policy in the Horn of Africa as a whole. It is I believe the policy of the United States to support the Ethiopians as the only stable force in the Horn of Africa and, as long as the United States continue to take a pro-Ethiopian line in all circumstances, it is very difficult for us to bring much pressure upon the Ethiopians. Yet, unless effective pressure is brought upon them over the Haud and Reserved Area there is a serious danger that the Somalis both in the Protectorate and in Somalia will be estranged and they will be driven into the arms of Egypt. If this should happen we shall probably be faced in the early 1960's or before with an extremely serious situation in the Horn of Africa: an, as always, unstable régime in Ethiopia will find itself ringed by hostile Islamic peoples, widely subverted by Egyptian influence, from Eritrea right round to the Somalis in the Northern Province of Kenya; as a result traditional Sudanese hostility to the Ethiopians will without doubt be stimulated; British and indeed Western influence among the Somali peoples is likely to have been reduced to negligible proportions, because we will have shown ourselves in Somali eyes to have betrayed their interests and to have been incapable of recovering their territory for them; the measure of Egyptian and possibly Soviet influence which will by then exist in the Somali area of the Horn of Africa will constitute a grave threat to our strategic interests in East Africa and of course in Aden; similarly it will constitute a grave threat to our potential oil interest in the Somaliland Protectorate, Somalia and even in the Ethiopian Ogaden.

31. This is clearly a situation which must be avoided. One way of avoiding it might be to back the Ethiopians wholeheartedly and to allow and even assist them to absorb the Somalis, which is what they themselves would like to do. This however would constitute a major betrayal of people whom we are bound to protect, a betrayal which in itself seems to me quite unthinkable and which would be so manifest that it might have serious repercussions in other Colonial territories and in other Islamic countries. If this view is accepted the only alternative would appear to be to assist the Somalis to achieve their own real ambition which is a united Somali State, either completely independent or within the Commonwealth. There are risks and difficulties in this policy also:—

(a) to implement it, pressure will have to be put upon the Ethiopians to give up the Haud and the Reserved Area. The Ethiopians will certainly dislike this and the Americans may dislike it;

(b) the French are opposed to the idea because they fear it would create a demand in Jibuti for incorporation within the new State;

(c) the Italians would not oppose an independent Somali State but would strongly resent it coming within the Commonwealth;

(d) unless oil is found neither Somalia nor the Protectorate are viable and money would have to be provided from somewhere. An Anglo-Italian-Ethiopian consortium is the obvious solution but the inclusion of Ethiopia would not be acceptable to the Somalis. An Anglo-Italian consortium is a possibility but would not be acceptable to the Ethiopians. In any case our financial commitment would inevitably be greater than at present. When I was in Rome I tried to find out from the Italians how much money they would be prepared to put up after 1960. The impression I got was that although they would be prepared to put up some money they would not be prepared to put up anything like the amount which they are at present contributing. On the other hand if you do not have a consortium of friendly Powers there is a grave risk that you may get a new State financed by, and under the influence of, unfriendly Powers.

32. On the assumption however that an independent Somali State is what we are aiming for and that these difficulties and dangers could be overcome, we are still confronted with the greatest difficulty of all. If we turn down the Somalis latest appeal over the Haud there is a definite risk that they will turn elsewhere for assistance. It is true that on the last occasion Egypt refused to support their application at U.N.O. but there is no guarantee that the Egyptians may not change their mind. It is therefore of the first importance that we should do something about the Haud and the Reserved Area

Future policy—Haud and the Reserved Area

33. If we are to pursue this policy something must be done to solve the problem of the Haud and the Reserved Area. We cannot allow the Protectorate Treaties with the Somalis to become the subject of an advisory opinion by the International Court, because this would open the way to demands for the submission to the Court of all and any Protectorate Treaties, including those on which is based our position in the Aden Protectorate and Uganda. Nor can we admit the competence of the United Nations to interfere in any way in respect of the 1987 Treaty between Ethiopia and ourselves. Since we ourselves maintain that this Treaty is valid in international law, the only grounds on which we could justify or defend an appeal to the United Nations would be that the situation which has arisen since the Treaty was signed is inequitable. This, however, would be very dangerous to us in other interests. For example, it is exactly what the Greeks have been saying in the case of Cyprus. I do not see any form of international arbitration which we could accept and we must face having to make this clear to the Somalis.

34. Is there any alternative method of persuading the Ethiopians to give up their sovereignty over the Haud and the Reserved Area? There is an area in the Northern Province of Kenya which we might be able to offer to the Ethiopians in exchange for all or some of the Haud or the Reserved Area. However in any further negotiations I am convinced that the Americans must be enlisted on our side. As long as the Ethiopians can count upon American support against us nothing will be achieved. If an approach were to be made to the Americans it could be on the following lines:—

(a) the historical background to the situation, including all the efforts we have made since 1944 by friendly diplomatic means to achieve a satisfactory solution with the Ethiopians;

(b) a full explanation why, if the general Somaliland/Ethiopia (and Somalia/

Ethiopia) frontier cannot very soon be placed on a satisfactory footing, we shall find ourselves faced in the early 1960's or before with a disastrous situation in the Horn of Africa;

(c) our own policy for the Horn of Africa; this briefly being the eventual establishment of some sort of Somali Union in the area under either British or Western influence, and at the same time the maintenance of friendly relations with an Ethiopia which we hope can be persuaded to divert the energies at present directed towards external expansion into the more fruitful fields of internal consolidation and development;

(d) our own offer, if it can be made, of the exchange of Kenya territory for the Haud and Reserved Area.

35. I realise that this proposal is open to objection. It will be argued that the Americans are unlikely to agree and it may be argued that the only result of further pressure on the Ethiopians would be to drive them into the Russian camp. On neither of these points do I feel qualified to express an opinion. What does seem essential, however, is:—

(a) that we should have a definite policy which can be implemented by our representatives in Addis Ababa, Hargeisa and Mogadishu. Close co-operation between them is I believe essential;

(b) that the aim of the policy should be to keep both the Somalis and Ethiopians within the sphere of Western influence;

(c) that in view of the necessity of giving the Somalis a reply regarding their latest demand to be allowed to take their case to the International Court, we should take an early decision as to what we intend to do.

Appendix B to 97: Policy statement for Somaliland Protectorate (issued in the Protectorate on 29 May 1956)

Government is aware that recent political developments have made the people of the Somaliland Protectorate keenly desirous to learn the future policy of Her Majesty's Government towards the Protectorate and in the Somali area in general. I have accordingly obtained authority of the Secretary of State to make the following statement. The details of policy still remain to be examined in many important matters, particularly in regard to finance, but this statement will provide an indication of the general intention of Her Majesty's Government. The details of implementation of the policy to be followed within this general framework will be subject to consultation with responsible Somali leaders from time to time.

2. (a) The aim of Her Majesty's Government is to press ahead with economic, social and political progress in the Protectorate. In particular Her Majesty's Government has decided that steps must be taken to accelerate development of education and economic resources within the limits of the physical capacity of the territory to undertake them.

(b) In the field of education plans already exist for expanding elementary, intermediate and secondary education and technical training facilities; they will be discussed with the Secretary of State's Educational Adviser when he visits the Protectorate this autumn. Up to 200 overseas scholarships and training courses, in addition to those originally planned for the period ending 1960, will be provided subject to there being sufficient suitably qualified candidates. These scholarships are intended to cover all branches of education and include university and professional training of Somali students, technical training and apprenticeship overseas and provision for administrative and technical courses for serving Somali members in all branches of the Civil Service.

(c) In the development of economic resources particular attention will be paid to providing adequate water supplies both in the towns and in the interior, and to agricultural, irrigation, forestry and soil and water conservation projects by which grazing and natural vegetation will be improved and the Protectorate made less dependent on imported foodstuffs. It is hoped to improve outlets for livestock, skins and other livestock products, and schemes for an abattoir and cold store at Berbera are being investigated. Berbera port will be developed, and the search for oil and minerals of economic value encouraged. Every effort will be made to develop a stable and self-supporting economy and modern social services within the limits of Protectorate resources.

3.   The primary object of all of these developments is to make the Somalis of the Protectorate ready for internal self-government. Her Majesty's Government is not, however, laying down a definite time-table for political advances, and indeed it is believed that responsible Somalis themselves would not wish this to be done. Her Majesty's Government will, however, review the position in consultation with the people of the Protectorate within a reasonable time after 1960.

4.   Her Majesty's Government will therefore take every practical step to encourage Somalis to assume greater political responsibility. A Legislative Council with certain powers over legislation and finance will be introduced within the coming twelve months and local government councils will be progressively established throughout the Protectorate. The expansion in educational services and particularly the increase in oversea scholarships have been planned to secure among other things an acceleration of the process of the Somalis entering into posts in higher branches of the Civil Service.

5.   Somali leaders in the Protectorate have made enquiries concerning the views of Her Majesty's Government in regard to the possibility of some form of association between Somaliland and Somalia sometime after 1960. When the time comes to consider such matters the views of the Somalis concerned will be one of the factors of decisive importance in determining Her Majesty's Government's attitude towards any proposals which may be put forward on this subject. Her Majesty's Government would certainly discuss any such proposals with representatives of the people of the Protectorate; and, if political and economic conditions were propitious, and the proposals were both well-conceived and favoured by the Somalis concerned, Her Majesty's Government would be ready to support them in principle.

6.   The Protectorate's territorial integrity is guaranteed for as long as the territory remains under the protection of Her Majesty's Government and indeed Her Majesty's Government wishes to emphasise that she will certainly not withdraw her protection as long as the Somali people require it.[4]

---

[4] The onset of the Suez crisis prevented Cabinet consideration of this memo. In a memo of the same title several weeks later (CAB 129/83, CP(56)231, 5 Oct 1956), Lennox-Boyd pointed out that relations between Ethiopia and the Somaliland Protectorate had continued to deteriorate, making the problem even more urgent. Cabinet accepted his recommendation that the problem should be referred to a committee of

officials (CAB 128/30/2, CM 70(56)4, 9 Oct 1956). In 1960 the Italian trust territory and the British protectorate both gained independence, and united to form the new state of Somalia. French Somaliland became the independent state of Djibouti in 1977.

98 CO 936/337, no 43   25 Oct 1956

'Anglo-French ministerial discussions Oct 25th 1956': CO record of a discussion between Mr Lennox-Boyd and Monsieur G Defferre;[1] exchange of views on the Somali question   [Extract]

. . . The two Ministers exchanged views on the Somali question. M. Defferre indicated that the French Government could not but regard with apprehension any encouragement given to the "Greater-Somalia" movement. Such encouragement would certainly involve risks to French interests in Djibouti and to the territorial status quo in the region, such risks being of direct concern to Ethiopia. The French Government considered that to support Pan-Somalism would be to support the establishment of an Arab State which could not be other than an Egyptian Satellite. Western interests were bound up with Ethiopia in that part of the world and it was the responsibility of the West to take steps to prevent an eventual alignment of Ethiopia with the Randoeng [sic: Bandoeng] group, since such a course could only be a desperate last resort for her.

Mr. Lennox-Boyd in reply stated that the independence of Italian Somaliland had already been decided upon by the United Nations and the Greater Somalia Movement existed: account had to be taken of these facts. Her Majesty's Government had no desire to encourage any increase of Egyptian or Arab League influence in the Horn of Africa. They would do nothing which in their view would have that effect and would talk further with the French Government before making any further announcement of policy. It was a regrettable fact that the Ethiopians had not been observing their undertakings under the 1954 Agreement, under which Her Majesty's Government had handed the Haud and the Reserved Area back to Ethiopian administration, and that this was causing difficulties in Anglo-Ethiopian relations and providing opportunities for Egyptian intrigue. He earnestly hoped that the French would use their influence to persuade the Ethiopian Government to observe the 1954 Agreement.

In reply to M. Defferre's enquiry about the possible association of British Somaliland and Italian Somaliland after 1960, Mr. Lennox-Boyd referred to the statement made by Lord Lloyd which indicated that the views of the local people in British Somaliland would be a very important factor in the final decision.

M. Defferre said that the French Government were anxious to do what they could to improve Anglo-Ethiopian relations and reduce the risks of Egyptian influence in Ethiopia or amongst the Somalis. They would use their influence to the maximum with the Ethiopians in order to persuade them to observe the 1954 Agreement, though he felt that the United Kingdom Government might have over-estimated the strength of French influence with the Ethiopians. In any case, the problem of improved relations was complicated by the Ethiopian fears of a Greater Somaliland.

---

[1] G Defferre, ministre de la France d'Outre-Mer, 1956–1957.

It would be helpful if the French were in a position to assure the Ethiopians that the United Kingdom Government desired no more than observance by the Ethiopians of the 1954 Agreement and did not wish to put forward proposals affecting the territorial integrity of Ethiopia. The French delegation added that it would not be practicable to make any *démarche* for about two months since the Ethiopian Emperor with his Foreign Minister would not be available before then.

After M. Defferre had recalled that the communiqué published on the occasion of the recent meeting in Paris of the two Prime Ministers mentioned the necessity of eliminating the elements of Anglo-French disagreement and that there was no doubt that the Somali matter was one of these, the two Ministers agreed to regard it as important that contact be maintained between the British and French Governments on the subject of their policy in the Horn of Africa. . . .

99 FO 371/118677, no 39   31 Oct 1956

'French views on the Communist threat to Africa': despatch no 370 from Sir G Jebb (Paris) to Mr Selwyn Lloyd. *Minute* by W N R Maxwell[1] (10 Nov 1956)

In your despatch No. 307 of the 21st of April you drew my attention to the danger of Communist subversion in Africa and instructed me to take a suitable opportunity to discuss this problem with the French Government.

2. I now have the honour to transmit a copy of a Note[2] from the French Ministry of Foreign Affairs in reply to an aide mémoire, based on your despatch, which was communicated to the Ministry on the 9th of May. The French authorities entirely accept the reality of the threat of Soviet Communism in Africa, and have noted a number of signs of increased Soviet interest in the area in addition to those listed in your despatch.

3. It is evidently easier to diagnose this danger than to prescribe for it. The Ministry do not suggest how the Communist threat is to be combated, except by proposing that there should be continual contacts on the subject between the French and British authorities, at the meetings regularly held between colonial officials of both countries. I understand that there may be some difficulty, from the security point of view, in taking the French entirely into our confidence; but I hope that it may be possible for rather fuller exchanges on this subject to take place at these meetings than in the past.

4. The French Note concludes with a reference to the probability that the Soviet Union, or a Satellite country, will attempt to set up a mission at Accra soon after the Gold Coast has been metamorphosed into an independent Ghana. The French Government have reason to think, after the recent visit of the Liberian President to Paris, that the opening of a Soviet mission at Accra would cause the Liberian Government to succumb to Soviet advances. Presumably the same would be true of an independent Nigeria. The establishment of Soviet missions along the West Coast of Africa would clearly greatly facilitate the extension of Soviet influence there; and the danger to which the French Government have drawn attention seems a very real one. If you have any indications of the attitude that the Government of Ghana are

---

[1] W N R Maxwell, African Dept, FO.   [2] Not printed.

likely to adopt on this question, or any hopes that Her Majesty's Government will be able to persuade them to resist Soviet pressure, I should be grateful if I might be instructed to inform the French Government accordingly.

5. I am sending copies of this despatch and its enclosure to Her Majesty's Ambassadors at Washington, Brussels and Lisbon.

Minute on 99

The French authorities entirely accept the reality of the threat of Soviet penetration of Africa as we see it, even if the Colonial Office and C.R.O. still have doubts; but all they can suggest to counteract it is continued Anglo-French contact at the regular meetings between Colonial officials. Even at these talks the security risk involved has hitherto prevented much effective collaboration.

2. The danger to which the French draw attention (see paragraph 4 of the despatch) that the Russians will attempt to set up a Mission at Accra as soon as the Gold Coast becomes independent is serious, and so are the consequences if they succeed.

3. The chances of Soviet economic penetration of the Gold Coast and a forecast of Gold Coast foreign policy were set out in Mr. Cumming-Bruce's[3] memoranda which he sent to C.R.O. and to C.O. and F.O. on July 18 (entered and minuted on J11017/1 – in circulation – a further copy without covering letter received from C.R.O. is at J11017/3 attached).[4] We copied Mr. Cumming-Bruce's papers to Paris in August, but unfortunately we cannot yet tell the Embassy that economic support for Ghana on the lines he proposed has yet been approved by C.R.O.; action there is being taken by the Economic Department who are putting certain economic proposals to Mr. Cumming-Bruce next week and will send us a copy of their letter.

4. The proposal for a "Colombo Plan" for Africa on which a Working Party has had its first meeting may lead to effective counter measures against economic penetration but only if sources of new money can be found without unacceptable conditions.[5]

5. On the political side we have already been considering whether we should not initiate periodical meetings between the Foreign Office and the Quai d'Orsay to discuss the international political aspects of these problems which have been considered as mainly colonial hitherto. Here the difficulties are:—

(a) that although the dangers of Soviet penetration in Africa are increasingly recognised we have no agreed policy for dealing with them; and
(b) the security risk involved in detailed exchange of information and a thorough study of appropriate counter measures.[6]

---

[3] F E Cumming-Bruce, assistant secretary, CRO, 1948–1955; adviser on external affairs to the governor of the Gold Coast, 1955–1957.

[4] cf part II of this volume, 277. For Cumming-Bruce's views on the risk of Soviet economic penetration of the Gold Coast, see BDEEP series B, R Rathbone, ed, *Ghana*, part II, 238, 271.

[5] See part III of this volume, 446.

[6] Subsequent minutes on this file advocated referring the problem to the Brook Committee on Counter-Subversion in Colonial Territories. This was a secret committee and its papers have been retained by department.

CHAPTER 2

Colonial policy in Britain's international relationships

Document numbers 100–172

100   FO 371/101383, no 7   3 July 1952
'Anglo-American talks on colonial questions': minute by C P Hope[1]

The Colonial Office have now furnished us with their ideas for the forthcoming talks. As in previous years they are anxious to limit the talks to discussion of tactics in specific cases and to avoid any general policy education of the Americans. They have therefore produced a list of subjects covering the colonial sphere which they suggest should be sent with a written memorandum on each issue to the State Department some little time before the talks are due. The Colonial Office hope to get the State Department's comments so as to dispose of some of the subjects in writing and before the talks begin; thus narrowing the talks to issues where there is disagreement.

2.   While I think we can probably accept this procedure in principle, I feel (and I am sure Sir O. Franks would feel the same) that there must nevertheless be some basic discussion with the Americans on points of policy. The Colonial Office clearly hope to tie the Americans down and get written assurances from them, but in view of American liberalism I doubt if they will succeed in all cases. Furthermore discussion on tactics, however detailed, cannot cover every eventuality. Last year, for instance, the occasions on which we felt ourselves let down by the Americans could hardly have been foreseen and were not covered in pre-Assembly talks.[2]

3.   I can readily appreciate the Colonial Office point of view. Their main anxiety is to prevent the U.N. weakening our hold on our colonies. I think it is true to say, however, that the Americans take quite a different view. They regard the United Nations as a major instrument of their foreign policy and they are anxious lest dissension on colonial questions will so divide the United Nations as to weaken it seriously. Thus the Americans urge the administering powers to join in taking a propagandist forward line while the administering powers (at any rate the Continental ones) hope to join together to put pressure on the Americans to support their resistance to U.N. intrusions into their colonies. The Colonial Office sympathise with the latter view.[3]

4.   It seems, therefore, that we in the Foreign Office have an important role to

---

[1] C P Hope, UN Dept, FO, 1950–1953.
[2] See BDEEP series A, R Hyam, ed, *The Labour Government and the end of empire 1945–1951*, part II, 193, 194.
[3] See 158.

play in the talks and that they should open with a general discussion where H.M. Ambassador or whoever represents the Foreign Office point of view should take the lead. To do this would put the Colonial Office memorandum on specific issues into perspective and enable us, I would hope, to secure American support for Colonial Office tactics, not so much for the selfish motive of administering powers to protect their interests from United Nations interference but as part of the policy of preventing dissension in the United Nations on colonial issues and consequently strengthening the Organisation as an instrument of Anglo-American foreign policy. The talks even offer a chance to make some slight impact on the basic American dislike of colonialism which harms us quite apart from the U.N. (e.g. in the Persian oil dispute).

5. The Colonial Office are suggesting in a different context the circulation of their proposed memorandum for the State Department to the Governments of France, Belgium, Australia, New Zealand, the Netherlands, Denmark and South Africa. This would be simultaneous to its despatch to Washington and perhaps reflects the desire to put joint pressure on the Americans. If I am right, I think we should dissuade the Colonial Office from circulating their memorandum to other administering powers.[4] (I ought also to add that so far the C.R.O. are inclined to oppose the inclusion of Bechuanaland in the list submitted. They would, however, like unofficial discussions outside the agenda on S.W. Africa. African Department[5] dislike mention of the Sudan).

6. I would therefore suggest that we speak to the Colonial Office in this sense and in particular offer to prepare Part I of the memorandum "The Prospect before us and General Policy" ourselves.

---

[4] Higher authority in the FO agreed with Hope on this: 'If the U.S. Govt. got to hear, we should be accused of ganging up' (FO 371/101383, no 7, minute by P Mason, assistant under-secretary of state, FO, 1951–1954, 3 July 1952).

[5] ie, African Department of the FO.

101   FO 371/101386, no 85   6 Oct 1952

'Anglo-American conversations on the United Nations 22nd-26th September 1952': despatch no 466 from Sir O Franks (Washington) to Mr Eden. *Enclosure*: summary report of conversations, 22–24 Sept

[Extract]

I have the honour, with reference to your despatch No. 1131 of 19th September, to enclose a summary report, agreed with Sir Gladwyn Jebb and Sir John Martin (Colonial items only), on the Anglo-American conversations on the United Nations, which took place from 22nd–26th September in Washington. From the point of view of this Embassy, there are one or two aspects of these talks to which I would draw your special attention.

2. The first is . . . about the need of the United States Government for some assurance of United Nations cover for certain aspects of their foreign policy. Although it is true that many sections and individuals in the State Department are still imbued with a somewhat naïve spirit towards the United Nations ideal,

(stemming probably in part from American lack of League of Nations experience and consequent inability to appreciate the present limitations on international planning), in others a more realistic and responsible attitude is slowly growing. The curious truth, however, is that although the two schools may be wide apart in theory in confronting particular problems, they quite frequently come up with the same answer. The realist school recognises that for many years to come the Federal Government will be faced with periodic waves of revulsion on the part of the American public against the sacrifices which the rise of their country to world leadership imposes on them. At any given moment an emotional wave of this kind might sweep over Congress and make it impossible for the reigning Administration to take the kind of decisive action which Mr. Truman took at the outbreak of hostilities in Korea, unless they had United Nations cover and backing. It is, I think, a fair guess to say, therefore, that amongst this school the true objective behind the pressure exerted by the United States for bigger and better plans for collective resistance to aggression, involving all United Nations members, is to ensure that should the moment for action come, the United States itself may not be found wanting. This feature in the political evolution of the United States is one for which other Governments may be wise to make some allowance for in the next few years.

3.   The second point I should like to make [is that although] we have long realised that the American conception of what international problems could or could not be profitably handled in the United Nations in its present stage of development, differed from our own, the breadth of the division between us has never before, to my knowledge, been quite so openly expressed as it was during these recent talks. To have given the subject a thorough airing in the extremely friendly atmosphere which prevailed throughout the discussions can have done nothing but good. It would at the same time be misleading to say that we had succeeded in altering the State Department's views to any noticeable extent. Unfortunately some of the higher officials who we had been lead to believe would take part in the talks (notably Mr. Perkins and Mr. Matthews), were away from Washington and so unable to attend. Since Mr. Hickerson[1] himself is amongst the *inconvertibles*, the absence of these other senior representatives was particularly regrettable. Possibly only the passage of time and a few more unfortunate experiences on the "Indians in South Africa" pattern, will succeed in moderating the present United States conviction that, even if discussion can do no good, lack of it is certain to do harm. The background of this attitude seems to lie in five converging lines of thought: (i) the inherent American belief in the intrinsic merit of free speech and the basic right of every man, no matter what his status, to a hearing before the Court; (ii) a determination to give no substance to complaints that the United Nations is an instrument of the Great Powers, run by them for their own benefit, and that the rights of smaller members are being denied to them; (iii) a hope that by placating the smaller nations in matters like the Tunisian case, they will gain their confidence and support for programmes in which the United States have a special interest—such as the organisation of collective measures (cf. paragraph 2 above); (iv) a conviction that once the smaller states lose their present sense of frustration they will soon learn by experience how impotent the United Nations actually is to deal with their internal disputes and so come to exercise more restraint in the type of problem which they choose to bring

---

[1] J D Hickerson, assistant secretary of state, US State Dept, 1949–1953.

before the Assembly; (v) belief that a too inflexible resistance to discussion of certain questions on legal grounds, even when it may in cases be impossible to prevent it, generates so much bitterness that the evils it creates are in the end greater than those it was designed to prevent. Each of these arguments has a strong emotional as well as intellectual pull in the State Department and influence on their policy which I think it will be very uphill work to moderate by argument.

4. So far as the "Colonial" part of the talks was concerned, the Americans once again maintained that their history, their traditions, and indeed their self-interest as a world power made it impossible for them to align themselves openly with the Colonial Powers. They must seek the confidence of the new and the "emergent" nations; if they succeeded in obtaining and keeping it, they would, in their view, be in a stronger position to help us because they could act as "honest broker" in resolving difficulties between the Colonial and anti-Colonial powers. If they allowed themselves to be identified with us, and, worse still, with the French and the Belgians, they would lose their powers of conciliation and the rift in the Assembly on Colonial questions would be greater than ever. Moreover, public opinion in the United States, which always sided with the underdog and against colonialism, would be outraged. They continued to feel that the question of their own dependencies was in some mystical way irrelevant.

5. State Department officials are by no means unanimous in their thinking on Colonial questions. Depending to some extent on the sub-Department as well as the background of the official concerned, at least three approaches to the problem can be detected. There are a few staunch supporters of our policy, there are others who would like to support it on strategic or other grounds but who are not convinced by its soundness, and there is a third group which to a greater or less degree shares the point of view of the "under-developed" countries. For our supporters, the discussions provided a useful, up-to-date briefing on our position. The uncommitted were given an unusually cogent and detailed exposition of our case, and the remainder were at least clearly impressed with the sincerity of our policy.

6. Expressions of admiration for our enlightened Colonial policy, and admission that General Assembly discussion of many Colonial and analogous subjects could never solve anything, were unfortunately not translated into any definite undertakings to stand with us at any of our sticking points. All that was promised was a clearer understanding of our problems and a desire to avoid causing us any unnecessary embarrassment.

7. Nevertheless, we feel that the Colonial Talks were very valuable. There was a full and frank exchange of views on Fourth Committee items which should make the task of our Delegation somewhat easier during the Assembly. Finally, we were able on our side to gain a valuable insight into the inner workings of the State Department in arriving at policy decisions and an appreciation of the reasons for the sometimes unpredictable change of front on questions to which the American public traditionally reacts emotionally rather than rationally.

8. A copy of this despatch with the enclosures has been sent to Sir Gladwyn Jebb in New York and to Her Majesty's Ambassador in Paris.

Enclosure to 101

. . .

Nationalist and racial problems

69. *Mr. Hickerson* said that the ground swell of Nationalist emotion and supposedly frustrated nationalist aspirations was the most delicate and explosive movement with which the Western Powers would be faced for some while to come in all United Nations meetings. There was at the moment a dangerous tendency amongst the majority of United Nations members to think that dependent peoples must, just because they were dependent, always be right. Whether questions of internal politics were raised in connection with non-self-governing territories (and so under the protection of Chapter XI of the Charter) or not, we were still faced with the growing need to define our respective interpretations of Article 2 (7).[2] In the United States view there was a sharp distinction between "discussion" and "action". They did not consider that Article 2 (7) precluded the Assembly from debating any issue, since debate did not of itself constitute intervention. Mr. Hickerson alleged that for its part the United States Government would never resist inscription on the Assembly agenda or debate in the United Nations, of any question concerning American internal affairs. The State Department Assistant Legal Adviser (Mr. Tate) even went so far as to say that no resolution adopted by the United Nations just so long as it stopped short of sanctions, would constitute "intervention" within the meaning of Article 2 (7). (This should not however be taken as representing the considered view of the State Department who are still engaged in hot internecine warfare on the subject.) Mr. Hickerson admitted that the United Nations was in fact impotent to take any effective action either in regard to the domestic affairs of its individual members or in differences between a non-self-governing territory, and the metropolitan power responsible for its administration. He further admitted that debate would almost invariably do more harm than good. At the same time it was the considered view of the State Department that to resist the rising tide of opinion for open debate on all these questions would do even more harm than the debate itself. To resist inscription or try to stifle debate was now doomed to failure and the act of resistance would in itself so vitiate the atmosphere and foster irresponsibility that the course of wisdom was to "roll a little with the punch", so disarming the ferocity of the attack and retaining some chance of controlling the outcome. The best hope in the coming period was, he therefore suggested, to play for a position when the smaller States, which at present had an inflated view of the General Assembly's powers, would come to realise its impotence and the little benefit they could expect from bringing their troubles before the United Nations.

70. *Sir John Martin* outlined the United Kingdom position in regard to both infringement and interpretation of Chapter XI and of Article 2 (7) of the Charter. He pointed out that the evolution of a territory from dependent to independent status was the most delicate political transition conceivable, which had in history only rarely been achieved without bloodshed. Our responsibility for the peaceful evolution of our Colonies, therefore, made it essential for us in all honesty to resist interference from any quarter which might prejudice beyond repair our basic aim of leading all these territories towards ultimate independence. Experience in the South-West African case and in the case of "Indians in South Africa" had shown that

---

[2] For the substance of these sections of the UN charter and the UK interpretations thereof, see eg 164.

open discussion in an irresponsible atmosphere engendered only heat without light and made a solution more and not less difficult. If, once we permitted the thin end of the wedge to be driven into our strict reading of the Charter, there was no knowing where we should afterwards logically or actually be able to call a halt, and it was possible that the success of our whole colonial policy might be fatally undermined.

71.   Whilst it was obvious that Sir John Martin's exposé made a real impression on both Hickerson and many of his officials, he still said that he could see no other way for the United States to stop the gathering snowball of pressure for universal discussion, than by persevering in their role of "honest broker". They would continuously try to impress on the smaller powers that if the General Assembly was to be a responsible action body, they could not use it for a periodical emotional binge just to get things off their chests. *Sir Christopher Steel*[3] pointed out that this middleman's role was not one which the United States would long be able to maintain. America was, after all, the greatest force in the world today and had 20th Century pattern colonial problems of its own developing – he instanced Okanawa [sic] and Panama. The State Department position on Article 2 (7) seemed to him untenable. If discussion of a United States domestic issue in the United Nations did not constitute "intervention in their domestic affairs", why should a debate on, for instance, the outcome of the American Presidential election in the British House of Commons be any different, and yet they would be the first rightly to stigmatize this as in precisely those terms. The question we all had to decide was how and where we could draw the line. *Sir Gladwyn Jebb*, seizing on Mr. Hickerson's admission that a debate on e.g. Tunisia and Morocco would do more harm than good, made a strong appeal to the State Department to take an appropriate opportunity at the next session of the General Assembly (probably in the debate on Tunisia), of making clear their honest opinion that the Assembly was impotent in cases of this kind and that although it might not be *ultra vires* to hold a debate, it was futile and could do no good. The response to this was not very encouraging.

Tunisia

72.   In the light of the foregoing general statement of position, *Mr. Hickerson* said that the State Department intended to continue pressing the French strongly not to resist inscription of the Tunisian item on the Agenda, and merely to reserve their position, but not to fight or force a vote on the question of competence. A majority vote for inscription was certain and to resist it would only build up prejudice against the colonial powers in the ensuing debate. The State Department considered that the French were in a strong position as the reform proposals they had made were reasonably good. Since Tunisia was a protectorate established by treaty, State Department Legal Advisers considered that an international relationship existed and the Assembly was therefore competent to deal with the case.[4] Attempts to block discussion would only feed the emotional appetite of nationalist opinion both in Tunisia and elsewhere. If it could be shown that the Assembly was in fact powerless

---

[3] Sir C Steel, minister, British embassy, Washington, 1950–1953; permanent representative on North Atlantic Council, 1953–1957.

[4] The British government wished no precedent to be set of UN competence to deal with colonial issues, and was accordingly extremely perturbed at the US position on Tunisia. The issue went up to Cabinet level ('UN. Handling of colonial questions', CAB 128/25, CC 93(52)3, 6 Nov 1952).

to help the Tunisian case, prospects for a future bilateral settlement would be improved, since so long as there was a misguided hope of action by the United Nations, the Tunisians would show no disposition to settle direct with the French. . . .

102   CO 936/95, no 93   [Oct 1952]

'Informal note on Anglo-American discussions on the handling of colonial and trusteeship questions in the United Nations (held in Washington 26th—28th September, 1952)': note by Sir J Martin

1. Talks on colonial and trusteeship issues arising in the United Nations have been held with the State Department before the 1950 and 1951 General Assemblies. At the 1950 talks the aim of the United Kingdom delegation was to obtain United States support for the new tactics the United Kingdom proposed to follow in the discussion of such issues in the General Assembly and Trusteeship Council. The 1951 talks were in effect a review of the success of this policy and the 1952 talks both continued this review and examined the particular problems likely to arise at the 1952 Assembly.

General

2. The United Kingdom delegation restated United Kingdom policy towards the United Nations. The United Kingdom recognised the considerable world interest in colonial affairs, although it realised that in certain cases this interest was malicious. It therefore took advantage of the opportunities for giving publicity to its own colonial achievements which debates in the United Nations afforded, and hoped by this means to bring world opinion to a more realistic appreciation of the problems with which we are faced and the danger of uninformed intervention in the intimate and complex relationship through which the United Kingdom was leading the territories concerned to self-government. Pursuit of this policy in the United Nations always involved the risk that the anti-colonial members would demand that the Administering Powers should be accountable to the United Nations for the administration of their non-self-governing territories. United Kingdom tactics were to turn such attacks and to avoid having to take direct issue with the Assembly on this question. As a means to this end considerable attention was being paid to the education of moderate opinion in the Assembly, and this was especially important in view of the revision of the Charter in 1955. At the forthcoming Assembly the United Kingdom delegation would seek to lower tension in debate and to adopt a positive role which would occasionally be expressed in putting forward resolutions. In general, by the exercise of moderation in replying to critics, the United Kingdom hoped to discredit the extremists. There were, however, certain issues on which the United Kingdom could not afford to yield without undermining its authority in the non-self-governing territories and hampering their progress towards self-government. These were:—

(1) Discussion of the political affairs of non-self-governing territories.
(2) The making by the United Nations of recommendations on any subject relating to specific territories.

(3) The right of the United Nations to receive and examine petitions from non-self-governing as distinct from trust territories.

(4) The grant of oral hearings to persons with petitions or information about non-self-governing territories, as distinct from trust territories.

(5) The despatch of United Nations visiting missions or the holding of United Nations plebiscites, except with the consent of the Administering Authority.

The Governments of France and Belgium agreed with the United Kingdom on these points.

3. The United States delegation welcomed the positive line the United Kingdom proposed to follow. The United States had not yet finally determined its 1952 Assembly policy, but they were, in principle, prepared to agree with points (3), (4) and (5), though not with (1) and (2). Their attitude was most clearly demonstrated in discussion of the Tunisian item which was considered at the end of discussions on general political subjects between the two delegations and at the beginning of the talks on purely colonial questions. The State Department considered that the United Nations were competent to discuss the Tunisian issue although they were not certain how far the United Nations could go in making recommendations after discussion. The United States "had sympathy with all peoples "struggling" for independence" and also felt that discussion of such matters was a convenient means of reducing international tensions. The United Kingdom delegation could not accept these premises.

In the specific case of Tunisia it seemed improbable to the United Kingdom that a public and most likely intemperate debate would in any way help towards an agreement being reached between the French and the Tunisian nationalists. The same would apply if the affairs of colonies were discussed during the last and most difficult stages of their progress towards self-government. It would be only too easy for elements in the colonies to seek to play off the United Nations against the administering power instead of working with the latter towards sensible and workmanlike solutions. It was apparent to the United Kingdom delegation that the State Department was not at all clear in its own mind as to the actual scope of Article 2(7) of the Charter. Nevertheless, the United States agreed that they would do their best in the lobbies to prevent difficult subjects coming up for discussion. For example, the State Department were anxious that nothing should be done to weaken the strategically vital position held by the United Kingdom in Cyprus. In the case of the Kenya land question they felt that in exceptional circumstances they might agree to an oral petitioner being heard, but they were not clear as to the nature of these circumstances. The United Kingdom delegation expressed a firm belief that a direct clash with the Assembly on these points might be avoided, but if the political affairs of United Kingdom non-self-governing territories were discussed Her Majesty's Government would have seriously to consider withdrawing the United Kingdom delegation from the relevant proceedings of the United Nations. The United Kingdom delegation explained that this statement was made as a result of careful consideration of the matter at the highest United Kingdom level[1] and was a firm and pre-determined policy framed in the light of our assessment of the likely course of debates at this year's Assembly.

---

[1] See 159, 160.

4. *Trusteeship questions*

(1) *Administrative unions*. On the problem of administrative unions the United States expressed themselves as being satisfied by the report of the Standing Committee. They hoped that it would be possible to suppress the Assembly's Committee on Administrative Unions, which seemed to them an unnecessary body. This view is shared by the United Kingdom.

(2) *The Ewe problem*. The United Kingdom delegation explained that the Ewes in northern Togoland wanted union with the Gold Coast. The unificationists,[2] who were all in the south, were a minority. The Joint Council had held its first meeting in August but had been adjourned because the representatives from British Togoland had walked out when their proposal for equal representation from both territories was rejected. The State Department inclined to the view that the ultimate solution might be for both Togolands to unite and then to join the Gold Coast. The United Kingdom delegation explained that they thought the unification of British Togoland with the Gold Coast was a natural development, but they could not entertain the idea of French territory being absorbed into a British Colony.

(3) *Cameroons unification*. The State Department were less hopeful than the United Kingdom Delegation that this artificial agitation would die a natural death.

(4) *Participation of indigenous inhabitants in the work of the Trusteeship Council*. The United Kingdom delegation recalled that the United Kingdom had supported the Trusteeship Council's resolution on this question. The State Department said that they felt that the resolution would probably have to be amended before the Assembly would be prepared to accept it. The United Kingdom delegation made it clear that the form in which it was adopted in the Trusteeship Council represented the limit to which the United Kingdom was prepared to go.

(5) *Timetables for self-government*. The United Kingdom delegation said that they considered any such arrangement both undesirable and impracticable. The State Department had open minds on the matter. They were inclined to think that the question of laying down a timetable could not arise on a practical matter until the territory concerned was clearly in the last constitutional stage before the attainment of self-government or independence.

5. *Non-self-governing territories*

(1) *Future of the Special Committee*. The United Kingdom delegation said that they were opposed to a permanent committee but would acquiesce in its continuation for three years on existing terms. The United States were also against a permanent committee.

(2) *Factors determining whether a territory is non-self-governing*. The United Kingdom considered that the United Nations was not competent to say when a metropolitan state might cease transmitting information under Article 73(e) in respect of any particular territory. The United States firmly agreed with this view.

---

[2] ie, those who sought the unification of British (northern) Togoland and French (southern) Togoland. See BDEEP series B, R Rathbone, ed, *Ghana*, part I, 80; part II, 150.

(3) *Participation of non-self-governing territories in the Committee on Information*. The State Department agreed with the United Kingdom Delegation that proposals for associate membership or any other form of "dual representation" should be opposed. They suggested that Administering Members might include indigenous experts in their delegations.

(4) *Human Rights – self-determination*. Both the American and United Kingdom Delegations were agreed that the Administering Powers were under no obligation to transmit political information, but the former remained obdurate in their support of "self-determination", as a general principle worthy of inscription in the Covenants on Human Rights.[3]

6. *Inter-delegation contacts*

The United Kingdom Delegation suggested that western and other friendly powers should make a practice of meeting informally to discuss Fourth Committee matters. The Americans, however, were reluctant to attach themselves to any particular bloc, though they agreed on the value of inter-delegation contacts on specific issues.

7. *Conclusion*

The discussions were conducted, as in previous years, in a most cordial atmosphere. Unfortunately the State Department had not yet chosen the members of their delegation who would be handling the various colonial questions. Both sides were, however, fully seized of the other's views, and the United Kingdom's attitude on certain questions involving the competence of the General Assembly were made plain to the State Department.[4]

---

[3] See 155, 163.

[4] Martin later minuted to Sir T Lloyd that Britain could hardly hope for a more sympathetic American line on colonial questions so long as the Americans' main desire was ' "to cast a succulent fly over the uncommitted third" i.e. the U.S. wooing of the Arab-Asian bloc.' Lloyd felt that there was little evidence 'to conclude that talks of this kind have more than a negative value, i.e. that if they did not take place the Americans might act even more stupidly than they at present sometimes do in relation to Colonial matters in the United Nations.' But in Martin's view 'this year's talks were really more valuable than last year's because this year we got closer to grips with actual questions arising in the Assembly and so brought out differences which were previously concealed under an appearance of *general* understanding' (CO 935/95, minutes, 28 & 29 Oct 1952).

103   FO 371/107032, no 1   12 Jan 1953

[Anglo-American relations and the UN]: despatch no 4 from Sir G Jebb (New York) to Mr Eden

The adjournment of the Seventh Session of the General Assembly and the imminent advent to power in Washington of a Republican Administration provide a convenient occasion for reviewing our general attitude toward the United Nations. I hope also that the short appreciation which follows may be of use as background in any discussions which may take place in the next few months with the new figures in American public life regarding United Nations problems. Both General Eisenhower and Mr. Dulles have, I believe, stated publicly and privately that it will be their intention to support the United Nations. But expression of a general intention is one thing and a positive policy is another. Moreover many of the American experts who have up to now been dealing with United Nations questions will soon be leaving for other fields. For instance, the entire senior staff of the United States Mission to the United Nations will, I understand, shortly be changed. Excellent though Senator Lodge[1] will no doubt prove to be, he may well therefore suffer from a certain lack of experienced advice. For these reasons, if for no other, our own ideas, based as they will be on a greater continuity, may be of considerable value in moulding American opinion. Naturally everything that I say in this despatch regarding America and American opinion is subject to correction by Her Majesty's Ambassador, to whom I am sending a copy of this despatch. Subject to that, I venture to submit the following propositions for your consideration and, as I should hope, your approval.

Collective resistance to aggression

2. Clearly, we can only rely on the Security Council for this purpose if the aggression should take place in some part of the world not directly affected by the Cold War. There might conceivably be such an aggression in South America, though it would presumably be dealt with there within the framework of the Treaty of Rio. It is, I suppose, still possible, though perhaps unlikely, that the Soviet Union would not block action by the Security Council in the event of a renewal of the war between Israel and the Arab States. Or conceivably in the event of war between India and Pakistan. But even if she did not do this her offer of assistance in suppressing the aggression might prove to be still more embarrassing. Apart from these instances it is difficult to think of any area where aggression would not be viewed in a different light by the Five Permanent Members and consequently result in failure on the part of the Security Council to take the necessary action.

3. However, even though the Security Council were paralysed, it would still be possible, in theory at least, to cope with some further aggression in accordance with the "Uniting for Peace" resolution of the General Assembly. It is quite conceivable that, even though the Soviet Union and the Western Powers were on opposite sides, this machinery could come into play and the conflict still be localised. For instance, even if the Soviet Union were to veto action by the Security Council in the event of renewed hostilities in Palestine, the "Uniting for Peace" machinery might be successfully invoked in the Assembly. Or it might even be successfully invoked in the event of a conflict between Yugoslavia and a Soviet satellite or satellites not overtly supported by the Soviet Union.

4. In practice, of course, if such situations as these developed, almost everything would depend on the extent to which the United States was prepared to commit itself, including, if necessary, its own armed forces. But even so, the existence of the United Nations and of the "Uniting for Peace" machinery might encourage the United States to make the necessary effort, and in any case the moral obligation on Member States to support the action of a two-thirds majority of members of the Assembly might prove of some material benefit to the Great Powers who would undoubtedly have to bear the main burden of the struggle. It can certainly be argued that we should not have enjoyed even the limited support which a country like India has given to the resistance to aggression in Korea if it had not been for the fact that the

---

[1] H C Lodge, US ambassador to the UN, 1953–1961.

Republic of Korea was under United Nations tutelage and that a United Nations Commission, of which India was a member, was on the spot when the aggression took place. During the course of the fighting there has also been some advantage, which was demonstrated most clearly at the present Session of the Assembly, in being able to associate the Arab and Asian countries, through the debates in the United Nations, with the attempt to achieve a settlement. If the Korean action had not been conducted under the auspices of the United Nations, the moral, if not the material, support for it among the countries of the Free World, including the United States itself, would almost certainly have been less widespread and less clearly demonstrated.

5. Should some local aggression develop into World War III, however, it would be quite foolish to place any particular reliance on United Nations machinery. The initial decision to resist the aggression having been taken, it would certainly help to have the support of a large majority in the United Nations. Even if the conflict developed into a World War, there would no doubt be some continuing advantage for the Free World to make use of the United Nations flag and to assert that it was standing for United Nations principles. But the course of the war would not really be affected very much one way or the other by such developments as these, and it is not perhaps too pessimistic to think that the bulk of United Nations Member States would try to preserve some kind of neutrality until, at any rate, they were pretty certain which side was going to win. In any case, World War III would signify the end of the United Nations as we know it. If it were reconstructed after the War, it would presumably, in the prevailing radio-active atmosphere, be on rather different lines.

6. Nevertheless, we can, I think, legitimately assume that, on balance, it is in our interests, as well as in those of the United States, to preserve the United Nations machine for the help, for the most part moral, but in some part material, which it might be able to afford us in the event of another aggression. Without it, it seems certain that a great part of the non-Communist nations, in particular what has come to be known as the Arab-Asian bloc but also probably most of Latin America, would stand aside from what might seem to be not so much a conflict between Right and Wrong as a morally meaningless struggle between rival groups of Great Powers for the physical domination of the world. I suggest that it is well worth while putting up with quite a deal of nonsense to preserve this particular advantage.

Peaceful settlement

7. It may be argued that, particularly of late, efforts by the United Nations to achieve peaceful settlement of international, or allegedly international, disputes have merely resulted in worsening the situation. The discussion of Tunis, Morocco and Apartheid at the last Session of the General Assembly might be held up as an example of this unfortunate tendency. But we maintain that the ventilation of such questions at the United Nations is an abuse of its machinery, and it is to be hoped that their relative lack of success at the Seventh Session may induce in those responsible a greater sense of restraint. Although there may be a tendency for the machinery to be abused, it does not follow that the machinery itself is at fault and must be scrapped. Where genuine disputes of an international kind have arisen, it is a fact that the United Nations has certain real, if limited, successes to its credit. The evacuation of Iran by Soviet troops, the end of the indirect aggression of her northern neighbours against Greece, the settlement of the dispute between Indonesia and the Dutch, the

Armistice Agreements in Palestine, and (subject to greater reservations) the Kashmir issue, all represent situations which almost certainly would have been worse, had it not been for United Nations intervention. It may, of course, be held that United Nations successes in this field are becoming progressively rarer as the Cold War is intensified. This may be so, but just as it is still possible to conceive of aggressions which are not directly affected by the Cold War, so it is possible to conceive of international disputes which are not affected or only slightly affected, by Cold War circumstances. It would certainly seem desirable to maintain United Nations Machinery for coping with such situations as these. For instance, it might be in our own interest, one day, to have recourse to United Nations procedures to deal with claims by Saudi Arabia on the territories of some of the Trucial Sheikhs or by the Yemen on the Aden Protectorate.

8. I know, of course, that United Nations procedures for dealing with disputes may in the future be employed to our disadvantage. Recent events in Iran, for instance, have not been such as to encourage one to put much faith in United Nations solutions when our own interests are at stake. But as a general proposition it seems safe to assert that no great harm can come to us in the Security Council, and even in the General Assembly so long as we can count on the support of the United States of America and consequently of those States which politically follow in her train. Whereas, if we cannot count on such support, it is difficult to see how we should not be in difficulties even in the absence of any kind of World Organisation. In sum, if it has done nothing else, the United Nations has certainly evolved a technique for dealing with international disputes in accordance with certain defined rules of procedure. And on the whole it seems probable that both we and America might be in a rather weaker position if no such facilities as these existed.

Colonial matters

9. Here it must be admitted that, from our point of view, there are few apparent advantages in maintaining the existing machinery. In spite of all the investigations, appeals, petitions and Visiting Missions organised during the last few years, it is not apparent that the Trusteeship Council has anywhere actually bettered the lot of any of the inhabitants of the Trust Territories supposed to be under its special care.

10. In any case the activities of the Fourth Committee have been almost wholly undesirable as far as we are concerned. The majority of Members of the United Nations indeed seem to be much keener on abolishing the whole colonial system than on doing anything which might conceivably have the effect of improving it. The danger that the constant demands for independence for every Colony, however backward, may result in increasing anarchy is considerable, and there seems little doubt that if both the Trusteeship Council and the Fourth Committee were abolished tomorrow nothing but good for our non-self-governing territories would result.

11. As against this it may perhaps be said that, whether we like it or not, the gradual process of industrialisation and education is resulting in a kind of colonial revolution and that, in these circumstances, the United Nations can act as a kind of safety valve. But as the elements which seek and gain United Nations support are invariably the most extreme, United Nations intervention can only result in a violent disintegration rather than a controlled revolution. Therefore it is difficult to see how this particular argument can be sustained. As has been said above, the majority of the Members of the United Nations do not want the United Nations to act as a safety

valve; they want the revolution to succeed and do not like to forego any chance of promoting it.

12.   Perhaps the most hopeful feature of this part of the picture is that if the Colonial Powers show that they cannot be pushed beyond a certain point, the anti-Colonial Powers may simply lose heart, and the debate in the United Nations therefore eventually peter out. Moreover we may perhaps legitimately hope that the new American Administration will see the folly of on the one hand spending dollars through the Mutual Security Agency for developments in Uganda and on the other of encouraging anarchy in East Africa by adherence to out of date "anti-colonial" policies in the United Nations. Still, in general, it must be admitted that the colonial activities of the United Nations represent for us purely a debit.

Economic

13.   Though one should not exaggerate its importance, it seems fairly clear that some useful work is being accomplished by the United Nations as distinct from the work of the Specialised Agencies. UNESCO apart, it is unlikely that there will be any popular demand to wind up any of the latter, most of which are doing purely technical jobs in connection with aviation, health, food and agriculture, labour and so on. The Technical Assistance Administration and the Technical Assistance Board are both undoubtedly of some value and are of direct assistance to the Free World in its efforts to combat communism by, so to speak, prophylactic methods. The quiet and on the whole efficient work of the United Nations Children's Emergency Fund has also served to strengthen the belief of many countries that direct practical benefits result from the economic and social activities of the United Nations. Measures of land reform introduced by some countries, improvements in the collection of agricultural and industrial statistics, better fiscal arrangements, improvements in other branches of public administration, and the fostering of a climate of opinion favourable to the development of backward countries are only some of the results of the activities of the Economic and Social Council and its subsidiary Commissions, when looked at over a period of time. Changes in the world economic situation, however, are not generally sufficiently spectacular to warrant public discussion twice a year in the Economic and Social Council and once a year in the Second Committee. This is probably why these meetings, and more particularly those of the Second Committee, tend to waste time and energy.

14.   It would be gratifying if technical aid, and the work of the Economic and Social Council's functional and regional Commissions were to result in an improvement of relations between the under-developed countries and the governments and private interests of the countries at whose expense aid is chiefly provided. To some extent this may prove to be the case, even in the short run. But the under-developed countries seem to be coming to the view that they have a right to assistance, for which nothing like gratitude should be expected and which must not be allowed to undermine their entire freedom of action in regard to the industrialised states. The support for the resolution passed at the Seventh Session on the right to nationalise foreign enterprises was, I think, typical of this state of mind. Irritating as it is to us, however, this does not in itself demonstrate that present aid is wasted, or even that it might not with advantage be increased. For the basic aim of the pro-technical assistance programme is to prevent the spread of communism by strengthening the economic structure and thereby to improve the social structure and standard of

living of the more backward countries. An early improvement in their relations with the industrialised states, if it came about, would be a by-product.

15. In a word, the economic activity of the United Nations must undoubtedly be recorded as a credit rather than a debit.

Social

16. It is, I fear, my considered view that, in practice the continued efforts to achieve international agreement on Human "Rights" and "Freedoms", and thereafter to enforce them do, in themselves, more harm than good.

17. The world is still so divided from the point of view of religion and philosophy that it is clearly not ripe for the general acceptance of legal or moral maxims, however obvious these may appear to the Western mind. Moreover, even if nominally accepted such imperatives would undoubtedly be disregarded by many nations in practice. Unfortunate though it may be, we must also, I think, realise that the great Liberal conceptions of social progress, freedom of man, intellectual integrity, freedom of thought and so on have been perverted by the Communists for their own purposes. The religious content of these ideas that once moved the masses has been largely drained and extracted. What is left is the utilitarian bone which is grist for the Communist mill. Reason, though still nominally enthroned, has really abdicated. In a sense, we have moved back as it were from the eighteenth to the seventeenth century. What is needed is some new formulation of the basic truths of the Western Democracies with which to combat the religious appeal of a Communism which falsely represents itself as the heir to the Liberal, and hence, ultimately, to the Christian tradition.

18. And yet, until such a formulation is made, if it ever is, we certainly cannot abandon our efforts to spread Liberal conceptions throughout the world, even if we have to do so with intellectual weapons that are rusty and out of date and which are anyhow used against us by our adversaries. For to do this would simply mean declaring that we were without any world philosophy capable of countering the undoubted world appeal of Communism, specious and illusory though it is. This is another way of saying that the Social activities of the United Nations must proceed and that until we have discovered the formulae which can rally and unite the Free World we shall deprecate these activities only at our peril.

General

19. The more general activities of the United Nations have admittedly resulted in almost total frustration. Disarmament makes no progress at all, nor is there the slightest likelihood that it will progress as long as the Cold War continues. All that can be said is that, here also, a certain technique has been evolved which can be applied if circumstances make this possible. The control of atomic energy has now (rightly) been discovered to be simply a facet of Disarmament. Its discussion is therefore equally unproductive. But it also stands to reason that on these two fronts the situation would not be any better if the United Nations ceased to exist or were disrupted.

20. Among the general activities of the United Nations must presumably be included the waging of the Cold War itself. A forum has been provided by the United Nations for both participants in this struggle. It has been alleged that this forum is of greater use to the Communists than to the Free World. It is extremely doubtful

W

whether this proposition is true. On the contrary, the United Nations provides an unrivalled stage for combating Soviet lies and propaganda and indeed for preaching the principles of true democracy. It is standing proof of our willingness, through methods of "open diplomacy" (by which Americans set such store), to seek agreement with the Soviet Union and a peaceful solution of the Cold War. Undoubtedly also, the sense of comradeship between members of the Free World is stimulated by their being jointly attacked in New York by representatives of the Communist areas. This sense of solidarity is of great importance in the general struggle to prevent members of the Free World from breaking away and seeking refuge, either in neutrality or in the protection of the Soviet system.

Provisional conclusions

21.   It seems to follow from the above that, though it has many defects from our own point of view, and a good many even from the point of view of the United States as well, the United Nations as a whole is something which it is in our joint interest to foster and preserve, not only as a machine which might be used in happier days, but also as something which is of practical and definite use in the present unfortunate international circumstances.

Wider considerations

22.   There is, however, a powerful additional argument in favour of preserving the United Nations as a more or less "universal" machine, that is to say, a body containing States representing different and conflicting ideologies.

23.   If indeed the Soviet Union and its friends withdrew from the Organisation, or if they were expelled, or if the United States itself weakened in its support, or even if the United Kingdom, perhaps owing to Colonial circumstances, became a rather non-active Member, there is reason to suppose that what are sometimes referred to as the "isolationist" elements in American public life—but which could equally truly be described as the extreme nationalistic, xenophobic, or even Fascist elements— would be considerably strengthened. Members of the outgoing Administration here have always argued that United States foreign policy must be based on the United Nations because they could not otherwise justify the predominant role which the United States must now play in international affairs and carry American public opinion with them in support of it. I see no reason to doubt this considered judgment. We must hope that the new Administration will share the same objectives, and they may well feel that they must also adopt essentially the same tactics. As a generalisation, I suggest that those in America who most fear war and who are most in favour of peaceful settlement, are those who are most in favour of maintaining the Free World and of working in close conjunction with foreigners and more especially with the British. If such elements became discouraged owing to the disappearance or too obvious enfeeblement of what they believe, rightly or wrongly, to be the main hope of peaceful settlement in the future, there seems little doubt that the policy of the United States, as expressed in Congress and indeed in the Administration, might become much more intransigent and much less sensitive to European suggestions. During the next few years when World War III may well break out, or be avoided, as a result of some American decision, we should do well, I think, constantly to reflect on this grave possibility.

24.   Nor will it do, I am convinced, for us to shrug our shoulders and say that if

the United Nations folds up we shall always have N.A.T.O., which is what we must rely on for our practical defence in any eventuality. For if extremist policies were, as suggested above, to become more popular in the U.S.A. as a result of a collapse of the World Organisation, the resultant conflicts between the United States and her N.A.T.O. allies might well result in a collapse of N.A.T.O. itself. Then indeed we might see a recrudescence of real isolationism in America and a revival of the old MacArthur slogan that the United States must have no regard to her allies but simply "go it alone".

Final thought
25. If World War III is to be avoided it can only be as a result of:—

(a) An economic or political collapse of one side or the other.
(b) A successful ultimatum addressed by one side to the other, resulting in the achievement of desired objectives.
(c) A process of negotiation on outstanding issues or
(d) An indefinite continuance of the *status quo*.

(a) and (b) appear to be highly unlikely, though (b) may be attempted. We must not abandon hope of (c) but progress at the best will be slow and difficult. Bad therefore though it may be (d) is therefore perhaps the best guess. But if we are in for a long period of "co-existence" it is all the more important to have an organisation on which both sides are at least represented. The United Nations cannot of course prevent the outbreak of World War III, but so long as it exists in its present form it can at least do a little to assist the process of prevention.

104 CO 936/96, no 114   17 June 1953
[Forthcoming Anglo-American talks on colonial questions]: letter from M S Williams[1] to Sir C Steel (Washington)[2]

We have begun to think about the talks which we now usually hold with the Americans about United Nations affairs in preparation for the regular meeting of the General Assembly. You made some reference to this in paragraph 8 of your despatch No. 192 of the 29th of April.

2. In theory, the talks this year should be of particular value. There is a new administration in Washington and presumably many new faces among the higher officials in the State Department. It therefore seems to us that we should make a special effort this year to enlighten the United States Government as to our position on the most contentious United Nations issues. The talks last year covered both our general conceptions of the rôle the United Nations should play in the field of international affairs, as also the attitude our two Delegations should adopt in regard to specific questions likely to come before the General Assembly. With a new administration in Washington there may be advantage this year in concentrating rather on the general principles and leaving discussion of detailed co-ordination of our policies in practice to the Delegations in New York. The only doubt in our mind

---

[1] M S Williams, FO, 1952–1956.   [2] See 101, note 3.

is that if Hickerson should still be in charge of United Nations affairs in the State Department it may be rather a waste of time to hold discussions of a general nature with the State Department before his successor takes over.

3. The general line of our thought in regard to the rôle which the United Nations should play is already well-known. It was expounded during last year's talks and in many of Jebb's recent speeches in the United States. But we think there would be every advantage in repeating it. Our views on the handling of colonial affairs in the United Nations are equally well-known, but we think that this year there would be advantage in making a special effort to explain them clearly to the new administration before the Assembly. Further, apart from the general explanation of our point of view, it has occurred to us that it would be desirable this year to inform the Americans closely about our various policies in Africa. There have been indications that attempts will be made to discuss the internal affairs of Kenya and Central African Federation, while there will of course be discussion of various questions affecting the Africa [sic] Trust Territories. There is no weakening in our determination to do everything possible to prevent the discussion in the United Nations of the internal affairs of particular colonies (other than trust territories) or their political development, and there is no question of the United Kingdom Representatives participating in discussions in the United Nations on such subjects. It therefore seems to us important that the United States Government should be reminded of our standpoint, and that we should at the same time try to convince them that the policy we are in fact pursuing in our African territories is the right one and that our determination to brook no interference from the United Nations in no way means that we have anything to hide. Our aim would be to convince the Americans that our position is reasonable and to persuade them to adopt an attitude of sympathetic understanding in the United Nations.

4. It may be that it will be unusually difficult to reach an understanding with the Americans on colonial affairs this year if as seems to be forecast by Mr. Dulles' speech on his return from his trip to the Near East the United States Government are proposing to give more active support to dependent peoples seeking political independence. We think, nevertheless, that the effort would be worth making.

5. We had wondered whether it would be practicable to separate the talks on colonial affairs from the more general pre-Assembly talks with the Americans. The colonial battle is however now being carried into the First, Second and Third Committees as well as the Fourth Committee, and it seems unrealistic to try to separate discussions about colonial issues and the interpretation of Article 2(7) of the Charter from the main body of the talks. In fact, it is only by relating colonial questions to the other matters that come up for discussion in the Assembly that they can be seen in their proper perspective and that the reactions on other discussions in the United Nations of particular politics in regard to colonial affairs can be properly appreciated.

6. As regards the timing of any talks we had been thinking, on the assumption that the Assembly will meet on its appointed date, September 15, that the end of July would be the most suitable period, and the Colonial Office would in any case prefer this. If, however, owing to the resumption of the Seventh Session to deal with the Korean question, the opening of the Eighth Session is postponed until October, as now seems quite probable, the talks with the Americans should perhaps be held over until mid-September.

7. In your despatch No. 192 you infer that the talks this year should be in London, since they were held in Washington last year. For our part, we should very much prefer that the talks should be held in Washington. We can hardly expect that the Americans would send abroad a particularly strong team and certainly no one would be likely to represent the United States in the Fourth Committee. If the talks are held in Washington, on the other hand, we have a much better chance of reaching a wide and important audience in the State Department. If therefore the Americans agree, we would like the talks to be held again in Washington.

8. If it is agreed that the talks should be in Washington, we should like them to be on the same basis as last year. That is to say, they should be held under the patronage of the Embassy, with Jebb as the principal spokesman on the United Kingdom side. He would be supported in regard to colonial matters (as well perhaps by Mathieson)[3] by one or two Assistant Under Secretaries of State from the Colonial Office. Normally, Sir John Martin would represent them, but in view of the importance they attach to enlightening the Americans on African developments the Colonial Office might also send the Assistant Under-Secretary dealing with African affairs, Gorell Barnes. No decision has been taken on this point, and the Colonial Office would particularly welcome your views on it.

9. I am sending a copy of this letter to Jebb, and I should be grateful for the views of yourself and the Delegation in New York on the various matters raised therein. We should have no objection to your discussing the question with the State Department should you so desire before replying. If you do so and if the State Department favour the holding of talks you might say that we would welcome their suggestions for a draft agenda.

---

[3] W A C Mathieson, assistant secretary, CO, 1949–1958; counsellor (colonial affairs) to UK delegation to UN, 1951–1954; minister for education, labour and lands, Kenya, 1958–1960.

105   CO 936/317, no 13   [June 1954]
'Notes on colonialism for Washington talks': note prepared in the CO for use by Sir W Churchill and Mr Eden

Reports from *The Times* Washington Correspondent and in various American newspapers ascribe to Mr. Dulles and the State Department an intention to discuss with the Prime Minister and the Foreign Secretary the disadvantages which United States alignment with the "Colonial Powers" has brought to the United States in her relations with the backward and recently independent countries of the world. The State Department feel that by condoning the colonial activities of Britain and France the United States has lost the respect of these countries who are consequently less friendly to her general foreign policy.

It is the case that, especially since the advent of the Republican Administration, the State Department has been markedly more sympathetic towards the colonial policies and activities of H.M. Government and especially in the United Nations. We believe that this has been the result of an increasing American realisation that the grant of premature self-government to colonial peoples, and attempts to apply in practice such catchwords as "self-determination", would merely increase the areas of political instability in the world and expose any newly independent but economically and socially unstable countries which might emerge from it to infiltration by communism.

It would be a serious embarrassment to us in handling colonial questions on the international plane (and especially in the United Nations) if the tacit support we have received from the United States were to be withdrawn and be replaced by the unrealistic and often irresponsible idealism which characterised United States policy on colonial matters in the immediate post-war years.

To avert this risk, the following points might usefully be made:—

(a) It is a fallacy to assume that American difficulties with the under-developed countries, and especially those in South Asia, stem from a disgust at American abandonment of anti-colonialism. The fact of the matter is that the United Kingdom, which is the major Colonial Power in the world, has close and friendly ties with the South-Asian countries, closer than the Americans have hitherto been able to establish. This seems to indicate that colonialism itself is not, in the last resort, a factor which blinds the under-developed countries to the need for maintaining friendly relations with the Western Powers. It is extremely doubtful whether an American *volte face* on colonialism would appear to such countries as India as more than a tactical move.

(b) Even if the Americans feel impelled to make some re-statement of their attitude towards the advancement of under-developed countries, we hope that any pronouncement they make will take account of political realities. It is demonstrably absurd to describe current British colonial policy as oppressive and procastinating. Apart from our actions in South Asia since the war, we have now brought the Gold Coast to the last stage before independence and we are introducing in Nigeria, a land of 30 million inhabitants, a constitution based on adult suffrage, with an undertaking that in 1956 the peoples of Nigeria will have an opportunity freely to state their own views on the future which the component parts of the territory wish to enjoy. In Kenya, despite the disturbance of Mau Mau, we have made a start on the introduction of multi-racial government of a kind not before tried in practice anywhere in the world. We have suggested to the United Nations that British Togoland should be accorded full self-government at the same time as the Gold Coast so that, under our tutelage, a British-administered territory will be the first Trust Territory to reach maturity under the International Trusteeship System. In British Honduras, despite the risks involved, we have decided to work with the elected representatives of the people in an effort to establish a popular and contented administration in an area, Central America, which is at present exposed to anti-western infiltration. In Malaya we could not have damped down the communist insurrection had the people of Malaya not been fundamentally well-disposed towards us and appreciative of the benefits which British tutelage can bring. Upon that goodwill we are attempting to build a system of popular government based on a combination of the elected representatives of all races and on the traditional authority of the Sultans.

(c) It would be impolitic, in our view, and would serve no American interest, if they were to revert to the sort of easy statement of ideologies which bedevilled international discussion of colonial questions in the immediate post-war years. Whatever their deep-seated repugnance to the concept of colonialism may be, all responsible governments, including that of India, recognise that British colonial policy is still an essential feature of the advancement of many of the under-developed peoples of the world. Any American attempt to hasten the pace of our progress in colonial political development would appear to those Governments as little more than an empty gesture.

106   CO 936/317, no 62   31 July 1954
'Record of Anglo-American conversations on colonial affairs in the United Nations held in Washington on 26th and 27th July, 1954': CO note   [Extract]

Preliminary discussion
1. The talks were opened by *Mr. David Wainhouse* (U.S. Deputy Assistant Secretary for United Nations Affairs) who spoke of the firmness of Anglo-American understanding in spite of the differences of opinion which arose from time to time. He then went on to express appreciation for the help rendered to the U.S. by the U.K. in the Trusteeship Council when the Marshall Islanders' petition was being examined. Also he stated how glad the U.S. Government had been to be able to take the lead in supporting the U.K. proposals for the future of Togoland. Mr. Wainhouse concluded by emphasising that although it was not necessary to reach agreement on the matters to be discussed it was hoped that as a result of the talks an identity of policy would emerge in most cases. In reply *Mr H.T. Bourdillon* (Assistant Under-Secretary of State, Colonial Office) remarked how grateful he was for being given this opportunity to meet representatives of the State Department in informal talks. He appreciated that this was not a formal conference, but he hoped that the agenda prepared—especially Part II—would provide the framework to enable both sides to obtain a better understanding of what the other was doing, and of the problems which had to be reckoned with. He reciprocated *mutatis mutandi* Mr. Wainhouse's remarks on the treatment in the Trusteeship Council of the American bomb tests in the Pacific and on the U.K. proposals for Togoland.

Item 1. Review of the attitude of "blocs" in the United Nations on colonial questions, including consideration of diplomatic action on particular issues: possibilities of bringing about a larger bloc of moderate opinion
2. In opening the discussion Mr. Bourdillon presented the views in the U.K. brief emphasising that it was the British wish to exchange ideas with the Americans, particularly with a view to obtaining advice on the attitudes of the Latin American countries. The U.K. did not want to adopt a negative "hands off" attitude in dealing with her colonial problems in the U.N. The objective was to induce an atmosphere which would enable colonial questions to be discussed with less emotion and in a more realistic and moderate way. This might in its turn lead to decisions being taken by U.N. committees based upon the merits of a case and not upon dialectics and prejudice.
3. After some detailed discussion *it was agreed*:—

(a) that the attitudes of the different blocs often varied from committee to committee. On occasion for example, countries which took a moderate line in the

First Committee were far from being equally temperate in the Fourth Committee; (b) that within delegations there was frequently a lack of "discipline" or clear-cut direction. Individual delegates were often found to be "free wheeling". For this reason the United States had not decided yet whether to make diplomatic representations in Latin American capitals before the next Session of the General Assembly. In the past acceptance by the Latin American governments of a U.S. line had often not been reflected in the attitude of their delegations. Consequently irrespective of what diplomatic action might be taken, British and American delegates at the U.N. would still have to work on their opposite numbers in the lobbies in all matters of importance. For their part the U.S. were thinking of concentrating more this year on the heads of delegations who were frequently more reasonable than their subordinates;

(c) that moderation in speech was not always reflected in the vote. Unfortunately resolutions aimed specifically against either France or Belgium were often couched in general terms which made them distasteful to all the administering powers. This was however probably a necessary evil which must be accepted as at least preferable to resolutions directed at specified administering authorities. No one wished to see continuous attacks developing on any one State or colonial territory;

(d) that the attitudes of all non-administering countries opposed to colonialism varied widely and was difficult to pinpoint. In Latin America, Haiti, Peru, the Dominican Republic, Cuba and Costa Rica seemed to be becoming increasingly objective in their approach. The State Department thought Brazil had recently become less reliable as a moderating influence. Argentina and Mexico were rabid opponents, and it remained to be seen to what extent the Guatemalan attitude of hostility would be modified by the change in regime. The statement by *Miss Salt* that the United Kingdom was announcing recognition of the Junta that day was welcomed by the Americans. They felt that this might have a salutary effect on the Guatemalan attitude at the U.N. later in the year.

It was not expected that the Arab nations would change their ways. The recent tendency of some Arabs to vote in unison with the U.S.S.R. presented a dreary prospect which probably flowed from continuing Arab/Israel hostility. Lebanon had not come up to expectation as a moderating force. Pakistan was becoming more moderate, but her influence was limited. There was little hope that Burma would improve on her disappointing record. Indian tactics were unlikely to change although her influence was perhaps declining. The State Department suggested that the U.K. should press Canada to take a more active part in colonial issues. Her respected, independent position might carry weight with India. Indo-Canadian relations were close and, if properly briefed and inspired, Canada might contribute much towards Indian moderation.

After examining Yugoslavia's ominous activities it was noted that the new look in U.S.S.R. policy was fraught with danger. By moderating the tone of its anti-colonial speeches and resolutions the U.S.S.R. could attract "neutral" support for a line inimical to the administering powers. Mr. Gerig[1] felt that occasional attacks in the U.N. on Russian imperialism and colonialism would not be valueless. The value of

---

[1] B Gerig, director of the Office of Dependent Area Affairs, US State Department, from 1949.

these tactics was doubted by Mr. Gidden[2] who thought that a policy of ignoring Soviet sallies paid off more successfully.

Item 2. Review of the basic principles motivating our respective attitudes to colonial questions in the United Nations, and Item 13—Review of current and future developments in the major colonial territories—West, East and Central Africa, Malaya, the West Indies

4. In the course of presenting the United Kingdom views on colonial basic principles *Mr. Bourdillon* gave a review of current and future developments in the major British colonial territories (original Part II of the agenda). In his opening remarks Mr. Bourdillon made it clear that the United Kingdom's stand on the question of accountability and on the legal interpretation of Article 2(7) of the United Nations Charter had not changed. The United Kingdom was entirely open to moderate and informed criticism, but deplored the emotionalism and recklessness exhibited in the Fourth Committee. It was in an effort to keep down the emotional temperature that the United Kingdom had gone to the greatest limits possible, without jeopardising the welfare of her dependent peoples, to co-operate with the United Nations. Nevertheless the United Kingdom must insist that any discussion of the political affairs of colonial territories in United Nations bodies constituted an infringement of the Charter which she could not tolerate. Irresponsible discussion in the United Nations could not fail to exacerbate those racial and colour antipathies in colonial countries which it was a prime aim of United Kingdom policy to remove. In reply *Mr. Gerig* (U.S.) made reference to the differences of background—historical, philosophical and geographical—between the United Kingdom and the United States, which coloured the thinking of all in America who were concerned with the problems of colonialism. He referred particularly to the United States suspicion of Colonialiam exhibited in the American press in recent months, and indicated that American representatives at international meetings were bound to reflect such expressions of domestic public opinion. Mr. Gerig quoted from recent statements by Mr. Dulles on the necessity for the early abolition of colonialism. He admitted the dangers of granting premature independence to colonial peoples, and said the United States also were opposed to the fragmentation of colonial areas. It was recognised that small islands or territories would often be incapable of standing on their own feet as independent nations. He concluded by urging the United Kingdom not to adopt too negative an attitude in its dealings with the United Nations even though it was a body which the United States recognised as being far from perfect as an international forum. *Mr. Wainhouse* considered that United Kingdom delegations were too modest in showing the world at the United Nations the best colonial asset which the United Kingdom had—her record in the colonial territories. From time to time during Mr. Bourdillon's review of progress in British colonial territories the Americans returned to this theme. They obviously felt it was up to the United Kingdom to find a remedy. Mr. Wainhouse quoted as possibly a helpful precedent the practice in the First Committee where certain Security Council reports are tabled for information only—i.e. not subject to debate. *Mr. Gidden* pointed out that the Fourth Committee was far more irresponsible and undisciplined than the First Committee

---

[2] B O B Gidden, assistant secretary, CO, 1951–1954; counsellor (colonial affairs) to UK delegation to UN, 1954–1958.

Committee and made it clear that detailed political information about British colonial territories could easily be made available to all interested powers. The trouble in the United Nations was that critics of the colonial powers were not objective. They did not wish to be informed but were concerned with launching attacks for national or ideological reasons. Moreover our interpretation of Articles 73(e) and 2(7) of the Charter and our attitude on accountability virtually precluded us from taking any initiative to publicize our political achievement to United Nations bodies.

5. In subsequent discussion the following suggestions were made:—

(i) that the legal advisers to the United States and United Kingdom delegations to the next General Assembly might try to reconcile the conflicting advice they customarily gave their Governments on Articles 2(7) and 10 of the United Nations Charter;

(ii) that an effort should be made to consult individual non-administering members of United Nations committees dealing with colonial matters on the economic and social problems of their own territories.

Item 3. Possibility of discussion in the Fourth Committee of the political affairs of particular territories

(a) *Cyprus*[3]

6. *Mr. Bourdillon* introduced the Cyprus problem by notifying the meeting in confidence of the constitutional proposals which Her Majesty's Government had agreed to for Cyprus. Having given a resumé of the economic and social progress made in the island during recent years, as well as drawing attention to the United Kingdom's financial assistance towards implementing past and present plans for Cyprus, Mr. Bourdillon explained Her Majesty's Government's reasons for deciding to introduce now a modified form of the constitution offered to the Cypriots in 1948. He emphasised that owing to the imperative need to give the rising middle class of Cyprus a chance to participate in the political control of the island without at the same time opening the door to the Communists, it had been necessary to restrict the number of elected members in the proposed legislature. As a balancing factor when comparing the proposed constitution with that suggested in 1948 he drew attention to the proposals for associating by means of a ministerial system the representatives of the people in the executive side of the government to an extent greater than had been planned previously. Mr. Bourdillon rehearsed all the arguments in Intel. No. 140 and made a strong appeal for United States support to prevent inscription of a Cyprus item on the agenda of the next session of the General Assembly. In particular the United Kingdom was convinced that a bitter and biased debate in the United Nations would help to kill all chance of success which the new constitution might have. It could not be denied that when the affairs of Tunis and Morocco were being discussed in the United Nations lawlessness and incidents resulting in bloodshed had suddenly increased. Her Majesty's Government was grateful for the line which the United States had taken in this matter so far, and Mr. Dulles' approaches and advice to the Greek Government were greatly appreciated. If, however, these efforts failed Her Majesty's Government most earnestly hoped they might count on United States

---

[3] On Cyprus, see BDEEP series A, R Hyam, ed, *The Labour government and the end of empire 1945–1951*, part III, 229–247; also part II of this volume, 321–333.

support in a question which more closely affected British interests than any other. Cyprus was for the United Kingdom the touchstone of the ninth General Assembly. If in spite of our (we hoped joint) opposition the item were nevertheless inscribed, not only would the U.K. Delegation withdraw when it was discussed in Committee, but Her Majesty's Government would have to make "an agonising re-appraisal" of her present policy of co-operation with the United Nations on colonial matters. Her Majesty's Government felt they should be able to rely on the United States Government in an issue so crucial to both countries, particularly since the weight of the United States Delegation influence would almost certainly be decisive.

7. The State Department feigned surprise that the United Kingdom would go to such lengths in this matter. *Mr. Wainhouse* was not alone in expressing his dismay at the prospect of the United Kingdom boycotting any discussion in Committee. He cited the South African example as showing that it was wiser to remain in a committee and to continue to fight for one's principles. In reply *Mr. Ramsbotham*[4] pointed out that, judging by the resolutions which had been passed in the Assembly, the argument was not convincing as the South Africans had certainly fared worse than the French who had walked out over Tunis and Morocco.

8. Other points made by the United States representatives were that the new constitution for Cyprus would be criticised on the grounds that there had been no prior consultation with the Cypriots, and that, since it was not as liberal as the 1948 offer, it would be considered retrogressive. After discussing in general terms the various tactics which might be followed both in the General Committee and the Plenary Assembly, Mr. Ramsbotham showed what an awkward and embarrassing precedent maladroit handling of the Cyprus question would create for all U.N. members. It could always be quoted as an example by any nation which wished to discuss or interfere in the United Nations in the domestic affairs of another nation. When asked if the United States was in a position to indicate what stand it would take in this matter, *Mr. Wainhouse* reiterated that all efforts would be made to try to persuade the Greeks not to insist upon trying to place Cyprus on the United Nations agenda. The final decision on how the United States would vote would have to be taken by Mr. Dulles. The State Department said they would try to let the United Kingdom have an early indication of what this decision might be. . . .

Conclusion

21. In closing the meetings *Mr. Wainhouse* and then *Mr. Gerig* remarked on behalf of the United States Government how much such talks on colonial problems were appreciated. Although there was a divergence of view on the interpretation of Article 2(7) of the United Nations Charter, and even though neither side had entered into any commitments during the talks, the exchange of views had shown a pronounced drift in the same direction. In spite of the Americans' uneasy conscience regarding colonialism it was obvious that over vital issues the United States and the United Kingdom could reach agreement. In reply *Mr. Bourdillon* expressed his pleasure at being able to attend their exchange of views, adding that the unity of interest to which reference had been made would, he hoped, result in satisfactory solutions being reached to the two problems foremost in the minds of all who had attended the talks.

---

[4] P E Ramsbotham, member, UK delegation to UN, 1953–1957.

107   CO 936/317, no 64   31 Aug 1954

[US attitude towards colonialism]: letter from J H A Watson (Washington) to M C G Man[1]

One aspect of the general re-appraisal of foreign policy now going on here (see our recently weekly political summaries etc.) which has concerned us is the attitude of the press and public to "colonialism".

2.   The trend of the general discussion has been towards a less entangling foreign policy and a rueful realisation that America cannot expect to run all the world—or even all the "free world"—its own way. But there has been a recrudescence of reports about anti-colonialism in a number of metropolitan newspapers (set off usually by the visible failure of French colonialism in Indo-China) which seemed to run counter to this trend. Of the papers concerned the *New York Times* and the *Washington Post* have led the field in stressing the view that colonialism is obsolete, that Asian and African nationalism is the force with which the United States should associate itself, and that the United States can expose Soviet imperialism more effectively if it opposes colonialism of any kind. And they have gone further than most in implying or even alleging that "the State Department" holds similar views. This was particularly the case during the Geneva Conference and during the visit of the Prime Minister and the Secretary of State to Washington. Indeed there is substantial evidence that Dulles, though at first less anti-colonial than Acheson,[2] has become more inclined to see "colonialism" as an obstacle to uniting the "free" world against Communist aggression. In this he has been encouraged by certain groups in the State Department (especially the Policy Planning Staff) and at the Pentagon; who have been impressed by the unwillingness of the Indo-Chinese to fight for "freedom" if this meant continued French domination.

3.   The danger of this attitude seriously influencing United States policy is a real one; and it will not grow less when Hoover[3] takes Bedell Smith's[4] place. At one time we became a little worried by the mood in Washington. But we rather doubted whether "anti-colonialism" was a major issue with the public outside the rather intellectual circles in New York and here which read such articles in the big newspapers. So we thought it as well to ask superintending consular posts what their impression was. We are encouraged to find that our Consuls have almost unanimously (Hadow[5] being the big exception) reported that they have not noticed any significant strengthening of the ever present but now rather latent traditional American bias against "colonialism", the metropolitan dailies notwithstanding. Most Americans have at best a vague understanding of the objectives and achievements of British colonialism and are usually quick to criticize any policy that smacks of "imperialism". Cyprus may give us some trouble; but so far Her Majesty's Government's colonial policies appear to have weathered the storm of criticism launched at the French over Indo-China and Morocco. This does not mean to imply that a government policy of opposing "colonialism" outright as a tactical measure in the

---

[1] M C G Man, head of American Department, FO, 1954–1956 (for Watson, see 85, note 2).

[2] D G Acheson, US secretary of state, 1949–1953.

[3] H Hoover Jr, special adviser to US secretary of state, 1953; under-secretary of state, 1954–1957.

[4] W B Smith, director, CIA, 1950–1953; US under-secretary of state, 1953–1954.

[5] British consul in San Francisco.

cold war would meet with public disapproval: but it does indicate that there is no spontaneous grass roots demand for it. It would however be well to keep in mind that among the thousands of Colonial students in this country there are many vigorous and effective speakers championing the cause of anti-colonialism.

4. Some typical extracts from the consular reports are enclosed.[6] Hadow's comments from San Francisco are taken from his despatch No. 22 to us, which we sent you under cover of our despatch No. 406 of August 10.

5. I enclose a copy of this letter for the Colonial Office, and I have sent one to John Russell at the B.I.S., New York.

---

[6] Enclosures not printed.

---

108   CO 936/317, no 115   [Aug 1955]

'Pre-General Assembly UK–US talks on colonial questions': report by CO on talks held in Washington on 23 and 24 Aug 1955   [Extract]

These talks were held in the State Department on August 23 and 24. The United Kingdom representatives were Mr. H. Bourdillon, Assistant Under-Secretary of State for the Colonies; Mr. B. Giddon, Counsellor, United Kingdom Delegation to the United Nations; Mr. A. Campbell, Colonial Attaché, and Mr. R. Parsons, Third Secretary, British Embassy, Washington. The chief participants on the State Department side were Mr. David Wainhouse, Acting Assistant Secretary of State, and Mr. B. Gerig, Director of the Office of Dependent Area Affairs. Mr. Mason-Sears,[1] United Nations Representative on the Trustee Council, was also present.

Introductory

2. In his introductory remarks of welcome, Mr. Wainhouse said that in his view the three most important new factors which had emerged in this field during the last year were the Bandoeng conference, the "anti-colonial" resolution passed by the United States Congress and the crisis in French North Africa.

Effect of the Bandoeng conference upon the attitude of delegations towards colonial questions

3. *Mr. Bourdillon* and *Mr. Gidden* thought that the effects of Bandoeng were not necessarily unwelcome. Although the conference had passed a strong anti-colonial resolution, some qualified comfort could be drawn from the fact that the main aim of several of the sponsors was to show that communism represented a threat that was just as unwelcome to them as Western colonialism. On the whole there had been a notable absence of anti-Western bias. There was unlikely to be any significant change in the attitude of the Fourth Committee, where all the Bandoeng Powers who were members of the United Nations had voted anyhow before the conference on the anti-colonial side. But we should not discount the possibility that Bandoeng might result in greater cohesion among the anti-colonials on such specific issues as the Yemen and the Aden Protectorate.

---

[1] P M Sears, US representative on the Trusteeship Council, 1953–1961; president of Trusteeship Council, 1955–1956.

4. *Mr. Gerig* agreed generally. He thought it possible that these Bandoeng Powers who were members of the Fourth Committee might produce an anti-colonial resolution there. Another possibility was a resolution in the Fourth Committee against the colonial tendencies of international communism, sponsored by the anti-communist Bandoeng countries; in view of the Congressional resolution this year, the United States delegation would be under strong pressure to support such a resolution, even if it were accompanied by a preamble unsatisfactory to the non-communist Administering Powers.

5. *In discussion* it was pointed out that it would be a new departure for resolutions of so broad a scope as the two possibilities envisaged by Mr. Gerig to emerge from the Fourth Committee. In view of the importance which the anti-colonial powers attached to this question and in view of the fact that they were not represented at a very high level in the Fourth Committee, they might try instead to introduce a resolution in the First Committee. Another possibility was an anti-colonial resolution in the Third Committee arising out of the discussion of self-determination in a Human Rights context.

Review of the basic principles motivating our respective attitudes to colonial questions in the United Nations

6. *Mr. Bourdillon* and *Mr. Gidden* expounded the policy of Her Majesty's Government along familiar lines. In particular they stressed the willingness of the United Kingdom to cooperate with the United Nations as far as possible, as was shown for example by its attitude towards the Committee on Information. But constitutional development at a rapid pace was a complicated and difficult process, which might be disastrously interfered with if Her Majesty's Government ever abandoned their stand on United Nations competence. The two chief dangers of interference arose from the interpretation of Article 73 of the Charter as a contract between the Administering Powers and the United Nations and the concept of self-determination as an over-riding human right. The Administering Powers had to be particularly careful, because a precedent once set in the Fourth Committee was set for all time.

7. *Mr. Gerig* began by saying that there was a strong instinctive reaction in the United States against one people being ruled by another. *Mr. Campbell* interjected that he had found a good deal of sympathy in the United States for the quite different line taken in a public speech by Mr. Byroade[2] two years ago; that the United States should give no blank cheques to Administering Powers but should also not support anti-colonial agitations without a very careful examination of the true facts. He thought that the United Kingdom/United States differences on colonialism did not concern basic principles but only the pace at which constitutional development should proceed. This intervention seemed to have a salutary effect on *Mr. Gerig*, who admitted that the instinctive anti-colonial reaction of the American people did not necessarily reflect their considered view. The President and Mr. Dulles in public speeches had laid emphasis on the orderly transition which was essential before dependent peoples could ultimately achieve self-determination.

8. *Mr. Sears* thought that the question of pace was paramount and that many

---

[2] H A Byroade, US assistant secretary of state for Near Eastern, South Asian and African affairs, 1953–1955.

anti-colonial powers were beginning to realize this. More might be done to educate them in the Fourth Committee. This work of education could not be accomplished by the Administering Powers, who were automatically suspect, but might be entrusted to some other Power such as the Philippines. *Mr. Bourdillon* and *Mr. Gidden* did their best to discourage this. They pointed out that, by trying to use the Fourth Committee for educational purposes, we should be giving it a direct invitation to inroads in the political sphere. It would be better not to attempt a conscious exercise in the United Nations, but rather to try to influence governments in their capitals, as Her Majesty's Government had attempted before[3] and were doing again this year. When *Mr. Campbell* suggested that, if we were trying to influence the anti-colonial powers at the United Nations, the United States were the best people to undertake the task, the State Department showed no enthusiasm for pursuing the subject.

9.   On the question of United Nations competence, *Mr. Gerig* pointed out that the United States view that discussion was not necessarily intervention in the sense of Article 2(7) differed from the United Kingdom view. *Mr. Bourdillon* and *Mr. Gidden* thought this difference more theoretical than practical, since discussion was likely to lead at least to a resolution, which might well constitute intervention in the view of the United States as well as the United Kingdom.

Review of the attitude of blocs in the United Nations on colonial questions
10.   *Mr. Gidden* said that with the composition of the Fourth Committee as it was last year, it had been possible for the United Kingdom to influence in advance the tactics of the anti-colonial powers on several specific issues. (He was not of course referring to a consciously didactic operation of the kind suggested by Mr. Sears.) The United States had even better opportunities for useful influence of this kind, which might stop our being caught short by surprise anti-colonial moves.

11.   *In discussion* the point was made that it would probably be dangerous to try to exert too much influence on India at present. In any case representations in New Delhi would not do much good if, as was feared, Mrs. Menon[4] should be the Indian representative in the Fourth Committee. Owing to the influence of General Romulo,[5] the Philippines were likely to be protagonists of timetables for constitutional development, but might be amenable to approaches on specific issues. *It was agreed* that there would be considerable danger to the Administering Powers if the Soviet delegation should change their tactics without a corresponding change of heart and decide to take a lead along a moderate anti-colonial line. *Mr. Gerig* wondered whether it would be possible in the Fourth Committee to turn the fire of the Bandoeng Powers against communism. But *Mr. Bourdillon* thought this would be dangerous to the Administering Powers on the competence front. . . .

---

[3] See 161, 164.
[4] Lakshmi N Menon, alternate delegate from India to UN General Assembly.
[5] C P Romulo, Philippine ambassador to the UN, 1952–1953, to the USA, 1954–1962.

109   CO 936/318, no 162A   [Sept–Oct 1956]

'Colonial questions in the UN, 1956': CO brief for conversations with US and Canadian officials in Washington and Ottawa, Oct 1956

[Extract]

Introductory note

As in previous years, the Washington talks will be more formal than those in Ottawa. However, the points discussed in both places will in general be the same, and the guidance provided in this brief, although mainly applicable to the Washington talks, will serve for the Ottawa talks as well. . . .

2.   For the purpose of this brief, Cyprus is considered to be *sui generis* and not a colonial question: it is being dealt with through diplomatic channels.

Part I: General

(1) *Review of basic United Kingdom principles*

3.   A feature of the past year has been the expression of views by Mr. Chester Bowles[1] and others to the effect that the Administration should take more positive action to align itself with nationalism in Colonial territories, in order to avoid being identified with the Colonial powers in the United Nations and so losing ground to Communist propaganda. Such a belief finds a ready response in those sectors of American public opinion which are influenced by anti-Colonial prejudice, but they are not held by the State Department, and the year 1956 saw a further authoritative pronouncement by a senior State Department official (Mr. Allen)[2] expressing understanding for the problems of Colonial powers and the importance of questions of timing and orderly evolution towards self-government. We have also been encouraged to see the recognition of the need to hasten slowly shown in Mrs. Frances P. Bolton's[3] report on her tour of Africa.

4.   The existence of this pressure tends nonetheless to encourage the Administration's tendency to compromise in practice on Colonial issues in the United Nations, and the position has been made more difficult by the behaviour of Mr. Mason Sears in the Trusteeship Council.[4] Mr. Sears has placed himself at the head of those anti-Colonial delegations seeking to press the Administering Powers into the acceptance of "intermediate target dates" for the attainment of self-government or independence by Trust Territories; the effect of his sustained initiative which has been undertaken without prior consultation with the United Kingdom Delegation and in the face of the opposition of other Administering Delegations has been an unfortunate breach between the United States and the other Administering Powers

---

[1] C A Bowles, special assistant to the UN secretary-general, 1946–1948; US ambassador to India, 1951–1953.

[2] A B Allen, 2nd secretary, US embassy, Libya, 1954–1957.

[3] F P Bolton, Republican Congresswoman, 1939–1966.

[4] Sears, the US representative on the Trusteeship Council, had angered the CO before. As a member of the Council's visiting mission to Tanganyika in 1954 he had clearly sympathised with the African nationalist point of view. Para 5(d) of this document can be read as referring by implication to Sears. Later in the brief (para 47), UK delegates were enjoined to ask the State Department to keep Sears off the Trusteeship Council's 1957 mission to Tanganyika on the grounds that he had been in contact with 'subversives' in that country. (The State Department declined to meet this request.)

and the passage of a series of recommendations relating to individual Trust Territories which are expected to cause serious embarrassment in the Fourth Committee.

5. Against this background, we are justified in reminding State Department officials of the keynotes of our Colonial policies, and our main objective at the talks may be summarised as follows:—

(a) To emphasize that the basis of our policy is and must remain Anglo/American partnership. The added difficulties that both delegations must expect in the United Nations with the arrival of the new members make it all the more essential that the exchange of views should be frank and wide-ranging.

(b) To reinforce State Department belief in the sincerity of our paramount aim to establish in our dependent territories stable and democratic self-governing communities; to stress once again that this is a creative, not a negative, task, and one in which timing, as Mr. Allen recognised, is all-important and something which we alone can judge.

(c) To stress the dangers of United Nations intervention in matters of detailed administration (and especially in political relationships that are necessarily delicate); not only in Colonial but also in Trust Territories.

(d) To emphasize the special need for close alignment of United States and United Kingdom policies in questions of Trusteeship where United Nations intervention-ists are in a position to do most damage. The territory of Tanganyika (a fuller account of whose problems will be given under Item (13) provides as good example as any of the need for care and caution in the task of building a Nation out of a complex of tribes and races with, as yet, only the beginning of a sense of common destiny. Both in political and economic development, Tanganyika has far to go before our present aims come to fruition, and in the meantime, it is essential that we should be left in peace, and not harried, while we evolve the constitutional process in the manner we think best, even if concepts like qualitative democracy and multi-racial parity—which represent the stage for which Tanganyika is now fitted—do not chime with United Nations political ideology. Our reaction to United Nations pressure for time limits and timetables reflects the seriousness with which we view our task in Tanganyika and our determination to carry out our responsibilities in our own way.

(e) In general, we must make it clear that successful erosion of our position by anti-Colonial forces in the United Nations, even when inspired by altruistic motives, directly serves communist interests since it militates against our primary aim to hand over power to communities that are stable and strong enough to hold their own as independent states. Any attempt by the Americans to outbid the Russians to win anti-Colonial support will, even if successful, only result in a weakening of our position and so in the attainment of a communist objective. . . .

110　CO 936/318, no 176　　　　　　　　　[Oct 1956]

'Pre-General Assembly UK-US talks on colonial questions': CO report on talks held in Washington on 11–12 Oct 1956　　　[Extract]

Meeting on morning of October 11th

1. *Review of basic principles*

At the invitation of the Chairman, *Mr. Bourdillon* gave a review of the basic principles underlying the United Kingdom attitude towards colonial questions and of the principal developments in the past twelve months in major United Kingdom territories. As far as the United Nations attitude towards colonial affairs was concerned, Mr. Bourdillon stressed that we were anxious to co-operate with the United Nations and to get from them what help we could. We had no desire to stifle criticism of what we were doing in our colonial territories. We did, however, see serious dangers of United Nations intervention in political and constitutional developments in colonial territories as opposed to trust territories and we were not prepared to tolerate any United Nations attempts to send visiting missions, to hear petitioners or to discuss the affairs of specific territories.

There was a general welcome from the American side of the exposition, *Mr. Mason Sears* in particular expressing his appreciation of what the British had accomplished. He suggested, however, that we ought to give more publicity to our achievements before the United Nations and stressed the urgency of finding a solution to the racial problems of East and Central Africa.

Meeting on the afternoon of October 11th

Mr Phillips[1] opened the discussion with a review of the basic United States attitudes towards colonial questions. He said that United States responsibilities in the colonial field were, of course, neither as broad nor as direct as those of the United Kingdom. United States thinking on colonial questions, however, started from the premiss that the weight of world opinion was against the colonial relationship even in its most enlightened form. It was therefore a relationship which could have only a limited duration. At the same time, the United States appreciated that there were many areas where it could be abruptly terminated. The problem was how to terminate it under conditions which would ensure stability and secure good will.

The current crises in a number of colonial fields gave opportunities to the Communists to make mischief. They had everything to gain by fishing in troubled waters and the baits which they could employ were irresponsible promises and the ability to identify their own economic experience with the aspirations of African and Asian powers, while concealing their own exploitation of subject peoples. As a result of this, colonial issues had become the principal battleground between East and West. This made it especially important to the United States to adopt policies which would retain the sympathies of the colonial peoples. In the opinion of the United States, it was psychologically better to err, if at all, on the side of acting a little to early rather than a bit too late.

In the discussion of colonial matters at the United Nations and elsewhere, clear differences had emerged between the administering and the non-administering

---

[1] C H Phillips, deputy assistant secretary of state, US State Department, 1954–1957.

powers on the question of the time factor in the attainment of self-government. These difference had been brought into the open by the discussion on time limits and target dates. The United States was still opposed to long-term target dates but intermediate target dates seemed to them both reasonable in themselves, a good way to ward off more extreme demands in the U.N. and a practicable administrative technique.

The United States regretted the differences which had arisen between themselves and the United Kingdom over this question but in their view these very differences should lead to a strengthening of our respective positions *vis-a-vis* the rest of the world since they showed a flexibility of approach and an absence of a monolithic front which gave clear evidence of independent thinking. It was not to the interest of the U.S. (nor indeed to U.K. and French interest) that the United States should become stereotyped as an out-and-out defender of the colonial system.

The United States were anxious to see the development of progressive common policies between themselves, the United Kingdom and other European powers as a means of eliminating friction with Asia and Africa over colonial issues, and promoting the cohesion of the free world. They were convinced that the nationalist tide would in the long run prove itself irresistable [sic]. Intelligent accommodation was the only answer. This view, they felt, was shared by the British but not by all the other colonial powers. They believed it was important for the United Kingdom and the United States to work together to influence the colonial policies of their NATO allies in such a way as to prevent an irreparable cleavage between the free nations of the East and the West. The United States had absolutely no interest in supplanting the present colonial powers in any part of the world, but American public opinion, for historical reasons, could not assist in discouraging or suppressing *bona fida* national movements, except in the rarest case where a broader security interest might temporarily be at stake. The United States was bound to weigh its attitudes on colonial questions with the very great care because of its history, its ethnic composition and its own racial strains.[2] While recognising clear limits, the United States were, at the same time, very alive to the dangers of going too far in thwarting impulses towards applying the principle of self-determination. Their aim was to channel these impulses in the right direction rather than to suppress them and they hoped their friends would give further thought to this concept.

Mr. Bourdillon replied that, in the light of the Chairman's remarks, he felt there was a good deal of fundamental agreement between the United Kingdom and the United States on colonial issues. The United Kingdom realised that the United States attitudes could not and indeed ought not to be identical with ours. The United Kingdom also agreed that, particularly in the United Nations context, too much identity of view looked too artificial to be convincing. On the other hand, the United Kingdom felt it would be dangerous if differences went too far and hoped that there would be a progressively increasing approximation to a similar approach to colonial problems.

On the question of timetables, *Mr. Bourdillon* said that our policy was not one of

---

[2] Later in the meeting, Gerig pointed out that US policy on South-West Africa—specifically, its view that the UN's Committee of Seven should hear oral petitioners from the territory—'was in fact forced upon the United States Government in part by the existence of its own negro population. This prevented the United States from accepting the application of the apartheid laws to Southwest Africa' (item 4). (Britain opposed on principle all attempts to bring oral petitioners from dependent territories before UN agencies; see 166).

"go slow". Though in some areas it looked that way sometimes, there was clear evidence to the contrary and indeed in at least one case (British Guiana)[3] the United Kingdom had quite clearly gone to fast. Moreover, the United Kingdom did not look on what it was doing as a withdrawal or an abandonment of responsibility. We were, by contrast, consciously engaged on perhaps the most positive and constructive political task of the 20th century era.

As regards our Western allies, however, it was impossible for the United Kingdom to lecture them on their colonial policies. United Kingdom objectives were traditionally different from those of the continental powers. Our aim had always been to turn colonies into independent sovereign states and not to regard the metropolitan power as the fountainhead of all law and authority. The continental way was different and it was too early yet to say that they were wrong. On the other hand, the French "Loi Cadre" might mark the beginnings of a radical change in French policy in the direction of greater devolution of powers. But if this were so, it was because the French had themselves concluded that this was the right line to take and was not due to any pressure brought to bear upon them by the British.

Mr. Gerig asked whether the United Kingdom shared the United States view that there were advantages in our respective countries having an independent position. *Mr. Gidden* replied that, in his view, it was not possible to decide this question in the abstract. There was a danger that in a search for visible independence, decisions might not be taken objectively.

Mr. Sears said that in his view there was no danger in differences over things that did not go too deep. Moreover, differences were inevitable. He cited as an example the question of French Togoland where it would be far more embarrassing to the United Kingdom than to the United States to vote against the French.

2. *Review of attitude of blocs*

Mr. Bourdillon and *Mr. Gidden* maintained that the advent of new members emphasised the importance of preserving unity. The new members would undoubtedly make the tasks of the colonial powers more difficult. We had made some progress, however small and slow, in making the existing members aware of the true nature of our aims and policies in colonial matters. This process would have to start all over again in the case of the new members. However, the anti-colonial attack had not shown much cohesion so far, and there was a possibility that the advent of the new members would make it more diffuse.

Mr. Gerig pointed out that the colonial powers had already lost the "blocking third" on trusteeship questions. There could be little doubt that the anti-colonial pattern of the General Assembly would be strengthened by the new members. The United States were interested in encouraging the development of a moderate middle group and hoped that this could be achieved by energetic lobbying.

Mr. Mason Sears said that in his view India held the key as far as influencing anti-colonial powers was concerned. He wondered whether the United Kingdom could not do more to educate India and to get them to use their influence on our behalf. *Mr. Bourdillon* agreed that the Indian position was often crucial. Approaches to them in the past had often been made in vain although, as *Mr. Gidden* pointed out, the Indian attitude had changed very considerably for the better during the past four years. . . .

---

[3] See part II of this volume, 336, 337.

111 DO 35/6953, no 32 29 Oct 1956
[US attitude towards colonialism]: letter from B Salt (Washington) to J D Murray[1]

I enclose six copies of a record of the pre-Assembly talks with the State Department about colonial questions which were held here on the 11th and 12th October.[2] This record was not cleared with Harry Bourdillon before he left for Ottawa, nor has it been cleared with Barry Gidden in New York. I must apologise for the delay due to pressure of other business in Chancery. Douglas Williams,[3] our Colonial Attaché, who kindly took the record, finished his part of the work over a week ago, but the draft then got held up in my office.

2. A few general comments on the talks may be of interest. By and large the Americans this year appeared better educated on what we are trying to do in our colonial territories and more sympathetic to our aims and policies than they have been in previous years.

3. On the vexed question of intermediate timetables, we were not able to budge them from their position. This was perhaps too much to hope for. Nevertheless, we all feel that Harry Bourdillon's trenchant exposition of the grave dangers which attended this device created a deep impression even on Mr. Mason Sears, and several members of the United States team have since confirmed that this is true. The State Department will, of course, still want to press the idea for purposes of window dressing in the United Nations and for propaganda in the world at large, and they will presumably use the timetable technique in their own dependent territories. But the memory of Harry Bourdillon's remarks may at least tend to moderate their favour on the subject in future.

4. The other main impression which emerged, not perhaps so much from the talks themselves as from the discussions that took place outside them, was the growing American concern about the situation in East and Cental Africa. Partly because of their own racial situation in this country and partly because of the increasing amount of American investment in this area (particularly in the Central African Federation), they are becoming increasingly concerned about the problem of race relations. We understand this is a point to which Harry Bourdillon intends to draw the attention of the Colonial Office on his return.

5. I am copying this letter, with enclosure, to Harry Bourdillon in the Colonial Office and to Barry Gidden in New York.

---

[1] J D Murray, UN Dept, FO, 1955–1959.   [2] See 110.
[3] D Williams, principal, CO, 1949–1956; colonial attaché, British embassy, Washington, 1956–1960.

112 DO 35/6953, no 36 17 Dec 1956
[US attitude towards colonialism in Africa]: letter from J E Marnham to C E Diggines[1] [Extract]

Many thanks for your letter of 10th December (reference WES 21/41/16) about the growing American interest in East and Central Africa.

---

[1] C E Diggines, principal, CRO, 1956–1958 (for Marnham, see 6, note 3).

2. I have shown your letter to Harry Bourdillon, who asks me to apologise on his behalf for not having made special noises in the direction of the C.R.O. about this aspect of his Washington talks. He adds, however, that there is not a great deal to say. As the major territories or groups of territories in other parts of the world (South-East Asia, West Africa, West Indies) either reach full self-government or draw close to it, the only remaining area which can give rise to controversy between us and the Americans on the issue of "colonialism" is East and Central Africa. We had already foreseen, therefore, that in future discussions with the Americans about colonial policy the problems of East and Central Africa would occupy an increasing share of attention on the American side, and what happened in the October talks was really no more than a fulfilment of this forecast. Bourdillon did not himself say anything of substance about Central Africa (bearing in mind that this is primarily a C.R.O. responsibility), but he did think it advisable to give the Americans a particularly full account of constitutional progress in East Africa and of the special difficulties which force us to move cautiously in this area if we are to build something really solid for the future. On their side the Americans listened with great interest and showed no lack of sympathy. Whilst, therefore, what Barbara Salt says is true and important,[2] we would not ourselves regard the development to which she refers as untoward or unexpected. . . .

---

[2] See 111.

113   FO 371/95757, no 5   13 Nov 1951

'French proposals for Anglo-French conversations at ministerial level': record by C P Hope of an FO inter-departmental meeting with the CO[1]

Mr. Martin opened the meeting by recalling that the Quai d'Orsay had recently invited the Colonial Office to agree to a meeting between the Secretary of State for the Colonies and the Minister of France d'outre-mer to discuss African questions. The Secretary of State for the Colonies had agreed that such a meeting was desirable and had in his distribution of duties for the Colonial Office asked that the Minister of State, Mr. Lennox-Boyd, should be responsible.

2. Mr. Cohen said that he had recently spoken to M. Jurgenson [sic: Jurgensen] of the Quai d'Orsay, who had suggested that it would be desirable for him (Mr. Cohen) to take part in the Ministerial talks.[2] As, however, he was leaving to take up his post as Govenor of Uganda on the 16th January, this would mean holding the talks before this date, a course which would not be possible since the Minister of State would be away between the middle of December and the middle of January on a tour around West Africa.

3. Jurgenson [sic] had also suggested that there should be talks in Paris at the official level before Christmas, at which he hoped the Colonial Office, the Foreign

---

[1] The CO's representatives were J M Martin (chair), A B Cohen (head of Africa Division, 1947–1951), T B Williamson (assistant secretary, 1948–1961), and B O B Gidden; the FO's representatives were C A Lockhart and C P Hope.
[2] The French 'laid particular importance on this as they regarded him [Cohen] as the chief planner of present British policy in Africa' (letter from C P Hope to B O B Gidden, FO 371/95757, no 7, 16 Nov 1951).

Office and Mr. Cohen could participate.

4. *It was agreed* that arrangements should be made to hold these preliminary talks in Paris at some time mutually convenient to Mr. Cohen, the Quai D'Orsay and the Foreign Office.

5. *Mr. Cohen* then asked what was to be discussed between Ministers. Jurgenson [sic] had told him that the Ministère de la France d'outre-mer was favourably inclined to the talks and that the Quai D'Orsay considered that both sides should prepare agendas and exchange them at the meeting of officials in December. Mr. Cohen suspected that the Quai D'Orsay were hoping to induce a change for the better in French colonial policies as a result of the talks and would probably wish to cover the last three years of colonial development and then lead on to deeper things. He was doubtful, however, whether we should allow ourselves to be drawn into such a discussion.

6. *Mr. Hope* said that he felt that the French were concerned at our policies on the political level in West Africa. Our colonial policies are fundamentally different and the French would consequently almost certainly wish to discuss fundamentals. They were known to be worried at the speed of development in the Gold Coast, they were concerned at the gradual incorporation of British Togoland into British colonial territory; to a lesser extent they felt the same way about Nigeria. They would probably ask that we should restrain Nkrumah, the present Prime Minister of the Gold Coast. They would want to know whether we intended to ask the United Nations to cancel the Trusteeship Agreement in respect of British Togoland. Finally, while they were not likely to raise this directly, they were worried at the threat which our policies caused in their eyes to Dahomé and they were still harping on the British Intelligence Service and the activities of the United Africa Company.

7. In general terms therefore they would probably ask us to slow up the speed of development in these areas. If we replied that we could not do this, or that it was outside our power, they would probably ask for safe-guards such as prior information.

8. There was then a general discussion, in which *it was suggested* that no papers need be prepared until after the official meeting with the French, and that we should thereafter decide what we should do.

9. *It was finally agreed* that it was necessary to decide now what line we should take with the French on the basis of a probable agenda. This meant that we should need to draft policy papers and decide therein how much should be said to the French. These papers should be joint Colonial Office-Foreign Office papers and put to Ministers before the meeting of officials.

10. *Mr. Cohen* expressed the hope that there would not be recommendations from the Foreign Office that present Colonial Office policies in West Africa should be slowed up or halted. The fact was that whatever might have been done a year ago, events had to-day taken charge. Not only was it therefore impossible to change the present course of events, but future developments could not be accurately forecast.

11. *It was furthermore agreed* that a basic historical paper should be prepared on the basis of the Anglo-French Agreement of 1948.[3] This would summarise the steps agreed, describe those steps taken and provide evidence to show how events in the

---

[3] See BDEEP series A, R Hyam, ed, *The Labour government and the end of empire 1945–1951*, part II, 177, 180.

territories had moved forward since that date. A second general policy paper would be prepared by Mr. Cohen on present British intentions in West Africa, showing where they bore on French administration. Appendices would be prepared to this paper, describing particular issues such as the Ewe Problem, the future of British Togoland, etc. arguing the British case as fully as possible.

12. *It was agreed* that the general tone of these papers would inevitably show that present British policies in West Africa could not be changed. They might therefore leave the impression that French policies in the area were not only inconsistent with present day conditions but that, if they were to be acceptable to the indigenous inhabitants, they would need amending to bring them more into line with British policies.

13. There was then a further general dicussion as to what offer we could make to the French to sweeten this unpalatable pill. *It was suggested* that some sort of West African defence organisation might be put to them. Mr. Lockhart pointed out that this could not be done without the inclusion of the Union of South Africa. The character of the Gold Coast Government and the attitude of the Union towards Aparteid [sic] presented such complications that it was decided not to pursue this idea.

14. *Mr. Cohen* suggested that we should offer the French a joint Anglo-French secretariat in Accra. This Secretariat could be at the official level and the Colonial Office already had an incumbent in the shape of Mr. Galsworthy.[4] If the French agreed to post an officer of suitable rank, the Secretariat could be set up at once without extra cost to His Majesty's Government. He suggested that it should foster co-operation between the two countries and avoid friction by exchanging informa-tion of a political and administrative character on the territories concerned. Mr. Cohen said that he expected the French to ask for prior consultation. This might present certain difficulties to us, but we might go a little way to meet them.

15. *Mr. Martin* concluded the meeting by asking his side to prepare draft papers, copies of which would be sent to the Foreign Office for consideration.

---

[4] A N Galsworthy, assistant secretary, CO, 1947–1956; chief secretary, West African Inter-Territorial Secretariat, 1951–1954; assistant under-secretary of state, CO, 1956–1965.

114   CO 537/7148, no 17   20 Nov 1951
'Anglo-French relations in West Africa': memorandum by A B Cohen

The British and French territories in West Africa are closely linked geographically, the British territories forming enclaves along the coast in most cases entirely surrounded by French territory. Although the area of French West Africa and French Equatorial Africa is much greater than the four British territories, the population of the British territories is greater (approximately 30 million people against approx-imately [21.7][1] million people). There has moreover been a steady migration of people from the French territory of Niger into Northern Nigeria.

---

[1] Editorial insert; population of the French territories left blank in the original. In 1951 the population of French West Africa was estimated at 17,208,000; that of French Equatorial Africa at 4,484,000. *Statistical Office of the United Nations Department of Economic Affairs: Demographic Yearbook, Fourth Issue, 1952* (New York, 1952) p 89.

2. The economic ties between British and French territories are in general not close, because all the West African countries as producers of raw materials have parallel rather than complementary economies. Road and air links exist between the territories, but the main roads are from the interior to the ports and the French hinterland is linked with French ports by railways entirely within French territory. Chad and Niger use British transport routes and Senegal uses the Gambia River; but in all three cases only to a limited extent.

3. Politically the contacts between the territories are very limited, except in the case of Togoland where the Ewe tribe lives on both sides of the border. The organisation of the West African territories has hitherto been tribal and the African people have not had wider contacts except to a limited extent in trade. The territories have therefore grown up separately within the British and French spheres. Contacts between officials have been limited by language difficulties and have been mainly confined to exchange of visits between frontier officers. Africans have always lived in a parochial atmosphere and there is comparatively little interest in what goes on behind the frontier. Even among advanced politicians contacts have been very infrequent. Recently a policy of Anglo-French co-operation has led to closer contacts between the local Governments, but the watertight compartments have by no means been broken down.

British and French policy

4. British policy in West Africa, in accordance with the accepted traditions of the British Commonwealth, is to build up each of the West African territories as a country with its own political institutions, the aim being self-government within the British Commonwealth. It is clear that this means something different for Nigeria and the Gold Coast, which can look forward to full responsibility for their own affairs, and for Sierra Leone and the Gambia, which cannot expect to go beyond full responsibility for their internal affairs, leaving such matters as defence and foreign relations to the British Government. Recently there have been striking constitutional advances in all four West African territories. The Gold Coast has progressed very far towards self-government in internal affairs and is now governed by an Executive Council with a majority of African Ministers drawn from the Legislature, each of whom is responsible for the administration of a group of departments. The Executive Council is presided over by the Governor, who has reserve powers, but normally policy is settled by a majority decision of the Executive Council. There are three *ex-officio* members of the Executive Council who are European officials; their portfolios cover external affairs, defence and security, the civil service, finance and justice. The Legislative Assembly consists almost entirely of African members directly or indirectly elected by popular vote. A similar constitution is about to come into force in Nigeria, although this will go slightly less far than in the Gold Coast in that Ministers will not be responsible for the administration of departments but will work in consultation with the official heads of those departments; all decisions of the Council of Ministers will be collective and Ministers will themselves have no power of overriding the heads of departments. The Nigerian constitution will be on a federal basis with the three regions of Nigeria having Legislatures and Executive Councils of their own with responsibility over a wide field of administration. New constitutions have just come into force in Sierra Leone and the Gambia generally similar to the Gold Coast and Nigerian constitutions. There will be no African Ministers, but

African members of the Executive Councils will in both cases have not only general policy-making functions but special functions in relation to particular departments of Government.

5. All these reforms place a large degree of power in the hands of primarily African Legislatures and Executive Councils in which African members drawn from the Legislatures play a substantial part (in Nigeria and the Gold Coast in the majority). All the constitutions, however, retain *ex-officio* members (i.e. European officials) in key positions in both the Executive and Legislative Councils. The Governor remains the utlimate authority for the administration of each territory and is armed with the necessary reserve powers to secure this position. Although these reserve powers can only be used sparingly, their existence is an important factor in the Governor's dealings with his Ministers and with the Legislative Council. The constitutions are in fact designed to secure a system of administration by consent and consultation between the Governor, his Executive Council and the Legislative Council. Simultaneously with these constitutional developments the system of local government in West Africa is being reformed and modernised, increasing numbers of Africans are being appointed to senior positions in the Civil Service, while representative Africans are taking an increasing part on public boards and corporations concerned with economic development. The Nigerian Government are converting their public utilities, ports, railways, electricity service and coal production from Government departments to public corporations with substantial African representation on their boards. The same applies to the industrial and agricultural development corporations in the Gold Coast. The boards which are responsible for marketing the crops on which the economy of West Africa depends also have substantial African membership.

6. These reforms are based on the following principles; that a sense of responsibility can only be created by giving responsibility; that no constitution which did not provide for full participation by Africans would have any chance of success under present conditions in West Africa; and that such a constitution provides the best defence against Communism in West Africa, the only chance of friendly co-operation between this country and the West African territories and the best chance when the time comes of securing a favourable decision by the Gold Coast and Nigeria to stay within the British Commonwealth. Our policy has been criticised by the French as moving too fast. We cannot for the reasons just given accept this criticism if it means that we have gone too far in reform. If on the other hand what is meant is that reform started too late and has therefore had to move more quickly than we should have liked, then we can agree, since it would certainly have been better if the changes which have taken place during the last three years could have been preceded by more adequate preparations. We can moreover reassure the French generally about the results of our policy. The recent constitutional changes in Sierra Leone and the Gambia are likely to satisfy public opinion there for a considerable time to come. There is little nationalism in these two countries such as is known in the Gold Coast and Nigeria and they are likely to be quite content with a large say in the running of their own internal affairs. In Nigeria, which is less advanced politically than the Gold Coast, rapid advance beyond the new constitution is not likely to be demanded by a majority of opinion for some time to come. Although there is a vocal political party in Lagos and the south which demands early self-government, the balance of power at present lies heavily with the more backward rural areas, particularly in Northern

Nigeria; here there is strong opposition to rapid change. It is in the Gold Coast that our policy is likely to meet its greatest challenge. Here all the political parties are pledged to Dominion status at the earliest possible moment; but the Convention People's Party, which won a resounding victory at the last election, is finding that the country is not ready for substantial advance in the immediate future. The leaders of this party will be pressed by their own extremists and by their opponents to demand further advances, but if full confidence can be maintained between them and the Gold Coast Government, as well as H.M. Government, it may well be that they will be satisfied with a slower pace. It is significant that Moscow has written off Dr. Nkrumah as a bourgeois politician.

7. The key to future relations between this country and the Gold Coast (as well as the other West African territories) is the maintenance of confidence between the political leaders on the Coast and ourselves. The Gold Coast needs above all a period of stability to consolidate its recent political gains; whether it will get it depends primarily on the extent to which there is general popular pressure for advance and the extent on the other hand to which we can satisfy the political leaders of our good intentions. If we can satisfy public opinion in the Gold Coast, and the rest of West Africa, that we are behind them in their ultimate objective of Dominion status and that we will assist them forward towards that objective, if we can make them sure in fact that there is no doubt about the ultimate goal to be reached, then they may be much less insistent on the pace of advance. We must therefore allow nothing to happen which would destroy their confidence in our good faith.

8. There have been in the past quite unjustifiable fears that we might allow our policy in West Africa to be deflected by pressure from South Africa. Our recent actions in West Africa provide the answer to these fears. South Africa is in any case far away from West Africa, whereas the French territories are on their borders. It would be fatal to our policy of building up confidence with the West African leaders if any impression were created that we were allowing our policy of political advancement to be slowed down by pressure from France. While, therefore, we must take the French into our confidence and make then understand our policy and the reasons for it, we must avoid any suggestion that the French could secure a position in which they could influence the substance of that policy or the pace of its execution. We are in fact committed to our present policy by statements from both political parties in this country and the facts of the situation in West Africa itself make it necessary that we should adhere to that policy.

9. Whereas we aim at developing political institutions in colonial territories and gradually handing over power to them, the French, while they administer West and Equatorial Africa through groups of territories each with its own Government and Assembly, seek to link these territories constitutionally to France itself through the Union Française. French colonial policy, moreover, has always had as one of its principal objectives to create good Frenchmen; hence the emphasis on the rights of the individual as a citizen of France as opposed to our emphasis on the political advancement of each colonial territory as a whole. The French have Assemblies in West Africa and in French Equatorial Africa and in each of the territories which compose them; these Assemblies have considerable powers in finance but only limited powers of legislation. Control over finance, administrative action and legislation is to a great degree concentrated in Paris. Each of the territories selects deputies to both Houses of the French Parliament and to the Assembly of the Union

Française in Versailles.

10.   We and the French thus have quite different policies in West Africa. We aim at establishing self-governing institutions in each colonial territory; the French aim at strengthening the organic link between the territories and France. Our policy in the constitutional sphere is to devolve; theirs is to centralise. Clearly the French and British policies cannot be harmonised unless one of then is modified and, for the reasons given in paragraph [?6] above, ours could not be modified without endangering our whole position in West Africa and departing from the well accepted method of political evolution of the British Commonwealth. It may seem arrogant to suggest that British policy is right and French wrong and it may be argued that the French policy equally with ours is in accordance with the traditional system of French overseas development. There is some truth in the second point, but it is not completely true. French policy might well have developed in a different direction after the war. Gouverneur Eboué, the black West Indian Governor of Chad during the war, tried very hard to persuade the French to adopt something like the British system of political evolution. But his French colleagues were strongly influenced by the need which they felt at the time to bolster up metropolitan France and the Brazzaville Conference of 1945 adopted the policy of the Union Française. There is much sceptism [sic] among intelligent French officials both in Paris and in French West Africa about the success and even the future of this policy. These people admit that the African Deputies who go to Paris and take part in Parliamentary life there are at the present time well satisfied with their position; but they take the view that these African Deputies will soon learn the futility of devoting themselves primarily to what are after all the politics of France and not the French Empire. Sooner or later, these French officials say, the Africans will realise that effective power for them can only lie in their own countries. They will then demand progress towards self-government in French West Africa and Equatorial Africa and greater powers in the local Assemblies. It is thus by no means impossible that the French themselves will sooner or later realise that their own policy must be modified. We cannot, of course, tell them this. We can only seek to explain our policy to them and to convince them that at any rate in British territories it is the only policy with any chance of success. There is certainly still very much to be done in this process of persuading the French of the rightness of our own policy; this should be one of the purposes of the forthcoming discussions.

11.   This leaves unanswered the question of the ultimate relationship between British and French territories in West Africa. Some Frenchmen—although not, I think, the Ministry of Overseas France—are inclined to say that West Africa as a whole should ultimately become a single political unit (presumably a federation) closely linked to Western Europe as a whole. This is an attractive proposition on the face of it, but should in my view be treated with reserve, at any rate unless and until a European federation, including this country, is created. Our task in West Africa is to make sure that the British territories remain on the friendliest possible terms with ourselves and eventually become self-governing countries within the British Commonwealth. Any suggestion at this stage that there should be some link even in the future with the French territories so that France would have a direct say in the political development of the British territories would be likely, to say the least, greatly to increase the difficulties of maintaining good relations between this country and the British West African territories, thus prejudicing the smooth political

development of these territories towards self-government. Ultimately it may be that there will be some definite political connection between the French and British territories; but we must leave this to the future. All that we can do now is to keep in the closest touch with the French, seeking to understand their problems and to make them understand ours and at the same time seeking to promote co-operation between the French and British territories in West Africa in all useful spheres, thus to some extent breaking down the present parochialism of all the territories.

Co-operation

12.   At present we co-operate with the French in technical, economic and political questions. Technical co-operation, which has been developed since 1945, has been very fruitful. Conferences whether covering the West African region only or the whole of Africa south of the Sahara have been held on a large number of technical subjects. Useful contacts have been established and valuable practical recommendations have emerged. In 1950 the Commission for Technical Co-operation in Africa South of the Sahara was set up to co-ordinate and direct these activities. In the economic sphere it was agreed early in 1948 that there should be close co-operation between the British and French in West Africa and this has been pursued mostly through the Overseas Territories Commitee of the O.E.E.C. These forms of co-operation are important, but the present note is concerned with political matters.

13.   In June 1948 agreement was reached between ourselves and the French for the exchange of information and the development of closer contacts both in Europe and in West Africa in the political and economic field. It was agreed in particular that information should be exchanged between the two Governments, and between the local administrations, over a wide range of constitutional, local government and other political questions; that Studies Branches should be maintained in the two Colonial Ministries for this purpose; that there should be close contact between those concerned with political matters in West Africa and these two Ministries; that contacts should be developed at all levels between the territories in West Africa; and that for this purpose not only exchanges of visits but exchanges of postings should take place.

14.   A further meeting to discuss political co-operation in West Africa was held in May 1949; it was recognised that we should not seek to arrive at a common policy, but we intended to see how far we could harmonise our long-term objectives. We on the British side intended to propose the setting up of an Anglo-French Secretariat in Accra which would promote co-operation and the exchange of information. At the last moment the Ministry of Overseas France decided not to allow the French representatives to participate effectively in this discussion, with the result that the meeting was largely abortive, although further useful agreement was reached as to methods of promoting closer contact and exchange of information.

15.   The agreement of 1948 was not an ambitious one; its principal objective was to secure much closer personal contacts and understanding between those responsible for British and French policy in Europe and in West Africa. This aim has only been achieved to a very limited extent but the agreement has had useful results. In West Africa there have been frequent exchanges of visits between Governors and senior officials and some very valuable discussions on matters of common interest. On the British side the Chief Secretary of the West African Council at Accra is responsible for co-ordinating our relations with the French; he has on his staff an

officer who deals exclusively with this. We also have an officer on the staff of the Colonial Consul at Dakar. The French have no senior co-ordinating officer but maintain Vice Consuls at Dakar and Lagos who are specially concerned with co-ordination. There have been very close contacts between the Gold Coast Government and the Government of French Togoland over the Ewe question and political information is exchanged between the Chief Secretary of the West African Council and the French Consul-General in Accra, although the latter has many other duties besides co-ordination. What is mainly needed now in West Africa if further progress is to be made is some formal machinery for promoting co-ordination. For this purpose I suggest that the proposal of 1949 for an Anglo-French Secretariat in West Africa should be revived.[2] This would simply consist of the Chief Secretary of the West African Council on the British side and a new senior officer specially appointed for the work of co-ordination on the French side. The Secretariat would promote and co-ordinate co-operation in all these fields and would also arrange for the exchange of information in technical, economic and political matters. The establishment of such a Secretariat could either be published or kept confidential, if that was preferred by the Gold Coast Government, as I think might well be the case.

16.   In the metropolitan field the close contact and understanding which existed up to the end of 1948 between the Colonial Office and the Ministry of Overseas France has been largely lost. This is no doubt partly due to our having not paid enough attention to the matter since 1948; it is mainly due to changes of personnel in the Ministry of Overseas France and the fact that the present senior officers there take a somewhat narrow view. We for our part have always been ready to supply information from the African Studies Branch of the Colonial Office, but the French have no corresponding organisation and are not in a position to reciprocate effectively. We have sent the French every month extremely informative political intelligence reports but they have sent us nothing in exchange. If closer contacts in the political sphere are to be established it will be necessary, I suggest, to hold fairly frequent meetings either in London or Paris to exchange information and views about current policies and developments. These meetings to be effective should be completely informal. They ought not to be regular but should probably take place about twice a year. We should not, however, accept any obligation to consult together in advance about proposed constitutional developments. Such an arrangement would be bound to sooner or later to become known to the African leaders on the Coast. They would strongly object and would be most suspicious and resentful of any such obligation to the French. Moreover if disagreements arose on matters which were entirely within the responsibility either of ourselves or the French, this could not fail to cause embarrassment. It was agreed between us and the French in 1948 that we should not bind ourselves to prior consultation; we should certainly adhere to this. But if fairly frequent informal meetings took place between us, that would bring us much closer together and would help us to understand each other's points of view. Other measures which might usefully be taken would be closer contacts between French and British journalists interested in West Africa through exchanges of visits or possibly periodical dinners in Paris and London; and the establishment of some Anglo-French body through which Members of the British

---

[2] See BDEEP series A, R Hyam, ed, *The Labour government and the end of empire 1945–1951*, part II, 182.

and French Parliaments interests in West African affairs could periodically meet. To remove mutual suspicions and to promote understanding it is not sufficient to bring officials together; the basis of co-operation ought to be broad.

17. To sum up I suggest that the following line should be pursued in the talks with the French:—

(1) We should explain as fully as possible the nature of our policy in constitutional matters in West Africa and the reasons for it and should seek to show the French that it is the only practicable policy in the circumstances of the British territories. We should make it clear that there is no chance of our modifying this policy.
(2) We should agree to any reasonable measures which the French may propose for promoting closer contact and the exchange of information in political matters; but we should not agree to prior consultation about political developments.
(3) We should review the results of the 1948 agreement and see how the machinery for carrying this into effect could be improved.
(4) We should propose the establishment in Accra of an Anglo-French Secretariat for the promotion of co-ordination.
(5) We should propose the holding of fairly frequent informal meetings between those concerned with political development in the British and French Colonial Ministries.
(6) We should discuss the possibility of closer contacts between the British and French journalists and British and French Members of Parliament interested in West Africa.

115   FO 371/10360, no 33   2 Apr 1952
'British and French colonial policies in Africa': minute by C P Hope

[Successive French Cabinet crises delayed the convening of the Anglo-French ministerial talks, but they were eventually held in London on 31 March 1952 with Mr Lyttelton in the chair. The main concrete outcome was an agreement to establish joint consultative machinery in West Africa as proposed by Cohen at the CO-FO meeting of 13 Nov 1951 (see 113) and in para 15 of his paper of 20 Nov 1951 (see 114). A copy of the official record of the meeting, 'Anglo-French ministerial discussions on colonial policy in Africa', is at FO 371/101360, no 28].

The Secretary of State for the Colonies and the Minister of Overseas France held a one day meeting on March 31st in the Colonial Office and in that day more than covered the agenda which had been agreed between officials at last December's preparatory meeting in Paris.

2. It was clear in the course of the ministerial meeting that the French were much preoccupied with British policy and future intentions both in the Gold Coast and in Nigeria and that this was mainly reflected in two ways:

(i) The local effect in adjacent territories firstly of the rash statements of African Ministers in the Gold Coast and secondly of the extension of British policies of self-government to the trust territories of Togoland and the Cameroons.
(ii) The effect that these policies had on Anglo-French attitudes towards the United Nations and the need for the British and the French anyway to alter their attitude to the United Nations because of the tendency of that Organisation to encroach on the colonial field.

3.   The talks were extremely useful in that pertinent questioning by the French caused the Colonial Office to explain their double policy in Togoland concerning which we have separately expressed Foreign Office doubts.[1] While the French were content to think that we intended ultimately to incorporate British Togoland in the Gold Coast as a unit in the Commonwealth, they were clearly surprised at this since we had earlier emphasised so strongly the need for a Joint Council for the two Togolands (thus appearing to favour a policy of unification of the two territories). The French felt that in the light of this new information there should be futher talks about our policy towards the Joint Council. A second issue on which the French appeared to be much less happy was that of the Cameroons. They assumed that in this territory as in Togoland it was our ultimate intention to make the present frontiers between the two trust territories the ultimate permanent frontiers between Britain and France. It became, however, clear in the course of the talks that the French feared the present embryo movement for Cameroons unification and, noting that this stemmed from British territory, requested positive action on our part to suppress it. They were not pleased to notice a certain sympathy in respect of this movement on the part of the Colonial Office.

4.   These same issues dominated discussion about the United Nations because the French wished to take our ultimate policy into account when considering this question (they themselves made it clear that it was their own intention ultimately to see both French Togoland and the French Cameroons as separate members of the Union française). Parallel to and separate from this question, the French pressed for firmer action on the part of H.M. Government towards the policy of the Fourth Committee. They were alarmed at the intention of this Committee to secure the same rights and powers in respect of colonial territories as they now enjoyed for trust territories. On this question all the familiar arguments and fears were brought forward. Much play was made of the fact that in so doing the Fourth Committee were acting outside the Charter. The activities of the Special Committee and the various obligations under Article 73(e) were stressed. Generally the French felt that we should call a halt now to this development in the Fourth Committee. They also felt that we should contain the new Committee on Petitions, even to the extent of trying to make its work less effective even than is allowed by the terms of the resolution setting it out. They similarly wanted to reduce the number of Visiting Missions or at least to prevent any extension of them. They were also perturbed at the question of "factors". They felt in a way that the sooner we could establish factors which would show that more rather than less dependent territories were self-governing the sooner we could get them out of the hands of the General Assembly.

5.   These preoccupations were comparatively latent during the Ministerial meetings on the first day, but they became a source of friction on the second day when

---

[1] 'We are thus pursuing two mutually incompatible policies. A short-term one of agreeing with the French in the handling of the administration of the two Togolands by means of the Joint Council, and a long-term policy of self-government which can only end in the absorption into the Gold Coast of British Togoland and the suppression of the Trusteeship Agreement with the United Nations' (memo, 'French concern at British colonial policy in Africa', by P Mason to Sir W Strang, FO 371/95757, no 13, 16 Nov 1951). Mason had earlier been asked by Strang to take responsibility for co-ordinating FO and CO policies towards France on colonial issues. The FO was diplomatically concerned at the fact that CO policy, by providing 'an undesirable attraction for the native inhabitants of French colonial territories', was embarassing the French (*ibid*). See also part II of this volume, 175, note.

officials attempted to agree a record of the Ministerial exchanges. In fact a deadlock was reached on this so that it was necessary at mid-day to inform Ministers that officials could not agree a record. The French Minister, who had to leave immediately by plane for Paris, was plainly distressed so I took the opportunity of suggesting that, as was usual, use should be made of the diplomatic channel to agree a record which could thereafter be signed by Ministers.

6. On this basis further meetings were held in the afternoon and early evening and with some difficulty an agreed record was finally produced. Much of the trouble arose from the lack of confidence between the two Colonial Offices and the various efforts made on both sides to read more into what each other's Minister had said than was agreeable to officials. A compromise record of a fairly satisfactory nature was finally agreed by representatives of the Quai d'Orsay and myself and accepted by both Delegations.

7. The main points of discord on the French side were:

(a) A demand that the Colonial Office should restrain Africans in the Gold Coast from criticising French policy in French Togoland. The Colonial Office were only prepared to speak gently to Nkrumah about this.

(b) The French asked for suppressive measures to be adopted both against the Pan-African Congress in the Gold Coast[2] and the development of the Unification Movement in the British Cameroons. The Colonial Office could only undertake "not to encourage."

(c) The French asked for guarantees that we would join them in resisting the United Nations on the various points described above even to the extent of refusing to accept Visiting Missions, refusing to supply information to the United Nations and in various other measures of non-cooperation. Given our support for the Charter and our general policy towards the United Nations I did not feel able to advise the Colonial office to accept this.

Future action

8. Ministers have agreed that there shall be a further meeting between officials in Paris towards the end of April to discuss matters arising out of this meeting. They have also agreed that there shall be tripartite talks with the Belgians thereafter to discuss the policy of administering powers towards the United Nations, so that a joint approach can later be made to the Americans before the next Assembly. It is suggested that the talks in Paris shall take place on the 29th and 30th April and that they should cover matters affecting the Cameroons, the Togolands and a preliminary draft for later discussion with the Belgians. It is suggested that this meeting should take place in Brussels towards the end of May and that both we and the French should meanwhile warn the Belgians that we intend to talk to them.

9. These Ministerial agreements make it more urgent for us to agree with the Colonial Office a basic policy towards the United Nations. The Colonial Office have already put to us two drafts in respect of this, neither of which we felt inclined to accept in toto, since they are built around a "walk out" as a basic element of policy. I had an opportunity of discussing this separately with Sir J Martin and Mr. Gidden,

---

[2] Nkrumah was planning to convene a Pan-Africanist congress in the Gold Coast later in 1952, in succession to the fifth congress held in Manchester in 1945. In the event he waited until 1958, when he was able to convene the sixth congress as prime minister of an independent African state.

Y

who told me that they would be disinclined to accept from us a policy which did not give comparable prominence to the walk-out. They are nevertheless prepared to be convinced that it is not possible at this stage to define every circumstances in which a walk-out could be staged.[3]

10. At the final meeting of officials, it was requested that the Foreign Office should be represented at the Paris and Brussels meetings and the officials from the Quai d'Orsay separately asked me whether I could secure agreement from the Foreign Office to my own presence at the talks. I undertook to put this forward in the Foreign Office.

---

[3] See 159, 160.

116 CO 936/192, no 195   [May–June 1953]
'Anglo-French discussions': report by CO of official talks on colonial policy held in Paris on 22 and 23 May 1953   [Extract]

. . .

3. *General questions: comparisons of colonial policies; reforms in progress, mutual information, possibilities of co-ordination*
In the absence of the political authorities responsible[1] there followed simply an exchange of information on the policy being followed by each Government.

Taking into account the repercussions of reforms and of political events in one territory on another, the two delegations agreed entirely on the necessity for a constant exchange of information and documents on these questions, both on the local level as well as on the metropolitan level.

4. *Communism*
The delegations considered that communist activity functioned especially in the French and the British territories through the medium of trade union organizations who were in touch with the W.F.T.U. A stricter supervision of these organizations and a constant exchange of information between the local governments were indispensable.

The comparative study of the controls in each territory in respect of the Press, of meetings and of passports, might be undertaken either locally or on the metropolitan level.

5. *Trade unionism*
The British delegation made known its views on the activity of I.C.F.T.U. in Africa, which it considered a good means of defence against the penetration of the unions by communism. It believed that the anti-colonial declarations of certain members of this confederation were only the expression of personal ideas and that they were not to be considered as the doctrine of the confederation, which itself had been denounced as an imperialist movement.

---

[1] 'Owing to the fall of the French Government after my arrival in Paris on the evening of the 21st May', as Lyttelton put it, 'the talks were held only at the official level' (circular despatch 663/53 from Lyttelton to African governors, CO 936/192, no 195, 17 July 1953).

The French delegation, whilst recognizing that the action of I.C.F.T.U. could be favourable to the expansion of trade unionism in the British territories, since it was perfectly suited to the policies which govern their formation and activity, had, however, to record its great reserve towards this confederation.

The creation of purely African trade unions recommended by this confederation went in fact against the principles of non-discrimination which were at the basis of French trade unionism and which are exemplified by the existence of local unions forming part of the metropolitan bodies.

The Secretary of the Office of I.C.F.T.U. at Accra, who had just arrived in the Gold Coast and who was perhaps unaware of the peculiarities of French trade unionism in Africa might usefully be informed of them.

6. *Moslem questions*
The French delegation stressed that its Government considered it particularly important that African Islam, which up to the present had remained unreceptive to outside influences, should not now be penetrated by the modernist and xenophobic ideas coming from the Middle East. Thus, in order to put a check on the harmful propaganda of the University at El Azhar,[2] the French authorities had set up the Franco-Arabic School at Abéché to implant in the Tchad a modern Franco-Arabic education. The attention of the British delegation was drawn to the importance of taking action so far as was possible against the use of Arabic at the expense of the vernacular languages and to the dangers of the Amadhya Pakistani Sect in Nigeria and the Gold Coast.

The two delegations welcomed the enquiries conducted by M. Mangin.[3] The British delegation stated that it would be pleased to welcome M. Mangin to London and that it would be equally willing to ask local governments to facilitate any missions carried out by officers dealing with Moslem affairs. Aware of the dangers which an Islamic xenophobia would present, the two delegations agreed to keep in close liaison on the whole subject of Moslem questions.

7. *National movement: Pan-African Congress; Pan-African movements*
There followed an exchange of views and information on these questions which had, moreover, been raised in the course of the examination of other points on the Agenda.

8. *United Nations questions*
Very satisfactory results had already been achieved following the exchange of views on the 5th and 6th May which was devoted to the examination—with Belgian delegates—of the principal Colonial problems which would be raised from now until the end of the year in the various bodies of the United Nations. The two delegations took note of the recommendations already adopted, which were based on the principles laid down last year.

A synthesis of two matters of concern had been proposed and this appeared acceptable to the two delegations: the first was the necessity of maintaining the principles on which there could be no compromise and the importance of following a

---

[2] In Egypt.
[3] Directeur d' affaires Musulmanes, Ministere de la France d'Outre-Mer.

policy of firmness which proved itself last year, and the second the advisability of employing in tactics a certain flexibility which was called for by the world situation and the very nature of the United Nations bodies.

The two delegations agreed to recommend that the diplomatic representatives of their Governments at Brussels should endeavour to ascertain the final views of the Belgians on questions on which the delegation was unable to commit itself during the discussions at London (participation in the work of the Committee on Information). The joint declaration relating to the resolution of the 20th December regarding the Joint Council in Togoland had been communicated by each of the Governments to the local authorities responsible. They had been informed that the publication of this declaration should take place, as agreed at London on the 7th May, during the fourth week of May on a date to be mutually agreed.

9. *Anglo-Egyptian Sudan*

The French delegation recalled the reasons why the French Government was following attentively the evolution of the Anglo-Egyptian Sudan and drew attention to some anxieties which certain aspects of the Anglo-Egyptian Agreement of February, 1953, caused them, notably the disappearance of the greater part of the guarantees concerning the peoples of the Southern Sudan. The French Government hoped that contacts between the French and English administration should be instituted both on the metropolitan and the local level. Its wish was in fact to be kept informed as much as possible of the progress of events on the doorstep of the A.E.F.

The British delegation gave an account of the events, both internal and external, of the Sudan which led up to the present situation and analysed the Anglo-Egyptian Agreement of February, 1953. It pointed out that it was now thought in London that the change of attitude of General Neguib on the subject of the Sudan was only a purely tactical move. The friendship recently established between the Egyptians and the Sudanese party which favoured independence was already hanging fire. At the same time the fears expressed by the French were not completely shared in London. The Sudanese in the great majority were solely preoccupied with their own problems and their horizon did not stretch beyond the frontiers of the Sudan. The idea of a "Greater Sudan" had no meaning for them. Finally, it was hoped in London the Sudanese would continue in the future to turn to Great Britain, and seek her assistance.

10. *Technical co-operation*

Before dealing with the several practical questions listed under points 10 and 11 of the Agenda, the French delegation stated that its Government was inclined to raise larger questions in the future as well as other specific matters. The two delegations agreed to recommend to their Governments that co-operation should be established to prevent costly and useless duplication in the field of road works, ports and power distribution. The French delegation informed the British delegation of the satisfactory results of co-operation of this nature with the Belgians. Further meetings of French and British experts could be envisaged, it being understood that they would be preceded by the distribution of detailed notes on each point of the Agenda.

The two delegations recommended also the exchange of publications by experts. The officers responsible for liaison between the French and British territories as well as between the two metropolitan departments concerned were asked to give particular attention to this question. The French delegation here stressed the keen interest it attached to the work of British experts on the national revenue and economic development of British territories.

The French delegation suggested the submission of a list of economic questions to experts, possibly within the framework of the Franco-British Joint Economic Commission, which met periodically at London and in Paris. . . .

117 FO 371/108108, no 3   25–28 Jan 1954
[FO interest in Anglo-French talks on colonial policy]: minutes by Mr Dodds-Parker and J E Jackson[1]

Monsieur de Beaumarchais of the French Embassy brought Monsieur Jurgensen, who is head of the African Department at the Quai d'Orsay, to see me this morning. In the course of a general talk on African affairs it became clear that both ministerial and official French opinion wanted closer contacts with us on colonial matters. Monsieur Jurgensen fully agreed when I observed that there was a fundamental difference of approach between us and the French on policy in overseas territories; he felt that the French were dragging their feet in the face of dependent territories' desire for self-government and that we were going too quickly. It was, therefore, all the more necessary, particularly in those areas of Africa where our dependent territories adjoined, that the British and French should at least have some chance at a fairly high level of studying each other's problems and of finding out what each other had in mind to solve them. This was surely the logical way to avoid cutting across each other's paths. The occasional meetings between the British and French Colonial Secretaries were too short and too infrequent to be of much value. He remarked, incidentally, that his talks in Paris with Sir Anthony Rumbold,[2] although interesting, were mainly limited to an informal and personal exchange of views, since the latter was naturally not empowered to discuss colonial matters.

Monsieur Jurgensen made the point that hitherto our colonial experts, including Ministers, had worked too much in ignorance of each other's plans, and at the best, when an exchange of views had been possible, had agreed to differ. This is probably true. I said that when the Colonial Secretary next had a meeting with his French opposite number I should much like, if possible, to come along and thereby associate the Foreign Office with the Colonial Office. This suggestion was well received, for Monsieur Jurgensen felt that some attempt should be made to bring the Foreign Office and the Quai d'Orsay more in touch with each other on African affairs and also more in touch with their respective Colonial Offices.

If the Secretary of State and the Colonial Secretary did agree to my accompanying the latter when he next sees the French Colonial Secretary, I might well take the opportunity of suggesting that the Brussels Treaty Permanent Commission would be a suitable forum for exchanging views at the official level on British and French problems and policies in dependent territories. I do not think this would embarrass us, and by getting the ball rolling in the direction that the French obviously want, it would at least please them.

A.D.D-P.
25.1.54

---

[1] J E Jackson, 2nd secretary, FO, 1952–1956.   [2] Counsellor, British embassy, Paris.

M. Jurgensen's approach is, I am certain, concerned chiefly with basic colonial policy as opposed to Anglo-French co-operation in colonial matters with an international flavour. Certainly from U.N. (Pol.) Dept. point of view—and I believe that this holds good for African Dept.—our contacts on the official level with the French are as close and effective as we could wish them to be.

2. With the growing importance of colonial affairs in foreign policy (Mr. Jamieson of P.U.S.D. is at present preparing a paper on this general problem), there would obviously be advantage in having a Foreign Office Minister at the talks between the French and British Colonial Ministers. The key to M. Jurgensen's thoughts, however, is given in his comment that we are going too quickly in colonial matters. What he really means is that we are going too quickly for the French, and I do not for one moment doubt that the purpose of closer co-operation with the French on colonial matters at a high level would be, from the French point of view, to try to persuade us to slow down the tempo of our whole colonial policy, which at the moment certainly shows the French at a disadvantage. I think it would be highly unfortunate if we were, as the result of such increased co-operation, to revise our colonial policy in a negative way, and I am equally certain that our international reputation on colonial matters would suffer if the fact that co-operation had now been intensified at a high level were to become publicly known. I believe that the Colonial Office would share my views on all these points.

J.E.J.
28.1.54

118   FO 371/108108, no 7   9 Mar 1954
'Anglo-French colonial co-operation in Africa': minute by B J Garnett[1]

M. Jurgensen's approach to Mr. Dodds-Parker on January 25 (J 1041/3)[2] in which he stated the French desire for closer contact with us on African affairs, represents a sincere desire on the part of the French for better co-operation. At the same time, I suspect that it indicates a line of thought which we have previously encountered from Quai d'Orsay, namely, that the *Quai* itself is anxious to play a leading part in all this rather than to leave it to the Ministry of Overseas France.

2. The various existing and possible methods of co-operation with the French on African affairs and the possibilities of improving them are summarised below:—

(1) *Ministerial talks*

The talks between Colonial Ministers (which were laid for the first time in March, 1952,) have proved on the whole satisfactory as far as they go, but M. Jurgensen told Mr. Dodds-Parker that they were "too short and too infrequent to be of much value". There is no doubt that what is desired is a more continuous form of contact between these talks. The French have, however, welcomed Mr. Dodds-Parker's suggestion (J 1041/3) that at future meetings between Colonial Secretaries there should be Foreign Office ministerial representation on both sides. This fits in with the Quai d'Orsay desire to play a greater part in these exchanges. Hitherto, there has been an official from the Foreign Office attending these talks. It is submitted

---

[1] African Dept, FO.   [2] See 117.

that Mr. Dodds-Parker's suggestion should be taken up now with the Colonial Office. Provided that the Colonial Office agree, we would then inform the French that Mr. Dodds-Parker will attend the next ministerial meeting. This is due to take place next May.

(2) *Annual talks between Foreign Office and Quai d'Orsay assistant under-secretaries*

The French suggestion that these regular talks on Middle-Eastern subjects should be extended to include discussion on Black African matters was put into effect by the inclusion of an item on "Black Africa" in the agenda for the talks which have just taken place between Mr. Allen and M. de Courcel. (The French, however, did no more than to urge briefly that there be closer collaboration on policy, greater exchange of information in advance on important developments, and attendance of junior Ministers of the Foreign Office and the Quai at the annual meetings of Colonial Ministers). While we have no objection to a general exchange of views at these meetings of Under Secretaries, we would not wish it to develop into a detailed discussion of colonial policy, since we are not involved in the day-to-day matters of Colonial policy in Africa to the same extent as the Quai d'Orsay. It is submitted that we should agree to a general exchange of views at the meetings of Foreign Office and Quai d'Orsay Assistant Under-Secretaries, but that this should be in addition to regular meetings between Assistant Under-Secretaries of the two Colonial Ministries (see paragraph 6 below).

(3) *Normal diplomatic channel*

There is close and frequent day-to-day consultation between the French Embassy in London and the Foreign Office, not only with African Department on general Black African matters and CCTA, but also with United Nations (Political) Department on African matters, such as Togoland, which involve the United Nations. (There are also pre-session Anglo-French meetings, attended by officials of Foreign and Colonial Ministries on both sides, to agree so far as possible a common line in CCTA and the various United Nations' organs.) M. Jurgensen, however, told Mr. Dodds-Parker that talks in Paris with Sir Anthony Rumbold were limited since the latter was not empowered to discuss colonial matters. The real point of course is that neither the French Embassy in London nor our Embassy at Paris include anyone who is fully *competent* to discuss colonial matters in detail. This could be overcome by the establishment of Colonial Attachés (see sub-paragraph 7 below) but little could be done effectively simply by authorising the Embassy to become involved in detailed discussion of colonial matters.

(4) *Brussels Treaty Permanent Commission*

Mr. Dodds-Parker mentions in his minute (J 1041/3) that he might suggest that the Brussels Treaty Permanent Commission would be a suitable forum for exchanging views at the official level on British and French policies in dependent territories and he was due to discuss this with Mr. Hopkinson. (See submission at (J 1022/1)). While the Brussels Treaty Permanent Commission is certainly a forum in which such a discussion might take place, it is very doubtful whether this suggestion would be welcome to the French who have shown an increasing desire recently for the establishment of close *bilateral* contacts between the United Kingdom and the French Governments. This fits in with their desire to be recognised as a great power and they would like to think that we would be prepared to discuss our colonial problems with them direct. The Brussels Treaty Permanent Commission on the other hand is regarded by many as a useful outlet for the expression of views by the smaller powers. It is submitted that while we would have no objection to using the Brussels Treaty Permanent Commission for this purpose, it would be unlikely to satisfy the French and they might indeed be inclined to resent this idea if it were put to them. It is therefore suggested that unless the French raise it themselves no further action should be taken on these lines.

(5) *Contact between officials in neighbouring territories*

Since the war, there has been a great improvement in the establishment of close contact between officials in neighbouring British and French colonial territories. This contact has been furthered by the provision of a British Colonial Attaché at Dakar and a French Colonial Attaché at Accra. (M. Jurgensen, however, is more concerned with furthering co-operation on a policy-making level.)

(6) *Direct contact between the Colonial Office and the Ministry of Overseas France*

Since the war, it has become established practice for the two colonial ministries to maintain direct contact on matters of common interest. At the ministerial talks of March, 1952, it was decided that an official in each colonial ministry should be specially charged with maintaining liaison between the two ministries on matters affecting Anglo-French co-operation in West Africa. Correspondence between these two officials, however, has been largely confined to routine matters. There has also been occasional contact on the Assistant Under-Secretary level between the Colonial Offices, but here again the Quai d'Orsay likes to interpose itself. For example, Sir John Martin has been surprised to receive replies from M. Jurgensen at the Quai d'Orsay to letters which he has addressed to M. Deltail at the Ministry of Overseas France. Neither the Foreign Office nor our Embassy at Paris, nor again the Under-Secretaries in the Foreign Office and the Quai d'Orsay, are, however, really the most suitable and competent people to discuss colonial policy and developments. It is therefore considered that we should try to persuade the French to keep to the agreement that there should be *direct contact between the two Colonial Offices* on matters of mutual interest, and urge them only to add the additional diplomatic channel when matters affecting foreign policy, or likely to come before the United Nations, are involved. It should, of course, be made clear that both the Foreign Office and the Quai d'Orsay should be consulted on all exchanges involving major policy since this will always impinge to some extent on Franco-British relations in general. It is submitted that we should suggest to the Colonial Office that there be regular meetings, say six months after each meeting of Colonial Ministers, between officials of the respective Colonial Ministries of Assistant Under-Secretary level, with suitable Foreign Office and Quai d'Orsay representation, to discuss colonial matters of mutual interest and supplement the annual ministerial meetings. We should add that on colonial issues likely to come before the United Nations, we should wish to continue existing arrangements for consultation through the diplomatic channel, and at meetings attended by suitable Foreign Office and Colonial Office officials on both sides, and, where desirable, representatives of other interested governments.

(7) *Colonial attachés*

M. de Crouy Chanel in his letter to Mr. Dodds-Parker of February 6 (J 1041/5) suggests that the French Embassy in London and our Embassy at Paris should each have a Colonial Attaché who would be competent to follow colonial affairs in liaison with the appropriate departments. The only Embassy which has a Colonial Attaché in London at present is the Belgian. We have one in Washington. It is submitted that there would be advantage from the Foreign Office point of view in having such Attachés, provided they were allowed direct access to the respective Colonial Offices. This is, however, a matter primarily for the Colonial Office to decide, as they are best able to judge the probable extent of the work to be done. If we appoint a Colonial Attaché to Paris it would be desirable for him also to cover Brussels; and possibly the Hague also, as the Dutch would no doubt resent the suggestion that Belgium is now a more important Colonial Power than they. It is suggested that we should pass the French proposal, with this addition, to the Colonial Office. We could, meanwhile, seek the views of Her Majesty's Ambassador in Paris who should be consulted before we reply to the French.

(8) *Recommendations*

The Department recommends that Mr. Dodds-Parker should discuss this whole matter with Mr. Hopkinson, mentioning, incidentally, that we are particularly anxious at present to be as forthcoming as possible with the French in connexion with our efforts to secure their ratification of the European Defence Community Treaty.[3]

In speaking to Mr. Hopkinson, it is suggested that Mr. Dodds-Parker should:—

(a) recommend that a Foreign Office Minister should attend the next meeting of Colonial Ministers;

(b) say that we agree to there being a *general* exchange of views on African colonial matters at the periodic meetings between the respective Foreign Office Assistant Under-Secretaries;

(c) recommend that we strengthen the *direct* links between the two Colonial Offices and, in particular, suggest to the French regular meetings at the Colonial Office Assistant Under-Secretary level, say six months after each meeting of the Colonial Ministers;

(d) pass on to the Colonial Office the French proposal to exchange Colonial Attachés, adding that if it is agreed to appoint such an Attaché to Paris he should also cover Brussels, and possibly the Hague.[4] It is recommended that we should not pursue the suggestion to use the Brussels Treaty Organisation in this connexion.

(9) The foregoing has been cleared with Western and Southern, Western Organisations, United Nations (Political) and Personnel Departments.

---

[3] See 2, note 2 & 28, note 1.

[4] Both the CO and the British embassy in Paris opposed the 'colonial attaché' proposal, the latter on the grounds that it would tangle the lines of communication. The idea was pursued no further.

119   CO 936/327   21 Apr 1954

[Differences between British and French colonial policies]: minute by H T Bourdillon   [Extract]

... 4. These annual talks with the French present us with a difficult problem, largely because of the fundamental difference of approach between the two metropolitan powers. The French are, as we know, anxious to strengthen the links of consultation and collaboration over the whole field of Colonial activities, and they evidently hope by this means to curb in some measure the speed of constitutional advance in British territories, particularly in West Africa. To the French mind it seems obvious commonsense that the two major Colonial powers should lay their plans in common and should form a defensive alliance against the hostile world. They regard this as a major objective not only of Colonial policy but of foreign policy—hence the desire that Foreign Office Ministers should be associated with the talks. We on our side regard the whole matter in an entirely different light. We welcome technical co-operation where it really has a useful function to perform, though even within this field I think we are conscious that co-operation cannot easily go beyond a certain point without becoming a political matter. On political questions themselves the whole idea of subordinating Colonial policy to foreign policy or of forming a defensive alliance with other Colonial powers is repugnant to us—and this goes for the Foreign Office as much as for the Colonial Office, although the former do not perhaps see the issue in quite such an uncompromising light. On the other hand we are anxious to maintain our general good relations with the French and to give them no reasonable cause for complaint. In consequence we have no alternative but to acquiesce cheerfully in the talks, though we may doubt their positive value.

5. I have not, of course, been present on previous occasions. Last year's talks in any case resolved themselves into discussions at the official level, since the French Government of the day had fallen just before the talks were due to take place. Mr. Williamson has told me, however, that his impression of previous occasions is that the British side are somewhat on the defensive and that the French, though studiously polite, are inclined to be critical of our unwillingness to come forward. In the circumstances described above this may be inevitable. All the same, I think we must do our best, in putting forward our proposals for the agenda, to give the impression of being forthcoming without in fact selling any passes. Another danger which we must try to avoid is that of cluttering up the agenda with trivialities with which Ministers never ought to be bothered at all. This is not too easy, partly because of the French tendency to drag in everything and partly because of our own unwillingness to consult the French about fundamentals. The best way out of the difficulty seems to be to show as much readiness as possible to give the French full *information* about important developments in our own territories. By doing this we may even succeed in establishing a certain initiative. . . .

120 CO 936/327, no 8   22 Apr 1954
[FO representation at Anglo-French ministerial talks on colonial policy]: letter from Mr Eden to Mr Lyttelton

My dear Oliver

The French have recently been hinting that they would like closer co-operation between us in colonial matters in Africa. A few suggestions as to how this might be done have come up in conversations with them, and Dodds-Parker has already mentioned these to Hopkinson. There is, however, one suggestion which I should like to put to you myself—Dodds-Parker is writing separately to Hopkinson about the others. This concerns the annual talks which you have with the Minister of Overseas France and which I understand are this year proposed for May 27.

We are often taxed by the French with not paying enough attention to the international effects of our colonial policy, especially in Africa where it affects them most. It has occurred to us that one way of convincing them that we are alive to the international aspect of our colonial policy would be to have a junior Foreign Office Minister assist at your annual talks with the Minister of Overseas France. We have already sounded the French (in the Quai d'Orsay) on this suggestion and they have re-acted very well to it. Clearly it would give them great pleasure and I imagine you might also find it useful yourself as I see that the agenda for the two meetings held so far included the Sudan, on which a Foreign Office official spoke. If you accept this suggestion, the junior Foreign Office Minister I have in mind is Dodds-Parker.

I am sorry that this proposal was not brought to my notice earlier so that we could have talked it over before I left for Geneva, but I hope you will feel able to accept it. If you do, you will no doubt wish to say in the formal invitation you send to Monsieur Jacquinot[1] that Dodds-Parker will also be attending the talks. We should like to be able to tell the French Embassy at the same time.

Yours ever
Anthony

---

[1] L Jacquinot, ministre de la France d'Outre-Mer, 1953–1954.

121 FO 371/108108, no 10   23 Apr 1954
[FO representation at Anglo-French ministerial talks on colonial policy]: letter (reply) from Mr Lyttelton to Mr Eden

My dear Anthony,

Thank you for your letter of April 22nd, about the Anglo-French Colonial talks.[1]

As the idea of associating a Foreign Office Minister with the talks has already been put to the French, I think it would cause us more embarrassment to try to go back than to go forward. The formal invitation to Monsieur Jacquinot will therefore go on the lines you suggest, and I note that you will be telling the French Embassy at the same time. All the same I am afraid I am not very happy about the proposal, and I am

---

[1] See 120.

rather sorry that your people didn't consult me before the Quai d'Orsay were sounded.

I realise that the French have often taxed us with not paying enough attention to the international effects of our Colonial policy, and I am not at all surprised that they should have reacted well to the present suggestion. The trouble is that the Colonial policies of the two countries are entirely different. The French desire for greater political co-ordination in Colonial matters springs largely from an anxiety about the effects in French territories of the constitutional advances which are taking place on our side, particularly in West Africa. But we are committed to our policies, and they are so different from the French way of looking at things that I am afraid there is nothing to "co-ordinate". Any attempt at co-ordination on the political front could in fact only lead us into a very embarrassing position.

This is the main difficulty which we have had to face in trying to make these Anglo-French Colonial talks a success. We have surmounted the difficulty as far as possible by trying to keep an intimate and informal atmosphere. This has enabled us not only to make the most of co-operation at the technical level, which we have always tried to foster to the limits of its real usefulness, but to give very frank explanations to the French about political developments (which have been much appreciated) and to encourage the same treatment from them. My fear is not of course that the presence of a Foreign Office Minister on our side will do anything to upset this informal atmosphere—on the contrary, we shall be delighted to have Dodds-Parker with us—but that the presence of a French Foreign Office Minister may make it difficult to be as frank and forthcoming with the French as we have been in the past. In other words I am afraid of the whole thing being inflated by the French into a formal conference, a development which can only be embarrassing to us and will not in the long run be helpful to themselves.

However, we must hope for the best. I am sure that all of us on our side will do everything to keep the talks informal and—within the limits imposed by the facts—fruitful.[2]

Yours ever
Oliver

---

[2] A junior FO minister, Mr Nutting, inscribed on Lyttelton's letter: 'S/S agrees. Does not want formal colonial confce w French at present time. Could we get out of it? Consult Selwyn.'

---

122   CO 936/327, no 29   7 May 1954
[FO representation at Anglo-French ministerial talks on colonial policy]: letter (reply) from Mr Eden to Mr Lyttelton

My dear Oliver,
Thank you for your letter of April 23 about the Anglo-French Colonial talks.[1]

I have now looked into the question of Foreign Office representation at these talks and I should like to say at once that I am very sorry indeed that the Colonial Office were not consulted before the possibility of a junior Foreign Office Minister

---

[1] See 121.

attending the talks was mentioned—even tentatively—to the French.

Your point about preserving the informality of your talks with the Minister of Overseas France made me wonder whether it would in fact be a good thing for junior Foreign Office Ministers to be present. We have thought this over and now agree with your that the presence of Foreign Office Ministers might make it more difficult to keep these talks as informal as you rightly wish them to be and might expose us to the danger of having them inflated by the French into a formal international conference. This might in turn be misrepresented in the Muslim and anti-colonial world as a deliberate ganging-up of the French and British involving British support for French policy in Morocco and Tunisia in return for French support of British policy elsewhere in Africa.

I have therefore decided that we should tell the French that we do not agree that Foreign Office Ministers should attend your talks. I understand that you have not yet sent your invitation to M. Jacquinot so it will be possible for you to avoid all mention of Foreign Office Ministers. Unfortunately, the French had already heard unofficially of your agreement that Foreign Office Ministers should attend but we have now taken steps to disabuse them on this point. I hope that they will not make any further difficulties and that the atmosphere of your talks will not be harmed. I am only sorry that we should have put you in a rather embarrassing position.

Yours ever
Anthony

123 CO 936/327   11 May 1954

[French proposals for Anglo-French ministerial talks on colonial policy]: minute by H T Bourdillon   [Extract]

. . . I am, however, slightly alarmed by one or two points in M. Jurgensen's very latest letter of May 10th (which came in after I began dictating this minute). This letter is about the agenda for the talks, and it urges that we should include not only an exchange of information on recent constitutional developments but also "a confrontation between the two policies and an examination of their bearing on each other". This sounds very much like at attempt to secure our agreement to a process of *consultation* on constitutional matters. M. Jurgensen claims the 1952 talks as a precedent, but my understanding is that we have always strenuously resisted such a development. I have an uneasy feeling that the French are trying to drive in a wedge, and it may not be fanciful to interpret the pressure for Foreign Office Ministerial representation as part of the same process. If so, I think we and the Foreign Office will need to do some careful joint thinking on this whole matter. It is essential that the two departments should be in line, and recent indications are not entirely reassuring. It is true that the Foreign Office have come into line with our way of thinking on the matter of Ministerial representation, but only at the eleventh hour and at the cost, I fear, of some irritation and disappointment on the French side. . . .

124 CO 554/1288   7 July–4 Aug 1954
[Anglo-French economic co-operation in West Africa]: minutes by J D B Shaw[1] and W A C Mathieson[2]

After the earlier generalities they have canvassed on this topic, this latest French document is agreeably specific in its proposals, though I note the recurrence of some of the perennials in the field of Anglo-French co-operation, particularly under the transport co-ordination head.

2. What we are asked to agree to is evidently the establishment of a joint committee of experts sitting in London and Paris, and presumably supplying the initiative and periodical impetus for an examination of these problems at the local level. The question of railings of French groundnuts on Nigerian railways is quoted as an example of the difficulties of dealing with problems of this kind, if they are left entirely to negotiation on the spot.

3. I have no doubt that the French have some justification in thinking that consideration of problems of Anglo-French interest proceeds slowly and often without noticeable enthusiasm if left entirely to the discretion of West African Governments. The truth of the matter is that—as the present list of suggested subjects shows—we have on balance little to ask the French for ourselves, whereas they have a number of projects on which they believe there is scope for co-operation. But the major difficulty is that in our own territories responsibility of [sic] the problems in the economic sphere rests with the local Government. The extent to which we are able to direct pressure on to West African Governments to consider, for example, questions such as the import of salt manufactured in French West Africa, is limited and likely to become increasingly so under the new constitutions in the Gold Coast and Nigeria. We can bring matters of this kind to their notice and invite comment, but I cannot believe that the establishment of standing machinery in London and Paris will help materially to sustain interest and attention on the part of local Governments, or necessarily be more effective than the present arrangement by which we bring to the notice of Governments specific matters as, and when, they arise.

4. If a joint Anglo-French committee of economic experts is to be established, a more useful contribution might be the establishment of local regional machinery at the Daker-Accra level, bringing in W.A.I.T.S. and the Colonial Conseil at Dakar, and competent, if it so wished, to call on the services of metropolitan experts.

5. I am not sure how far the last Ministerial talks resulted in a firm commitment to establish a joint committee of experts, but I take it that we are not expected, at this stage, to pursue in detail the various matters listed in the note, in advance of the committee coming into being, but merely to note them as illustrative of the field it might cover.

J.D.B.S.
7.7.54

I agree ... that the points suggested by the French for discussion by an Anglo-French Committee of economic experts are not new. They fall into two general

---

[1] Principal, CO.   [2] See 104, note 3.

categories. The first covers questions of inter-territorial trade and the movement of persons which are a feature of every day economic relations between adjacent territories and should be regulated through local contacts between consular officers and the governments concerned. In the second category come large and well identified problems in the economic field resulting mainly from the geography of West Africa, for example, navigation problems on the Benoue and the evacuation of French produce by the Nigerian railways. I agree with those who say that both these categories of problems are essentially for local discussion and settlement. In dealing with these matters with the French I have always found that their system of centralised control in Paris leads them to expect the Colonial Office to be able to do more to influence such local negotiations and also to be more fully informed of their details than is our custom. Discussions between the two metropolitan Governments can, in my view, be fruitful only if local negotiation has disclosed some well-defined points of difference on which metropolitan arbitration may be possible, or if agreement has not been reached because of the failure of one side or the other in West Africa to make arrangements for local discussions. . . .

W.A.C.M.

4.8.54

125   CAB 128/27/2, CC 80(54)5   29 Nov 1954
[Spanish policy towards Gibraltar]: Cabinet conclusions

The Cabinet considered a memorandum by the Colonial Secretary (C. (54) 360) seeking the views of his colleagues on the expediency of applying economic sanctions against Spain in response to Spanish restrictions directed against Gibraltar.

The Colonial Secretary said that the Spanish Government had introduced a series of restrictions on travel and trade between Spain and Gibraltar with the evident intention of impairing the economy of the Colony. He had considered what means were open to us to bring pressure to bear on the Spanish Government. In trade relations we were not in a position to do Spain more harm than she could do to us; and on balance he thought it would be wiser to concentrate our efforts on building up the economic strength of Gibraltar in order to reduce its present dependence on Spain. He hoped that it would be possible to accelerate the construction of new barracks which were to be built by the Army, to encourage both naval and merchant vessels, British and foreign, to call at Gibraltar, and to assist the projects for constructing new harbour works and improved bunkering facilities at Gibraltar. It was, however, for consideration whether it would also be expedient to reduce Spain's share of the British tourist trade by adjustment of the travel allowances.

The Foreign Secretary said that in his view political issues should not be introduced into the trade talks which were now opening in Madrid. We should do nothing to discourage the flow of trade between the two countries, which now stood at a level of about £40 million a year. The best means of countering Spanish threats to Gibraltar was to reduce Gibraltar's economic dependence on Spain and at the same time to demonstrate our determination to retain British sovereignty over the Rock. Our policy should be to show ourselves reasonable in our trade relations but firm in our support of the Colony. This policy would involve some immediate expenditure but would prove economical in the long run.

The Cabinet:—

(1) Agreed that it would be undesirable to introduce political issues into the forthcoming discussions with the Spanish Government on trade and payments arrangements in 1955.

(2) Invited the Colonial Secretary, in consultation with the Chancellor of the Exchequer and other Ministers concerned, to consider what measures should be taken to render the economy of Gibraltar less dependent on Spain.

(3) Invited the Foreign Secretary to consider the legal issues raised by the encroachment of the Spanish authorities in the "neutral" zone surrounding Gibraltar.[1]

---

[1] Lennox-Boyd visited Gibraltar in Oct 1955 for talks with local political leaders. They 'spoke with strong feeling of the effect of Spanish restrictions which are being maintained without relaxation and which seriously affect the economy of the Colony. . . . There was emphatic general support for the view that in the long run the best hope for Gibraltar lay in a re-establishment of friendly relations between the United Kingdom and Spain and support for Spain's admittance to United Nations would be one way of fostering this. They emphasised, however, that it would be essential to couple this with a clear-cut statement of Her Majesty's Government's firm intention to maintain sovereignty over Gibraltar' ('Spain', Cabinet note by Lord Lloyd, CAB 129/78, CP(55)157, 18 Oct 1955).

126   FO 371/123714, no 1   5 Mar 1956
[Relations with Italy, Portugal and Spain in connection with colonial policy]: letter from E G G Hanrott[1] to R Scrivener[2]

We have been giving some preliminary thought to the question whether it would be wise to extend invitations to the Administering Governments among the New Members—i.e. to Italy, Portugal and Spain—to join our annual fraternal discussions with the Belgians and French in preparation for the Fourth Committee. The thought began as a preparation for the C.C.T.A. Conference at Salisbury, since it seemed that the French might then raise the subject; in fact it was not mentioned, but we think all the same that it would be useful to come to some provisional conclusion.

The purpose of this letter is to suggest to you that this conclusion should be that no invitation should be extended, at least for the present. Our main reason is that we do not consider that the Italians, the Portuguese or the Spaniards are sufficiently close to our thinking about colonial problems in the U.N. to make a meeting of minds profitable—indeed the effect might, we think, be to spoil the existing tripartite talks without any counter-balancing gain. We and the French and the Belgians have now had close on ten years' common experience of the peculiarities of the Trusteeship Council, the Fourth Committee and the Committee on Information. There are of course differences between us, but we should not allow these to camouflage the fact that on fundamentals we share a great deal of common ground. Thus, although we talk of the Belgians as being diehards, we do not mean by this that they are less aware than we are of the subtlety and savoir faire necessary for life in the U.N.; it is merely that it suits their interests as an important but minor Colonial Power, and that, having a smaller commitment, they can get away with being

---

[1] E G G Hanrott, principal, CO, 1948–1959; Malayan Civil Service, 1951–1953.
[2] R S Scrivener, diplomatic service, 1945–1976.

relatively intransigent, whereas we could not. In fact of course their intransigence suits us, since it adds an element of toughness to our common colonial position.

The position of Italy, Portugal and Spain on the threshold of the U.N. is fundamentally different. The Italians arrive shorn of their imperial responsibilities and with their only claim to be entitled a Colonial Power their temporary hold on the Trust Territory of Somalia, a hold which they are apparently to relinquish voluntarily in the near future. We think it unlikely that, placed as they are, they will be particularly eager to be too closely identified with the group of Colonial Powers, that they will be very interested in Fourth Committee affairs or, if they do become interested, they would be much more reliable than, say, Turkey.

Portugal similarly is not technically an Administering Power—not because she does not possess Colonies but only because she does not give them that name. There is little doubt that Portuguese colonial administration would be sharply attacked, and Portugal will no doubt enlist our support and that of the other Administering Powers. This help we should give, and the time may come when we shall want to draw the Portuguese into our inner counsels in the same way as in C.C.T.A. But we think that it is too early to do this, partly because of their ignorance of U.N. affairs, partly because of their present uncertainty as to how they should handle their Chapter XI responsibilities (if they acknowledge them), and partly because the advent of a delegation with a position much more uncompromising than our own may make it more difficult for us to induce the French and Belgians to adopt realistic and flexible tactics. Although, therefore, we do not rule out the possibility that it may later suit our book to bring Portugal into the talks, we think that we must wait until the Portuguese are more in tune with us and until the advantages to us of such an association are more obviously indicated.

I need not say much about Spain since several of the objections to Portugal apply even more strongly in her case. We obviously could not invite the Spaniards without the other two. (We must also bear in mind that if we bring in the Portuguese, they may themselves feel that Spain ought to come in, because of the close relations existing between them on account of the (fairly reactionary) plantation interests in San [sic] Tomé and Fernando Po.

I have not mentioned a further serious disadvantage of enlarging the present small family circle, namely that the talks would inevitably lose something of the easy informality which is such a valuable feature of them at present. This is a major disadvantage and one over which we should wish to think fairly hard before we disregarded it.

Our conclusion does not mean that we should not have, as and when the need arises, bilateral talks with both the Italians and the Portuguese. There are obvious advantages in doing so, as we are to some extent already doing with Portugal about general Fourth Committee procedure (see New York despatch 1987/4/56 of the 3rd February). We are also of course contemplating discussions with the Italians over Somali affairs, which will have their U.N. implications. It seems to us clear that we should carry on with such talks on specific issues and so pave the way for closer collaboration later over the whole U.N. field.

We should be interested in your views and whether you agree with this conclusion—one which is not, we think, seriously affected by the risk of the Portuguese or Italians getting to know of the existence of the tripartite talks and wanting to butt in.

Z

We should also like to know whether the Foreign Office have heard anything from the French and Belgians about their attitude to co-operation with these New Members over colonial questions in the U.N.[3]

---

[3] The FO was persuaded by the arguments in this letter (letter from Scrivener to Hanrott, 21 Mar 1956, FO 371/123714, no 1).

127   FO 371/123714, no 7   21 June 1956
[Consultations with Portugal on colonial policy]: despatch no 117 from Sir C Stirling (Lisbon) to Mr Selwyn Lloyd

You were good enough to send me under cover of your despatch No. 170 of the 6th of June, a copy of your despatch No. 403 to Paris of the 28th of May concerning the proposal to hold consultations with the French and Belgian Governments on colonial issues which are likely to arise at the General Assembly of the United Nations. I appreciate your misgivings about including Portugal in these consultations, but I regret none the less the decision to exclude her, and I could wish that I had been given an opportunity to express my views before it was taken.

2. In face of the additions to the strength of the anti-colonial forces in the United Nations as the result of the recent new elections, it would appear to be in our interest to do all we can to make Portugal a useful ally. It is true that her attitude to colonial questions is in some respects different to our own, that she may not always be willing to adopt the tactics we favour, and that her presence among the colonial powers may even at times be an embarrassment to us; but, whether we like it or not, she is in the colonial camp and it is surely in our interest to see that her tactics conform as far as possible to what we think is in the common interest and that she does not too often give a handle to the opposition.

3. Portugal is clearly in quite a different category to Italy, who has very limited colonial responsibilities, and to Spain, who, owing to her interest in Gibraltar and her links with the Arab States, may well be inclined to vote against us on colonial questions. Portugal is a colonial power *par excellence*, a member of N.A.T.O. and an ally of the United Kingdom, and, above all, a member of the Commission for Technical Cooperation in Africa. As such she has in the past pressed us, the French and the Belgians to agree to political consultations on colonial questions. If she is excluded from the talks in November she will undoubtedly hear of it and will very likely be told that we have taken the lead in excluding her. To say the least of it, this will not improve Anglo-Portuguese relations generally or dispose the Portuguese Delegation to follow our lead in New York.

4. Colonial items will interest Portugal more than any other questions on the Assembly agenda. Ministries here have not yet given any serious thought to the policy they should follow on these items. The official in charge of the United Nations Department at the Ministry of Foreign Affairs recently gave his opinion that the attitude of the Portuguese Delegation will be discreet and unassuming at their first appearance at a General Assembly; but reticence on colonial matters, on which they feel intensely, would not be altogether in keeping with the Portuguese character: if only for domestic consumption their representatives may be tempted to adopt certain firm attitudes. It may therefore be to the interest of the other powers having

colonial responsibilities that Portugal should be warned against taking positions on colonial matters which might be regarded with disfavour in New York.

5. You point out, Sir, that the Portuguese Government are not prepared to admit in public that their overseas territories are colonies, but this is largely a tactical position comparable, to some extent, to the position of the French Government in maintaining that their relations with Algeria are an internal question. In any case I see no reason to suppose that the Portuguese would not be willing to discuss their relations with these territories on a realistic basis in private consultations. They are, I am sure, deeply sensitive of the exposed position they will occupy at New York and I have no doubt that they would welcome advice, if they could be sure it was disinterested and sound. On the other hand they would regard with suspicion any direct suggestion from us that they should adopt a conciliatory attitude towards interference or criticism by the United Nations, since they disagree with our liberal colonial policy and regard what they consider our weakness as being partly responsible for the strength of the nationalist and anti-colonial forces in the world. The best possible way of initiating them in advance into the realities of United Nations colonial politics would, it seems to me, be to allow them to sit in at a frank discussion between the colonial powers who know the New York atmosphere on the situations which will arise in the Assembly and the best way of meeting them. The Portuguese representatives may not be able to contribute anything useful to the discussion and they may not always agree with the tactics suggested, but I do not see that their presence can do any harm. There can be no question of their loyalty in this connexion, and I feel strongly that any trouble taken to enlighten them would be well repaid by making them better allies at New York. I venture to call attention once again in this connexion to Portugal's close relations with Brazil, which may enable her to exert a useful influence on members of the Latin American *bloc* if we can enlist her in our team.

6. For all these reasons I very much hope that it may be possible to reconsider our attitude and, if necessary, to press the French and Belgian Governments to agree to the inclusion of Portugal in the conversations which it is proposed to hold in November on these questions.

7. I am sending a copy of this despatch to Her Majesty's Ambassadors at Paris, Brussels, Rome, Madrid, Rio de Janeiro and to the United Kingdom Permanent Representative in New York.

128   FO 371/123714, no 11   3 Aug 1956
[Consultations with Portugal on colonial policy]: letter from
I T M Pink to Sir C Stirling (Lisbon)   [Extract]

[The CO remained firmly opposed to holding multilateral talks on political subjects in Africa at which the Portuguese would be present, but did not object to holding bilateral discussions with the Portuguese on UN matters. 'I realise that this may be rather galling for the Portuguese, but I should have hoped that the offer of bilateral talks would go a long way to satisfy their *amour propre*', minuted C O I Ramsden of the FO on 17 July (FO 371/123714, no 9). The CO's point of view was expounded in a letter from H T Bourdillon to J D Murray on 24 July (*ibid*, no 11). This letter from Pink (see 96, note 2) to Stirling was based very largely on Bourdillon's letter.]

I am now back in the Office and have seen your further letter 2222/20/56 of July 16 to

Dalton Murray about Portuguese participation in talks on colonial affairs at the United Nations. Let me say at once that I think there is a great deal of force in what you say; if other things were equal we would certainly want to bring the Portuguese into these talks straight away. We want to associate ourselves as closely as possible with the Portuguese in all United Nations matters and particularly of course in colonial affairs; and it is clearly in our interest that the Portuguese should look to us in the first place for help in the United Nations.

As you recognise, the Portuguese will be a problem in any case. But I do not think it is necessarily true that they will be more of a problem if they are left out. The experience of the Colonial Office in the Commission for Technical Co-operation in Africa South of the Sahara unfortunately shows that the Portuguese, realising the extreme vulnerability of their position in Africa, tend in multilateral discussions about colonial matters to adopt attitudes of the utmost rigidity and to try and play off the other participants against each other. If this were to happen at the pre-Assembly talks, the whole spirit of intimacy and common purpose which we have succeeded in establishing with the French and Belgians would be jeopardised. We should in fact have lost everything and gained nothing by bringing the Portuguese in.

Moreover this year it is expected that the tripartite talks will include an item extending their scope to cover wider political issues in Africa. Hitherto, the talks have been concerned only with colonial affairs at the United Nations and discussion of wider issues in Africa was confined to meetings between the French and ourselves. The intention now is to bring the Belgians in on this. We doubt very much if it would be wise to invite the Portuguese to take part in talks which included these wider questions since Portuguese views on such topics are greatly different from our own.

Although it need not be a decisive argument in considering our attitude, the French are pretty emphatic that we should wait and see how the Portuguese shape in the United Nations before inviting them to join the tripartite talks. It would be difficult to persuade them to the contrary.

We think also that the system of bilateral talks would, to start with, have definite merits in itself. They would be more intimate because there would be only two parties involved, and only thus would we find out just how much common ground on colonial matters there is between the United Kingdom and Portugal. They would also enable us to discuss freely with the Portuguese the awkward question of the transmission of information from non-self-governing territories under Article 73(e) of the United Nations Charter. On this, the Commonwealth Relations Office, Colonial Office and ourselves think it would be in the general interests of the Colonial powers if Portugal were to agree to co-operate with the work of the United Nations in this field and with the Committee on Information as we do, despite our doubts about the Committee's legal standing. Our fear is that if the Portuguese tried to evade transmitting information there would be long and bitter arguments in the 4th Committee, and, while the mere fact of transmission would not stop India from raising the Goa question, it might make the Indians a little less hostile. Were this question discussed at the tripartite meetings in the presence of the French we should run into difficulties. The French have themselves stopped transmitting information in respect of certain of their dependent territories, arguing that they have been incorporated in the metropolitan area. I fully understand that we should have to use the greatest tact in discussing this matter with the Portuguese and indeed that we may be unable to convince them that our view is the right one. But we and the

Colonial Office think we have a better chance of explaining our attitude to them on a bilateral rather than on a quadripartite basis. The question of how we would in fact cast our vote on questions of this sort would have to be considered in the light of the talks.

We think therefore that we should now take the initiative by inviting the Portuguese to join us in bilateral pre-Assembly talks on colonial problems arising in the United Nations. We could tell them we would hope to be able to give them the benefit of our experience in these matters, and that we on our side would hope to profit from their close relationship with the Latin American countries. It seems to us that this would be the best way of avoiding the dangers which you fear and at the same time of testing the ground before considering further steps. It seems to us that it would be as well for the talks to be held as soon as possible—perhaps in the early part of September. This would have the advantage, amongst others, that we would go to the tripartite talks with the French and Belgians with advance knowledge of what the Portuguese attitude in the Assembly would be likely to be. Our present assumption is that they will take place at the beginning of October and not in November. After having our bilateral talks with the Portuguese and seeing how they perform at the General Assembly we would re-open next year after the Assembly the question of making the tripartite talks into 4-power meetings. We are assuming, of course, that no difficulties would arise with the Spaniards if we were to invite the Portuguese without them, and this would perhaps have to be gone into nearer the time.

I hope you will think these arrangements go at least some of the way to meeting the points raised in your despatch and letters. . . .[1]

---

[1] Bilateral talks with Portuguese officials, extending over three days, were held in London in Sept, with J D Murray and H T Bourdillon as chairmen. Bourdillon emphasised that 'although there were differences between our approaches Portugal had the complete support of the United Kingdom in resisting the encroachment of the United Nations into the political affairs of colonial territories. The United Kingdom, however, still looked upon the question of taking a more positive line with an open mind' ('Record of a meeting of United Kingdom and Portuguese officials at the Foreign Office on September 19, 20 and 21', para 30; FO 371/123715, no 29). Selwyn Lloyd commented on the talks in despatch no 148 of 1 Oct to Stirling (ibid): 'Although the Portuguese Government may be expected to take the stand that they administer no non-self-governing territories and will not therefore transmit information, I hope that the suggestions we put forward, designated to add weight to this Portuguese contention, will be of use to the Portuguese when, if they do indeed decide not to transmit, they face inevitable criticism and hostility at the General Assembly.'

129   CO 936/337   18–19 Oct 1956
[FO interest in Anglo-French ministerial talks on colonial policy]: minutes by J E Marnham and H T Bourdillon

Mr. Bourdillon
You should know of two points which have arisen during our preparation for these talks on 25th October.

(1) You will notice that the agenda includes our old friends "Communist Penetration" and "Egyptian Influence in Africa". These were put on at the instance of the Foreign Office after we had said that we had no particular grounds ourselves

for doing so and that if they (the F.O). wanted them included, it was up to them to produce the material for a brief which would make it clear to our Secretary of State what the object was and what it was hoped he would put across to, or extract from, the French. The F.O. have agreed to do this; I.S.D. are content that the item should be included, and we await the F.O. material.

(2) This may or may not be connected with a phone call I had yesterday (Wednesday) from Mr. Adam Watson on his return from New York. He told me that M. Negre had suggested to him that, in view of the increasing international importance of Africa, the Quai d'Orsay and F.O. should play an increased part in the series of what have hitherto been predominantly inter-Colonial Office exchanges, of which next week's talks are the next example. M. Negre thought that the level of F.O. and Quai d'Orsay representation should be substantially higher than in the past, and he had suggested that next week's talks might even be attended by Sir Ivone Kirkpatrick.

Mr. Watson volunteered at once that he didn't think the last suggestion appropriate. Nor did he want to countenance any proposals which would seem to be stealing our thunder. Nevertheless, he had some sympathy with the French view that Africa is going increasingly to throw up questions of international concern ranging wider than straight questions of colonial administrative policy. It will, he thinks, become necessary before long for the two (and possibly more) F.O.s to put their heads together about these, and it is desirable that we should be in on this process.

Without denying this, I suggested that the best way of achieving it called for more thought than was possible between now and next week. We valued very highly our direct contacts with the Rue Oudinot,[1] not because we should feel the slightest impediment *at this end* if the F.O. were to take the front seat, but because we believed that relations between the Quai d'Orsay and Ministry of Overseas France were less close than ours with the Foreign Office and it was an enormous advantage to us to be able to confer direct with M. Pignon[2] without going through the Quai d'Orsay. It was therefore important to us that, whatever else might be added under them, by, for example, prolonging them, dividing them into separate sections or even holding extra talks on different occasions, our own series should continue not to be swamped by "F.O.-type" agenda and overwhelming F.O. representation.

Mr. Watson professed to see the force of this and was inclined to agree that any substantial attempt to shift the emphasis of next week's talks should be avoided. He also accepted the lesser, but still important, argument that this will make it easier to skate over Somaliland problems, which we are not yet ready to discuss further with the French.[3]

Thus relieved, I readily accepted that once these talks are over we should join the F.O. in considering M. Negre's suggestion at more leisure. I also volunteered that, whilst I was sure that our Secretary of State would be happy to look to Mr. Watson as his F.O. adviser at the talks, it seemed to me entirely reasonable that for talks of that level the Foreign Offices should be represented by Under-Secretaries if such a proposal would please the French. This would not in the least detract from the

---

[1] ie, the Ministère de la France d'Outre-Mer.

[2] L Pignon, directeur des affaires politiques au Ministère de la France d'Outre-Mer.

[3] They were discussed, however; see 98.

inter-C.O. atmosphere of the talks, and if Mr. Ross[4] were to attend, with or without his French opposite number, we should be delighted to see them.

We left it that either Mr. Ross or Mr. Watson would come and that they would consider further whether to tell the French that we should welcome the equivalent of an Under-Secretary from the Quai d'Orsay.[5]

So, far so good. But I imagine that M. Negre or whoever comes next week from the Quai d'Orsay may pursue this. If so, I suggest that our line (which we should agree beforehand with the F.O.) should be to express interest in the suggestion that there are wider ranging international questions coming to the fore in Africa, and to say that we were giving further thought to how they could best be dealt with. If you agree, one of us might have a word with Mr. Watson in that sense.

J.E.M.
18.10.56

Mr. Marnham

Thank you very much. This is of course a hardy annual. I entirely agree with the line you have taken, and I also agree that once the impending talks are over we can join the Foreign Office in considering the matter at greater leisure. If in the meanwhile you think it desirable to have a further word with Mr. Watson (and I agree that this might be a good idea), I suggest you should merely tell him that you have reported the affair to me, that I have agreed with the line you have taken and that we trust that the Foreign Office, like ourselves, will avoid any commitment, pending our further consideration of the matter, if the French return to the charge next week. I suggest this slight variant of your final paragraph because I think the F/O, with their newly found and perhaps hyper-sensitive Africa-consciousness, might regard as a bit ostrich-like the idea that we should merely "express interest" in the suggestion that there are wider ranging international questions coming to the fore in Africa.

H.T.B.
19.10.56

---

[4] A D M Ross, assistant under-secretary of state, FO, 1956–1960.

[5] In the event the FO was represented by Ross, Watson and W N R Maxwell; the Quai also sent three representatives.

130   DO 35/3087   8 Jan 1952

[Indian interest in colonial policy]: minute by S F StC Duncan[1]

[Extract]

[Since 1947 the Indian government had taken a lively interest in problems and policies affecting Indian communities in British colonial territories. It had made representations to the British government concerning, for example, Indian migration to East Africa and Aden; education and franchise in Kenya; pyre burial in the West Indies and British Guiana; land settlement and taxation in Fiji; and the situation of Indian traders in Gibraltar. While dealing with Indian representations on Kenyan electoral law in 1951–1952, CRO officials decided that it was necessary to work out general guidelines for assessing what constituted legitimate Indian interest in colonial matters.]

. . . There are two considerations which we should be clear about. Firstly how far the

---

[1] Executive officer, CRO.

principle of [India] making any sort of approach is justifiable, for I do not think we can say straight out that it is or it is not, and secondly the way in which the principle, in cases where it is concerned permissible, might be applied.

Since the display of interest in all overseas communities is a major feature of India's foreign policy, whether we like it nor not, she is unlikely to conform with our ideas as to what constitutes legitimate interest. There is no reason however why we should not make our attitude towards her dependent upon the degree to which we consider her interest in each case justified.

A certain degree of justification for the principle can be found in:—

(a) *The practice of the free interchange of views and information within the Commonwealth.* This can be interpreted widely but cannot be said to cover domestic policy in any Commonwealth country unless such policy directly affects other member countries. Nevertheless, whilst the U.K. alone carry responsibility for internal constitutional developments in Colonies dependent upon her, we recognise the interest of the Governments of other members of the Commonwealth and are publicly committed to the statement that it is our practice to keep them informed of major developments in that sphere.

(b) *Religion.* While the strongest argument for resisting Indian interest in Indian communities in the Colonies, (and one that is admitted by India) is that these peoples should cease to look to India as their homeland and should concentrate on becoming citizens of the country in which they are living, the ties of religion are natural and cannot be dismissed so effectively. There is justification therefore for both comment and criticism of any colonial legislation which admits, or seems to admit, of religious discrimination.

(c) *Practice of the former Government of India.* Interest in Indian communities overseas is not new; several matters, still the subject of correspondence with the Indian Government, were originally raised by the former Government of India. It would be undesirable therefore to effect a change in the attitude already adopted towards India over colonial afairs affecting Indian communities in which the Government of India were interested before 1947.

(d) *Immigration legislation.* It is of course the right of any country to impose its own immigration laws but it cannot be denied that where these discriminate against Indians, not so much in the case of would-be settlers but in the case of travellers and merchants, the Government of India are not only directly concerned but have justification for making representations.

(e) *Expediency.* It is generally desirable to avoid as far as possible irritating India on petty issues which might result in losing her co-operation over matters of major importance.

The form Indian "interest" may be permitted to take in such matters is also worthy of some definition.

(i) There are few circumstances in which we can, or should, refuse to meet a general *request* by India *for information.*

(ii) It would be difficult not to grant *permission to express* India's *views* on a subject before any decision is taken even though it was justified only under (a) or (e) above.

(iii) *Representations* from the Government of India should only be countenanced if justified under (a) to (e) above.

(iv) *Discussion* of colonial policy with the Government of India should be avoided except in very exceptional cases.

If this attempt at analysis can be accepted it proves the weakness of India's case in trying to interfere over the electoral law in Kenya by the manner of their approach and the subject of it.

There are some eleven recent cases of Indian interest displayed in various aspects of colonial policy but again on the basis of the above analysis most of these do not compare with that now under consideration. . . .

131   DO 35/5340, no 12   17 Apr 1953
[Speech on Kenya by Mr Nehru]: letter from Sir T Lloyd to Sir P Liesching

Please refer to telegram No. 429 from the United Kingdom High Commissioner in Delhi reporting a speech made by Mr. Nehru on the annual commemoration of Jallianwla [sic] Bagh.[1]

2. There have been several occasions in the last few months on which Mr. Nehru has made remarks about "colonialism", and particularly about the situation in Kenya. These remarks have been improper, provocative, and sometimes, as in the latest case, intolerable. Their general tendency has been to criticise "colonial (European) rule" as 'ipso facto' an oppressive anachronism, leading inevitably to race war, to place the responsibility for disorder and violence entirely on the European elements including Government in the territories, to refer to any necessary special measures such as any Government, including the Indian Government itself, is sometimes obliged to take to preserve law and order, as unjust repression, and to declare India's intentions of opposing "colonialism" and "racial suppression and inequality" wherever they exist. As regards Kenya, although the usual Indian homilies about the Indian example of non-violence are sometimes thrown in, the tendency of the speeches has been to avoid criticism of Mau Mau, to treat it as a legitimate and justifiable protest against unjust and extreme European oppression, and to give the impression that the Indians and Africans in Kenya are united in a common struggle against the Europeans.

3. The Colonial Office have already asked on various occasions that suitable representations should be made to the Government of India about particular speeches on these lines. . . . In the past, we have not wished to push matters too far, realising that Mr. Nehru is apt to become emotional and unguarded in his public speeches, particularly on important occasions, and that nothing we say will eliminate the apparently ingrained "anti-colonialism" of Mr. Nehru and his followers, based as it apparently is on sincere conviction, historical prejudice, and possibly also on political opportunism. We hope that we might have been justified in our attitude when we saw Clutterbuck's[2] reports on the results of his representations to Pillai,[3]

---

[1] ie, the Amritsar massacre of 1919.

[2] Sir A Clutterbuck, high commissioner in India, 1952–1955.

[3] Sir R Pillai, secretary-general, Ministry of External Affairs, India, 1952–1960.

whose reactions as recently reported in his letter of the 12th March, 1953, to you were apologetic and reassuring.

4. Mr. Nehru's latest utterances, if accurately reported, however, seem to reveal that he has changed for the worse. They go further in calumny and provocation than anything that has gone before. There is reliable evidence that considerable feeling has already been aroused in responsible quarters here and throughout East Africa by such speeches and complaints are being made that such abusive and untrue statements are going unanswered by H.M.G.

5. In the circumstances, Mr. Lyttelton feels strongly that H.M.G. should make immediate and forthright representations to the Government of India about this speech, and furthermore that suitable publicity should be given to the fact that they have been made. He hopes that Lord Swinton will agree that these steps should be taken with the least possible delay.[4]

---

[4] On 17 Apr Swinton summoned the Indian high commissioner, Mr Kher, to the CRO, and delivered a verbal protest (whether he had seen Lloyd's letter of the same date before doing so cannot be ascertained). The record of the meeting appears as Annex II to 'Mr Nehru's speech' (Cabinet memo by Swinton, CAB 129/60, C(53)138, 23 Apr 1953), and was also sent as tel no 598 of 17 Apr 1953 to the British high commissioner in New Delhi. But on CRO advice, Swinton decided that 'it would be undesirable to give publicity to these representations' as requested by Lloyd (letter from Liesching to Lloyd, DO 35/5340, no 14, 20 Apr 1953).

132   DO 35/5340, no 19   20 Apr 1953
[Mr Nehru's speech on Kenya]: personal minute (M 89/53) by Mr Churchill to Lord Swinton

I am in entire agreement with your spirited reply[1] which I hope will be conveyed to Nehru. I never expected anything better from a Congress governed India. I used to try to tell this to the Baldwin-Macdonald Government. However, we have to make the best of what is left. It is about less than half of nothing. In fact it may well be that they only maintain a formal association with us because of the Sterling balances.

I am told, however, that the British in India get on very well with the Indians now that they have put aside their racial superiority. I am glad you said what you did.[2]

---

[1] ie, Swinton's rebuke to Kher, see 131, note 4.
[2] Swinton received Kher again on 23 Apr. On 28 Apr he reported to Cabinet that a reply had been received from Nehru 'which was conciliatory in tone' (CAB 128/26/1, CC 29(53)9, 28 Apr 1953).

133   DO 35/5340, no 47   11 June 1953
'Interview with Mr Nehru': note by Mr Lyttelton

Because of the violent and inflammatory statements that are appearing in the Indian press about Kenya I thought it advisable to seek an interview with Mr. Nehru. I saw him this morning and we talked for about three-quarters of an hour. I reviewed the Malayan situation and showed him how we had not only reduced the terrorism and banditry to very small proportions but how we had also won over the minds of the people. I described Operation Service to him (which is the name given in Malaya for the campaign designed to show the population that the police are their friends.) This campaign I said was being a striking success: the badges which are given out for acts of service are now to be seen far beyond the ranks of the police and are worn widely by the population. The number of reported instances when the police are of assistance to the civil population outside their ordinary duties is still about 20,000 a month.

I then said I was only giving Malaya as an illustration of the kind of thing we were trying to do and reminded him that all parties were agreed that our Colonial policy must be directed towards giving a greater amount of responsibility for the management of their own affairs to the peoples of all Colonial territories.

I then turned to Kenya. I told him that the population was coming over to the side of the Government in ever increasing numbers. At the request of the Asian community, conscription had been applied to them; that they were overwhelmingly on the side of the Government and had been most helpful. There were to be no constitutional advances during the acute phase of the Emergency. The reason for this was largely to meet the views of both Africans and Asians who feared that the Emergency might be used by the Europeans for getting a greater share in the Government than might be gained from any constitutional talks, between representatives of the three principal races.

Pandit Nehru interrupted once or twice, to emphasize his point that you could achieve nothing by force but had to win the confidence of the people. He gave me an interesting account of the largest public meeting he had ever addressed. He said that at one time about a thousand or two terrorists were holding up the whole life of the city of Calcutta and of its three and a half million inhabitants. He had addressed a meeting which he put at about 700,000 in the Maidan. He refused to allow guards or police intervention. The meeting opened by a bomb being thrown in the front row about 50 feet from the platform which killed a policeman and a civilian and wounded the thrower of the bomb. Afterwards a rifle shot was fired in the air at the back. He exhorted the people to see that they kept law and order themselves. After this meeting there were no further outbreaks in Calcutta. The people policed themselves. I had heard this story before and I said to him that the whole object of our policy was just that: to get the people to do these things for themselves. That was the object of organising the Kikuyu Home Guard and so forth. I told him we were dealing with quite a different kind of situation. He dismissed in one sentence the matter of law and order by saying that of course murder and banditry must be put down. He then went into a long homily about how the whole of Africa was embittered by British rule; that Kenya was perhaps the most startling example; that in the last year or so (sic) there had been a tremendous change in African opinion, which was now much inflamed; that people had to have something to hope for; that the Kenya troubles were due to a land hunger created by the Europeans who had seized the best land, and much more in the same style. It was quite clear that his opinions about Kenya were derived solely from the newspapers and that if he has had any official advice it has left a very wrong impression. From the Indian Commissioner it had been highly tendentious.[1] I told him in polite terms that his information was wrong and that I would be glad to supply the Government of India with a full report, weekly or

---

[1] Abu Pant, the Indian commissioner in Kenya. Pant became involved in local African politics and, at Britain's insistence, was recalled to New Delhi early in 1954. See 137, para 14.

monthly or whenever they liked, of what was really happening. He said he would like this, but it is quite clear that he is not going to read it, nor will any representations alter his view. He was polite and agreeable if somewhat didactic and I made about as much impression upon him as he made upon me. I think it is just possible that he may think twice before making quite such inflammatory speeches as the Amritzar [sic] day effort.

That is the most that I hope to expect from someone in whom the term Colonial or Colonialism produces a pathological and not an intellectual reaction.

134   CO 936/97, no 18   7 Aug 1953
[India at the UN]: letter from Sir J Martin to N Pritchard[1] advocating an approach to the Indian government to determine whether the Indian delegation intends to raise certain colonial issues at the UN

In recent years, we have made diplomatic approaches at this time to the Governments of Member States in the United Nations in the hope of diverting them from over-enthusiastic anti-Colonial attacks on us in the General Assembly. This year, as you know, the Foreign Office has already arranged preliminary soundings of select Governments and we shall shortly be writing to them to suggest that these might, in appropriate cases, be followed up by the representations on particular issues likely to arise in this year's Assembly.

2. So far, however, we have not considered an approach to India or Pakistan. I doubt if any useful purpose will be served by conveying a general exhortation to these Governments to be on good behaviour on Colonial matters—there is no evidence in our past experience that approaches on these lines have ever had any worthwhile results. Indeed, we doubt whether it is necessary to make any representations to Pakistan at all. The pattern of Pakistan behaviour in the Assembly seems to be that Zafrulla Khan, or some other leading spokesman, makes a single anti-Colonial speech on an important occasion (e.g. in Plenary Assembly) but that in the Committees, including the Fourth, the Pakistan delegation is usually quiescent and affable, if not exactly co-operative. It seems advisable for us to be content with this not altogether satisfactory state of affairs.

3. Equally, we are inclined to doubt whether any useful purpose will be served by attempting a general "softening up" of the Indians. Mr. Nehru's immovable prejudices on Colonial matters tend to make nonsense of our efforts to influence his officials and subordinates, and, in any case, the presence of Mrs. Pandit in New York as leader of the Indian delegation makes it unlikely that any cautionary words we might succeed in inserting in her brief will be interpreted in a spirit favourable to us. On the other hand, we have to reckon with two factors which, taken together, make it necessary for us to make some approach to the Indians.

4. In the first place, it is clear that the Indian Government, and particularly Mr. Nehru himself, are much concerned about events in Kenya and Central Africa, and it would be in keeping with previous Indian activity in the United Nations if they were to engineer, if not initiate, some discussion of these subjects in this year's

---

[1] N Pritchard, assistant under-secretary of state, CRO, 1951–1954.

Committee on Information and also, and more probably, in the Fourth Committee. Sir Alan Burns[2] has been privately warned by Khalidy of Iraq that the Arab/Asian group intends, in fact, to raise the Kenya situation in the Fourth Committee (the correspondence between the Foreign Office and New York in Foreign Office telegram 409 saving and its predecessors has some bearing on this). Also the Nyasaland chiefs and Michael Scott[3] have appealed to the United Nations to intervene in connection with Central African Federation and to seek an opinion from the International Court of Justice on the compatibility of the Federation Scheme with Article 73 of the Charter. We have succeeded in acquiring copies of the legal advice (by Dingle Foot and Sinclair Shaw) upon which this appeal is based, and it is evident that the appellants recognize that their only hope of getting Federation discussed in the United Nations is to persuade some influential member to raise it. They also recognize that India is the only member sympathetic to their cause with sufficient influence to organize a majority in favour either of discussion itself or of a reference to the International Court. It is true that in February this year Mr. Nehru stated publicly that India had not considered raising Federation in the United Nations, but that was before the opponents of Federation proposed reference to the United Nations, and before thay had any change of making the soundings of Indian Government feeling which it would be prudent to assume they have since made.

5.   The second factor is that India is much the most influential and persistent of the anti-Colonial leaders in the United Nations and, we believe, the brains of the Arab/Asian bloc when it comes to evolving ways of embarrassing the Colonial powers. She has had so much intimate experience of our susceptibilities on Colonial issues that she is able to put a finger on our weak sports with unerring accuracy. It is safe to say that if India can be dissuaded from initiating or supporting a particular anti-Colonial manoeuvre, her friends in the Arab/Asian bloc are either so clumsy or so lacking in genuine concern with Colonial issues that we should probably have no difficulty in killing that manoeuvre in the lobby.

6.   This year we could expect a fairly quiet Committee on Information and General Assembly (so far as Colonial questions are concerned) provided no attempt were made to discuss Kenya, Central African Federation, or self-determination in Cyprus. There is nothing legitimately on the agenda of the Committee or the Assembly which need create friction, but if any of these three subjects are raised, we shall be brought at once into a situation which we are anxious to avoid but which Cabinet memorandum C52(232)[4] envisaged, namely of having to use the threat of withdrawal in order to avoid discussion of the political affairs of Colonial territories.

7.   We are inclined to think that this danger can be minimized if we go to the Indian Government, and if practicable to Mr. Nehru himself, and enquire whether it is the intention of the Indian delegation or of any of its friends to raise Kenya, Federation or Cyprus in the Committee on Information or the Fourth Committee. If the answer is "yes" or non-commital [sic] we should make it plain that the raising of these issues would be regarded by us as a most unfriendly act which could not fail to damage very seriously our relations with the United Nations, and which we should have to oppose with the strongest sanctions available to us: for example, the discussion of these issues in the Committee on Information would compel us to

---

[2] Sir A Burns, UK permanent representative, UN Trusteeship Council, 1947–1956.
[3] Rev M Scott, co-founder and director of Africa Bureau (London).   [4] See 160.

withdraw from that Committee. There is no point, we feel, in talking to the Indians in this context about the effect of U.N. discussion in the territories concerned, or of embarking on persuasive argument about the merits of the issues. If the answer is "no" we should express gratification and say that we hope that the Indian representatives will be instructed to keep in close touch with the U.K. delegation should the possibility of discussion arise. If it can be borne in on the Indians that we are concerned to dissuade them not only from raising these matters themselves but also from working (as we know to our cost they do work) behind the scenes with the Secretariat and the other anti-Colonial delegations, so much the better.

8. We do not see any risk, that by such an approach we should put in the Indians' heads ideas which are not there already. It may be ineffictive [sic] but we do not believe that it would leave us worse off than if it had never been made. It is just possible that it might succeed. Before now there have been wars that might have been avoided if the enemy had known beforehand how strongly we should react to their aggression.

9. I trust that this suggestion of a particularized approach to the Indians on a specific topic will commend itself to you and that the Foreign Office will concur in the terms proposed in paragraph 7 above. If it is made, it ought to be made within the next week or so since the Committee on Information opens on the 18th August.

10. I am sending a copy of this letter to Paul Mason in the Foreign Office, and a copy is also going to Baxter[5] who will, I know, be interested from the point of view of his preoccupation with Central African Federation.

---

[5] G H Baxter, assistant under-secretary of state, CRO, 1947–1955.

135   CO 936/97, no 23   17 Aug 1953
[India at the UN]: letter (reply) from N Pritchard to Sir J Martin

Thank you for your letter of the 7th August (IRD 144/195/03) about the steps we might take to prevent the subjects of Kenya, Central African Federation and Cyprus being raised in either the Committee on Information or the General Assembly.[1]

2. Baxter is at present on leave, but I have consulted the other people in this Office who are concerned.

3. You may take it that we fully sympathise with your desire to prevent discussion of these subjects. As regards Central African Federation, Ministers have of course taken the firm line that discussion of it is outside the competence of either body. In the absence of any evidence that India intended to raise that item herself or to instigate its inclusion in the agenda we had not, however, contemplated raising the question with Delhi.

4. As regards your proposal for a general démarche in Delhi, it seems to me that there is a question of timing and a question of what should be said. We gather from the Foreign Office that, in their view, the chances of Federation, Kenya or Cyprus being raised in the Committee on Information are extremely remote. In the first place we have already made our attitude towards that Committee very clear, and I understand that our delegate at the forthcoming meeting is to re-emphasise that our

---

[1] See 134.

collaboration with the Committee is conditional on its good behaviour. Secondly, the membership of the Committee is such that an attempt by the anti-colonials to introduce any of these items into the agenda would seem too uncertain of success to be worth making. Is it not much more likely that, if the anti-colonials really want to raise any of these items, they will wish to do so in the Assembly rather than in this comparatively unimportant Committee, and will reserve their ammunition until then? In these circumstances our feeling is that it would be best not to make any approach to the Indians in the context of the Committee on Information. If our object therefore is to avert trouble in the Assembly there is not the same hurry; indeed it would probably be best to make an approach, if one is to be made, rather nearer the time.

5. As regards the substance of any approach, I understand that the Foreign Office could not agree to anything being said to the Indians that could be interpreted as a threat to withdraw from discussions in the United Nations without first getting the approval of their acting Secretary of State. They consider that the Cabinet approval given to C.P.52(232) would not necessarily cover the circumstances of an aproach at this stage to the Indian authorities. This would rather take the stuffing out of the sort of approach you have in mind.

6. In these circumstances our inclination is, a little later on—perhaps towards the end of the month—to authorise Middleton[2] to throw a fly over Pillai saying that we had heard rumours to the effect that these items might be raised in the United Nations and asking Pillai whether he also had heard them, and whether he thought there was anything in them. If Pillai were to indicate that any of these subjects was to be raised, he might then go on to say that, as Pillai well knows, we regard these matters as entirely within the sphere of our own domestic jurisdiction and therefore outside the competence of the United Nations, that we should of course have to make this very clear if such an attempt were made, and that he (Middleton) would have to report the information to Ministers here who he felt sure would be much disturbed.

7. If you are agreeable and the Foreign Office see no objection, I should be willing to ask Middleton to proceed accordingly. I realise that it is not altogether what you were asking for, but it would I think have the merit of clearing the air.

8. I am copying this letter to Michael Williams of the Foreign Office (in Paul Mason's absence on leave).

---

[2] G H Middleton, deputy high commissioner in India, 1953–1956.

136   CO 936/369   6 Oct 1954
[Indian anti-colonialism]: minute by W G Wilson[1] to W A C Mathieson

You have not, I think, seen these papers before. They were opened in 1953 (IRD.114/03 refers) in order to facilitate consideration of the impact of international anti-colonialism on public opinion in the colonial territories and also of the desirability, and feasibility, of taking account of the influence of anti-colonialism in determining our colonial policies in general. Put baldly, the I.R.D. thesis is that the

---

[1] W G Wilson, principal, International Relations Dept, CO.

antipathy towards "colonialism" among influential governments in the world is such that it is a concrete and important factor factor affecting H.M. Government's ability to maintain satisfactory foreign relations and to achieve the objectives of United Kingdom foreign policy. In addition, we were, and are, convinced that anti-colonial opinion is so strong in international affairs that it has created a climate in which it is no longer possible for the Colonial Office and Colonial Governments to pursue political, economic and social policies in the territories without taking account of the repercussions of those policies on international opinion, since to do so may very well, and often does, stimulate criticism and discussion which is fed back into the minds and attitudes of indigenous politicians and thus reacts on our ability to carry the policies themselves through. We felt, therefore, that it would be well if some means could be devised of providing the policy forming departments in the Office with useful and timely advice from those departments (e.g. I.R.D., Information, Defence) who are responsible for keeping in touch with international and public opinion on colonial questions, in order that the likely reaction of policies in contemplation on international and public opinion could be taken into account in the formulation of those policies.

2. To this end the paper at (50) on IRD.164/139/02 was prepared and was considered by a meeting of Under-Secretaries, the results of which are recorded in (52) on that file. Subsequent developments are recorded in the minutes by Sir J Martin and Sir T Lloyd of the 14th and 16th December, 1953. They amounted to the following:—

(a) A draft Cabinet Paper was to be prepared to apprise Ministers of the extent and dangers of Indian involvement in colonial politics.

(b) A minute was to be sent to Heads of Departments affirming the need to keep Information Departments and I.R.D. in close touch with the formulation and development of policy, and urging that these Departments should be closely associated with action, involving relations with the Foreign Office and the Commonwealth Relations Office, on disputes with foreign countries affecting colonial territories.

(c) A series of monthly meetings, to be attended by representatives of I.R.D., Information Department, Defence Department, Social Services Department and Geographical Departments currently in the news was to be instituted at the Principal level in order that the policies of these Departments in relation to specific problems might be co-ordinated and the experience of each Department made available to the advantage of the others. In his minute of the 16th December, 1953, Sir T Lloyd asked for a report, after six months, of the usefulness of these meetings.

3. In theory, these arrangements should have sufficed to accomplish the objectives indicated in the first paragraph of this minute. In practice, they have failed to do so. The draft Cabinet Paper was, in fact, prepared and constituted, in my view at least, a remarkable exposé of the extent and influence of Indian anti-colonialism on colonial political affairs, especially of East Africa. The main purpose of this paper (which you have seen on the relevant file) was to apprise the Cabinet of this situation: its recommendations for action were in themselves mild and conservative. They recognised that there was little prospect of bringing about any fundamental change in the attitude of the Indian Government or of taking any spectacular measures to

minimise the effect of Indian policy in the colonial territories. They consisted mainly in the suggestion that we should recognise the positive nature of the Indian menace and determine our policies accordingly, and also that we should engage in certain marginal diplomatic and information activities which might, in the very long run, bring about an improvement in the Indian attitude to colonial questions. The paper was referred to the Commonwealth Relations Office, where it raised the hackles of the pro-Indian element. A Commonwealth Relations Office redraft which consisted of little more than an apologia for Indian anti-colonialism was evolved and there the project has foundered for the time being.[2]

4. The minute to Heads of Departments issued over Sir Charles Jeffries' signature on the 27th February, 1954 and is registered at (54) on IRD.164/139/023. It cannot be said that this minute made any impact on Geographical Departments. Indeed, we have on two occasions been obliged to muscle in on certain issues which, under this minute, should have been referred to us in the normal course of events, and there is no doubt that our intervention produced, in each case, a significant change in tactics and averted what would otherwise have been the development of a serious situation.

5. The meetings of Principals were instituted in February and continued until August, but they were, it must be admitted, of little value and made no impact on departmental action. This may have been due to failure on the part of I.R.D. to bring home to the other participants the purpose and potential value of the meetings: it is much more likely that it was due to the fact that such ad hoc meetings cannot, in the nature of things, replace inter-departmental consultation of a more orthodox kind, e.g. on files and through inter-departmental meetings on specific topics. Possibly, also, the meetings would have served a more valuable purpose had they been held at a higher level: it rapidly became evident that few of the participants were willing to accept the validity of the thesis indicated in the first paragraph of this minute despite its implicit endorsement by Under-Secretaries and indeed, in the case of one Department, there was a decided reluctance, exemplified in absence from all but the first of the meetings, to participate in the exercise at all.

6. It seems, therefore, that there are few results to report from the somewhat elaborate exercise enshrined on these papers. Certainly the three bits of action taken have produced no direct results: a fact painfully demonstrated in the case of the minute by the two instances referred to above. There have, however, been certain indirect, but I think still tangible results. The very act of consulting the C.R.O. about the Indian Cabinet Paper cannot have failed to bring the C.R.O. out of the cloud-cuckoo land in which they determined their attitude to Indian policy on colonial questions before it was drafted, and though there are few signs that it induced any modification in the more staunch supporters of Mr. Nehru in that Office, the fringe of the Indian bloc there is visibly crumbling. So far as the meetings were concerned, although they themselves died an unsatisfactory death in August, they have left behind the beginnings of much closer consultation between I.R.D. and Information Department especially in the matters within the purview of Mr. D. Williams. I think too that our intervention in the two instances mentioned in paragraph 4 above was genuinely appreciated by the Geographical Department concerned, and we may hope that the help we gave there may become known to other Geographical Departments who will thereafter be willing to use our experience

---

[2] The paper went to Cabinet in Jan 1955, see 137.

2A

and knowledge to their own advantage when faced with similar problems. Outside the main stream of action on these papers, we have been able to sound a warning about anti-colonialism and its implications for United Kingdom interests and policies in the two speeches delivered by the Minister of State to the Conservative Commonwealth Council (see (1) and (3)) and there is a fair amount of evidence, not registered on the file, that the opinions there expounded have found their way, through the Conservative Central Office, into the thinking of journalists and politicians.

7. I am tempted, on leaving the Department, to set down some suggestions for continuing the development of the ideas behind the action on this file, but since it is apparent from our conversations that you accept the thesis outlined in the first paragraph of this minute, you may prefer to brood over these papers and to formulate fresh ideas in the light of the lessons learnt from the, generally speaking, abortive action hitherto taken.

137 CAB 129/73, C(55)10   20 Jan 1955
'Indian communities in the colonies': Cabinet memorandum by Mr Lennox-Boyd

Population growth

Indian interest in British Colonies dates from the last quarter of the nineteenth century, when large numbers of immigrants from the sub-continent of India entered Mauritius, Fiji, Trinidad, British Guiana and Malaya as indentured labour and East Africa as small traders and railway labourers. In the last quarter of a century immigration has become less important than prodigious natural increase as a factor in population growth. Immigration is also now controlled by legislation. In some territories Indians are the largest single element in the population, and often dominate the economic field. For instance, the Indian population of East Africa, where on the average each Indian woman has 6 children, has risen from about 5,000 in 1901 to 259,000 in mid-1954, a development unknown in most parts of the world, and on present trends it will double itself in the two decades between 1948 and 1968. In Fiji, the Indians who were a small minority in 1901, now outnumber the native Fijians. In Mauritius, the Indian population now has a absolute majority over the rest of the population and in British Guiana they are the largest racial group and nearly half the total population. Considerable Indian communities are to be found in Aden and Singapore. Smaller Indian communities, mainly of the merchant class, also exist in other colonial territories, *e.g.*, Gibraltar, Jamaica, Hong Kong, West and Central Africa. In nearly all territories the proportion of Indians who would now regard Pakistan as their mother country is small and they are the less vigorous element in the Indian population. (Illustrative statistics on the facts given above are to be found in the tables annexed to this paper.)[1]

2. There has been in the past and there still is a place in the economic life of the African territories at any rate which the Asian has filled because there has been no other race capable already to fill it. Thus in East Africa the Asians constitute a

---

[1] Annexes not printed.

number of essential cogs in the economic machine as clerks, technicians and petty shopkeepers and until Africans have been trained, their presence is indispensable. Moreover, as shown by recent constitutional developments in Kenya, Uganda and Tanganyika, it is accepted policy to treat Asian residents both in Africa and in other territories as citizens in the fullest sense of the word, since this is the only hope of attracting their wholehearted loyalty to the territory in which they live. Any other attitude would be unfair to people who have entered in good faith and of whom many have made a very substantial contribution to the economic development of the territories concerned. Colonial Governments in East Africa and elsewhere recognise that the rate of reproduction of the existing Asian population, coupled with the inevitable advance towards some form or other of representative government, must confer on the Asian population a steadily increasing importance in the politics of their territories. Any attempt to deny them political rights and opportunities similar to those given to other races will result in the very situation which we want to avoid, *i.e.*, that they will look to India for their protection.

3. However, their occupations, their religion, and for a long time the professedly temporary nature of their residence have all reinforced their tendency to resist assimilation. The experience of territories outside Africa where Indians have achieved both numerical superiority and substantial political rights indicates some of the difficulties which this is causing—difficulties which may be in store for the plural societies of East and Central Africa. In Mauritius the introduction of the 1947 constitution, with an extended franchise, has permitted Indo-Mauritians to exploit their great numerical superiority; and in the past 6 years they have, in conjunction with some of the coloured elements, achieved a coherent and predominant position as a political party. The danger in Mauritius is less the threat of direct Indian intervention in the affairs of the Colony than racial and social discord derived from the fear of Indian domination in the minds of the Franco-Mauritian population which for a century and a half, controlled the political, and still controls the economic, fortunes of the Colony.

4. In Fiji the rapid increase in the Indian population has caused an undercurrent of anxiety about the future in each of the main racial groups. The Fijians (and also the Europeans) resent the occupation of some of the most fertile and easiest worked land by the Indians, the prominent part played by Indians in public affairs and in commerce and the general influence which they appear to wield. The Indians fear that they will not have enough land for their growing numbers and are uncertain whether they will be able to continue to occupy the land which they at present lease from the Fijians. They also desire a greater share in the direction of public affairs commensurate with their numbers and capacity.

5. In British Guiana the East Indian element in the population has now shaken off its earlier lethargy, its increased self-assertiveness being particularly marked since India received her independence in 1947. Indians are tending to play a major part in the commercial and economic life of the Colony and the Civil Service, and to displace Portuguese, Syrians, Creoles and Africans from these occupations. The People's Progressive Party, which was responsible for the constitutional crisis in 1953, was not a racial party in that it contained both leaders and members of Indian and of African descent. (Its main racial bias was anti-white.) Its internal stresses were and are partly, but by no means wholly, on racial lines. In the Colony as a whole, however, racial tension has tended to increase and is likely to become a serious

political problem. In evidence given before the recent Constitutional Commission, Guianese of African origin stated their impression that many Indians looked forward to the day when British Guiana would be part not of the British Commonwealth but of an East Indian Empire.

6.   In Trinidad, the Indians, who for the most part arrived as coolies, now hold a much higher proportion of the wealth in land and property than other racial groups. They are already 35 per cent. of the total population, and as they grow in numbers and influence, they are organising themselves politically on racial lines through the Hindu Mahasbha. A strong East Indian political party is likely to emerge in the near future, both as the Colony approaches self-government and also in opposition to Caribbean Federation, which East Indians dislike because it would swamp them in a unit with an overwhelmingly African population. It is even possible that a racial East Indian party may hold the predominance of power in the Legislature after the next election. The development of politics on such lines can, of course, only result in an increase of racial tension in the Colony.

Policy towards Indian immigration into colonial territories
7.   The realisation of such dangers and the natural increase of population in the East and Central African territories has led the East and Central African Governments to the decision that Indian immigration should be severely curtailed, both in order that the political problems of plural societies shall not be aggravated and to permit the African to take his proper place in the economic life of his territory. This general policy is, therefore, to limit further Asian immigration to the minimum subject to:—

(a) the need to avoid clear-cut discrimination embodied in legislation, which would give the Indian Government reason for airing the matter internationally, particularly with regard to the Trust Territory of Tanganyika;
(b) the need to preserve the supply of skilled and semi-skilled artisans for which India remains the principal source.

8.   The effectiveness of immigration policy in East Africa largely depends on immigration machinery; under existing legislation it is difficult for the Executive to apply recognised policy with vigour and discretion. The desirability of amending East African legislation in order to provide for the necessary machinery to control further Asian immigration is recognised, and ways of doing it are now being worked out by the East African Governments and the Colonial Office.

9.   Indian immigration into Fiji, Mauritius and the West Indian territories has virtually stopped and is no longer a significant factor.

Policy of the Government of India on colonial affairs
10.   This policy may be summarized as follows:—

(a) to foster links between Indian communities in colonial territories and India itself (while paying lip-service in public to the principle that Indians should integrate themselves into the territories in which they live);
(b) to build up the position of India as a champion of coloured peoples everywhere, and as the leader of those who wish to throw off "imperialist" domination and achieve self-determination and independence. In pursuing this

policy, more especially in the United Nations, India stimulates and exploits the international hostility to the Colonial Powers which hampers the United Kingdom in foreign affairs generally.

11. Reports received from a number of Governors show that the two aspects of this policy together constitute the most persistent and most unsettling of the various external influences which stimulate anti-British, anti-government and the extreme nationalist feelings in Colonial territories.

(a) *Links between India and Indian communities in the colonies*

12. Since the earliest days of Indian immigration the Government of India has striven to exercise a "protective" interest in the large communities of persons of Indian origin now settled in a number of colonial territories. At the time when India became an independent member of the Commonwealth it was agreed, after consideration by Ministers, that it would not be possible to deny to her the usual Commonwealth privileges of representation of a consular character in colonial territories, provided it was clear that the Indian representatives could not intervene in local political affairs as the protectors of settled Indian communities or otherwise. Indian Commissioners were subsequently appointed for East and Central Africa, Fiji, Mauritius, the West Indies and British Guiana, Aden, and recently Hong Kong and West Africa (the Gold Coast and Nigeria). The position of the Indian representative (formerly Indian Agent) in Malaya (established many years ago) has been brought into line with that of Commissioners in other territories.

13. It is clear that the Government of India and its Representatives are still inclined to regard themselves as the protectors of such communities. Mr. Krishna Menon, when Indian High Commissioner in London, made a number of representations to my predecessors on questions affecting Indians in colonial territories, even where these matters were of political character entirely within the jurisdiction of the local government (*e.g.*, on education policy in Kenya and land and taxation policy in Fiji). More recent representations have been made (towards the end of 1953) in two formal aide-mémoires from the Government of India. The first dealt with immigration into Northern Rhodesia (which increased sharply before Federation) and the effects of Central African federation in this and other fields. Among other things, including criticism of the Federation scheme itself, this aide-mémoire alleged discrimination in immigration restrictions on Indians. The second dealt with events in East Africa, British Guiana and our general colonial policy. Such representations have in the past been treated with the tolerance fitting relations between members of the "Commonwealth family."

14. Until recently the only area in which the Indian Commissioner had given serious cause for complaint was East Africa, but the Indian Commissioners in Trinidad and Mauritius both appear to have contravened their instructions. Although no formal evidence is yet available against the former, the Governor has reported that there is no doubt that he has participated energetically in local politics and organised East Indian opposition to Caribbean Federation while the latter has circulated material critical of the South African Government. In East and Central Africa, the transgressions of Mr. Pant, the Indian Commissioner there, and his Deputy, Mr. Rahman, were frequent and often blatant. Reports of these activities revealed a correct attitude in public but in private a consistent meddling of varying

degrees of importance in the political affairs of East and Central Africa and association with persons of positive and potentially subversive tendencies. Mr. Pant and his Deputy were reported as advising Africans against Central African Federation, actively supporting the Kenya African Union, having contact with Mau Mau leaders, financing African politicians, organising an African political newspaper, and attempting to organise new political parties. These activites became so dangerous that representations were made to the Government of India, which resulted first in the recall of Rahman in the middle of 1953, and then the recall of Pant early in 1954. The new Commissioner is a great improvement.

(b) *Indian attitude at the United Nations*

15. Although there has been some abatement very recently, Indian representatives at the United Nations have been foremost in criticising the "evils of colonialism" and the "right" of dependent peoples to self-determination and independence, and they have fostered the idea that non-self-governing territories and those territories alone are characterised by denial of human rights, economic exploitation and race discrimination. They have also played a large part in attempts to establish the accountability of colonial powers to the United Nations for the administration of their non-self-governing territories, particularly as regards the development of self-government and the exercise of self-determination.

Conclusions and recommendations

16. (a) The best way of meeting the Indian problem and of reducing Indian interference in British colonial territories is through success in handling the wider problems of the plural societies of which the Indian communities form a part. The experience of Fiji, Mauritius and the West Indies shows the kind of difficulty which a policy of integration of resident Indian communities will necessarily involve, but there is no alternative policy. If we fail to retain the loyalty of the Indians settled in British colonial territories, we shall only aggravate the risk of interference from India. It should be the continued aim of our political and social policy to strengthen the link between Indian communities and the Government of their territory of residence and to strengthen their loyalty to the Crown.

(b) At the same time we should not aggravate the problem further by permitting any significant increase in the Asian population (other than the inevitable and formidable natural increase) through immigration. Efforts to improve East African legislation should be stepped up, and other Colonial Governments (*e.g.*, in West Africa) should, if necessary, be advised to exercise a similar control to prevent the emergence of an Indian problem there also.

(c) A careful watch should be maintained upon the activities of Indian Commissioners in colonial territories.

(d) Every opportunity should be taken to inform and influence the Government of India and Indian opinion generally on colonial questions.

(e) Suitably firm and public action should be taken in the United Nations and elsewhere to counter particularly tendentious and offensive speeches and actions by Indian representatives.

138 CAB 128/28, CC 15(55)1   17 Feb 1955
[Indian communities in the colonies]: Cabinet conclusions

The Cabinet considered a memorandum[1] by the Colonial Secretary on the problem presented by the growth of Indian communities in British Colonial territories.

The Colonial Secretary said that, although he sought no immediate decisions on this problem, he had thought it right to bring it to the notice of the Cabinet since it was one which Ministers should have constantly in their minds. There were substantial Indian communities in many of the Colonies, both in Africa and elsewhere, and their rate of natural increase was alarming. In some Colonies this was already giving rise to racial tension.

In discussion the following points were made:—

(a) The attitude of the Indian Government towards these communities should be closely watched. It was at present their professed policy that Indians settled overseas should regard themselves as members of the community in which they lived. It was, however, stated in paragraph 10 of C. (55) 10 that, while professing this policy, the Indian Government lost no opportunity to foster links between India and these overseas communities.

(b) Close attention should be given to the activities of Indian Commissioners in Colonial territories. The Indian Government had recognised that these representatives should not intervene in the domestic politics of the countries where they were stationed; and it was open to us to press, as we had done successfully in the past, for the recall of any Indian Commissioner whose activities transgressed this principle.

The title "Commissioner" gave these representatives a higher local status than that of the Trade Commissioners of other Commonwealth countries. It was for consideration whether those countries should not be asked to change the title of their representatives, so as to deprive the Indian Commissioners of the superior status which they now enjoyed.

(c) Colonial Governments could take steps to restrict further immigration of Indians. The Indian Government had not disputed the right of other Commonwealth countries to restrict Indian immigration into their territories.

(d) In paragraph 16(e) of C. (55) 10 it was proposed that public action should be taken in the United Nations and elsewhere to counter tendentious speeches and actions by Indian representatives. It was suggested that on most occasions it would be preferable, and more effective, to proceed by way of private representations to the Indian Government.

The Prime Minister said that, while he recognised the gravity of this problem, he did not think the time was opportune for any drastic action in respect of it which might given offence to the Indian Government. India was in a position to exercise a moderating influence in Asia; and it was specially important at the present time that she should maintain the closest possible association with us in the handling of the major international problems of the day. It need not be assumed that in all Colonies Indian communities would prove an embarrassment to us: in some they might even be a balancing factor. Thus, although the problem should be carefully watched, precipitate action should be avoided.

---

[1] See 137.

The Lord President doubted whether action could be long delayed. He was specially impressed by the considerations summarised in paragraph 10 of C. (55) 10. He believed that in this matter the policy of the Indian Government was likely to be influenced by their desire to champion coloured peoples and to encourage opposition to Colonial rule.

The Cabinet:—

Took note of C. (55) 10 and agreed to resume their consideration of this problem later in the year.

139   DO 35/5344, no 23   [7 July 1955]
'India and the colonial problem': note by R C Ormerod[1]

Indian attitude on colonial questions

The Indian attitude to colonial questions, and in particular to the U.K. Government's colonial policy, is deep-rooted and from time to time subjects our relations with the Government of India to a certain strain. In deciding on our policy for meeting the hostility with which India sometimes confronts us on colonial matters, it is important to weigh the good relations we enjoy with India in other fields. We must also consider the degree to which we may be able to influence Indian foreign policy, since in some areas India carries great weight. The co-operation of India in economic matters is also of great importance. Unsatisfactory though India's anti-colonial attitude may be therefore in a member of the Commonwealth, it must remain our policy so to defend our interests in the colonial field as to minimise the area of friction.

2. The emotions felt throughout India on colonial questions are comparable to, but go deeper than, the anti-colonial prejudice traditionally felt in the United States. Indian memories of "imperialism" are of course very recent. Few colonial problems are considered in India quite rationally or on their merits and Indian criticism is sometimes not only unfair and unconstructive, but leaves the impression that the Government of India are more concerned with urging natives everywhere to throw off the yoke, however unready they may be to govern themselves, than in finding solutions of what are, after all, the U.K.'s domestic problems. It is a deep-rooted conviction with Indians that it is a crime for one race to rule over another. They feel that a tolerable relationship between East and West is now by and large being worked out in Asia, largely as a result of their own long struggle for freedom but also because of our liberal policy in granting independence to dependent peoples, which they are ready to recognise. Thus they have not, as Mr. MacDonald will be aware, made any difficulties for us over Malaya. But when they look at Africa and see what they regard as every form of white domination, from French oppresion in the North to Apartheid in the South, they fear the danger of a very grave racial conflict. From this standpoint, Nationalist policy in South Africa (and our very proper refusal to interfere in its internal matters) has done us great damage. They feel that, racial discrimination being everywhere an evil, the fact that it should actually be enjoined

---

[1] R C Ormerod, CRO, 1953–1956. Ormerod's note is a condensed version of a document drafted by A F Morley (assistant under-secretary of state, CRO, 1954–1956; deputy high commissioner, Calcutta, 1956–1957) for the new S of S for Commonwealth relations, Lord Home, in Apr 1955.

by law in a certain country and made the basis of its internal policy is indefensible. Our enforced silence over South Africa, coupled with the violence in Kenya, has led to a feeling that we ourselves, in spite of our liberal professions, are not always free from an innate desire to keep natives in their place, at least in territories where there are permanent European settlers. With this background, Mr. Nehru's desire to play a leading part on the international stage and to build up the position of India as a champion of non-European peoples everywhere has inevitably resulted in much being said by Indians in public attacks on our Colonial record. At the same time there is no evidence at all of any deliberate Indian policy to supplant us in any colony as is sometimes alleged to exist, chiefly in East Africa. The Indian leaders regard themselves rather as responsible for handing on the torch of freedom and teaching others the lesson of their long, but eventually successful, struggle against white domination.

3. In these circumstances no radical change can be expected in the Indian attitude in the near future. But with increasing experience and understanding of the objectives of our policy and the practical difficulties which have to be met, the tone of Indian criticism may be considerably softened. This objective can be achieved only by methods of diplomacy and constant attempts to define and explain, both to the Government of India and through publicity channels to the Indian people, the policies which we are following in the colonial field. In the last two years the flow of information to the Government of India on colonial matters has grown considerably, though efforts are still needed, and are being made, to expand it. It is possible to detect some improvement in the attitude of the Indian leaders and Government during this period. Mr. Nehru, for example, has not recently made such forthright public criticisms of us as he did towards the end of 1953 and it is arguable that the full information which we gave the Indian authorities about the suspension of the Constitution of British Guiana in 1953 was an important cause of the unusually detached attitude which he and his government took towards Mr. Jagan[2] when, to their embarrassment, the latter decided to tour India.

Indian communities in the colonies

4. Closely connected with the problem of Indian views on colonialism is the problem of populations of Indian race in the Colonies. These communities present a number of difficulties. They generally increase more rapidly than the rest of the population. They tend to monopolise sections of the countries' commercial life and they resist full integration into the life of their territories. Their mere presence may give rise to local difficulties and to provoke emotional reactions, particularly among European settler populations. On the other hand, they not unnaturally maintain where they can close personal and cultural links with their mother country. The main communities go back to the middle of the last century and at the turn of the century many Indians were migrating overseas either as indentured labour or under their own arrangements. Such migration has now almost completely ceased but the local communities are in many cases expanding rapidly through natural increase. In Fiji the Indians, a small minority in 1901, now outnumber the native Fijians. In Mauritius the Indian population is now two-thirds of the whole. In East Africa in 50

---

[2] C Jagan, minister of agriculture, lands and mines, British Guiana, May–Oct 1953. See part II of this volume, 336.

years it has risen from 5,000 to over 200,000 and in another 30 years is expected to reach 500,000.

5. The policy of the Indian Government was outlined by the President in Parliament on 31st January, 1950, and has been frequently proclaimed by Mr. Nehru and others. The President said, "India has large numbers of her children living in countries abroad, notably in Africa and Fiji, in the West Indies, in the Island of Mauritius and elsewhere. Our advice to them has always been that they should ifentify themselves with the indigenous people and look upon their country of adoption as their real home". The President did not mention that his Government also consider that the Indian settler communities should strengthen their *cultural* relations with India. This strengthening is the firm policy of the Indian Government, promoted by intensive information and cultural activity by their representatives and by the provison of scholarships for study in India. We can take no exception to this in principle, though in practice it is not easy to forge cultural links without effect on political loyalties. As several Indian Commissioners in British Colonies have found, it is not always easy to know where cultural activity ends and political interference begins.

Indian commissioners in the colonies

6. The Government of India had, before 1947, Agents in Ceylon and Malaya who watched over certain interests of the Indian community. On the attainment of independence it was felt that we could not resist the wishes of the Indian Government to be allowed to appoint their own representatives in other colonial territories. It was agreed that a number of such appointments might be made, the functions of the Indian Commissioners (as they were now to be called) being defined by agreed Instructions which laid down that their protection extended only to Indians not permanently resident in the Colony in question, and that they should not interfere in local political affairs. Besides Malaya there are now Indian Commissioners in East and Central Africa, West Africa (the Gold Coast and Nigeria), Fiji, Mauritius, the West Indies, Aden and Hong Kong. These Commissioners are often in a difficult position where there is a large resident Indian population. Many of them have been inexperienced and the Indian settlers tend to look to them as their natural spokesmen. To act in conformity with the Instructions in these circumstances demands a clarity of judgment which not all Indian Commissioners have possessed. Though the Governors of some territories have had occasion sometimes to give an Indian Commissioner a quiet warning, most of the Commissioners who from time to time have held the eight posts have in fact caused no serious trouble. In East Africa, however, Mr. Pant had to be recalled at our behest after he had been found to have been infringing his instructions; only a few months earlier his second-in-command had also been withdrawn at our instance. Otherwise, until the end of last year, there had been few serious complaints.

The case of Mr. Nanda

7. At the end of last year as efforts were being made to coax the West Indies towards federation, the activities of Mr. Nanda, the newly appointed Indian Commissioner there who resides in the key territory of Trinidad, began to come to adverse notice. In view of his previous record it came as a surprise to us to hear reports from Trinidad that he had been acting as a focus for East Indian opposition to Caribbean Federation and had attracted [sic] himself some of the less desirable

Indian politicians with whom, so intelligence reports stated, he had been concocting plans for the organisation and policy of a new political party of Trinidad Indians opposed to Federation. He was also accused of approaching Indians of British Guiana to persuade them also to oppose Federation. While the Colonial Office were preparing their case for the C.R.O. to consider presenting to the Government of India, Mr. Hopkinson, the Minister of State at the Colonial Office, mentioned the matter "privately" to Mr. Krishna Menon on 30th March, 1955. Mr. Menon at once undertook to arrange for Mr. Nanda's early recall and on return to India raised the matter with Sir Raghavan Pillai. Sir R Pillai was indignant at this method of approach and informed Sir Alexander Clutterbuck that matters affecting his staff should only be raised through him. At Sir R Pillai's request, full particulars of the case against Mr. Nanda were sent him. Sir A Clutterbuck subsequently discussed the matter with the Commonwealth Secretary in Delhi, Mr. Dutt, who informed Mr. Nehru, whose reactions, as we have since heard, at this preliminary hearing were "comparatively restrained". Mr. Nanda's statement of his own case was obtained from the Indians and has been sent to Trinidad for consideration by the Government. There the matter still stands.

Indian publicity material

8. It is occasionally necessary to take up with the Government of India cases of tendentious or undesirable Indian publicity material affecting the Colonies. The only known case of a clear breach of proprietary by the Government of India was a pamphlet re-printing some comments on policy in East Africa by a correspondent of the *Hindustan Times*, which was distributed in 1953 in the U.N. by India House. The Government of India readily apologised and withdrew the pamphlet when the matter was brought to their attention. More frequently material comes to notice which would be harmless enough to Indian or British eyes but which, it is felt by Colonial Governments, could have a dangerous effect among more primitive peoples. Thus it was found necessary to prohibit the circulation in Nyasaland and Northern Rhodesia of an abridged version of Mr. Nehru's biography on the ground that it was liable to foment civil disobedience (which would probably not in Africa be non-violent) among the Africans of that territory. The occasional distribution of objectionable material through Indian official channels (e.g. Indian Commissioners, who have legitimate information functions) need not be attributed to sinister motives. We cannot, however, permit it when our colonial interests are thereby endangered.

9. Our policy in dealing with Indian anti-colonialism in its various contexts may be summarised as follows:—

(a) Since our relations with India in other fields are close and fruitful, it is our aim to minimise friction in the colonial field. In general we avoid public recriminations.

(b) By the supply of information on U.K. Colonial policy it is our constant endeavour to persuade the Indian Government and people to take a more reasonable and favourable view of our Colonial policy.

(c) We endorse the officially stated policy of the Government of India to encourage Indians in the Colonies in every way possible to identify themselves with the territory of their adoption and follow this policy ourselves. We cannot object to their retaining cultural links with India. We must hold Indian Commissioners to their Instructions.

140   DO 35/5344, no 27A   12 Sept 1956

**'India: Indian interest in colonial Africa': despatch no 149 from
G H Middleton (New Delhi)[1] to Mr Crookshank[2]**

I have the honour to report that a number of events in the past few months have seemed to quicken the interest, never quiescent for long, of Indians in the affairs of colonial Africa. The Afro-Asian Conference at Bandung was a strong stimulant. Other events have been the campaign by the Africans of Uganda against the proposal to appoint an Asian Minister to the Protectorate Legislative Council; the visit to East Africa of Mr. S.K. Patil, an influential member of the Congress Working Committee; the holding of an exhibition in Bombay on the "African Question" and the opening at Delhi University of a School of African Studies. To these may be added the activities of the growing number of Africans studying in India, which now provide a permanent stimulus of interest in African matters.

2.   In their approach to the affairs of the African continent, Indians are confronted with the fundamental problem of trying to reconcile two desires which are often mutually conflicting. One is an earnest wish to see as speedy an end as possible to the colonial system of government; the other is an understandable concern for the welfare of the large Indian communities in many of the African colonies to which Indians at home are linked by ties of kinship, language and custom. In the past, when neither the overseas Indian nor the African played a direct part in colonial government and the physical links between the two continents were less close and effective, the educated Indian in this country could happily be illogical and inconsistent in his views on these two basic issues. It is becoming increasingly difficult for him not to look at events more realistically.

3.   The hostility shown to the overseas Indians by the Africans in Uganda caused much concern in India and, both during his East African tour and on his return to Bombay, Mr. S.K. Patil referred in public speeches to their position. In Nairobi he was at pains to emphasise their goodwill towards the Africans and their desire to help them in the "fulfilment of their aspirations." In Bombay, the chief city of the State from which many of the Indians in Africa are sprung, he found it politic to put greater stress on the part these settlers had played in developing the territories in which they were now living and on their right to stay there. Since Mr. Patil's speeches the Indian newspapers have printed a number of letters from African students in India on Indian Government Cultural Scholarships. These letters were strongly critical of the past performance and the present attitude of the Indian settlers in Africa. The Bombay newspapers have in their turn published indignant denials of these charges from Indians at home who have connections with Africa.

4.   This emphasis on one of the two aspects of African affairs about which Indians are especially sensitive has naturally dampened down for the time being the fervour with which they usually prosecute their campaign on the other—the securing for the Africans of their "legitimate aspirations." It may have been for this reason that the "African Question" exhibition in Bombay proved to be something of a failure. Some of the usual techniques were certainly employed. The real significance of graphs and pictures was distorted by setting them among violently anti-colonial quotations and

---

[1] Acting UK high commissioner.   [2] H C Crookshank, lord privy seal, 1952–1955.

captions and the opening speech by Sardar K.M. Panikkar, the well-known Indian historian and one-time Indian Ambassador in Peking, was larded with the usual anti-colonial themes. A new development was the holding of a forum on race tensions in Africa between four Africa students—one from Ethiopia, one from the Gold Coast and two from Kenya. The exhibition was, however, poorly reported and badly attended, while some of the speeches, notably one by Mr. S.K. Patil, did much to counterbalance the effect of that delivered by Sardar Panikkar.

5. Well in advance of Indian public opinion as a whole the Government of India has been prepared for some time to express opinions on African problems that, at least in theory, are consistent and objective. Their declared policy in the case of overseas Indians is that they should be encouraged to acquire the citizenship of their country of domicile. Their views about the future of the multi-racial colonies, where so many of the problems are at their most marked, are that all the inhabitants, no matter what their racial origin, should co-operate on the basis of a common electoral roll in building up a system of government where there are no prejudices and no inequalities arising from differences of race, creed or colour. In practice, defending these policies has been no easy task when Indians at home signally fail to understand that, if their kinsmen abroad decide they wish to remain permanently in the territory in which they have settled, their affairs no longer remain the direct concern of the Government of India; and when, on the other hand, the Africans whose cause they are ready and eager to champion display so marked an antipathy towards those Indians who are living in their midst. The events of the past few months must have convinced Mr. Nehru that the conflicting pressures were becoming too insistent and that the time had come to indicate on whose side—the African or overseas Indian—his Government would come down should a decision ever have to be made. In a speech on August 6th at the formal opening of the School of African Studies at Delhi University, he made it quite plain that, so long as the present leaders remain in power in India, they will continue to follow the affairs of their kinsmen in Africa with sympathetic interest, but that pride of place will be given to assisting the African. To the latter he gave an assurance that India had no intention whatsoever of indulging in economic exploitation of their continent; to the former he said that if they could not live in harmony with the Africans then "the sooner they came home the better." The vast majority of Indians accept without question the policies followed by Mr. Nehru in the international field and so far there has been a marked absence of reaction to this part of his Delhi University speech. It will be interesting to see whether, in a case where the personal relationships of many of them are affected, they will be equally content to follow the path he has indicated.

6. Although much of Mr. Nehru's speech was couched in the impulsive language which he is sometimes apt to use in public, the Government of India have in practice tended more and more to show moderation in dealing with African problems both officially and in Parliament. It would, unfortunately, be idle to pretend that Indians in general have learnt as many lessons as the Ministers and officials who have had the practical experience in recent years which has undoubtedly helped to modify their former opinions. Much of the press—notably the influential *Times of India* and the *Hindustan Times*, which invariably follows the stock Congress Party lines—loses few opportunities of producing anti-colonial material and refuses blindly to see any merit in our colonial policies. The lesser politicians, still living in their emotional past, are equally unprepared at present to make any concessions to realities. As contacts

between Indians at home and Africans develop, however, it is to be hoped that Indian opinion too may take a less biased view. The presence in India of so many African students is already proving to be an interesting experiment. It is salutory [sic] for the Indians to discover that the former have a legitimate pride in the achievements of their own territories and are by no means willing to accept without question Indian ideas about the way their affairs should be managed. Visits to the African colonies such as that recently made by Mr. Patil are also valuable. Mr. Patil has in the past been as ardent an opponent of our colonial policies as most other Indian politicians. He was, for example, closely concerned with the visit to Bombay of Dr. Jagan and Mr. Burnham.[3] But in conversation with the Deputy High Commissioner in Bombay after his return from East Africa and subsequently in his speech at the "African Question" exhibition, he made comments about his visit which suggest that he learned a good deal whilst he was on his travels. He said for instance that the Indian idea of Africa was based on ignorance and often on misrepresentation and that racial discrimination was absent from territories such as Uganda and Tanganyika. Anything that someone of his influence is prepared to say about Africa is bound to make an impression here; from this point of view the visit can have done nothing but good.

7. For a long time, efforts to put across to the people of this country our case on the part we have played in the process of African development have been undermined because most of the leading figures in Indian public life and Indian public opinion as a whole have been unwilling to give any credit to those tainted with "colonialism." If, as now seems possible, India's own contacts with Africa lead gradually to a better understanding of the problems of that continent, it is not unreasonable to hope that in time we shall indirectly benefit as well.

[3] L F S Burnham, minister of education, British Guiana, May–Oct 1953; prime minister, 1964–1966; prime minister of Guyana, 1966–1980; president, 1980–1985.

141   CAB 129/55, C(52)306   24 Sept 1952
'Relations with the Union of South Africa in the context of the United Nations': Cabinet memorandum by Lord Salisbury

At the forthcoming General Assembly of the United Nations the South African Government will almost certainly be severely attacked on three questions: the question of the treatment of Indians in South Africa; the general racial policy of the Union Government, which has given rise to the current passive disobedience campaign; and the problem of South West Africa. The attack on the first two questions will probably be led by the Indian Delegation. It is necessary to decide the policy by which the United Kingdom Delegation should be guided on these issues. Brief notes on these three items are at Appendices I, II and III.[1]

2. Our policy on all these items should have regard to three basic factors. First, we must preserve our own rights as a Colonial Power *vis-à-vis* the United Nations: we cannot afford to allow that organisation to establish a "right" to intervene in any way in our colonial administration. In our view the political affairs of our dependent territories are essentially a matter within the domestic jurisdiction of the United

[1] Appendices not printed.

Kingdom and as such fall outside the scope of the Assembly by virtue of Article 2(7)[+] of the Charter. Secondly, we have a reputation to maintain as a champion of liberal Western civilisation. We would wish to maintain this reputation not only in the United Nations but also before our own public opinion and—what is perhaps even more important—opinion within our colonies. African and Asian opinion in our colonies is especially hostile to the Union of South Africa, and any move on our part which could be construed as endorsement of Union racial policy could bring us into serious conflict with that opinion, especially in West and Central Africa. We must also bear in mind the strength of opinion in India and Pakistan on this subject.

3. Thirdly, we must do all we can to preserve and strength [sic] our relations with South Africa. This is important not only on the general ground of the desirability of maintaining our Commonwealth links, but also for weighty strategic and economic reasons. The Nationalist Government's willingness to co-operate both in Middle East defence in wartime and in anti-Communist measures represents a change in traditional policy which must be encouraged. Moreover, our continued use of the Naval Base at Simonstown is of the utmost importance to us both in peace and in war. Further, South Africa is a source of supply for a number of raw materials of great importance to the United Kingdom in peace-time and vital to us in time of war. Economically the stability of the sterling area is dependent on the United Kingdom obtaining a substantial part of South Africa's gold output and equally the Union furnishes an important market for our exports. It must also be borne in mind that the High Commission Territories of Basutoland and Swaziland, and possibly the Bechuanaland Protectorate as well, can at any time be economically strangled if the Union Government chooses to deny them essential facilities. I suggest that each item might be considered in the light of these factors.

Persons of Indian origin in South Africa
4. This represents a direct clash between the Union on one hand and India (together with Pakistan) on the other. Clearly this debate will serve no useful purpose and the only helpful role that we can perform is to do our best to make it as short and as temperate as possible. We could not discuss the merits without offending either one side or the other. Apart from this, it would be most unwise to be drawn into such a discussion because the subject appears to fall clearly within the sphere of South Africa's domestic jurisdiction and therefore (by virtue of Article 2(7) of the Charter) outside the scope of the United Nations. In 1946, we proposed that the question of the Assembly's competence should be referred to the International Court of Justice for its opinion. This proposal was defeated and, since then, the line our Delegation has taken has been that before the item can be discussed, the Court's opinion should be obtained; but we ourselves have not again formally proposed such a reference. I recommend that we maintain our previous policy, subject to the modification that in future we should not advocate a reference to the International Court of Justice except as a last resort in an attempt to prevent the passage of a thoroughly objectionable resolution (e.g. one which sought to establish the principle that the United Nations was entitled to intervene in the political affairs of

---

[+] Article 2(7) of the Charter reads as follows:— "Nothing contained in the present Charter shall authorise the United Nations to intervene in matters which are essentially within the domestic jurisdiction of any State . . ."

non-self-governing territories). For there is this disadvantage in a reference to the Court, that we should not be able sufficiently to control the wording of the question that would be put to it. Thus the question might be phrased in such a way that the Court was asked to give an opinion of the general effect of Article 2(7) of the Charter with regard to the competence of the Assembly to discuss the political affairs of non-self-governing territories. The legal arguments are finely balanced on this issue and there is considerable danger that the Court as at present composed would tend to show a bias against the Colonial powers. Even if the question posed were carefully limited, the Court might well express some general views unhelpful to the United Kingdom on the effect of Article 2(7) in examining its relevance to the limited issue. An opinion of the Court therefore might well establish the competence of the Assembly to discuss not only this particular issue but also general problems arising from the presence of immigrant peoples in our own Colonies (e.g. Indians in Kenya).

5. The safest course for the United Kingdom Delegation to pursue, therefore, seems to be to do all they can, at the moment, to keep the idea of a reference to the Court in the background; to work for a moderate and short debate; to seek to get both sides to discuss their differences directly; to work for a moderately worded resolution; to play as inconspicuous a part in the debate as they can; and, in particular, to abstain on any resolution critical of South Africa.

South Africa's racial policies

6. This item encroaches even more obviously on the field of domestic jurisdiction. As Appendix II shows, we have already made our position clear to the Government of India. In reply to their request that we should intevene directly with the Union Government, we declined to do so on the ground that this was a matter which in our view clearly lay within the field of the Union's internal jurisdiction. *A fortiori* we could not support any attempt by the United Nations to intervene. To do so would be a *volte face*. Moreover, it would be against our colonial interests to support such an attempt, for we might then be regarded as having consented to a debate that might later be quoted as a precedent for the discussion of matters within our own domestic jurisdiction (e.g. in relation to a colony).

7. It must be remembered, however, that South Africa's racial policies have aroused strong emotions both here and elsewhere—especially in some of our colonial territories. These feelings will be played on to the full in New York and much will be made of the claim that this is a matter of human rights and therefore eligible for discussion in that context. Our reply must be that Article 2(7) of the Charter has over-riding effect and precludes discussion of the subject. We should therefore vote against the inclusion of the item in the agenda. If—despite our opposition—the item is debated, our delegation should make a formal reservation that they do not regard the debate as setting a precedent; should avoid commiting themselves to any expressions of opinion on the merits of the case, while making it clear that their opposition to the inclusion of the item on the agenda relates solely to the question of competence; and should be guided generally by the policy proposed in paragraph 5 for the item on people of Indian origin in South Africa. Since it is impossible to predict the manner in which the Assembly may decide to deal with the item, I recommend that our Delegation be given discretion to abstain on or vote against any resolutions that may be put forward.

8. I should warn my colleagues that if the Assembly does decide to include this

item in its Agenda—as it almost certainly will—the Union Government may well decide to withdraw their Delegation and take no further part in the work of this session of the Assembly. From time to time, South African Ministers have even gone so far as to suggest that South Africa might withdraw altogether from the United Nations if the Assembly continues its hostile treatment of issues affecting South Africa.

South-West Africa

9. There is, on the merits, something to be said in favour of the Union's point of view. In the first place she had a very reasonable case for incorporating the territory into the Union in 1946.[2] We then supported the Union Government, and it seems probable that, but for the fact that South Africa's racial policy was even then causing concern, the Assembly would have agreed to the proposal. In view of the Assembly's rejection of the proposal, South Africa admits that she remains internationally accountable for her administration of the territory. What she has not so far been prepared to admit is that her accountability is now to the United Nations. This is why she has not so far accepted that part of the International Court's opinion which advises that the United Nations has rights of supervision in respect of South-West Africa similar to those exercised by the League of Nations, including the right to receive reports on the Territory and to examine written petitions relating to it. This is the crux of the disagreement between the Union and the rest of the United Nations. The Union Government's attitude is based mainly on the belief that the opponents of their racial policy would seize the opportunities afforded by public debate of reports and petitions to criticise their domestic affairs.

10. We can have some sympathy with the Union's attitude in view of the hostile character of the Assembly's attitude in the past and in particular of the Fourth Committee (in which the South West African item would be debated). Moreover, the Court's opinion is only an advisory one and, as it has no binding force, the Union Government are within their strict legal rights in rejecting part of it; our own legal experts have always been doubtful of the legal soundness of this particular part of the opinion. Our predecessors however decided that advantage lay in accepting the Court's opinion *as a whole*.[3] My immediate predecessor also agreed with this view, which has accordingly been expressed by our Delegation at the last two sessions of the General Assembly. Even if it were desirable, I consider that it would be very difficult to follow a different course now.

11. In considering our policy, regard must be had to the fact that the debate on this item will take place in the Fourth Committee (which discusses colonial questions). Feeling in this Committee is strongly anti-colonial, and in recent years it has been endeavouring to enlarge its powers beyond the scope laid down by the Charter of the United Nations. The Colonial Powers have to be constantly on the alert to frustrate these attempts. Hitherto we have been reasonably successful in this contest. In particular we have been able to preserve the principles listed in the Annex to C.(52) 232[4] on which the Cabinet recently agreed that we could not yield (C.C.(52) 75th Conclusions, Minute 7). One of these principles is likely to be challenged during

---

[2] cf BDEEP series A, R Hyam, ed, *The Labour government and the end of empire 1945–1951*, part IV, 412–414.
[3] cf *ibid*, 427.   [4] See 160.

2B

the forthcoming debate on South-West Africa, since it is possible that the anti-colonials may make a further attempt to maintain their claim that the Fourth Committee is entitled to hear oral evidence from petitioners from South-West Africa. It would be but a short step from this to claim the right of the United Nations to hear oral evidence from petitioners from non-self-governing territories. We could not concede the latter claim; but our position would be undermined if even the former were re-asserted by the Fourth Committee and put into effect without protest from ourselves. To this extent our interests lie in the same direction as those of the Union Government.

12.   On the other hand, we must be careful to avoid giving the South Africans any encouragement to think that they can be sure of our support if they adopt an unconciliatory attitude to the Fourth Committee. If they were to do so, feeling in the Fourth Committee would become exacerbated, with consequent risk of danger to our own interests. Moreover, we must remember that much of the opposition to South Africa on this issue arises from the feeling that unless South Africa is made accountable to an internatioinal body like the United Nations for its administration of South-West Africa, the inhabitants of that territory will be exposed without any defence to the Union's racial legislation. We cannot ignore this sentiment and we must therefore avoid giving the impression by our actions in the Assembly that we are indifferent to the fate of these people. These two factors impose definite limits on the extent to which we can go in supporting South Africa.

13.   Taking all these factors into consideration, I feel that the best course for our Delegation to adopt would be to advise the South African Delegation (if it is still present when this item is discussed) to adopt a conciliatory attitude, and to counsel moderation generally while avoiding the impression that we are prepared to compromise the happiness of the inhabitants of the territory. If a solution is proposed which offers some hope of acceptance but which does not entirely comply with the Court's opinion, our Delegation should not reject it on that ground alone. They should not regard themselves as entirely fettered by our advocacy of that opinion as a whole. Should the South Africans directly challenge that opinion, however, we would have no alternative but to support it. If this policy is accepted, it is proposed to inform the South African Government in advance that this is the limit to which we can go in supporting them on this item.

14.   It is therefore recommended:—

(i) *On the problem of people of Indian origin in South Africa* that our policy should be to work for a moderate debate; to seek to get both sides to discuss their differences directly; to work for a moderately worded resolution; to play as inconspicuous a part in the debate as possible and to abstain on any resolution critical of South Africa.

(ii) *On South Africa's racial policy*

(a) that we should vote against the inclusion of the item in the Agenda on the ground that it is a matter of domestic jurisdiction, to which Article 2(7) of the Charter applies;

(b) that if it is included in the Agenda our intervention in debate should be limited to a restatement of our views, including the point that our opposition to

---

⁴ See 160.

the inclusion of the item on the agenda relates solely to the question of competence;
(c) that the Delegation should be given discretion to abstain on or vote against any resolution.

(iii) *On the problem of South-West Africa*

(a) that the United Kingdom Delegation should work for a moderate debate in order to prevent points of principle arising affecting our own vital interests; defend our interests should such points arise (e.g. the hearing of oral petitioners) while avoiding any implication that in doing so we necessarily agree with South African policies; help the South Africans by counselling moderation; and endeavour to persuade them to make concessions to the majority view that the opinion of the International Court of Justice must be accepted as a whole, including the obligation to submit reports to the United Nations and of acknowledging their right to receive written petitions;
(b) that if, in spite of our efforts at moderation, a head-on clash were to occur on the question of the validity of the International Court's opinion, we should make it plain that we adhere to the view that it should be accepted as a whole;
(c) that the Union Government should be told in advance the limits within which we are prepared to support them.

15. The Secretary of State for the Colonies and the Minister of State have seen this memorandum and are in general agreement with my recommendations.[5]

---

[5] Cabinet approved these recommendations. Selwyn Lloyd, who as minister of state served as ministerial leader of the UK delegation to the UN, felt that South African withdrawal from the UN would be regrettable, 'since they were playing an active part in the Korean war and South Africa's vote in the Assembly was often of considerable value to the Atlantic Powers'. Lyttelton made the point that if South Africa's racial policy came up for discussion, the 'only safe course' for the UK would be to deny UN competence and stay out of the debate: 'Any other course would involve us in serious difficulties either with South Africa or in the Colonial Empire' (CAB 128/25, CC 81(52)7, 26 Sept 1952).

142 CAB 129/61, C(53)165   5 June 1953

'Relations with South Africa': Cabinet memorandum by Lord Swinton reporting a conversation with Dr Malan on 31 May 1953

I dined alone last night with Dr. Malan and the South African High Commissioner, Dr. Geyer. Though we talked for three hours the conversation was more noticeable for the matters Dr. Malan did *not* raise than for those which he did.

2. Dr. Malan's only reference to a Republic was to ask what was the position in Pakistan. He said that Nazimuddin[1] had said at the last Conference (presumably to Havenga) that Pakistan would become a Republic. I told Dr. Malan that this was not at all certain under the new régime; and that I thought Mohammed Ali[2] would very much wish to leave things as they are. I felt sure Mohammad Ali realised that if Pakistan were to declare a Republic at this time, when everywhere there was a

---

[1] Sir A-H K Nazimuddin, prime minister of Pakistan, 1951–1953.
[2] M Ali, prime minister of Pakistan, 1953–1955.

spontaneous upsurge of love and loyalty to The Queen, that would be regarded as a direct rebuff to the Queen, and would forfeit all the public sympathy that Pakistan enjoyed here today. The whole climate was quite different from the time when India became a Republic. In spite of this obvious opening Dr. Malan said nothing about his own position or intention.

3. Although he talked a great deal about Africa and Africans Dr. Malan did not raise the question of the Protectorates.[3] At the end of the evening when we were leaving, the High Commissioner said "We have not talked at all about the Protectorates. I think the Prime Minister will want to talk to you about that some time." Dr. Malan said nothing.

4. I was particularly interested in what Dr. Malan said about the future of the Commonwealth. He introduced the subject. He emphasised the importance of the old Dominions in defence and in common outlook. That was where the real strength of the Commonwealth lay—and the real unity too. When Mr. Gordon Walker[4] was in South Africa, he said to Dr. Malan that the Gold Coast, the West Indies and perhaps Nigeria would before long attain Commonwealth status. What was the position of the United Kingdom Government with regard to that? I said our position was perfectly clear and had been publicly stated. It was the responsibility of the United Kingdom Government to decide what measure of self-government should be given to Colonial territories. But even if a Colonial territority attained complete self-government, that did not carry with it automatically full Commonwealth status. The attainment of that full status would be a matter for all the existing Members of the Commonwealth. Dr. Malan was very pleased and said that that was entirely satisfactory.

5. Dr. Malan then asked me how I thought we could in fact meet the situation, which would arise sooner or later. I emphasised that it would be most unwise to say anything publicly in advance. But I thought it might be possible to arrive at a position where there was in practice a difference in fact, if not in status. For example, there were matters like defence in which the position of Commonwealth countries was in fact different. Dr. Malan said that he thought this was a good line of approach. There was that sort of differentiation now. On some matters the old Dominions were given fulll information and taken into full consultation, while there was more limited information and consultation with the Asiatic countries.

6. Dr. Malan then went on to talk about what he called the African problem. He said that it affected the whole of Africa, and we all had to face the position of whether the Africans sooner or later were to dominate. This affected every Colonial Power as well as the Union of South Africa. I said it was not the same problem everywhere. For example, West Africa was not a white man's country. On the other hand when you came to Rhodesia, that was as much the home, generation after generation, of the white population as of the black. What would be a suitable constitutional development in West Africa would be wholly unsuitable in Rhodesia. Dr. Malan knew the lines on which we were proceeding there. Dr. Malan had no criticism of what we were doing in Rhodesia. He seemed indeed quite friendly about it. He only asked whether we were going forward with Federation, to which I replied emphatically "yes".

[3] The high commission territories of Bechuanaland, Basutoland and Swaziland; see 143 and part II of this volume, 304.
[4] P C Gordon Walker, S of S for Commonwealth relations, 1950–1951. For his visit to South Africa, see BDEEP series A, R Hyam, ed, *The Labour government and the end of empire 1945–1951*, part IV, 433.

7. Dr. Malan's next point was the activities of Africans who wanted and were planning complete African domination. He said for example that he had read in a newspaper that Nkrumah was organising a pan-African conference of leading Africans from every country in Africa. I said this was the first I had heard of it and it sounded to me most unlikely. Nkrumah had his work cut out for him in the Gold Coast. There was no unity in West Africa, and Nigeria which is itself far from united would not follow a Gold Coast lead. I hoped Dr. Malan would not believe all he read in the papers. This led both Dr. Malan and the High Commissioner to say that it would be very helpful if they could have more factual information about what was going on in our African territories. We give them complete information about foreign affairs, defence, trade and other subjects and also tell them of our ideas and plans on these matters; but they really knew nothing authoritative about what was happening in West Africa or East Africa or of our policy. I said I thought it was very desirable that they should have correct information about this, and that I would certainly talk to the Secretary of State for the Colonies who, I was sure, would feel the same way. I have since spoken to Mr. Lyttelton, who entirely agreed.

8. Dr. Malan then suggested that it would be a good thing if the Colonial Powers could get together more and discuss their common problems. Not only the United Kingdom and South Africa, but the French, Belgians and Portuguese as well. He then adumbrated the rather alarming idea that these countries might all meet and formulate an "African Charter." I said that I did not think it would be a very good idea that we should meet with the declared object of discussing how we were to treat Africans: but there were a lot of other questions, trade, railways, air transport, health, &c., on which we could very usefully meet in some way or another and exchange ideas. And when you met for one object, you could talk about other things on the side and off the record. Dr. Malan chuckled and said: "You English are very illogical, but you have a lot of commonsense."

9. Dr. Malan then got on to the continual attempts by the United Nations Organisation (U.N.O.) to interfere in native affairs and domestic policy. I said that our line on this was clear and consistent. We maintained that it had been agreed at San Francisco and laid down in the Charter that it was no business of the U.N.O. to interfere with matters which were the domestic concern of any country. Our representative had consistently taken this line at the U.N.O. I had already been approached more than once by the Indian Government on this matter. I had told the Indian Government that we should firmly maintain this line over any affairs of our own or the affairs of any other Commonwealth country. Dr. Malan was appreciative of the line we had taken.

10. Dr. Malan then proceeded at length to talk about Indian interference in African affairs. This went far beyond any proper discussion of the position of Indians in his territories or ours. In Dr. Malan's opinion Mr. Nehru was determined to play an ambitious and dangerous rôle in Africa. He thought Nehru wanted to off-load surplus Indian population on Africa. But, even more dangerous and insidious was his aim to become the Protector of Africans everywhere in Africa. Nehru had started with the idea that he and India would be the supreme power in Asia. Nehru had been beaten in this by Mao Tse Tung in China. Having failed in China Nehru wished to extend his empire to Africa.

11. We talked for three hours; and as our talk went on I thought Dr. Malan talked more and more without reserve, though no doubt he selected his topics. To-day, Dr.

Geyer, whom I have found to be a frank and trustworthy friend and who is very close to Dr. Malan, told me that Malan had been very well pleased with our talk. Geyer said that Malan had talked without any reserve and with great freedom and that they were both glad I had done the same.

143 CAB 129/61, C(53)169   12 June 1953

'Relations with South Africa': Cabinet memorandum by Lord Swinton reporting a conversation with Mr Havenga on 10 June 1953

Mr. Havenga came to see me this morning. He said that Dr. Malan and he ought not to leave without our having had some talk about the Protectorates and the question of Transfer. There was a strong feeling among all their followers that nothing had happened in forty years, and the prospects of Transfer did not appear to get any better. What was to be the position? Was it to recede further into the background? It was the one question which could embitter relations between our two countries and make our co-operation on other things more difficult.

2. I said that Mr. Havenga was a realist and he must realise that there could not be a worse moment to raise this question. As a Government we had scrupulously maintained the position that South Africa's internal policy was her affair. We had maintained that position not only in this country but at the United Nations Organisation; Havenga assured me that they fully appreciated that. But, I went on, there was no doubt about what people in this country felt about the native policy South Africa had adopted. The United Kingdom Government could not possibly contemplate Transfer at the present time and even if the Government were prepared to consider it, which they were not, they would not get ten votes in the House of Commons if they proposed it. It was much better to speak frankly. Havenga said that, being a realist, he appreciated that this was the position. But what about the future? Was Transfer to be ruled out for ever? I said that the worst possible thing would be to raise it now. If it were raised now, things would be said which must make the whole future more difficult.

3. Havenga said that not only his own Party, which had a good majority in Parliament, but many of the Opposition were in favour of the policy of Apartheid. While South Africa was firmly determined that political power should rest in the hands of the white men, their policy was to do a great deal for the material advancement and prosperity of the natives, and to do their best for them in the native reserves. It was not realised here how much they were doing for native welfare. I said that neither of us could prophesy what would happen in the future. If the policy of Apartheid succeeded, in the sense that it were proved that the native population were well treated and prospered under it, public opinion outside South Africa, though they would not think this Apartheid the right way, might come to think better of it in practice.

4. Havenga pointed out that the Territories depended a great deal on the Union. I said that there was close economic co-operation and that the more that was developed the better. In a number of ways that was working well to-day, and that was the best means of practical co-operation. Havenga then asked what would be the attitude of our local administrators, and how would they advise the native populations. I said that so far as economic co-operation went they would do all they

could to further it, but that I certainly could not instruct our administrators to try and influence the Africans in the Territories in favour of Transfer.

5.   In the end, Havenga said that his Government would not raise the question of Transfer with us at the present time. They must be free to say that they thought Transfer was right, and ought to be conceded, but Malan and he would do their best to avoid a head-on collision. He thought they could do that for the time being, but they were old men nearing the end of their course and their successors would be less realistic. He must emphasise again that while they would do their best to avoid a collision of this kind, the Transfer question was a constant source of friction and was likely to become more so as time went on.

6.   Havenga then went on to talk very frankly about the Republic. He said that this certainly was not an issue at the present time. He did not think it would come in his lifetime. On this Malan and he had full support in their Cabinet. Even Strydom [sic][1] had agreed that there could be no question of a Republic unless the white population of the Union expressed a decisive opinion on that specific question. It had not been an issue in the election. It was Havenga's personal opinion that if a secret ballot was taken to-day, two-thirds of the white population would vote against a Republic. Havenga added that one of the strongest forces making Afrikaners inclined to a Republic was the attitude of some of the people in Natal in trying to claim as it were, a special property in the Queen and saying that the Crown would protect them.

7.   Havenga then said that the least helpful thing over both the Republic and the Territories was when newspapers wrote that Dr. Malan was going to raise these issues actively. I assured Havenga that I had done and would continue to do my best with the Press and that I had told them that the surest way of getting these issues raised, which I hoped and believed could lie dormant, was to ventilate them in the Press here.

8.   Havenga also referred with a good deal of unhappiness to a statement which had appeared in the foreign supplement of the *Economist* that he had said he was in favour of leaving the sterling area. This really was a bit hard. He had been such a staunch partner and had now brought the whole of his Cabinet round to his point of view. He said he would mention this to the Chancellor. I said we had all appreciated enormously his loyal and generous support and that this sort of thing was intolerable, but he was an old politician and he would realise that we all of us suffered alike from time to time, and some of us very frequently, under misrepresentations in the Press.

---

[1] J G Strijdom, prime minister of South Africa, 1954–1958.

144   DO 35/5343, no 14   11 Jan 1954

'South Africa: attitude of the Union government to United Kingdom policy in colonial territories': despatch no 2 from A W Snelling (Pretoria)[1] to Lord Swinton. *Annex*

I have the honour to refer to the despatch No. 297 of 11th December from the Acting High Commissioner in India transmitting an Aide-mémoire giving the views of the

---

[1] A W Snelling, UK deputy high commissioner in South Africa, 1953–1955.

Government of India on United Kingdom policy in British Colonial territories. The views in that Aide-Mémoire, as might be expected, differ in many respects from those of the Government of the Union of South Africa. As it would obviously be inappropriate to ask the Union Government to set out their own views, and as these have undergone quite a considerable change since Sir John Le Rougetel[2] last summarised them in his despatch No. 459 of 28th December, 1951, I have attempted in the attached memorandum to describe what I believe to be current South African opinion upon this topic. In this memorandum I have concentrated almost exclusively on the African Colonies because these are the territories of by far the greatest interest to South Africa.

2.   The principal difference between Indian and South African views seems to be, in brief, that whereas the Government of India implicitly, and in certain instances (*e.g.*, over British Guiana) explicitly, support the policy of the Labour Party, the South African Government are broadly sympathetic with the Conservative Government, both in the latters' general outlook upon Colonial questions and in their handling of specific issues. Another difference between the two Commonwealth Governments is that the Union Government would certainly expect that a good deal more attention would be paid to their views than to those of the Government of India on questions relating to the African continent. The Government of India, I believe, sometimes claim a special right to be heard on Asian affairs; the Government of South Africa similarly expect that if the United Kingdom Government are going to take notice of what any other Government says about policy in African Colonies, they will pay particular attention to the opinions of the only member of the Commonwealth in Africa.

3.   The South African Government and people fear both the policies advocated for this continent by the Government of India and the fact that that Government is interfering in African affairs. They think that India cannot possibly have anything to fear from Africa. They do not believe that India is genuinely animated by deep feeling against racial discrimination. Their newspapers give a good deal of publicity to the failure, allegedly admitted by Indian Ministers themselves, of the attempt to bring to an end, by means of legislation, discrimination against 50 million Untouchables. On the other hand, the South Africans themselves fear that, unless a firm policy is followed in the African Colonies, Mau-Mau and worse will spread throughout the continent. They feared, during the Labour Government in Britain, that self-government would be granted to many territories prematurely, and that corruption, disorder and either communism or anarchy would inevitably follow and would spread rapidly from one part of Africa to another so that before long the whole continent would be aflame. They feared that native governments in Africa, even if they did not go communist would at any rate turn neutral, as India herself has done, and so diminish South Africa's security. However exaggerated these fears may be, they are held by almost all Europeans in the Union. They have been allayed to a considerable extent since the Conservative Government came into power.

4.   Sir John Le Rougetel reported two years ago that he considered our Colonial policy in Africa to be the most important factor, in the minds of South Africans, affecting their relations with us. It cannot be doubted that this is still true. The European and particularly the Afrikaner section of the population of the Union is

---

[2] Sir J Le Rougetel, UK high commissioner in South Africa, 1951–1955.

haunted by the thought that, if things go wrong in Africa, it has nowhere else to go. South Africans have a renewed and growing confidence in us and believe that we are not now afraid to govern. This confidence could be endangered if we were to lean perceptibly towards the Indian point of view.

5. I am sending copies of this despatch to the United Kingdom High Commissioners in New Delhi and Salisbury.

Annex to 144

1. The volume of criticism of the United Kingdom Colonial policy has diminished sharply in the Union during the last two years. South Africans in general, and Dr. Malan in particular, almost invariably draw a distinction between what they characterise as Labour policy and what they regard as Conservative policy in this field.

Labour policy

2. Towards the end of the life of the Labour Government, scarcely a week went by without its Colonial policy being condemned by South African Ministers and newspapers. They regarded the Gold Coast experiment as Socialist Utopianism, and as being doomed, like the groundnut scheme, to certain failure. Dr. Malan has spoken of the Gold Coast many times in forthright terms: "The previous British Government simply applied the democracy of Western Europe to that territory. Ninety per cent. or more of the population who are entitled to vote are illiterate. Democracy is a good thing, but to make democracy successful it must be based on the ability of the enfranchised masses to exercise their right to vote with a sense of responsibility and with knowledge. . . . How can an illiterate people with so little civilization and knowledge assume the responsibility of governing itself? It cannot be done. It leads to chaos . . . . and to a dictatorship."[a]

3. Dr. Malan objected also to the alleged intention of the Labour Government, on the basis of certain statements by Mr. Griffiths, to admit some of the Colonies to membership of the Commonwealth when they reached a state of self-government. He staunchly maintained that the agreement of all existing members of the Commonwealth was required for new admissions. Labour policy, he said, signified "nothing less than the undermining of the foundations of the Commonwealth and its gradual liquidation. . . . We who value its survival may regret it, but the problem is fortunately not ours."[b]

4. Labour Party leaders are condemned as strongly for their statements since they lost the election as for their actions when in power. Their policy then and now is regarded as being based upon sentimentality. They are described as possessing a neurotic sense of guilt towards native peoples, and as not having the guts to govern. They are accused of failing to distinguish between methods of government appropriate for those areas in Africa that are suitable for permanent white settlement and for those that are not. They are alleged to regard Europeans in Africa as intruders—a view which is particularly annoying to South Africans whose European ancestors established themselves in large areas of what is now the Union before the Bantu arrived there.

[a] South African Hansard, 4.3.52., Col. 2197.   [b] Statement to the press, 24.2.51.

Conservative policy

5. In contrast, the Conservative Government is far more often praised than criticised for its Colonial policy. Its current problems, whether in Kenya or elsewhere, are regarded largely as springing from the unhappy legacy it inherited from its predecessor. Its handling of the British Guiana situation met with universal South African support. Dr. Malan stated with approbation that "when the present British Government came into power a statement was issued that the Commonwealth should be regarded in the light of a club, and that nobody should in future be allowed to belong to it without the approval of all members."[c] The Afrikaans press endorsed Mr. Lyttelton's statement that many of the ideas which were forced on people who were still emerging from the darkness of primitive man were positively dangerous for them. Mr. Hopkinson was congratulated for distinguishing between policies suitable for East and Central Africa on the one hand and for West Africa on the other, when he told Native representatives at Livingstone that, with or without Central African Federation, Native self-government in the full sense was impossible in countries with mixed communities, whatever the case might be in a wholly African country like the Golf Coast.

6. Above all, the Colonial policy of the present United Kingdom Government is welcomed in South Africa as representing a reversal of the "abdication spirit" of the Labour Party. The only trouble, in Union eyes, is that the Conservatives' majority is not big enough. "The present British Government is not made up of abdicators, but because of internal political circumstances they have done little as yet to make the colonial peoples of Africa realise this, as other colonial powers and the present South African Government make it abundantly clear to their non-European populations. In its own interests, in the interests of its own colonial subjects, and in the interests of other states in Africa, Britain should make it clear to the meanest intelligence that it is not packing up."[d] Even though South Africans now mostly realise that federation in British Central Africa has been inspired partly by a desire to contain the Afrikaner, they support the United Kingdom Government for pushing ahead with this plan, undeterred by either criticism from the Native population on the spot or by sentimentalism and opportunities for vote-catching within the United Kingdom.

South African policy

7. Dr. Malan's basic points in regard to African policy are summarised in his proposed "African Charter." The idea of such a Charter has been germinating in his mind for several years, and its latest expression was in the Union Parliament on 11th August, 1953. He then said that such a Charter should include the following four points:—

(i) the indigenous population of South Africa must be protected against penetration by the peoples of Asia;
(ii) Africa must be led along the path of European civilization;
(iii) Africa must be protected against communism;
(iv) Africa must be prevented from militarisation, and in particular Natives must not be armed.

8. At present, Dr. Malan's mind is most occupied by the first and third of these

[c] South African Hansard, 7.7.53, Col. 57. [d] *Die Burger*, 2.12.53.

points: he regards communism and India as the main dangers to the peace of Africa. Of his opposition to communism little need be said: to help to stop the Russians from trying to carry their doctrines from Asia to Africa, his Government have, for the first time in South African history, entered into a commitment in peace-time to go to war, if it becomes necessary, in alliance *inter alia* with the United Kingdom. Of the menace of India he is equally convinced. He says, for instance, that "India's claims in Africa are very clear and she does not hide them. India stands for anti-colonialism. In other words, the white man must leave Africa. In practice, India intervenes wherever there is trouble and takes sides against the Europeans. Nehru has openly called upon the Indians in South Africa to join up with the natives and defy the law of the land. Nehru has interfered in the same way in Kenya, encouraging the Indians to remain friends with the Mau Mau and the natives. . . . ."[e] On another occasion he said: "the cry that 'the white man should quit Africa' is only one half of the slogan; the other half is 'and let India enter in.' "[f] To stop Indian infiltration he wishes to secure the co-operation of all governments in Africa. "What," he asks, "is the spirit motivating India?" He sees the answer as a new form of Imperialism, "India," he says, "is a danger to Africa and the peoples with possessions in Africa."[g]

9. Apart from resisting Indian infiltration and interference in Africa, the Union Government would like to see a sharper demarcation between the policies which the United Kingdom Government adopt in different parts of the continent. The official definition of apartheid includes a reference to the desire to furnish non-Europeans "with the opportunity to develop in their own areas in accordance with their natural genius and capacity. . . ." A continent-wide application of this doctrine would suggest the appropriateness of a measure of African self-government in areas, *e.g.*, in West Africa, where Europeans do not settle. This is, indeed, Dr. Malan's view. He is definitely not opposed to all political development in those areas. He said not long ago "I have no objection to it if any member, any European power, with possessions in Africa wants to develop its possessions in a judicious manner. . . . . It is their right to do so. . . . . But what I want to emphasise is that they should exercise their rights judiciously."[h] Recent events in the Sudan have confirmed South Africans in the belief that it is no use expecting primitive people to vote wisely when they are confronted with a decision whose form they do not understand between alternatives they understand even less. Many statements by Dr. Malan on these issues boil down to the proposition that he would like to see the United Kingdom, in developing its Colonies, pay closer attention to its own constitutional history, and ensure that the universal franchise should be roughly contemporaneous with universal literacy.

10. South Africa maintains that she has a right to be heard on these topics because she believes that events in other parts of Africa have quick repercussions throughout the continent. The experiment in the Gold Coast, according to Dr. Malan, resulted in the whole of Africa to-day being in a turbulent state, and had its influence in Kenya, Nyasaland, Northern Rhodesia and even in the Union.[i] The newspaper that reflects closely the views of Dr. Malan's heir-apparent, Mr. Strydom, [sic] said that "the greater majority of the British people are obsessed with the idea that their own future is linked with the granting of political privileges to the immature non-Europeans of Africa. It is undoubtedly the right of the British people

[e] South African Hansard, 11.8.53, Col. 1326.
[f] At an official lucheon in honour of Mr. Menzies in Cape Town on 9.7.53.   [g] Ditto.
[h] South African Hansard, 7.6.53, Col. 58.   [i] South African Hansard, 7.7.53, Col. 58.

to look after their own safety, but this does not give them the right to criticise other peoples who consider that the British way of acting is endangering their own safety."[j] So South Africans fear for themselves as a result of British policy which, in uncharitable mood, they see as "oscillating dangerously between the extremes of sentimental liberalism and the greatest heavy-handedness—constitutions and bullets are equally freely doled out, and it is difficult to say which of the two is doing the greater damage to relations in Africa."[k]

11.   Most of these views are held as strongly by English-speeking as by Afrikaans-speaking South Africans. The United Party differs from the National Party on United Kingdom Colonial policy only in that it is less vituperative about "Socialist excesses." It was Mr. Harry Lawrence, speaking for the United Party, who said that "the Gold Coast elections startled the European communities in Africa like the crack of a whip."[l] On all matters concerning Natives, English-speaking South Africans smart under criticism from "the British of Britain, who," according to a Southern Rhodesian, "distrust their fellow-Britishers of Africa, and consider their mentalities to be of a lower order so that they cannot distinguish between good and evil."[m] Over a year ago an Afrikaans newspaper said that "anyone looking at the Portuguese and Belgian territories in Africa will notice at once that in comparison with the British territories . . . . things are strikingly peaceful."[n] The English-speaking South African, albeit with regret, would agree. He hopes that the Colonial policy of 1945–51 was only an interlude, and that his safety, his prosperity and the prospects for his descendants, no less than for those of his Afrikaner fellow-citizens, will not be endangered by the growth "in West Africa of a succession of Liberias under the leadership of black demagogues, in East Africa of a number of nominally black states with the better-equipped Indians as rulers,"[o] and in South Africa of a régime under which every person has the vote, irrespective of his standard of civilization, and which thereby condemns the European to a permanent position of inferiority on the fringe of a dark continent.

[j] *Die Transvaler*, 24.4.53.   [k] *Die Burger*, 1.12.53.   [l] South African Hansard, 4.3.52, Col. 2199.
[m] Mr. Muirhead, Chairman of the Chamber of Industries in Salisbury quoted in *Die Transvaler*, 30.10.52.
[n] *Die Burger*, 30.10.52.   [o] *Die Burger*, 26.2.51.

145   FO 371/113513, no 2   16 Mar 1955

'A proposed pan-African conference': note by A W Snelling (Pretoria) to Sir P Liesching (Cape Town)[1] on Mr Louw's proposal   [Extract]

You told me that when you paid your first call on Mr. Louw, he made some brief and vague remarks to you about organising some counterpoise to the forthcoming Afro-Asian Conference at Bandung in Indonesia. I understand that Mr. Louw has also seen separately on this subject the French, Belgian and Portuguese Ambassadors and the High Commissioner for the Federation, and that he spoke to them with rather more precision than to you about what was involved. The reason for this is that he had meanwhile asked Mr. Forsyth[2] to suggest what the subjects of such a conference might be, and Mr. Forsyth had jotted down on paper for him a number of topics

[1] Liesching had recently taken up appointment as high commissioner in South Africa.
[2] D D Forsyth, permanent secretary, South African Department of External Affairs.

which might form an agenda. The Minister had this before him when he saw Mr. Chataway [sic][3] and the foreign Ambassadors.

2. This idea for a proposed Pan African Conference seems to be the same as that put forward on a number of occasions by Dr. Malan for what he called an "African Charter". I attach a note[4] by Mr. Mills summarising briefly public references in recent years to such a Charter. It was a pet idea of Dr. Malan. You will see that the United Party, sharing to some degree the Government's sense of isolation, also back the idea of a Pan African organisation, though not to cover exactly the same subjects. Mr. Forsyth told me that some of the subjects he had suggested to Mr. Louw were as follows:—

(i)   Common measures against Communism.

(ii) A common line on United Nations interference on matters of domestic policy.

(iii) A common policy on stopping Indian immigration and infiltration into Africa.

(iv) Defence.

Mr. Forsyth told me that he had added at the end of his note to Mr. Louw that the Minister would be well advised to get the backing of the United Kingdom Government first or the idea would be still-born!

3. This proposal, is I think, quite distinct from that for an African Defence Organisation[5] except that if we pour cold water on the idea of A.D.O. we may find that the same suggestion bobs up again as part of the content of a proposed Pan African Conference.

4. The geographical scope of the proposed Conference or Charter is, I know, a point very much exercising the minds of the Union officials. Apparently both Mr. Erasmus over A.D.O., and Mr. Louw over the Pan African Conference started with the idea that the area concerned and the membership should be the same as those of the C.C.T.A. But Mr. Cuff[6] has pointed out to his Minister that the C.C.T.A. area includes West Africa. Apparently neither Mr. Erasmus nor Mr. Louw want the Gold Coast, Nigeria, etc., in their pet organisations.

5. It is also quite clear that there is a good deal of rivalry between Mr. Erasmus and Mr. Louw over their pet ideas. Mr. Erasmus wants to see A.D.O. created (as well as to obtain Simonstown) in order to bolster up his waning political prestige. Mr. Louw's idea is that defence, as well as many other things, are primarily questions of External Affairs, and that he should exercise an overlordship over them. Mr. Louw is therefore evidently not enthusiastic about A.D.O., but wants it mopped up in his Conference.

6. In the meantime my understanding is that the Department of Defence and of External Affairs are working in fairly water-tight compartments on two separate documents. . . .[7]

---

[3] A D Chattoway, high commissioner of the Federation of Rhodesia and Nyasaland in South Africa.

[4] Not printed (F Mills was on the staff of the UK High Commission in South Africa).

[5] See 72–74, 76–81.   [6] H F Cuff, South African secretary for defence.

[7] The FO recommended 'that we should avoid if possible committing ourselves to participation in either of the South African proposals. If, however, for reasons of Commonwealth relations, this is not possible, then Mr Louw's proposal should be ridden off but Mr Erasmus should be listened to rather more sympathetically when he comes to this country in late May/early June. We should aim at keeping Mr Erasmus in play and use this as a reason for not proceeding with Mr Louw's proposal' (minute by C O I Ramsden, FO 371/113513, no 3, 25 Mar 1955). In taking this view the FO concurred with other departments, see 77.

146 CO 1032/51, no 8   24 May 1955

[South Africa and the admission of the Gold Coast to Commonwealth membership]: letter from Sir S Garner to Sir P Liesching (Cape Town)

Would you please refere to paragraph 4 of Laithwaite's letter, CON.32/40/6, of the 1st March about the admission of new Members of the Commonwealth? The handling of this problem with the Union Government, which will be crucial, is full of difficulties and is very present in our minds. We had some discussion about it before you left and you then told me that it would help you to have some indication of the likely time-table.

Since Laithwaite wrote to you on the 1st March, we have been examining, with the Colonial Office and in consultation with the Governor, whether we could give you any fairly detailed idea of the time-table which is likely to govern the whole question of Gold Coast Membership. For a number of reasons, including the recent course of events in the Gold Coast itself, it is not at the present moment feasible to do so. But, though Nkrumah is not at present thought likely formally to ask for a transfer of power before July, 1956, we must expect such a request at any time after that date, and no doubt this would be accompanied by a request to sponsor an application for Commonwealth Membership. The only safe assumption is that it may well be necessary to reach a decision on this question during the second half of 1956.

If this proves so, we shall not have had a great deal of time on which to work on South African Ministers. This underlines the desirability, which I know you have in mind, of broaching matters with South African Ministers at a relatively early date. They are bound to have initial "tantrums" and the sooner they get these over, the longer will be the interval before a final decision is required, and thus the greater the chance of getting their acceptance in the end. We should not, however, wish you to take any initiative with the Union authorities until you have received specific instructions to do so. The Secretary of State would, of course, wish to consult his colleagues before authorising you to act. This does not, of course, mean that if you were to be questioned on the subject by Union Ministers you should not deal with the matter in the light of your own knowledge. But naturally, if you were to get such an opening, you would not reveal that the matter had been the subject of Ministerial consideration here or had been already mentioned informally to some other Commonwealth Governments.[1]

Before seeking the authority of his colleagues to instruct you to open the question, the Secretary of State would wish to have before him your estimate of the South African reactions, together with your advice as to the best way of handling matters with Union Ministers. Naturally, when the time comes we shall do our best to supply you with the fullest information about the situation in the Gold Coast itself and our estimate of how things are likely to work out. Other things being equal, it would seem desirable for the necessary Ministerial consultations about your instructions to

---

[1] Swinton had discussed the matter very fully with Mr L St Laurent (prime minister of Canada, 1948–1957) in Oct 1954; Swinton and Lennox-Boyd had discussed it no less thoroughly with Mr R G Menzies (prime minister of Australia, 1949–1966) and Mr S G Holland (prime minister of New Zealand, 1949–1957) in Feb 1955. See 'Anglo-Canadian relations', Cabinet memo by Swinton, CAB 129/71, C(54)327, 28 Oct 1954; 'Commonwealth membership', Cabinet memo by Swinton, CAB 129/73, C(55)43, 15 Feb 1955.

take place before the Summer Recess. As soon, therefore, as you have had time to feel the temperature and perhaps take some discreet soundings, we should be glad to receive an expression of your views. If you could let us have these before the end of June, it would, I think, be very helpful.

147   CO 1032/51, no 12   8 June 1955

[South Africa and the admission of the Gold Coast to Commonwealth membership]: letter (reply) from Sir P Liesching (Cape Town) to Sir S Garner

Thank you for your letter of the 24th May about the admission of new Members of the Commonwealth.[1] I need hardly tell you that I agree with everything you say about the crucial difficulties we shall meet in handling this problem with the Union Government. For a number of reasons, which will be obvious to you from our reports on the political situation here, it will be even more difficult to handle with Mr. Strijdom's government than it would have been if Dr. Malan had been in power. Moreover, the transfer of responsibility for External Affairs from the Prime Minister to Mr. Louw increases the difficulties in several ways. As this is Prime Minister's business, the first approach, if and when I am authorised to undertake it, would be to Mr. Strijdom, with whom Forsyth, our best friend and only confidant on this subject, has now no contact or influence.[2] Mr. Louw, temperamental, impetuous and fundamentally obsessed by anti-British bias, is not only grossly overburdened with his two portfolios but is, more than any of his colleagues, excited and embittered by the attacks of the anti-colonialists upon South Africa. (See, for example, his recent outburst recorded in paragraph 2 of my telegram No. 185 about the U.N.O. Conference for a revision of the Charter). It is Mr. Louw who, as soon as Mr. Strijdom consults his colleagues on the question, will be the first to be called in and will have a very big say in the matter.

It was with thoughts such as these in mind that I saw Forsyth yesterday for a private conversation, which can be guaranteed to be completely off the record. I put my first thoughts to him and he fully confirmed everything I have said in the preceding paragraph, but added a number of helpful comments on the timing of an approach which, as he recognised, must inevitably be made before long.

Forsyth has for some time been working on Mr. Louw and has in fact, had some limited success in moving him towards better policies in relation to the Union's African neighbours to the North. Forsyth now has a powerful committee on African affairs under his chairmanship comprising the heads of practically all the Government Departments, and has succeeded recently in getting from Mr. Louw approval of a unanimous report, recommending the offer of bursaries to the Council for Technical Co-operation in Africa South of the Sahara (C.C.T.A.) to be held by Africans from outside the Union for study at some of the Universities, Medical Institutions, the C.S.I.R. and similar bodies in the Union. The recommendations included the setting up of one—Forsyth had hoped for more—hotel or hostel on a

---

[1] See 146.
[2] Forsyth was one of the few anglophile foreign ministry officials of the Smuts period who retained his post when Malan came to power. He was replaced in 1956 by G P Jooste, an Afrikaner nationalist.

kind of extra-territorial basis with special provisions so that "apartheid" should not apply to it.

Apart from this limited progress on the general front, Forsyth already intends to advance on Mr. Louw after the Session ends with proposals more directly connected with the Gold Coast itself. He told me that Africans from the Gold Coast in contact with the representative of the Union at C.C.T.A. meetings (both that held at Lourenço Marques and the one on housing held in the Gold Coast) had made friendly and informal approaches to the South African delegates, with whom they got on well, urging that South Africa should set up some form of permanent representation in the Gold Coast where, they said, the educated African was faced with somewhat similar problems to those which arose in the Union in dealing with backward and uneducated Africans. (The latter part of the foregoing sentence seems to me far-fetched, but I record what was said to me). Forsyth was planning, after the tumult and the shouting of the present session has subsided, to work on Mr. Louw in favour of the appointment of a South African Commissioner to the Gold Coast. At this point I mentioned in confidence to Forsyth the initial steps which we had already taken in the appointment of Cumming-Bruce.[3] It is clear that Forsyth hopes, though he knows the difficulties, to persuade Mr. Louw to the view that, instead of trying to ignore or affront the Gold Coast in its advance to full self-government, he should deal with it in a practical way. Forsyth, I should add, is himself convinced that, in spite of the immense difficulties for South Africa, the right policy is to keep the Gold Coast within the Commonwealth circle, and he realises, moreover, that if South Africa opposes this policy she is likely to find herself in a minority of one.

This does not mean that he is not greatly anxious and far from optimistic about the prospects of getting Mr. Louw into a frame of mind where he will advise that the membership pill should be swallowed. Mr. Louw's violent fretfulness about the anti-Colonial attacks on South Africa, and his intense bitterness against Mr. Nehru's attitude and utterances will all, no doubt, be heard, and will be supported by re-assertions that the dangerous non-cooperation movement, which was started here among the non-Europeans but was firmly suppressed, was fomented by Indians and inspired from Delhi. We discussed whether it would be wise or unwise to try to take advantage of Mr. Louw's forthcoming absences from the Union to get the Prime Minister's ear and attune it to this subject. (Mr. Louw will be away on his expedition to San Francisco from the 10th June until about the end of July. He will be away again for the International Monetary Fund Meeting at Istanbul during a good deal of September). We agreed that it would be most unwise to do so. Mr. Strijdom would probably by nature react pretty fiercely against a proposal to admit the Gold Coast to full membership and it might be difficult afterwards to get him to modify or retract his opposition.

My conclusion is that we should hold our hands for the next four months or so and thus give Forsyth—on whom my conversation will have impressed a sense of urgency—an opportunity to see whether he can get Mr. Louw into a better frame of mind on future policy towards the Gold Coast in the context of the suggestion that a South African Commissioner should be appointed to Accra. Forsyth may be able to start on this during August and he could continue the process after the Minister's

---

[3] Cumming-Bruce (see 99, note 2) was appointed as adviser on external affairs to the governor of the Gold Coast in Feb 1955.

return from Istanbul. I would maintain close contact with him to discover what he had been able to do, and, in the light of this, could send the Secretary of State further advice which might lead to a decision that our approach to Mr. Strijdom should be made, say, during November. This, I think, is the best advice that I can offer at the present time. There are, as you say, going to be initial tantrums to be got over, but we must try and ensure that they are not too severe and, if possible, that the issue is not treated by the present Government as one which can be exploited for political ends.

There is one further point of some delicacy on which I will touch now, although it does not arise at present. When the time comes and the approach is made it will be a tragedy if the present Government should stampede the opposition into wholly uninformed reactions which might play into their hands. You may remember that when I was sent out in 1949 to broach the question of Indian membership with Dr. Malan, I had a long and completely secret talk with General Smuts,[4] who was then leading the Opposition, and was himself in favour of the two-tier solution. This is dangerous ground and I do not wish to anticipate the course of events. But it seems to me that when the time comes there may well be an occasion when I find myself in conversation with Mr. Strauss[5] and when the conversation turns to Colonial affairs, and that things could then be said to him in strict confidence to throw sufficient light on the subject to enable him to avoid taking up a mis-guided attitude through ignorance of some of the weighty considerations in favour of accepting new candidates within the Commonwealth fold.

---

[4] Field-Marshal J C Smuts, prime minister of South Africa, 1939–1948; leader of the opposition, 1948–1950.
[5] J G N Strauss, leader of the opposition, South Africa, 1950–1956.

148   FO 371/113513, no 15   12 July 1955
'Visit of Mr Louw': brief by T E Bromley for Mr Macmillan on Mr Louw's proposals for a Pan-African conference

Mr. Louw, the South African Minister for External Affairs, will be paying an avowedly courtesy call on the Secretary of State at 10.45 a.m. on July 13. It is possible that he may raise the subject of his proposals for a pan-African conference.

Argument
2.   Mr. Louw is known to be very anxious to secure the calling of a conference of all countries interested in Africa South of the Sahara to discuss matters of common concern. The topics which Mr. Louw has suggested might be covered by this conference are set out in an aide mémoire given to the United Kingdom High Commissioner in Pretoria on March 21, 1955 (*Flag A*).[1] A covering despatch from Sir P. Leisching, and the comments of the High Commissioner's Office on the suggested agenda, are at *Flags B and C*.
3.   The list of subjects shows a strong anti-United Nations and anti-Asian bias, and

---

[1] The documents flagged with this brief are not printed.

2C

also suggests a concern with white supremacy. It is believed that in putting forward these proposals Mr. Louw may have two motives:—

(a) To reduce the sense of isolation which has been produced in the minds of South Africans by the hostile reaction of world public opinion towards *"apartheid"*;

(b) To strengthen his own position within the South African Government and particularly *vis-à-vis* Mr. Erasmus, the Minister of Defence.

4. Mr. Louw's proposals were brought to the attention of Lord Reading at the end of March and his views are contained in a minute at *Flag D*. The Commonwealth Relations Office are known to share Lord Reading's dislike of the proposed conference though the matter has not yet been put to Ministers.

5. Mr. Louw had a conversation with M. Spaak, the Belgian Foreign Minister, at San Francisco, in the course of which he sounded M. Spaak about the Belgian Government's view of his proposal. According to our Embassy in Brussels M. Spaak gave Mr. Louw a fairly dusty answer: this information has subsequently been confirmed by the Belgian Embassy here. The Portuguese Government are also reported to view the idea of a Pan-African conference with much distaste.

6. I suggest that from the point of view of Her Majesty's Government there would be few, if any, advantages, and very many disadvantages in attending a conference to discuss the topics suggested by Mr. Louw. It would certainly have a bad effect on our relations with India, on our influence with the emergent states of West Africa, and in general on our relations with the anti-colonial countries within the United Nations. We have moreover only just concluded an agreement with Mr. Erasmus by which we have undertaken to sponsor a conference to discuss communications and logistics on the African lines of communication.[2] We have yet to see whether our partners in the Nairobi and Dakar conferences will be prepared to fall in with this idea, and if we were to agree to a further political conference there is no doubt that Belgium, Portugal, France and Italy would be extremely suspicious of our motives. We do already engage in international co-operation on technical matters South of the Sahara through the Commission for Technical Co-operation South of the Sahara (C.C.T.A.), of which South Africa is a member. We have, however, no desire that C.C.T.A. should be used for political ends, since to do so would detract considerably from its value in the eyes of the African populations which it has been set up to serve. Point 8 of the proposed agenda suggests that Mr. Louw may have exactly this in mind. For all these reasons I suggest that no encouragement should be given to Mr. Louw to believe that we are prepared to attend a conference of the type which he proposes.

Recommendation

7. That should Mr. Louw raise the topic of his proposed conference he should be given no encouragement to believe that H.M.G. would be prepared to attend.[3]

---

[2] See 81, note 2.

[3] Sir I Kirkpatrick minuted, 12 July 1955: 'I agree . . . . Let us first see how the Erasmus meeting works' (FO 371/113513, no 15).

149   CO 1032/53, no 1   15 Dec 1955

'The Gold Coast and Commonwealth membership—conversation
between the United Kingdom high commissioner and the prime
minister of the Union of South Africa': despatch from Sir P Liesching
(Pretoria) to Sir G Laithwaite. *Enclosure*

[In Nov 1955 Lord Home advised Cabinet that Liesching considered the time was ripe for
him to speak to Strijdom about the admission of the Gold Coast to Commonwealth
membership. Liesching sought permission 'to make a generalised and provisional
approach in which he would deploy some of the arguments most likely to secure a
favourable response from the Afrikaaner mind'. Home recommended that Liesching
should be so authorised ('Commonwealth membership', Cabinet memo by Home, CAB
129/78, CP(55)182, 28 Nov 1955). Cabinet approved this recommendation (CAB 128/29,
CM 44(55)5, 1 Dec 1955).[1]]

With reference to my telegram No. 472 of the 13th December, I enclose a note
recording the conversation which I had on that day with Mr. Strijdom and Mr. Louw
on the subject of the Gold Coast.

In my opinion the results were as good as, if not rather better than, we could have
hoped for. Both Ministers listened with very close and serious attention to the
observations which I offered, and in their own questions and comments they were
much less reticent than I should have expected.

It struck me at the time as particularly significant that their first question—that
about the position of the Federation—should have based on the assumption that the
Gold Coast had been admitted. One can be mistaken, of course, but, not only then,
but throughout the discussion I got the impression that, while they were facing a
very unpalatable dish, they were at present of the mind that they would have to gulp
it down. I was surprised that they did not show more signs of distaste at the prospect,
for distasteful it certainly is to them.

I was confirmed in my impression by the Prime Minister's remark recorded in
paragraph 7 of the note. I consider he interjected this because there had been so little
counter-argument from them against the case for admission and because he thought
I was finding it all a bit too easy.

I think that the record speaks largely for itself. We must not yet take anything for
granted on a question which is extremely tricky for any South African Government
and not least for this one. We must also, if we are to carry them with us, pay
particular attention to the two points on which they concentrated so heavily:—

(a) The position of the Federation if the Gold Coast is admitted. This could
become a real stumbling block if the point is not met. It is from her own point of
view, not for love of the Federation, that South Africa would not be content to see
a "white country" (I do not speak of numbers) walking behind an African
"non-white country."

(b) The procedures to be adopted when the question comes up for discussion.
Much may turn on this.

As you will see, the argument likely to count most heavily with the South Africans

---

[1] For Cabinet's approval of this recommendation, see part II of this volume, 197. Home's memo is
reproduced in BDEEP series B, R Rathbone, ed, *Ghana*, part II, 202.

is the danger that a rejected Gold Coast will fall into the hands of the Communists or the Bandung Group.

But an argument which may count heavily is the strategic one. I used it (*vide* the last sentence of paragraph 6 of the note). I had not at the time seen C.O.S. (55) 275, which shows the important defence facilities we should wish to retain in the Gold Coast.[2] More should be made of this point on a future occasion.

Enclosure to 149

The Prime Minister received me at 10.30 a.m. on the 13th December. I had thought it wise to tell Mr. Louw that I was due to see Mr. Strijdom on this subject, which fell within his field of responsibility and interest, and, as I expected, he joined the Prime Minister for the interview.

2. I started by explaining to the Prime Minister the various stages of constitutional advance which had already taken place in the Gold Coast. I went on to describe the difficulties which had made their appearance recently, and were causing uncertainty about the time at which, with the abolition of the reserve powers of the Governor and the assumption of responsibility for external affairs and defence, the Gold Coast would attain its full independent constitutional status. But, I said, it was possible that this stage might be reached at the end of 1956 or during 1957; and, though it was at present impossible to say whether the subject would be ripe for discussion between Commonwealth Prime Ministers when they were in London next June, the Secretary of State had thought it right that I should have a purely provisional and preliminary talk with Mr. Strijdom on the subject.

3. I took care to emphasise that, although they were conscious of the problems which would then arise and of the various arguments for and against enlarging the circle of the full Members of the Commonwealth, United Kingdom Ministers were taking no view of their own on the subject yet, since it was one for collective decision; and that they would not be attempting to reach any conclusions until they had had an opportunity of hearing the views of others and contributing their own.

4. Mr. Strijdom intervened at this point, and was supported by Mr. Louw, in asking what would be the position of the Rhodesia and Nyasaland Federation if and when the Gold Coast was admitted. Mr. Strijdom said that he could hardly contemplate a situation in which the Federation with a comparatively large established European community should be called upon to take a place behind a purely native African state. I told the Prime Minister that this matter was very much in our minds. I was bound to admit that certain reservations in the constitution of

---

[2] These defence facilities were defined by the COS in COS(55)275, 21 Oct 1955 as follows. *Royal Navy:* in war-time it was considered desirable but not essential to have the right to set up a Naval Control of Shipping Organisation at Takoradi and similar rights in Tema when the construction of the port was completed. *Army:* the retention of the wireless station at Accra as an essential link in Commonwealth communication with Canada in both peace and war, and the retention of the recently completed Command Training School at Teshie as the main training centre for the forces of other British West African colonies as well as those from the Gold Coast itself. *Royal Air Force:* the right to stage aircraft through the Gold Coast both in peace and war, and the right to station a small maritime reconnaissance force in war should this prove necessary (CO 968/488, no 14). J S Bennett of the CO described these requirements as 'relatively small'.

the Federation represented a formal derogation from the status of the other full Members, and indeed from the status which, in the circumstances contemplated, the Gold Coast would enjoy. But I reminded him of the constant attendance by invitation enjoyed first by Southern Rhodesia and subsequently by the Federation over the past years, and went as far as I could to assure him that this particular problem would be properly looked after. I went so far as to express the personal view that public opinion in the Federation and, indeed, I thought, in the United Kingdom would not readily accept a situation in which the Federation was obliged to take a place behind the Gold Coast. Mr. Strijdom and Mr. Louw were both emphatic in their view that they themselves would find it difficult if not impossible to accept a situation in which the Gold Coast enjoyed precedence.

5. I then developed some of the considerations which would, I suggested, have to be weighed when the matter came up for decision. I acknowledged the hesitations which might be felt at the prospect of a dilution of the intimate relationships which existed in varying degrees between the existing Members of the Commonwealth. I touched on the idea of the "Second Tier" and discounted hopes that it could provide a satisfactory answer or one which would be accepted by a country which had achieved full constitutional independence.[3] I mentioned the discreet discrimination which was practised in the exchange of top secret information on difficult international matters, and said that a newly-established African state, while receiving suitable information on all matters concerning it, could not expect to be introduced to all the complex and delicate matters with which older Members were deeply concerned. Mr. Louw interjected some remarks based upon the unofficial use of the words "old Members of the Comonwealth," which were helpful to me in dealing with this point.

6. I referred to the important industrial and agricultural potential of the Gold Coast in the event of war, and went on to the argument which, I judged, was most likely to count with South African Ministers. I spoke of the difficulties of an adolescent nation launched upon a turbulent world. Such a nation must find friends and help and would be inclined to look for the hand of friendship from those with whom she had been associated in the past. If those hands were withheld, where would friendships be formed? If independent and outside the Commonwealth such a nation might fall into strange company in its international relations, not least if she were admitted, as might well be, to the United Nations Organisation. There was Russia looking for opportunities of making mischief in Africa, and there was also the danger that an African people, frustrated in its aspirations, might turn wholehearted-ly to the Bandung group. It was a question largely of where our interest and our best hopes lay in dealing with an independent country which was exposed to these dangers and lay across the important lines of communication to South Africa.

7. The Prime Minister then made various comments which showed that he no longer questioned the inevitability of the Gold Coast reaching an independent status. He said that he would have preferred a policy of *festina lente*, but agreed with me when I said that frustrated nationalism was one of the best seed-beds for Commun-ism. He went on to say that whereas before 1945 it might have mattered little, to South Africa at any rate, whether a country such as the Gold Coast became independent and went out of the Commonwealth, all things had changed since the rise of Russia as a great world Power, and these matters could no longer be regarded

---

[3] See part II of this volume, 192.

with indifference. There was, he agreed, much force in what I had said about the possibility of undesirable affiliations being formed.

8. Mr. Strijdom then referred to the speech which he had made about cultivating relations of friendly co-existence with non-European states to the north in Africa. He said that when he made this speech he was not thinking of such places as the Gold Coast but rather of such countries as Egypt and Ethiopia. I did not challenge this, except to say that I thought the Egyptians would probably not have read his speech as applying to themselves. Nor did I think it wise to refer to the significant leading article which appeared on the 3rd December in his own newspaper, the *Transvaler*, about which I wrote to Sir Gilbert Laithwaite on the 5th December.

9. The Prime Minister then turned with some signs of anxiety to the question how, if the subject was to be discussed among Commonwealth Prime Ministers, the discussions would be handled. He very much hoped that they would be canvassed first among the "old" Commonwealth countries and not be made the subject of a full and prolonged debate in Plenary Session. I said that speaking personally and in the light of my experience at a good many meetings of Prime Ministers, I thought that subjects of this kind would almost certainly first be the subject of quiet conversations—separately or jointly—between himself, United Kingdom Ministers, and such other Prime Ministers as Mr. St. Laurent and Mr. Menzies, and that it might well be that as a result of a series of discussions of this sort, in which the Asians were sometimes joined and sometimes not, the subject would not be brought to a Plenary Session until it was known that agreement had been reached. Prime Ministers might then simply be able to make speeches formally expressing such views as they wished to place on record. Mr. Strijdom and Mr. Louw in what they said on this point showed that they were anxious to avoid the kind of collision of views which can be foreseen if they became involved in discussions of this question with Mr. Nehru. They clearly wished to avoid any form of Plenary debate in which acrimony or dissension might find a place.

10. This conversation lasted for about forty minutes, and at its conclusion I left with the Union Ministers copies of the Colonial Office Memorandum on the Gold Coast dated the 25th October, 1955, copies of which were sent to my Deputy under cover of Commonwealth Relations Office letter Con 141/13 of the 3rd November.

150   DO 35/6176, no 45   28 June 1956

[Commonwealth prime ministers' meeting]: note by Sir G Laithwaite of a conversation with Sir N Brook about the Gold Coast

Sir Norman Brook told me yesterday that he understood that Mr. Strijdom had indicated to the Prime Minister that he would be quite prepared to accept the Gold Coast contingently as a Commonwealth member but was most reluctant that the matter should be discussed in Plenary Session.

2. The Prime Minister hand, it appeared, replied that he broadly accepted this on the understanding that Mr. Strijdom was prepared definitely to commit himself, but had indicated to Sir Norman Brook that it would be well that we should ensure that there was no doubt about this.

3. Sir Norman agreed that if this embargo on discussion in Plenary was to stand,

it would mean that we should have to approach the other Prime Ministers individually and obtain their concurrence in our intentions as regards the Gold Coast.

4. I said I would tell the Secretary of State how things stood. If the decision were to stand it looked at first sight as though we might have difficulty in bringing up the question of the future of the Rhodesian Federation. But Lord Malvern had given us a card of entry by his remarks at the opening Session about the desirability of getting the position of his successor regularised.[1]

5. Sir Norman said he thought that was the answer and that we could hook a discussion about the future of Rhodesia on to any discussion about the status of the Prime Minister.

6. We discussed the desirability of a general talk in Plenary on the position of colonies which were moving towards Commonwealth status, on which the Secretary of State had asked me to ascertain Sir Norman Brook's feeling. Sir Norman thought that, by and large, it would be better not to broach this subject. If even the Gold Coast were not to appear in Plenary Session it would be much more difficult to have a general talk about emergent colonies and there was a real risk of our getting back into an argument of [sic] anti-colonialism of the type that had been under discussion in connection with the briefing of Ministers.[2]

7. I have let the Secretary of State know the position. He is not very happy at having no discussion of the Gold Coast in Plenary and will probably speak to the Prime Minister to find out more precisely how things passed between him and Mr. Strijdom. As I understand it, he is content, however, not to take up the question of a general "Colonial" discussion and would agree too that even if, for whatever reason, the Gold Coast were not to be discussed in Plenary, we could still use Lord Malvern's remarks at the opening Session as the peg on which to hang specific proposals about the future of the Rhodesian Federation.

---

[1] Sir G Huggins (Lord Malvern 1955), prime minister of Southern Rhodesia, 1933–1953; prime minister of Central African Federation, 1953–1956. Malvern had attended meetings of Commonwealth prime ministers by invitation since 1934. The question now was whether his successor as prime minister of the Central African Federation would attend prime ministers' meetings 'as of right'. See part II of this volume, 305–310.

[2] 'Anti-"Colonialism"': note by the CO for Cabinet Committee on Commonwealth Prime Ministers' Meeting (CAB 130/113, GEN 518/6/14, 14 June 1956).

---

151   PREM 11/1367   5 July 1956

[Admission of Gold Coast to Commonwealth membership]: letter from Mr Strijdom to Sir A Eden. *Minute* by Lord Home (6 July) to Eden on Strijdom's letter

[On 3 July Eden wrote to the Commonwealth prime ministers, who were assembled in London for the prime ministers' meeting, to sound them out on the question of admission of the Gold Coast to full Commonwealth membership (for the text of Eden's letter, see part II of this volume, 279). A key paragraph is quoted by Strijdom in this response which was sent from the South African High Commission.]

In your letter of the 3rd July, 1956, you state:—

"If the present Prime Minister of the Gold Coast, Dr. Nkrumah, is returned, we know that he will introduce a motion calling for full self-goverment within the Commonwealth. The United Kingdom Government are committed to give effect to such a motion if it is passed by a reasonable majority".

In view of the above undertaking of your Government, it would appear that we are confronted with a fait accompli, and that refusal to agree at this stage would place the United Kingdom Government in a very embarrassing position.

If it were merely a matter of granting self-goverrment or full independence to a colony or dependency of the United Kingdom, that would of course be a matter for the decision only of the United Kingdom, but where as in the case of the Gold Coast the granting of independence is coupled with an undertaking to admit such a new State into the Commonwealth, then in my opinion it is a matter in regard to which prior consultation with Member States should take place before your Government commit themselves. In this case your High Commissioner in South Africa informed us that the Gold Coast would probably ask to be admitted to membership of the Commonwealth but the Union Government was not asked to express their views, with the resultant predicament in which we now find ourselves.

I would therefore very strongly urge that in future, and in the case of a similar request from any other dependency of the United Kingdom, prior agreement be arrived at between your Government and other Member States before your Government commit themselves.

Our fear, well-founded I think, is that the population of the Gold Coast, except for a small minority, is as yet so undeveloped and politically immature that the granting of full independence and concurrent admission to the Commonwealth would create a dangerous position for all concerned. In any case it creates an undesirable precedent. We are of the opinion that in the case of a political immature and largely undeveloped country like the Gold Coast, which has been granted independence with full power to manage its own affairs, there should first be a testing period, before the following step is taken of admitting it to membership of the Commonwealth.

In view of the fact, however, that your government are committed not only to grant full self-government, but also concurrent admission to the Commonwealth, and that refusal by us at this stage would place your Government in a very awkward position, the Union Government are prepared to give their consent, although we are convinced that the proposed action is for the reasons stated above, both premature and ill-advised.

In view of the importance of this matter I shall be glad if you would kindly bring the view of the Government of the Union of South Africa to the notice of the Prime Ministers of Canada, Australia, New Zealand and the Central African Federation respectively.

Minute on 151

Prime Minister
Mr. Strijdom's letter of the 5th July about the Gold Coast shows a serious misunderstanding of the United Kingdom position. I should have thought your letter of the 3rd July made it perfectly clear that you were in fact following the very procedure which he advocates, *viz* consulting the Union Government, along with the

Governments of all other Member countries of the Commonwealth, about the admission of the Gold Coast to Commonwealth Membership.[1] I attach a draft letter which I suggest you might send to him in reply.[2]

You will no doubt be agreeable to sending copies of the correspondence to the Prime Ministers of Canada, Australia and New Zealand, in accordance with Mr. Strijdom's request; Lord Malvern was not consulted in the first place, because the Federation is not a Member of the Commonwealth, and I do not recommend that the correspondence should be sent to him now.

I am sending a copy of this minute to the Colonial Secretary.

---

[1] It should be noted here that the British government customarily drew a distinction between 'self-government within the Commonwealth' and 'Membership of the Commonwealth'. All colonies were assumed to be 'within the Commonwealth' and to remain so at independence unless they opted to leave; but they could not attain full 'Membership', which entailed among things the right to attend prime ministers' meetings, until all existing Members had approved. Many people found the distinction difficult to grasp, and even senior British officials sometimes differed on how best to express it (see 154 and *ibid*, note 6). In his letter of 5 July Strijdom was clearly treating 'self-government within the Commonwealth' and 'Membership of the Commonwealth' as synonymous; what is less clear is whether he took this line because he misunderstood British constitutional doctrine or because it suited him politically to do so.
[2] Lord Home's draft (in fact drafted by I M R Maclennan, assistant under-secretary of state, CRO, 1955–1957) was couched in somewhat apologetic terms: 'I realise that I failed to make clear in my letter of the 3rd July what we had in mind . . .'. Eden would have none of this: 'Strijdom sent me an offensive letter, even an insulting one. We require no lesson from him in how to treat blacks. We must send a firmer reply. We shall not be respected by these bullies if we do not' (manuscript annotation on Home's draft, PREM 11/1367). For the revised version, see 152.

---

152 PREM 11/1367   11 July 1956

[Admission of Gold Coast to Commonwealth membership]: letter (reply) from Sir A Eden to Mr Strijdom

> [Lord Home sent a revised draft to Eden on 10 July with a covering memo: '. . . I attach a stiffer version with which I hope you will agree. We have got our point of substance out of them, and the drafting in this case is, I am certain, not Strijdom's but Louw's. I have no very strong feeling about sending copies to the other Prime Ministers but, on the whole, I would prefer to do so. The South African letter is so misconceived that it will do South Africa no good and the reply that you will be sending will again put the correct constitutional position on the record . . .' (PREM 11/1367).]

Thank you for your letter of July 5.[1] I am glad to know that the Union Government are prepared to give their consent to the granting to the Gold Coast of Membership of the Commonwealth once that country has achieved full self-government.

You mention in the second paragraph of your letter that you recognise that the granting of full self-government is a matter for the decision of the United Kingdom Government alone. In the case of the Gold Coast the United Kingdom Government are committed to the grant of full self-government and, as I indicated in paragraph two of my letter, once this stage has been reached, the question that will have to be faced is not whether the country is to remain in the Commonwealth (the Gold Coast

---

[1] See 151.

2D

is already in the Commonwealth as are all other United Kingdom dependencies) but whether it is to become a Member of the Commonwealth. As regards the latter status, the United Kingdom Government, of course, agree that admittance to Membership of the Commonwealth is a matter in regard to which there must always be prior consultation with existing Member countries, and it is in accordance with this principle that I wrote to you on July 3 seeking your view as Prime Minister of the Union of South Africa, and, concurrently, the views of the Prime Ministers of other Member countries.

In accordance with the request which you make in your final paragraph, I am sending copies of your letter and of this reply to the Prime Ministers of Canada, Australia and New Zealand, but I am not sending copies to the Prime Minister of the Federation of Rhodesia and Nyasaland, since Lord Malvern was not among those to whom my letter of July 3 was addressed.

153   PREM 11/1367   8 Aug 1956
[Admission of Gold Coast to Commonwealth membership]: letter (reply) from Mr Strijdom to Sir A Eden

This is really the first opportunity I have of replying to your letter of July 11, which was delivered to me immediately before my departure from England on the 12th July.

In so far as the Union Government's consent to the admission of the Gold Coast as a member of the Commonwealth is concerned, I wish to emphasize that such consent was given in the circumstances set out in the penultimate paragraph of my letter of the 5th July, which reads as follows:—

"In view of the fact, however, that your Government are committed not only to grant full self-Government but also concurrent admission to the Commonwealth and that refusal by us at this stage would place your Government in a very awkward position, the Union Government are prepared to give their consent, although we are convinced that the proposed action is for the reasons stated above both premature and ill-advised."

I want to repeat that the granting of independence to a dependency of the United Kingdom, if admission to membership to the Commonwealth thereafter were not involved, would be a matter of decision only of the United Kingdom, but that the admission of such a new or independent state as a member of the Commonwealth, is a matter with which each member State is vitally concerned, and that the United Kingdom Government should therefore, before committing themselves, consult with and obtain the consent of the other member States.

Consultation with member States, by letter in this case, as late as the 3rd July, 1956, after your Government had already committed themselves in so far as the Gold Coast was concerned, in effect amounted to the other member States being confronted with a fait accompli, as stated in my letter of the 5th July.

It was in view of this fact that I so strongly urged in my letter of the 5th July, that in the case of a similar request for independence and membership of the Commonwealth from any other dependency of the United Kingdom, your Government should, before committing themselves, consult with and obtain the consent of the Governments of the other member States.[1]

---

[1] Eden's manuscript annotation on this letter was 'Still obstinate, rude and purblind'.

154   DO 35/6176, no 70A   29 Aug 1956
[Admission of Gold Coast to Commonwealth membership]: letter from Sir G Laithwaite to Sir P Liesching (Pretoria)

In his letter to Garner of 9th August, about the attitude of Union Ministers to the Gold Coast, Belcher[1] said that the chances were that a further letter from Mr. Strijdom would come to London. I send you herewith a copy of a further letter from Mr. Strijdom to Sir A Eden dated 8th August.[2] The Prime Minister has decided, after consulting the Secretary of State, to send no reply or further explanation to Mr. Strijdom. As to the request in Mr. Strijdom's last paragraph the Secretary of State's position is already sufficiently on record in Sir A Eden's letter of 11th July. There seems no profit in rejecting in even blunter terms the suggestion that we should obtain the consent of other Commonwealth Governments before granting full self-government to one of our Dependencies.[3]

We were much interested in Belcher's comments on this matter; and in view of the care which you have taken in your communications with Union Ministers on the conceptions of self-government and membership of the Commonwealth, it looks distinctly probable that for domestic reasons, Mr. Strijdom and Mr. Louw may be taking advantage of an admittedly complex point to keep a misunderstanding alive.[4]

There is nothing more that we wish to do about this at present, though we look forward with interest to any further light you can throw on the South African attitude, since we are not out of the wood yet in the case of the Gold Coast, and the Federation of Malaya will, we expect, be not long behind. We are looking carefully into the amount of information which we have been able to send to other Commonwealth Governments about developments in Malaya, and we shall try to ensure that no one has cause to complain of being left in the dark.[5]

Belcher reported that the phrase "self-government within the Commonwealth" may have given rise to genuine misunderstanding. The normal significance of this

---

[1] See 85, note 3.   [2] See 153.

[3] Strijdom's final paragraph could indeed be read as suggesting that not only membership of the Commonwealth but also the granting of independence to a colony should be subject to the approval of Commonwealth members.

[4] Somewhat later, however, Louw informed Liesching that he and Strijdom had genuinely misunderstood the British constitutional doctrine (letter from Liesching to Laithwaite, PREM 11/1367, 19 Sept 1956).

[5] The force of this remark can be gleaned from a minute which Laithwaite had earlier sent to Home: 'The South Africans have been tedious about this. . . . But there is, I think, for all that just a shadow of substance in the point which Mr Strijdom made. . . . I am not sure that we are not ourselves to some extent to blame over the Gold Coast.' The point of substance was that Eden's letter of 3 July had come so late that Commonwealth prime ministers had the sense of being confronted with a fait accompli; Canadian officials had privately confirmed this point in talks with Laithwaite (minute by Laithwaite to Home, DO 35/6167, 23 Aug 1956).

phrase is not so much to represent a transitional state[6] as a theoretical goal. Self-government means neither more nor less than it says. The words "within the Commonwealth" are customarily appended in order to indicate and emphasise that the objective of our policy, and the goal which we are setting before the dependency in question, is that of a fully self-governing state remaining in the Commonwealth, a situation which we would welcome, though Belcher is, of course, right in implying that a country which has achieved this goal has the power and liberty to leave the Commonwealth thereafter.

The phrase "self-government within the Commonwealth" on the other hand does not in itself mean or convey anything as to the recognition by the existing members of the Commonwealth of the new country as one of themselves. Self-government is a matter for the United Kingdom; recognition as a Member is a matter for all the existing Members; and this distinction implies the theoretical possibility that the one status might be achieved without the other. We are very conscious, however, that it is more a theoretical than a practical possibility, and the situation is one which we must do our utmost to avoid in any particular case. To that end we obviously must ensure that Commonwealth Governments are fully informed of progress in U.K. dependencies. I have already mentioned Malaya in this connection, but we shall hope to cover in the same way all candidates for Commonwealth membership as they emerge.

---

[6] This was in fact the construction that Belcher had put upon the phrase (letter from R H Belcher to Sir S Garner, DO 35/6176, no 67, 9 Aug 1956).

155 CO 936/100   11–18 Feb 1952
[Proposed UN covenants on human rights]: minutes by W A Morris,[1] Sir H Poynton and B O B Gidden

Sir H. Poynton

I am sorry to trouble you with this subject, which you will recognise as a familiar spectre from the time when you used to deal with this group of subjects. But I think that I must report one development over Human Rights to you, under the arrangements for submission of papers during Sir T Lloyd's absence.

2. The Human Rights Commission is due to meet again in April. Meantime, the Third Committee have been passing some more Resolutions to guide the Commission in its work. They have, for example, decided to ask the Commission to draft two Covenants on Human Rights, one to contain civil and political rights, and the other economic, social and cultural rights; but I need not bother you with these details. On the 25th January, however, they passed a Resolution to include in the Covenant an article on the right of all peoples to self-determination, mentioning twice the obligation of colonial powers to promote the realisation of that right in relation to peoples of non-self-governing territories. This was the work of the Russians, and a number of oddments, but it gained acceptance despite the opposition of the U.K., the other Colonial powers and the U.S.A.

3. The formal reasons for objecting to this Resolution are threefold:—

---

[1] W A Morris, assistant secretary, CO, head of International Relations Dept 'B'.

(a) It brings into a document purporting to deal with the fundamental rights of individuals a right which has reference only to States or collections of people.

(b) In pretending to reaffirm the principles of the Charter of the United Nations, it goes further than anything which is in the Charter.

(c) It particularly singles out the Colonial powers.

The whole thing is a vexatious piece of tactics directed to making the Colonial powers appear as opponents of the principle of self-determination. The Resolution calls for the Commission on H.R. to prepare recommendations inviting members of the United Nations to avoid manoeuvres frustrating the right of peoples to self-determination, including the obstruction of the free expression of the peoples will, etc., etc. If this were adopted, it would manifestly give a handle to tactics in the United Nations over ENOSIS, and so on.[2]

4. I understand from the Foreign Office that this Resolution was bound to be endorsed by the Assembly, and that the U.K. representative would confine himself to saying that the U.K. was in favour of all good things and against all bad things, but regarded this Resolution as misplaced in the Human Rights Covenant. There is nothing more to be done until the Whitehall Working Party on Human Rights considers what line should be taken at the meeting of the Commission in April. At that stage, it will probably be necessary to submit the matter again; but as the present Assembly Resolution is something that affects us so closely, I thought that I could not let it pass without reporting to higher authority at this stage.

5. Of course, there is some way to go before the question will arise of whether the U.K. can sign the Covenant on Human Rights. As far as I have been able to see, the present drafts are in much to woolly a form for H.M.G. to be able to sign up. Incidentally, there is no Colonial Application Clause, which is another stumbling block for us.

W.A.M.
11.2.52

Seen with alarm, but not despondency. The important thing, to my mind, is that we must avoid recognising any right of any international body to interfere in the political and constitutional relationship between the U.K. and our n.s.g. territories (other than "Trust Territories" to the extent of Caps XII and XIII & the Trusteeship Agreements).[3] That is why information on "political" conditions was deliberately excluded from Article 73(e)—and our refusal to supply such information is still, I believe, a matter of regular and perennial controversy. I am very much afraid that the

---

[2] As I Wallace of the CO put it in a letter to A A Dudley of the FO: 'I will not weary you by recalling the long history of Colonial Office reluctance throughout the years of discussion there have been about this subject of human rights. We have always been, or tried to be, the brake on the U.K. chariot, not because we have colonial horrors to hide, but because we have always recognised the opportunities offered by international conventions on human rights to dangerous outside interference in the delicate and changing relations between H.M.G. and the Colonial Governments and peoples' (letter from Wallace to Dudley, CO 936/108, no 3, 19 Dec 1951).

[3] Britain's UN trust territories (formerly League of Nations mandated territories) were Tanganyika, British Cameroons and British Togoland. Under ch. XII of the UN charter, the Trusteeship Council had certain powers of supervision over Britain's administration of these territories. Colonial affairs more generally were normally discussed in the UN's Fourth Committee, a committee of the whole which received reports from the Trusteeship Council and the Committee on Information from Non-Self-Governing Territories.

inclusion of a provision about self-determination of peoples in the Convention on H.R., especially if accompanied by provisions for implementation, would give the U.N. precisely that right which we must continue to refuse. The arguments advanced against the proposal have been in my view perfectly sound; though arguments influence few votes in the UN 'racket'. If we cannot vote it down, our only remedy will be not to ratify this Convention. I gather we may have to refuse ratification anyhow because of some of its other provisions. I cannot deny that our position would be more easily defensible if we could apply the Convention (without "self-determination" to lead it astray) to all our "n.s.g.'s". But that is another story.

It would, by the way, be worth checking whether there is any reference to "self-determination" in the Trusteeship System provisions (Charter or Agreements). If not (and my recollection is that there are not) it is manifestly absurd for the U.N. to insist upon more rigorous provisions for n.s.g.'s generally than they have thought necessary for those of them over which the U.N. itself exercises some responsibility of supervision—though I suppose a cantankerous critic could argue the opposite.

Anyhow let us stand on Chaps XI and XII.

A.H.P.
11.2.52

Please see Sir Hilton Poynton's minute. It occurs to me that it is not only the inclusion of provisions about self-determination, but also the arrangements to be made about implementation of the Covenant, which we shall have to watch closely to ensure that we do not bring to life the right of the U.N. to obtain information about the political conditions in our territories. I should be grateful if Mr. Gidden could confirm Sir H. Poynton's understanding that there is no reference to self-determination in the Trusteeship System provisions.

W.A.M.
12.2.52

There is no mention of "self-determination" either in the Trusteeship Agreements or in Chapter XII of the Charter (or, for that matter, in Chapter XI of the Charter).

However, Article 76(b) of the Charter does refer to "the freely-expressed wishes of the people concerned" and I think there can be little doubt that this phrase means very much the same as "self-determination"; "self-determination" is referred to in Article 1(2) of the Charter. I understand that the reason why "self-determination" is not repeated in Article 76(b) is because when that Article was drafted in 1945 the Palestine question was very much in peoples' minds and both Arabs and Jews could have claimed the right to self-determination if it had been.[4]

B.O.B.G.
18.2.52

---

[4] Morris and others in the CO felt, and continued to feel, that the FO was partly responsible for Britain's predicament on this issue: 'the F.O. are disposed to consider . . . that the U.K. has already implicitly recognised, by its actions in the U.N., *vis à vis* Russia, that human rights have an international character. . . . The F.O., in the early stages, were so anxious to dish the Russians that they did not think ahead to all the implications for ourselves, especially in relation to the Colonies, of a weakening of Article 2(7) of the Charter' (minute by W A Morris, CO 936/108, 16 July 1952).

156   FO 371/101383, no 4   16 Feb 1952

'Colonial questions in the United Nations: analysis of the Sixth Session and proposals for the Seventh Session': memorandum by C P Hope

Introduction

Although the specialist departments of the French and American Governments and the Colonial Office have not yet completed their analysis of events in the Fourth Committee of the recently completed Sixth Session of the General Assembly, we already have some indications of the way in which the views of these departments are forming. This has, for instance, already led both the French and the State Department to make unofficial enquiries in the Foreign Office about our thinking. Both Governments clearly anticipate more trouble next year and want to consult with us about this.

2.   The French are perhaps the more worried because they feel that the United States are grudging in support for their policies and because they recognise that we ourselves are not prepared to take as tough a line in the United Nations as they would wish.

3.   The State Department feel that they have perhaps let us down by their policy of "liberalism" and they are clearly concerned that the harmony achieved in the pre-Assembly Anglo-American Colonial Talks did not bear more fruit in Committee.

4.   The Colonial Office on the other hand are not so concerned about the future. They feel we have benefitted from the failure of the United States to maintain their leadership in the Fourth Committee. Our prestige has been further enhanced by comparison with the intransigent and unpopular policies which the French have pursued. They believe we have emerged from an admittedly difficult debate with enhanced credit and probably because the Colonial Office believe we could again successfully threaten to withdraw from the Committee if it showed signs of exceeding its functions, they are at the moment not to perturbed.

5.   It seems, however, inevitable that events in this year's Assembly are a pre-cursor to renewed pressure next year by the non-administering powers rather than an abortive attempt which has failed once and for all. The anti-Colonial spirit in the Fourth Committee has now been coupled with the rise of nationalism, particularly in the Middle East, and consequently a number of member states have national objectives to pursue which conveniently fit into the anti-Colonial movement. As a result, efforts to lessen the influence of Colonial powers, particularly in the Middle East, have become more open. There have been overt references to Aden, to Cyprus and much enthusiasm over Morocco and Tunisia has been whipped up. It would therefore seem quite unrealistic to argue that pressure in the Fourth Committee has been stopped for good by threats from the administering powers to leave it or that this pressure will not gather momentum next year.

What went wrong in the Fourth Committee?

6.   A broad analysis of recent events shows that in fact no real harm was done to our interest this year in the Committee. On the other hand, a number of resolutions were passed where we have had to make it clear that we do not intend to implement them. This necesary if undesirable development does not, however, harm us much if we can give good reasons for our actions and if we have on our side native opinion.

An example of this is the call made by the Fourth Committee to suppress corporal punishment, a call which has been resisted more strongly by the native chiefs than by the administering power itself.

7. Our position would of course have become prejudiced were we to refuse to follow the recommendations of the Fourth Committee on an issue supported by the local population. This might well have been the case over the Ewe problem had unificationists been able to apply concerted pressure on the Fourth Committee. Paradoxically, however, the influence of Nkrumah, the present Prime Minister of the Gold Coast, which has tended to embarrass us in the United Nations has also had the effect of dividing the Ewe movement so that a risk of the character described above has so far been averted.

8. This risk, however, becomes more real in the case of some of our Colonies, e.g. Cyprus. Support at the United Nations to local dissidents might give rise to trouble in the territories. It is for this reason that the movement in the Fourth Committee to take a hand in the political affairs of non-self-governing territories undoubtedly represents for us a real risk.

9. This is perhaps the only respect in which the proceedings of the Fourth Committee were worse than last year because the principle of discussing the political affairs of non-self-governing territories was nearly established.

10. It is true that the move was defeated for the time being by:—

(a) the intervention of the Americans behind the scenes with the Secretariat. It is significant that even Dr. Bunche[1] realised that the Fourth Committee were pushing the administering powers too far, and
(b) because we publicised our threat to leave the Committee.

11. If we have had our own difficulties in the Committee so have the French and so, of course, have the South Africans. Our support of the French, our efforts to prevent the Assembly from considering Morocco as well as our defence of the complaint by the South African Government that the Fourth Committee had exceeded its legal functions in agreeing to hear petitioners from S.W Africa before it had assumed international responsibilities for the territory, have not perhaps harmed us. Our reactions were not unexpected but they equally did not gain us sympathy. The non-administering powers however were disgruntled at the way in which they had been deflected and debates on these subjects consolidated their ranks.

Possible courses of action

(1) General

12. We have in the past to some extent neglected intensive lobbying amongst other member states on colonial issues. We have done this because we firstly thought that we could anyway rely on our friends (particularly the Western Europeans) and because we felt it would be useless to lobby amongst the rest (particularly the South

---

[1] R J Bunche, principal director, Department of Trusteeship, UN, 1947–1954. C C Parrott commented: 'I should have thought that the decisive factor was the Secretary of State's frank speaking with Mr Trygve Lie [UN secretary-general, 1946–1953] which in its turn led to Bunche practically being given orders to stop the rot in the Fourth Committee. I still think that high level intervention in private is far more effective than dramatic moves in public' (minute by Parrott, FO 371/101383, no 4, 19 Feb 1952).

Americans) unless we were assured of benevolent neutrality from the United States Delegation. For reasons given below it seems doubtful if we can continue this policy.

13.   It is consequently suggested that we should consider one or more of the following lines:

(a) *Diplomatic approaches.* It would perhaps be more dignified and equally effective not to circulate as we have in the past a general self-adulatory despatch on our achievements, but to lobby actively and do this more concisely and more categorically. We should not be deterred from lobbying amongst the Europeans and at least some of the South Americans whatever the U.S. attitude.

(b) We should attempt to concert tactics with other administering powers. If it however came to a walk-out, a joint walk out, or a threat to do this, would clearly be more effective. At the same time we must be careful not to call "wolf, wolf" too often and it may be difficult to reach agreement under what conditiions threats for a walk-out should be made.

(c) We should make a really determined effort this year to ensure the election of a more effective Chairman of the Fourth Committee. The incumbent at the recent session was a weakling.

(d) We should endeavour to prevent the early debate of unpleasant issues. Difficulties in the Fourth Committee have arisen from the outset because other powers have spoilt the atmosphere there. The South Africans did it this time.

(e) We should try to see if we could not prevent the solidification of the Arab-Latino bloc. The question of the Italian Colonies was at one time an issue which divided them. It may be that Morocco is one on which they could now be split.

(f)   We should endeavour to list not only subjects which are likely to appear on the agenda of the forthcoming session, but also subjects which may be put forward by anti-Colonial powers. There were, for instance, some ingenious attempts made to undermine the position of the administering powers mainly by deriding the standing of the Trusteeship Council and by attempting to destroy the equal balance between administering and non-administering powers on that Council and its bodies. (It might, for instance, be possible to expose such proposals and to say that if the balance in these bodies were destroyed the administering powers would not be prepared to take their recommendations so seriously.)

14.   The suggestions made above have been put forward after examination of the Fourth Committee in vacuo. It has been assumed that so far events in that Committee have not affected other Committees. It is, however, possible that in time the Committee may provide a training ground for lining up majorities against, say, the Atlantic Powers. An obvious counter to this would be to break up any Arab-Latino bloc as best we might. Rifts in the Arab bloc are now visible and we should not despair of breaking up the Latinos.

(2) *Action with the Americans*

15.   It is in a way the U.S. Government which provides the key to our problem in the Fourth Committee. Without at least their benevolent neutrality our position in that Committee is a difficult one. Lobbying with the more reasonable members of it becomes harder and the split disclosed amongst the administering powers is exploited to the full.

16. The U.S. position this year has been dominated by the spirit of liberalism which has been more apparent amongst their delegates than officials. Mrs. Roosevelt[2] and Mr. Channing Tobias[3] (their Delegate in the Fourth Committee) have carried the day with the result that the U.S. Delegation has been reluctant to be too closely associated with efforts by the remaining administering powers to contain the Fourth Committee and keep its activities within the powers given to it by the Charter.

17. In the past we have felt that we could not expect United States co-operation on specific issues unless we convinced them of the justice of our general policies in the Colonial field and consequently of the need to limit as far as possible undesirable activities of the United Nations which might undermine these. We have recognised that it would be difficult to persuade the Americans entirely, but we have hoped at least to prevent them from accepting plausible proposals by anti-Colonial powers. It is, however, very doubtful if we can this year hope to continue this policy. Elections in the United States must inevitably weaken the hand of the State Department since they will occur at the time of the opening of the Seventh Session. Whichever way these elections go it is very doubtful if we can get whole-hearted American support for our policies. We will either be faced with the continuation of this year's "liberalism" or there may be objections to our policies simply because we represent a Colonial power.

18. These considerations apply with redoubled force to the French who will find it even harder to secure support for their claims of domestic jurisdiction and their efforts on these grounds to prevent, say, Tunisia or Morocco from appearing on the Assembly's agenda.

19. In these circumstances it would seem more profitable for us to lobby thereby to secure agreement on tactics. These specific issues should, however, not only be those likely to appear on the agenda but should also include the difficult and contentious problems which have been raised above. Cyprus, Morocco, the Ewes, etc., are examples where U.S. tactics generally differ from our own. Even if exchanges of this sort do not result in agreement the foreknowledge of U.S. intentions would be of great value and might on certain issues enable us to take useful steps to meet such a situation.

20. If the general considerations described above meet with approval a first step might be to prepare a fairly general paper for H.M. Embassy, Washington, to be used as a basis for a high level démarche with Mr. Hickerson. Such a démarche might lead to further exchanges at a working level in Washington concerned with specific questions and aimed at agreeing joint Anglo-U.S. tactics on this. It would seem most important that these working level discussions should be concluded in an uninhabited atmosphere. Matters on which we and the U.S. do not see eye to eye should not be left on one side, but on the contrary probed very fully perhaps even on the understanding that exchanges of this sort will only result in agreement to differ.

21. A slight complication in these proposals arises because it seems, at any rate at the moment, as if the Colonial Office are less concerned than we about the Fourth Committee at the next session of the General Assembly. This difference of emphasis,

---

[2] Mrs E Roosevelt, US representative, UN General Assembly, 1945–1952.
[3] C Tobias, director, Phelps-Stokes fund, USA, 1946–1953; visited several African countries on behalf of fund.

however, is not likely to prevent exchanges of the type described above, though it may mean that the Foreign Office will wish to take a greater part in the exchanges than they did last year.

157   FO 371/101363, no 48   [Mar 1952]
'The Fourth Committee': memo by D I Dunnett[1] analysing anti-colonialism in the UN

1. In what ways have proceedings at the United Nations damaged our position in colonies and trust territories?

(i) By tending to edge us into a position in which we have to give an account to the United Nations of our administration of our colonies. This point is amplified in the Colonial Office draft.[2] It may be remarked that we have all along been accountable for our administration of trust territories, i.e. we have had to allow petitions, visiting missions, etc. This does not seem to have impaired our hold on these territories so far. Presumably, however, there are different factors present in our colonies, as a result of which our hold on them would be weakened if petitions, visiting missions, etc. were allowed.

(ii) It passes resolutions tending to tie the hands of our administrators, e.g. calling for the abolition of corporal punishment.

(iii)   It encourages unrest in colonies by:—

(a) Weakening respect for British authority, e.g. by calling for the flying of the United Nations flag in trust territories, and for the dissemination of information about the United Nations.

(b) It provides a forum where speeches encouraging agitation are delivered.

(iv) By its handling of South-West Africa it has made it less likely that African countries, after attaining independence, will agree to remain within a Commonwealth of which South Africa is a member. It may even have made more probable the exit of South Africa itself from the Commonwealth.

2. It is not only in the Fourth Committee that things detrimental to our interest have been going on. The United Nations as a whole is responsible for creating examples of colonial territories attaining independence, e.g. Libya, Indonesia, Somaliland, and these have an unsettling influence on other dependent territories. The discussion of human rights in the Third Committee and the general ventilation of ideas of racial equality and self-determination also tend to under-mine our position.

3. We may seek to arrest these tendencies either by:—

(a) Altering the motives of those who make these attacks on our position, or

(b) By denying them the means by which to make their attacks effective.

---

[1] D I Dunnett, UN (Political) Dept, FO.

[2] 'United Nations General Assembly: note on United Kingdom policy towards the Fourth Committee', draft memo by CO (principal author W G Wilson), FO 371/101363, no 48, Mar 1952.

4. The motives prompting various countries to assail our position in this way are varied:—

(a) Some countries are openly predatory, e.g. Guatamala-British Honduras, Yemen-Aden, Greece-Cyprus.

(b) Some countries are seeking to extend their power in a more subtle way, e.g. Egypt's attitude to Africa, in particular North Africa, and the attitude of India to East Africa. China has also a natural interest in the Chinese minorities in South-East Asia.

(c) Ideological. On colonial issues the liberal and the Communist come close together; it cannot be forgotten that the Atlantic Charter proclaims respect for the right of all peoples to choose the form of Government under which they will live, and that the United Kingdom was herself largely responsible for Chapters 11 and 12 of the United Nations Charter.

(d) The general rise of the under-privileged against the privileges [sic]. This is directed as much against the U.S. as ourselves. c.f. the demands for funds for undeveloped territories.

5. While predatory designs may be exposed and discredited it is unlikely that in the present climate of world opinion any appreciable impression can be made on the widespread feeling that the dependence of one people on another is morally wrong.

6. The line in which we think the best chance lies is to point out that the maintenance of our position is in the interest of the state whose support we are seeking, e.g. Turkey desires our retention of Cyprus. India by no means desires us to evacuate East Africa. The maintenance of our position is probably in the general strategic interest of the U.S.A. While something may be achieved on these lines it is unlikely that such appeals will prevail against the ideological motives for weakening our position.

7. We must therefore consider how countries impelled by these motives can be denied the means of giving them effect. Two proposals have been put forward:—

(A) The Belgians have proposed that they should take our stand on the principle that whatever is applicable to the inhabitants of non-self-governing territories should equally apply to the inhabitants of self-governing states. There are the following arguments against this course:—

(i) We have considered it ourselves in the past and decided not to employ it on the grounds:—

(a) the material which we could collect is not particularly effective;
(b) feelings in the Fourth Committee would be inflamed, whereas it was our policy to keep tempers low.

(ii) If this policy were launched by the Belgians, the most extreme reactionaries, it would be damned from the outset.

(iii) It is not in accordance with the Charter. The Belgians have to look back to the Covenant of the League for very doubtful authority for it. It would in effect contravene Article 2(7) of the Charter (on Deomestic [sic] Jurisdiction).

(iv) It would be ultra vires the Fourth Committee, though perhaps within the competence of the Third Committee to consider the kind of questions the Belgians would wish to raise.

8.   There are, however, the following points in favour of the Belgian idea:—

(i) It is probably the direction in which we could most usefully encourage American thinking to develop. The Americans have already asked us to supply political information about our Colonies in the hopes that the example will be followed with the eventual result that all countries allowed all their affairs to be discussed.

(ii) Discussions on the Human Rights Covenant may afford us an opportunity to act on the Belgian thesis, though perhaps not in the Fourth Committee. We could find ways of making it clear, e.g. to the Guatemalans, that attacks by them on us in the Fourth Committee would produce attacks by us on them in the Third Committee.

(iii) There is a general principle in law that "he who comes for equity must come with clean hands". It was on this principle that the Russian attack on the American Mutual Security Act with its encouragement of subversive elements in Communist countries was rejected by the First Committee. A limited appeal to this principle might be possible in the Fourth Committee.

(B) The French and the South Africans have adopted the policy of walking out of the Committee when the Committee has challenged principles which they regard as fundamental. The objects which it is thought that a walk-out might achieve are:—

(i) the shock of seeing one or more administering powers walk-out would pull the Committee up with a jerk and "bring it to its senses";

(ii) if the administering powers walked out en masse, the Fourth Committee would be put out of business.

9.   However:—

(i) The walk-out by the South Africans and the French had a negligible effect on the Fourth Committee's proceedings. It may be argued that a walk-out by the United Kingdom would be more seriously regarded. Since the Committee has experienced the walk-out of the French and South Africans and felt no ill effects it is doubtful whether the shock of a walk-out by the U.K. would by itself have more than a passing effect.

(ii) It is not clear how the absence of the administering powers would prevent the Fourth Committee functioning. It is true that the resolutions they might pass would not be implemented by the administering authorities. But the Committee well realises that, like the U.N. as a whole, its effectiveness lies not in the resolutions which it passes, but in the platform which it affords for propaganda and publicity. There seems no reason why the Committee should not hear the Archbishop of Cyprus and the Kenya Africans in our absence.

10.   There are the following further arguments against a walk-out:—

(i) The Secretary of State for Foreign Affairs is on record as saying that he is against any ostentatious action. It is true that he did agree on one occasion that we should walk out of the Fourth Committee. While the interpretation of this incident may be doubtful it appears that the Secretary of State was more incensed by the Guatemalan attack on His late Majesty than by the issues of principle, and it was the knowledge that public opinion would strongly support a resolute attitude to such irresponsible rudeness.

(ii) A walk-out would have far-reaching repercussions on our whole position at the U.N. The guiding principle seems to be that we might in certain circumstances walk-out, but as at the last Assembly it would have to be on an issue over which opinon both at the United Nations and in this country would be solidly in our favour. This would not necessarily be the case on any particular issue which from the constitutional point of view we might regard as essential, e.g. opinion might not support us if we walked out simply because the Fourth Committee was asking us to abolish corporal punishment in Basutoland, although we object to the naming of any particular Colonial territory in Fourth Committee resolutions.

11. The conclusion seems to be that in certain circumstances which cannot be foreseen in advance, the policies of the Belgians and of the French might be appropriate, but that we cannot plan ahead to use these instruments in the normal shaping of our policy. The most that can perhaps be done now is to list the various instruments which we might employ and the considerations for and against their use. Our difficulties in the Fourth Committee are likely to continue for many years and it is unlikely that any dramatic victory can be achieved by either side in the foreseeable future.

12. Possible tactics which we might consider are:

(i) Limited denial of co-operation to the Fourth Committee, e.g.

(a) declining to implement Fourth Committee resolutions;
(b) declining to supply information under 73(e) on the grounds that it was merely being used as ammunition against us.
NOTE: The Americans would take a very grave view of both these steps. It would have to be decided in the light of circumstances whether public opinion would support such action.

(ii) More carefully planned diplomatic approaches. It is suggested that this should be designed to secure specific commitments from those addressed, e.g.

(a) that they would issue instructions to their representatives in the Fourth Committee and not give them a free hand;
(b) that they would instruct their delegates to keep in touch with ours.

(iii) Procedural measures in the Fourth Committee, e.g. election of efficient Chairmen, arrangement of business to keep contentious items to the end.

158 FO 371/101363, no 49 24 Mar 1952
[CO and FO attitudes towards the UN]: minute by C P Hope on a CO draft memorandum

[The CO's lengthy draft memo 'Note on United Kingdom policy towards the Fourth Committee' (see 157, note 2) had opened with references to 'deep-rooted anti-colonial feeling' and 'prejudice' among the majority of UN members: 'the conception that colonialism in all its forms (whether direct colonial administration as exemplified by the British Empire, or interference by one State in the affairs of another e.g. British influence in Iran and Egypt) is evil'. Arguing that 'The need to maintain our position in the Colonial

Empire . . . is a paramount of interest of H.M.G. and, we believe, of the Colonial peoples', the memo advocated selective use of the tactic of walking out of UN proceedings.]

By ascribing the motives of non-administering Powers to "prejudice" the C.O. have ignored many valid and understandable reasons which cause so many members of the U.N. to be anti-imperialist. Lobbying against prejudice is not likely to succeed. If we are to safeguard our colonial interests from undesirable interference by the U.N. we must recognise & counter real motives e.g. Greek aspirations in Cyprus, Arab desire to see us out of Aden & the Canal and French influence removed from N. Africa, etc. etc.

2. To fall back on a Walk out as a major instrument of policy in such circumstances will do little good even in the 4th cttee and wd. be oddly at variance with our policy on parallel political questions in cttees I and the Ad hoc.

3. So far the 4th cttee has not really embarrassed our Colonial policies— therefore our aim is surely to continue to string the cttee along. It can only cause real trouble if it extends its powers outside the Charter (which we largely wrote ourselves). We can counter this by showing legal reasons (a) for non-implementation and (b) if necessary, for a formal demonstration i.e. the Walk out.

159   FO 371/101363, no 49   10 May 1952
[Question of withdrawal from UN proceedings]: minute by Mr Lyttelton to Mr Eden

I have now read with much interest the Minister of State's minute of April the 16th, which you enclosed with yours of April the 22nd,[1] about our policy towards the Fourth Committee of the United Nations General Assembly.

2. I am glad to see that the Minister of State agrees that the principles set out in paragraph 8 of the Colonial Office draft memorandum must be preserved.[2] I myself feel strongly that the leader of the United Kingdom Delegation should have prior authority to withdraw from the Fourth Committee, and therefore to use the threat of withdrawal, if any of these principles are threatened. We have no other effective sanction.

3. I understand from Selwyn that, provided that authority to withdraw is given only to himself and Sir Alan Burns and is not transferable to anyone else, he will be quite satisfied. I hope that you will agree to this. Burns is now a very experienced conférencier and has done extremely well for us. I am sure that he may be relied upon not to use this authority save in extremis.

4. I understand that our officials are due to meet those of the French and Belgian Governments in Brussels towards the end of the month for an exchange of views on United Nations matters and it would be useful if our policy could be settled before then.[3]

---

[1] Minute by Selwyn Lloyd to Eden, 16 Apr 1952, enclosed with minute by Eden to Lyttelton, 22 Apr 1952 (FO 371/101363, no 49). Selwyn Lloyd's minute was critical of the CO draft memo (see 157, note 2), expressing doubts in particular about the advisability of the 'walk out' tactic. This tactic, Lloyd felt, 'tends to make the "walkers out" look ridiculous' and was likely to be counter-productive.

[2] For the list of principles, see 160, annex A.

[3] Eden remained less than convinced of the merits of walking out, and decided to refer the matter to Cabinet; see 160.

160　CAB 129/53, C(52)232　　　　　　　　　　　　8 July 1952

'Handling of colonial questions at the United Nations: the question of withdrawal in certain circumstances': Cabinet memorandum by Mr Eden. *Annex* A

At the last Session of the Assembly some of the anti-colonial Powers tried to establish the right of the United Nations to discuss the political affairs of colonies, and to assert, at least by implication, that Administering Powers are accountable to the United Nations for the administration of their colonies. If such a principle were established our position as an Administering Power would be seriously impaired.

2. Our best hope of diverting the General Assembly from such courses is to increase our general influence and that of other moderate members. Our policy is to keep down the temperature in debates, to make reasonable and constructive contributions and to present our policies in a clear and positive manner. Approaches through diplomatic channels have also a useful influence on certain countries.

3. These methods, however, take time to bear fruit. Other methods must be considered of dealing with attempts which may well be made at the forthcoming Seventh Session of the General Assembly to establish principles which would impair our ability to maintain our position in the colonies. (There is attached at Annex A a note of the main principles which we cannot afford to see established.)

4. We must therefore be prepared to consider the possibility of threatening to withdraw and, if necessary, actually withdrawing from any proceedings in the Assembly arising out of a decision to discuss matters of the kind referred to in paragraph 1 above, particularly in cases where no other redress is open to us (*e.g.*, (a) and (b) (ii) and (iii) of Annex A).

5. In favour of this course it may be said:—

(i) The French and Belgian Governments, which are our closest allies in these matters, are strongly in favour of it.

(ii) A threat of withdrawal proved effective during the Sixth Session of the General Assembly in helping to avert the passage of a resolution affirming the right of the Fourth Committee (which deals with matters relating to trust and non-self-governing territories) to discuss the political affairs of non-self-governing territories.

(iii) It might make States which proposed to discuss matters of the kind referred to in paragraph 1 hesitate if they knew that in those circumstances we (and those who think like us) should withdraw.

6. On the other hand:—

(a) It is arguable that withdrawal is not by itself a sanction at all. However much we dislike the proceedings, our withdrawal might well fail to arrest them. It might, for example, be decided to hear oral petitioners, *e.g.*, from Cyprus, even in our absence. During the last session of the Assembly both the South African and French Delegations (for different reasons) staged withdrawals which were ineffective. Yet once they found we were prepared to do the same they (or the Belgians) might well press us to join in some similar demonstrations for their benefit which we would find awkward to refuse.

(b) It is from a threat to withdraw rather than from actual withdrawal that we should hope to derive benefit. But it seems unwise to base our policy on a bluff which may be called.

(c) The whole policy of withdrawal is not only publicly identified with the actions of the Soviet Government, but is objectionable as conflicting with the view of the United Nations as a forum in which differences may and should be discussed.

7. *Recommendations*

Although the manœuvre of withdrawal is distasteful and its effectiveness cannot be gauged with certainty, we must be prepared to consider the possibility of threatening or using it, as an extreme course, if an attempt is made to discuss matters vitally touching our colonial position. I therefore recommend that the leader of the United Kingdom Delegation to the Assembly should have prior authority to threaten to withdraw our representative from any such discussion. This authority should, however, be given on condition that the threat would not be carried out without prior reference to London, except in *extremis*.

Annex A to 160: Basic issues

(a) The right of the United Nations to discuss the political affairs of non-self-governing territories.

(b) The principle of accountability to the United Nations, as exemplified in the following forms:—

(i) the right of the United Nations to make, or attempt to make, recommendations on *any* subject relating to *particular* non-self-governing territories;

(ii) the right of petition in relation to non-self-governing territories;

(iii) the granting of oral hearings to persons with complaints regarding non-self-governing territories (as distinct from trust territories);

(iv) the sending of Visiting Missions to non-self-governing territories;

(v) the holding of plebiscites in non-self-governing or trust territories except with the consent of the Administering Authority.[1]

---

[1] Cabinet accepted Eden's recommendation (CAB 128/25, CC 75(52)7, 31 July 1952). For subsequent developments, see 168.

161 FO 371/101383, no 23   22 Aug 1952

[Approaches to foreign governments concerning colonial questions in the UN]: circular despatch no 072 from Mr Churchill to UK ambassadors

Mr. Attlee's circular despatch No. 082, dated 29th August, 1951, requested you to renew the diplomatic approaches which had in the previous year contributed to an improvement in the atmosphere in which Colonial and Trusteeship questions had been discussed at the Fifth Session of the United Nations General Assembly.

2. It is unfortunately not possible to report that this improvement was sustained

at the Assembly's Sixth Session in 1951. Although the number of objectionable resolutions carried was small, a determined effort was made to establish the principle that the political affairs of non-self-governing territories may be discussed by the General Assembly and these efforts were only narrowly prevented from achieving success. The issue over which this question arose was the affairs of Morocco. This issue may be raised again and the Tunisian question will also come up and will provide at least as favourable an opportunity for these efforts to be further pursued at the forthcoming Seventh Session of the Assembly. There is also a possibility that Guatemala may raise the question of her claim to British Honduras, and the Argentine that of her claim to the Falkland Islands; but if this possibility material-ises, separate instructions will be sent to you.

3. Should the Assembly succeed in establishing the principle that the political affairs of non-self-governing territories may be discussed, the ability of Her Majesty's Government to maintain their position in parts of the Colonial empire would be gravely impaired. Political stability in a number of Colonial territories depends upon a delicate balance which could be only too easily upset by exposing their affairs to the blasts of controversy at the United Nations.

4. It is thus of the utmost importance to Her Majesty's Government to maintain the principle that the Assembly has no mandate to discuss the political affairs of non-self-governing territories. Unfortunately this view is not shared by the great majority of member states, and no direct arguments designed to persuade them to accept it are likely to make much impression.

5. I have set forth the above considerations to show the great importance which attaches to securing as favourable an initial attitude as possible to Colonial questions on the part of as many delegations as possible. I shall therefore be glad if, without referring to the considerations set out above, you will renew the approaches made last year on the same general lines. The references to an improvement in the atmosphere of discussion at the United Nations which were suggested, for example, in paragraph 6 of Mr. Attlee's despatch, would not this year be appropriate.

6. The considerations set forth in the Appendix to Mr. Attlee's despatch are still generally applicable, although it is less appropriate this year to attempt any such classification of countries into those deserving a "congratulatory" or a "regretful" approach. The references to the attitudes of particular countries should also now be read in the light of United Nations (Political) Department letter UP 243/30 of 1st March, 1951, enclosing an account of the proceedings in connexion with trusteeship and colonial questions at the Sixth Session of the General Assembly, of which I attach copies[1] to all recipients of this despatch for ease of reference, although it has already been received by certain posts. In certain cases there will also have been subsequent changes in the attitude of particular governments to these matters, which should be taken into account in appropriate cases.

7. Middle Eastern posts will find further guidance in the report on the attitude of the Arab States at the Sixth Session of the Assembly, enclosed with my despatch to Cairo No. 75 of 27th February. In the case of Saudi Arabia no further approach should be made for the time being pending further instructions.

8. Latin American posts may find similar guidance in the report on the behaviour of Latin American delegations enclosed in Mr. Meade's letter from Washington No.

---

[1] Not printed.

22218/6/52 dated 26th March, 1952 (copied direct to all Latin American posts).

9.   In approaching the Government to which you are accredited an endeavour should again be made to ascertain whether they will authorise their delegation to maintain contact on these questions with the United Kingdom delegation.

10.   Since the co-operation of other administering powers may be assumed in these matters, this despatch is sent for information only to Her Majesty's Representatives at Washington, Paris, Copenhagen, Brussels and The Hague.

11.   I leave to your discretion the timing and manner of your approach though you will no doubt bear in mind the need to influence the Government to which you are accredited before they have finally decided their policy and briefed their delegates.

162   FO 371/107076, no 10   [Mar 1953]
[UN questions]: draft FO brief for UK representatives at Anglo-French ministerial talks on 30 March 1953   [Extract]

The two principal features of current U.N. interest in Colonial questions are:—

(a) The concerted activity of the Arab-Asian bloc; and
(b) Colonial questions are increasingly discussed in Committees other than the Fourth (e.g. Tunis in the First, Self-Determination in the Third).

2.   We shall act as follows in 1953:—

(a) The first essential is for the Administering Powers to work closely together. Talks between French, Belgian and U.K. officials are being arranged in early May to examine detailed issues arising in 1953. We hope to send a representative to ascertain, and if possible to influence, the policies of the U.S.A. and Canada. (The French may suggest a joint approach in Washington but we believe that separate approaches will be more effective.)
(b) To undermine anti-Colonial solidarity we have asked our Ambassadors etc. to work on foreign Governments and public opinion. We shall try to detach "marginal" countries (e.g. Brazil, Colombia, Chile, Peru) from automatic allegiance to their respective blocs. We hope to modify the hostility of countries (e.g. Cuba and Yugoslavia) with whom we have good relations on all except Colonial issues.
(c) Subject to the situation in the territories concerned we shall try to ensure that our actions at the time of the Assembly in Central Africa, Kenya, and other trouble spots give no pretext for U.N. discussion.
(d) We hope to take the initiative in debate in both the Committee on Information and the Fourth Committee, by making full statements on our achievements, by trying to convert anti-colonial resolutions into resolutions of universal applicability, and by refuting particularly malevolent anti-Colonial speeches. We shall encourage the Belgians to develop their thesis on every possible occasion (the Belgian thesis is that if the U.N. has responsibility for any dependent people it has

responsibility for all, including the aboriginal inhabitants of South America, South-East Asia and the Soviet Union[1]). . . .

[*paras 3–6 on Togoland and the Cameroons: omitted*]

Non-self-governing territories

7. General aspects of U.N. discussion of Colonial questions are dealt with in paragraph 1 and 2. The Ministers may wish to reaffirm the agreement at the 1952 talks on general policy towards the U.N. (see Annex).[2] For the rest, discussion could usefully concentrate on two aspects: first, the attitude of the Administering Powers to the Committee on Information; and, secondly, the possibility of specific Colonial issues being raised in the Assembly.

8. On the first point, France and the U.K. only agreed to participate in the Committee (which was re-established for three years by the 1952 Assembly) if its terms of reference remained unchanged. The French considered that the Assembly, by subsequently asking the Committee to examine information concerning the exercise of the right of self-determination, has extended those terms. In our view this development can be arrested if the Administering Members insist on refusing to allow the Committee to discuss the political affairs of non-self-governing territories. For our part we intend to participate in the 1953 Committee and we are sending an educational expert (Mr Ward)[3] to filibuster on his subject.

9. There are many subjects which the anti-Colonials might seek to raise in the 1953 Assembly: Central African Federation, Mau Mau, Cyprus and a renewal of the Tunis item. In each case the possibility exists that oral hearings may be requested by such persons as the Rev. Michael Scott, the Archibishop of Cyprus etc. While it will be necessary for our respective Governments to handle each of these issues as it arises, or to prevent any of them arising, it would be useful if Ministers were to reaffirm the determination of the two Governments to support each other in rejecting these attempts to interfere in the domestic affairs of individual non-self-governing territories.

---

[1] The 'Belgian thesis' is discussed at length in 'The Belgian approach to the discussion of colonial questions in the United Nations' (note by CO, CO 936/315, no 11, Mar 1954).

[2] Not printed   [3] W E F Ward, deputy education adviser, CO, 1945–1956.

---

163   FO 371/107142, no 13   19 June 1953
'Human rights covenants': letter from S Hoare[1] to E R Warner[2]

At the last Session of the Human Rights Commission the French representative, on instructions from his Government, abstained in the vote on the Commission's report, the first time he has ever done so in seven years' work on the Commission, because of the inclusion of the provision for special implementation of the Article on self-determination. We voted for the report, but, for the record, expressed entire

---

[1] S Hoare, assistant under-secretary of state, Home Office, 1946–1961; head of International Division, 1950–1961.

[2] E R Warner, FO, 1951–1956.

agreement with the French objections, which in fact were fairly mildly expressed, and in a tone more of sorrow than of anger.

I have been wondering whether the time has not come to take a stand on the question of the inclusion of anti-colonial provisions in the Covenants, of which this last provision is the crowning folly. There were good reasons for refraining from taking a strong line on the inclusion of the "anti-colonial" clause, but the accumulation since then of the article on self-determination, the General Assembly's resolution about self-determination, and now this article on special implementation of self-determination, alters the situation. I am not, of course, suggesting that H.M.G. should, like the U.S. Government, disown further interest in the Covenants. What I have in mind is that a statement might be made indicating that H.M.G. has observed with growing concern the use of the draft Covenants as a repository for provisions directed against the states administering non-self-governing territories and relating to political issues which are outside the scope of a Covenant on Human Rights, and that H.M.G. wishes to make it quite clear that, while continuing loyally to participate in the work of the framing of the Covenants, it will not sign or ratify a Covenant containing these provisions.

The advantages of making such a statement seem to me to be the following:—

1. It is already an open secret that all this stuff has made it virtually impossible for H.M.G. or other colonial powers to sign. But the discussions in the Commission proceed in a more or less objective and dispassionate way; the anti-colonials score their triumph and a few remarks, never amounting to a firm statement, as to its possible consequences, are made on explanation of vote. They are not brought up hard against the fact that they have been doing too well and have sunk the Covenants. To bring them up against this could do nothing but good for the future course of anti-colonialism in the United Nations. Some of them privately realize that they may have been too successful, but they have never had any public intimation of this.

2. There have already been suggestions that the whole question of self-determination should be taken out of the Covenants and made the subject of a separate instrument. Sweden and China have both at various times made statements to this effect. If we wanted to get these excrescences removed, a firm statement might stimulate attempts to do so, whether by dumping them in a separate instrument (to which we need not adhere) or otherwise.

3. A statement of this kind would act as a brake on the enthusiasm of our own non-governmental organizations in submitting proposals for the remaining stages of work on the Covenants.

The possible disadvantages seem to me to be the following:—

1. We might be accused of letting our colonial interests take precedence over our concern for human rights. I do not myself think that there is any risk of this. The accumulation of provisions in the Covenants deliberately discriminating against administering powers is now so great that we should have public opinion in this country solidly behind us, and the anti-colonials abroad could be left to rave as they liked.

2. A statement, even in this conditional form, dissociating H.M.G. to some degree from the Covenants as they stand, might play into the hands of the Americans,

who are seeking to give a new direction to the Commission's work. I believe this objection to be unfounded, because the American proposals have got to be considered anyway; the Commission's work on the Covenants, even if it goes on (and nothing in our statement would prevent it going on) cannot occupy more than another Session, and the future work of the Commission is an issue which the Americans have now brought into the fore-front of discussion, and which will have to be settled in the light of their proposals, or any better ones that may be forthcoming. This will have to be done either at the next Session of the Commission, or by ECOSOC before then. Our statement would not kill the Covenants any more dead than they are already.

3. It is possible that a statement on these lines might lead to concessions by the anti-colonial bloc, e.g. the removal of these provisions to another instrument, which would embarrass us by depriving us of our main reasons for an ultimate refusal to sign or ratify the Covenants. I recognise that this may be a substantial objection. On the other hand it is difficult to envisage the present procedure of discussion of these Articles on their so-called merits continuing indefinitely through the final stages of the Covenants, without an eventual show-down, e.g. in the Assembly, on the question whether, if these provisions remain in, we will sign or not. And if we are to be forced into a statement, it is better made early on our own volition, than late, under pressure. If on the other hand we do succeed in avoiding any specific declaration on this point, and continue the policy of deploying arguments, already over-familiar, against provisions for which we know there is an automatic majority, without ever committing ourselves on the question whether their inclusion definitely precludes our signature, we run the risk of our attitude being interpreted at the end of the day, and rightly, as a form of shadow boxing designed to secure that we have sufficient grounds for defending, before public opinion, refusal to sign or ratify the Covenants.

The balance between these considerations may not be easy to strike. The question of policy is one for your Office and the Colonial Office to determine. I am really only concerned as representative on the Human Rights Commission to raise the question, which I think deserves careful consideration.[3]

---

[3] In a minute to Selwyn Lloyd on 23 June. Warner expressed sympathy with Hoare's argument but doubted that the time was yet ripe for a 'show-down' on the convenants; Lloyd minuted his agreement on 25 June (FO 371/107142, no 13).

164 CO 936/325, no 14   25 Aug 1954
'Colonial questions at the United Nations': circular intelligence telegram no 187 from Mr Eden to UK ambassadors explaining UK policy

Instructions have already been issued to the majority of Her Majesty's Representatives accredited to Governments of states members of the United Nations to inform those Governments that, if the General Assembly decides to inscribe an item on Cyprus on its Agenda, the United Kingdom Delegation would very probably not be present in discussion of the substance of this item by any organ of the Assembly and that Her Majesty's Government would feel obliged to consider whether it would be necessary to limit to the strict requirements of the Charter the extent to which the

United Kingdom could continue to cooperate with the United Nations on Colonial Questions. This Intel explains the background to this decision and gives arguments that may be used in defence of our general colonial position at the United Nations.

2. Chapter XI of the United Nations Charter contains a general declaration concerning the obligations of those member states which administer non-self-governing territories towards the peoples who inhabit them. In addition, under Article 73(e) these states accepted an obligation to transmit regularly to the Secretary-General, for information only, technical information on economic, social and educational conditions in these territories. The Charter creates no obligation to transmit political information and in our view Article 2(7) thereof denies the United Nations competence to discuss any of the information transmitted since this relates to matters within the domestic jurisdiction of the administering power. It was on this understanding that the United Kingdom signed the Charter. As a gesture of goodwill, however, we have cooperated in the work of the Committee on Information from Non-Self-Governing Territories set up by the General Assembly to examine the information transmitted, provided that it does not consider political matters, but confines itself to general examination of the technical matters covered by Article 73(e). We have set an example by staffing our delegations to its meetings with experts, and at the Eighth Session of the General Assembly we successfully sponsored a resolution urging other delegations to do likewise. The Report of this Committee is considered by the General Assembly.

3. Ever since 1946, the anti-colonial members of the United Nations have been trying to extend its competence in the colonial field, and to establish the principle that the colonial powers are accountable to the United Nations for the administration of their dependent territories. Nothing in the Charter supports such an interpretation. This would involve discussion in the United Nations of every aspect of colonial policy. Experience in the past few years of United Nations discussion of the administration of Trust Territories suggests that as far as it has any effect at all it is rather to the detriment of the peoples concerned, of whom the members of the United Nations have little knowledge and for whose welfare they are not primarily concerned, preoccupied as they are with their own particular interests in international affairs. Such discussion could also in some territories have serious consequences for the political prestige and strategic position of the colonial power concerned.

4. The anti-colonial convictions of many member states are nevertheless sincere and probably unshakeable. We have, therefore, tried to avoid a test of strength in the United Nations on the issue of competence by maintaining a cooperative and constructive attitude on those subjects of colonial interest which we feel that the Assembly can discuss without serious damage to our position, even though the letter of the Charter gives it no such right. We have participated in this spirit in the Committee on Information from Non-Self-Governing Territories and in the General Assembly debates on its Reports. These tactics have at times succeeded in moderating the attitude of some of the anti-colonial powers, who have become aware that our constructive participation in this work is conditional upon their relatively good behaviour.

5. We have always realised that at any time a determined attempt might be made to establish United Nations competence in the colonial field, probably in connexion with some particular political issue over which world opinion would be against us (cf.

my Intel No. 214, 1953). To counter such attempts we had contemplated threatening to withdraw the United Kingdom Representative from the United Nations body concerned. If necessary we should have carried out this threat. This action would have been taken in the event of a move which would clearly establish our accountability to the United Nations either as a general principle or in a particular case. Such a move might take the form of an assertion of any of the following:—

(i) The right of the United Nations to discuss the political affairs of non-self-governing territories.

(ii) The right of the United Nations to make recommendations on any subject relating to a particular non-self-governing territory.

(iii) The right of petition in relation to non-self-governing territories.

(iv) The right of the United Nations to grant hearings to persons with complaints regarding non-self-governing territories.

(v) The right of the United Nations to send visiting missions to non-self-governing territories.

(vi) The right of the United Nations to call for a plebiscite in a non-self-governing territory.

Threats of withdrawal would not of course be made lightly. Actual withdrawal would only be made as a last resort, and its duration would depend upon the subsequent actions of the United Nations body concerned.

6. The proposed Greek item on Cyprus invites the United Nations both to discuss and make recommendations for the political future of Cyprus. It is clearly an assertion of (i) and (ii) above and may well involve an assertion of (vi). If the item is placed on the Agenda it would form a very dangerous precedent for discussing matters affecting the political future of any other colonial territory. There are obvious and dangerous implications for the future of, for example, Aden, Hong Kong, British Honduras, the Falkland Islands and British Guiana. In our view it would also open the way for discussion by the United Nations of any minority in any country which might for one reason or another desire to pass under the sovereignty of another state—a position which a number of governments might do well to reflect [sic].

7. The following general arguments may be used in defence of the British colonial position at the United Nations, and in justification of the line we are taking to prevent a discussion on Cyprus:—

(i) The United Nations Charter does not make the colonial powers accountable to the United Nations for the administration of their dependent territories. Had this been intended provision would have been made when the Charter was drafted at San Francisco, as was done in the case of the Trust Territories, for which the administering authorities are specifically made responsible to the United Nations. The records show that this matter was discussed at San Francisco and that it was the deliberate intention of the signatories to the Charter that no such provision should be made. Although Her Majesty's Government have always shown themselves prepared to cooperate with the utmost goodwill in those colonial matters in which the United Nations has shown an interest, even in excess of their strict obligations, they cannot recognize any general responsibility towards the United Nations in such matters.

(ii) If the principle of accountability were accepted, each British colonial territory would be subjected to a further authority, over and above its local administration and Whitehall. This might complicate and delay the evolution of the territory towards self-government. There is no evidence that the more responsible native leaders in British non-self-governing territories desire such a development.

(iii) Disgruntled elements or political leaders representing minority opinions would be encouraged to exploit the external court of appeal provided in New York, and local political controversies would thereby be removed from the country concerned to a foreign arena. (This tendency has already been seen in the United Nations debates on Puerto Rico and the Trust Territory of British Togoland). This kind of subversion of the local democratic process is extremely unhealthy for the development of a national political consciousness and a responsible political atmosphere; it plays straight into the hands of the less scrupulous of local politicians, and has indeed been used by Communist elements in the French Cameroons.

(iv) There is always advantage in international consideration of such general technical problems as illiteracy, malnutrition, and labour conditions; the United Kingdom has always taken a lead in international collaboration in such matters. But this is properly the task of expert bodies such as the specialized agencies and should be carried out without regard to considerations based on political and constitutional status. The social and economic problems of non-self-governing territories cannot be dealt with in isolation from similar problems in sovereign states, and should be judged in relation to general standards of achievement and not against hypothetical standards of perfection in an atmosphere of political prejudice and suspicion.

(v) At present only eight members of the United Nations have declared that they have responsibilities for the administration of non-self-governing peoples. Although there are many others, in Latin America, in Asia, and in Eastern Europe, who have such peoples living within their frontiers, these eight—the "colonial" powers—are in a permanent minority; the rest cast their votes in the belief that they themselves will be in no way affected by the results. Consequently the majority of members of the United Nations have shown little inclination to try to understand the formidable nature of the task of guiding the backward peoples through the stages of social and political evolution which the great civilisations of the world have taken not years but millennia to pass. Instead they tend to propose superficial and impossible solutions which make good propaganda.

(vi) We are not in any way concerned to conceal what we are doing in our colonial territories. Indeed we are proud of the manner in which we are discharging the general obligations set out in Chapter XI of the Charter and we send to the United Nations Library every year most detailed and voluminous information on our activities. We are always ready to discuss our policies fully and frankly with any government.

(vii) We are concerned that the confidence of member states in the United Nations organization should not be weakened by attempts on its part to undertake activities which the signatories of the Charter did not intend that it should have, and which might be felt by them to threaten the sovereignty of their peoples.

165   FO 370/117530, no 2   4 Apr 1955
'The policy of Her Majesty's Government towards UNESCO': FO
minutes of an inter-departmental committee meeting with the CO
[Extract]

Mr. Bourdillon said that the Colonial Office felt that the time had come for Her
Majesty's Government to adopt a more positive policy towards Unesco. There were
now four British Colonial Associate Members which would look to Unesco for a good
deal of help. For this reason Her Majesty's Government's policy should not appear
too dominated by negative budgetary considerations (an attitude vigorously criticised by one of the non-official delegates to the recent General Conference upon
return to this country). It was desirable that the advice the Associate Members
obtained from Unesco should conform to our ideas. There had for some time been
signs, confirmed during Howard-Drake's recent visit to Paris, that Unesco was
anxious to draw on our experience of such subjects as community development and
formal and informal education. The Colonial Office thought it would be useful to
develop direct contact with the Unesco Secretariat, such as they had with the
Secretariats of other Specialised Agencies.

Mr. Howard-Drake said that M. Maheu, the Assistant Director General, had
suggested that the United Kingdom (and France) were missing opportunities of
using Unesco as a means of exerting influence in areas of the world otherwise closed
to us. Mr. Howard-Drake had also found Unesco's Secretariat willing to accept a lead
from us on technical questions. Since many countries, for example in Latin America
and the Middle East, had a great regard for Unesco, they were willing to accept ideas
and techniques from Unesco and we should make sure that so far as possible those
ideas were British. In this way we could exert an influence which could not be
exerted direct[;] for example the organisation of American States wanted Unesco to
co-sponsor their forthcoming conference on Free and Compulsory Education in
Latin America. The OAS, following a line customary in Pan-American gatherings,
wanted to exclude the United Kingdom and the British Caribbean Associate Member.
Unesco proposed to make their co-sponsorship conditional on invitations being
extended to all Member States with responsibilities in the area, and to the Caribbean
Associate Member. The influence of Unesco could thus make it possible for us to
participate in Conferences which would otherwise be closed to us and where
anti-colonialism would otherwise go unopposed.

2. *Mr. Pink* said that a distinction should be drawn between the political question
inherent in our relations with the international organisation and the use of that
organisation for propaganda purposes. We should only try to disseminate through
Unesco ideas which would make their way on their own merits. *Mr. Bourdillon*
agreed. *Mr. Thompson* said that in the fields with which Unesco was concerned the
United Kingdom had much to offer and Unesco might come to draw upon our
techniques as extensively as did the Social Welfare Division of the United Nations
Secretariat. At present this was impeded because the Colonial Office had no direct

---

[1] The committee's members were, from the FO, I T M Pink (chair) E R Warner, K Kenney and H F
Bartlett; from the CO, H T Bourdillon, J K Thompson (assistant secretary, CO, 1953–1959), W E F Ward,
E M West and J T A Howard-Drake (principal).

contact with Unesco but went meticulously through the United Kingdom National Commission. *It was agreed* that the Colonial Office would develop direct contact with Unesco.

3. *Mr. Ward* suggested that more than the supply of information about United Kingdom experience and techniques was required. He gave instances of foreign delegations having had the impression at past conferences that not merely were we interested in obtaining Unesco services for ourselves, but we wanted to prevent others getting them. Unesco work had improved year by year; the greater part of it was now useful and we should take this into account in framing our policy towards the organisation. . . .

166   CAB 128/30, CM 20(56)7   8 Mar 1956
[UN competence in South-West Africa]: Cabinet conclusions

The Cabinet had before them a memorandum by the Commonwealth Secretary, the Colonial Secretary and the Minister of State for Foreign Affairs (C.P. (56) 72)[1] seeking approval of a proposal that Her Majesty's Government should intervene in proceedings before the International Court of Justice on the admissibility of oral hearings of petitioners from South-West Africa.

The Cabinet were informed that the purpose of such an intervention would be, not to support the South African Government in resisting the claim of the United Nations to exercise supervision over South-West Africa, but to ensure that no ruling was given by the International Court which might imply that the United Nations had some supervisory jurisdiction over dependent territories within the Commonwealth.

The Attorney-General[2] said that the Law Officers had not in fact advised, as stated in paragraph 5 of C.P. (56) 72, that the International Court ought on merits to rule that oral hearings from South-West Africa were not admissible. The advice which they had given was that a fairly strong argument could be put before the Court in support of this view. Information was now available about the line which the United States Government were proposing to take at the hearing. They proposed to argue that, as the South African Government were unwilling to furnish to the United nations the information about South-West Africa which they would have been required to give to the Mandates Commission of the League of Nations, the United Nations were entitled to use other means of informing themselves of conditions in South-West Africa. At first sight it seemed that this was an argument which we need not oppose. A ruling based on it would not carry any implication that the United Nations had some supervisory jurisdiction over dependent territories within the Commonwealth. It might therefore suffice if a United Kingdom representative attended the hearing before the International Court with a watching brief. He could argue the construction of the opinion given by the Court in 1950 and could, by emphasising the special status of South-West Africa, make it clear that the decision on this case would have no application to dependent territories within the Commonwealth.

---

[1] 'South-West Africa', Cabinet memo by Lord Home, Mr Lennox-Boyd and Mr Nutting (CAB 129/80, CO(56)72, 7 Mar 1956).
[2] Sir R Manningham-Buller, attorney-general, 1954–1962.

The Cabinet:—
Agreed that a United Kingdom representative should attend this hearing before the International Court with a watching brief authorising him to intervene, if necessary, to argue the construction of the opinion given by the Court in 1950 and in order to stress the difference in status between South-West Africa and the dependent territories of the Commonwealth.

167   CO 936/316, no 77   10 Mar 1956
'Formation of the European Group[1] in the United Nations': circular savingram no 36 from CRO to UK high commissioners

Until recently the only systematic attempts at co-operation between the United Kingdom and the Western European members of the United Nations on United Nations questions have been occasional meetings on colonial matters and an annual meeting of officials from the Western European Union Powers. This has been in strong contrast to the regular meetings and close co-operation of the Commonwealth Group, the Bandoeng Powers, the Latin-American caucus and the Soviet Bloc.

2. With the admission of 17 new Members, the chances of the United Kingdom and other interested powers obtaining a blocking one-third vote on anti-colonial resolutions, or a two-thirds majority vote on anti-communist questions, have considerably diminished. It was therefore felt that a greater effort must be made to rally the Western European votes.

3. On a United Kingdom initiative informal meetings of the United Kingdom and Western European Delegates will now be held in New York from time to time, when asked for by members of the Group. The United Kingdom is at present taking the chair.

4. There is no intention of trying to form a rigidly organised European caucus on the Latin-American model, even if this were possible. The subjects likely to arise will concern not only General Assembly matters, but also items arising in the Security Council, ECOSOC and other bodies, on which it is desirable to obtain the views of the members of the Group.

5. It is hoped that these arrangements will be useful to other Commonwealth countries as well as to the United Kingdom. United Kingdom co-operation with the new Group will not of course in any way detract from our special relationship with Commonwealth Delegations.

---

[1] Austria, Belgium, Denmark, Finland, France, Greece, Holland, Iceland, Ireland, Italy, Luxembourg, Norway, Portugal, Spain, Sweden, Turkey, United Kingdom and Yugoslavia.

168   CO 936/354, no 34   7 May 1956
'Intervention by the Fourth Committee in the affairs of British colonial territories: U.K. policy on withdrawal': note by E G G Hanrott

1951
The Prime Minister gave approval to the Delegation withdrawing if a certain Iraqi

resolution calling for discussion of the political affairs of non-self-governing territories were adopted. The use of this threat with Delegations effectively secured the withdrawal of the resolution.

1952

2. The Cabinet decision of 31st July, 1952, recommended that "the leader of the U.K. Delegation should threaten to withdraw, and if necessary should actually withdraw, from any proceedings in the Assembly which seem likely to establish" any of the following principles:—

(a) the right of the United Nations to discuss the political affairs of non-self-governing territories;

(b) the principle of accountability to the United Nations, as exemplified in the following forms:—

(i)   the right of the U.N. to make, or attempt to make, recommendations on any subject relating to particular non-self-governing territories;

(ii) the right of petition in relation to non-self-governing territories;

(iii) the granting of oral hearings to persons with complaints regarding non-self-governing territories;

(iv) the sending of Visiting Missions to non-self-governing territories;

(v) the holding of plebiscites in non-self-governing or Trust Territories except with the consent of the Administering Authority.

3. Two points about this decision are noteworthy:—

(a) it relates only to a withdrawal (in the clearer language of Cabinet Paper C(52)232 of the 8th July, 1952) "from any proceedings in the Assembly arising out of a decision to discuss matters of the kind referred to" above—i.e. a limited withdrawal;

(b) it was taken in relation with the Seventh Sesssion of the General Assembly, 1952, but it was subsequently extended with the approval of C.O. and F.O. Ministers to later sessions (see for example (26) on IRD 164/139/01).

1953

4. The highlight this year both at the briefing stage and during the Assembly's debates was Central African Federation. The brief (IOC(53)148) authorises withdrawal from the Fourth Committee in the event of an adverse vote on the question of the competence of the Committee to discuss the political affairs of non-self-governing territories or of a decision to discuss a written petition or to grant an oral hearing. There is no definition in the brief of the type of withdrawal involved, but the following quotation from a minute by Mr. Gidden of 7th August, 1953, indicates that, as in 1952, only a limited withdrawal was contemplated.

"As it stands the brief is not intended to go further than the Cabinet paper of last year which approved the use of the threat of withdrawal, and withdrawal itself. The threat of withdrawal, if it has to be used this year, would undoubtedly be more effective if we could say that we would not attend *any* of the discussions relating to non-self-governing territories and not merely discussion relating to the particular political item. But I do not myself believe that there would be any hope of securing

Ministerial approval at this stage of this extension of last year's decision; and if we tried and failed to secure such approval, that would perhaps leave the Delegation with even less latitude than is conceded by the terms of the Cabinet paper. It is, however, possible that if the crisis does arise in New York the Delegation may feel it advisable to seek approval for non-attendance at the Committee for a longer period than the discussion of the particular political item in question. I have in mind the difficult situation which would arise if the Delegation, having with-drawn, were forced to return to the Committee say within an hour because the Committee had gone on to another subject. I think that the way in which a difficulty of this nature should best be met can only be decided at the time in New York, and it is therefore for that reason that I recommend that the draft brief opposite should not attempt to extend the authority given by the Cabinet last year."

5.   Once debate was joined at New York we were, however, compelled to go rather further than this. Lord Hudson[1] on the 26th October, 1953, stated "Nevertheless, I must assert, in all solemnity, that if this matter is made the subject of debate here, it will raise in an acute form the question of the extent to which it would still be useful for my Delegation to continue to co-operate in this way". At a later stage (7th November) the Minister of State, Mr. Selwyn Lloyd, proposed to tell the Fourth Committee that if they decided to debate Central Africa we should "regard it as a parting of the ways with the Fourth Committee" and that our non-cooperation would take the following forms:—

"(a) we would limit to the absolute minimum the information in respect of all territories to be transmitted under Article 73(e);
(b) we would withdraw from the Committee on Information from Non-Self-Governing Territories;
(c) we would consider whether we could continue to take any part at all in the work of the Fourth Committee in relation to non-self-governing territories."

6.   Foreign Office approval for this significant extension of the authority in the brief was granted in F.O. telegram Build 1253 of 13th November which was approved personally by the Foreign Secretary. This telegram states that the decision to withdraw in the circumstances envisaged "was taken after full consideration of the implications by the Cabinet" (which appears to be something of a gloss on the Cabinet decision of 1952).

1954
7.   This year the briefing centred on the Cyprus question in which it was clear that the issues were as much international as colonial. The keynote for the briefing was struck in a letter from Sir J Martin to Mr. Ward[2] of the Foreign Office of the 13th August, 1954, which agreed on authorisation of the use of the threat of limited withdrawal in respect of the Cyprus issue and then went on to say: "We have considered whether this threat should not be reinforced by the additional threat of wider non-cooperation with the United Nations on colonial questions such as that for

---

[1] UK representative, UN Trusteeship Council.
[2] J G Ward, deputy under-secretary of state, FO, 1954–1956.

which Mr. Selwyn Lloyd successfully sought authority on the Central African issue.
. . . Our Secretary of State takes the view that he would rather reserve this greater
threat for an issue (e.g. one like that of Central African Federation) in which no other
member of the United Nations has a vital or even a direct interest, rather than use it
publicly on an issue over which many sections of public opinion would feel that,
since our ally, Greece, is so closely concerned, H.M.G. ought not to go to extremes in
an attempt to prevent her delegates airing their case in the United Nations".

8.   The brief (IOC(54)120) when drafted authorised the use of threats to individual
Delegations of the ultimate consequences of U.N. discussion of the Cyprus item
which comprises the same items as in paragraph 5 above, but which were described
in terms of possible eventualities rather than certain results.

9.   In the event, the Cyprus item was inscribed and, although we said that we
would not take part in any substantive discussion, we managed to get the item
disposed of without such discussion.[3]

1955
10.   The experience of 1954 had shown the need to collate instructions on
withdrawal in one master brief instead of having slightly divergent instructions in a
number of briefs. Another feature of the brief was a distinction between the "limited
withdrawal" and the "major withdrawal"; this was made necessary by the nature of
the Somali question which required the formulation of alternative policies according
to the terms of the reference to the International Court which the United Nations
might decide upon. (A reference to the Somali petition in "particular" terms would
require only a limited withdrawal; a reference in general competence terms would
require a major withdrawal.) Although this was the first occasion on which we had
attempted to describe the procedure to be adopted over the two types of withdrawal,
the distinction had, as has been shown, been implicit since the Cabinet decision of
1952.

11.   During the IOC discussions of this brief differences revealed themselves
between Foreign Office and Colonial Office understanding of the position reached in
previous years. These are recorded in the minues of I.O.C. meeting on the 30th
September, 1955, the points of difference being as follows:—
The F.O. stated:—

(a) that the 1952 Cabinet decision related only to the Seventh Session of the
General Assembly. (This is *not* true and is in fact contradicted by the fact of F.O.
approval of the 1953 and 1955 I.O.C. briefs which authorise a limited withdrawal,
in extremis without reference to London;)
(b) that generalisations could not be made on the basis of the specific instructions
to the Minister of State about Central Africa in November, 1953 (para 5 above).
(This we must accept;)
(c) that a limited withdrawal can be authorised, *in extremis* without reference
back home, but no threat of a major withdrawal can be made without such
reference, even *in extremis*, since no covering Ministerial authority for the latter
exists. (We had to accept this conclusion and the brief IOC(55)114 Revise is drafted
accordingly.)

---

[3] See part II of this volume, 322.

Conclusion

12. Apart from the minor point of difference about the continuing validity of the Cabinet decision of 1952 at 11 (a) above (due, probably to a mistake on the part of the Foreign Office which could quite easily be rectified when the need for clarification arose) the main outstanding point is whether we should take steps to obtain Ministerial authority for the use of the threat of major withdrawal, and for the major withdrawal itself on any occasion when colonial interests are threatened. We cannot appeal to the specific instructions of 1953 on Central Africa and if we want to obtain this covering general approval we must seek from the Cabinet a widening of their decision of the 31st July, 1952, which quite clearly is limited to a withdrawal limited to the item in question. The difficulty about this is that there is little likelihood of obtaining such Cabinet approval unless we can point to a particular burning question—another Kenya or Central Africa—which genuinely affects our whole colonial position (Cyprus is now so *sui generis* as to be largely irrelevant). Although the colonial scene is full of potential trouble internationally there is no such question at present and it looks therefore as if any extension of the measures at present authorised must await the development of some more imminent threat.[4]

---

[4] CO officials decided not to circulate this document to other departments; 'If we send it to the F.O. and the C.R.O. when there is manifestly no action to be taken, I fear they may suspect us of trying to drive in undisclosed wedges' (minute by Bourdillon, CO 936/354, 12 May 1956).

169 CO 936/321, no 16   24 Sept 1956
[Proposed General Assembly speech defending colonialism]: letter from H T Bourdillon to I T M Pink

In paragraph 15 of his secret despatch No. 15 of 10th April last, dealing with Soviet tactics in the United Nations, Bob Dixon[1] urged that we should make greater efforts at this year's General Assembly to publicise our Colonial record. In paragraph 4 of his reply (despatch No. 215 of 30th June), the Foreign Secretary pointed out that our failure hitherto to make the most of our Colonial achievements in the United Nations had been largely the result of deliberate policy, since experience had shown that attempts to do so were all too often seized upon by anti-Colonials as an implied admission of "accountability". He went on to say, however, that the time might be ripe for a reappraisal of this admittedly cautious policy and that the matter was being considered with the Colonial Office.

2. In point of fact I do not think there has been any further correspondence or discussion between the Foreign Office and the Colonial Office on this subject except in relation to the particular question of Cyprus. We on our side have, however, been giving the general question a good deal of thought.

3. It is true that we have in the past years failed, or rather refused, to publicise in the United Nations our political achievements in the Colonial territories. On the contrary, we have consistently attempted to restrict the discussion of Colonial questions to social and economic matters, and we have held that even this is not justified in terms of the Charter. It is equally true, however, that there have been

---

[1] Sir P Dixon, deputy under-secretary of state, FO, 1950–1954; UK permanent representative at UN, 1954–1960.

) *The American attitude.* This is likely to be affected by (a) and (b) above. As we now to our cost, the Americans have always been unsatisfactory allies as an administering Power and have sometimes dangerously upset the balance between the Administering and non-Administering side in the Trusteeship Council and the Committee on Information. The latest example is their attitude over "intermediate time-tables" in the Trusteeship Council. Unless we do something to check them, I am afraid they will feel impelled by the arrival of the new members and still more by the change in Soviet tactics to attempt to reassert their own moral position by associating themselves (in Colonial matters) more and more from the Colonial powers. This in spite of the fact that more and more thinking Americans are coming to recognise the real rights and wrongs of "Colonialism" and to adopt an attitude on these matters which is barely distinguishable from our own. On my pre-Assembly visits to Washington in 1954 and 1955 I tried to head the State Department off from going in the wrong direction by emphasizing to them that our Colonial policy was something which it was not only in the American interest to support but which they could support with a perfectly clear conscience. In support of this line I gave details of the latest political and constitutional developments in all parts of the Colonial Empire, with the object of showing that the march towards self-government was going on everywhere and was not confined to one or two places which had happened to reach the final stages. I was trying to lead towards the idea that the Americans might get out of their own dilemma by openly supporting British colonial policy on the grounds that it bore no resemblance to the "Colonialism" which is the object of so much American prejudice. I think this line of argument had some effect—certainly the State Department professed to be impressed by the progress that was going on and to be satisfied that our Colonial policy was everything we said it was. But on each occasion I was met by the objection that the Americans could not be expected to come out in support of our policy unless we did more to publicise it ourselves. Why did we not make much more of a splash about our achievements in the United Nations? Why did we not use this international forum to clear away misunderstandings and to put the matter in its true perspective? To these questions I was bound to reply with the familiar (and very cogent) argument about accountability; and there the matter rested. It may be too much to hope that the Americans would come out in open support of us even if we now changed our tactics in the sense indicated; but at least we should have removed the objection which they themselves have raised and should have thus presented them with a strong challenge.

If it is agreed that these points constitute a *prime facie* case for taking a more active line in the Assembly this year, the next question to consider is how this could best be done, bearing in mind the need to be effective on the one hand and to avoid the obvious dangers on the other. On this we have the following comments. In the first place, we agree with Dixon's suggestion that the subject should be tackled in the General Debate. This might be followed up, with the help of B.I.S., by publicity within the United Nations . . . and directed towards the American public. It might also be possible (though there are considerable dangers here, and very careful handling would be necessary) to follow up whatever was said in the General Debate *references* in subsequent speeches in the Committee which could be used to drive

strong reasons for this attitude, one of which is clearly stated in t
despatch referred to above. Nobody who has attended the debat
Committee can have any doubts about the avidity with which t
would seize on any overt attempt by the United Kingdom represen
Committee as a political shop window. Another reason for our retic
need for solidarity with the French and the Belgians, whose politica
least their methods of achieving them, for their overseas territori
very different from our own. There is little doubt that if we were
Fourth Committee an exposition of our own Colonial philosophy, v
invite the anti-Colonials to compare it with the French and Belgi
detriment of the latter.

4. The question is, are there now any compelling reasons f
cautious attitude? And if so, are there any means of surmounting
have just mentioned?

5. No one will deny that our present attitude imposes upon us s
Not only does our whole positive political case go by default in th
but by our insistence on the limitation of discussion to social and e
we actually encourage the belief, whether feigned or genuine, that p
something to hide. We thus indirectly help to perpetuate the myth
which thrives on the belief that the mere possession of things cal
some way disreputable and which bedevils almost every otherwis
(including Suez?) which comes before the United Nations. Thes
however, are not new, and in the past we have never felt that th
enough to overcome the difficulties in the way of taking a more
they today, on the eve of the 1956 General Assembly, reinforced by 1
might lead us to reconsider the whole question? Our view in the
that there are a number of such factors which may or may not be d
certainly need to be taken into account. They are as follows:—

(a) *Soviet tactics.* This was the subject of Dixon's despatch, and
general line of argument. In past years (even in 1955) the So
attacks on "Colonialism" in the United Nations have been crude
themselves. It may be that these sledge-hammer tactics will b
more subtle and dangerous approach which the Russians
international affairs in general. There is a case for saying that th
the only way of countering a new style Soviet offensive would b
the inherent strength of our own position.

(b) *New members.* We have been able to forecast the attitude of
Assemblies with reasonable certainty. This year we are dealing v
quantity. Since most of the new members are automatically "a
have assumed that from the Colonial point of view the mixture w
before. From the point of view of voting power this is almost certa
other hand the new members, from the mere fact that they c
United Nations, should be to a certain extent malleable. If we can
persuade some of them at the outset, by a clear and forceful
positive case, that the hallowed anti-Colonial doctrine simply doe
we may have done lasting good. At the worst we may have helpe
harm.

2F

the point home without constituting an admission of accountability. Secondly, we feel that the safest and at the same time the most effective way of going about the business would be to draw attention to our actual achievements and to leave the moral to speak for itself, rather than to launch out on a general disquisition about our Colonial philosophy. As it happens, we shall have a very striking tale to tell this year—"independence" for the Gold Coast and Malaya in the immediate future. We could point out that this is the fulfilment of British rule, the arrival at the goal which we have had before us for many years and towards which we have taken great strides in recent years. It would also be possible, no doubt, to give other examples of constitutional advance which would show that political progress in our Colonial territories is not confined to a few areas, though, equally, we might have to explain why in some other areas the pace has to be slower. Thirdly, we should have to be careful not to say anything which implied unfavourable comparison with the methods of other Colonial Powers. We might indeed make appreciative references to their achievements—a task which has been made rather easier by the latest political advances in the French territories.[2]

7.   The above represents our view of the way in which the matter should be handled if it were finally decided, in spite of the risks and difficulties, to go ahead. The Assembly, however, is still nearly two months off, and I do not suggest that any final decision should be taken now. What I should like to do is to discuss these ideas with the Delegation in New York when I go to America early next month and, subject to their views, with the State Department. I should be careful to restate the difficulties and I should emphasize to the State Department that if we went ahead it would be with the object, in part, of helping the Americans to resolve their own problems; we would therefore count on them to respond by backing us up both in more open support of our Colonial policy and in repudiation of "accountability". We could then consider the matter further, on my return to this country in the middle of October.

8.   I hope that you and Snelling, to whom I am sending a copy of this letter, will agree to my undertaking these non-committal soundings. I should be most grateful if you and he could let me have your views before the end of this month since I am due to leave for America on October 7th, and just before that we shall be having our pre-Assembly talks in London with the French and the Belgians.

---

[2] ie, the enactment of the *loi cadre*.

170   CO 936/316, no 114   [Oct 1956]
'Colonial questions in the United Nations': report by CO of Anglo-French-Belgian talks held in London on 1 and 2 Oct 1956[1]   [Extract]

Mr. Bourdillon welcomed the Belgian and French delegations. He suggested, and *it was agreed*, that as in previous years the talks should be entirely informal; no attempt would be made to produce agreed minutes, but the United Kingdom delegation, as hosts, would compile an informal record and circulate it later to the

---

[1] The British delegation was led by H T Bourdillon (chair) and I T M Pink; the French, by L Pignon; the Belgian, by C Dupont, inspecteur-royal des colonies, government of Belgium.

other delegations. It would not be in any way binding, but the United Kingdom would welcome any amendments or clarifications which the French and Belgian delegations might wish to suggest.

Item 1(a). Anti-colonialism in general

Mr. Bourdillon said that from the U.K. point of view the past year had been quite successful, with the satisfactory handling of the British Togoland problem and the avoidance of substantive discussion of Cyprus. The anti-colonials on the Fourth Committee had not evolved any novel technique of significance, and the Committee on Information had behaved itself with fair docility. However, the adoption of the "target date" recommendations on virtually all Trust Territories had been a real setback, especially serious because of the disagreement between the United States and the other Administering Powers.

M. Pignon and M. Dupont agreed, and *M. Pignon* added that anti-colonialism was a major factor in world politics outside the United Nations as well as within it. For example, a congress of "black" artists and intellectuals had been held in Paris last month, and the moderate and responsible element had not been able to stand up to the Marxists and nationalists. The United Nations was an ideal forum for dressing up anti-Colonialism in quasi-juridical form.

Item 1(b). Consequences of admission of new members

Mr. Bourdillon noted that the admission of sixteen new members had brought about a radical shift in the balance of strength in the General Assembly. The Latin American group was much less powerful and no longer provided the United States with a blocking third; while the Afro-Asian group and the Soviet bloc had both substantially increased. A provisional assessment of Assembly voting on a major colonial item showed 44:52 anti-colonial votes against 24:16 and 8 abstentions. Although this meant that it would prove virtually impossible to prevent the inscription of an item, this was balanced to some extent by the fact that it would prove more difficult for any one group to be sure of passing a resolution, unless it was watered down. This might result in increased peddling of compromises by moderate delegations which should be guarded against. *M. Pignon* agreed with Mr. Bourdillon's analysis of the situation and added that the number of "uncommitted" States was very small. With regard to inscription, items were proposed with propaganda motives and nothing much could be done to defeat these. A possible tactic to combat this new situation would be the creation of numerous committees and sub-committees. Several countries which were compelled to follow an anti-colonial line in public might be more amenable to private persuasion in such small committees; Laos and Cambodia were examples. In addition, we should endeavour to have Portugal elected on to United Nations bodies. With the help of such delegations it might often be possible to water down hostile resolutions into comparatively harmless shape. Admittedly there were cases in which a thoroughly bad resolution which could be wholeheartedly opposed might be better than a plausible compromise. But the compromises, particularly in concrete cases concerning specific territories, might sometimes be worth working for from the point of view of their effect on African opinion.

Mr. Dupont welcomed M. Pignon's suggestion regarding committees, though he felt that Portugal could not be counted on to align herself completely with us. Our attitude towards compromise resolutions should depend on the nature of the individual question: on some matters there could be no compromise. *Mr. Bourdillon* agreed that on fundamental issues it was essential for the Administering Powers to hold their positions and it was better to oppose a bad resolution than to accept a watered-down one. *Mr. Pink* thought there might be something to be said for accepting the inscription of most items. It was not good tactics to use up our reserves of good-will fruitlessly in attempting to defeat inscription when we were certain to lose. In such cases it was more dignified to accept defeat gracefully, while making it clear that the item was nonsense. *M. Pignon* said that in his personal view he agreed with this and felt that "filibuster" tactics could be used in such cases. . . .

171   CO 936/321, no 21/22   30 Oct 1956
[Proposed General Assembly speech defending colonialism]: letter from H T Bourdillon to I T M Pink

Please refer to your letter of 2nd October, about the possibility of our adopting a more positive attitude in the United Nations on Colonial questions. I can now report the results of my soundings on this subject in the United States and Canada.

2. I am happy to say that the general State Department attitude, which I discussed at some length in paragraph 5 (c) of my letter of 24th September,[1] seemed on this occasion to be better than I had expected and to have improved rather than deteriorated since last year. My impression, which I think is shared by Barabara Salt and Barry Gidden, is that in addition to the usual friendliness there was a greater frankness in the discussions on the American side and an increased realisation both of the merits of our Colonial policy and of its importance for United States interests. On the question of "intermediate target dates", the Americans, while obviously unable to eat their words in the Trusteeship Council, showed what I could only regard as signs of a guilty conscience and seemed unexpectedly ready to admit the justice of our demand for complete flexibility. I say this with great diffidence, since the unaccountable Mason Sears was very much in evidence, and while he is about the place nobody can tell what is going to happen next. All the same, I think I can allow myself the remark that so far as general good understanding between ourselves and the Americans on Colonial matters is concerned, this particular round of talks was mildly encouraging.[1]

3. That does not mean, however, that the dangers mentioned in paragraph 5(c) of my letter of 24th September were altogether absent. On the contrary, there was a good deal of talk on the American side about "the British and the Americans not being too afraid to show some divergence in the United Nations on Colonial matters where fundamental issues are not at stake". Whilst this attitude may to some extent be due to pre-election pressures, and whilst I hope we succeeded in battering it a certain amount during the talks, it cannot be written off as a mere passing phase. I would judge that the State Department, with their well known capacity for wishful thinking at other people's expense, are to some extent indulging the vain hope that they can draw closer to us on essentials, and satisfy us into the bargain that they are doing so, while at the same time meeting the new pressures in the United Nations by

---

[1] See 169.   [2] See 100, 111.

emphasizing a certain aloofness from the Colonial Powers. I have therefore come back from Washington reinforced in my view that it is important for us at this stage to give the Americans something positive to catch hold of, thus helping them to solve their own dilemma without damaging our joint interests.

4. My conclusion from the Canadians talks is fundamentally similar. Rather to my surprise, I found the Canadians obsessed with the idea that this year's General Assembly was going to be, in a big way, the worst ever from the anti-Colonial point of view. In support of this thesis they adduced certain admitted facts, such as the net voting effect of the new members and the change in Russian tactics (though I pointed out that this had not yet become evident in the Colonial sphere); but their main thought seemed to be that the effect of the Suez crisis would be to divide the world more irreconcilably than ever into the "Colonial" versus "anti-Colonial" camps. I was not of course qualified to express any authoritative view about Suez, but I did go so far as to say that I thought the Canadians were over-simplifying its probable effect, if any, on the alignment of Powers in the United Nations. In general I attempted, without indulging in counter-prophecies, to allay unnecessary alarm and to give due weight to the more hopeful features in the situation. I think this had the desired effect. The Canadians seemed genuinely relieved by what I said, and finished up by promising to keep in close touch with us on Colonial matters in the U.N. and to support us to the best of their ability. There is no doubt, however, that they like the Americans are impressed (perhaps unduly) by the changes which are likely to take place in the United Nations as a result of the new members and of the alteration in Russian tactics. In addition to this, we have got to reckon with the increasing Canadian desire, shown so clearly last year, to play a big part in United Nations affairs. I was specifically told before I left that in 1956 the Canadians intended to show increased activity in the Colonial field as well as in other United Nations matters. I conclude, therefore, that the need to give the Americans something positive to catch hold of goes to some extent for the Canadians as well.

5. I should add, in honesty, that I got no express reaction either from the Americans or the Canadians about the extent to which they would be able to support us more openly in the U.N. on Colonial matters in the event of our deciding to take a more positive line. In the time available I could only have got to snap reaction at best, and I did not think it would be wise to press for this—particularly as I had to be studiously non-committal about our own intentions. I therefore left the thought to sink in. It is possible that we shall get some expression of view, at least from the State Department, before the General Assembly begins. Meanwhile I must emphasize that my conclusions as given in this letter spring entirely from my own assessment of the present American and Canadian attitude.

6. I had of course discussed the matter with the Delegation in New York before going to Washington. I was unable to catch more than a fleeting glimpse of Bob Dixon, who was immersed in Suez, but I discussed the question at length with Barry Gidden. He was in full agreement with the proposal that we should take a more positive line on Colonial matters in this year's General Assembly, subject to the following conditions which he and I agreed to be essential;

(a) As suggested in paragraph 6 of my letter of 24th September, the only safe and effective way of launching out is in the General Debate. The only place in which we can *not* in any circumstances launch out is the Fourth Committee. This does not, of course, rule out the kind of follow-up action suggested in my previous letter. On the contrary, it has been emphasized here that publicity follow-up would be essential if any lasting effect were to be achieved.

(b) It is no use thinking that a passing reference or two to Colonial matters in the course of the United Kingdom speech in the General Debate will have any effect. This has in fact already been done in previous years. What is needed is a whole section of the speech, textually approved in advance and not subject to excision or drastic reduction when the time comes owing to pressure of other material. Unless we can decide on this, we may as well drop the whole exercise.

(c) The suggestion in paragraph 6 of my previous letter that we should draw attention to our actual achievements is correct, but we must be ready to go a little further than this. If we *merely* talk about the forthcoming independence of the Gold Coast and the Federation of Malaya, with perhaps a word about the establishment of the Caribbean Federation, we shall not materially increase the impact which these events will make of their own accord. On the other hand we are likely to give the impression that we are parading these undoubted achievements in order to cover up less reputable activities elsewhere. It is therefore essential for us to say enough to show that we are pursuing a sound and progressive policy everywhere—with full allowance, of course, for the wide difference in circumstances. This need not involve us in making incautious statements about East Africa—which is, of course, by far the most tricky British colonial area (together with Central Africa) from the United Nations point of view. On the contrary, we can make use of the occasion to emphasize (if only by implication) both the need for caution in the East African territories and the reasons for not allowing U.N. interference in their political affairs.

7. On the basis of the above points I have prepared the enclosed draft.[3] It has been vetted here at the official level, but we may still have some amendments to make. Meanwhile, I am sending it to you as it is since time is so short. I very much hope that you and Snelling, to whom I am sending a copy of this letter, will be able to let me know in the very near future whether you concur in the terms of the draft. Apart from the actual wording, the most important requirement at this stage is, of course, firm Ministerial appoval from the Foreign Office (subject only to the views of Bob Dixon and the Delegation, who have not seen the draft and who will want to say what they think of its suitability in the light of the atmosphere in New York when the Assembly opens) for the inclusion of the passage in the United Kingdom speech in the General Debate.

8. Before concluding this letter, I should add that I took an entirely private and unofficial sounding of Pignon during our tripartite talks with the French and the Belgians before I went to Washington.[4] I was not, of course, able to give him any close indication of what we would actually say in any statement which we might make in the General Debate, but he was in support of the idea of such a statement. He added that he himself had tried to get a statement on similar lines included in the French speech in previous years, but that this had always been thrust out at the last moment. You will notice that I have included an appreciative reference to the other Administering Powers in the last paragraph of the enclosed draft.

---

[3] Not printed.   [4] See 170.

172 CO 936/321, no 25/26 7 Nov 1956

[Proposed General Assembly speech defending colonialism]: letter
from H T Bourdillon to I T M Pink abandoning the idea [Extract]

Please refer to my letter of 30th October,[1] under the above references, about the possibility of our adopting a more positive attitude in the United Nations on Colonial questions. Snelling wrote to me on the subject on the same date, and I assume that a copy of his letter was sent to the Foreign Office. The Commonwealth Relations Office reference is WES 21/33/2. Please see also Jasper's letter to Marnham of 2nd November, copied to Dalton Murray.

2. I have now spoken to Snelling about these proposals, and we are agreed that they cannot be pursued in the immediate future. Our view is that so long as the General Assembly maintains its recent hostile mood towards the United Kingdom as a result of the Suez operation, any attempt to draw attention in the United Nations to our Colonial policy would merely result in a furious onslaught. I assume that the Foreign Office would not disagree with this assessment. On the other hand it must be hoped that the dust will settle and that the operation in the Middle East will increasingly come to be recognised, in retrospect, as a necessary step for the maintenance of world peace rather than an act of "Colonialist" aggression. If and when the tide begins to turn in this way, it may be expected that there will be a greater readiness, both in the United Nations and elsewhere, not only to dissociate the Middle East operation from "Colonialism" but to take an objective view of United Kingdom Colonial policy as such. At that stage it may become more necessary than ever to take whatever opportunities may present themselves of speaking up for our Colonial record. I suggest, therefore, that the draft statement enclosed in my letter of 30th October should be kept on the stocks for possible use in anticipation of a more favourable turn of events. In the meantime I doubt if there is any point in trying to perfect the draft, since it will probably need amendment in any case, when and if it comes to be used, in order to fit in with circumstances at the time. . . .[2]

---

[1] See 171.

[2] The text prepared by Bourdillon in defence of Britain's colonial record was shortly afterwards used in the preparation of a speech delivered by Selwyn Lloyd at the annual dinner of the English Speaking Union in New York on 26 Nov 1956. The main theme of the speech however was a defence of the British action at Suez. The text of the speech is at CO 935/321, no 32.

Index of Main Subjects and Persons

This is a consolidated index for all three parts of the volume. It is not a comprehensive index, but a simplified and straightforward index to document numbers, together with page references to the Introduction in part I, the latter being given at the beginning of the entry in lower-case roman numerals. It is designed to be used in conjunction with the summary lists and chapter headings of the preliminary pages to each volume-part. It provides a quick finding-aid to the main references to the principal subjects (countries and broad themes) and the leading British policy-advisers and decision-makers. As far as persons are concerned, only in the case of key figures (Eden, Lennox-Boyd, Lyttelton and Macmillan) are the entries subdivided by subject; a preceding asterisk indicates inclusion in the Biographical Notes at the end of part III. Where necessary (eg, in particularly long documents), and if possible, paragraph numbers are given inside round brackets. The following abbreviations are used:

> A – appendix or annex
>
> n – footnote

Documents are divided between the volume-parts as follows:

> nos   1–172   part I
>
> nos 173–357   part II
>
> nos 358–526   part III.